DAVID BASKERVILLE

Professor Emeritus, Late of the University of Colorado, Denver

TIM BASKERVILLE

MUSIC BUSINESS HANDBOOK

AND CAREER GUIDE

edition

11

SAGE

Los Angeles | London | New Delhi
Singapore | Washington DC

Los Angeles | London | New Delhi
Singapore | Washington DC

FOR INFORMATION:

SAGE Publications, Inc.
2455 Teller Road
Thousand Oaks, California 91320
E-mail: order@sagepub.com

SAGE Publications Ltd.
1 Oliver's Yard
55 City Road
London EC1Y 1SP
United Kingdom

SAGE Publications India Pvt. Ltd.
B 1/I 1 Mohan Cooperative Industrial Area
Mathura Road, New Delhi 110 044
India

SAGE Publications Asia-Pacific Pte. Ltd.
3 Church Street
#10-04 Samsung Hub
Singapore 049483

Staff for the Eleventh Edition

Editor: Tim Baskerville
Project Manager: Deborah Barber
Senior Contributing Editors: Robert Marich,
Dave Laing, Lynne Dundas
Contributing Editor: Peter J. Strand of
Leavens, Strand & Glover, LLC
Photo Editor: Deborah Barber
Editorial Consultant: Roberta Baskerville

SAGE Staff for the Eleventh Edition

Acquisitions Editor: Maggie Stanley
Associate Editor: Abbie Rickard
Editorial Assistant: Nicole Mangona
eLearning Editor: Katie Bierach
Production Editor: Olivia Weber-Stenis
Copy Editor: Gillian Dickens
Typesetter: C&M Digitals (P) Ltd.
Proofreader: Sue Irwin
Indexer: William Ragsdale
Cover Designer: Janet Kiesel
Marketing Manager: Ashlee Blunk

Printed in the United States of America

ISBN 978-1-5063-0953-8

This book is printed on acid-free paper.

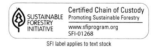

SFI label applies to text stock

16 17 18 19 20 10 9 8 7 6 5 4 3 2 1

This publication is designed to provide accurate and authoritative information in regard to the subject matter covered. It is sold with the understanding that the publisher is not engaged in rendering legal, accounting, or other professional service. If legal advice or other expert assistance is required, the services of a competent professional person should be sought.
—From the *Declaration of Principles* jointly adopted by a committee of the American Bar Association and a committee of publishers and associations.

Solo Musician's Monthly Album Sales Target to Earn U.S. Minimum Wage

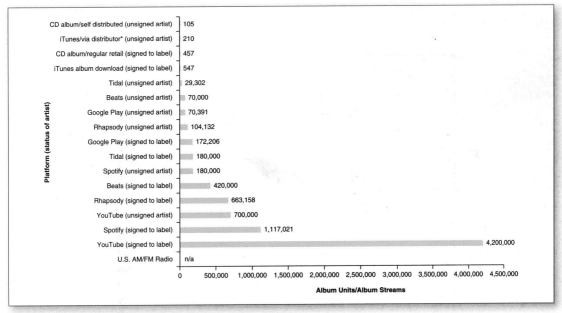

Platform (status of artist)	Album Units/Album Streams
CD album/self distributed (unsigned artist)	105
iTunes/via distributor* (unsigned artist)	210
CD album/regular retail (signed to label)	457
iTunes album download (signed to label)	547
Tidal (unsigned artist)	29,302
Beats (unsigned artist)	70,000
Google Play (unsigned artist)	70,391
Rhapsody (unsigned artist)	104,132
Google Play (signed to label)	172,206
Tidal (signed to label)	180,000
Spotify (unsigned artist)	180,000
Beats (signed to label)	420,000
Rhapsody (signed to label)	663,158
YouTube (unsigned artist)	700,000
Spotify (signed to label)	1,117,021
YouTube (signed to label)	4,200,000
U.S. AM/FM Radio	n/a

*Distributors include CDBaby, Reverberation, TuneCore.

Notes: The benchmark monthly minimum wage is calculated at $1,260/month from $7.25/hour.
Figures assume a solo artist playing own compositions.
Individual streams are considered one-tenth of an album.
Excludes broadcast, performance, mechanical, and other publishing income.
Unsigned Artist assumes all production, manufacturing, and other costs.
"Signed To Label" figures are calculated from typical label deal, though deals vary greatly.

Source: Derived primarily from InformationIsBeautiful.net, 2013 and 2015.

U.S. Recorded Music Revenue 1999–2014

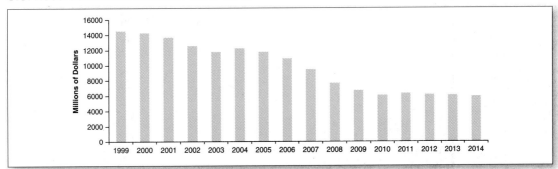

U.S. Recorded Music Revenue 1999–2014

Millions of Dollars

	1999	2000	2001	2002	2003	2004	2005	2006	2007	2008	2009	2010	2011	2012	2013	2014
On Demand Streaming—Ad Supported	0	0	0	0	0	0	0	0	0	0	0	0	113.8	170.9	220	294.8
Digital Subscriptions	0	0	0	0	0	0	149.2	206.2	234	221.4	206.2	212.4	247.8	399.9	639.2	799.1
Digital Downloads	0	0	0	0	0	183.5	502.7	876.2	1336.6	1708.8	1957.2	2245.4	2625.6	2849.2	2816.4	2574
Music Videos	376.7	281.9	329.2	288.4	399.9	607.2	602.2	451.1	484.9	227.3	209.6	177.6	151	116.6	104.7	90.5
CDs	13038.7	13357.2	12988.8	12063.7	11268.0	11461.5	10531.1	9380.3	7464.5	5474.8	4321.9	3392.3	3104.2	2488.8	2125.9	1857.9
Cassettes	1109.6	630.6	363.4	209							0	0	0	0	0	0
Vinyl LPs & Singles	59.7	54	58.8	45							66.3	91.2	124	165.4	213.7	320.8
TOTAL	14584.7	14323.7	13740.2	12607							6761.2	6118.9	6366.4	6190.8	6119.9	5937.1

Notes:
- All figures are retail dollar value from record-label reports of shipments (net of returns).
- On-demand streaming includes ad-supported audio and music video services not operating under statutory licenses.
- Subscription includes streaming, tethered, and other paid subscriptions not operating under statutory licenses, with counts averaged throughout the year.

Source: Recording Industry Association of America (RIAA).

To my family, and to those in the business who care about the music, too

Brief Contents

Detailed Contents

Foreword

Nile Rodgers

■ Artists Need to Be Good Listeners, Too

I'll never forget what David Bowie told me was his objective when I produced his album *Let's Dance.* He said, "Nile, darling, what we've got to do is come up with something that's the same but really quite different."

Don't laugh, because David is the consummate artist with an impresario's keen sense of the market. He knows the audience wants new musical sensations, but not so new that they are completely alien. Keeping your eye on the audience has been my philosophy ever since I was a skinny kid with glasses from the streets of New York, a musician who broke into the business playing in the house band at the Apollo Theater in Harlem.

Photo by Roy Cox.

My advice to the next generation of musical talent is to explore with an open mind and discover the musical world that's out there. Don't assume that you are so smart and talented that the world is absolutely going to find you on your terms.

The music business, after all, is business. And business requires focus. I make my songs for the specific gatekeeper that I see just in front of me. The gatekeeper could be an A&R dude, who I know will then take my song to the label boss. I'm not looking way down the road like when I drive a car. This philosophy focuses creativity on a simple and achievable objective.

I've never had a manager because I always want to figure out the marketplace myself and then plot my next move (although not having a manager is right for me, it may not be right for others). When I started out, it was the age of the rock star—the Rolling Stones, Yes, and Jimi Hendrix. I knew that I'd never make it as a rock star because I didn't look the type. So I wrote songs that were catchier and more commercial than theirs.

When I broke into the business, all we could hope for was that our records would get on the radio and land on the *Billboard* charts. The business was like a distant fortress with high walls and just a few gatekeepers. As artists—the musicians, producers, and songwriters—we had to figure out how to get over that fortress wall.

In today's digital age, music is everywhere, creating a flat, wide landscape with many points of entry. It's not just record labels and radio stations anymore. In recent years, retailers ranging from coffee shops to clothing stores have sold select CDs, giving them national distribution. Clothing manufacturers, liquor marketers, tobacco companies, electronics companies, and other consumer product outfits sell and sponsor music in deals with artists, creating whole new classes of music financiers and enablers.

James Taylor, who is a friend of mine, made one of the single smartest moves of his entire career—and he has an incredible career going—when he did a Christmas album distributed through Hallmark Cards stores. This album sold over a million copies; Hallmark covered the cost of the recording, and James kept ownership of the master. Now that's what I call knowing the audience and working the system!

Years ago, the business was more combative and appeared punctuated with endless battles between artists and labels. Today, the environment is much more collaborative, with fewer battles. That transformation requires listening with an open mind but doesn't mean agreeing to what doesn't sound right. Once, I was in a disagreement with a label over one of my songs. The label was slow to come around to my view but finally agreed to destroy hundreds of thousands of singles that were just about to ship and replaced them with *Good Times,* the song my band CHIC wanted. It ultimately went on to become one of our most influential songs and No. 1 on the *Billboard* chart.

That incident illustrates the big stick of leverage that the artist—who often is portrayed as powerless—actually wields in dealing with labels and other big entities that are partners in the music industry. Despite their armies of executives and their mounds of corporate money, the big companies know deep down that they don't *really* know. It's the artist who has a feel for the music, and—if listening to my advice—it's the artist who makes the effort to understand the audience.

The late Ahmet Ertegun—the legendary label executive known for his eye for up-and-coming talent—confided this little secret when I first met him. He told me, "Kid, the reason I'm letting you do whatever you want to do is because I learned early on that *I* am not the ultimate consumer."

The lesson: Listen to the audience, and the audience will listen to you.

Nile Rodgers is a recording artist, songwriter, video game scorer, and record producer who has collaborated with David Bowie, Eric Clapton, Madonna, and Diana Ross. His guitar-driven CHIC funk recording "Le Freak" is Atlantic Records' biggest single of all time. He is a trustee of The Recording Academy and founder of the We Are Family Foundation. Read more about him in his memoir, *LeFreak: An Upside Down Story of Family, Disco and Destiny.*

Preface

I t's still big. One estimate from consulting firm PwC is that the global music market today is worth about $46 billion, a lot of money any way you count it. But, when you do count it, it is not what it used to be. When the first edition of this handbook rolled off the press decades ago, a lot of people were making a lot of money from selling pieces of plastic in which were encoded the cultural touchstones of the 20th century: The music business was largely the *recorded* music business, and recorded music was monetized in physical form.

Then technology happened. Just as it roiled other media—from newspapers to magazines to over-the-air television—it upended the comfortably predictable principles that governed artists, record labels, retailers, radio broadcasters, and the other vital cogs in the vast recorded music business machine. In fact, most of the titans in the business today—think Apple, Spotify, Sirius XM, SoundExchange, YouTube, Pandora, Amazon—a few decades ago weren't even in the music business or weren't in business at all.

That upending, and the adjustments that have been reverberating through the business ever since, are what we explore in this 11th edition.

What's new, you ask?

Instead of buying particular pieces of music through a CD or download, consumers are doing more of their music consumption activity as an "experience." That experience might include attending a live concert (Chapters 16 and 17) or listening to a curated digital stream (Chapter 19).

Instead of subsidizing live performances to boost record sales, labels now routinely use concert profits to fatten their take of an artist's overall success through 360 deals (Chapter 12).

Instead of defining performance licensing as just the exploitation of compositions, the United States has significantly boosted the value of licensing the master recordings themselves (Chapter 7).

Instead of tracking the industry by looking at just retail sales charts and radio playlists, the quantitative analysts of today tap into a torrent of digitized behavioral data to spark discovery, shape tastes, and one way or the other squeeze more money out of the complex ecosystem that is the music industry of the 21st century (Chapter 15).

Our narrative in this edition has changed as well. We've reordered some chapters to recognize today's new alignment of the important issues. And we've added some more discussion questions to spark student inquiry.

Perhaps as important, we've humanized the story by offering vignettes illustrating how individuals in different industry roles are coping and indeed triumphing as the rules change. Notable examples include movie composer Jeff Beal (Chapter 21), music video producer Emmanuelle Cuny-Diop (Chapter 20), instrument merchants Stan and Jerry Keyawa (Chapter 24), and nonprofit venue executive David Asbell (Chapter 17).

Admittedly, with such fundamental changes, not everyone in every role is emerging unscathed. What these hundreds of pages illustrate, however, is with change can come genuine opportunity for players as diverse as the inventors of new digital tools as well as the DIY creators of the next big sound.

The band is tuning up. Let's enjoy the show.

Tim Baskerville
September 2015
Santa Barbara

Online Resources

Visit **http://study.sagepub.com/baskerville11e** for support materials that accompany the book.

Password-protected **Instructor Resources** include the following:

- A **test bank** by Tim Baskerville is available containing multiple choice, true/false, and essay questions for each chapter. The test bank provides you with a diverse range of pre-written options as well as the opportunity for editing any question and/or inserting your own personalized questions to effectively assess students' progress and understanding.
- Carefully selected, web-based **video links** feature relevant interviews, lectures, personal stories, inquiries, and other content for use in independent or classroom-based explorations of key topics.
- Editable, chapter-specific Microsoft® **PowerPoint® slides** by Tim Baskerville offer you complete flexibility in easily creating a multimedia presentation for your course.
- **Chapter-specific discussion questions** help launch classroom interaction by prompting students to engage with the material and by reinforcing important content.
- **Teaching tips** are designed for instructors to expand questions to students, or initiate class discussion.
- **Web exercises** direct both instructors and students to useful and current web sites, along with creative activities to extend and reinforce learning or allow for further research on important chapter topics.
- **Web resources** are included for further research and insights.
- General resources include **templates and forms** students can use in the music business.

The open-access **Student Study Site** includes the following:

- Mobile-friendly **eFlashcards** reinforce understanding of key terms and concepts that have been outlined in the chapters.
- Carefully selected, **video links** feature relevant interviews, lectures, personal stories, inquiries, and other content for use in independent or classroom-based explorations of key topics.
- **Web exercises** direct you to useful and current web resources, along with creative activities to extend and reinforce learning or allow for further research on important chapter topics.
- **Web resources** are included for further research and insights.
- General resources include templates and forms to use in the music business.

Acknowledgments

We wish to thank those people who were helpful in generously sharing their knowledge of many facets of the music and entertainment business during the preparation of this 11th edition and its predecessors.

Once again, our anchor reporting for this edition comes from Robert Marich, a veteran entertainment journalist (*The Hollywood Reporter, Variety*) who for years has set the standard for coverage of entertainment and media. Key contributors for this edition also include project manager and photo editor Deborah Barber, marketing professional Lynne Dundas, and U.K.-based author Dave Laing. We also acknowledge with fond memory Dave's writing partner, the late Phil Hardy, who contributed his knowledge of the global scene to many of our editions over the years.

Over time, a number of entertainment and music attorneys have kept us up to date with the shifting sands of law and regulation. Peter J. Strand of Leavens, Strand & Glover, LLC, served as a key adviser for portions of this 11th edition. In recent years, we're also grateful for input from attorneys Mark J. Davis, David Hirshland, and Susan Rabin. Among the notable legal contributors to earlier editions have been Alan S. Bergman and Robert Clarida.

Key contributors to this edition include music video executive Nicole Acacio, Caviar music video executive producer Kim Dellara, film composer Ron Grant, AEG Ehrlich Ventures' Renato Basile, Me Gusta Music owner Trina Smith, Kathy Marsh and Bill Archer of MusicNotes.com, Musical Merchandise Review editor Christian Wissmuller, NAMM Director of Public Relations Lora Bodmer, SAG-AFTRA historian Valerie Yaros, Mediabase VP of Marketing Dwight Douglas, and Phizzle VP of Marketing Jeffrey A. Ryznar.

Particularly helpful with the primary research we reference in these pages are the Future of Music Coalition; IFPI in London along with its U.S. affiliate, RIAA; professional services consultancy PwC; Russ H. Crupnick of MusicWatch; and numerous other sources that are credited within the text.

For help with our coverage of music and advertising, we thank the key players from ad agency Rubin Postaer and Associates: Senior VP, Chief Production Officer Gary Paticoff; VP, Executive Producer Isadora Chesler; Executive VP, Management Account Director Brett Bender; and Senior VP, Director Human Resources Lark Baskerville. We particularly appreciate that RPA and Honda allowed us to peek behind the scenes to excerpt the storyboard of their high-impact Matthew Broderick Super Bowl spot.

Other professionals, educators, and experts were generous with their time. Heartfelt thanks go to all of them: Santa Barbara community leader and philanthropist Jim Morouse of the Lobero Theatre Foundation, analyst Michael DeGusta, and digital music expert Anu Kirk.

As usual, we are grateful to the alphabet-soup collection of associations, performing rights organizations, unions, societies, for-profit companies, and nonprofits that have contributed input; their contributions are frequently referenced throughout the text.

Special thanks go to the many friends who gave us advice and information used throughout the book. We are especially grateful to Ira Mayer, Paul Sweeting, Ned Sherman, Joe Diamond, David Hazan, and Motion Picture Academy members Cathy Karol Crowther and Tee Bosustow. And, a grateful nod goes to close friend and industry veteran Barry Freeman, who contributed the quotation from Dinah Shore as well as his in-the-trenches insights from the Golden Age of the record business.

We have relied heavily through several editions for fresh insights from leading thinkers in music business education, most particularly Don Gorder of Berklee College of Music; Tim Hays of Elmhurst College; Kristel Kemmerer of Lamar State College Port Arthur; Carole Knisely of York College of Pennsylvania; Ava Lawrence of Northeastern University; David P. Leonard of TREBAS Institute; Stephen Marcone of William Paterson College; Richard McIlvery of the USC Thornton School of Music; Janet Nepkie of State University of New York, College of Oneonta; Catherine Fitterman Radbill of NYU Steinhardt; Kim Wangler of Appalachian State University; and Elizabeth Sellers, Professor and Director of Film Scoring, California State University, Northridge.

We'd also like to extend a great thank you to the reviewers who contributed their time and feedback to improve this edition. These reviewers include Michael Phillips, University of South Alabama; Carl Anderson, Bradley University; Denise A. Grupp-Verbon, Owens State Community College; Kim L. Wangler, Appalachian State University; Anthony McClure, Dallas Baptist University; Charles Denler, Colorado Christian University; Jason Vanselow, Anoka Ramsey Community College; Brian St. John, University of Evansville; Richard H. Bailey, Jr., University of Arkansas at Pine Bluff; and L. H. Dickert, Jr., Winthrop University.

Many people have contributed to the development of this book in earlier editions, including Dr. Alfred Reed, who, along with Dr. William Lee, established the first university degree program in music merchandising at the University of Miami. In more recent years, University of Miami's Rey Sanchez and Serona Elton have been leaders in advancing the field.

We're grateful to all those educators who have labored for decades to enhance scholarship and curricula in the field of music business education, notably Bruce Ronkin of Northeastern University and Jim Progris, retired from the University of Miami.

And, we are compelled to mention the ongoing role of the Music and Entertainment Industry Educators Association (MEIEA), which has trail blazed in the field—gaining respect in both the halls of academe and in the corridors of business.

To all of those mentioned here and to many other friends who have shared their knowledge of the music business with us—thank you.

About the Authors

Author David Baskerville (right) receiving ASCAP's Deems Taylor Award, given each year for outstanding books on music. The presentation is by Academy Award–winning songwriter Hal David, representing ASCAP.

David Baskerville

Author **David Baskerville** (1918–1986) received a PhD in music from UCLA. His background included staff composer-conductor for NBC-Hollywood; arranger for Nelson Riddle, Paramount Pictures, and 20th Century Fox; television producer for BBC-London; conductor at Radio City Music Hall; trombonist with the Seattle Symphony, Los Angeles Philharmonic, and NBC-Hollywood orchestra; Executive Vice President of Ad-Staff, Inc.; producer of award-winning broadcast commercials; Executive Editor of Tor Music Publishing Company; and President of Sherwood Recording Studios, Los Angeles (subsequently operated by Warner Bros. Records).

He also served as a consultant to companies in the entertainment industry, such as Walt Disney Productions, and to research and marketing firms, such as Vidmar Communications, Los Angeles.

As an educator, Dr. Baskerville created and directed the music management program at the University of Colorado at Denver, where he became professor emeritus. He was a guest lecturer, consultant, or clinician at USC, UCLA, Chicago Musical College, Hartt School of Music, the Ohio State University, University of Miami, and Trebas Institute, Canada.

He was a featured speaker at national conventions of the Music Educators National Conference, College Music Society, National Association of Jazz Educators, and the National Association of Schools of Music.

Tim Baskerville

Author **Tim Baskerville** has a diverse background in entertainment and media. He began his career in broadcasting after receiving a BA in theater arts from UCLA. Early affiliations included CBS and Cox Broadcasting, where he served as a staff writer-producer. The first TV documentary he created for CBS TV stations was nominated for an Emmy.

As a publisher and entrepreneur, he launched business periodicals on the home video software industry, global film distribution, and multinational broadcasting. Today, a publishing company he founded in London in the 1990s is one of the world's leading providers of data on mobile entertainment (www.informatm.com).

In recent years, he served as President of what is now the SNL Kagan unit of McGraw-Hill Financial, the leading provider of financial analysis on the media industry, and CEO of JupiterResearch (acquired by Forrester Research), a key source of consumer research on Web behavior and new media.

As a consultant, Baskerville's clients have included the Motion Picture Association of America, *Variety*, Time Warner, IBM, International Data Corp., Young & Rubicam, JVC America, Apple, and The Rockefeller Foundation. He has been both a strategy consultant and weekly columnist for *Billboard*.

Baskerville was Vice President of the Music and Entertainment Industry Educators Association (MEIEA); member of the Writers Guild of America, West; and chapter founder of the Overseas Press Club of America. He has served on the boards of both public and private companies that publish and distribute business information.

SAGE was founded in 1965 by Sara Miller McCune to support the dissemination of usable knowledge by publishing innovative and high-quality research and teaching content. Today, we publish over 900 journals, including those of more than 400 learned societies, more than 800 new books per year, and a growing range of library products including archives, data, case studies, reports, and video. SAGE remains majority-owned by our founder, and after Sara's lifetime will become owned by a charitable trust that secures our continued independence.

Los Angeles | London | New Delhi | Singapore | Washington DC

Setting the Stage

PART 1

CHAPTER 1

Overture

"I never cared much for poverty."

—Igor Stravinsky

Did someone say "music business"? What happened to the art of music? The shortest possible answer is, "Billions!"—the windstorm of money swirling around the art and business of music. But the question of what is happening to musical art in the modern marketplace calls for a serious answer, particularly when that marketplace is changing so rapidly. That is what this book is all about.

How much has the music business changed since the 20th century gave way to the 21st? More than many could have imagined only a few beats back. What remains the same? More than you might expect, given the chorus of questions about its future direction and shape. Yes, the music industry looks radically different today, having been reshaped by a still-evolving digital landscape, but the fundamentals of the business—the creation, publishing, packaging, marketing, distribution, and sale of music—are constant. Creators still create at one end, artists and merchants continue to "monetize" a music product at the other, and an array of equally passionate, talented individuals—agents, managers, producers, sound engineers, **label**[1] executives, bookers, **promoters,** broadcasters, business advisers, lawyers, accountants—perform their vital roles throughout the process. The differences, of course, are in the details.

That, then, is what will be laid out in the following chapters: the core fundamentals of the *music business* (the term is used here to include the art, the profession, and the business of music), along with the industry's current state of the art (those 21st-century details). Not only do we examine the major changes in music and its audiences, but we also set forth in detail just who produces the music, who "consumes" it, and how the artists, merchants, and others in that long music chain divvy up the

Left: Radio City Music Hall, New York.

Photo © Jeff Hunter.

billions of dollars that the industry produces. Armed with a thorough understanding of both, a music-industry hopeful will be well prepared for a career not only in today's music business but also in the music business of tomorrow—one in which the next seismic shifts are surely only a few more beats away.

Music and Society: We've Got Music in Us

Prepare for some surprises: Perceptions of the profession and business of music are usually at wide variance from reality. This is partly because the field is so diverse and changes so rapidly, but it is also because its public face—the major record label and chart-topping superstar—reveals such a small piece of the whole picture. But it can be understood. It is argued that the music business, particularly the recording industry, is fundamentally irrational. But most of what really goes on in the business and the profession does submit to rational analysis.

We can begin to understand the music business, or any large and diverse activity, once we examine each of its components. That is our method here. But before we do this, let's consider the overall magnitude of the industry today. These facts can provide some perspective:

- Some 164 billion songs were streamed in just the United States during 2014 via audio and video platforms, according to researcher SoundScan, reflecting the consumer affection for free and flat-fee subscription media services.
- Some 1.1 billion legal digital music downloads were sold in the United States in 2014. Although this figure experienced erosion in recent years, downloads today are still sharply higher than the 19 million tracks bought as recently as 2003.
- The scourge of music piracy is declining as 62% of Internet users surveyed in nine countries employed legitimate digital music services in 2013, according to researcher Ipsos MediaCT.
- From the format's introduction in 1982, several hundred billion music **CDs** have sold worldwide, although this format is now in decline.
- One of five Americans plays a musical instrument. These musicians spend more than $6.8 billion a year on instruments, accessories, and **sheet music.**

The love affair starts young—listening to music is cited as the most popular activity among teens—and it's not exactly monogamous: Our passion for music is not limited to any one **genre,** although a cursory glance through the major-media pop-culture lens might suggest so. The American Symphony Orchestra League reports that approximately 36,000 symphony concerts are given every year. This particular audience now numbers around 26.5 million patrons each season. Opera continues to attract its loyal audience, now being served by more than 1,800 professional, semiprofessional, and youth companies in this country.

Nor is the desire strong only in the United States: Recorded music is one of the primary forms of entertainment worldwide, ringing up more than $15 billion in annual trade-level sales.

Meanwhile, ever-cheaper digital production tools, along with the wide-open world of the Web, have combined to spark an explosion of choices for every possible music taste (or lack thereof), and those options are often only a click away from being pumped into the many varieties of pocket-size digital media devices attached to eager ears around the globe. Musicians are no longer restricted in their expression by the laws of acoustics—new electronic ways to make music are invented every year, offering a composer or video producer more controls than 10 fingers can handle. The people with access to newer technology are limited in their expressive capacities only by their imaginations.

In short, the *music* side of the music business is booming.

Art Versus Commerce: Music Changes Everything

What about the business side of the music business? A straight line between a strong consumer appetite for music and a fat, happy music industry is inarguably less certain than it once was. The early explosive growth of peer-to-peer file sharing in the 1990s, a shift toward nontraditional and online retail, the introduction of single-track downloads rather than full (more expensive) albums, and the acceleration of streaming have all altered the old equation. These new realities have spurred (some would say forced) new ways of thinking about how to connect "making music" with "making money."

Art and commerce, of course, have always made strange bedfellows. This ever-present linkage is inherently tense, for musicians and merchants are, in many respects, natural enemies. They seem to hold generally conflicting views on what music should be and do. Musicians want their music to break creative boundaries and to be heard and appreciated by as many people as possible; they want to "connect" with an audience.

Music merchants and businesspeople want music to fit the mainstream sales taste of the moment and to make as much money as possible; they want to "connect" with an audience's wallets. "Good" does not necessarily equal "popular." Perhaps the reason so many hit songs sound bad is that they are. (One irony of the opening up of the creative process through cheaper digital tools and the Web is that there is more bad music being made than ever before—and more that is mind-blowingly good.)

Great music does still break through, as it always has, and great business is still being done. It is simply being done somewhat differently. The major recorded music companies that continue to control the lion's share of the U.S. **market** are exploring new business models and alliances, different types of artist contracts, and previously untapped **licensing** opportunities for current hits and their all-important **catalog** ("old") titles. Musicians and recording artists—newcomers and veterans alike—are discovering that there are more ways than ever to "do-it-yourself": build a fan base, book shows, record music, and support themselves by selling music on the Web. Many artists are picking and choosing those areas where they need or desire professional muscle and those segments of their art or business that can be done better or cheaper with some **DIY** sweat.

Indeed, the very definitions of artist, label, retailer, and even "music product" are blurring and changing. An "artist" increasingly may be his own label—and his own retailer with direct online sales to consumers. A "composer" might compose music for a symphony, a commercial, a film, and a videogame. A "music store" might be a location in a local strip mall, a streaming service, a merchandising section in a **big-box** retailer, a site on the Web, or an app on a cell phone. These "stores" may sell music in the form of albums or singles, physically or digitally, or they may sell access to it for a fee. The "product"—the recorded music itself—can be a direct source of revenue for artists and labels, or it might be viewed more as a method of promotion for bringing in revenue from touring and merchandise (it's hard to download and "share" a T-shirt).

The positives for the music business in this latest reinvention—for those already in it and those just starting out—are many. New technologies naturally equal new challenges. But, as the music industry has shown from its infancy, new technologies also bring vast new opportunities to evolve and expand—whether the technology in question is the Web, music-video **channels**, CDs, TV, radio, or the LP. History's overarching lesson: The industry has been rocked by waves of always new technologies for more than a century, and after rocky adjustments, the business has always emerged healthier and more prosperous.

Historical Development

Finding a Paying Audience

History books provide only spotty information on how the musician fared in earlier times as a professional. We can assume that in the beginning, music making was undertaken by individuals and groups simply for their own pleasure. The performer was also the composer. If there was an audience, it was a social or religious gathering; it did not occur to the early musicians that they might develop an audience that would pay to hear them sing their songs.

Among the first important professional musicians in Western civilization were the mimes of the Greek and Roman theater. They were singing-dancing actors. Roman law held them to be disreputable types, calling them *infami* (outlaws). In the Middle Ages, the minstrels of Germany and the jongleurs of France were the first professionals. Accounts of their activities read like a review from *Variety*. These musicians were actually vaudevillians, and their acts might include not only singing and dancing but also juggling, card tricks, and even knife throwing and trained animals. Show business had begun—in the Middle Ages!

A handful of musicians involved in secular music managed to earn at least part of their livelihood during the Middle Ages and Renaissance. But in the religious sector, almost no musicians enjoyed real professional status. The choirboys and men of the Western church performed in the cathedral choirs as just another part of their Christian service. Professional composers in the religious field seem to have first appeared in Paris around 1100 AD at Notre Dame Cathedral. But musicologists cannot provide a satisfactory account of how the profession of composing music took shape in the following centuries. To this day, church musicians in most communities are either unpaid or paid below professional rates.

Conditions for the working musician were somewhat better in Germany in the 15th and 16th centuries. The tradition of **guilds** included the music trade. Musicians' guilds influenced not only working conditions but also creative and artistic standards. These early guilds were active in organizing composition and singing contests and formulated elaborate rules for them (an accurate account of these proceedings may be found in Richard Wagner's opera, *Die Meistersinger Von Nürnberg*).

In the following period in Europe, increasing numbers of artists were employed by the nobility as house musicians. Composers and performers were put on the royal payroll to make music in the salons, ballrooms, and chapels for their wealthy patrons. But nobility looked on these artists as servants, and they were expected to use the rear entrances to royal buildings. In addition, musicians' royal patrons would frequently pay them later than promised or not at all. Despite considerable advances in status, modern-day musicians sometimes complain that they still do not receive appropriate respect for their talents and professional stature.

In our own time and place, the champion for elevating the status of the music profession is the American Federation of Musicians (AFM), a labor union with members in the United States and Canada. AFM **locals** receive requests regularly from sponsors of civic events, political rallies, and community benefits. These requests are usually sung in the same key: "Please, would you just send over some musicians for our event? They'll really enjoy it and, of course, we'll have some nice refreshments for them." Most musicians have been willing to play benefits, but they have also been exploited by those who would have them "share their art" just for the inherent pleasure of it. AFM locals have developed an effective response for unreasonable requests of this kind: They offer to supply union musicians without fee, provided the other trades and professions—stagehands, waiters, teamsters, bartenders—also work without pay. It is a fair offer; there are few takers.

Gradually, musicians acquired recognition as professionals with the development of a new phenomenon, the paying audience. This first occurred in the musical theater and opera, particularly in Italy and England. When the public began to pay its way into a room to hear music, the *music business* had begun. By the 1800s, the public had accepted the idea that you had to buy a ticket to hear a professional. Increasing numbers of paid concerts developed, not only in European cities such as Vienna, London, and Paris but also in New York, Philadelphia, and Boston.

We lack reliable accounts of who organized and promoted the earliest paid employment for professional musicians. Perhaps the earliest notable artist's manager or agent was Mozart's father, Leopold Mozart, who discovered his son's talent before the youngster had barely graduated from diapers. When Wolfgang was 6 years old, father Leopold started presenting his son to all of Europe. But Mozart's father did not teach his son much about career management. Mozart junior earned considerable sums in his short lifetime but seems to have died a pauper. Mismanagement of money and careers is not unique to recent decades.

A more recent ancestor of today's music entrepreneur was the circus genius, P. T. Barnum. In 1850, when opera singer Jenny Lind, "The Swedish Nightingale," came to America, Barnum presented her around the country as if she were a star acrobat. Barnum's bookings earned the artist $150,000 in her American tour, big money indeed in those days.

Barnum understood that the public likes a good show, and the music business grew, even in the classical field, in a razzle-dazzle, show-biz atmosphere. At the same time Barnum was touring Jenny Lind, other entrepreneurs were developing enthusiastic audiences for that unique American contribution to theater—the minstrel show. This is not the place to treat the racist aspects of that phenomenon; our interest in minstrelsy here must be limited to how it fostered the development of the popular music business. As early as the Middle Ages, musicians from Africa were in Europe entertaining whites. But it was not until the mid-19th century, with the development of the minstrel show, that blacks began to find a place in the white musical world as full professionals. Although most of the performers were white, increasing numbers of blacks began to take part. This development turned out to be of historical significance, for it would be impossible even to conceive of music in the 20th century without the pervasive influence of black musicians.

The increasing popularity of minstrelsy in the 1850 to 1900 period enlarged public awareness and appreciation of popular music and the entertainment business. Near the end of the Reconstruction period, the size and affluence of the middle class grew. By the 1890s, the piano was a standard adornment in the parlors of upper-middle-class families. On thousands of piano racks across the land, one would probably find, in addition to some Stephen Foster songs and a hymnal, a copy of *After the Ball.* The year was 1892, and this song was the first to sell more than a million copies in a 12-month period.

By this time, a number of large publishing houses had developed, such as E. B. Marks, Witmark Bros., T. B. Harms, Leo B. Feist, Mills Music, and Shapiro, Bernstein & Co. These popular music publishers took pride in being able to spot potential hits. When they couldn't find them, the publishers wrote the songs themselves or put composers on weekly salaries to work **in-house.**

These late 19th-century publishers developed the merchandising methods that prevailed until radio became a key music marketing platform in the 1920s. Songs were introduced in a number of ways. In the final days of minstrelsy (which died around 1900), song pluggers would attempt to persuade performers to use material coming off the presses. When vaudeville and burlesque began to displace minstrel shows, pluggers contacted headliners and even lesser acts to try to get them to use the songs their firms were pushing at the time. A publisher who could come up with a piece of material that some vaudeville headliner like Al Jolson or Eddie Cantor would sing was almost ensured a hit, for these were the superstars of their day.

At this point in the music business story, technology stepped in to play a starring role, not unlike the one it occupies today. And also not unlike today, many in the industry first feared that it might be more villain than hero. That hot new innovation? Radio.

Mass Media: Yesterday, Today, and Tomorrow

The world has always been full of music lovers, but it was not until the development of mass communication technology that so many "new" audiences were discovered. Until the 1920s, most professional music making was addressed to a small, elite audience that was accustomed to buying tickets to attend the opera, the symphony, perhaps a Broadway musical. When radio (and, later, records and television) came along, that elite audience not only continued but also grew. But now it was joined and immeasurably augmented by whole new audiences for folk music, country and western songs, blues, and jazz. Mass media forever changed the size and composition of the music audience, and merchants were quick to respond to the new millions of paying customers.

Not that this tremendous upside was clear from the start. Industry leaders misjudged radio broadcasting: When it started in the 1920s, the publishers fought it, believing that "giving music away" through this medium would hurt sheet music sales. Overexposure via radio broadcasting, they argued, was killing songs in 6 weeks; potential customers could not get down to the store to make a purchase before the song's popularity had waned. It should be pointed out that publishers' income from broadcast performances at that time was zero.

Another significant technological development in the entertainment field occurred in 1927 when the "talkies" began. Movie producers discovered, with the very first sound film (a musical titled *The Jazz Singer,* starring Al Jolson), that audiences would buy a lot of theater tickets to hear songs sung on "the silver screen." The major studios began scrambling for **synchronization rights** to enable them to add music to films and turn out musical films in rapid succession.

During the Great Depression of the 1930s, million-selling records disappeared, and sales of sheet music collapsed. Attendance at vaudeville theaters dropped, too, with the growing popularity of the movie musical. Concurrent with these depressions in the music market, radio broadcasting grew rapidly. Music publishers now shifted their attention from plugging vaudeville performers to the new stars of radio. The **network** broadcasts at that time emanated mostly from New York, Chicago, and Los Angeles. Publishers closed their regional offices across the land and focused their plugging efforts on these new broadcasting centers. It worked. The publishers quickly discovered that they should point their promotional efforts toward the big bands and their singers who had weekly, sometimes nightly, radio broadcasts (which, at that time, were referred to as "remotes"). Song-plugging had grown from a local to a national enterprise with the development of network radio.

Publishers were not the only ones to benefit from the coming of network broadcasting. Big bands became name bands because of network radio. Then the name bands became the record stars. Management noticed that the best-selling big band **records** featured the band's singer. Alert talent handlers pulled the singers off the bandstand (Frank Sinatra, Doris Day, Ella Fitzgerald, etc.) and started them working alone—for much more money. This was the beginning of the present era of the dominance of the popular singer; they became the new stars and superstars, with the help of recordings and films.

During World War II, the whole world seemed to discover the appeal of America's popular music, enchanted by its glossy, up-tempo big-band tunes. Much of this worldwide popularity was fostered by the Armed Forces Radio network. With over 90 **stations** broadcasting American-made records around the world, millions of listeners, not just the GIs for whom the broadcasts were intended, heard the great entertainment available from this kind of music. By the late 1940s, the American style had become a world style.

When the GIs returned home, they bought large quantities of records. Music instrument factories, which had been shut down earlier to produce weapons, were now spewing out guitars, organs, pianos, and wind and percussion instruments in quantity. The music industry was reaching a mass market.

Record companies were moving millions of singles in the 1940s. When Columbia came out with the long-playing (LP) vinyl platter record, the music business again experienced a development of overwhelming significance. Now, instead of two songs per record, songwriters and publishers could place 12 songs on each release. On the new LP, record buyers could hear an entire Broadway show; opera buffs could carry home an entire opera in a box; complete symphonies could easily fit on one LP. The dollar volume of classical records grew to 10% of the market (versus 2% these days).

Concurrent with the growing popularity of LPs was the increasing availability of low-cost tape recorders. Add to this the boom in high-fidelity sound. For a relatively low cost, consumers could hear recorded or broadcast music with a quality of sound that was better, audiophiles believed, than that offered at their local concert halls.

The music business began to attract a new breed of merchants, inventors of new distribution and merchandising methods. The most significant marketing development at the time was the discovery that people would buy records wherever they shopped. Enter the **rack jobber.** This new kind of music merchant set up record racks in supermarkets, variety stores, department stores—anywhere shoppers passed by.

Large corporations began to notice that people in the music publishing and record business were making lots of money. They decided to buy in. By the 1970s, even conservative bankers got the message: Music enterprise was now an acceptable risk. They began making loans to music publishers, record producers, and artists' managers—types of people they used to classify with street vendors. The main attraction to these new investors was record production. In what other kind of business enterprise could someone invest, say, $20,000 in a **master** tape, then receive from it **royalties** one hundred times that amount for distribution rights, if the record hit? To the inexperienced investor, the music business began to look like a money tree. By the 1970s, the buying and selling of music companies resulted in the majority of industry revenue becoming controlled by a handful of giant corporations (to become the long-time "Big 6," a number that would shrink further in later years).

This belief in a "money tree" seemed almost justified when another game-changing innovation was introduced in 1982: the compact disc. Labels shook their **analog** catalogs, and out poured dollars as consumers replaced their record collections with the digital discs and then scooped up new CD-only releases. Although audiophiles initially balked, the CD soon overtook both the LP and the previously unveiled "new" format, the music cassette; that complete symphony now fitted on *one side* of one disc. Music television was simultaneously taking root—having become a cultural force with the debut of MTV in 1981—and the two together helped usher in a period of creative and business growth.

Cue new technology once more, and underscore the arrival of the MP3 format onto the scene in the 1990s with a somewhat unsettling composition. When digital music was further compressed into files that could be distributed over the Internet freely (in every sense of the word), a new form of mass media became, in part, a medium controlled by the masses. The ability of consumers to make duplicate recordings shattered the grip that labels held on music when play-only media such as the LP were the standard. The most fervent of music fans were now tastemakers, although not yet hit-makers, as they sought out, chatted up, and "distributed" songs online. Musicians were quick to tap into this newfound promotional base, and record labels followed.

The Internet, vast and far-reaching as it is, allowed a direct, intimate, and interactive connection with fans in ways never before possible outside of a small concert. If the 20th century was about discovering new audiences, the 21st may prove to be about finding new, better, and—here is the still-open billion-dollar question—*profitable* ways to connect with them wherever they are and through whatever medium they desire—live venues, streaming, downloads, music stores, TV, radio, film, social networking sites, cellular phones, videogames, and whichever *next* new thing is just over the horizon. In the next chapter, we examine the implications of the nascent digital millennium.

Note

1. Words in **boldface** type indicate inclusion in the glossary section.

Chapter Takeaways

- Despite the upheavals of transformational change, global recorded music sales (in all forms) remain impressive, amounting to more than $15 billion to record labels alone.

- Tensions have always persisted between artists who want to connect with audiences and business enablers who want to connect to an audience's wallets.

- The rise of the middle class in the late 19th century made possible the first blockbuster music publishing hit, *After the Ball,* which sold more than a million units in 1892.

- Technology, in its many forms, has been a consistent driver of the changing business—from the invention of radio, to movies, to TV, to vinyl LPs, to CDs, to the Web.

- Transition to a new legal recording medium, such as cassette tapes being supplanted

by CDs, created short-term prosperity for record labels. That's because consumers bought their favorite tunes in the new format, even as they owned the same music in the old format.

Key Terms

- infami   (p. 6)
- label   (p. 3)
- LP   (p. 6)

- MP3   (p. 10)
- rack jobber   (p. 9)
- singles   (p. 5)

- synchronization rights (p. 8)

Discussion Questions

1. Discuss the evolution of music into a formal "business," from church choirs of the Middle Ages to the modern enterprise in the 21st century.

2. In terms of creativity and distribution models, what's changed in the music business in recent years and what remains the same? Hint: one thing hasn't altered much but the other has experienced a radical upheaval.

3. What are some of the changes that have come about in the music industry as a result of new technology?

4. Discuss areas of the music business that still need to evolve in order to adequately adapt to the changing ways people are creating and accessing music.

CHAPTER 2

The Digital Millennium

For nearly a century, the modern music industry was forged by two then-new technologies—the phonograph record and broadcasting. In the late 20th century, a third force—digital technology[1]—emerged to shake the industry's foundations. Digital technology radically altered not only the business of music but also its creation, manufacture, distribution, and consumption. Furthermore, it changed the very culture of how music is created, with inexpensive technologies to record, present, distribute, promote, and play music, fashioning a unique artistic and commercial digital democracy, which drew music creator and music consumer closer even as it blurred the boundary between them.

> "The future is already here—it's just not very evenly distributed."
>
> —William Gibson

Digital's power was most graphically illustrated in the arena of distribution. When Philips and Sony collaborated on the development of the compact disc (**CD**) in the 1980s, no one could have predicted the extent to which digital technology, in combination with the Internet, would revolutionize the business. A few years later, the unauthorized **digital distribution** of music via early peer-to-peer (**P2P**) networks like Napster and Grokster, and by websites like The Pirate Bay and LimeWire, were big drivers behind the music industry sales slump that began with the new millennium. Global recorded music sales dropped by nearly half in the following decade. As a result, the digital millennium heralded an era of financial pain for the music industry.

Left: Steve Jobs unveils Apple's iPod Mini, 2004.

The Double-Edged Sword

From the onset, **digital recording** and distribution created a quagmire of conflicting benefits and disadvantages for the recording industry. On one hand, those making the actual recordings—recording artists, producers, and **engineers**—found in the digital medium freedom from the technical constraints of analog tape, including tape noise and limited dynamic range. Furthermore, as digital audio technology progressed, musicians and producers were given powerful new tools, such as digital signal processing systems (DSP)—digital reverbs, delays, samplers, looping, pitch-tuning, and editing capability—that vastly enhanced their ability to create and assemble sounds.

Record labels equally benefited. The CD was initially an expensive proposition to manufacture, and replication was concentrated in factories owned mainly by major record labels. The cost of a manufactured, packaged CD dropped quickly, from an estimated $2 per disc in 1988 to less than $1 by 2000. Thanks to sustained demand for CDs and early players being unable to record, however, the labels managed to maintain their retail prices and their substantial profit margin to a large extent throughout this period. At the same time, the labels' marketing strategy of releasing popular album titles from their vast catalogs was encouraging consumers to replace entire vinyl and cassette tape collections with the CD version, further stimulating sales of CDs and CD players (Sony and Philips, which then owned both record labels and consumer electronics divisions, derived double benefit from retail sales of CD players and from CD patent licensing royalties). Furthermore, when the CD was introduced in 1982 but was still unproven as a successful consumer format, labels were able to demand sales-royalty rate reductions from recording artists, ostensibly to help mitigate the legitimate cost of fostering the new technology but simultaneously increasing label profits.

However, digital's dark side quickly became apparent. While analog cassette tapes could be copied fewer than a dozen times before generational fidelity loss rendered them unusable, digital music, on a CD or in the form of an electronic file, could be copied—"cloned"—infinitely and distributed instantly with the click of a mouse anywhere in the world. Songs "**ripped**" from a CD that was paid for once could be redistributed an unlimited number of times for free. Understandably, this led to the double-digit percentage declines in record sales that decimated what had come to be known as the "legacy" (i.e., pre–digital era) music industry.

Internet Synergy

The growth of the Internet in the 1990s created a volatile proposition, providing a virtually unregulatable yet broadly accessible channel to distribute digitized music files between computers, known as P2P file sharing. Music **piracy** mushroomed, engendering financial losses in the hundreds of millions of dollars for labels, music publishers, and the artists, producers, musicians, and songwriters who depended on music sales for their livelihood.

A lengthy series of legal battles and buyouts left the major recording corporations in control of some of the most well-known file-sharing entities, including Napster, but the giant corporations had little in the way of innate organizational or entrepreneurial skills to turn these newly acquired entities to their own advantage. In fact, it would not be until 2011 that the decline in aggregate music sales would abate somewhat, thanks to digital download and streaming revenue rising to make up for much of the decline in physical media sales. However, piracy continued to negatively affect the music market, since according to the IFPI and Nielsen, one in four Internet users worldwide regularly accessed unlicensed services.

▪ Labels Sow Seeds of Self-Destruction

As the digital Pandora's box began to open years ago, the music industry fought back using legislation, litigation, and market propaganda. Several key pieces of digital technology legislation were passed in the United States. The Audio Home Recording Act (AHRA) of 1992 stipulated by whom and for what purposes digital copies could be legitimately made. The Digital Millennium Copyright Act (1998) was more comprehensive, particularly in establishing a mechanism for securing copyrighted music online. But legislation proved too weak to address the issue and furthermore revealed a growing divide between the digital Zeitgeist and legacy entities that had built fortunes on the foundation of inviolate **intellectual property.** Case in point: In 2012, the Stop Online Piracy Act (SOPA), whose provisions included allowing copyright holders to request court orders that would bar access to alleged infringing websites and far stricter penalties for infringers, was successfully blocked by a consortium of entities ranging from Google to library associations, who asserted that SOPA would lead to wholesale censorship of the Internet.

In 2007, the Record Industry Association of America (RIAA) turned to mass litigation. It sued colleges, universities (their central servers had become a popular file-sharing nexus among students, the largest cohort of early illicit downloaders), and individuals. The civil litigations were tactically successful but strategically dubious, causing public relations damage to the record industry as a whole. The RIAA eventually shifted to publicity campaigns to raise awareness about the implications of illegal music distribution.

The RIAA's efforts may have gone as far as they could. Digital rights management (**DRM**), file encryption, and the threat of litigation were deterrents to some casual file sharers, but they did little to affect the apparent hard-core file-sharing users who were likely to continue downloading illicitly. This legislative/litigious game of technological cat-and-mouse made one thing clear: The mechanisms of law and regulation simply could not keep up with the rapid innovation that digital technology brought to music. An on-demand mind-set was fostered among music consumers, who now wanted music whenever and wherever they decided, and thus ultimately changed the economic structure of the music industry. *The labels would have to adapt—if they could.*

▪ Smaller, Cheaper, Faster, Better (?)

At the heart of the digital music revolution is how digital technology changed the process of making music, from the relative confines of analog technology to the potentially infinite realm of digital's nonlinear universe.

In the late 1980s, computer-based **multitrack** recording and editing platforms began to proliferate, from companies including Steinberg (Nuendo, Cubase), Apple (Logic, Garageband), and Avid (whose Pro Tools system eventually came to dominate the field). Within a decade, software-based audio recording became ubiquitous. Analog tape, on which modern music recording had been founded, had become simply an expensive niche.

This had serious implications for the music industry. For one thing, it lessened the need for conventional recording studios. Records that once had to be made in multi-million-dollar facilities with complex acoustical designs and expensive equipment could now be made in homes and other personal spaces, using an expanding universe of inexpensive software-based recording and processing systems. Simultaneously, the ability to distribute and promote independent records using the Internet was greatly enhanced. This chipped away at the major labels' other putative advantage—their promotion, manufacturing, and distribution infrastructure. The independent record sector of the music business, which by the turn of the century accounted for nearly a quarter of all reported sales, began to threaten the power of the larger labels. Here are the consequences: The digital revolution enabled high-quality, low-cost recording and inexpensive online distribution that improves economics for aspiring and semi-professional musicians. But at the same time, digital technology is the catalyst for piracy that cut into recorded music sales of globally popular major-label artists. Digital democracy, indeed.

The Economics of Digital Distribution: Change and Evolution

Starting in the 1960s, the rise of pop music as a multi-million-dollar enterprise and the transformation of record production from a relatively straightforward process into a complex subculture created an economically distorted landscape. As rock music and later hip-hop genres became a larger force in popular culture, recordings were transformed into artistic sojourns, and the now lightly supervised recording process sometimes stretched into months and even years. Costs spiraled upward. With a larger array of technologically advanced and geographically diverse recording facilities, and a growing cadre of independent record producers to guide them, rock and pop music artists gained more autonomy over the making of their records. Record label **A&R** departments, which once routinely assigned producers to artists and chose their recording studios, transitioned to advancing artists lump-sum amounts to pay for their choice of producer and recording location(s) and as an advance on royalties (they hoped) to be earned back from the sale of those records. (Today, some even argue, who needs the expense and bureaucracy of A&R talent hunters when promising amateurs are showcased on TV talent shows and YouTube? TV shows instantly expose talent to a large audience and viewership data counters reveal who is a hit online.)

The numbers game of music production evolved into one that seems, in retrospect, odd, to say the least: Most of the thousands of recording artists signed by what were once a dozen or so major labels in the past nearly 50 years never recouped their costs. However, contracts almost always stipulated that the advanced monies could be recouped only from the sales of artists' records; that is, if an artist was dropped from a label, the debt remained with the recording, not the artist, who was free to sign with another label, if he or she could, and start the process all over again.

In a very real sense, record labels were acting as banks that, when they made "bad loans" (in the form of monetary advances for failed albums), forgave the debt; when they made successful products, those seemingly lucky artists found themselves relegated to a sort of decently paid sharecropper status (in a typical recording contract earning between 12% and 15% of wholesale). Nonetheless, despite the fact that record budgets continued to increase—particularly after the music video (which could sometimes cost as much as the album to produce) became an accepted part of artist promotion in the 1980s—the system worked—profits from successful records paid for the losses of failed ones with enough left over, most of the time, for a profit to the label. That is, until music file sharing undermined that economic model with its own undeniable logic: The more successful a recording was, the more it became the target of illicit downloading. Legacy record labels have implemented variations on this business model as they seek to offset these losses. One of these is a "**360 deal,**" which gives a label participation in the artist's revenues from concert-ticket and merchandise sales in exchange for larger advances and broader marketing support.

The New Economic Order

Digital technology and the Internet created a new economic paradigm for recording artists, one that enables far more artists to actually earn a living from making and selling music as independents outside the framework of the traditional business architecture. Digital recording technologies reduce the artist's reliance on major label funding, and the Internet creates a pathway for artists to directly market and distribute their recordings.

Digital democracy comes at a price, however. While the power implicit in the software tools of digital music and the unprecedented reach of the Internet have created a "backstage pass" past the music industry's traditional gatekeepers, like A&R executives and managers, some argue that what has been lost is the filtering process that the legacy record industry offered. In the previous era, bands and artists had to run a gamut of self-financed steps—demos, club **gigs,** and so on—to attract initial record label interest. From there, artists had to prove themselves to successive levels of label hierarchy, at the same time pursuing business management, agency representation, and other necessities. As economically anomalous and inflexible as the old record industry business model had become, it had also served as a development ground for several generations of well-trained "ears" who knew what it took to make a hit record and recognize talent—executives like Doug Morris, who once sold records for his independent label from the trunk of his car and later became chairman and CEO of Universal Music Group, or Clive Davis, former president of Columbia Records and later founder of Arista Records. As the influence of these gatekeepers receded, vastly greater numbers of records have been released into the market even as overall unit sales decline—the flip side of digital democracy. To many, this inversion has actually undermined the perceived value of music itself.

iTunes Arrives

Near the turn of the century, the most robust new business model for the music industry emerged from a computer company, which was both appropriate and ironic, given the computer's central place in the upheaval of the music business. Apple's iTunes was a way to legitimize and monetize music file downloading.

The economics were cut and dried: Labels received a fixed amount from each sale, approximately two-thirds of $0.99 single-song downloads, with that formula more or less extrapolated for complete digital album sales. However, the labels lobbied vigorously for Apple to raise its prices, a move that Apple resisted until 2008, when a reformulated agreement between iTunes and the labels resulted in both sides compromising on two key points: Apple would for the first time permit a variable pricing scheme, keeping the $0.99 128-KB-resolution single-song download and adding a

$1.29 price point for higher quality downloads at 256 KB, as well as a $0.69 price for back-catalog songs, applicable at the labels' discretion. For their part, the record labels agreed to let Apple remove embedded DRM code from the song files.

iTunes created the template for an entirely new music distribution system, one followed by other retailers, including Amazon.com and Wal-Mart. But it also established another trend that was ultimately detrimental to conventional record labels, which had built much of their revenue from the sale of CDs to consumers who often bought a CD just to access one or two favorite songs. Now consumers could simply buy the few songs they really wanted. Thus, even though music unit sales began to slowly rise, as legitimate single-song downloading increased, overall record-label revenues continued to stagger along an uncertain path.

Streaming

The iPhone was the vanguard emblematic of a wave of synergy between music and mobile devices that continues unabated, generating billions of dollars annually for a web of stakeholders, including device makers, operating system developers, wireless network providers, record labels, and content producers, including music creators. Today, all major mobile service providers offer access to online music via apps from **streaming** music providers such as Spotify and Pandora. This represents a transitioning from the download model, in which consumers buy individual songs as downloads and store them on their devices or in "cloud"-based **digital lockers** (remote servers often operated by third-party companies) to a streaming model in which consumers can access all the music available from a specific content aggregator at any time through any of their devices for a monthly subscription fee. Digital lockers allow users to permanently store and then endlessly access their owned music via all their authenticated devices. Streaming offers a large inventory of music that is essentially rented.

The streaming business model (or rental), however, continues the trend of reducing revenues for music rights owners and artists—whereas copyright owners would earn about 70% of the proceeds of a $0.69 to $1.29 sale per **track** through iTunes, they earn a few cents or fraction of a cent per streaming play, as do recording artists. According to data compiled by former JupiterResearch analyst Mark Mulligan, music artists must rack up 80 to 200 music streams to earn royalties equivalent to one download, leading some major artists to refuse to license their music for streaming. However, while that represents a significant decrease in per-play revenue for songwriters and publishers compared to what they earn through terrestrial radio **airplay,** it's found money for nonauthor artists, who in the United States earn nothing directly from radio airplay.

Music—its creation, realization, and distribution—is now almost entirely a digital proposition. Companies and individuals who understand the dynamics of digital commerce are best poised to exploit that dramatically changed paradigm.

Consolidation

Merger and acquisition activity has been common within the music industry throughout its history. It accelerated in the 1970s as existing major labels acquired smaller ones to increase their market penetration (such as Sony Corporation's buy of Columbia Records in 1988), acquire its catalog assets (such as the sale of Motown to MCA that same year), or as a creative resource (a role David Geffen's Asylum Records played for Warner Bros. in the 1970s). This trend continued into the 21st century, although it was fueled more by the need to reduce costs in the face of the digitally driven music business. In 1998, there were six majors: Warner Music Group, EMI, Sony Music, BMG Music, Universal Music Group, and PolyGram. By 2012, Universal absorbed PolyGram, Sony merged with BMG, and Universal Music Group acquired EMI Records' recorded music assets.

On the concert side, it's the same story. Live Nation and AEG dominate the business of promoting national concert tours after being consolidators. They control a big chunk of concert venues, but it doesn't stop there. Live Nation owns national ticketing behemoth Ticketmaster and has gobbled up over 100 personal managers that guide careers of music acts that headline in its arenas. That's *vertical integration,* putting many different facets of the same business (the vertical part) under one roof (integrated together). With size, Live Nation is a magnet for $300 million a year in advertising and sponsorships and also controls huge online consumer traffic with its website properties.

The benefits of consolidation are greater efficiency as more business gets funneled through a single sales organization, and costs of administration are better supported by a large underlying business. In the music business, many act on the belief that size does matter.

Where the Money Is Today

Not all the recent changes that have reshaped recent music business economics are bleak. The concert business remains healthy, and lucrative niches have opened up. Britney Spears took an artist-in-residence gig at Planet Hollywood in Las Vegas, reportedly earning $15 million a year. Her booking is part of a trend of recording artists getting big paychecks as regular performers in the growing field of gambling casino theaters (more states and municipalities have legalized gambling). Not a musical headliner? No problem. Get a job as a performer for cruise lines that regularly mount musical stage productions at sea, letting you get a paycheck and see the world.

Trending opposite the downturn in recorded music, music publishing income actually has been growing as movies and TV programs, commercials, and other audiovisual productions license underlying rights to popular tunes. Synchronous rights—using the original hit version—also generates some fat paydays. Nissan paid $1 million for Harry Chapin's hit version of "Cat's in the Cradle" for one of the automaker's Super Bowl TV commercials. Also springing up amid recorded music's economic funk is the boom in electronic dance music (**EDM**), which made millionaires out of the most talented disc jockeys dishing out recorded music to concert audiences and spawning mammoth music festivals. Music is on the lips and in the hearts of consumers around the world, so it's no surprise these pockets of economic strength emerge.

The Digital Future

The upheaval that the music industry experienced in recent years is in some ways rather familiar. Every technology-led revolution of the past two centuries—railroads, telephones, electricity, the Internet—experienced similar stages of evolution: an embryonic, high-tech stage (limited accessibility, technology rapidly evolving), an entrepreneurial stage (technology stabilizes and attracts capital), an explosive growth stage (numerous commercial startups and multiple business models appear, a stage many consider the music industry to be occupying now), and a consolidation phase (the participants are fewer but the entities are larger because of mergers and acquisitions, a stage legacy record labels exploited successfully in decades past).

But the digital revolution, while following familiar business patterns, has also changed the attitude of more than a generation of music consumers, perhaps irrevocably. For instance, the ease with which digital distribution made music freely accessible has created a culture in which music is often perceived as being free of cost. The public often perceived a legal conflict as one between corporate hegemony and individual rights, a situation that encouraged a widely held perception that the cost of music product was out of proportion to the cost of making it.

Ultimately, as the encrusted shell of the old music business disintegrates, digital technology has made the music business an entrepreneurial one once again. With access to affordable production of music and digital distribution less encumbered by the capital and logistical requirements of manufacturing and physical distribution, the music industry has become less mythical and more accessible to more people. As a result of digital, the music business may have shed some of its mystique and glamour, but in the process, it has become a viable career choice in more ways and for more people than ever before.

Note

1. While the term *digital* was originally only used to contrast with *analog,* many in the industry today use it informally to embrace all forms of new, nonphysical media and their associated business models. Strictly speaking, the CD, the leading physical format of the age, is itself a digital format and distinct from the analog LP and cassette formats it supplanted.

Chapter Takeaways

- Digital technology has been a double-edged sword, improving the ability to produce new sounds but threatening the established order of distributing recorded music.

- Overwhelmed by the free-on-demand mindset sweeping cyberspace, record labels eventually backed away from antipiracy mass litigation and digital rights management (DRM) as enforcement tools.

- The democratization of the music business has diminished the importance of the gatekeeper function of key record label personnel.

- Streaming subscription services rose in importance and popularity in the early years of the 21st century.

- The major labels were largely caught flat-footed in the digital age, watching with alarm as technology companies such as Apple, Pandora, and Spotify pioneered disruptive business paths.

Key Terms

- 360 deal   (p. 17)
- electronic dance music (EDM)   (p. 19)
- digital lockers   (p. 18)
- digital rights management (DRM)   (p. 15)
- intellectual property   (p. 15)
- P2P   (p. 13)
- piracy   (p. 14)
- streaming   (p. 18)

Discussion Questions

1. With the shift to digital media, explain why aspiring and semi-pro musicians with recording aspirations were helped and why the major recorded music labels suffered.

2. Recorded music revenue slumped with the advent of digital media, but what other parts of the music business have enjoyed good economic times in recent years?

3. What changes do you anticipate in the digital music business in the next decade?

4. What can record labels change in order to profit through digital media?

CHAPTER 3

The Music Business System

The music industry can be described as having two essential elements: the musician and the audience. Drawing them together is the business of music. Despite the distracting spotlight of changing technology, the music industry continues to operate much like other large, multifaceted commercial activities. A main difference between the music business and most other industries is, of course, its artistically driven "product" and the constant tug of hair-trigger cultural shifts. In examining the business aspects of music, it is the rapid change of product that makes this business almost unique.

> "I would rather play 'Chiquita Banana' and have my swimming pool than play Bach and starve."
>
> —Xavier Cugat

▰ Help Wanted!

Over the years, transformational technology has reshaped the way people in the music business organize themselves to make a living. A century ago, a music publisher manufactured and shipped vast quantities of paper to retail stores throughout the land. Today, a publisher might be the part-time vocation of a songwriter, whose assets reside entirely on a hard drive. A half-century ago, a record company exploited just about the only path to putting recorded music, for a fee, in the hands of consumers. Today, some idiosyncratic artists—either with no recording contract in the offing or disenchanted with their last contract—might record in a home studio, manufacture on a CD burner, and sell the resulting handiwork via download or mail order

---

Left: Riffs that make the crowd go wild.

Photo © PeopleImages.

through their own website. A few decades ago, the nuanced performance of a large ensemble required having dozens of musicians on the payroll. Today, one or only a handful of musicians and **MIDI** controllers might provide a similar performance. The economists call this trend increased productivity. The old guard fears it, for jobs are jeopardized and investors traumatized. But with change also comes opportunity.

Even if aided by semiconductors and the Internet, a human being must still make the music, a human being must market and promote it, and human talent is the key ingredient all along the **value chain** between the original creative idea and the ears and eyes of a fan.

Getting Through the Maze

To analyze that value chain in detail, let's consider two different ways of viewing the industry as a whole. First, study the flowchart shown in Figure 3.1. It graphically illustrates the music business system and its principal subsystems.

A second way of grasping the big picture is to examine the sequence of events that often occurs as a new song finds its way to market. As you will observe, the following list sets forth much of the same information appearing on the flowchart in Figure 3.1.

1. The composer—who sometimes is also the performing artist—writes a song and signs with a publisher.

2. The publisher persuades an artist (or that artist's producer) to record the song.

3. Lawyers (at several stages) negotiate contracts between parties and specify terms for varying forms of usage and exploitation, such as **mechanical rights** and **synchronization licenses**.

4. The record company produces a recording and, possibly, a video version of the song.

5. **Promoters** persuade programmers to broadcast the audio recording and the video.

6. The record company uploads the song for online sale and ships the merchandise to **distributors,** who sell it to retailers.

7. In cases where artists retain distribution rights, artists sell music from their websites and negotiate deals directly with download and/or streaming digital platforms.

8. If the song becomes popular, a second wave of **exploitation** can occur—licensing of ringtones and merchandise connected to the song and/or artist.

9. A talent agency contacts promoters and books a concert tour.

10. Concert promoters enlist cosponsors and sell the tickets.

11. The road manager moves the people and the equipment.

12. The concert production manager dresses the stage, lights it, and reinforces the sound.

13. The artists perform.

14. The performing rights organizations collect performance **royalties**.

15. The accountants count the money; the participants pay their bills.

16. The government collects the taxes.

Figure 3.1   The Music Business System and Selected Principal Subsystems

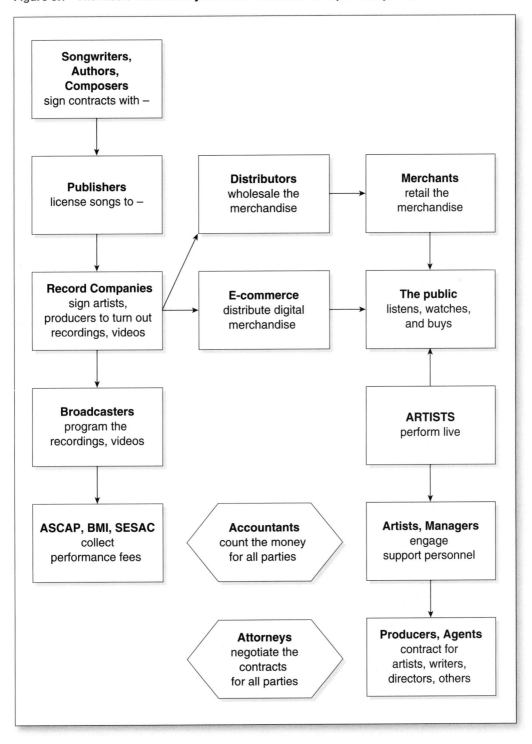

Figure 3.2 U.S. Music Industry Revenue: Select Segments (Estimate of Billions of Dollars Annually)

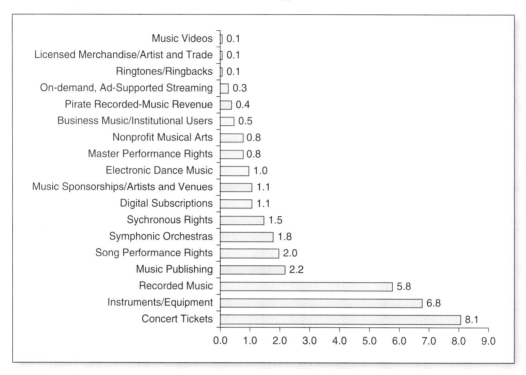

Sources: Compiled in part from Billboard, Recording Industry Association of America, Pollstar, National Association of Music Merchants, National Music Publishers Association, PwC's Entertainment & Media Outlook 2015–2019, SoundExchange, and other industry sources.

Notes: Figures include double counting of some revenue in overlapping categories, rounded to nearest hundred million dollars. Receipts for U.S. consumption or exploitation only, except where noted otherwise. Recorded Music is consumer revenue estimate of all audio-only physical and digital formats. Instruments/Equipment is consumer-spend revenue. Concert Tickets includes the face value of tickets for national tours as well as sales in the secondary market. Business Music covers services piping in recorded music to businesses and institutions. Song Performance Rights are fees to publishers and composers for using their copyrighted works that are handled primarily by collection agencies ASCAP, BMI, and SESAC. Synchronous Rights are U.S. licenses (which may include some worldwide rights) for use of copyrighted audio recordings embedded in such media as films, TV programs, and commercials. Master Performance Rights are fees to artists and labels for public performance of recordings, collected in the United States by SoundExchange. Nonprofit Musical Arts are independent music and dance entities. Pirated Music estimates money changing hands and does not impute value lost from all pirate activity. Ringtones/Ringbacks include a variety of categories sometimes referred to as personalization services. Sponsorship revenue excludes bartered or in-kind services.

Show Me the Money

Many people would say the making of music hasn't changed much in centuries—since it's still all about a catchy tune performed by talented artists. Placing aside the obvious changes wrought by technology, the big transformation has been in the scale of the business. The music industry has mushroomed into an interconnected series of segmented multi-billion-dollar businesses in the United States (not even counting the intertwining of an even bigger business abroad!). These businesses range from traditional recorded music to live concerts to sale of musical instruments and equipment to cell phone **ringtones.** As we'll learn in the pages to come, success often springs from moving back and forth from one business "silo" to another. But in order to understand the industry, we'll want to examine, chapter by chapter, each silo for the role it plays and the unique career opportunities it presents. Figure 3.2 shows just a sampling of the scores of segmented businesses. Many billions of dollars flow from business to business, as one sector's revenue (such as a composer's royalty receipts) is another sector's expense (a publisher's royalty expense). Thus, the same "music dollar" may at one time or another end up in the pockets of multiple industry participants.

Tools of the Trade: Everybody's Gotta Learn Sometime

Now that we see how big the industry is, and how diverse, how do we stay on top of it? Although being—and staying—informed has always been important in the music industry (or any industry, for that matter), in times of rapid change, it is vital. A new trend, technology, or development that seemingly has little to do with a particular segment of the business may well suggest a new means of promotion, a potentially profitable new partnership, or an additional income stream to pursue. New types of licensing deals and previously unheard-of music distribution methods bring with them new twists and turns on **copyright** and royalties issues—issues that could mean money in (or out of) the pockets of numerous music business players. And, of course, job seekers looking for an "in" will need to know what new doors might be open to them and how best to educate and market themselves.

It is one of the great mysteries of the contemporary music scene, then, that many of those involved in it—composers, performers, businesspeople, educators—do not understand how it really works. Worse yet, much of what they believe they "know" is either out of date or incorrect. The result of this pervasive ignorance about the business

Students in MIDI Lab at the University of North Alabama.
Photo by Dr. Robert A. Garfrerick.

and the profession has been tragic. Top graduates of conservatories fail to get their careers even started. Aspiring business-side candidates lack the big-picture smarts and specialized savvy to succeed in a competitive label environment. Musicians navigating the DIY waters fall victim to sharks and their own lack of knowledge when relying solely on their own ingenuity.

So what does the artist or the business executive do to get the information needed to function effectively in this field? Take the time to regularly read about music business, professional, and creative developments that are readily available online. Bookmark the websites that consistently deliver relevant information. Another source is the various professional meetings. These national (and international) affairs are sponsored by industry associations, trade magazines, and sometimes by artists' unions. Most have websites (you'll find a listing of the major associations and their sites inside the back cover of this book), offering industry overviews, news, and information, along with current research and publications to download or request (some free of charge, others for a fee). Specialized information can also be found in books on subjects such as copyright and pop songwriting; many of the industry associations' sites offer sector-specific suggestions.

The Web offers a wealth of information, although you'll need to wade through a lot of junk to find the truly helpful gems (something to which anyone who has gone trolling for music online can attest). The best bets are a handful of well-respected blogs, some of which focus on the creative and others on the business side of music. Because websites come and go, asking around for recommendations—from fellow musicians, instructors, industry-connected friends of friends—can point to the cream of the current crop.

The most reliable sources of information for the serious student can be found in a select group of colleges, universities, and specialized institutions.[1] Following the leadership of the University of Miami in the mid-1960s, increasing numbers of accredited institutions are offering courses and degrees in the music business field. Course offerings include studies in music, certainly, but also in areas as diverse as business administration, accounting, marketing, business law, copyright, arts administration, and recording technology. Graduates of these programs cannot know it all, of course. But they are far better prepared than others to meet the wide-ranging demands of today's music industry.

And then there is the option of going to the source. Qualified professionals in the business can be found throughout North America, although many are concentrated in one of the three major recording centers—New York, Nashville, or Los Angeles—where the big music companies have their U.S. headquarters. Most of the music business, even today, is based on the star system—specifically, the recording star system—and these cities remain the high-powered nexus.

• • • The Musician-Entrepreneur: Prospering by Constantly Adapting

While our analysis of the music business necessarily presents a close-up view of the many specializations—from songwriting, to producing concerts, to monetizing downloads—the untold story of the industry is that sustained career success often is *not* due to mastery of one specialized garden of knowledge. Frequently, success over the years and decades comes from an adaptability to hop from specialty to specialty.

That's the case for Gene Perla, who has made a living in the many nooks and crannies of the music industry available to a jazz bassist throughout his career—Broadway show sound designer, music publishing company founder, recording studio entrepreneur, songwriter, studio musician, and music teacher.

"Sure, I like to sit back and come up with the 'grand concepts,'" he says of what drove him to work in so many music segments. "But I also like to deal with the nuts and bolts as well. I like to do the futzing and fudging about with things so I really understand them."

Gene Perla
Photo by Richard Stopa.

After several years of musical instrument higher education, Perla broke onto the New York jazz scene as a bass player in the 1960s. Hoping to distribute the music of friends who could not get a record deal, he decided he needed to know how albums are made, so he enrolled in a technical school in Manhattan to study recording engineering. One night after class while relaxing in a night club where he sometimes performed, a stranger who recognized him from recording performances offered him a job at Todd Rundgren's famous Secret Sound Studio. It was at Secret Sound, not formal classes, that Perla really learned recording through a series of from-the-ground-up jobs.

Years later, another chance meeting with a stranger led to a teaching job at another New York multimedia school, where Perla took advantage of a faculty perk that allowed teachers to take other classes free of charge. He learned video production and computer graphics, among many skills.

Still a performing musician making contacts in gigs around town, Perla eventually played bass and had two of his songs recorded for the Blue Note jazz album, *Genesis,* by Elvin Jones (famous as the drummer in the band of the late John Coltrane). Perla had already registered those songs with the U.S. Copyright Office—which was and remains a simple process—but then went the extra step of creating his own publishing company to license the songs. Today, his Perla Music is a money-maker and has a catalog with 100 compositions, for which he sells sheet music at $3 a PDF download from his website. ASCAP administers other aspects of Perla Music.

Along the way, with skills learned in jobs, in schools, and from personal contacts as a working musician, Perla established the Red Gate recording facility just outside of New York. His partner in this venture was Jan Hammer, keyboardist for the Mahavishnu Orchestra and composer of the *Miami Vice* theme song. Perla also established a small music label, PM Records. After another chance meeting, he was called to make an emergency rescue of a Broadway production just hours before show time. His tech knowledge enabled him to untangle a Musical Instrument Digital Interface (MIDI) setup whose otherwise bright software engineer messed up with improper cabling.

With that experience, he and partner Bernard Fox started their own sound design business for other stage productions such as *Beauty and the Beast, The Lion King,* and *City of Angels.* Sound designers provide equipment, billing shows weekly for service. Some $125,000 of microphones were purchased to service a show that promptly closed after just seven performances, but Perla wasn't fazed. "It worked out all right because we were doing other shows," he says.

(Continued)

(Continued)

He left Broadway for a lucrative business rerecording dialog in a studio for prime-time network TV series, fixing street scenes with audio problems in what is known as automatic dialog replacement (ADR).

Today, Perla operates a computer services consultancy from his home in Easton, Pennsylvania, from where he commutes to teach and perform. He teaches music business, Sibelius software, and bass at the New School for Jazz and Contemporary Music and Lehigh University. Perla also still plays gigs locally, regionally, and internationally with several of his own bands and other artists.

Perla is nonchalant about his dizzyingly diverse career, saying only, "I am persistent," while also crediting education and some chance meetings.

Comparing the music landscape today versus when he broke in, Perla says that universities are churning out so many skilled jazz bassists that the competition for live gigs—where he got his start and made a living—is intense and the pay is therefore miserable. His advice to freshly graduated jazz musicians is not to be afraid to take jobs on the technological edge of music—such as telecom and multimedia companies—which are the Wild West frontier for music today. The graduates "may not be performing, but they will still be connected to the music," he says.

Only a limited number of performers can attain star status, of course, so it is fortunate that the music business system offers many opportunities for individuals needed to help make the system function. No performer today can ascend to stardom or hang there in orbit without an array of qualified supporting satellites.

Whether as a star or as one of the myriad categories of supporting players, many (although not all) ambitious newcomers do make it. Why: Luck? Timing? Education? Networking skills? These factors have helped launch many successful careers in both the creative and business ends of the field. Four other factors contribute to the success of those who "win" in the music business:

1. They are strongly motivated; they really want to win.

2. They are talented—and they surround themselves with talented associates.

3. They persevere; they hang in there until they succeed.

4. They study the business for insights on the creative process, career trajectory, and industry economics.

The first three items depend totally on you. This book deals only with Item 4. The music business offers excellent career opportunities for the really talented individual, provided that individual gets the important information—and acts on it. The essential core of that information is offered here.

Note

1. A valuable source displaying educational institutions in the field is the listing of member schools on the website of the Music and Entertainment Industry Educators Association: www.meiea.org.

Chapter Takeaways

- The music industry can be viewed as a series of sectors and distinct types of businesses that feed off each other, such as record labels and live concerts.

- The same "music dollar" often passes from one industry participant to another.

- Over the course of a career, people in the business often move back and forth from one work category (composer) to another (publisher).

- Music business students should seek out a wide range of information, from different sources, to stay on top of a field that shifts rapidly.

Key Terms

- copyright   (p. 27)
- exploitation   (p. 24)
- mechanical rights   (p. 24)
- royalties   (p. 24)
- synchronization licenses (p. 24)
- value chain   (p. 24)

Discussion Questions

1. Outline areas where music is a dollars-and-cents business and not an art.

2. Discuss technical areas where someone entering the music business can gain a foothold.

3. What are some ways in which different areas of the music business depend on each other?

4. What are some changes that are happening in the music business today? What changes might happen in 10 years?

Copyright, Songwriting, Publishing, and Licensing

PART 2

Music Copyright

Every serious student of copyright should acquire a complete copy of the Copyright Act, together with other special publications and bulletins relating to copyright. In addition to the act, Circular 1 (Copyright Basics) and Circular 50 (Copyright Registration for Musical Compositions) are especially useful. These documents are available on the Copyright Office website at www.copyright.gov. The Copyright Office Public Information Office number is (202) 707-3000. If legal advice or other expert assistance is required, the services of a competent professional should be sought.

"Music is spiritual. The music business is not."

—Van Morrison

Background

Songwriters, recording artists, music producers, performers, and almost all others in the music industry care about copyright. As much as anything else, it provides the statutory structure that enables creatives in all aspects of the business to put food on their table, sometimes amounting to a generous banquet. Copyright is a form of protection provided by the laws of the United States for **intellectual property**, including works of literature, songs, recordings, art, and other forms of creativity. Copyright literally means "the right to copy." The term has come to mean that body of exclusive rights granted by law to authors for protection of their work. Article I,

---

Left: Congressman Sonny Bono. The singer-songwriter had a major change in copyright law named after him months after his death in 1998.

Photo © Jeffrey Markowitz/Sygma/Corbis.

Section 8 of the Constitution gives Congress the power to enact laws establishing a system of copyright in the United States, and Congress enacted the first U.S. copyright law in 1790. Comprehensive revisions were enacted in 1831, 1870, and 1909, and the current Copyright Act, enacted by Congress in 1976 (U.S. Code, Title 17, Copyrights), became generally effective on January 1, 1978.

As we'll see throughout this book, copyright issues have an enormous effect on many of the essential components of the music business, including the writing, publishing, recording, and performance of songs and other musical material. While no work can be automatically copyrighted worldwide, two international treaties have brought cooperation from countries on copyright matters. The United States became a party to the Universal Copyright Convention in 1955 and to the Berne Convention in 1989, both of which have greatly enhanced the protection of its copyrights internationally (see Chapter 31).

Tempered by the political jostling of powerful adversaries in the 1970s, the goal of Congress was to seek a balance of interests between copyright owners and users.[1] This search for fairness took place under the watchful eye and with the vigorous participation of a number of special interest groups representing the motion picture, music, radio, and TV industries as well as educators, librarians, the cable industry, and others. When ultimately enacting the 1976 Copyright Act, Congress stated its intent that the implementation of the law "would minimize any disruptive impact on the structure of the industries involved and on generally prevailing industry practices."[2]

The 1976 act has been interpreted in widely varying ways by the different courts, and it is useful to remember that copyright law involves not only examining the "letter of the law" but also developing persuasive *interpretations* of the statute. Copyright law has also evolved through new statutes written by Congress and through interpretations by the courts in previous cases (legal precedent). The ultimate authority in all matters relating to U.S. copyright law is, of course, the U.S. Constitution as interpreted by the Supreme Court.

To explore the broader landscape of copyright law, it is necessary to first become familiar with the law's basic terms and provisions.

Essential Provisions

Following are seven essential provisions of the 1976 act and subsequent amendments:

1. The statute preempts nearly all other copyright laws—both statutory and **common law.** Therefore, only the federal Copyright Act can provide protection for most types of works. One notable exception is pre-1972 sound recordings, which are not protected by the Copyright Act. This class of recordings can only be protected under state law.

2. The duration of copyright has been lengthened over the years and now conforms closely to practices prevailing throughout most of the rest of the world: generally, life of the author plus 70 years for works created on or after January 1, 1978.

3. There is no exclusive right for the public performance of sound recordings. That is why under the 1976 act, no royalties for use of sound recordings are paid to copyright owners of sound recordings. However, the act was amended in the 1990s to provide a **digital transmission** right for sound recordings. This addition to the act provides that the copyright owners of sound recordings are paid

for performances by digital transmission such as on satellite radio or webcast. (The act does provide an exclusive public performance right for musical works, also known as *songs*, and any performance of a song—live, on broadcast radio and TV, and venues from churches to arenas—earns performance royalties.)

4. Public broadcasters, cable systems, and jukebox operators were compelled to begin paying for the use of copyrighted music, as were schools and colleges. As a by-product of accession to the Berne Convention in 1989, the law was later amended to provide for **negotiated licenses** between jukebox operators and music copyright owners (through performing rights organizations) rather than statutorily mandated **compulsory licenses.**

5. Certain uses that would otherwise be copyright infringement are excused as "fair use" under the act, which codified the principles previously enunciated in case law. Four distinct factors (detailed later in this chapter) are considered by the courts in determining the applicability of the fair use defense, and courts may also look to other factors as appropriate to a particular case.

6. Policies and rates of music use licenses were to be periodically reexamined.

7. Some formal procedures, such as copyright notice and renewal, were treated more permissively, and others were eliminated.

Key Terms

An understanding of copyright—as with all legal issues—depends on awareness of how the current law defines its terms. Most of the definitions that follow are quoted directly from Section 101 of the Copyright Act. (Language not relating to music has been deleted.)

"Audiovisual works" are works that consist of a series of related images intended to be shown via projectors, viewers, or electronic equipment, together with accompanying sounds, if any.

The **"best edition"** of a work is the edition, published in the United States at any time before the date of deposit, that the Library of Congress determines to be the most suitable for its purposes.

A **"collective work"** is a work, such as a periodical issue, anthology, or encyclopedia, in which a number of contributions, constituting separate and independent works in themselves, are assembled into a collective whole.

A **"compilation"** is a work formed by the collection and assembling of preexisting materials selected, coordinated, or arranged in such a way that the resulting work as a whole constitutes an original work of authorship. A compilation can also be a collective work.

"Copies" are material objects, other than phonorecords, in which a work is fixed and from which the work can be perceived, reproduced, or otherwise communicated, either directly or with the aid of a machine or device.

"Copyright owner [proprietor]," with respect to any one of the exclusive rights comprised in a copyright, refers to the owner of that particular right.

A work is **"created"** when it is fixed in a copy or phonorecord for the first time; where a work is prepared over a period of time, the portion that has been fixed at any particular time constitutes the work as of that time, and where the work has been prepared in different versions, each version constitutes a separate work.

A **"derivative work"** is a work based on one or more preexisting works, such as a musical arrangement, dramatization, fictionalization, motion picture version, sound recording, or any other form in which a work may be recast, transformed, or adapted. A work consisting of editorial revisions, annotations, elaborations, or other modifications that, as a whole, represent an original work of authorship is a derivative work.

A **"device," "machine,"** or **"process"** is one now known or later developed.

A **"digital phonorecord delivery"**[3] is a delivery of the content of a phonorecord by digital transmission that results in an identifiable reproduction by any recipient, whether via a public performance of the recording or a nondramatic musical work. This does not include real-time subscription transmission of a recording where no reproduction is made.

To **"display"** a work means to show a copy of it, either directly or by means of a film, slide, television image, or any other device or process or, in the case of a motion picture or other audiovisual work, to show individual images nonsequentially.

An **"establishment"** is a store, shop, or any similar place of business open to the general public in which the majority of its nonresidential space is used for the primary purpose of selling goods or services and in which nondramatic musical works are performed publicly.

A work is **"fixed"** in a tangible medium of expression when its embodiment in a copy or phonorecord, by or under the authority of the author, is sufficiently permanent or stable to permit it to be perceived, reproduced, or otherwise communicated for a period of more than transitory duration. A work consisting of sounds, images, or both that are being transmitted is "fixed" for purposes of this title if a fixation of the work is being made simultaneously with its transmission.

A **"food service or drinking establishment"** is a restaurant, inn, bar, tavern, or any other similar place of business in which the public or patrons assemble for the primary purpose of being served food or drink in which the majority of the gross square feet of space that is nonresidential is used for that purpose and in which nondramatic musical works are performed publicly.

To **"perform"** a work means to recite, render, play, dance, or act it, either directly or by means of any device or process, or, in the case of a motion picture or other audiovisual work, to show its images or to make the sounds accompanying it audible.

"Phonorecords" are material objects in which sounds, other than those accompanying a motion picture or other audiovisual work, are fixed by any method now known or later developed and from which the sounds can be perceived, reproduced, or otherwise communicated, either directly or with the aid of a machine or device. The term *phonorecord* applies to the material object, such as a CD, in which the sounds are fixed.

A **"pseudonymous work"** is a work of which the author is identified under a fictitious name.

"Publication" is the distribution of copies or phonorecords of a work to the public by sale or other transfer of ownership, or by rental, lease, or lending. Publication is also the *offering* to distribute copies or phonorecords to a group of persons for purposes of further distribution, public performance, or public display, although a public performance or display of a work does not constitute publication.

To perform or display a work **"publicly"** means the following:

1. to perform or display it at a place open to the public or at any place where a substantial number of persons outside of a normal circle of a family and its social acquaintances are gathered; or

2. to transmit or otherwise communicate a performance or display of the work to a place specified by clause (1) or to the public, by means of any device or process, whether the members of the public capable of receiving the performance or display receive it in the same place or in separate places and at the same time or at different times.

"Registration" means a registration of a claim in the original or the renewed and extended term of copyright.

"Sound recordings" are works that result from the fixation of a series of musical, spoken, or other sounds but not including the sounds accompanying a motion picture or other audiovisual work, regardless of the nature of the material objects, such as discs, tapes, or other phonorecords, in which they are embodied.

A **"transfer of copyright ownership"** is any conveyance, such as an assignment or license, of the exclusive rights comprised in a copyright, whether or not it is limited in time or place of effect, but not including a nonexclusive license.

A **"transmission program"** is a body of material that has been produced for the sole purpose of transmission to the public in sequence and as a unit.

To **"transmit"** a performance or display is to communicate it by any device or process whereby images or sounds are received beyond the place from which they are sent.

A **"work made for hire"** is (a) a work prepared by an employee within the scope of his or her employment or (b) a work specially ordered or commissioned for use as a contribution to a collective work, as a part of a motion picture or other audiovisual work, as a translation, as a supplementary work, as a compilation, as an instructional text, as a test, as answer material for a test, or as an atlas, if the parties agree in writing that the work shall be considered a work made for hire. A "supplementary work" is one prepared for publication as a secondary adjunct to a work by another author for the purpose of introducing, concluding, illustrating, explaining, revising, commenting upon, or assisting in the use of the other work, such as a musical arrangement.

Coverage

It is important to note that copyright protection does not extend to ideas themselves, but only to the expression of those ideas. For example, no one can copyright the idea of "reggae music," but a particular expression of that genre (say, a reggae song by Ziggy Marley) may be protected. The fact that no one can copyright an idea itself (the beat, the general concepts defining the genre, etc.) allows the normal development of musical forms, which always includes elements borrowed from other sources. It is the unauthorized exploitation of a particular artist's expression of an idea that is prohibited.

Copyright protection is granted to original works of authorship. As noted above, such works must be "fixed in any tangible medium of expression, from which they can be perceived, reproduced, or otherwise communicated, either directly or with the aid of a machine or device." Works of authorship include the following categories:[4]

Literary works

Musical works, including any accompanying words

Dramatic works, including any accompanying music

Pantomimes and choreographic works

Pictorial, graphic, and sculptural works

Motion pictures and other audiovisual works

Sound recordings

Architectural works

The works listed above are subject to protection under the law even if unpublished, without regard to the nationality or domicile of the author.

Copyright protection can also cover compilations and derivative works, but this protection does not apply to material that has been used unlawfully. Also, copyright in compilations and derivative works extends only to the material contributed by the author of such work (as distinguished from preexisting material employed in the work) and does not imply any exclusive right in the preexisting material. The copyright in compilations and derivative works is independent of and does not affect or enlarge the scope, duration, ownership, or subsistence of any copyright protection in the preexisting material.

Copyright does not extend to publications of the U.S. government. An individual may reproduce or quote from such publications without concern for copyright infringement.

Exclusive Rights

Section 106 of the Copyright Act specifies six distinct exclusive rights vested in the author of a protected work. Subject to certain limitations,[5] the act states that the owner of copyright has the exclusive right to do and to authorize any of the following:

(1) to reproduce the copyrighted work in copies or phonorecords;

(2) to prepare derivative works based on the copyrighted work;

(3) to distribute copies or phonorecords of the copyrighted work to the public by sale or other transfer of ownership or by rental, lease, or lending;

(4) in the case of literary, musical, dramatic, and choreographic works, panto-mimes, and motion pictures and other audiovisual works, to perform the copyrighted work publicly;

(5) in the case of literary, musical, dramatic, and choreographic works, panto-mimes, and pictorial, graphic, or sculptural works, including the individual images of a motion picture or other audiovisual work, to display the copy-righted work publicly; and

(6) in the case of sound recordings, to perform the copyrighted work publicly by means of a digital audio transmission.

These are often referred to as the **bundle of rights.**

Fair Use of Copyrighted Material

With this law, Congress sought to reconcile the rightful interests of the copyright owners with the interests of society in reviewing, studying, commenting on, and reporting on copyrighted works. Much of the act, particularly Sections 107 through 112, concerns the limitations of the bundle of rights.

Since the 19th century, the courts have held that certain uses of copyrighted material are "fair," within reason, and not an infringement of or materially damaging to a copyright owner. This tradition was largely validated and codified in the 1976 act, which offers examples of fair use.[6]

The fair use of a copyrighted work, including such use by reproduction in copies or phonorecords, or by any other means specified by Section 106 of the law, for pur-poses such as criticism, comment, news reporting, teaching (including multiple copies for classroom use), scholarship, or research, "is not an infringement of copyright." In determining whether the use made of a work in any particular case is a fair use, four criteria have been established by prior court actions and are incorporated in the act:

1. The purpose or character of the use, including whether such use is of a com-mercial nature or is for nonprofit educational purposes

2. The nature of the copyrighted work

3. The amount and substantiality of the portion used in relation to the copy-righted work as a whole

4. The effect of the use on the potential **market** for or value of the copyrighted work

The **fair use doctrine,** a legal defense to a copyright infringement claim, essen-tially allows minimal reproduction of copyrighted material for purposes such as scholarship, research, and news reporting. Any substantial taking is likely to be seen by the court as an infringement.

Some analysts point out a potential conflict between broad First Amendment free speech rights and the more limited fair use doctrine of copyright law. Although copyright law provides an incentive for authorship, some critics say it gives creators monopoly rights that may conflict with public interest in the dissemination of infor-mation. A counterargument runs that copyright protection extending only to the expression of ideas (as opposed to the ideas themselves) allows free speech to flourish. In addition to fair use, which requires a case-by-case analysis, the law also identifies certain kinds of performances that are always considered to be exceptions to the copyright owner's exclusive rights. These performances are not infringements:[7]

1. The performance or display of a work by instructors or pupils in the course of face-to-face teaching activities of a nonprofit educational institution

2. Performance of a **nondramatic** literary or musical work, display of a work, by or in the course of a transmission, if

   a. the performance or display is a regular part of the systematic instructional activities of a governmental body or a nonprofit educational institution
   b. the performance or display is directly related and of **material** assistance to the teaching content of the transmission
   c. the transmission is made primarily for reception in classrooms or similar places devoted to instruction

3. Performance of a nondramatic literary or musical work or of a **dramatico-musical** work of a religious nature in the course of religious services

4. Performance of a nondramatic literary or musical work (otherwise than in a transmission to the public) without any direct or indirect purpose of commercial advantage and without payment of any fee or other compensation for the performance to any of its performers, promoters, or organizers, if

   a. there is no direct or indirect admission charge; or
   b. the proceeds, after deducting reasonable costs of production, are used exclusively for educational, religious, or charitable purposes and not for private financial gain

5. Communication by an establishment of a transmission or retransmission embodying a performance or display of a nondramatic musical work intended to be received by the general public, originated by a radio or television broadcast station, or, if an audiovisual transmission, by a cable system or satellite carrier, if that establishment contains less than 3,750 gross square feet, or, for those establishments containing more than 3,750 gross square feet, if (1) their audio use is via six or fewer speakers with not more than four in any one room or (2) their audio/visual use is via not more than four TVs, of which no more than one TV is in any room unless a direct charge is made to see or hear the transmission, or the transmission thus received is further transmitted to the public. Those non–food service and beverage establishments that contain more than 2,000 gross square feet must meet the requirements of (1) and (2) above in order to be exempt.

6. Performance of a nondramatic musical work by a vending establishment where the sole purpose of the performance is to promote the retail sale of copies or phonorecords of the work or of the devices used in performing the work

Copyright Ownership

Copyright ownership vests initially and exclusively in the author of the work[8] and includes the six exclusive rights under copyright (the bundle of rights enumerated earlier).

Where there are multiple authors, ownership of the copyright is shared. In the popular song field, it is customary for the composer(s) of the music to share ownership equally with the lyricist(s). Unless there is a written agreement to the contrary, coauthors—whether composers or lyricists—will share equally in the ownership of a copyright. Multiple authors may, however, set up, through a written agreement, disproportionate shares of ownership in a work in which they collaborated. Examples:

Composers' Share (50%)	Lyricists' Share (50%)
Example 1. One composer and one lyricist, sharing equally:	
One composer: owns 50%	One lyricist: owns 50%
Example 2. Two composers splitting their share equally, three lyricists dividing their share unequally:	
First composer: owns 25%	First lyricist: owns 25%
Second composer: owns 25%	Second lyricist: owns 15%
	Third lyricist: owns 10%

Ownership Limitation

Ownership of copyright, or any of the exclusive rights under a copyright, is distinct from ownership of any material object in which the work may be embodied, such as sheet music, discs, or tapes. Transfer of ownership of any such material object does not convey any rights in the embodied copyrighted work. For example, the ownership of the physical master tapes on which a song is recorded does not carry with it any ownership of copyright in the underlying song (see First Sale Doctrine below).

Collective Works

Copyright in each separate contribution to a collective work (such as an album of songs) is distinct from copyright in the collective work as a whole and vests initially in the author of the contribution. In the absence of an express transfer of the copyright, the owner of the copyright in the collective work is presumed to have acquired only the privilege of reproducing and distributing the contribution as part of that particular collective work, any revision of that collective work, and any later collective work in the same series.

Film Music

Copyright in music, and accompanying words, written for theatrical films and TV movies is often covered by the overriding copyright in the movie itself as an audiovisual work; however, additional copyrights may preexist for music that a film producer licenses for inclusion in this production. In this situation, the two copyrights coexist. The film producer would be required to obtain a synchronization license for use of the preexisting copyrighted music. But even in this situation, the complete audiovisual work—the movie itself—could still be protected by a blanket copyright covering its particular combination of component parts.

Transfer or Assignment

Although all six exclusive rights of authorship vest initially in the author(s) of a work, the law states that any or all of these rights may be transferred or assigned to other persons. As a matter of fact, most original copyright owners find it necessary to transfer or assign some or all of their rights to generate income from their properties. Some writers own their own publishing companies and record labels, but the great majority assigns publishing and recording rights to others, usually through the granting of exclusive licenses (see Chapter 7). Transfers must be in writing to be effective, but nonexclusive licenses may be oral or even implied from conduct.

The law even permits subdivisions of individual rights. As explained elsewhere, this often occurs with publishing rights, where authors "split the publishing."

Recordation of Transfer

As just noted, when copyright owners assign or grant an exclusive license for any of their copyrights, the action does not become valid until the parties (or their agents) execute a written agreement confirming the transfer. This written instrument may then be filed with the Copyright Office in accordance with procedures set by that office, although such filing is not necessary for the transfer to be effective. Filers must also pay the specified fee (the latest forms and fees are available on the Copyright Office website, www.copyright.gov). Following these actions, the Copyright Office issues a Certificate of Recordation.

This recordation serves to provide all persons with what lawyers call "constructive notice" of the facts stated in the Certificate of Recordation.

Occasionally, a situation arises where two transfers are in conflict. In such instances, the first transfer to be properly executed prevails (see Title 17, Section 205 for instructions for proper recordation).

Termination or Recapture

In the case of any work other than a work made for hire, the exclusive or nonexclusive "grant of a transfer" or license of copyright or any right under a copyright, executed by the author on or after January 1, 1978, is subject to termination under the following essential conditions, cited in Section 203:

1. Termination of the grant may be effected at any time during a period of 5 years beginning at the end of 35 years from the date of execution of the grant; or

2. If the grant covers the right of publication of the work, the period begins at the end of 35 years from the date of publication of the work under the grant or at the end of 40 years from the date of execution of the grant, whichever term ends earlier.

3. Advance notice of intent to terminate must be in writing, signed by the number and proportion of owners of termination interests required under Section 203 or by their duly authorized agents, served upon the grantee or the grantee's successor in title. The notice shall state the effective date of the termination, which shall fall within the 5-year period specified in Section 203, and the notice shall be served not less than 2 or more than 10 years before that date. To be in effect, this notice must be recorded in the Copyright Office before the effective date of termination. An individual intending to file a notice of termination must comply with the form, content, and manner of service prescribed by the Register of Copyrights.

4. Termination of a grant may be effected notwithstanding any agreement to the contrary, including an agreement to make a will or to make any further grant.

5. Upon the effective date of termination, all rights under this title that were covered by the terminated grant revert to the author(s).

6. Unless and until termination is effected under Section 203, the grant, if it does not provide otherwise, continues in effect for the term of copyright provided by law.

Section 203 thus establishes the outer limits of copyright assignability by providing statutory termination guidelines. In practice, however, writers and publishers may negotiate a shorter term (typically, 1 to 5 years) to balance the writer's interest in recapturing copyrights that have not been effectively "worked" by the publisher against the publisher's interest in controlling the property long enough to promote it.

In the case of any copyright **subsisting** in either its first or renewal term on January 1, 1978, other than a copyright in a work made for hire, the exclusive or nonexclusive grant of a transfer or license of the renewal copyright or any right under it, executed before January 1, 1978, by an author or any statutory successors, is also subject to termination.

The termination of the grant may be effected at any time during a period of 5 years beginning at the end of 75 years from the date copyright was originally secured. Termination of the grant may be effected notwithstanding any agreement to the contrary, including an agreement to make a will or to make any future grant.

Work Made for Hire

The term *work made for hire*[9] has special meaning under copyright law and is of great significance to composers, publishers, and movie producers. Whenever a composer is engaged on a work-made-for-hire basis, the employer is considered under the law as the author of any resulting creative work. And the "author," under copyright law, is the owner of the works.

In music, this arrangement was first fully developed in the 1920s and 1930s in the **Tin Pan Alley** days, when large publishing companies employed salaried songwriters to work in-house on a full-time basis. Songwriters today typically operate as **independent contractors** with much less supervision.

Occasionally, however, a music publisher will attempt to claim authorship rights in a work produced by a writer who is effectively working as an independent contractor. To protect against this kind of conflict, before signing a work-made-for-hire agreement, it's advisable to run it by an attorney.

Section 101 describes (but does not clearly define) conditions in which certain "creations" are to be considered works made for hire:

1. Work prepared by an employee within the scope of employment; or

2. Work specifically ordered or commissioned for use in one of several categories, the most relevant for composers being "as part of a motion picture or other audiovisual work." Even if the work falls into one of the defined categories, the parties must sign an agreement saying the work is made for hire.

Some disputes center on the language of the first condition. To resolve these disputes, bills are periodically introduced in Congress that attempt to clarify the meaning of *employee* by, for example, attaching Social Security benefits and withholding of taxes to the definition, as the courts have often required. In 1989, the Supreme Court spoke to the question of when a creative artist may be considered an employee, listing no less than 13 factors to be considered.[10] The case dealt with whether ownership of a sculpture rested with the sculptor or the group that commissioned its creation. Although the original court decision found for the organization, that decision was reversed on appeal and the Supreme Court affirmed the reversal, **finding** the sculptor to be the owner of copyright in the commissioned work.

As one provision of the law shifts, it can often have significant spill-over effects. Once Congress granted a copyright in sound recordings, it triggered a slow-motion legal war over the right of the author to terminate that copyright, potentially depriving labels of substantial revenue. The conflict arose because the law didn't define precisely who is the author of a sound recording, although there is evidence in congressional debate of the intent that a featured performer would at least be one of the authors. Labels have insisted the recordings were works made for hire and thus the label itself was the author. What about the producer? Congress or the courts, or both, will have to settle the matter.

Musical Arrangements

Copyright law provides that the original holder of the copyright has the exclusive right "to prepare derivative works based upon the copyrighted work." Because musical arrangements are usually considered derivative (or supplementary) works, arrangers must obtain permission of the copyright owner before scoring their own version of the material. In practice, this permission is sought and granted only under particular circumstances, especially when the proposed arrangement might substantially alter or distort the original. But music publishers are usually delighted that anyone is interested in recording one of their songs and welcome the potential exposure and income from a **cover record.** Most publishers issue a negotiated mechanical license (see Chapter 7) to record one of their properties. Implicit in this license is the understanding that the record producer may create a new arrangement consisting of minor changes that will suit the style of the recording artist. Copyright law provides that when a compulsory (mechanical) license is issued, that license "includes the privilege of making a musical arrangement of the work to the extent necessary to conform it to the style or manner of interpretation of the performance involved" for the recording. This industry practice is not so much a specific permission to create such an arrangement as it is a tacit agreement by the publisher not to raise any objection to it.

With respect to arrangements made primarily for educational use, many publishers give their approval by accepting the standard form, Request for Permission to Arrange, which states that the publisher owns the arrangement made and limits its use.

Arrangers' Rights

The role of the music arranger is often as creative as that of the original composer of the song. Arrangers usually create work for hire, receiving a flat, one-time fee based on the American Federation of Musicians (AFM) **scale** for "orchestration," or negotiating whatever the traffic will bear. Except for work on music in the public domain—when the underlying work is not owned or controlled by anyone—arrangers who work under such agreements generally enjoy no rights of copyright ownership and receive no royalties from record sales, nor do they share in income generated for composers and publishers from licensing of performances of their arrangements.

Public Domain

A different condition prevails when an arranger creates an original **chart** of a work in the public domain. The arranger's publisher of such material may demand and receive mechanical royalties from the label releasing the recording of the song and usually splits one half of such receipts with the arranger. In respect to performance income, ASCAP, BMI, and SESAC are accustomed to paying (often reduced) royalties to authors and publishers of arrangements based on works in the public domain. Arrangers of such works may also receive royalties from their publisher's sale of printed editions.

Arrangers are accorded more privileges in some European countries, where they are not always required to secure publishers' approval to render new arrangements of copyrighted material. Furthermore, arrangers are often accorded parallel rights, which provide a share of royalties derived from mechanical licensing and performances of their charts.

■ Sound Recordings

As noted at the beginning of this chapter, a potentially confusing aspect of the 1976 Copyright Act and subsequent amendments is that a musical work (the underlying song with lyrics) is categorically differentiated from a sound recording. The record company typically holds the copyright in the sound recording, while the publishing company, which sometimes is a division of the same company, holds the copyright in the musical work.

The owner of a sound recording, under Sections 106 and 114, has these exclusive rights:

1. To reproduce the copyrighted work to duplicate the sound recording in the form of phonorecords (or copies of motion pictures and other audiovisual works). Note that this right is limited to duplicating the actual sounds fixed in the recording.

2. To prepare derivative works based on the copyrighted material—to make and distribute phonorecords that are new arrangements or versions of the copyrighted work (sound recording).

3. To distribute phonorecords to the public by sale or other transfer of ownership, or by rental, lease, or lending, or by digital phonorecord delivery (downloading).

4. To perform by digital audio transmission.

Performance Right Exclusion

The 1976 law specifically excluded **performance rights** in sound recordings, and owners of sound recordings still do not enjoy the level of protection common in many other parts of the world, including more than 50 Western countries.

From the standpoint of the music industry, progress in chipping away at this long-standing U.S. regulatory bulwark has been slow and patchy. It took years for the Recording Industry Association of America (RIAA) to achieve a partial victory when Congress passed the Digital Performance Right in Sound Recording Act (DPRA) in 1995, which gave copyright holders in sound recordings the exclusive right "to perform the copyrighted work publicly by means of a digital audio transmission." This allowed record companies to collect a royalty on digital performances of the sound recording on digital cable and satellite television, the Internet, and satellite radio.

Except for this narrowly defined right, owners of sound recordings for many years did not receive performance royalties when music from these recordings was broadcast or otherwise performed. Congressional sparring over this policy has illuminated a longstanding battle between the intellectual property community (including labels and artists) and users of creative works (notably broadcasters).[11] But, as we'll see in Chapter 7, the rising importance of digital performances has begun to give those who have rights in the recordings (primarily labels and featured artists) a growing slice of the economic pie.

Imitation Exclusion

The exclusive rights of the owner of copyright in a sound recording with respect to the preparation and reproduction of derivative works do not extend to the making or duplicating of another sound recording that consists entirely of an independent fixation of other sounds, even though such sounds imitate or simulate those in the copyrighted sound recording. In other words, imitations that mimic the original recording are legally permissible, but the imitative recording cannot simply be a recorded copy of the original. Furthermore, it is not legal to market the mimicked recordings as if they feature the original artists or in any way that might confuse the public about who performed the song.

Compulsory Mechanical License

One of the most important copyright provisions concerns the conditions under which a person is permitted to produce and distribute phonorecords of nondramatic musical works. The law provides that copyright owners of nondramatic music have complete control over recording rights of their properties until they license the material for the first recording. But after this first recording is distributed to the public, they are compelled by law to license any other person to produce and distribute recordings of the copyrighted music in exchange for a fixed statutory royalty, which is adjusted periodically. This provision stems in part from an important goal in copyright law: the increased dissemination of works to the public.

According to Section 115, copyrighted songs become "subject to compulsory licensing" after they have been released on record for the first time. This kind of licensing requires special conditions, the most important of which are the following:

1. "A person may obtain a compulsory license only if the primary purpose in making phonorecords is to distribute them to the public for private use, including by means of a digital phonorecord delivery." This sentence is very significant and clearly excludes from compulsory licensing all recordings that are generally classified under the term **transcriptions.** In the music field, the

term *transcriptions* is not applied to phonorecords intended for purchase and use by the public but to recordings sold for special uses, such as theme music for broadcast programs or wired music services such as Mood Music.

2. "A person may not obtain a compulsory license for use of the work in the making of phonorecords duplicating a sound recording fixed by another, unless (i) such sound recording was fixed lawfully; and (ii) the making of the phonorecords was authorized by the owner of copyright in the sound recording or, if the sound recording was fixed before February 15, 1972 [the date when sound recordings first became subjects of federal statutory copyright protection in the United States], by any person who fixed the sound recording pursuant to an express license . . . for use of such work in a sound recording." (The purpose of this provision was to prevent pirates and counterfeiters from availing themselves of the compulsory license.)

3. "A compulsory license includes the privilege of making a musical arrangement of the work to the extent necessary to conform it to the style or manner of interpretation of the performance involved." But the law also states that the arranger shall not change the basic melody or fundamental character of the work. Furthermore, the new arrangement shall not be subject to protection as a derivative work, except with the express consent of the copyright owner.

4. The person planning to obtain a compulsory license must notify the copyright proprietor of this intention before or within 30 days after making, and before distributing, any phonorecords of the work. If the person cannot locate the owner of the work, "it shall be sufficient to file notice of intention in the Copyright Office." Failure to serve or file notice forecloses the possibility of a compulsory license and, in the absence of a negotiated license, renders the making and distribution of phonorecords actionable as acts of infringement.

Compulsory License Bypass

Compulsory mechanical license provisions in the copyright statute are so stringent, particularly in respect to notice and accounting requirements, that the industry often uses an alternative, the negotiated mechanical license. This alternative kind of license is permitted by law and is explained in Chapter 7.

Royalty Payments (Section 115[c])

After permitting the initial recording of a song, publishers are limited as a practical matter by the statute as to what royalty rate they may charge record makers. The **statutory rate** provided in the 1976 act was "2.75 cents, or one-half of one cent per minute of playing time or fraction thereof, whichever amount is larger" for each work embodied in a phonorecord. Rates are adjusted periodically. For physical formats, the rate designated through 2017 is the larger of 9.1 cents or 1.75 cents per minute.

To be entitled to receive royalty payments under a compulsory license, the copyright owner must be identified in the registration or other public records of the Copyright Office. The owner is entitled to royalties for phonorecords made and distributed after being so identified but is not entitled to recover for any phonorecords previously made and distributed.

Except as provided above, the royalty under a compulsory license shall be payable for every phonorecord made and distributed in accordance with the license. "For this purpose, . . . a phonorecord is considered 'distributed' if the person exercising the compulsory license has voluntarily and permanently parted with its possession." This language helps reduce the ambiguity prevalent until 1978 relative to liability for royalty payments. It appears that the manufacturer is not liable for royalty payments on records returned to it that have not been sold, for such records did not leave the manufacturer's possession permanently, as the law provides. "Giveaways" such as free goods and promotional copies do, however, trigger royalty payments, as the definition doesn't require a sale.

Duration of Copyright

Copyright protection obtained prior to enactment of the 1976 act could last no more than a total of 56 years: a 28-year initial term, followed by an optional 28-year renewal term. Under Section 302 of the Copyright Act, this was changed so that copyright in a work created on or after January 1, 1978, was to last for 50 years from the author's death. But that did not settle the matter.

In 1998, the Sonny Bono Copyright Term Extension Act (named after singer-turned-congressman Sonny Bono) added 20 years to the term of protection of works protected by copyright. A song that had previously been protected for the life of the author plus 50 years was protected after 1998 for the life of the author plus 70 years. Works for hire receive even longer protection (see Table 4.1).

Subsisting Copyrights in Their First Term on January 1, 1978 (Section 304)

Copyrights still in their first terms continue, under the 1976 law, for their original 28 years. At the expiration of the original term of copyright, the copyright shall endure for a renewed and extended further term of 67 years

1. if the application to register a claim to such further term has been made to the Copyright Office within 1 year before the expiration of the original term of copyright, and the claim is registered, shall vest in the proprietor of the copyright who is entitled to claim the renewal of copyright at the time the application is made; or

2. if no such application is made or the claim is not registered, shall vest, upon the beginning of such further term, in the person or entity that was the proprietor of the copyright as of the last day of the original term of copyright.

Renewal Registration

As the result of a 1992 renewal amendment to the Copyright Act, there is no longer a requirement to register a renewal of a pre-1978 copyright during the 28th year to keep the work from falling into the public domain. It is, however, advisable to make such renewal registration to enhance the enforceability of the copyright during its renewed and extended term. Renewal registration will also determine who has the right to use derivative works prepared under a grant of a transfer or license made before the expiration of the original term.

Table 4.1   Duration of Copyright Term After Sonny Bono Act

Date of Work	When Protection Attaches	Term of Protection
Created in 1978 or later	Upon fixation	Unitary term of life + 70 (or if anonymous or pseudonymous or work for hire, 95 years from publication or 120 years from creation, whichever is shorter)
Published[a] or registered 1964–1978	Upon registration or publication with notice	95 years (28 + automatic 67-year renewal)
Published or registered 1923–1963	Upon registration or publication with notice	28 years + 67 years renewal term, if renewal was made before end of first term
Published or registered before 1923	Upon registration or publication with notice	Work is now in the public domain; although term of protection is now at 85 years for works covered in the 1909 act, works made from 1922 and earlier were already public domain in 1998 when the Sonny Bono Act was passed, and the act does not revive them. Thus, status cannot be determined simply by counting back 95 years from the present date.
Created but never published before 1978	Upon creation	Unitary term of at least life + 70; earliest possible expiration is December 31, 2002, if work remains unpublished. If work is published prior to December 31, 2002, earliest possible expiration is December 31, 2047.

Source: Adapted by Robert Clarida, Partner, Cowan, Liebowitz, and Latman, from chart on p. 275 of Latman, A., Gorman, R. & Ginsburg, J. (1989). *Copyright for the nineties.* Charlottesville, VA: Michie.

[a] To start the term running, the publication must be authorized by the copyright owner. An unauthorized publication, even with notice, has no legal effect.

Subsisting Copyrights in Their Renewal Term

As Congress stated, the 1976 law creates an entirely new property right in the renewal term. The 1909 law provided a maximum of only 56 years of protection for pre-1978 works, which was later extended to 75 years by the original 1976 act. The current law provides, for these works, a total of 95 years of protection. The significant monetary value of many popular songs written before 1978—which have come to be known as "standards"—gives authors and publishers a strong incentive to establish claims on the additional 20 years of protection to which they are entitled.

After 75 Years

Properties whose 75-year protection would otherwise expire under the original 1976 act are, under the new amendments, automatically granted copyright protection for a total of 95 years. If a writer wants to recapture a composition from a publisher to whom the renewal term has been assigned, the writer may, within a 5-year period following the original 75-year—or 56-year—protection, terminate the grant of renewal term to the publisher by serving a notice of termination. This notice of termination must be given to the publisher not less than 2 years or more than 10 years ahead of the termination date decided on by the author. Once an author has thus reclaimed the publisher-owned renewal copyright, ownership by the author is free and clear. Failure to exercise the option to terminate within the 5-year period will permit a copyright to remain with the publisher to the end of the renewal period.

After January 1, 1978

Copyright protection in works created on or after January 1, 1978, extends to a work from its creation and, except as provided under certain conditions, endures for a term consisting of the life of the author and 70 years after the author's death.

Joint Works. Where two or more authors prepared a joint work (and did not do the work for hire), they enjoy copyright for a term consisting of the life of the last surviving author and 70 years after such surviving author's death.

Work Made for Hire. In a work made for hire, copyright exists for 95 years from the date of its first publication or a term of 120 years from the year of its creation, whichever expires first. Works made for hire are not included in the provisions concerning termination of grants for the 20-year extension period.

Works in the Trunk (Section 303)

Copyright in a work created before January 1, 1978, but not theretofore in the public domain or copyrighted, subsists from January 1, 1978, and endures for the life of the author and 70 years after the author's (or last surviving coauthor's) death. "In no case, however, shall the term of copyright in such a work expire before December, 2002; and, if the work is published on or before December 31, 2002, the term of copyright shall not expire before December 31, 2047."[12]

In summary, songwriters generally leave the task of taking care of renewals and terminations to their publishers, attorneys, or administrators. But it's not infrequent that these representatives fail to act in a timely manner, resulting in headaches and lost income. Songwriters should therefore keep track of their copyrights as a check against such outcomes.

Formalities

The term *formalities* is used around the world in reference to the specific actions a claimant must take to validate claim to copyright.[13] These formalities include notice of copyright, deposit of copies, and registration of claim to copyright. The 1976 law is permissive in respect to some kinds of mistakes in following through on formalities. After March 1, 1989 (the effective date the United States joined the Berne Convention), these formalities for U.S. works became almost entirely optional. But to be on the safe side, claimants should put a proper notice on copyrighted material (see below).

Notice on Printed Music

The term *notice of copyright* refers to the public display of information concerning the date the work was published and who registered the claim. On printed editions, the law stipulates the following:

1. Notice may be placed on all publicly distributed copies. The notice imprinted should be the symbol © or the word *Copyright* or the abbreviation *Copr.* and the year of first publication of the work. The type of notice most often seen is this:

   © 2010 John Doe

   Although not required by the Copyright Act, the language "All Rights Reserved" should also accompany the statutory notice to provide additional protection in some foreign countries under the Pan-American Convention.

2. In the case of compilations or derivative works incorporating previously published material, the year of the first publication of the compilation or derivative work is sufficient.

3. The notice must also include the name of the copyright owner. A recognizable abbreviation of the owner's name may be used.

4. The position of the notice shall be affixed to the copies so as to give reasonable notice of the claim to copyright.

Notice on Phonorecords (Section 402)

Whenever a sound recording protected under the 1976 law is published in the United States or elsewhere by authority of the copyright owner, a notice may be placed on all publicly distributed phonorecords of the sound recording. It is still prudent to do this. The form of the notice consists of three elements:

1. the symbol ℗,

2. the year of the first publication of the sound recording, and

3. the name of the owner of the copyright in the sound recording. A recognizable abbreviation may be used. If the producer of the sound recording is named on the phonorecord labels or containers, and if no other name appears in conjunction with the notice, the producer's name shall be considered a part of the notice.

Position of Notice. The notice shall be placed on the surface of the phonorecord, or on the phonorecord label or container, in such a manner and location as to give reasonable notice of the claim to copyright. A typical notice for a phonorecord is as follows:

℗ 2010 Smith Records

Audiovisual works do not require the symbol ℗ but rather the symbol ©, because they are not phonorecords.

Notice Errors or Omissions

For works first published between January 1, 1978, and March 1, 1989, as detailed in Sections 401, 402, and 403, omission of notice from copies or phonorecords does not invalidate the copyright in a work (Section 405) under any of the following conditions:

1. The notice has been omitted from no more than a relatively small number of copies or phonorecords distributed to the public.

2. Registration for the work has been made before or is made within 5 years after the publication without notice, and a reasonable effort is made to add notice to all copies or phonorecords that are distributed to the public in the United States after omission has been discovered.

3. The notice has been omitted in violation of an express requirement in writing that, as a condition of the copyright owner's authorization of the public distribution of copies or phonorecords, they bear the prescribed notice.[14]

Deposit (Section 407)

Deposit of works in the Library of Congress and registration of works are separate formalities. Neither action is a condition of copyright, yet both are important. With respect to published copies, Section 407 states that the copyright owner (or the publisher) must deposit, within 3 months after the date of publication, two complete copies of "the best edition" of the work. The deposit for sound recordings shall include two complete phonorecords of the best edition, together with any printed material or other visually perceptible material published with such phonorecords. Under the Berne Convention, notice of copyright is no longer required in deposit copies.

Under certain conditions, deposits made prior to any attempt to register the work may be used to satisfy the deposit requirements called for when the author (or the publisher) undertakes to register the work. If the author desires to have the initial deposit satisfy the deposit requirements specified on the registration forms, a letter must be enclosed with the initial deposit specifically directing the Library of Congress to hold those deposits for later connection with the author's registration application. If such a letter is not enclosed, the Copyright Office will require separate, additional deposits of a work, as specified on the registration form.

Congress has authorized modifications of deposit requirements from time to time, at the discretion of the Copyright Office. Although failure to deposit copies or phonorecords according to current regulations does not actually endanger the copyright, the Register of Copyrights does have the authority to demand copies and impose fines of up to $250 per work on laggards and levy additional fines up to $2,500 for willful and repeated refusal to comply.

Registration (Section 408)

Although deposits and registration are referred to in the law as "separate formalities" and a deposit can be made independently of registration, it is important to note that registration of a claim to copyright must be accompanied by the deposit specified on the application form. Registration is strongly advised because, under certain conditions, an author's work left unregistered lacks certain advantages the work would otherwise enjoy. Most important, a work must be registered in order for the statutory damage provision of the Copyright Act to be triggered.

A work may be registered at any time during the term of the copyright, whether it is published or unpublished. The registration may generally be made by the author as copyright owner or the publisher, as exclusive licensee.

The acceptance of sound recordings, not just sheet music, in claims to copyright the underlying music was a significant advance over the 1909 law. In the popular music field, many songwriters lack the ability to render their material in music notation. Now all they have to do is make a simple recording and submit it in lieu of sheet music. The acceptance of sound recordings also provides important advantages to persons desiring to copyright jazz improvisations, many of which are not easily transcribed into conventional music notation.

If the Register of Copyrights determines that all legal and formal requirements have been met, a certificate of registration will be sent to the applicant. If the claim is found invalid, the register will refuse registration and notify the applicant in writing of the reasons for such refusal. (The Copyright Office has formulated an appeal procedure for applicants whose claims have been found invalid.) The effective date of copyright registration is the day on which an application, deposit, and fee have all been received in the Copyright Office.

If the author or the author's publisher made a mistake in an original registration of claim, or if either party wants to modify it, the Register of Copyrights has established procedures and set fees to accommodate these matters.

Fees (Section 708)

The Copyright Office charges fees for certain services, such as registration of claims and recordation of transfers. For current rates, contact the Copyright Office, Library of Congress, Washington, D.C. 20559, or consult the Copyright Office website, www.copyright.gov.

Copyright Royalty Board

The 1976 Copyright Act provided for the establishment of an instrumentality of the Congress to serve that legislative body in matters concerning copyright. That instrumentality was the Copyright Royalty Tribunal (CRT). The CRT set and periodically adjusted compulsory royalty rates and held hearings to determine whether rates and royalty distribution were fair and equitable.

The CRT was abolished in 1993 and replaced with ad hoc Copyright Arbitration Royalty Panels (**CARP**s), administered by the Librarian of Congress and the Copyright Office. CARPs were phased out beginning in 2005, when the Copyright Royalty and Distribution Act of 2004 replaced them with the Copyright Royalty Board (**CRB**). The CRB comprises three Copyright Royalty Judges who determine rates and terms for copyright **statutory licenses** and make determinations on distribution of statutory license royalties collected by the United States Copyright Office of the Library of Congress. Royalties within its jurisdiction include the following:

cable and satellite retransmission,

digital performance and phonorecord delivery,

mechanicals, and

educational broadcasting.

Infringement, Remedy

Copyright infringement is widespread, most of it going unnoticed and unpunished. Where infringement is of little or no financial consequence, courts may limit assessment of statutory damages (see below) to a nominal amount. Where a library or school is involved with an infringement arising out of a lack of full understanding of the law, sometimes no damages at all are awarded.

Remedies. When infringements are not innocent offenses, the following remedies are available following a successful court action:

1. Injunction: A temporary or final injunction can be sought from any court having jurisdiction to prevent or restrain infringement of copyright.

2. Impoundment: The court may order impoundment of articles alleged to be involved with infringement. The impoundment can hold pending court determination of the merits of the claim of infringement. Impoundment could include printed copies, phonorecords, masters, and even duplicating, manufacturing, and packaging equipment.

3. Destruction: The court could order, as part of a final judgment, destruction of inventories, such as printed copies and phonorecords.

4. Damages:

   a. The infringer is liable, except as the law otherwise provides, for (1) actual damages suffered by the copyright owner as a result of the infringement and (2) any additional profits gained by the infringer as a result of acts of infringement.

   b. The copyright owner may elect, before final judgment is rendered, to seek statutory damages instead of actual damages and profits for all infringements in a sum not less than $750 or more than $30,000, "as the court considers just."

   c. In a case where the copyright owner sustains the burden of proving, and the court **finds** "that infringement was committed willfully, the court at its discretion may increase the award of statutory damages to a sum of not more than $150,000." Lesser awards are made where the court finds the infringer was not aware and had no reason to believe the actions constituted infringement, and even in cases of willful infringement, a statutory damage award is not supposed to provide a windfall for the copyright owner.

   d. Costs and attorneys' fees may be recovered by the prevailing party, at the court's discretion. At today's legal rates, this amount is usually substantial.

   e. Copyright owners may choose to sue for actual damages or statutory damages and may change to the latter course at any time before final judgment of the court. Successful artists with significant dollars at risk will often seek actual damages; multi-million-dollar cases are not uncommon.

Neither statutory damages nor attorneys' fees can be awarded, however, if the copyright was not registered before the infringement began. This is the most important reason to register copyright in a work before making it available to potential infringers, whether within the music industry or the public at large.

Record Counterfeiting, Penalties

The 1976 law imposed strong penalties for counterfeit use of the copyright symbol on phonorecords. Owners of copyrights in sound recordings complained that the threat of fines and imprisonment were not adequate deterrents. Violators seemed to view threatened sanctions simply as "the cost of doing business." Subsequently, Congress strengthened the penalties by passing the Piracy and Counterfeit Act of 1982. This law made both piracy and counterfeiting a felony. Among its other provisions, the 1982 law provided a maximum penalty of a $250,000 fine along with jail terms. A person would receive this maximum penalty if found guilty of illegally manufacturing or distributing within a 180-day period at least 10 copies or phonorecords or one or more copyrighted works with a retail value of more than $2,500.

The trend in the United States and abroad is toward increasing penalties for copyright infringers.

Changing Laws

Laws governing copyright have never been able to keep fully abreast of changes in the way music is produced, communicated, bought, and sold. This time lag is most damaging to copyright owners when it comes to matters of counterfeiting, home taping, direct satellite transmissions, or other alternative distribution via the Internet, cable, or cellular technology.

As technological change thrusts new issues into the spotlight, two economic coalitions traditionally line up against each other, trying to persuade Congress and the courts to rule in their favor. On one side is the creative community: authors, composers, filmmakers, and those who hold copyrights on their creations— publishers, recording companies, movie producers, and so on. On the opposite side are the users of copyrighted properties: broadcasters, hardware manufacturers, software merchants, and the consumer, who is understandably reluctant to pay for music uses and the royalties that may be demanded.

First Sale Doctrine

The principle of "first sale" was carried over from the 1909 statute to the 1976 copyright law (Section 109[a]). Simply stated, the first sale principle provides that the copyright owner is entitled to compensation for the first sale of the copy or phonorecord embodying the copyrighted work. Thereafter, the owner of the physical copy may dispose of it or transfer it as the owner sees fit, with only a few exceptions such as prohibitions on duplication. Later, Congress passed what is known as the 1984 Record Rental Amendment, clarifying that transferring a musical phonorecord through rental (as opposed to sale) was generally not permitted. The first sale doctrine, developed to facilitate dissemination of creative works, prevents copyright holders from exercising unreasonable control over the physical product once it has left the distributors. This doctrine became the legal basis for the video software rental business.

The Audio Home Recording Act of 1992 (AHRA)

In 1992, Congress enacted the Audio Home Recording Act, which amended the 1976 Copyright Act by allowing home audiotaping and by implementing a royalty payment system and a serial copy management system for digital audio recordings. As a direct result of the passage of this act, home taping is no longer an infringement of copyright, and certain additional copyright infringement actions were prohibited.

The Digital Performance Right in Sound Recording Act of 1995 (DPRA)

As detailed earlier in this chapter, the DPRA, after years of fierce negotiations, gave record companies the exclusive right "to perform the copyrighted work publicly by means of a digital audio transmission," paving the way for them to collect audio-only digital performance royalties from digital cable and satellite television, Internet, and satellite radio providers.

The Digital Millennium Copyright Act of 1998 (DMCA)

Congress further explicated and extended the reach of copyright law by adopting the Digital Millennium Copyright Act of 1998. A key provision of the act requires that "webcasters"—such as Internet radio stations and **webcasting** services—pay licensing fees to record companies. It also criminalizes production and dissemination of technology, devices, or services intended to circumvent measures that control access to copyrighted works. This is commonly known as digital rights management (DRM). (In certain circumstances, exemptions from anti-circumvention provisions are provided for nonprofit libraries, archives, and educational institutions.) The law also generally limits Internet service providers (ISPs) from copyright infringement liability for simply transmitting information over the Internet. However, ISPs are expected to remove material from users' websites that appears to constitute copyright infringement. In addition, the DMCA heightens the penalties for copyright infringement on the Internet.

Revival From Public Domain

In 2012, the Supreme Court upheld a federal law that restored copyright protection to a class of foreign works that had entered the public domain in the United States. The law applied principally to works first published abroad from 1923 to 1989, including some Alfred Hitchcock films, C. S. Lewis writings, Prokofiev symphonies, and Picasso paintings. Justice Ruth Bader Ginsburg, writing for the majority, said the law had merely put "foreign works on an equal footing with their U.S. counterparts." The Court did not overturn the general principle that most works entering public domain lose U.S. copyright protection in perpetuity.

Rights in Names and Trademarks

Rights in trade names and trademarks are not covered under copyright law in the United States, but such rights are related. Company names and professional names of performers cannot be protected under copyright law but are covered under a broader branch of law concerning unfair competition. In some states, it is a criminal offense to infringe on someone else's name or mark. (For more information, see the Federal Lanham Act, U.S. Code, Title 15.)

Individuals seeking federal registration of a name or mark must apply to the U.S. Patent and Trademark Office. Before proceeding, write to the Government Printing Office in Washington, D.C. (www.gpo.gov) for the pamphlet *General Information Concerning Trademarks,* and consult the Trademark Office website at www.uspto.gov. Table 4.2 provides a summary of information regarding trademarks, copyrights, and patents.

Table 4.2   Summary Table Comparing Trademarks, Copyrights, and Patents

	Trademarks	Copyrights	Patents
Nature	Commercial identifications of source such as words, designs, slogans, symbols, trade dress	Original literary and artistic expressions such as books, paintings, music, records, plays, movies, software	New and useful inventions and configurations of useful articles
Scope	Protects against creating a likelihood of confusion or diluting a famous mark	Protects against unauthorized use or copying	Excludes others from making, using, offering for sale, or selling the invention in the United States or by importation into the United States
Purpose	Protects owners and public from unfair competition	Encourages and rewards creative expression	Encourages and rewards innovation
How to obtain rights	Use mark in commerce or apply for federal registration	Create work and fix it in tangible form. Registration confirms rights	Be the first inventor to file
Principal advantages of registration	Nationwide priority rights; possibly conclusive evidence of validity and ownership; U.S. Customs recordation; increased anti-counterfeiting remedies	Statutory damages and attorney's fees; prima facie evidence of validity; U.S. Customs recordation	Protection for nonsecret inventions
Basis for registration	(1) Bona fide intention to use in commerce followed by actual use; (2) non-U.S. owner's country of origin registration or application filed within 6 months prior to U.S. application, or extension to the United States of international registration, plus bona fide intention to use in commerce; or (3) actual use in commerce	Originality	Novelty, unobviousness, utility
Notice requirements	Optional. "TM" or "SM" if unregistered; "®" or "Reg. U.S. Pat. & Tm. Off." if registered	Optional after March 1, 1989. © or "Copyright" with year of first publication and name of owner	Optional. "Patent applied for" or "Pat. Pending" after application; "Patent" or "Pat." plus registration number after grant
Term of rights	As long as used; registrations must be maintained by filing use declaration before each 6th and 10th anniversary; renewal required every 10 years	Creations after January 1, 1978: author's lifetime plus 70 years, or if anonymous or work made for hire, earlier of 95 years from publication or 120 years from creation	20 years from filing date (or sometimes 17 years from grant) for utility or plant patents, subject to periodic maintenance fees; 14 years from registration for design patents

(Continued)

Table 4.2   **(Continued)**

	Trademarks	**Copyrights**	**Patents**
Infringement prerequisites	Registration optional	Registration required for U.S. nationals; optional for foreign nationals	Issued patent required
Infringement standard	Likelihood of confusion, mistake, or deception as to source or sponsorship; or dilution by blurring or tarnishment	Unauthorized use or copying (access plus substantial similarity)	Unauthorized manufacture, use, sale, or offer for sale of devices or processes embodying the invention
International protection	(1) Individual countries; (2) Community Trade Mark registration; or (3) Madrid Protocol centralized filing	Usually protected without registration through international treaties	Usually granted on a country-by-country basis with centralized filing available under the Patent Cooperation Treaty or European Patent Convention

Note: This summary is highly simplified and should be used only for a general comparison. A PDF with detailed information and examples is available at the website of Cowan, Liebowitz & Latman, P.C. Please call (212) 790-9200 for more information, or go to http://www.cll.com/clientuploads/2015PTC.pdf © 2015 Cowan, Liebowitz & Latman, P.C.

Selection of a Name

A new performing group should select its professional name with care to avoid duplication and possible confusion with another group using the same, or similar, name. Because most performing groups will have to register their professional names as "fictitious," they may discover at their own county and state government levels if any other group in that geographic area has already registered the same name or a similar one (for details, see Chapter 27, "Starting Your Own Business"). To confirm the uniqueness of the group's name on a national level, the group should inquire of organizations such as artists' unions, ASCAP, BMI, and SESAC. Libraries often have publications such as the Index to the Trademark Register that can be consulted, as can the USPTO website, www.uspto.org. In addition, the group's attorney can provide the names of firms specializing in searches of this kind and can offer guidance on time restrictions for any filing that might be required under the Trademark Act.

Rights in a Name

Performing groups should, at the very outset, draw up a written agreement that explicitly states who owns the professional name, how the ownership is shared, and under what circumstances shares of ownership end or are modified when individual performers join or leave the group. Signing a basic agreement of this kind should help the artists avoid the kinds of costly lawsuits that have hurt less organized groups.

A Final Note on Law

Just as knowing how the law protects you is vital to success in the music business, so is an understanding of when the law will not protect you. Copyright protection extends to "expressions" but not "ideas." Anyone who is considering entering the recording and publishing part of the music and entertainment industry should be familiar with the Copyright Act, the Lanham Act, and issues of unfair competition, rights of privacy, and First Amendment issues relating to free speech. Contract law provides for additional remedies in many circumstances. No matter how well you may understand the law, however, court delays and attorneys' fees may effectively prevent access to a judicial decision on your issue.

■ Notes

1. 1976 Copyright Act, Chapter 8. Section references throughout this chapter are from the 1976 act, unless otherwise noted.
2. 1976 Copyright Act, Chapter 8.
3. This definition from Section 115(d).
4. Section 102.
5. As laid out in Sections 107 through 122.
6. Section 107.
7. Section 110.
8. Section 201.
9. Section 201(b).
10. *Community for Creative Nonviolence v. Reid*, 490 U.S. 730, 109 S.Ct. 2166, 104 L.Ed.2d 811 (1989).
11. Congress has repeatedly, and unsuccessfully, attempted to establish a broad-based performance right in sound recordings that would require broadcasters to pay royalties to labels and artists.
12. Section 303(a).
13. Chapter 4 of the 1976 Copyright Act.
14. For pre–Berne Convention works (prior to March 1, 1989), an error in the date appearing in the copyright notice does not invalidate the copyright. For example, when the year in the notice is earlier than the year in which the publication first occurred, any period computed from the year of first publication under Section 302 is to be computed from the year of the notice; or when the year is more than 1 year later than the year in which the publication first occurred, the work is considered to have been published without any notice and is governed by the provisions of Section 405.

Chapter Takeaways

- Beginning with the first U.S. copyright law of 1790, Congress has sought to balance the conflicting interests of creators with the rights of users of intellectual property.

- A bedrock principle is that copyright does not to extend to ideas themselves but only to new specific expressions of ideas fixed in a tangible medium such as sheet music or sound recordings.

- With some exceptions, new copyrights remain in effect for the life of the author plus 70 years.

- The bundle of rights reserved to authors regarding their works generally includes the exclusive right to reproduce, prepare derivations, distribute copies, perform, and display.

- Congress and the courts permit "fair use" of copyrighted works, particularly for some limited educational, nonprofit, and scholarly activity.

- The copyright in a song (music and lyrics) is categorically different from a copyright of the recording of the song—with different rights and benefits accruing through these distinct types of works.

- Copyrighted sound recordings typically do not generate performance royalties for exploitation in most U.S. media, such as radio and TV, but royalties from digital performances can be lucrative.

- By paying a compulsory license fee, anyone may make a cover record of a work that has been legitimately released.

Key Terms

- bundle of rights   (p. 41)
- Certificate of Recordation (p. 44)
- collective work   (p. 37)
- compulsory license   (p. 37)
- copyright owner (proprietor)   (p. 37)
- derivative work   (p. 38)

- dramatico-musical work (p. 42)
- fair use doctrine   (p. 41)
- first recording   (p. 48)
- fixed   (p. 38)
- intellectual property (p. 35)
- negotiated license   (p. 37)

- performance rights (p. 47)
- public domain   (p. 47)
- sound recording   (p. 39)
- subsisting   (p. 45)

Discussion Questions

1. For how long should a music creator be entitled to royalties before a work goes into the public domain?

2. How can law enforcement keep up with technologies that allow music users to easily get free music, thus depriving writers and publishers of royalties?

3. Discuss why a music creator might transfer or assign rights of a work to another entity.

What steps must the songwriter take to recapture rights to that work?

4. How is the DIY (do-it-yourself) movement affecting copyright procedures and royalty payments?

5. Who is the author of a sound recording released by a major label? Why do you think so?

CHAPTER 5

Professional Songwriting

The Market

Everything begins with the songwriter. Before anyone else in the music business can make a sound—or a dollar—the songwriter must create a unique melody and lyrics. No songwriters, no music industry—it's that simple. Songs are the fuel that powers the global music business machine, and frequent fill-ups are essential. The great standards of the past, songs that have stood the test of time, are always there to be mined, but a steady stream of new works is also crucial. Over the decades, the relentless rise of new forms of media, from radio to films to video games to the Internet to satellite radio to cell phone ringtones, has expanded both the audience for music and the commercial demand for new "product" to supply new business niches. Great songs, and the writers who create them, will always be the foundation of the music industry.

That, of course, is the good news. The bad news is that only a fraction of aspiring songwriters will ever find commercial acceptance for their material, and fewer still will be able to build sustainable songwriting careers. This is partly a matter of ability (some talent, after all, is required) and partly of desire—an unwillingness to work at songwriting as a serious business enterprise. But it is also a matter of math: Music publishers are inundated with submissions, their mailrooms and email servers littered with thousands of unsolicited songs each week. Eager young songwriters descend on the recording centers like locusts. Probably 10% of the people flowing through the bus stations in Nashville and Hollywood are carrying a suitcase full of demos, while

"I've outdone anyone you can name—Mozart, Beethoven, Bach, Strauss. Irving Berlin, he wrote 1,001 tunes. I wrote 5,500."

—James Brown

Photo © Jupiterimages/Bananastock/Thinkstock.

countless iPods and hard drives in New York and Miami are stuffed with original songs, raps, or beats, all competing for the limited attention of executives who are in a position to turn dreams into reality. Add in the networking angle— preferential treatment for the lead singer's cousin, the band manager's neighbor, or the label VP's friend of a friend, all with songs "perfect for Big Label Act's new album"—and the difficulty getting a hearing increases exponentially.

That doesn't mean that there isn't a hearty appetite among labels and publishers for new songs from newcomers or that there aren't do-it-yourself (DIY) options for promoting your music (see the DIY Toolkit in Chapter 26), but it does mean that finding a way to stand out amid the clutter to connect—to actually catch the eye and the ear of the people who can move one's work from a song on paper to a record on the charts—is a game of long odds. The payoff can be enormous, however, for everyone concerned. To achieve it, a writer must know the craft and the business, both the art and the commerce, of songwriting.

Predictors of Success

Is it possible to define a "good" song? Yes, if you know what to look for. Can anyone predict professional acceptance? Sometimes, if you know how. Does anyone know which songs will become lasting hits? Not on this earth. In a perfect world, a good song and a hit song would be one and the same. Good songs would become hits, and hits would be good songs. That's not always the case (just ask any songwriter), so it is perhaps easier to look at the two concepts separately.

A hit song is one that gets significant radio airplay, streaming, and downloads. Those metrics are quantifiable. By contrast, a *good* song is harder to define, but at a minimum, it must be well crafted musically and, if it's not an instrumental, lyrically as well.

How far can we go in predicting how any song will fare in the marketplace? Until The Beatles came along and turned the world on its ear, musicians and merchants had a working understanding of what a "popular song" was. They knew what made a C&W (**country** and western) song or an R&B (**rhythm-and-blues**) song. A certain set of songwriting criteria—this type of lyric, that type of beat—could be counted on to resonate with a certain segment of the music-buying audience when matched up with the right artist. Today, these tidy classifications don't serve nearly as well, because many songs incorporate various styles and straddle multiple genres. Tastes are not easily predictable, and trends can be born fast (and die faster). One thing, at least, has stayed constant through the centuries: From 11th-century chansons to this week's charts, the all-time favorite is the love song. So *that's* a good bet for success, right? But even within the love song genre, it's difficult to classify songs or to predict what might be successful. Hits come from everywhere. This unpredictability both frustrates and encourages writers. Sometimes you know you've nailed it, and sometimes you just get lucky.

There *are* some patterns to be found, however. Some lessons to be learned from the past, as well as some newer approaches described in Chapter 15, can help predict what might work in the future. Although it is difficult to identify specific ingredients that might bring a song artistic or commercial success, we *can* critically examine great songs and see what they have in common. What makes a Franz Schubert, a Richard Rodgers, or a Duke Ellington stand out above the rest? Is there a common denominator to be discovered in the works of Joni Mitchell, Randy Newman, Billy Joel, and Diane Warren? Can we identify the elements in their songs that make us love them?

Consider these general criteria and you'll begin to see that all good songs tend to exhibit the following characteristics:

1. The song is memorable; it sticks in the mind. This is often accomplished by use of a **hook,** a catchy phrase or refrain that repeats several times during the song.

2. The song has immediate appeal.

3. The lyrics contain an overall theme and employ vivid phrases or imagery. For example, not "Your beauty makes me love you," but perhaps, "Your touch makes me tremble."

4. The song is well crafted and exhibits an arc: It has a discernible beginning, middle, and end.

Even if a song has these basic characteristics of a *good* song, it still has only the potential to become a *hit* song. Achieving that breakthrough will involve a number of other elements beyond the songwriter's control. Traditionally, these included the following:

1. The song gets an appealing initial performance, hopefully by a well-known performer, that is captured in a recording session.

2. The record company gets behind the project and promotes strong airplay for the recording.

3. The song and the recording suit the taste of the current market.

4. The recording is distributed effectively.

The Craft

OK, so now you have a general idea of what a good song is. How do you go about writing one? Not all songwriters are endowed with creative gifts, and there is little evidence that creativity can be taught. But the craft of songwriting can be learned through formal study and/or private instruction. All colleges accredited by the National Association of Schools of Music (NASM) offer at least 2 academic years of theory study—harmony, ear training, music reading, orchestration, and counterpoint. Some colleges offer composition classes that teach popular songwriting as well as classical fare. These are good options to explore. What about the various "how-to" books addressed to songwriters? Many contain useful information. Some are lightweight, get-rich-quick publications. And what about private instruction? Excellent, if you can find good teachers and can afford it.

Perhaps nothing could be more useful to a songwriter, amateur or pro, than to select 100 of the leading standards and then study them phrase by phrase, line by line, and chord by chord. To guide you in this kind of analysis, you might study Alec Wilder's excellent book *American Popular Song: The Great Innovators, 1900–1950.* Wilder, himself a first-rate songwriter, theorist, and contemporary music historian, studied not just 100 songs but several thousand. Borrow Wilder's technique: If you can examine the internal workings of 100 great melodies, 100 great lyrics, you will have at least begun a serious study of the songwriting craft. If you lean more in the pop or rock and roll direction, do a similar analysis of the masterpieces of Lennon and McCartney, Bob Dylan, and Paul Simon. For country, choose Willie Nelson or Merle Haggard; for soul or R&B, Smokey Robinson or Holland-Dozier-Holland. Talk to songwriters and read interviews with writing legends in books, magazines, and online songwriter forums, and you will likely get the same message from them: Serious songwriters never stop studying their craft.

Songwriters, particularly those just starting out, will also do well to open themselves up to all the advice and feedback they can get on their early writing efforts, which might not exactly be world class right off the bat (they may, for instance, include lyrical clichés such as "right off the bat"). Here again, listen and learn. Don't become discouraged and don't take any one opinion as gospel—remember that The Beatles were turned down by every label in America before finally getting a deal—but keep an eye out for patterns: Are there particular points of criticism that keep coming up? Are your lyrics confusing to people, your hooks not snagging attention? Address those shortcomings via rewrites and new songs.

Collaboration

Some of the most creative artists in the history of popular music have managed to write both brilliant words and hummable music. If you can do this as well as Irving Berlin, Cole Porter, Bob Dylan, and Paul Simon, the world awaits. But if your strong point is melody, find yourself a lyricist. If you are good at lyrics and lack musical talent, don't try to fake it as a composer. If you write only words or only music, join the club that includes Rodgers and Hammerstein, George and Ira Gershwin, Lennon and McCartney, and so many others. In most cases, two complementary talents can be greater than the sum of their parts.

There are no formulas for locating a collaborator. Try hanging out with other writers and performers. Get the word out around town that you are looking. Contact the regional offices of performing rights organizations (ASCAP, BMI, or SESAC). Check local clubs for songwriting nights. Some good writing teams got started through placement of classified ads in trade papers or on social networking sites. Whatever you do, don't pay someone to be your collaborator. Don't respond to ads soliciting song poems. Don't give money to any so-called publisher to "publish" your songs or add music or add words. *Legitimate publishers never charge writers a dime.* They pay *you*.

When coauthors are ready to approach publishers, they should have worked out a clear understanding, preferably in writing, of the terms of their relationship. The agreement should provide answers to these questions: Is all income generated by the collaboration to be shared equally? May one writer make changes in the material unilaterally? Under what conditions may one writer withdraw the words or music from the collaborative work if the work remains unpublished or otherwise unsuccessful? Under what circumstances will the collaborative relationship terminate? May the writers concurrently write alone or with a different collaborator? If a potential collaborator refuses to discuss these issues or does not show an interest in compromising, consider this an early warning sign of impending partnership problems.

A special kind of working relationship exists between a composer who doesn't read or write music and a chosen arranger. Some naturally gifted songwriters get by with their intuitive talent for inventing appealing, commercially viable melodies. They usually sing their tunes into a recorder, then hire an arranger to clean up the rhythm, fix the phrasing, add the harmony, and transcribe the results onto **lead-sheets.** (Be very clear on the copyright issues in these cases; such a relationship may be viewed as a cowriting arrangement, and some are indeed set up this way.) Such a composer should, however, endeavor to gain command of the songwriting craft, thus legitimizing the claim to be a professional composer. Computer "notation" software also is available that can help writers who haven't learned that skill.

Copyright Registration

Whether it is a solo or joint effort, a finished song raises a question for its creator(s): Should it be registered with the U.S. Copyright Office? Some writers file an application only when a song is ready to be used on an album or in another public forum, when such registration becomes necessary for the collection of royalties. Many other writers exercise caution and register all their songs upon completion. The only downside to this is the fee. Details of the latest fees and forms are on the Copyright Office's website (www.copyright.gov).

The Business of Writing

An ability to write good songs is only part of what it takes to make it as a professional songwriter. Anyone who aspires to a songwriting career must treat the job as a business, which of course it is. The details of the business will vary depending on the type of writer one is (for instance, a singer/songwriter vs. a "pure" songwriter) and the type of publishing arrangement one has (e.g., staff writer vs. single-song contractor vs. publishing company owner). The one constant is that a writer can expect to spend as much time and energy promoting his or her product as was devoted to creating it. Writing and promoting, promoting and writing: This is the professional songwriter's life. A writer will be successful only if those songs he or she creates are exploited—published, licensed, recorded, aired, and performed. A commitment to ensuring that this happens—and that the resulting royalty revenue streams keep flowing in—is what separates a songwriting hobby from a songwriting career.

From Tin Pan Alley to the Brill Building . . .

In the earlier days of the record industry, when music was released on black vinyl records, songwriting was very much a job in the more traditional 9-to-5 sense. In fact, songwriters were in great demand as workers well before records existed, hired by publishing companies to create popular songs for sale as sheet music. These were the heady days of Tin Pan Alley, a nickname given to the New York City street where many music publishers worked from the late 1800s into the early 1950s and in whose offices many of the greatest standards were created by composers and lyricists.

By the 1950s, the music business was changing, and the concurrent rise of radio's popularity and expanding record sales put the focus on writing hit songs to feed to recording artists, largely targeted at the fast-growing teenage market. The roles remained highly compartmentalized, however: Songwriters wrote; artists performed. The legendary Brill Building, on Broadway in Manhattan, became the epicenter of this vital new songwriting scene—a virtual "hit factory" where prolific and talented songwriters all but punched a clock. Output from teams such as Goffin and King, Barry and Greenwich, and Mann and Weil was staggering, and their songs remain classics of that era.

The mid-1960s saw another change in the songwriter's role, as Bob Dylan and The Beatles led a new generation of artists from folk troubadours to soul singers to rock bands, who increasingly wrote their own material. The solid wall between the songwriter and the performer was breached. As the 1960s ended, Carole King, one of the most brilliant of the Brill Building composers, led the way by embracing the new singer/songwriter concept, reveling in the freedom to write more personal material.

. . . To the Home Studio

Today, of course, the singer/songwriter is an industry mainstay, and few songwriters toil away in offices, cranking out tunes on demand (the commercial **jingle** business excepted). The job description of a songwriter is now a highly flexible one, encompassing diverse working styles, business affiliations, and creative approaches. In addition to writing songs for the record industry, songwriters can be found plying their trade for the film industry, TV shows, video games, websites, and advertising agencies.

Where a writer actually writes is a matter of personal preference. The key is to find an environment that works for you—whether that is completely away from distractions in a quiet home studio, perhaps, or surrounded by fellow scribes in a convivial workshop setting.

Pace, too, is an individual decision. Most successful songwriters write all the time. They write not dozens but hundreds of songs. Many professionals like to work out a schedule, perhaps setting aside every morning for creative work. They isolate themselves for several hours, not permitting anything or anybody to distract them. Others are more productive working in spurts. They might stay away from their studio for days or weeks. Then they get inspired or have to meet a deadline and work around the clock.

When not writing, the creator is working at promoting what has been written. Some professionals divide their workweek nearly equally between writing and selling. Professional songwriters not only help their publishers and recording

The Brill Building, New York.
Photo by Robert Marich.

companies push their material but are also on the street and in the studios, and around the watering holes where the pros gather. They spread the good word. If they don't, who will know what they have written lately? And how will the writer learn what people are looking for?

The Performer's Dual Role

One whose "business" comprises performing as well as songwriting will have a somewhat different job focus. Many writers begin as performers, particularly in the fields of rock, folk, and country music. In the rock field especially, almost every successful group includes instrumentalists and singers who also write for the act. Although this would seem to limit opportunities for writers, many aspiring writers have made initial inroads by cowriting with members of bands already under label contract.

Not all singer/songwriters draw the line between the two disciplines in exactly the same place. Some see their performing careers in nightclubs and on independent label releases primarily as a valuable showcase for their songs—and as an additional revenue source. Others are performers first and foremost, and write solely with their own label deals and recordings in mind. Still others move seamlessly between the two sides, actively writing hits for others even as they score with their own releases. Where you draw the line will affect how you spend your time and how you juggle your writing and performing workloads.

■ Income Sources

The type of writer one is—whether a sole songwriter, a cowriter, or an artist/songwriter—will naturally have an impact on the bottom line. Table 5.1 gives a concise summary of the various revenue streams that flow to writers, and Figure 5.1 shows how writers' and publishers' incomes are related.

Income From a Recording

One of the main sources of income for a writer is mechanical royalties, which is keyed to the sale and distribution of recorded music. Another source of income is **performance royalties.** These and other terms relating to a writer's licensing royalties are defined in the chapters that follow, but it's helpful here to keep in mind that a writer always gets 50% of the **mechanical** royalties ("the writer's share"); the other 50%, "the publisher's share," may sometimes be shared with the writer, depending on the writer's publishing arrangement and the contract in effect.

Here is a preview of what a songwriter might earn from just mechanicals on a hit record. Assume the following: (a) The recorded song is on an album that goes "gold," selling 500,000 copies; (b) the writer in question is the composer of two songs on the album, each under 5 minutes in length; and (c) the statutory mechanical royalty rate (it changes from time to time) is 9.10 cents per song for songs 5 minutes or less or 1.75 cents per minute or fraction thereof over 5 minutes.

500,000 albums sold × 9.10 cents per song × two songs = $91,000.

50–50 split between publisher and writer = $45,500 each.

If this same writer wrote all 10 songs on an album that went gold (500,000 copies sold), the math dictates that the writer would earn $227,500 from that hit album.

Table 5.1   Writer's Potential Income Sources

Type of Music Use	Who Pays the Writer
Broadcast performances (TV—commercial and noncommercial)	Writer's performing rights organization
Nonbroadcast performance (clubs, hotels, stadiums, business music, in-flight music, gyms, dance studios, etc.)	Writer's performing rights organization
Mechanical royalties (CD sales)	Recording company pays publisher, which shares 50–50 with writer
Sheet music sales	Publisher pays pennies per song or percentage on "paper" sales
Synchronization of music to film or tape (movies, videos)	Publisher shares 50% of fees received with writer
Special permission, licenses (merchandising deals)	Users pay publisher, who shares with writer
Jukeboxes	Performing rights organization pays publisher, who shares 50–50 with writer
Dramatic (or grand) rights	Publisher shares with writer (unless writer or agent retains dramatic rights)
Digital MP3 downloads, cell phone ringtones, streaming interactive subscription services, satellite radio, Internet radio stations, and other webcasts	Varies. Licensees pay writer's performing rights organization, or licensees pay publisher directly, which shares with writer

Note: All these uses are for *nondramatic* music, except dramatic (or grand) rights.

Figure 5.1   Songwriters' and Publishers' Income Sources

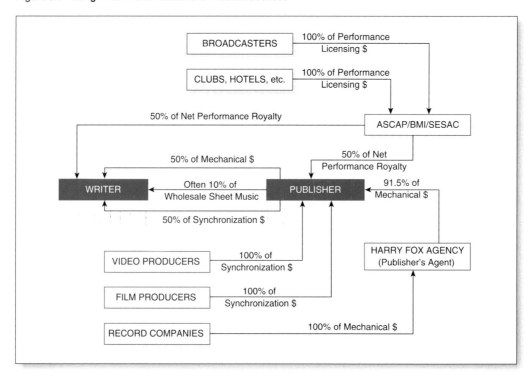

Don't start seeing big dollar signs, however. First of all, few albums sell that well. Even when they do, writers, and singer/songwriters in particular, routinely negotiate a rate lower than the statutory figure with their labels, which also often contractually "cap" the total mechanicals that will be paid on any one album (more on this later). Such categories of releases as "budget lines" and compilations may also carry reduced rates. The bottom line, then, is more like this: To generate a steady living wage, the writer must write and write and then write some more—and must find ways to get the material published and recorded on as regular a basis as possible.

Performance Royalties and New Revenue Streams

The other main source of income for songwriters is performance royalties, which are generated by the broadcast or performance of a writer's works. This income can equal or surpass that of mechanicals; a hot single, for instance, may receive tremendous radio airplay even when the album it is drawn from rings up only lackluster sales. This royalty is collected by the writer's affiliated **performance rights organization** (ASCAP, BMI, or SESAC), which issues blanket licenses to broadcasters and others for the performance of music from its catalog and then remits monies collected to the writer based on his or her songs' use in the marketplace. In addition, a writer may collect income from a variety of other music uses, ranging from the old standard of sheet music and folio sales to the newer arena of digital MP3 downloads, video downloads, satellite radio, Internet radio, digital subscription services, and ringtones.

■ Publishing Options

Before a writer can begin collecting any income, he or she must first get some songs published. A writer with a portfolio of marketable material has a number of options to consider. These are among the most common publishing arrangements:

1. *The writer can search out an established publisher and sign a contract with that firm.* Here, the writer participates only in writer's income. An unknown writer may begin with a single-song contract.

2. *The writer can negotiate a contract with a publisher in which the writer gets a piece of the publisher's share of the income.* This kind of deal is often called **copublishing** or "splitting the publishing"—the two parties usually share equally in the publisher's income. This option is obviously more appealing to the writer, and thus it generally takes a strong writer track record or a performer/writer's clout—such as having an existing album deal with a label—to negotiate this arrangement.

3. *The writer can set up a publishing company.* This option is often appealing to singer/songwriters who will record their own material. The writer will then own the copyrights and may make an agreement with an established publisher to administer his or her copyrights, for a fee.

4. If the writer is also a recording artist, the personal manager under contract (or an attorney) might set up a publishing company owned by the writer and administered by the manager for a commission.

5. *The writer might enter into a partnership or set up a corporation with others to operate a publishing company.* If the writer in a corporate structure is a full-time

professional writer, the corporation might pay the writer as a regular employee. Whether the writer also receives a salary "override" on writer's royalties is determined by the provisions of the employment contract.

6. The writer might be offered a staff job by a publisher.

Staff Writers

A small and decreasing number of publishers will sometimes place promising writers on staff and demand their exclusive services on a full-time basis. Most staff writers receive a weekly salary; it may be just a token payment or a living wage. Whatever its size, the payment is treated as an advance on the writer's future royalty earnings. Remember, the bigger the advance, the more may have to be paid back or done without when the royalties start coming in—*it's not free money.*

Another kind of staff writer is also on salary, often full-time, for exclusive services. But the big difference here is that the writer is engaged to perform work made for hire for the publisher—meaning that the songs remain the exclusive property of the employer, and the writer can never claim copyright. The writer still receives the standard writer royalty from all sources of income but cannot benefit from the copyright reversion provisions in the Copyright Act. If any work-for-hire songs become standards, this forfeiture of the right to recapture could represent a substantial financial loss for the writer and the writer's heirs.

Still another "staff" position at some publishing companies is that of a "song doctor." These writers rearrange and fix songs that the publisher owns an interest in to make the work more palatable to a certain audience. For example, the song doctor would rearrange a song to sound "modern country" in order to present it to a Nashville producer. The song doctor also makes small adjustments in the work to improve its overall condition. These positions are often salaried.

Early in a career, a writer might be so hungry that accepting a work-made-for-hire job is the only option. But it would be wise to seek a more attractive long-term alternative as soon as possible.

It's important to note that the above-described positions are becoming rarer and rarer in today's marketplace. But there are still a few mid-size publishers that engage writers in these kinds of roles.

Label-Affiliated Deals

As shown, multitalented songwriters can boost their marketability and their income by presenting themselves not just as writers but as performing artists. The monetary upside is easy to see: Singer-songwriters can earn both writer's royalties and artist's royalties. In addition, performing artists who write their own songs may be viewed as more attractive prospects by publishers, because they eliminate one of the efforts publishers must make with a "pure" songwriter—convincing a recording artist to use one of the writer's songs. An artist with an album deal already lined up is a particularly hot property.

Because of this potential for big earnings, everybody in the business wants a piece of that pie. A small label will pressure, sometimes coerce, a prospective writer-performer to assign some or all the publishing rights to the label's publishing arm. If the writer declines to share at least administration rights, the firm may **pass** on that writer—decline to sign a recording contract. Similar pressure on the singer-songwriter comes from many independent production companies. Typical dialogue:

"Hey kid, we're gonna make you a big star, but it'll be expensive. We must have your publishing rights to help us recoup our recording costs and promotion expenses." The aspiring singer-songwriter has been cautioned to "hang on to your publishing" but may have to choose between signing it away to a production company and not getting signed as a recording artist.

There *is* a royalty downside to being a performer who writes one's own songs. As noted earlier, record companies generally include a **controlled composition clause** in their artists' agreements. This states that the recording company will pay only a percentage (typically, 75%) of the current mechanical royalty rate to the composer and publisher for any song written or coauthored by that artist/ composer. In addition, a contractual "cap" on total mechanicals payable on an album (such as, 10 times 75% of the statutory rate) may require the artist to further lower his or her rate—for instance, if the album contains more than that number of **cuts**; alternately, the performer who uses both controlled and outside writers' songs may ask outside writers to reduce their rates in return for being included on the album.

In recent years, some publishers in Nashville have also been successful in contractually drawing from a songwriter's performance royalty, as well as from mechanical royalties, to recoup advance money. This point can be negotiable, if the writer is willing to take less in the way of an advance.

■ Evaluating Publishers

A writer who does not sign with the publishing arm of a record label or a production company, or who is not a recording artist, needs to pursue another business model, either by setting up a publishing company or by locating a publisher independent of affiliation with a record company or production company.

How does a thoughtful writer evaluate a prospective publisher? Very carefully. Sharks and wolves abound where big dollars are available. Let us assume the writer is unknown. If there has been a struggle to gain the interest of a publisher, the writer may be tempted to sign on any terms with just about any firm that shows interest. An unpublished writer should think twice before rushing to sign the first contract offered.

The following questions can help inexperienced composers judge a prospective publisher:

1. What is the publisher's reputation for integrity? Is your information objective, trustworthy, and current?

2. How good is the firm's leadership? How competent? How stable?

3. What is the firm's long-term track record? Is it coasting on its catalog of golden oldies, or is it currently active with contemporary material?

4. Is the company making money? Says who?

5. Who in the company cares about you and your material? Do you know the professional manager, or are you dealing with a subordinate person in the firm? Is there at least one individual in the firm who likes your songs enough personally to exert real effort on your behalf? This kind of personal enthusiasm, rare in today's market, is sometimes the key to successful promotion.

6. What are the firm's resources? Do the professional manager and field promoters have valuable contacts with record producers and other important people in the business, such as film and TV music supervisors? Does the company agree to produce high-quality demos of your songs? Does the company have enough **working capital** to carry it over lean periods?

7. If your songs hit, does the company understand the print business and the income available from licensing for sale a variety of different editions?

8. If your songs hit, does the company know how to set up licensing arrangements abroad to maximize foreign income?

9. If your songs hit, does the company have experience in negotiating the whole range of digital uses?

An unknown writer on the verge of signing a first contract with a publisher may be afraid to pose such pointed questions for fear of blowing the deal. But the writer risks being taken advantage of if the questions aren't asked and answered.

Whatever publishing arrangement the writer ultimately pulls together, the decision should be based on which person or firm can best exploit the music over the long term. Is the publisher a genuine professional with the know-how and contacts to exploit those copyrights internationally? Or are they only posing as a publisher, functioning merely as a collection agency for the writer's royalties? These days, a high percentage of so-called publishers function primarily as banks, collecting and disbursing money with little commitment to the writer or the music.

Richard Rodgers seated at piano with Lorenz Hart on right.
Photo by World Telegram staff photographer.

◼ The Songwriters Guild of America

One of the veteran organizations representing the songwriting community is the Songwriters Guild of America (SGA). The organization bearing this name was originally formed in 1931 as the Songwriters Protective Association. For many years, it was called the American Guild of Authors and Composers (AGAC); it changed to its current name in the 1980s.

The organization provides a variety of useful services to its members: (a) offers a standard writers' publishing contract; (b) collects royalties; (c) reviews members' publishing contracts, free of charge; (d) audits publishers; (e) maintains a copyright renewal service; (f) administers writer-publishers' catalogs (CAP, the Catalog Administration Plan); (g) provides a collaboration service; (h) maintains the Songwriters Guild Foundation; (i) operates an estates administration service; (j) provides financial evaluation of songs and catalogs to members and nonmembers; (k) offers workshops for writers; and (l) lobbies in Washington, D.C., on behalf of songwriters.

The Songwriters Guild of America Contract

The guild urges its members to attempt to negotiate acceptance of its Popular Songwriters Contract. As one would assume, it is heavily weighted in favor of the writer. Many publishers refuse to sign it. But writers can use it at least as a negotiating document. These provisions should be studied in tandem with the draft contract provisions in Chapter 6.

The SGA and its contract language argue for the following provisions:

1. The writer warrants that the composition is the writer's "sole, exclusive, and original work" and that the writer has the right and power to make the contract and that "there exists no adverse claim to or in the composition."

2. If the publisher agrees to pay an advance, it will be provided in the agreement, and the advance will be recoupable from the writer's royalties.

3. Royalties on printed editions are not less than 10% of the wholesale selling price on the first 200,000 copies sold in the United States and Canada, not less than 12% on sales in excess of 200,000, and not less than 15% on sales in excess of 500,000.

4. The publisher pays the writer 50% of the publisher's receipts from all sources outside the United States and Canada.

5. The writer shares 50–50 with the publisher on income derived from all other sources—for example, mechanical royalties, synchronization rights, transcriptions, and block licenses. The publisher may discount any payments made to a collecting agent, such as the Harry Fox Agency, Inc.

6. The publisher must obtain the writer's consent before granting use of the composition in a movie, broadcast commercial, or dramatico-musical presentation or for any other new use.

7. The writer's royalties must be held in trust by the publisher and not used for any other purpose.

8. If the publisher fails to get a commercial recording of the composition within a specific number of months, the contract normally terminates. But the

publisher may pay an additional specified sum to extend its window to secure a commercial recording.

9. The publisher must print and offer for sale regular piano copies or provide such copies or leadsheets to the writer.

10. The publisher must pay the writer 50% of foreign advances received by the publisher on a single song or a group of songs by the same writer.

11. Unless terminated earlier under other provisions, the term (length) of the contract may be for any number of years but not more than "35 years from the date of first release of a commercial sound recording of the composition."

12. When the contract terminates, the publisher revests in the writer all rights in the composition.

13. The publisher supplies a royalty statement at least every 6 months. The writer may demand an audit of the publisher's books upon supplying appropriate notice.

14. All disputes between the parties are to be submitted to arbitration under the rules of the American Arbitration Association, and the parties agree "to abide by and perform any award rendered in such arbitration."

15. The publisher may not assign (transfer or sell to another publisher) the contract without the writer's consent (except on the sale of a full catalog).

16. The writer and publisher must agree on future use—the exploitation of a composition in a manner not yet contemplated and therefore not specifically covered by the contract.

Contract Reassignment or Default

The writer and publisher may negotiate at length to shape an equitable contract. The relationship may turn out to be mutually profitable, even congenial. But it is the nature of the business that writers and publishers frequently want to terminate contracts. This does not mean the songs under contract must then die for lack of promotion. Rather, the copyrights may be reassigned.

Reassignments are common and can be to the advantage of the writer even if the songs are included in a bona fide sale of the first publisher's catalog, in the event of a merger or if the **assignment** is to a subsidiary or affiliated company. In each of these circumstances, the writer should demand from the first publisher a written instrument that states that the assignee-publisher assumes all obligations of the original (first) publisher.

Songwriters must continually police their contracts to make sure all the terms are being carried out. **Default** is a common occurrence. Default does not always involve unfairness, dishonesty, or fraud. More likely, a publisher defaults for one of the following reasons: inability to get the song recorded, the royalty statements are incorrect or incomplete, the publisher can't come up with royalty payments when they are due, or the publisher becomes overburdened working on other properties. If the writer believes the publisher is guilty of default and if the publisher has been given the chance to **cure** the default if such cure was stipulated in the contract, whatever the reasons, there are several options. The first is to go to arbitration, if that option is provided for in the contract. Next is to break the contract unilaterally. Courts take a dim view of unilateral action of this kind, for it is the court that must determine if a contract **breach** is material and whether the publisher has flagrantly disregarded appeals from the writer for **remedy.** Third, a lawsuit can be filed asking to be released from the contract. Fourth, a letter of termination can be sent to the publisher, stating that the publisher is in default and that henceforth the rights to any songs that have not yet been delivered to the publisher (known as *future rights*) will go to another publisher.

▪ Breaking In

By now, you are probably both excited and terrified at the prospect of embarking on a career as a professional songwriter. (Don't worry—the contracts arena gets less intimidating over time.) You're likely also ready to begin. Breaking into the field is not as mysterious as generally believed. Many unknown writers are discovered every year, but few make it on luck alone. When we dig into the so-called overnight success stories, we learn that most of these individuals used certain promotion techniques. We cannot articulate a breaking-in "formula." But we can describe what works for many new writers (see Table 5.2).

To increase your chances of success, you should undertake four levels of self-promotion: (a) establish a local reputation and local contacts, (b) contact publishers by mail or email, (c) meet with publishers directly, and (d) network, network, network—both online and face-to-face.

But first, you will need to arm yourself with a **demo.**

Demonstration Recordings

If you are a writer looking to connect with a publisher, or simply to get feedback from local artists and professionals on your work, you will need to be able to present

Table 5.2 Seven Steps to Success

1.	The first step is the most critical. Before spending time and money seeking a professional career, first find out if the talent is there. Your songs may go over great with family and friends. These reactions can be heartwarming—and misleading. What you as an amateur need at this point is an objective appraisal of your creative talents.
2.	Make certain you know your craft. A writer needn't be a creative genius but can learn to be a craftsman.
3.	Arm yourself with professional leadsheets, lyric sheets, and demonstration recordings.
4.	Focus your promotion efforts on the specific market your songs fit.
5.	Promote your songs in your own locale before risking a trip to the "big city." But do plan to make forays into music city hubs once you have a strong portfolio of songs you are ready to showcase before industry professionals.
6.	Employ the promotion techniques outlined in these pages; learn the business, and develop and nurture music industry contacts wherever you can find them. Network.
7.	Be relentless. Most of your competition will become discouraged and give up. Don't take it personally if someone doesn't return your calls or emails. Try again, and then try some more. The persistent writer can beat the competition by hanging in there.

a demonstration recording (demo) showcasing your songs. This will be your calling card, perhaps your one chance to make a strong impression. Choose your best five songs and spend what you can to present them in their best possible light. (Some publishers can hear a diamond in the rough, but it's best not to count on that.) The first requirement? The vocals must be clearly heard above the music. If you are a talented singer, you can take the vocal yourself; if you doubt your ability and can afford to hire a professional—hungry singers abound—by all means do. The minimum accompaniment is piano or guitar. The maximum appropriate accompaniment would include a **rhythm section** and one or two frontline players. The singing should be straightforward; with a songwriter's demo, the listener wants to judge the song. Of course, if you are also a recording artist seeking a label deal, your demo should convey a representative performance.

A demo can be produced in a home studio if one has access to good-quality recording equipment and knows how to use it. Professional demo producers are also available at recording studios in many cities, at reasonable rates. They provide a professional singer accompanied by piano or guitar. Rates rise for more backup musicians, but producers offer special rates for more than one song. (See Chapter 13 for more information on recording studios and production.)

Demos are most commonly recorded on **CD-R**s, perhaps MP3s. Each demo should be clearly labeled, on the box as well as on the recording itself, with an accompanying log of songs: their sequence numbers, song titles, and full names of composers. Tape one copy of the log outside the case and fold another copy inside. Be sure your own name, address, and phone number are included on every piece of material you submit; often, these items get separated.

Demos may include two notices of copyright: the letter P in a circle (Ⓟ), to protect the **phonorecord,** and the letter C in a circle (©), to protect the music contained in the recording.[1] The demo should also contain language saying it is for demonstration purposes only and is not to be distributed, sold, or otherwise disseminated and that it should be returned or destroyed if the recipient doesn't wish to make professional use of it. Such notices offer some protection from unauthorized use. Demos are frequently lost due to inadequate identification (e.g., complete return address) and careless handling. If you are mailing one to a publisher, send it first class. Send copies, of course, not the masters.

Demos will likely also be recorded again when the writer is further along in the publishing process. A publisher, for instance, may want to produce a demo to showcase the new work of a writer under contract to persuade an artist or producer to record the songs. These demos can be much more polished and expensive than an aspiring writer's efforts. The upside is that a publisher will often pay at least part of the demo's costs or at least provide the money for it as an advance on the writer's future royalties.

Local Promotion

Demo in hand, you are now ready to take your first steps toward a professional songwriting career, and for this task there is no place like home. Prove yourself locally. The amateur needs a place to make mistakes, to experiment with different kinds of promotional efforts before moving into the harsher spotlight of a music industry hub.

Look within your own circle of family and friends for a connection to the music business, no matter how small. If you don't have one, start with professional performers in your area. Go to their gigs, visit their rehearsals. Hang out, get acquainted. If your songs suit their style, you may persuade them to try your material. At this stage, it doesn't matter whether these professionals are well known. Making their acquaintance now may provide a contact that will bear fruit later.

Contact your local radio stations and try to persuade program directors, disc jockeys, and music librarians to listen to your demos. Because radio, like music publishing, has become increasingly corporatized, with programming decisions made in far-off cities, they almost certainly will be unable to use your songs, but their evaluations could be valuable.

Now might also be the time to promote yourself on the Internet. It's easy to post your music on social networking sites. You can also set up your own website, complete with blogs and sample songs. This is a helpful tool to which you can refer interested parties. Remember to include your website address on all correspondence and on your business cards. If you are a singer/songwriter, you can also use these sites to sell copies of your CDs, offer downloads, and advertise upcoming club dates. Be sure to register your site with major search engines.

Keep an eye out for acts coming through town on tour. Traveling performers often pick up useful material on the road. With some performers, it is more effective to try to get your songs to people *around* the artist, such as the performer's musical director (**MD**), arranger, or manager, any of whom could be an influential song picker.

Some smaller cities are headquarters for publishing companies. Do not rule out small publishers—they may do more for you than the majors. If you evaluate them according to the guidelines listed in this chapter and if they measure up, go with them if you do not have a more attractive option at the time.

Contact local advertising agencies and commercial production companies. Communities with populations of 100,000 and up will generally have such firms. They are in constant need of melodies and musical ideas for broadcast commercials.

If you begin to receive favorable local reaction to your writing, you just might be ready for the next step in promoting your songs.

Promotion by Mail and Email

Amateur songwriters have sometimes been successful in landing their first publishers through an initial mail contact. This is a special technique, however, and efforts of this kind often fail because they are not handled effectively. But the writer who follows the procedures outlined has a chance of getting songs heard. All it costs is the price of postage and a few demo CDs or a few minutes at the computer. Here's how to proceed:

1. Study the record charts and find out the names of publishers who are currently active in handling the type of music you write.

2. Get the addresses and telephone numbers of these publishers. Google them or try your local telephone company or library.

3. Verify by phone the name of the appropriate contact person.

4. Write a letter or send an email requesting *permission* to send in some of your songs. The letter should be short, well written, and to the point. Briefly state what reception your songs have already experienced with professional

performers. If permission is received, follow the publisher's submission guidelines exactly (mail physical CD, email link to your music, upload to a dropbox, etc.) to send in only your three to five best songs. Your submission should contain a demo recording of each song *and* separate lyric sheets for each song, with your name, address, and telephone number on each sheet. Inclusion of professionally prepared leadsheets is optional with some publishers, but play it safe and include them too. If submitting a physical CD, in addition to your cover letter, include a self-addressed, stamped postcard. Send your package by first-class mail, not by certified or registered mail; some publishers feel that accepting such mail could mean trouble. Wait 3 weeks. If you receive no reply, call or email the publisher to confirm that your material has arrived. If your songs have been received but have not gained acceptance, continue the process with other publishers until you receive a favorable reaction.

Very few publishers today will open unsolicited mail; not only are they wary of being accused of stealing material, but a greater concern is that the vast majority of unsolicited songs and demos are mediocre or worse. Publishers cannot take time to dig through the piles of songs received every week in the hope that one in a hundred might be worth serious consideration. But when a writer has been professional enough to obtain permission from the publisher to submit material, whatever is mailed in is viewed differently. Take a look at the sample first-contact letter that follows:

Mr. John Doe, Professional Manager

XYZ Music Publishing Company

Address

Dear Mr. Doe: Date:

Please indicate your response to the following question and then mail this card back to me (it is already addressed and stamped).

Will you examine my songs for publication?

Yes _____   **No** _____

Your response will be sincerely appreciated.

Thank you.

(Signed here)

Austin Hopeful

Address/Telephone

A first-contact email will be very similar:

Dear Mr. Doe,

Please reply by return email your response to the following question.

Will you examine my songs for publication?

Your response will be sincerely appreciated.

Thank you.

Austin Hopeful

Address/Telephone

Direct Contact With Publishers

Even though some lucky amateur songwriters manage to create publisher interest through mail or email contacts, most songs get published following a direct, personal contact with the publisher.

Because popular music publishers have offices in the leading recording centers, the amateur writer who wants to go professional and doesn't live in New York, Nashville, or Los Angeles will need to spend time in one or more of these cities. Occasionally, publishers will see unknown songwriters, but it is unwise for the newcomer to walk directly from the bus station to the publisher's office. First, write a letter or send an email requesting an appointment, or call the office and talk to the receptionist about setting up a meeting (*always* be polite to this gatekeeper). If you can drop a name of someone in the industry who has referred you, your chances will improve dramatically.

If you are fortunate enough to have been granted a meeting with a publisher, be sure to write a thank you note afterward. Keep up that valuable contact even if you may not have new material. Then, when you are ready to submit more songs— whether in person or by mail—you will have an "in."

Network, Network, and Then Network Some More

If it hasn't become apparent by now, it's worth stating bluntly here: Industry connections and contacts, those all-important "ins," are the key to getting your songs noticed and, ultimately, recorded. Many publishers will take meetings based only on referrals by industry pros, for instance, and record producers heading into the studio with an artist will usually turn first to songwriters they know or who have been recommended to them.

The music industry is built on networking and relationships, and songwriting is no exception. The good news is that networking can be easy and fun. It simply means getting out there, getting involved, getting seen, and getting heard. A good place to start is by contacting your regional ASCAP or BMI membership representative, who may be open to reviewing and assessing your songs; if he or she likes them, the representative can provide that all-important referral to a music publisher or label contact. ASCAP and BMI also host workshops for young writers, as do many other songwriter, publisher, and music business organizations. Use online resources to find out what's happening, and attend as many events as you can; even if you are not (yet) invited to perform yourself—you can make invaluable introductions. Seek out organizations in your area and explore the many online music forums for relevant information.

Contests offer another avenue to get your name and your songs in front of industry professionals; even if you don't win, you may make an impression and a connection. The performing rights organizations sponsor some of the major ones, but others abound. Read music publications, search websites, and talk to other industry professionals for information, but exercise caution in making sure any such contests are legitimate and not moneymaking schemes keyed to entry fees or demo production charges.

Finally, of course, you can take the ultimate networking plunge and choose to immerse yourself in a songwriting hub city such as New York, Los Angeles, or Nashville. Particularly in Nashville, you will find yourself rubbing shoulders constantly with music industry insiders and wannabes—everywhere from coffee shops to clubs. If you can afford it, such a move can prove invaluable in many ways, including finding new collaborators. Even if not, a serious songwriter will try to schedule regular visits to any (or all) of these cities to attend workshops, forums, and meetings.

Note

1. Some attorneys have suggested not using the ℗ symbol on a demo for fear its presence would create the legal presumption that the recording is "published," thus leaving the composer vulnerable to an unwanted compulsory mechanical license.

Chapter Takeaways

- Songwriting is the essential ingredient of the music industry, but the crush of competition makes success challenging.

- Successful songs tend to exhibit similar characteristics, notably a hook—a repeated catchy phrase or refrain.

- A songwriter can expect to spend as much time promoting songs as writing them.

- Main sources of songwriting income include mechanicals, performance royalties, and synchronization fees.

- There are many ways to publish a song, ranging from signing as a singer-songwriter with the publishing affiliate of a label to establishing a publisher sole proprietorship.

- Carefully prepare a demo recording to woo publishers to offer a songwriting contract.

- Networking in the music industry is essential, particularly in the profession of songwriting.

Key Terms

- controlled composition clause   (p. 75)

- cure   (p. 78)

- default   (p. 78)

- demos   (p. 79)

- hook   (p. 67)

- leadsheet   (p. 68)

- mechanicals   (p. 71)

- performance royalties (p. 71)

- revenue streams   (p. 69)

- song doctor   (p. 74)

- Tin Pan Alley   (p. 69)

Discussion Questions

1. What defines a good song? How does this differ from a hit song?

2. Why would you bother to have a written agreement with a songwriting collaborator if you've never published a song?

3. Explain the difference between networking and promotion.

4. How should a songwriter react to a publisher's proposal to deliver a work for hire?

5. What are some reasons a songwriter may want to get out of a contract? Discuss different ways to go about ending a contract.

6. Discuss specific ways a songwriter can promote his or her work. Which of these ways would be easy for you?

CHAPTER 6

Music Publishing

Decades ago, music publishers made a living by printing copies of sheet music and placing them in local music stores or the "five and dime" for sale to the public. Today, of course, few families spend their evenings singing songs around a piano, and the business of music publishing has responded to the changes and challenges wrought by radio, records, and a parade of ever-changing technologies—the new means of exposing music to the public. In the popular music field, the great majority of new songs are no longer printed commercially at all but may be available in digital formats (that users can print out on paper). When publishers believe that printing their copyrighted works for sale to consumers might prove profitable, they usually license that right to dwindling numbers of specialty **print** publishers whose sole function is to provide these services (see Chapter 4 for more information on copyrights).

> "Music is everybody's possession. It's only publishers who think that people own it."
>
> —John Lennon

Today, the heart of the music **publishing** industry lies not in the print business but in the marketing and administration of rights to songwriters' compositions. For the contemporary music publisher, success is keyed directly to how well the publishing company exploits music and generates mechanical royalties (from recordings), performance royalties (from broadcast or live performance), and other licensing fees (such as using an already existing piece of music in a film or other visual work). In recent years, the Internet and digital revolutions have created a world of new uses for garnering royalties. Among the myriad applications, online services pay publishers a fee for providing consumers access to copyrighted music made available through authorized streaming and downloading.

Left: The Universal Music Group building in Santa Monica, California.

Photo by Ryan V. Bitinis.

Those with long experience in the music business know publishing to be a lucrative and steady source of income that can bring in revenue long after a hit song has faded from the airwaves (or even when it doesn't "hit" at all). "Keep your publishing" has become a mantra for copyright owners all over the world, and just about everyone in the performing and recording fields is involved in music publishing in one way or another.

To gain a perspective on how this field has become such a colossus, Table 6.1 shows how the industry developed historically.

Table 6.1   Development of Music Publishing

1640	The first book published in America—and it happens to be a music book—is *The Bay Psalm Book*, which first used musical notation in its 1698 edition.
1770	The first native-born American composer, William Billings, gets his music published.
1790	First U.S. Congress passes the first copyright law.
1850–1900	Minstrel shows are widely popular and increase public interest in popular music. Publishers begin to prosper.
1890s	The player piano becomes popular, creating a demand for player piano rolls. Large music publishing firms are established during the last two decades of the 1800s. Merchandising methods develop, and publishers begin to discover that if enough people hear a good song, it will probably be a hit. The most effective song promoters now are the performers in various theaters and vaudeville houses that develop around the turn of the century.
1900	Popular music publishing becomes big business, and for the next 40-plus years, music publishers are the most powerful people in the music industry. In this first decade of the 20th century, an estimated 100 songs each sell a million copies or more within a 1-year period, at a time when the population of the United States is about 90 million. The U.S. Congress passes the historic 1909 Copyright Act that, for the first time, provides publishers with mechanical rights in recorded music. Initially, this revenue derives largely from player piano rolls.
1920s	The American Society of Composers, Authors and Publishers (ASCAP), established in 1914, becomes a major force as a performing rights organization (PRO). For the first time in this country, publishers and writers begin to receive income from performances of their music. Radio broadcasting begins and is initially fought by publishers who believe radio hurts sheet music sales. Sound movies ("talkies") begin. Film producers negotiate fees for music synchronization rights. The Harry Fox Agency is established as a broker between publishers and third-party licensees. Sheet music sales drop with the rise of radio. Publishers close most of their branch offices to concentrate promotion efforts on the radio network broadcasting centers that, at this time, are New York City, Chicago, and Los Angeles.
1930s	The Great Depression severely hurts the music publishing business, but increasing income from movie producers helps mitigate the losses. The "big bands" develop and become the most important source of plugs for new songs, particularly if the band has a remote wire for radio broadcasting. National Music Publishers' Association (NMPA) expands the Harry Fox Agency to include mechanical licensing of copyrights. SESAC is formed, as a New York–based PRO, in response to European publisher concerns about being underrepresented in the United States.
1940s	During and after World War II, people spend more of their incomes on music, instruments, records, and movies. The LP (for long playing) record appears in 1948, now producing publishers' royalties on 10 to 12 songs per record, not just 2. National Association of Broadcasters (NAB) forms Broadcast Music Inc. (BMI) in reaction to increasing revenue demands from the ASCAP. The big band singers (Perry Como, Frank Sinatra, Doris Day, and others) go solo and become the dominant source for introducing new songs. American gospel music becomes a mainstay of SESAC representation.

1950s	Rapid growth of television kills live music on the radio. Disc jockeys, who play records, become the new hit-makers. Rock and roll comes to dominate popular music, greatly expanding the market for records. BMI succeeds in capturing representation for the majority of copyrights in the rock and country fields. SESAC's repertory expands to include country music.
1960s	Increasing dependence of publishers to break new songs on radio. The Beatles and other pop groups begin recording mostly their own material. The print business improves, particularly editions for the amateur and the educational field. Harry Fox Agency becomes a wholly owned subsidiary of the NMPA.
1970s	Radio broadcasters shorten their playlists below the Top 40, forcing companies to promote airplay in secondary and tertiary markets located in smaller cities. The print business in the pop song folio and educational field continues to grow, but inflating costs cause many publishers to quit all print activity and assign such rights to subpublishers and licensees here and abroad. Publishers' incomes from ASCAP and BMI continue to rise. Record sales boom, and so do publishing revenues. New musical genres continue to develop.
1980s	Old copyrights enjoy financial boom due to widespread popularity of CDs. Huge mergers and acquisitions dominate the publishing business and the music industry in general. Licensed popular music becomes an even more significant part of films, television programs, and commercials. MTV begins broadcasting music videos 24 hours a day and becomes a key promotional tool for increasing sales. Increased music use via new media, particularly home videocassettes, computer games, and video jukeboxes, increases publisher revenues.
1990s	The beginning of the Internet revolution spurs publishers, recording companies, and other music users to contemplate new ways to exploit their product. What is now called the European Union eases restrictions between its member countries, and the United States makes trade agreements to remain competitive. New musical genres, including rap and alternative, challenge rock and roll for market dominance. Success in foreign markets remains critical to the overall success of an artist as a performer or composer. Media and entertainment companies, including their music publishing arms, consolidate.
2000s	The industry grapples with technological issues such as file sharing and complex transmission standards for delivering digital audio. Mechanical royalties decline significantly, mainly from slumping CD sales due to unauthorized file sharing and changes in consumer habits. Music rights revenue surges from sources such as video games, DVDs, film, TV, and commercial synchronizations. Digital opportunities such as Internet downloading, satellite radio, online subscriptions, micro-subscription services, and cell phone ringtones open new vistas for publishers to expose their material and generate incremental revenues.
2010s	Music publishers experience an even more dramatic shift of revenues away from mechanical royalties in favor of performance and synch fees. While performance revenue stays strong, synch fees become more of a challenge because buyers can get more and more music free or very cheaply via the Web and generic music creators. SESAC acquires the Harry Fox Agency to offer both mechanical and performance rights management under one umbrella organization.

Types of Publishers

The term *music publisher* includes everything from the one-person company devoted to the writings of a single artist/writer to the multinational affiliates of record companies, film companies, and media giants. Publishing companies can be publicly owned, artist/writer owned, or owned or administered by managers, lawyers, or even songwriters' relatives or friends. Some publishers are "full service," with huge catalogs covering a broad range of music styles. Others restrict their business to single genres, such as jazz or classical music, or deal only in educational, religious, or printed publications. All large music publishers have affiliates or licensees abroad, and these relationships afford opportunities for reciprocal sharing of royalties in foreign territories.

Music publishers have learned a valuable lesson from movie producers, who discovered decades ago that foreign receipts may equal or even outstrip domestic revenues.

Not too many years ago, there were as many as 30 major music publishers. Today, there are only a handful of major publishers, and they dominate the industry domestically and throughout most of the developed world. Through an unprecedented surge of mergers and acquisitions, a few companies currently boast catalogs of more than a million copyrights. Clearly, it takes vast resources to effectively administer these catalogs. At the same time, new markets around the world and emerging new media have changed the face of the music publishing industry. Publishers, both large and small, realize that their future depends not only on finding and publishing new material but also on growth in new markets and effective administration and exploitation of rights in existing catalogs.

Major Companies

Prior to the great expansion of the recording industry in the 1960s and 1970s, many of the older music publishers included a wide range of musical styles in their catalogs—classical, educational, movie, pop, and show music. Today, new firms with this broad a repertoire are scarce, but a few major publishers are still active in multiple genres. Some are affiliated with record labels and, in some cases, major media companies as well. Major publishers trace their origins to the music of Hollywood, Broadway, or the great pop writers of Tin Pan Alley. These companies provided a "full line" of services such as printing and selling copies of sheet music, "plugging" songs to performing artists, and developing long-term relationships with writers. Each major firm has developed its own corporate structure, but Figure 6.1 shows a typical organization of this scope. Department names and reporting relationships vary from company to company.

Recording Company Affiliates

Full-line publishers affiliated with major labels generally have their own staff and budgets and operate independently of their affiliated labels, although it is not unusual for a label and its affiliated publisher to negotiate with an artist/writer simultaneously. Label publishing affiliates, many of which are among the largest publishers in the world, also acquire catalogs from other publishers or writers, which may be purchased outright for substantial payments. A recording artist may have an existing catalog of previously recorded compositions, which might be acquired by a label's publishing affiliate as part of an overall record/publishing deal. Linkages such as these can make it difficult for the independent label or publisher to compete for a sought-after artist/writer. Of course, the argument can be made that these interlocking companies create a conflict of interest or an unfair negotiating advantage. Artists/writers are sometimes required to place their copyrights with the label's affiliated publisher; those who refuse to do so may find it more difficult to get recording deals.

Despite the reduced mechanical payments and potential conflict issues, publishing/recording deals, when fairly handled, are a way for a new artist to maximize advance income and marshal the publisher's (and label's) resources to establish a successful recording and writing career.

Figure 6.1   **Major Music Publisher Departments and Their Functions**

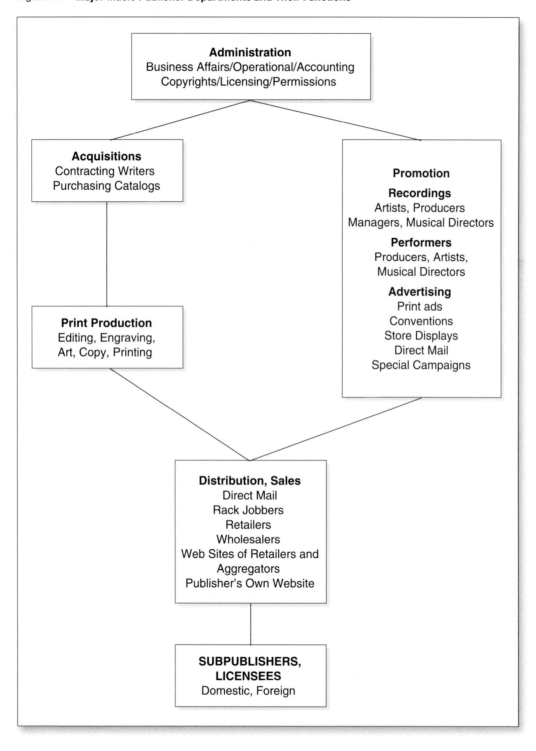

Independent Publishers

Firms not affiliated with either a multinational publishing organization or a **record label** are often referred to as independents. Independents range in size from the one-person operation to firms controlling multi-million-dollar catalogs. Many independents are members of the Association of Independent Music Publishers (AIMP). Some independent publishers perform only basic administrative duties in return for a percentage (generally 10% or 15%) of the publishing income they administer. Responsibilities of such administrative publishers include registering new copyrights with performing rights societies and mechanical societies worldwide, licensing the use of copyrights, collecting and tracking royalties, and royalty accounting. Most do little or no exploitation, which is not a problem for their clients, who are usually artists or writers who promote themselves. A significant number of independents offer more than administrative services, however. Some of these are based in Nashville, where old-style music publishing and song-plugging still exists and indeed flourishes.

Artist-Owned Companies. Many recording artists who write their own material form their own publishing companies. The reason is simple: They see no need to hand over the publishing income, especially when they themselves are the catalysts for the success of the works in the marketplace. Royalties to the publisher of the copyrights accrue from record sales, so artists, usually with assistance from their managers and attorneys, set up publishing companies to keep control over their music and its revenue stream. Because most artists are principally concerned with recording and performing, they generally publish only their own compositions. They rarely get involved in the print business. Once they achieve some international presence, they can arrange **subpublishing** deals abroad, usually negotiated by their attorneys or administrative publisher.

Writer-Owned Companies. A large number of very small publishing operations are owned by individual writers. These firms are set up either by writers who want to control their copyrights from the beginning or by writers unable to get their music accepted by labels or other publishers. Some writer-owned firms have been established by composers who were previously under contract to a publisher but came to believe their material was not receiving sufficient promotion to justify the loss of a percentage of income and a degree of control required in a publishing deal. See Figure 6.2, which shows how very small music publishing firms can be structured.

Educational Publishing

Some publishers in the United States limit their catalogs primarily to music intended for use by students and schools from elementary grade levels through college. The biggest sellers are for piano and guitar, followed by strings and percussion. Part of these sales is known as bench packs—educational materials such as lesson books given by the equipment manufacturer to the customer upon sale of a new keyboard. The instrument manufacturer pays the copyright owners for these materials. The biggest-selling editions for schools are scored for choirs, marching bands, and concert bands.

Specialty Publishers

Many publishers limit their catalogs to one kind of music. Publishers active only in the country field, for example, are among the nation's largest independent publishers,

Figure 6.2 Writer-Owned Publishing Company

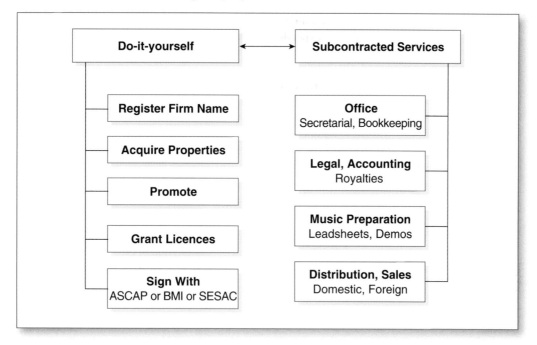

although most major publishers also maintain active offices in Nashville. Most specialty houses are, however, relatively small, preferring to restrict their activities to the field they understand best, such as choral music, gospel, children's music, or so-called stage band (big bands in schools and colleges playing pop and jazz music). One example of this is the publisher devoted solely to what is called "Christian music." Many prosper not only through sales of their music on records but also from a good-sized print business.

Concert Music

Concert (or classical) music is that repertoire generally associated with opera, symphony, ballet, recital, choral, and religious music. Only a handful of publishers limit their catalogs to these fields. Representative concert music publishers include G. Schirmer, C. F. Peters, Boosey & Hawkes, Carl Fischer, and Theodore Presser.

Classical music publishers produce and distribute an array of special editions of the classics for school orchestras and choirs, as well as studies for keyboard, strings, solo instruments, and voice. Much of the income of classical publishers derives from the rental and licensing of **scores** and instrumental and vocal parts.

Besides maintaining catalogs of older music, nearly all of it from Europe, these houses provide a special service. They also publish the works of serious contemporary composers from the United States, Russia, and China whose works are copyrighted. Music publishers in the classical category may offer dramatic works and extended pieces through the rental of the parts rather than the sale of printed editions.

Some classical publishers emphasize contemporary serious (classical) and avant-garde music. Many of these publishers are subsidized by a foundation or university, and they may have sizable catalogs of foreign copyrights that they administer for the U.S. territory. Recordings of their music are also largely subsidized.

Print Licensees

Few popular music publishers in the United States print, market, or distribute printed editions of their copyrights; instead, they license this function to another company. Most print deals provide that the licensee (the print firm) will bear the full costs of preparing, printing, and distributing the printed edition; the licensee then pays the licensor (the publisher controlling the rights) a royalty on sales, often in the range of 12.5% to 20% of the wholesale price. In deals of this kind, the licensee is sometimes called a **selling agent.** In past years, a major publisher with deep pockets sometimes prepared printed material itself, in exchange for a higher chunk of the proceeds. But as sales in digital formats shrunk sales of print, major publishers simply farmed out the opportunity.

Subpublishing

The publishing business is increasingly a global one, and many American publishers receive a large percentage of their income from foreign exploitation of their American catalogs. The foreign exploitation of copyrights via a license from the original publisher is referred to as subpublishing.

Subpublishing Agreements

Some large U.S. companies have branch offices in foreign countries that fill the subpublishing role for their affiliated publishers, functioning much like the American parent firm. First, they try to exploit the American catalog in their territory by promoting the original recording; getting cover records; selling printed editions; securing synchronization licenses for film, TV, and commercials; and collecting mechanical and performance royalties. As part of this effort, the branch office may arrange for translations of English lyrics into the local language. Second, branch offices often acquire compositions created in their own territories.

An independent American publisher lacking branch offices abroad may seek out licensees in those territories. Those subpublishers may be foreign independents or they may be affiliates of multinational companies that are seeking outside catalogs in addition to their own. The latter aggressively pursue successful U.S. catalogs.

Independent publishers lacking the resources to set up subpublishing deals can also choose to retain U.S. licensing firm, the Harry Fox Agency (now part of SESAC), to meet many of their basic needs for services in foreign territories through the agency's reciprocal agreements with foreign societies (see Table 31.1, Foreign Affiliates).[1]

Although royalty splits vary from company to company and country to country, a common arrangement between the original publisher and a subpublisher is 80% to 90% of the gross earnings in the territory paid to the original publisher and 10% to 20% retained by the licensee. Advances are usually paid by the foreign subpublisher to the original publisher based on the projected success and U.S. activity of the song. Usually, the larger the advance, the larger the commission kept by the subpublisher. Most subpublishing deals are usually for 3 to 5 years. The American company will expect the subpublisher to exploit the American copyrights through securing release and handling promotion of the original recording, arranging cover records, providing printed editions, and collecting performance royalties. The performing rights organization functioning in a given territory will forward the writer's share to ASCAP, BMI, or SESAC, but the American firm's subpublisher is usually allowed to collect the publisher's share and apply that to outstanding advances. It is also an advantage for the original publisher to have the publisher's share collected by the subpublisher in the licensed territory because the periods of time otherwise involved with transmitting that payment from the local territory to the performing rights organization (PRO) in the United States might involve a delay of up to 2 years. In addition, the subpublisher is in a better position to make sure the accountings are accurate based on activity of the catalog in that territory.

With regard to foreign collections, a distinction should be made between a collection deal and a subpublishing deal. In a collection deal, the subpublisher is merely expected to collect the income earned from the copyright, taking 10% or 15% as an administrative fee. In a subpublishing deal, the percentages are more favorable to the local publisher and usually involve advances to the original publisher supplying the catalog and more aggressive commitments for exploitation of that catalog in the territory, as outlined previously.

A writer's decision about what kind of foreign deal to make can have far-reaching implications, especially because currency fluctuations in various territories can cause the percentage of foreign income to skyrocket or plummet.

At-Source Deals Versus Receipts-Basis Deals

In choosing a subpublisher, the original publisher (the company to which the writer originally assigned the copyright in the United States) can make a deal with independent subpublishers in various territories or with a multinational subpublisher for a group of territories.

While many factors will play into that decision, the choice of a multinational publisher offers an advantage to the original licensor's bottom line. The reason lies in the distinction between an "at-source" deal and a "receipts-based" agreement. Payment of royalties earned at the source is a concept more favorable to the original publisher and writer, and such setups are usually available only from publishers who have wholly owned affiliates in foreign territories, such as multinational companies.

In an at-source deal, the publisher and writer's share is calculated on income earned in the foreign territory, or "at the source." The original publisher (who accounts to the writer) gets paid as if it were in the country where the money is earned without any deductions by the subpublisher. The writer, in turn, gets his or her 50% share (or more, depending on the deal in effect) of the income earned in the foreign territory, before deductions for subpublishers are made, no matter what money is eventually remitted to the United States. In an at-source deal, if $100 is earned in Australia, the writer's share would be $50.

In contrast, in a receipts-based agreement common among independent subpublishers, the publisher and writer's share is calculated only on income received by the publisher in the United States, *after* payments or deductions to a subpublisher have been made. In a receipts deal, the writer would get royalties based on monies received by the original publisher. If that same $100 is earned in Australia under this type of agreement and the publisher had a 75/25 deal with the Australian subpublisher, the subpublisher gets $25, the American publisher would receive $75, and the writer's share would be $37.50 (50% of $75).

On a positive note, independent subpublishers often give more attention to writers, have better contacts, and work harder to get covers and synch licenses than do the branch offices of multinational conglomerates.

Agreements for Multiple Territories. American firms usually contract with subpublishers to cover more than one country. For example, it is common for a subpublisher based in Germany to cover Germany, Austria, and German-speaking Switzerland, which makes up the territory of GEMA, the German performance rights society. French-based subpublishers would probably service the French-speaking territories in Africa and, quite possibly, the French-speaking radio stations in Luxembourg and Switzerland, which is the territory administered by the French performing rights society, SACEM. A Scandinavian subpublisher would probably have jurisdiction over Norway, Sweden, Denmark, Iceland, and Finland.

There is no one "right" deal for a U.S. publisher looking for overseas exploitation, since different approaches may suit different needs. Some independent U.S. publishers have chosen to become direct members of the foreign societies, for example. Any subpublishing situation, however, should ideally include a person "on the ground" in the country who understands the language and knows the ways of the region's music business, especially with regard to registering copyrights with local societies and collecting performance royalties.

Administration

Administration of publishing companies varies greatly according to the size of the firm. Independent companies may have a small staff, with each individual performing a variety of tasks. In some cases, a small, independent publisher might have only one employee: the owner-songwriter. Contrast this type of operation with the management structure of a major publisher (see Figures 6.1 and 6.2).

Large publishers will have a central administration consisting of a president (or vice president in charge of administration), department heads, and support personnel. Firms vary in the names they apply to departments. What follows is a description of the administrative structure of a typical major publisher.

Royalty Department

The royalty department is managed by an individual, usually an accountant or finance person, who supervises assistants handling receipts and disbursements, and fields inquiries from writers, among other duties.

Copyright Department

Most publishers have at least one employee who handles copyrights. Larger firms have a copyright division, with a department head over a number of staff people. A qualified copyright department head must know the U.S. Copyright Act of 1909, the 1976 revisions and subsequent changes, and basic international laws and agreements ("conventions") covering foreign copyrights.

The firm's copyright department performs a number of essential tasks. Among the most important are the following:

1. Conducting title searches. The copyright department must first determine who really owns a work. The Library of Congress will assist in this research. Copyright ownership can get complicated. If the work has coauthors, what are their claims of ownership and are the claims valid? Have the melody and/or the lyrics fallen into the public domain? What if the work was published before?

What if the music or the lyrics have been revised? How does a publisher determine if some of the rights have been assigned to another firm or individual or estate? After the copyright department has performed this research, questions remaining unclear are referred to a copyright attorney, who may or may not be on the publisher's staff.

2. Registering claims of copyright.

3. Recording transfers of copyright ownership.

4. Forming a liaison with the Harry Fox Agency to issue and administer mechanical licenses. Publishing firms occasionally choose to issue their own mechanical licenses or to go through the American Mechanical Rights Agency, Inc. (AMRA).

5. Keeping records of subsisting copyrights and their pending expiration and termination dates. Recommending renewal, extension, sale, or abandonment of subsisting copyrights. Proper timing is essential as valuable rights could be forfeited.

Legal and Business Affairs

Well-run music publishers must have lawyers with expertise in both copyright law and music publishing. They also need to be versed in tax law, artist management, and the recording industry. Nearly all publishing transactions are based on contracts, and the ongoing services of qualified attorneys are essential in negotiating them. Small firms employ these specialists by the hour or on a monthly retainer basis. Larger firms not only retain counsel part-time, as needed, but also employ one or more lawyers as full-time staff. Attorneys from outside firms may also be employed for specific projects, such as litigation or to facilitate a major acquisition.

Print Publishing Operations

Print publishing requires additional resources. After a copyright title has been cleared and the author is signed to a contract, and after the arrangers and editors have performed their tasks, the music must go through a number of additional operations before it can be distributed and sold. Many firms group these activities, such as printing, warehousing, inventory control, and shipping, under an operations department.

Editing for Print Publications. Nearly all music submitted for print publication needs editing. Few composers, even those classically trained, know how to prepare a manuscript for dissemination. Even a simple leadsheet should be prepared by an arranger qualified in this specialized field. At the outset, the arranger-editor must correct errors in notation and perhaps even rewrite portions that do not make good musical sense. In some cases, editors or "song doctors" are called on to polish lyrics. Print publication has changed dramatically in recent years as digital technology has transformed the processes to create the reproducible master and to distribute the final result to the reader.

The Print Production Line. In the classical and specialty print business, once a publisher determines that a newly acquired piece of music should be offered for sale in printed form in a digital format, on paper, or both, the music goes down a production line. Here is a typical line of production for a piece of printed music headed for the marketplace:

1. The publisher's acquisitions committee (or an authorized individual) determines that the piece of music or a specific arrangement, instruction book, or other proposed publication should be accepted for publication.

2. The publisher's copyright department determines that the title (ownership) of the music is clear (**unencumbered**).

3. The publisher registers a claim to copyright with the U.S. Copyright Office and places copies on file with the Library of Congress.

4. If the composition is an original composition or group of compositions, the publisher's arranger (or a freelance arranger) scores a piano-voice version of the music. The editor makes sure it is in an acceptable form. At some point, it is usually submitted to the writer for approval.

5. After proofreading, if the editor approves the completed work, the printer (in-house or external) duplicates the music. First printings in the educational field are normally 1,000 copies. In the case of popular song folios, a first printing may run as high as 25,000 copies, but usually it's less.

6. Meanwhile, the publisher's or licensee's promotion/advertising people try to generate sales both here and abroad. If they succeed, purchasers put down their money and everyone is happy.

7. The publisher pays the author royalties based on sales volume of the printed editions.

Distribution

Publishers vary in how they handle the distribution and sale of printed editions. As previously noted, most publishers sublicense the print area entirely and merely receive a royalty or share of income that they share with their writers under their overall agreement. The distribution trail generally goes from publisher to print publisher to rack jobber (the middleman between manufacturer and retailer) to retailer to customer.

As consumers have become Web-centric, publishers sell the bulk of their "print" products as digital downloads. Consumers can search, listen, and sample everything from single sheets to choral arrangements to folios to **fake books** to piano and guitar books. If they like what they see, they can either order the music to be mailed to them or purchase and download their music on the spot.

Audit/Tracking

Monitoring sales activity, the audit/tracking department collects payments from licensees and makes sure that they are conforming to limitations of their licensing agreements (for instance, not selling outside of a specified geographic territory). The main task is to make sure music sellers are paying the full amounts due. The biggest music publishers also handle auditing and tracking of digital media in-house. Smaller publishers may outsource tracking of digital media because it is technology intensive and complex. The audit/tracking function can be pushed into the spotlight when trackers became "detectives" to investigate unauthorized lyrics websites that rip off copyrighted lyrics. Millions of dollars in legal settlements can result.

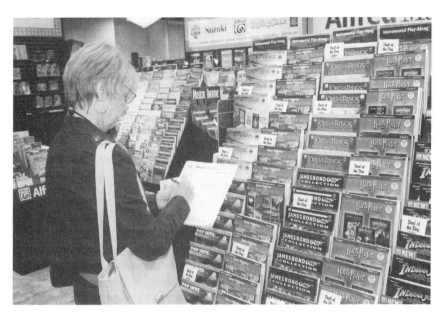

A delegate makes notes at the NAMM show.
Photo courtesy of NAMM (International Music Products Association).

Creative Department

There was a time when all publishers in the popular music field employed what were known in the late 1940s as "song-pluggers." Their place in the world of show business has been portrayed colorfully in the movies and other media. Gradually, they came to be known as professional managers, and later the terms *creative* and *A&R* (artist and repertoire) were used as well. Since World War II, the professional manager has had to assume a role much broader in scope than song-plugging. Here are the principal responsibilities of the creative department:

1. Discover and sign new writers.

2. Maintain good working relationships with writers under contract, pairing writers with compatible cowriters and producers.

3. Persuade artists and producers to record the writer's music.

4. Convince film, TV, and commercials to buy synch licenses; negotiate favorable rates when licensing uses of the copyrights.

5. Search out ancillary uses of those copyrights, such as jingles and merchandising tie-ins.

Acquiring New Material. Although some music publishers have chosen to save costs by foregoing new signings so they can maximize immediate cash flow, the most important enterprise for growth-oriented publishers is to locate new music and sign writers. The relentless search for new talent and new material is essential to the success of these companies, which cannot manufacture their own raw material. There is no shortage of new songs; the challenge for publishers is to discover talented writers among the thousands of composers who think their music is just what the market wants.

The most lucrative source of new material is from writers recently hot on the charts. These writers can be as sought after as recording stars and can pick and choose their own publishers. To persuade writers to place their new songs with them, publishers offer a variety of inducements. In fact, many successful writers change publishers frequently, ever seeking a better contract, stronger promotion, and more fruitful relationships.

A second source of good writers for publishers comes through the recommendation of those in the music business whose musical judgment appears trustworthy or whose track record in the field has been impressive. Producers, label A&R executives, and other writers are among the most frequently tapped insiders.

A third source of usable new material is writers already under contract, either on a work-made-for-hire basis or as writers paid a royalty advance in exchange for the rights to publish their output. (See Chapter 5 for more on publisher-songwriter working arrangements.) Professional managers often need to prod their own staff writers to keep turning out material for the insatiable market.

Often the recording company and publisher are seeking the same talent. Many new writers signed by publishers are potential recording artists who have not yet come to the attention of the label A&R staff. At this stage, the publisher can sign the artist or group to a publishing deal with the intent of then placing them with a label. This has two important advantages: (a) The publisher getting involved at this early stage usually pays less in advances, and (b) the artist/writer is getting some much-needed money at a crucial time while establishing a relationship with an influential ally who can provide creative as well as business assistance. On the other hand, lawyers and managers usually prefer to sign an artist to a label first and then either make a bigger publishing deal for the now more-valuable artist or have the artist retain the publishing rights, at least in the United States.

Acceptance Criteria. Successful popular music publishers have developed criteria that often serve well to distinguish acceptable material. Most publishers, knowingly or intuitively, seem to judge material based on these criteria:

1. Does the demo hit you right off the bat? If the music doesn't appeal to you in the first eight bars, that demo probably will never be heard to its end.

2. What has the composer done lately? Audiences are more fickle than ever, so a publisher may have better odds going with a currently charted writer than with someone with an impressive history but no recent success.

3. Which artists might record the song? What projects are going on at the moment, and who are the right producers, managers, or other key decision makers to pitch?

4. Does the material fill a current need in the publisher's overall catalog? Most publishers seek, over a period of time, some kind of balance among the types of songs they accept. Someone might submit an attractive piece of material, but if that particular publisher is loaded with that kind of song, it may be rejected.

5. Does the material show inherent quality? Most of the decision makers in the business love music. Although they can go broke if they pander too often to their own personal tastes, many music publishers know that the best way to build a catalog of lasting value is to continue searching not just for the surface appeal of a new song but also for music that has inherent quality and might also appeal to listeners of the next generation.

Catalog Acquisitions. The purchase and sale of entire catalogs has always been common in the industry. If the firm on the block is small and headed by a successful writer or manager, the buyer may seek to contract for the ongoing services of the management team that developed the firm's early success. More often, the buyer has its own team in place and simply wants to own the copyrights. The price of an acquisition is usually based on a multiple of the average annual net publisher's share (NPS) over a 3- to 5-year period. This multiple is generally between 5 and 10, but it can be lower or higher. The wide range for multiples is due to variables such as the overall economic climate, perceived ongoing popularity of songs, the steadiness of earnings, and the remaining copyright life of the compositions. For instance, a catalog may have one hit song that made a huge amount of money in the 2 years prior to the acquisition, which would skew the 3- or 5-year average NPS in the seller's favor. In that case, the multiple would be significantly reduced.

When whole catalogs are bought, the seller normally assigns all rights of copyright and ownership, including subsisting contracts with writers. This means that if the first publisher has contracted with a composer to publish that composer's music for the next several years, the new publisher must honor that contract. The new publisher also, of course, assumes all obligations for payment of royalties.

Contracts With Writers

In Chapter 5, we discussed the Songwriters Guild of America (SGA) contract, which is weighted in favor of the writer. Not surprisingly, publishers want a contract with terms favoring their position. Although the SGA contract is a single-song agreement, it would be useful to bear in mind the issues presented in the SGA agreement when considering an exclusive-term contract between a writer and publisher.

In an ideal world, writer and publisher would work out a contract that balances the interests of both parties. The draft that follows might serve as a model for two parties coming to the table with comparable bargaining power. They give and take and just might end up with something like this draft agreement:

• • • Assumptions

Any **consideration** of contract negotiations requires knowledge of the background of the parties and their relative bargaining strengths. In this draft contract, we make the following assumptions:

About the Writer: This is a creative person who writes both songs and instrumental pieces in the popular music genre. Prior to entering into these negotiations with our imaginary publisher, the writer enjoyed some publishing success through modest sales of recordings of music and has some music "in the trunk," compositions not yet copyrighted or published, that could be assigned to the publisher for the right kind of deal. Wanting to advance in this career, not only as a writer but also as a recording artist, the writer can be persuaded to assign copyrights in works covered by the contract to the publisher exclusively if the offer is good enough.

About the Publisher: The firm is well established and moderately successful, an ancillary operation of a parent recording company with multinational distribution. The label's publishing wing has

(Continued)

(Continued)

not yet fully established its operations in foreign territories. The publisher farms out all its printed music activity. The publisher has strong faith in the potential earning power of the prospective writer and seeks the writer's exclusive services.

Draft Contract

This condensed draft is for study purposes only. It covers the essentials of a hypothetical exclusive publishing agreement. It incorporates some of the concepts of the SGA single-song agreement described in Chapter 5. We recommend that each party entering into contract negotiations retains its own legal counsel to recommend the actual language of any agreement.

AGREEMENT made (date) _____ by and between _____, the Writer, and _____, the Publisher

1.0. **Appointment.** The Publisher engages the Writer as a composer, lyricist, arranger, orchestrator, and/or music editor, and the Writer's services as a writer shall be rendered exclusively for the Publisher. Services performed under this agreement shall not be deemed to be work made for hire as defined under U.S. copyright law.

2.0. **Term.** This agreement starts on (date) _____ and ends on (date) _____.[2] The Publisher is granted options to extend this agreement, by 1-year increments of extension for additional years, but not to exceed an aggregate total of _____ years,[3] on the identical terms and conditions of the initial term. The foregoing notwithstanding, the Writer retains the option to deny these extension options unless the Publisher has obtained, directly or indirectly, _____[4] commercially released recordings of the Controlled Compositions during the time period of _____. This shall be referred to hereafter as The Recording Goal.[5]

The writer would not have the option to deny extensions of the initial term if advances had been paid and unrecouped. The same agreement could be negotiated to provide a reversion of copyright after a period of years but only if all advances have been recouped.

2.1. If the Publisher's affiliated recording company terminates the Writer's contract as a **royalty artist,** this Writer's contract shall be **coterminous** with that recording contract.[6]

In situations where there is an affiliated recording company, the publishing deal will often be a copublishing deal rather than the 50/50 writer-publisher split described below. Copublishing deals are explained later in this chapter.

3.0. **Assignment.** The Writer assigns to the Publisher all rights throughout the world in the compositions listed on Schedule A attached hereto (prior compositions).[7] Throughout this contract the word *composition* shall include music, words, and title. During the term of this agreement, the Writer agrees to deliver _____ songs a year.

The assignment language might require a portion of the songs delivered by the writer to be recorded on demos. This obligation of the writer is a different "recording requirement" than one the publisher might undertake elsewhere in the contract in order to demonstrate to the writer the eventual economic viability of the publishing deal.

3.1. The Writer also assigns to the Publisher all rights in the compositions created by the Writer during the term and under the conditions of this agreement. The foregoing notwithstanding, these works are offered to the Publisher on a first-refusal basis only. If the Publisher does not agree to accept them for publication and exploitation within 60 days of their being offered, the Writer reserves the right to assign them to any other publisher.

A first-refusal deal would be made only if no advances were paid. If the writer has been paid an advance by the publisher, the publisher will not allow the writer to sign with another publisher.

All works listed on Schedule A, together with all works described under 3.1 that the Publisher accepts, are referred to hereinafter as the Controlled Compositions.

4.0. **Warranty.** The Writer warrants that the Writer has the right to enter into this agreement and that the Controlled Compositions are original and that as the sole author and composer, the Writer has not paraphrased or otherwise used any other copyrighted material for them.

4.1. The Writer indemnifies the Publisher against loss or damage and attorney fees arising out of a breach of warranty, including a situation where any copyright infringement action is settled with the Writer's consent.

5.0. **Advances and Royalties.** In consideration of this agreement the Publisher agrees:

5.0-A. To pay the Writer $ _____ in twelve (12) equal monthly installments, and the receipt of the first installment is hereby acknowledged, as a nonreturnable advance against royalties, and these payments shall be deductible only from payments becoming due the Writer under this contract. Payment of such advances is dependent upon the Writer's prior delivery of the agreed-upon number of compositions, and in the event of nondelivery, the Publisher shall have the right to suspend payment of advance installments hereunder.

Advances are a critical part of writer-publisher agreements. The publisher usually needs to provide a healthy enough advance for the writer to live while his or her works are in the initial stages of exploitation but not so generous an amount that the publisher risks losing significant money if the advance is never recouped.

5.0-B. Subject to Paragraph 5.1 below, to pay the Writer one half of the Publisher's net receipts in the United States from all other licenses of Controlled Compositions under licenses relating to uses now known or hereafter developed.

5.1. The Writer shall not be entitled to receive any income from any performing rights organizations anywhere in the world designated as a Publisher's share nor shall the Publisher be entitled to receive any income from any performing rights organization anywhere in the world designated as a Writer's share.

(Continued)

(Continued)

5.2. The Publisher shall not grant any mechanical license at a rate lower than the prevailing statutory maximum to any individual or company with whom the Publisher has any affiliation or financial interest.[8]

If the artist has signed a recording contract that has record contract controlled composition language, the lower mechanical rate might apply despite this prohibition in the publishing contract. The writer's attorney must reconcile this provision with that contract.

5.3. To pay the Writer 10% of the wholesale price on the sale of all printed editions in the United States and Canada.

5.4. No **cross-collateralization** is permitted the Publisher in respect to any royalties or other payments made to the Writer by the Publisher's affiliated recording company.

If limitations are not put on so-called cross-collateralization language, the recording company and the publishing company affiliate may treat advances under the publishing agreement as being recoupable from royalties payable from the publishing agreement and/or the recording agreement. It could even be extended to allow recoupment of recording costs and advances under the record agreement from royalties payable under the publishing agreement. This cross-collateralization is obviously extremely favorable to the publisher/record company and would be agreed to only by an artist/writer who had very little bargaining power and over the vehement protests of the artist's entertainment attorney.

5.5. Where a Controlled Composition has more than one author, the shares of royalties among them shall be apportioned in relation to the creative contributions of each Writer as these apportionments have been negotiated by the parties. The Writer will have final approval over which additional cowriters or arrangers are used.

5.6. If the Publisher engages the Writer as an arranger, orchestrator, editor, or copyist, the Writer, if a union member, will be paid the appropriate AFM union scale for such services, and such payments shall be over and above all other advances and royalties provided for in this contract and shall not be recoupable from royalties hereunder.[9]

6.0. **Foreign Rights.** Publisher shall have the right to designate subpublishers, foreign licensees, or affiliates outside the territory of the United States on such terms as the Publisher in its reasonable business judgment shall determine pursuant to **arm's-length** negotiations, provided that in no event shall the percentage paid to the Publisher of income earned at the source be less than 75%.[10]

An arm's-length agreement is negotiated between two unaffiliated parties acting in good faith to reach an understanding that benefits both parties. Such a stipulation would avoid the possibility of one party having an undue advantage over the other. An agreement between a parent company and its affiliate or a subsidiary company that favors the parent company at the expense of the subsidiary company is not an agreement negotiated at arm's length.

7.0. **Promotion Expense.** The Publisher shall be solely responsible for all promotion expense, including the production of audio and video demonstration tapes or discs.

The extent to which promotion expenses are recoupable is subject to negotiation. The demo costs are normally 50% recoupable.

7.1. If the ownership and copyright of any Controlled Composition should revert from the Publisher to the Writer, all demos on that composition shall also become the property of the Writer.

8.0. **Right to Audit.** The Publisher grants to the Writer the right to engage a qualified accountant to examine the Publisher's books and related financial documents, following receipt of reasonable notice. The cost of any such audit is to be borne entirely by the Writer except that if the Writer is found to be owed a sum equal to or greater than _____ %[11] of the sum shown on that royalty statement as being due the Writer, then the Publisher shall pay the entire cost of the audit, but not to exceed _____ %[12] of the amount shown to be due the Writer.

9.0. **Creative Rights.** The Publisher acknowledges that the Writer's reputation and potential income relate importantly to the originality and quality of the Controlled Compositions as well as to their use. The Writer acknowledges, however, that the Publisher has the right to make minimal changes in the compositions and has the day-to-day responsibility of determining the best way to exploit the compositions. To balance these interests of the parties in this respect, it is agreed that the Publisher has the right to do any or all of the following in this context only with the consent of the Writer:

9.0-A. Engage a lyricist to alter the Writer's lyrics materially or to write new lyrics.

9.0-B. Make substantive changes in the Writer's music.

9.0-C. Grant a synchronization license for a Controlled Composition when the usage does not comport with reasonable standards of taste and decorum, such as sexually explicit or violent content, or content offensive or demeaning to any race, class, or gender.

9.0-D. Use the Writer's likeness, photograph, or name to exploit a product or service, in respect to appropriateness and good taste, and without paying the Writer a royalty commensurate with the exploitation value.

9.0-E. License a Controlled Composition for use in connection with a broadcast commercial, print advertisement, or merchandising of a product or service.

9.0-F. Grant a Grand or Dramatic Right in connection with part of the production and performance of a Controlled Composition as a dramatic musical work.

Grand rights *are often excluded in publishing contracts.*

10.0. **Right of Assignment.** The Publisher reserves the right to assign this contract to another fully qualified publisher. The Writer consents to this right of assignment only if such assignment is part of a sale of a substantial portion of publisher assets and provided the assignee assumes all the responsibilities and obligations of the first publisher hereafter.

(Continued)

(Continued)

11.0. Reversion. If the Recording Goal is not reached, the Writer will grant the Publisher an extension period of six (6) months beyond the initial term set forth under Item 2.0 of this contract. If, by the end of the extension period, the Recording Goal has still not been reached, and if no advances have been paid by the Publisher to the Writer, or if paid, recouped or repaid to the Publisher, all rights in any Controlled Composition not released or recorded revert to the Writer.

12.0. Default, Cure. If either the Publisher or the Writer asserts that the other party is in default or breach of this contract, the aggrieved party shall provide written notice setting forth the nature of the default or breach. The accused party is then allowed 30 days to cure the alleged default, during which period no default or other grievances shall be deemed incurable.

13.0. Arbitration. The parties agree to submit all disputes to the American Arbitration Association and be bound by and perform any award rendered in such arbitration.

_____ Publisher _____ Writer

_____ Date _____ Date

County of _____ State of _____

Split Publishing, Copublishing

Nowadays, many songs on the pop charts are copublished by two or more publishers. In reality, nearly all these **split publishing** deals are simply a number of persons or firms agreeing to share the publishing income, not the publishing responsibilities.

In a traditional arrangement, publishing money is divided equally between the songwriter and the publisher; that is, the songwriter gets 50% of the publishing income and the publisher gets the other 50%. In this case, the publisher usually owns all of the copyright.

If an artist/songwriter who already has a record deal signs a publishing agreement, the publisher is often willing to give half of its publishing income and half of the copyright ownership to the artist/songwriter. In one kind of common copublishing deal, the parties are co-owners of the copyright, and the artist/songwriter receives 75% of the income (the writer's 50% plus 50% of the publisher's share). The administration of the copyright remains with the publisher.

When ownership of a copyright is split, administration of the property can be difficult. Where coauthors are involved, ASCAP, BMI, and SESAC will honor directions from the co-owners to divide performance royalties among the writers and publishers involved. With respect to mechanical royalties and synchronization fees, the Harry Fox Agency is accustomed to splitting monies in accordance with instructions it receives from copyright owners.

Joint administration of copyright requires specific contractual arrangements for sharing of synchronization fees. Synchronization rights apply worldwide, but differences of opinion prevail on how income from this source should be shared. In the past, most publishers have believed it equitable to attribute 50% of synchronization fee income to the United States and the balance to foreign sources. Administration of copyrights outside this country should be assigned entirely to one co-owner or the other, because sharing of the responsibility can lead to confusion and lack of oversight. This is particularly important because in some foreign countries, a unilateral commitment by one co-owner may be binding on the other.

Where a work has two authors, and two publishers split the copyright, one writer's share comes from one publisher, the other writer's share from the other publisher. Unless otherwise provided in a joint administration agreement, mechanical royalties will be equally divided by the two publishers, and each publisher will then pay its writer.

Sometimes the copyright proprietor does not split ownership but instead offers income participation or **cut-in** from the copyright. If a new artist/writer lacks the funds to rent a preferred studio or to hire a favored producer, the artist/writer may offer a cut-in to the studio or producer in place of, or in addition to, payment upfront. Under controlled circumstances, the cut-in can be fair and work even better than joint administration; a single administration is generally preferable to one that is shared. But a cut-in agreement should be limited to payments on mechanicals derived from a particular record by a specified artist for a finite period. If a work is recorded but never commercially released, the cut-in deal should be automatically voided or the proprietorship and copyright income should return to the original owner.

In yet another kind of cut-in, some songwriters or publishers agree to add the name of a prominent recording artist to a song in exchange for the artist's recording the song.

Copyright Protection: Sampling

As digital technology evolves, new concerns about copyright protection inevitably arise. For example, anyone who has access to modern playback equipment can easily make perfect digital copies of an entire recording or simply sample part of a song. Artists and disc jockeys can quickly stitch together bits of existing songs in mashups in what is called **sampling.** Thus, the **interpolation** of part of an existing song—but not the original master—pops up in a new recording. The **new use** may be instantly recognizable to the listener, or it may be changed or altered to such an extent that it is very unlike the original.

No matter how previously recorded sounds are used, permission to sample must be obtained from the publisher and the recording company of the original recording. Thus, two licenses are required: one for the recording and the other for the underlying music composition. Deals licensing rights for sampling are sometimes individually negotiated, so there is no single template.

Since small snippets of music are used, it's not always obvious what previously recorded music is lifted and so some samplers don't license music, hoping they won't get caught. If music is identified as being sampled without the permission of the publisher and recording company, the sampler is then subject to various penalties, including payment of actual or statutory damages, impoundment of recordings, and an injunction against further release of the infringing recording.

Revenue from sampling has become a significant part of the earning power of many copyrights. The legitimate use of a sample can take the form of one-time, flat-fee licenses, royalty participation in the new recording and/or the new underlying composition (i.e., the copyright of the song), or a combination; there are no set standards. However, unauthorized use of samples in new recordings is even costlier when lawsuits ensue, as has often been the case. The clearance of sampled portions of recordings for use in other recordings has become a lucrative legal and administrative subsector of the music industry.

Promotion, Advertising

Popular Music

The main concern of a publisher of popular songs is getting music recorded and broadcast. Although the promotion methods discussed here are ultimately meant to encourage the public to consume more music, much of the promotion process is initially aimed at professionals within the music business. Publishers generally persuade artists and record producers to record their music through direct, personal contacts. Even though the publishing and recording industries are huge, much of the power and control are in the hands of a relatively small number of insiders, including major recording artists, record producers, established writers, and important managers.

Song Casting. A critical function of a publisher is to attempt to match songs with performers. Creative departments and staff analyze songs carefully and search out recording artists they believe have a performing style that matches the material. This is often called song casting; it is as crucial as casting a TV show or Broadway play. This matching of artist to repertoire used to be the principal concern of staff record producers—hence their appellation, A&R producers. Those who do this well are scarce, in high demand, and well paid.

One of the largest popular music publishers has said that the song-casting process often works in reverse for prestigious publishers: Record producers will contact the publisher, listing their current needs, and ask the publisher to supply material the publisher believes right for a particular recording project. A publisher enjoying this kind of prestige has an edge with producers and artists who believe the firm has good casting judgment and strong material.

Experienced publishers understand that, at the outset, only a select number of recording artists will even consider their material because so many acts in popular music are **self-contained**—the individual performer or group uses only its own material. Rarely do self-contained acts accept outside songs.

Cover Records. The publisher who has a self-contained act under contract understands, or should understand, that once the material is initially recorded by that act, the publisher's job has only begun. One major concern is getting cover records—inducing other artists to record the song. Whatever the size of a publisher's catalog, the long-range income of the firm is tied in part to the number of quality covers generated over the years.

Given the unending need for potential hit material, it might be assumed that getting cover records is relatively easy, but nothing could be further from the truth. In addition to the difficulty of getting self-contained artists to record covers, many acts that are open to cover material tend to make their own decisions about which songs they will record. In fact, as record sales have slowed and revenue from synch performances has increased as a percentage of overall income, many publishers now devote only minimal time and energy to pursuing covers.

Because online sites have widened the opportunities for consumers to purchase one song at a time, song promoters seeking covers generally limit the material they submit to songs they believe might make it as singles. Most recording artists already have available, from their own hands or from insiders and friends, all the album-cut material they believe they can use. Of course, no one can consistently predict which songs will be hit singles, but the most talented publishers, especially in the country area, often have very good track records.

Another aspect of publisher promotion is offering services directly to recording companies, who share some of their economic interests. One manifestation of this is cooperative promotion campaigns for new material, frequently in connection with personal appearances of recording artists.

Digital Promotion. The digital medium has become a key marketing vehicle and income source for sheet music, as well as a listening post to ascertain musicians' tastes. An obvious resource to start in selecting sheet music to sell is the charts of hit recordings, which take the pulse of popular music. In addition, more sophisticated charts are compiled by music research firms for a fee (see Chapter 15).

But perhaps the best indicator is social media buzz among musicians—who are the actual buyers of sheet music. Perhaps a sheet music publisher wants to know who is the chart topper among choral classical composers at the moment . . . Bach or Handel? For that insight, listen to buzz on ChoralNet, which is an Internet destination for the American Choral Directors Association. Marketers good at reading tea leaves from multiple sources can anticipate the next hot sheet music hit with reasonable accuracy.

Paid search advertising in digital media is popular if it delivers an audience of musicians and can be directed to promote specific, relevant songs. The more on target the keywords selected, the more effective the campaign. Web banner ads directed to relevant prospects are less expensive than search ads and may also be effective if carefully targeted.

Sheet music sellers also place general corporate advertising with the evergreen message that we-have-it-all for sheet music. Another wrinkle is sheet music sellers partnering with music publishers or artists and songwriters for tie-in promotions. The sheet music outfit buys advertising featuring the talent or buys jointly with music publishers.

Synchronization Promotion. As we noted earlier in this chapter, film, TV, and commercial synchs are bringing in a greater share of publishers' revenues than ever before, as much as doubling the percentage in the span of a few years. Large- and mid-sized publishers have "synch experts" who pitch material to music supervisors and ad agencies. Smaller publishers may retain independent promoters to pitch their catalogs, generally paying these firms a monthly retainer and a percentage of synch revenues.

Educational Field

Publishers promote printed music intended for student and school use in several ways. The first is via direct mail campaigns. Music educators receive promotional mailings on a regular basis. Along with recordings of arrangements, printed samples of new releases are included in these mailings in the form of thematics—short samples of themes from complete works. The educator, when "sold" by such mailings, places an order through a store or by telephone, fax, mail, or the Internet.

A second promotional avenue involves publishers placing display advertisements in music education journals such as *Music Educators Journal, The Instrumentalist,* and *Down Beat.*

A unique promotional device used in the educational and church fields is the reading clinic. A large retailer or an educational group will cohost daylong readings of new publications. Educators attend these readings (school ensembles are commonly used) and subsequently place orders with their dealers to cover their needs for the school or church year.

Significantly, publishers are turning more and more to the Internet, including social networking sites such as Facebook and Twitter, to promote their products. Email blasts, promotion on publisher websites of sheet music and songbook aggregators and retailers, and direct promotion on publishers' own websites are among the tools that have become commonplace.

Classical Field

Publishers of chamber music, art songs, operas, and ballets have their own ways of acquainting potential buyers with their music. Unlike the pop and educational fields that focus on new music, classical music publishers are usually engaged in reminding customers of the great music of the past. They periodically enliven their catalogs with new compositions and arrangements, but the bulk of their sales comes from reprints and new editions of the classics.

New serious works of any length are rarely printed, because anticipated sales seldom produce enough money to cover production costs. In lieu of direct sales, large-scale works such as new operas, ballets, and symphonic pieces are made available through rental of the scores and parts for performance and recording. With regard to dramatic musical works like opera and ballet, publishers often get additional income by charging performance fees. Dramatic works by major contemporary composers can produce fairly good income for both publishers and writers, especially when works are revived by companies beyond the original commissioner.

Classical music is also promoted through display ads placed in music journals. A large part of the classical and semiclassical repertoire spills over into the educational field, and most publishers sell to schools and colleges either the original scores or parts or arrangements scored specifically for school use.

Income Sources

Publishing revenues continue to be strong because they are generated from so many diverse sources. The most important ones are shown in Table 6.2. The rise of new distribution technology has led to the shrinking of the revenue pie slice representing traditional mechanical royalties, as illustrated in Figure 6.3. Over the long term, one of the all-time money earners is probably the Broadway musical. If we were to aggregate the income of a dramatic musical work such as *South Pacific* or *A Chorus Line*— including grand rights, performance income of hits from the show, print rights, movie rights, mechanical royalties—these receipts would exceed all the money generated by the stage production at the inflation-adjusted box office.

Not all publishers control these kinds of multi-million-dollar properties, but standards of lesser value and current hits are in demand for tie-ins for such diverse uses as computer software, cell phone ringtones, musical greeting cards, apparel, posters, and stationery. Licensing fees, individually considered, for uses of this kind will rarely

Table 6.2   Publisher's Potential Income Sources

Type of Music Use	Who Pays the Publisher
Broadcast performance (TV, radio, cable, Internet)	Publisher's performing rights organization, which collects from the broadcasters
Nonbroadcast performances (clubs, hotels, stadiums, environmental music, in-flight music, aerobic and dance studios, etc.)	Publisher's performing rights organization, which collects from the venues where the music is played
Mechanical royalties (disc, tape, and CD sales)	Recording company
Sheet music sales	Publisher's print music licensee
Streaming online	Publishers' performing rights organization, which collects from the digital platforms
Synchronization of music (to films, videos, advertising, Internet, DVD, and video games)	Movie, video, advertising or game producers
Special permissions, licenses (merchandising deals such as musical greeting cards, toys and dolls, lyrics used in books and magazines, cell phone ringtones, etc.)	Publisher's licensee
Jukeboxes	Publisher's performing rights organization
Dramatic (or grand rights)	Producer of the dramatic performance
Foreign rights	Subpublishers, licensees abroad; reciprocating performing rights organizations (through ASCAP, BMI, and SESAC)

Figure 6.3   Publishing's Diverse Revenue Streams: Percent of Revenue by Type

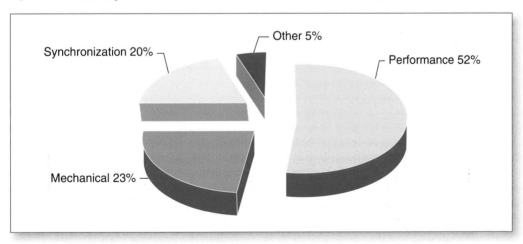

Source: National Music Publishers' Association (NMPA) data for 2013.

Note: Not all publishers classify revenue sources the same way.

be high, but when aggregated, money from these ancillary sources can generate a respectable share of a publisher's annual income.

Except where a compulsory license is involved (see Chapter 4), a publisher has the option of granting permissions-to-use either on a royalty basis (a percentage of sales) or for a one-time flat fee.

Trade Associations and Rights Administration ▰▰▰

National Music Publishers' Association

The trade association most representative of publishers in the popular music field is the National Music Publishers' Association (NMPA). The NMPA provides leadership for the music publishing/songwriting community, advocating for a variety of issues, including the protection of copyrights in an age of advancing technology and the payment of royalties for electronic delivery of music throughout the world.

The Harry Fox Agency

The NMPA established the Harry Fox Agency, Inc. (HFA) in 1927 to provide an information source, clearinghouse, and monitoring service for licensing musical copyrights. The HFA operated under the wing of the NMPA for nearly a century, eventually being acquired by SESAC in 2015. With over 48,000 music publishing clients, the HFA issues the largest number of mechanical licenses for the use of music in both physical and digital distribution formats. The HFA's service offering also includes a suite of outsourced technology solutions designed to facilitate the administration of intellectual property rights. The online tools are suitable for small do-it-yourself publishers and also small-scale users.

The HFA provides the following services in the United States on behalf of its publisher principals:

1. Mechanical licensing: The licensing of copyrighted musical compositions for use on commercial CDs, records, tapes, permanent digital downloads, interactive streams, limited downloads, ringtones, and digital background music services.

2. Royalty collection and distribution: The collection of royalties from licensees using copyrighted musical compositions and the distribution of these royalties to publishers.

3. Royalty compliance: The periodic review and tracking of the books and records of licensees using copyrighted musical compositions based on the license issued, as well as the identification of the unlicensed product.

4. Micro-licensing: Consolidated monetization services on social video networks, automated license verification with RADKey, and premium YouTube Content ID administration services through SESAC subsidiary Rumblefish.

The HFA does not act in the area of licensing grand and dramatic rights, print rights, and derivative uses (music arrangements). It discontinued mainstream synchronization licensing services in 2002. However, the HFA does offer eSynch, which is its specialty synchronization licensing service for noncommercial uses such as wedding, corporate, personal website video, background music for websites, and movies destined just for film festivals. Refer to Chapter 7 for further information on how the agency functions and Table 31.1 for a list of its foreign affiliates.

Association of Independent Music Publishers

The Association of Independent Music Publishers (AIMP) was formed in 1977 by a group of Los Angeles music publishers and now has chapters in Los Angeles,

New York, and Nashville. The organization's primary focus is to educate and inform local music publishers about industry trends and practices via monthly meetings, forums, and workshops. The AIMP includes in its membership not only independent music publishers but also publishers that are affiliated with record labels or motion picture and television production companies, as well as individuals from other areas of the entertainment community, such as songwriters, artist managers, and members of the legal and accounting professions.

Notes

1. Because certain foreign societies—Germany's GEMA, for instance—will not pay mechanical royalties directly to an American publisher, it is important in some countries to have a subpublisher or be affiliated with the Harry Fox Agency, which can collect these monies in most territories.

2. This kind of exclusive-term contract in earlier times was often limited to 1 year. Now, however, even enterprising publishers are often unable to develop acceptance of a composition in the first year of a contract.

3. In California, a contract for personal services cannot normally be enforced for a period longer than 7 years. Five-year-term contracts are probably the most common today, whatever statutory limitations might prevail.

4. The SGA contract allows the publisher 1 year to obtain a commercially released recording of the particular song under contract, unless the publisher pays the writer a sum of money to "buy" 6 additional months' time to attain that goal. Failing this, all rights to the song revert to the writer.

5. A reasonable "recording goal" might be getting recording deals for half of the Controlled Compositions. See 11.0 for the consequences if the recording goal is not reached.

6. Although coterminous contracts are often inadvisable for the writer, in this instance, the writer would want to be released from the publishing contract to be free to negotiate a new publishing deal with another recording company.

7. This list would probably include all the works the writer had in the trunk prior to signing this contract that had not been previously published or otherwise encumbered by prior commitment. Some lawyers recommend their clients grant only administrative rights to a writer's available works composed prior to a term contract.

8. This clause prevents the publisher from offering anyone a "sweetheart" deal and helps guard against the three-fourths statutory rate commonly found in controlled compositions clauses in artist recording contracts.

9. If the income of the writer under this contract fails to aggregate a reasonable amount, the contract may not be enforceable in some states in that the publisher has the writer completely tied up as exclusive writing "property," thus denying the writer the opportunity of finding additional outside writing income. California law makes personal service agreements unenforceable if the artist or writer has failed to achieve a certain minimum level of income from entertainment contracts.

10. The parent contract is left open-ended here to provide the parties an opportunity to remain flexible in response to rapidly changing foreign markets. Although the parties might agree on a worldwide 50–50 split of income, equity might be better served by negotiating deals territory by territory.

11. The SGA contract calls for 5% here. Between 10% and 15% might be reasonable, at least from the publisher's point of view.

12. The SGA contract calls for 50% here.

Chapter Takeaways

- In the early part of the 20th century, music publishers were the most powerful people in the music industry—shaping tastes and reaping substantial revenues from printing sheet music.

- Today, the heart of the music publishing business is exploiting rights in songs through mechanical, performance, and synchronization royalties and fees.

- Publishers range in size from multinational giants affiliated with large labels, to medium-size independent companies, to in-your-hat operations run by songwriters who want to control all forms of exploitation.

- Print publishing of music is a profitable niche business but is less important than publisher revenues from other forms of exploitation.

- Although there can be advantages in having one party administer exploitation of a copyright, it is commonplace for publishing royalties to be divided between one or more composers and one or more lyricists.

- Subpublishers in foreign territories help the original publisher (and songwriter) maximize royalties from overseas sources.

Key Terms

- at-source deal   (p. 95)
- bench pack   (p. 92)
- copublishing   (p. 102)
- cross-collateralization (p. 104)

- cut-in   (p. 107)
- NPS   (p. 101)
- print licensee   (p. 94)
- sampling   (p. 107)

- self-contained act   (p. 108)
- split publishing   (p. 106)
- subpublisher   (p. 92)
- subsisting copyright   (p. 97)

Discussion Questions

1. How has the role of the music publisher changed as a result of the increasing importance of the Web?

2. What are the implications of the shift in publishing revenues away from mechanical royalties in favor of performance fees and synch licenses?

3. Describe in brief how publishers administer songs written by more than one person and where copublishing (also called split publishing) occurs.

4. What's required in terms of licensing to legally obtain the right to incorporate existing recordings in a new recording, which is known as "sampling"?

CHAPTER 7

Music Licensing

Music Rights: An Overview

Under U.S. copyright law, protected music generally can be used only after permission is obtained from the copyright owner. This consent is customarily given by the granting of a license, which usually involves the payment of a fee. That path from creation of copyright to collection of cash is the heartbeat of the business of music, and the *music licensing system* is a critical—and occasionally complex—part of the process.

It is also omnipresent: If you have listened to a song on the radio, hummed along to a familiar tune hawking a car on TV, called up some favorite tunes on your subscription music service, tried to *avoid* humming along to a **classic rock** instrumental pumped into an elevator, tried to tune out a fellow diner whose blaring cell phone is repeating the melody of last week's chart-topper, melted to the strains of a favorite love song during a romantic movie scene, or ponied up a 20 for the film's CD soundtrack at the mall, you have brushed up against just a few of the many fruits of music licensing. In some way, a songwriter, music publisher, and/or recording artist is probably making money from the music that surrounds you every day and everywhere, often even when you don't pay directly for the music you hear.

"There should be a single Art Exchange in the world, to which the artist would simply send his works and be given in return as much as he needs. As it is, one has to be half a merchant on top of everything else, and how badly one goes about it!"

—Ludwig van Beethoven

Left: Ray Charles at the New Orleans Jazz and Heritage Festival, 1980.

Photo © C. Fishman/Woodfin Camp/PNI.

This is the highly lucrative world of music licensing, a system of permissions and payments keyed to copyrighted material. There are small exceptions and one limited exemption to copyright's airtight hold on music that is **fair use**, which permits very limited appropriation of small portions of copyrighted content for public comment (like music critics) or some educational purposes.

But for the most part, music must be licensed. *What* permissions are required, *how large* those payments will be, *with whom* the licenses must be negotiated, and *to whom* the license fees will be paid vary widely depending on how the music will be used and how eager the licensee is to obtain it, among other factors. Some licensing deals are done for a one-time flat fee, whereas others require this payment of royalties to be ongoing, depending on usage or sales. (We told you it could be complex!) The everyday examples cited above, for instance, involve a host of different license requirements, including the big three—**performance, synchronization,** and **mechanical**—and various combinations thereof.

These and other common types of license agreements are addressed in Table 7.1 and will be explored in this chapter, but first it is important to establish a basic distinction between the two different types of *music copyright* a music licensee might seek permission to use: the composition copyright, owned by the songwriter and/or music publisher, and the sound recording copyright, usually owned by the recording label. The former is the copyright in the song itself, encompassing the words and music; it's the © a songwriter affixes to the composition. The latter is designated by a ℗ and was established only in 1972 under federal law to encompass the actual recording of the song—the artist singing, the musicians playing, the entire production as put down on a CD or other recorded format. Meanwhile, rules governing licensing of pre-1972 recordings are murky and covered by a patchwork of state laws, triggering a raft of lawsuits pitting music talent, music labels, and their licensing intermediaries against music-playing platforms.[1]

Except where traditional business models are long established, licensees of music often complain about the difficulty of navigating music rights licensing, due to uncertainty over who controls exactly which of the many individual rights. "New digital services face a formidable challenge when attempting to license music," lamented a 2015 report from the U.S. Copyright Office. "One study showed that acquiring the necessary rights to offer a marketable digital music offering requires roughly 18 months of effort, with some entities never able to successfully negotiate the licenses needed to launch their services."[2]

The land rush in digital media creates another issue involving pay to creators. Record labels sometimes extract significant financial benefits from large music licensing deals, and talent doesn't always share in the bounty. For example, the big three record conglomerates received equity stakes in online streamer Spotify as part of music licensing deals; those combined stakes were soon worth hundreds of millions of dollars. The artists' share: zero.

The label-owned recording copyright is reflected in a **master use license**, because it represents the licensee's right to use the recorded master, not just the underlying song. This typically means the hit version of a song from the artist who made it famous, not less popular cover versions. Depending on the usage, this can take various forms, such as a master sample license or a master ringtone ("mastertone") license.

An understanding of this distinction and its implications is crucial, because it determines the type(s) of licenses needed for various purposes. A master use license would come into play in the earlier example of the hit love song recording reused in a movie. Use of a *preexisting recording* in a film, television show, commercial, and so on

Table 7.1   Music Licenses: Types Required for Different Uses

Type of Music Use	Type of License Required
Commercial radio broadcast of nondramatic music	Performance license and (often) transcription license
Nonbroadcast performance of nondramatic music	Performance license
Phonorecord (audiocassette, compact disc, LP)	Compulsory or negotiated mechanical license
DVD, videocassette, videodisc, AV downloads sold for private use	Negotiated synch license
Noninteractive digital broadcast (cable, satellite radio and online)	Digital performance license
Music video production used for broadcast or cable TV	Synch license by producer and performance license by broadcaster
Digital downloads	Statutory master-use performance license
Video (electronic) games	Negotiated fees
Motion picture for theatrical exhibition	Synch license that includes the right of U.S. theatrical exhibition[a]
Broadcast commercial	Performance license and, for some TV spots, synch license
Merchandising tie-ins, computer software applications, etc.	Negotiated fees
Business music (in stores, airports, etc.)	Transcription license that includes the right of performance
Dramatico-musical production (performed live)	Grand right or dramatic right
Public broadcasting station	Performance license and, for some shows, synch license
Jukebox	Negotiated license through performing rights organizations
TV programs	Synch license
Local TV channels	Either blanket or per program performance license for on-air promos and local content
Cable TV systems	Performance license and, for some shows, synch license. For digital audio channels, a compulsory performance license for recordings
Cell phone ringtone	Mechanical license if ringtone is a "mastertone" (i.e., derived from the actual master recording of the song)

[a] Performing licenses for theaters outside the United States are often obtained by foreign performing rights organizations directly from movie theater operators. Costs of these licenses are scaled to a share of the box office receipts. ASCAP and BMI members sometimes share in this income through foreign performing rights organizations with which they have reciprocal arrangements. There is no performance income derived from motion picture screens in the United States.

requires permission from both the music publisher *and* the record label—the appropriate © *and* ℗ owners. The music publisher will issue a synchronization license, and the record label will issue a master use license. A synchronization license gives permission for a composition to be used in synch with visual images. A master use license gives permission for a sound recording to be synched in the same manner. And here's a potential complication: For the resulting soundtrack album containing that previously released love song, the record company releasing it needs to go to the record label that owns the original recording copyright to obtain a master use license (if this was not negotiated as part of the original film license). It also needs to compensate the music publisher of the song via a mechanical license, giving the soundtrack label the right to reproduce the song in a CD or permanent digital download and sell it.

The level of permission involved in different kinds of licensing deals (in other words, the right to *refuse* to issue a license or to haggle over the terms of copyright use) is also a variable, depending on whether the licenses are designated as compulsory. Remember that mechanical licenses, as discussed in previous chapters, are *compulsory* after a song has been made commercially available once; that is, after the first recording, anyone can make a cover of a song and produce copies for sale by applying for a compulsory license and paying the statutory mechanical rate or, if the publisher cooperates, negotiating a lower rate with the publisher. That's to use the score and lyrics for a cover, not the original-artist sound recording. However, no one has the right to use copyrighted music in a movie or a commercial, for instance, without the express *permission* of the copyright holder, among others, for that particular use.

For the movie soundtrack album, the permission request would need to include information such as a royalty rate, SRLP (**suggested retail list price**), advance, territory, term, number of tracks, methods of sale, and release date to allow the record label that owns the recording copyright to decide if and on what terms it wants to take part in the project. (The same holds true for compilation albums.) Similarly, to obtain the synch and master use licenses for the *film's* use of the same love song, the film production company would be expected to detail in its permission requests the type of use (e.g., visual, vocal, background instrumental, instrumental), length of use (e.g., up to 30 seconds), territory (usually worldwide), term (length of time the resulting work will be distributed), a scene description, rights (e.g., free TV, basic cable, theatrical), and options. Recording artists, managers, and musicians unions may also be involved in these permission and payment processes for film music and soundtracks.

The permissions issue can be an especially thorny one in clearing music samples, because the copyright holders (the music publisher and record label) may insist on hearing how the sample of a preexisting recording is used in the new recording before considering the sample license request; that is, the artist has to record it before knowing if it can be used in the final recording. To clear a sample, one must send a copy of the new work to the music publisher that owns the copyright and the record label that owns the sampled track with an explanation of the proposed use. The rights requested typically cover inclusion of the song on an album and in a video, promotional uses, third-party uses (i.e., synchronization)—basically, whatever rights one would need to sell and promote the music. Once the publisher gives permission for the use, a copublishing deal can be negotiated between the publishers of the new song and those of the sampled song and a mechanical license issued. Once the owner of the sound recording gives permission, a master sample use agreement can be negotiated.

The digital distribution of music online and certain types of webcasting are two of the newer arenas where compulsory mechanical and master use performance licenses, respectively, have ballooned in recent years. These require writers and publishers to allow the use of their songs for sale as full digital downloads in exchange for payment of a statutory mechanical royalty rate; they also require labels to allow their masters to be used for webcasting in exchange for payment of a statutory rate negotiated within the industry or decided by the Copyright Royalty Board (CRB). Webcasters must meet a set of requirements to be eligible for the statutory master-use performance license. The Digital Performance Right and Sound Recordings Act of 1995 extended the compulsory mechanical copyright license to include the digital distribution of records at the full statutory rate (i.e., no reductions due to controlled composition clauses). The Digital Millennium Copyright Act of 1998 provided a compulsory license for the webcasting of masters.[3]

Complicated enough for you? Fortunately, a fairly well-established and regulated system of licenses and use permits that covers most situations has evolved over the years, smoothing the process considerably. There also are a number of organizations whose sole focus is on issuing licenses, monitoring licensees, and collecting and distributing monies from these licenses to the appropriate copyright holders.

Performing Rights Organizations

One of the important rights granted authors under U.S. copyright law is the right to control the performance of music creators' compositions in public. In practice, this means that most any venue or broadcaster that exploits a copyrighted composition must obtain permission from the copyright holder in the form of a license and must generally pay a fee. The largest source of income for many composers and publishers is from such licensed public performances of their music, including live concerts; broadcast over radio, TV, and the Internet; and other means of transmission. The creators—composers, lyricists, and musicians—typically contract with performing rights organizations (**PROs**), which collect money from music platforms on behalf of their client music originators.

The big three U.S. PROs for compositions are ASCAP, BMI, and SESAC, each with histories stretching back decades. Recently, industry trailblazer Irving Azoff started a competitor, Global Music Rights, promising to pass more money collected to music creators. Other smaller competitors have popped up using Internet-based technology to collect and distribute, also claiming to pay a higher cut to music creators. However, smallish outfits lack the reach to tag nonpayers and may lack the deep pockets to pursue litigation.

In the United States, recording artists historically have not received performance royalties for most public performances of their recorded works, such as on radio broadcasts. But attitudes toward this historical precedent have shifted somewhat over the past couple of decades. The limitation on sound performance rights first changed in the digital domain, where a limited public performance right for masters—such as under the webcast licenses mentioned earlier—was carved out. For writers and publishers—as distinct from labels and performers—the performing right has long been a bedrock of licensing income from a wide variety of sources. Webcasting struggled economically in its early years in part because of the unique burden of a sound recording royalty obligation, and pressure built up on key industry players to find a win-win solution. The problem: traditional broadcasters who operated separate digital outlets had to pay what they considered exorbitant recording royalties (a fixed amount per play) even if their nascent digital services were losing money. Labels and artists were hurting because as recorded music sales tanked, they were stuck with not a penny in royalties from the biggest outlet for their creative works—terrestrial broadcast radio. In 2012, group broadcaster iHeart Media (formerly Clear Channel) struck a groundbreaking direct deal with indie label Big Machine. Under that pact, iHeart agreed to pay a percentage of ad revenue to the label for plays on *both* digital and terrestrial radio—the first such deal in the United States. Big Machine (representing Taylor Swift, Tim McGraw, and Rascal Flatts) in turn would pay its artists their share of the newfound revenue stream. The deal was notable in that it bypassed the role of any PRO, the historical intermediary for distributing royalties. Such individualized deals can be an option between record labels that control music rights and users such as radio groups.

The reason for that intermediary role is obvious. From the beginning, it was impractical for thousands of licensees to send separate payments to thousands of copyright holders. Not surprisingly, then, several performing rights organizations were created with the express purpose of issuing performing rights licenses and then collecting and distributing royalties to writers and publishers that they represent. In the United States, the performance rights for most copyrighted compositions are handled by either the American Society of Composers, Authors and Publishers (ASCAP); Broadcast Music Inc. (BMI); or SESAC, Inc. SoundExchange, covered later in this chapter, collects and distributes performance royalties on noninteractive digital radio (again, *excluding* terrestrial broadcast performances) from statutory licenses on behalf of recording artists and *sound recording* copyright owners.

These organizations also lobby Congress on music copyright concerns, promote music scholarship, enforce their members' rights through infringement litigation, and host awards events. They do not publish music,[4] and they rarely promote individual copyrights.

ASCAP, BMI, and SESAC typically issue blanket performance licenses, which allow their entire repertoire to be used by broadcasters and others for an annual fee. Some entertainment companies that use only a small portion of the catalog or have a limited need for music performances may bypass them, seeking licenses at the *source* (through the program provider) or *directly* (from the copyright owner). For example, film or TV producers may get source and direct licenses by negotiating a single fee for performance and synchronization rights in the same transaction.

Although the Supreme Court's position on blanket licensing has traditionally been that PROs offer the most efficient and economical way of handling the large flow of information, lower courts and Congress may be getting more sympathetic to users' arguments against the practice and its inherent monopoly over song rights. In 1993, for instance, a lower federal court ruled that ASCAP must offer commercial television stations *per-program* licenses with surcharges for processing that approximate the cost of pro rata blanket licenses. Per-program licenses or low-cost blanket licenses to radio stations that use little music are typical.

How much money do ASCAP, BMI, and SESAC collect and distribute? More than $2 billion a year from all sources. The buoyancy of this income stream is supported largely by the vast economic scale of broadcasting and cable television. Other factors include (a) increasing acceptance by music users that they must obey copyright laws and pay up, (b) increasing efficiency of the collecting agencies, (c) rising licensing rates, and (d) more efficient, comprehensive collections from reciprocating foreign collecting organizations.

ASCAP and BMI, which operate on a nonprofit basis, retain about 10% to 15% of their gross receipts for overhead, then distribute the rest to their members and **affiliates**. SESAC, a for-profit business with income streams extending beyond performance rights, is privately held and does not publish its operating expenses or the amount of collections that it retains as profit. But SESAC maintains that its royalties to individual copyright holders are competitive with ASCAP and BMI.

Performance Licensing: The Nuts and Bolts

The licensing deals made by PROs with music users take many forms, and the fees range widely, from hundreds of dollars to hundreds of thousands and beyond. Some are based on a percentage of the user's revenue, others set a flat annual fee, others are keyed to the number of subscribers, and still others may be pegged to such factors as a venue's seating capacity or its weekly music budget.

The list of licensees is wide-ranging. The PROs license to practically all radio stations and most TV stations, as well as broadcast and cable networks, and satellite carrier systems. TV and radio generate the majority of their total performance revenues.

Between 10% and 15% of PRO income is generated by nonbroadcast sources. These include clubs, hotels, arenas, airlines, colleges, restaurants, taverns, concert promoters, symphony orchestras, skating rinks, circuses, and theme and amusement parks. The PROs also license background music services, websites, and cell phone ringtone providers. As noted earlier, if you hear music while you are out and about or surfing online, someone is probably paying a license fee to play or broadcast it.

Or, at least, someone *should* be! Prospective licensees—those who are legally obligated to take out a license—are initially contacted by a field representative from a PRO, who educates music users about the responsibilities that exist under U.S. copyright law. Most prospective licensees enter into licensing agreements at that time. If an agreement is not struck and the prospective licensee persists in using the music without permission, a lawsuit alleging copyright infringement is brought by the licensing organization, although sometimes in the names of specific music creators represented by the suing PRO. Licensing organizations almost always win these legal battles, through either persuasion or the courts, because copyright law is on their side.

Nonexempt[5] clubs, bars, and other such facilities that present live music performances are normally asked to sign a 1-year blanket license. Hotel and motel licenses cover a 5-year period. The setting of the license rate may take into account (a) the seating capacity of the venue, (b) whether it charges admission, (c) its live music weekly budget, and (d) the number of hours of musical entertainment provided. It may also factor in the estimated gross income of the facility or the amount the venue expends for entertainment.

Artists performing live on stage, as well as their agents and managers, normally are not expected to pay performance royalties to anyone. Rather, this responsibility and expense falls on either the venue owner or the entertainment promoter or producer.

When a venue, such as a stadium or arena, offers musical entertainment only occasionally, performance fees are typically collected from the promoter or producer renting the facility or sponsoring the event. When a facility offers entertainment on a regular basis, ASCAP, BMI, and SESAC normally look to the owner of the facility to pay for the performance license.

Keeping Track of the Music

To monitor the use of their repertoire by licensees and to properly credit royalties to their affiliated writers and publishers, ASCAP, BMI, and SESAC use techniques such as music logs sent by media outlets. But increasingly, they rely on electronic audio recognition software that logs music on an automated basis; the recognition software can identify songs without cooperation of media outlets. Service providers for such audio fingerprint recognition in music include Gracenote, Shazam, The Echo Nest, and Nielsen Broadcast Data Systems (BDS). YouTube also created its own technology (see Chapter 15 for more information). In some cases, the data are census level and in others just samples. A census refers to a complete count, whereas a sample looks at a statistically significant segment, and that segment is projected to represent the whole. Whatever the method, the totals are staggering: hundreds of billions of performances tracked annually.

To archive a uniform business identifier of represented music, ASCAP, BMI, and Canada's SOCAN formed MusicMark in 2014, enabling music creators to register their works with a single filing. It's a convenience for music creators because one piece of music can have coauthors who are represented by different PROs. Each of the partners in MusicMark continues to maintain their own separate databases.

PROs also compile song play from lists provided by media outlets in the form of **cue** sheets and program logs for movies and TV broadcasts from program producers and broadcasters. PROs also monitor TV program guides, random samples and censuses of radio broadcasts, reviews of radio logs, checks of actual programming recorded from TV and radio broadcasts, and censuses of performances transmitted by background music services or used online.

Directly surveying performances in venues such as clubs, hotels, skating rinks, or dance schools is cost prohibitive. The revenue generated by licensing such venues is generally distributed to members based on surveyed radio and television performances as a proxy. Distributions are also made based on surveyed performances by commercial music services as well as for live concerts.

With respect to concert music, PROs gather evidence of live performances of composers' works by scrutinizing printed concert programs or via performance activity reports received directly from the composer or artists. A recent innovation, started by BMI, with ASCAP following suit, allows online reporting by artists of music performed at very small venues, including house sets.

Royalty Distribution

Once a writer affiliates with its chosen outfit and has his or her works performed, the next logical question is, "What is my fair share of the total royalties collected?"

While specifics vary depending on the rights organization, a member's or affiliate's share of the total royalties collected is determined broadly by the number and kind of performances of his or her music in the marketplace, as tracked via the techniques laid out previously.

Some songs have more than one writer and/or more than one publisher. If they do not all belong to the same PRO, the parties can earn differing amounts from their respective representatives, because the three organizations use their own particular methods to determine royalty payments, which are usually paid quarterly.

Performing rights earnings vary tremendously for individual members and affiliates. The composers, authors, and publishers of widely performed copyrights earn royalties year after year, going into six figures and beyond.

Foreign Collections

Performance royalties generated outside the United States can add significantly to those total earnings and have increased rapidly as additional foreign markets open up to Western music, and surveys and accounting procedures have made it easier to collect what is due. U.S. adherence to the Berne Convention, under which member countries treat foreigners as nationals for protection purposes, was a significant development that facilitates greater ease and accuracy in foreign copyright royalty collections (see Chapter 31).

The foreign subpublisher remains the dominant source of foreign collections. For those publishers who cannot depend on subpublishers to collect performance fees, ASCAP, BMI, and SESAC perform this service through reciprocal agreements with the major music licensing organizations abroad (in excess of 90 territories). They receive performance royalties from these foreign organizations and then pay members their share, withholding a small service fee.

ASCAP, BMI, and SESAC generally need to deal with only one licensing agency in each country. Among the most lucrative foreign sources of income at this time are Japan, the United Kingdom, Germany, France, Canada, Italy, Spain, and the Netherlands.

Membership Options

Songwriters can affiliate with only one PRO, but how does one choose among them? There is no right or wrong choice, but an exploration of their differences can help writers find the best "fit" for their situation. License and royalty rates, policies on issues such as advance payments, and service to members and affiliates should be taken into consideration. In general, once a member/affiliate chooses, staying with that organization is usually wise, as the disruption in income flow resulting from changing organizations can be costly. In its Amended Final Judgment of ASCAP's **consent decree** (see below for more on this), the Justice Department attempted to lay the foundation for a "level playing field" approach that would provide more flexibility to writers and publishers interested in exploring a change in affiliation. But for the most part, PROs gain members through attracting new writers and publishers, not from raiding each other's rosters.

There are differences in the three groups' payment policies, organizational structures, ownership setup, member (or affiliate) benefits, sampling and survey policies, and rules for termination, among other issues. Snapshots of the three leading organizations follow.

American Society of Composers, Authors and Publishers

ASCAP, America's first PRO, was founded largely in response to the U.S. Copyright Act of 1909, which firmly established that the right to perform a copyrighted work belongs to the creator(s) of the work; others wishing to perform the work must obtain permission from the creator(s) or a designated representative. In 1914, a small number of the leading American music writers and publishers formed ASCAP to license and collect fees for the public performances of their works and to distribute the fees as royalties to the writer and publisher members.

The organization had a difficult time in its early days. Not surprisingly, music users were reluctant to pay for music performances they had traditionally enjoyed free of charge. Today, after decades of educating music users and after numerous court decisions in favor of copyright holders, the concept of payment of performance fees through music licensing organizations is now broadly, if sometimes reluctantly, accepted.

Income, Royalty Distribution. In addition to being the oldest U.S. PRO, ASCAP is also one of the biggest. In 2014 alone, ASCAP's revenues were $1.0 billion, and of

ASCAP President and Chairman Paul Williams with ASCAP Founders Award honoree Tom Petty and Jackson Browne at the 2014 ASCAP Pop Music Awards.
Photo by PictureGroup.

that, $883 million was distributed to its publisher and writer members, with the difference eaten up by operating expense. Foreign outlets account for about one third of ASCAP's revenue, while close to one third of ASCAP's licensed performances income comes from broadcast, cable, and satellite TV stations and networks. Radio generates another 18% or so of the total. The remaining roughly 15% of ASCAP's revenue is derived through the licensing of clubs, restaurants, hotels, and similar venues; new media such as websites, cell phone ringtones, and digital jukeboxes; symphonic and concerts; and member fees.

Membership. Until the mid-1940s, ASCAP's members were mostly composers and lyricists of Broadway shows, movie musicals, and pop songs. Charter members included Victor Herbert, John Philip Sousa, Jerome Kern, George M. Cohan, James Weldon Johnson, and Irving Berlin.

ASCAP's more than a half-million member songwriters and publishers do not pay annual dues but do pay a one-time initiation fee. ASCAP's repertory, numbering in millions of works, covers the entire spectrum of music.

ASCAP is distinct among PROs in being governed by its members. ASCAP's board of directors comprises 12 writer members and 12 publisher members, all elected to 2-year terms by its general membership. Many of the greatest names in American music have served on ASCAP's board, including Harold Arlen, Sammy Cahn, Aaron Copland, Oscar Hammerstein II, Morton Gould, Hal David, Cy Coleman, Marilyn Bergman, Virgil Thomson, and Paul Williams. Gould, David, Bergman, and Williams have each served as president.

From time to time, music users have viewed music licensing organizations' practices as monopolistic and in violation of antitrust law. The U.S. Department of Justice, in actions in 1941, 1950, 1960, and 2001, agreed to court-supervised control of ASCAP with ASCAP's consent. The arrangement is known legally as a *consent decree.*[6] Thus, a federal judge supervises a portion of ASCAP's affairs, mainly with respect to licensing music users.

ASCAP conducts a significant public relations campaign to create good will among its members and the music community. It offers prizes each year to composers and symphony orchestras. Its ASCAP Plus Awards Program provides cash and recognition for writer members whose performances are primarily in venues not surveyed or whose catalogs have prestige value for which they would not otherwise be compensated.

ASCAP also hosts a variety of songwriter workshops and showcases across the country to help aspiring composers improve their writing, as well as their awareness of how the music business functions, and to bring these talents to the attention of the industry. Since 1968, ASCAP has given its Deems Taylor/Virgil Thomson Award to authors and publishers for outstanding print, broadcast, and new media coverage of music. The second edition of this *Handbook* was honored with the award in 1980.

Weighting Performances. Licensing organizations use various formulas to calculate the relative value, or weight, of sampled performances of music in the marketplace. As part of its calculation, ASCAP takes into account, among other factors, the following:

1. The medium in which the performance takes place (e.g., **local** radio, local television, network television, online, live venues, etc.)

2. The revenue weight of the outlet carrying the performance; ASCAP describes this as its "follow-the-dollar" formula.

3. The time of day during which the performance occurs (e.g., prime-time network performances are accorded greater weight than performances earlier in the broadcast day or in the middle of the night)

4. The type of performance (whether it is a feature, theme, or background)

5. Vocal and instrumental background performances are treated the same. Background music underscoring a film is credited on a durational basis, and performances of serious longer works are also credited in this manner.

More detailed information about ASCAP, as well as access to its online registration forms and other documents, is available at www.ascap.com.

Broadcast Music Inc.

Concerned with ASCAP's dominance, 475 American broadcasters created BMI in the late 1930s to introduce competition into the field of music licensing. BMI has traditionally embraced songwriters of musical styles that may not have been previously represented by PROs. Its first affiliates worked in jazz, rhythm and blues (R&B), country, gospel, folk, and other indigenous American music. In fact, BMI represented more than 90% of the composers in these genres whose work served as the foundation for the "Golden Age of Rock" in the 1950s and 1960s.

Broadcast Music Inc. (BMI) is owned by stockholders, with a select group of stockholders serving on the board of directors, which monitors overall company performance. When formation of BMI was first proposed, the company prospectus stated that stockholders could anticipate no dividends, and none have ever been paid. It is managed day to day by its president and executive team.

Membership. BMI has no members; instead, it has writer and publisher affiliates. BMI accepts a writer affiliate if that applicant has written a musical composition, alone or in collaboration with other writers, and the work is either commercially published or recorded or otherwise likely to be performed. As for admission of new publishers, BMI states in part that affiliation with BMI will be of practical benefit only to publishers who have the ability and financial resources to undertake broad-based exploitation of their works. BMI does not charge its affiliated writers an application fee or dues. BMI publisher affiliates pay a onetime application fee.

BMI describes its attitude toward bringing in new affiliates as "the open door," and it is active in promoting awareness of the organization. Among its outreach efforts, BMI offers awards to school composers, unknown writers, and arts organizations such as symphony orchestras.

BMI also sponsors a number of workshops in which seasoned composers and performers help train a new generation of creators, such as supporting movie music activities at the Sundance Film Festival. The BMI Foundation, a separate nonprofit entity, aims to encourage the creation of a broad spectrum of music and to nurture the talent of young composers, artists, conductors, and musicians through scholarship grants. The foundation's awards include, among others, the Charlie Parker Jazz Composition Prize, the BMI Student Composer Award, and the Jerry Bock Musical Theater Award.

Paul McCartney and BMI's Phil Graham celebrate more than 6 million broadcasts of "Yesterday" as the most performed song in BMI's catalog.
Photo courtesy of BMI.

Sampling, Accounting. To avoid separate dealings with the many thousands of music users, BMI conducts overall negotiations with established trade organizations. For example, it periodically negotiates industry-wide rates with the American Hotel and Motel Association. In the classical field, BMI negotiates with the League of American Orchestras. Licenses for various venues are based on such criteria as the frequency of their use and seating capacity.

Following accumulation of data via logging or census procedures, the numbers are combined with information generated from the sampling process. These accumulated numbers are then used by BMI in a formula to determine royalty payments to its affiliated writers and publishers.

Income, Royalty Distribution. BMI collected $977 million in fiscal year 2014, of which $840 million passed through in payments to its members. BMI's standard contract with writers and publishers does not cite payment rates, but BMI does make its *Royalty Policy Manual* available on its website.

Commercial radio royalty payments are based on the license fees that BMI collects from each station that performs a work. Payments to music writers are higher for performances of songs that air on stations paying higher license fees and lower for stations paying lower fees. Statements and royalty checks are distributed four times annually in many categories.

Foreign collections are an important factor in BMI's total income, and it has reciprocal arrangements with the major music licensing organizations abroad. More information about BMI can be found at www.bmi.com.

SESAC

SESAC, Inc. was founded in 1930 by Paul Heinecke, making it the second oldest performance licensing organization in the nation. Although the acronym originally stood for Society of European Stage Authors and Composers, the company has been known only as SESAC since the 1960s. Unlike ASCAP and BMI, SESAC is a closely held, for-profit corporation. Private equity investor Rizvi Traverse Management bought a 75% stake in 2013, intent on disrupting a field long dominated by a non-profit ethos.

SESAC is the smallest of the three oldest U.S. performing rights societies, and the company maintains that staying small allows it to provide more personal attention to its members. The PRO charges no dues to writers and publishers it represents. SESAC says its strength is in "adult contemporary, urban, jazz, rock, Americana, contemporary Christian, Latin, country, gospel, dance and classical" music genres.

Sampling, Accounting, Income, Royalty Distribution. SESAC distributes royalties earned in the United States on either a monthly basis or quarterly basis, and timing for foreign royalties varies. Its royalty formula has various benchmarks such as revenue weight for TV and radio stations, time of day, and duration of play. "SESAC uses state of the art pattern recognition technology supplied by BDS to track performances of its repertory on more than 1,600 commercial FM and AM radio stations in the U.S.," says its website. "Monitoring on these stations occurs on a census basis thus enabling SESAC to collect over 14 million hours of radio air time annually." In 2014, SESAC acquired Rumblefish to offer micro-licensing services to online outlets such as channels on YouTube, representing online music creators for their original works, and also license verification. Rumblefish said it was licensing up to

100,000 songs a day to digital outlets after the SESAC acquisition. In 2015, SESAC acquired the Harry Fox Agency from NMPA, creating a diverse licensing power-house combining the administration of both performance rights and mechanical rights (see below) under one aggressive ownership structure.

SESAC conducts periodic song seminars for writers and writers' showcases for its affiliates and helps pair up potential collaborators. It has agreements for foreign representation with about 90 foreign counterparts. More information is available at www.sesac.com.

SoundExchange

SoundExchange was created in 2000 as an unincorporated division of the Recording Industry Association of America (RIAA) and spun off in 2003 as an independent, nonprofit PRO covering parts of the digital media landscape not addressed by the PROs founded in the 20th century. It is governed by an 18-person board of music industry executives. The big impetus for SoundExchange was the establishment of a performance right for sound recordings via digital transmissions established in the 1995 and 1998 copyright law revisions. The Copyright Royalty Board has designated SoundExchange as the sole entity in the United States to collect and distribute the digital performance royalties on behalf of featured recording artists, owners of mas-ter rights such as record labels, and independent artists who record and own their masters. By law, SoundExchange splits performance royalty distributions equally between the artist and the sound recording copyright owner. For the artist portion, most goes to the featured artists and a small slice to a fund for nonfeatured artists (session musicians, background singers, etc.) The featured artists' slice of the pie has become so lucrative that some labels now try to negotiate taking part of that piece, defying the more even split decreed by Congress. Besides music, SoundExchange also collects royalties for spoken-word performances, such as comedians.

SoundExchange collects statutory royalties for sound recordings from several thousand noninteractive outlets in Internet radio such as Pandora; cable TV audio music channels; webcasters, including original programmers and retransmissions of FCC-licensed radio stations by aggregators; satellite services such as Sirius XM Radio; and other digital platforms for streaming sound recordings. The media outlets report their music play. SoundExchange does not overlap with PROs such as ASCAP. Of course, a singer-songwriter might receive a royalty for a digital broadcast of a *com-position* from BMI and receive a royalty from SoundExchange for airing the *recording* of that same song from SoundExchange. The recipient could be the same, but the licenses are distinct.

SoundExchange does not administer royalties for interactive performances of sound recordings (e.g., "on-demand" services that allow listeners to select the tracks they wish to listen to and/or the order in which they wish to hear them), digital down-loads, or analog public performances (traditional radio and television).

The organization will negotiate direct-license deals outside the compulsory license framework. SoundExchange has administrative expenses, of course, which are lower than other collecting societies, benefiting from the ease of monitoring play in digital media. There is no membership fee. Payments are made on a monthly basis to those signed up for electronic funds transfer.

Collections and distributions by SoundExchange have skyrocketed, climbing to $773 million by 2014. SoundExchange has built reciprocal relationships with collec-tion societies around the world to receive royalties earned by U.S. artists and labels.[7]

Mechanical Licenses

A second significant source of licensing income for writers and publishers are mechanical royalties that encompass copies in physical media such as CDs and also digital copies that are retained by consumers such as digital downloads of ringtones and songs. A century ago, the term *mechanical* applied to songs performed automatically from mechanical piano rolls. Times changed; the nomenclature remains. As explained in Chapter 4, "Music Copyright," recording companies are required to obtain a mechanical license to manufacture and distribute phonorecords to the public. This type of license is limited to those who intend to make these recordings available only for private use—the kinds of recordings people buy and take home or, in the age of digital distribution, purchase and download.

The copyright law sets forth procedures and fees for record companies to obtain a compulsory mechanical license. The notion that music is "a business of pennies" likely has its roots in the statutory rate for mechanical licenses. The first change in that rate since 1909 occurred in 1978, when Congress implemented an increase from 2 cents to 2.75 cents for each work embodied in a phonorecord or one-half cent per minute of playing time or fraction thereof, whichever amount is larger. This rate has been periodically adjusted upward since then.

In actual practice, however, most licenses of physical recordings (phonorecords) for home use are *negotiated* mechanical licenses. Publishers and record companies generally bypass the compulsory licensing route and work out their own terms, although the prevailing statutory rate is often used as a benchmark (a de facto ceiling) in negotiating lower rates.

A negotiated mechanical license may differ from a statutory compulsory license in three ways:

1. The royalty rate may be lower.

2. Royalty accountings are usually quarterly rather than monthly as required under a statutory license.

3. The statutory requirement of "notice of intent" to record the copyrighted material is waived.

Most publishers use the SESAC-owned Harry Fox Agency (HFA) to issue mechanical licenses. After publishers instruct the HFA on the royalty to charge, the agency implements the license, collects the royalties, takes out a service fee, and forwards the balance to the publisher. The HFA absorbs the cost of conducting audits on behalf of its clients and has funded litigation efforts resulting in substantial settlements with the Internet's earliest copyright infringers. The HFA has also been active in evangelizing for licenses for ringtones and other innovations of the digital and new media realms. Along with co-marketing services offered by parent SESAC, it sells its Slingshot, SongFile, and eSynch software programs to the industry for music rights management.

Many publishers are not large enough to support strong branch offices in foreign territories to license their works and collect their international royalties. The HFA has reciprocal arrangements with most foreign collecting agencies, which normally charge the HFA about 5% to 20% for their collecting service. The HFA takes off its own service fee, then forwards the balance to the publisher client.

Table 7.2   U.S. Statutory Mechanical Rates: Selected Uses (2013–2017)

Type of Use	Examples	Per Download	Per Song: The Greater of		% of Revenue	The Greater of	
						% of Total Content Cost	Per Subscriber per Month
Phonorecord and downloads	CD and permanent digital		9.1 cents	1.75 cents/min			
Mastertone download	Cellphone	24 cents					
Paid locker service	iTunes				12%	20.65%	17 cents
Free locker storage with paid download					12%	22%	
Mixed bundle	Cell service including music				11.35%	21%	
Music bundle	CD combined with download				11.35%	21%	
Limited interactive	Genre-specific playlist				10.50%	21%	18 cents

Publishers choosing not to retain the HFA to collect royalties have a few alternatives. Publishers can arrange their own licenses—sometimes publishers will license some material through the HFA and issue their own licenses for other songs—or use other boutique entities as agents. Even before acquiring the HFA, SESAC collected mechanical royalties on a somewhat smaller scale.

As physical distribution fades in importance, the scope of the compulsory mechanical license has expanded to embrace newer forms of digital distribution. Table 7.2 compares some of the newer license categories to the phonorecord's benchmark rate. In a few instances, the U.S. practice is tiptoeing toward the concept of basing royalties on a percentage of revenue, an approach commonplace in others parts of the world.

Synchronization Licenses

Music copyrights also play a starring—and lucrative—role in another primary arena of licensing: movies, television programs, online video, and TV commercials. The use case is *synchronization,* referring to the right to use music that is timed to synchronize with, or relate to, the action on the screen. Movie synch revenues, as well as those for TV and commercials, have grown significantly in recent decades. Producers pay up for chart-topping music to incorporate in their audiovisual works to stand out in the crowded media landscape. Hit songs licensed for synch usage in Super Bowl commercials collect $75,000 to over $1 million for what often are only one-time telecasts (although commercials also end up in online galleries of all commercials from the championship football game).

Companies that provide services for synchronous music licensing are Corbis Entertainment (formerly GreenLight), CueSongs, Dashbox, and Rumblefish (owned by SESAC).

Movie Rights

A producer of theatrical motion pictures must acquire two kinds of licenses in the United States. The first one is the synchronization license. Often as part of the same negotiation, the film producer ordinarily also seeks a performance license for theater exhibitions in the United States.[8]

Not all the music requiring synch licenses is preexisting. If a composer who writes an original score retains all publishing rights, the producer of the audiovisual work must acquire a synchronous license to make use of the music. So the synch license is a consideration in hiring the composer.

Synchronization license fees vary and are largely determined by the market value of the music—whether the music is to be performed on camera or just **underscored,** whether it is to be sung, the nature of the scene, and the duration of the performance in the film. Record labels and publishers will likely also weigh the promotional upside of being featured in a particular motion picture in deciding on an acceptable fee (newer artists, for instance, may be willing to take less in exchange for a high-profile boost of exposure). In movies, a point of negotiating contention is a separate deal for including a hit song in the film's separate soundtrack album. Synchronous deals for audiovisual works just cover the full-length program. Even the usage of the same music in associated film trailers requires separate synch licenses.

It is very important for the film producer to obtain the broadest possible synchronization license, because a movie originally planned for theatrical exhibition in this country will probably be used in foreign theaters, TV globally, home video, online streaming, and digital downloads as well. The publisher may try to grant the film producer a limited license to maximize profits later when the film is used in different media. (This can be a sore spot for movie companies and a boon to writers of old standards. Because most licenses for old movies neglected to include a "universal" license, publishers and writers have been able to garner additional license fees when a new technology, such as was the case with DVDs, is introduced.)

With respect to performance licenses for film music, conditions in the United States differ from those in Europe. It is customary for film producers to acquire from publishers a performance license for theatrical exhibition of a film in this country. Outside the United States, each country's own performance-licensing organization generally grants to theaters in that country a blanket license for the performance of music accompanying films. These organizations usually derive their income from film music by charging a small percentage of the net box office receipts. Nearly all PROs outside the United States grant licenses for music controlled by ASCAP, BMI, and SESAC through reciprocal agreements. American composers sometimes receive substantial performance royalties from music they have scored for films that become popular in theaters abroad.

TV Program Rights

A different set of licensing challenges arises for television programs. The producer will go for the broadest possible synchronization license—including downloads within the context of the program, streaming on the Internet, and wireless distribution—in anticipation that the production will eventually be aired in other media and possibly foreign territories. The producer will normally not need a performance license for television broadcasts, as TV stations and networks already have blanket performance licenses with ASCAP, BMI, and SESAC. Broadcasters may, however, seek to use direct or source licensing to avoid paying for both performance and synchronization licenses.

New Use Rights

A film producer or TV movie producer frequently wants to use music already existing in a commercially released recording. This can be attractive to the producer because it is already known how the music will sound and how it has been received by the public. But obtaining permission to use a recording in a film score can be a complicated, expensive process. Negotiations of this kind involve not only the recording company but also the performing artists, the artists' unions, and music publishers. The recording company contract with the artist may prohibit use of that artist's recordings in another medium. If so, special waivers and artist's compensation must be negotiated. Both artists' unions—the American Federation of Musicians (AFM) and SAG-AFTRA (historically its AFTRA predecessor)—require new use payments. The music publisher seeks from the producer both a synchronization license and a performing license. For this reason, many music publishers have established methods of recording cover versions of their most popular songs, thereby facilitating "one-stop shopping" for producers.

Cable Television Licenses

Cable television systems rely on a hard-fought 1992 U.S. Supreme Court decision giving them the same status as TV broadcasters for "through the viewer" blanket performance music licenses. This status lessens their expenses on performance music licenses by giving them wide coverage without having to pick through individual music titles. Also, cable systems must get licenses for local commercials, local on-air promotions, community access channels, and audio-only channels. (The recordings aired on audio-only cable channels are subject to a license covered by SoundExchange.) The blanket licenses for cable systems do not cover music in nationally distributed TV, which obtain their own licenses. Cable TV operators with scattered holdings of wired communities are usually referred to as multiple system operators, or MSOs.

Cable TV Network Licenses

Cable networks telecast a mix of original programs and reruns that first appeared in other media. PROs negotiate separate licensing arrangements with program networks—for example, MTV, HBO, and Showtime. These network agreements are distinct from the compulsory licenses the law requires for cable TV system operators.

With respect to music bounced off satellites and picked up by earth stations, copyright laws were clarified in the Satellite Home Viewer Act of 1988. Section 119 of the Copyright Act generally requires a compulsory license for programming originating on superstations or network stations and distributed to the home by satellite.

Video Licenses

The music video market grew rapidly in the early 1980s with the launch of MTV and the increased availability and affordability of videocassette recorders and players. Initially, no industry standards were in place for licensing of these works, which was further complicated by the failure of the 1976 Copyright Act to address the question. Over the years, entertainment lawyers and industry leaders have gradually formed a consensus. Here is a summary of their views:

1. All videos, whether clips or albums, must be defined under copyright law as audiovisual works. As such, they are like small movies, and producers must acquire synchronization licenses from music publishers or their agents. It has become customary, however, for publishers to grant gratis rights for short-form videos produced by record companies for promotional purposes.

2. Performance rights in the musical portion of videos must be acquired from the publisher by the party who shows the videos to the public. When the video is shown through conventional (i.e., "free") TV or via cable (e.g., MTV, HBO), the broadcasters' blanket performance rights agreement is sufficient. If the video is shown in a club or other public venue, the venue's blanket performance license with ASCAP, BMI, or SESAC will suffice.

3. Video producers or manufacturers must pay publishers or their agents for the right to reproduce the videos as discs or digital downloads for home use. Unless addressed explicitly in an agreement covering television rights, this right is not automatically considered part of a synchronization license but must be addressed specifically and negotiated separately. For newer motion pictures and many television programs, these rights are now standard and included in the initial negotiation, but they can also be considered a separate right with separate payment. The parties or their agents can determine through negotiation whether the royalty is to be paid as a one-time flat fee or as a per-unit fee based on sales.

Transcription Licenses

The term **transcription license** is applied imprecisely to encompass music used by syndicated programs, background music companies (also known as business music), in-flight entertainment, and music **library services.** Transcriptions are a significant source of income. These kinds of music users require a mechanical license and a performance license. The two may be combined in one agreement or contracted separately.

A user seeking such licenses may negotiate directly with publishers or through the HFA. With respect to the collection of performance fees, users negotiate agreements with ASCAP, BMI, or SESAC.

User companies usually obtain a master license from the relevant rights organization, with fixed annual fees based on their current number of franchised dealers. Other transcription licenses may call, for example, for a payment of 5 cents per selection for each copy of a music package that is sold to users. This nickel might include 2 cents for the mechanical license and 3 cents for the performance right. The mechanical license is for duplicating CDs and downloads of music packages played on-site by institutions using business music.

A somewhat different kind of transcription license is obtained by program syndicators and broadcasters' library services such as those described elsewhere (see Chapters 19 and 25). The transcription licenses for these packages may be negotiated through the HFA or directly with the music publishers.

With respect to in-flight entertainment, the supplier of the music packages must obtain rights of synchronization and mechanical reproduction from copyright owners. Negotiations may be directly with publishers or through the HFA. In-flight program suppliers normally negotiate performance licenses directly with ASCAP, BMI, or SESAC, or else with overseas PROs in countries where air carriers operate.

Special Use Permits

As explained in Chapter 6, "Music Publishing," music is often licensed for a wide range of applications, including broadcast commercials, video games, and various merchandising tie-ins, such as music boxes and greeting cards with printed lyrics and even some with audio capability from embedded electronic chips. Licenses of this kind are referred to as permissions or special use permits. The music publisher will either negotiate a one-time fee or a royalty tied to sales.

TV Commercials

For many publishers, the highest earnings from special use permits are generated from broadcast TV commercials. An advertising agency or sponsor who wants to use all or part of a pop standard is often willing to pay many thousands of dollars for the privilege. (Microsoft famously paid millions for the synchronous use of the Rolling Stones' "Start Me Up" in a commercial, although that's at the high water market in pricing.) These kinds of music licenses often include the right to alter the words and music to suit the needs of the advertisers—a prospect that can cause resistance from some songwriters who don't want their lyrics tampered with.

For music composed originally for broadcast commercials, the composer usually has the option of granting the advertiser a **buyout** deal or, more likely, permitting unlimited performances of the music if the usage is confined to advertising.

Video (Electronic) Games

Video games are a multi-billion-dollar industry unto themselves, and the music licensed for them has also become a revenue source of synch-rights licensing for publishers and record labels, although one with ups and downs over the years. When music-based games like *Guitar Hero* and *Rock Band* were popular, game companies paid a per-unit royalty for hit tunes in what was a boomlet for music owners. For nonmusic game titles, music synch fees are usually quite modest because game companies license nonhit music, putting more spending emphasis on producing dazzling video and consumer marketing.

One PRO tells game companies that game royalties per unit "range from 8 cents to 15 cents per composition, and buyouts range from $2,500 to over $20,000" typically for terms running 5 to 10 years, and perpetual rights may be negotiated. Most video game deals convey global rights, since games sell around the world. Music licensing agreements usually address exploitation of music snippets in marketing such as advertising (typically, the answer is that strictly promotional usage is free to game companies).

Other issues affecting music rights pricing and allowed transmissions are whether a game is an inexpensive casual game that is free to users (for example, played on mobile phones) or an expensive physical cartridge for a dedicated game console. Other issues affecting music rights for video games is whether games can be bought online or are multiplayer games. As with other special uses, the agreement for any particular game is negotiated on the basis of, among many factors, the software manufacturer's need for a certain track, the length of usage, the manufacturing run, and the projected earnings of the game.

Jukebox Licenses

Since 1978, jukebox owners have been required to obtain a public performance license for so-called **nondramatic music** played on their machines (before then, jukeboxes were legally considered "toys" under U.S. copyright law and were not liable for payment). These licenses are negotiated between the jukebox operator and the copyright owner, often with the involvement of ASCAP, BMI, or SESAC.

In 1990, ASCAP, BMI, SESAC, and the Amusement and Music Operators Association (AMOA) created the Jukebox License Office (JLO), which contacts jukebox operators and offers them a blanket license to cover the use of music from all three PROs. The JLO deal offers one-stop shopping that "generally costs less, is more convenient, and is less of an administrative burden than . . . other options," says one of the big PROs. This **joint venture** handles the rebates and new jukebox registrations. Licensing fees are standardized.

Dramatic Music Rights

If you're wondering about that reference to "nondramatic" music previously, you should be: It's an important point because U.S. copyright law makes sharp distinctions between **dramatic music** and nondramatic music. Accordingly, the licensing of rights differs markedly.

Despite the way it sounds, this has nothing to do with a particularly heart-wrenching lyric or over-the-top vocal performance. The term *dramatic music* refers to compositions used in the context of a wider piece or in the telling of a larger story—including, for example, operas, musical shows, and revues, in whole or in part. The term may also include music that did not originate in a theatrical production but was written as part of a TV or radio show where the music was integral to the plot and where it contributed to carrying the drama forward. It is customary to refer to performing rights in dramatic music as **grand rights,** and grand rights must be negotiated with copyright owners separately from nondramatic rights, which are sometimes termed **small rights.** Grand rights are necessary to stage complete live musicals such as operas and Broadway musicals with multiple songs, as opposed to licenses for individual tunes.

With respect to Broadway musicals and similar productions, rights of authors, composers, and lyricists are set forth in contracts recommended by the Dramatists Guild, Inc. Under the guild's **Approved Production Contract (APC),** the separate rights in music and lyrics that make up the dramatico-musical work are retained by the composers and lyricists and their publishers, sometimes with certain restrictions, as in the sale of movie rights. Also, there may be restrictions with respect to when the music and lyrics can be recorded (e.g., there may be a prohibition against releasing recordings of a show's songs on a single prior to the release of the original cast album).

A show's composers receive royalties from ASCAP, BMI, or SESAC for performances of individual songs on radio and TV or in clubs and restaurants, and so forth. But when a dramatic musical work is performed as a whole or a substantial portion of it is performed—a scene including music and dialogue, for example—grand rights must be licensed. The copyright owner usually assigns that responsibility to one of the firms involved in grand rights licensing and rental of scores and parts. ASCAP and SESAC do not negotiate such rights, and BMI permits broadcasters only the limited right to perform up to 30 minutes of a full-length dramatic or dramatico-musical work or an insubstantial portion of a shorter dramatic or dramatico-musical work.

When a Broadway musical becomes a hit, its writers enjoy income from its performances long after its Broadway run. There are hundreds of regional theaters within the United States offering performances of these beloved shows. The author holds the so-called **subsidiary rights** to these shows, including motion pictures, band arrangements, live performance rights, TV usage, commercial jingle usage, and stage performance rights. Some agents specialize in the licensing of subsidiary rights such as stock and amateur productions of musicals. Stock and amateur rights of a play are those rights reserved by the authors of the play and licensed to organizations such as Samuel French, Inc.; Music Theatre International; R&H Theatricals (the initials are for famed musical creators Rodgers and Hammerstein); and Tams-Witmark Music Library. These companies, mostly based in New York City, represent authors for specific works rather than for every musical they write. The companies receive an agent's commission and handle the licensing of those shows to stock and amateur theaters around the country.

Each dramatic performance of this kind requires a license and royalty payment. Royalty rates are calculated on a percentage based on the seating capacity of the house, the number of performances, and the ticket prices. In addition to the license fee, the show's **book** (or script), score, and parts must be rented from the licensing agency. Professional performances of Broadway shows (following a Broadway run) require a license involving a weekly minimum guarantee (which sets a floor price) against 6% to 14% of the box office receipts (brisk ticket sales will trigger additional fees above the floor amount of money). Professional productions also must rent the show's book, score, and parts. The producers are generally charged higher rates than those for amateur groups, which often pay a relatively modest flat fee in addition to a percentage of ticket sales. A new wrinkle is gaining permission to video-record live stage plays, which Samuel French says must be requested in writing and may require an additional fee.

Performance licenses for touring companies vary. Some touring companies are under the aegis of the original Broadway producer; others are mounted independently. The original producer usually has many options and a period of time after the opening (or close) of the producer's production of the play in which to exercise them, such as the right to send out a touring company. If the producer doesn't send out a touring company, the rights to license a touring company revert to the authors (this is one of the subsidiary rights that include motion picture rights, touring rights, and foreign rights). If the original show has run long enough that the Broadway producer is entitled to a share of subsidiary rights, the authors would then pay the producer a portion of their receipts just as they do with stock and amateur rights.

■ Creative Commons

Some musicians choose to publish their songs under licenses from Creative Commons (CC), an American nonprofit corporation founded in 2001 to facilitate the distribution of copyrighted works with few strings attached. The typical CC license covers "baseline rights" to distribute the copyrighted work worldwide, without changes, at no charge, but only with the consent of the copyright holder.

A music creator might specify that its CC license allows the free legal sharing of songs online, duplication of songs for friends, use by nonprofits, and/or use in videos or other compositions. Working within the framework of statutory copyright laws, the creator also specifies rights that are not free. Websites that offer music published under CC licenses include BeatPick, CASH Music, ccMixter, Free Music Archive, Jamendo, Magnatune, SectionZ, and SoundCloud.

CC licenses require attribution of the original author. If the work itself contains copyright notices placed there by the copyright holder, those notices must be left intact or reproduced in a reasonable way. The work's title or name should be cited, noting if the work is a derivative work or an adaptation. Sampling licenses are easily issued. Creative Commons also offers a convenient way to release material into the public domain for music creators who chose to forgo copyright compensation on their original works.

Work licensed under a Creative Commons License, which is always nonexclusive and nonrevocable, is governed by applicable copyright law. In practice, it's rare that a music publisher would allow such a license, since it would potentially be forfeiting income, which means most music business attorneys don't familiarize themselves with the ins and outs of Creative Commons.

More information can be found at http://creativecommons.org/.

■ Notes

1. Settling one such lawsuit in 2015, Sirius XM caved in to pressure and agreed to pay labels for airing of pre-1972 recordings.
2. Passage from *Copyright and the Music Marketplace,* a report from the U.S. Register of Copyright, February 2015, p. 58.
3. In 2008, Congress passed the Webcaster Settlement Act, which led in 2009 to industry factions agreeing to a complex series of webcasting master use rates that any webcaster may agree to pay.
4. BMI did publish music for a while early in its history (1940s) but no longer does so. Neither ASCAP nor SESAC has ever published music.
5. There are some exceptions to the license requirement. The Fairness in Music Licensing Act of 1998, an adjunct to the Sonny Bono Copyright Term Extension Act mentioned in Chapter 4, exempts smaller businesses such as restaurants, taverns, and mall shops from paying royalties for the use of background music if their square footage is below a certain threshold. (According to the World Trade Organization, this put the United States in violation of the copyright protection rules it had agreed to as a signatory of the Berne Convention, an international treaty.)
6. BMI became the second PRO also operating under a consent decree, but it sets forth a different set of constraints than those governing ASCAP. In 2015 SESAC reached a legal settlement with radio broadcasters, agreeing to abide by some licensing rules that mirror limitations long enforced against the SESAC rivals.

7. In addition, another fund administered jointly by AFM and SAG-AFTRA distributes 5% of digital performance royalties collected in the United States as well as other performance levies from some foreign territories. This fund pays nonfeatured musicians and vocalists, regardless of their union membership. (Current information is available on the group's site: www.raroyalties.org.) And, multinational home taping, blank recording media, and rental levies generate royalties to labels and featured artists that are administered by the Alliance of Artists and Recording Companies (AARC).

8. For this license, the film producer usually goes to the publisher (or the publisher's agent) because a court decree has denied, to ASCAP at least, the right to require a performance license directly from movie theaters in the United States.

Chapter Takeaways

- Once a song is commercially distributed, other parties may release cover records after paying the applicable compulsory license fee. Commonly, they will attempt to negotiate a lower, noncompulsory fee with the publisher.

- Compulsory copyright rights do not extend to other uses such as inclusion of music in a movie soundtrack, commercials, TV programs, original online video, and so on; those usages must be negotiated.

- The largest source of income for many publishers and composers is broadcast public performance income paid through performance rights organizations. In the United States, the three leading PROs for compositions are ASCAP, BMI, and SESAC.

- A significant source of revenue for labels and performing artists is payment for noninteractive digital distribution rights administered by SoundExchange.

- A synchronization license granted by a music publisher gives a producer the right to use a composition in an audiovisual work such as a movie or TV show.

- A large variety of licenses and special use permits can increase the revenue of music owners, ranging from jukeboxes to grand rights for mounting Broadway shows.

- Clearing rights to samples is thorny because the publisher and label licensors may insist on hearing how the sample is used before granting permission.

Key Terms

- blanket performance license   (p. 122)

- buyout deal   (p.136)

- compulsory license   (p. 120)

- consent decree   (p. 125)

- copublishing   (p. 120)

- grand rights   (p. 137)

- Harry Fox Agency (HFA)   (p. 131)

- master use license   (p. 118)

- mechanical license   (p. 120)

- phonorecord   (p. 119)

- small rights   (p. 137)

- source license   (p. 122)

- SRLP (suggested retail list price)   (p. 120)

- synchronization license   (p. 132)

- transcription license   (p. 135)

Discussion Topics

1. What are the implications of smartphones and other digital devices on synch licenses?

2. With so many new forms of presentation online, how does one determine the difference between a nondramatic and a dramatic work?

3. Advances in technology have made tracking bits of information much easier. Is it time to revisit the suitability of the "blanket license"?

4. Do you think the thicket of different licenses in the industry is likely to become more complex or more streamlined as technology continues to change? Why?

Managing Artist
Relationships

PART 3

Agents, Managers, and Attorneys

Many professional artists find it desirable, even imperative, to call on others to assist them in handling their business affairs and the development of their careers. Partly because of the glamour of the music and entertainment fields, performers of even moderate success find themselves surrounded by individuals who claim they can help the artist find the path to fame and fortune.

> *"The first thing we do,*
> *let's kill all the lawyers."*
> — Shakespeare, *Henry VI,*
> Part 2, Act IV, Scene II

Artists have a long to-do list: Negotiate record deals and music publishing contracts, book live performances, arrange travel itineraries, license merchandise and product endorsements, maintain fan and press relations, and land movie and TV acting gigs. For all this, they engage a team of assistants and professional representatives, probably including a personal manager, agent, business manager, road manager, attorney, publisher, and publicist. The services that these support personnel perform often overlap and intertwine.

The job of these handlers is to maximize artist earnings and relieve the artist from directly overseeing complex financial and business activities. This can come at a cost of 20% to 30% of an artist's earnings, if a full array of representatives and handlers are hired at normal rates. Superstars with fat incomes often negotiate lower fees because their music paydays are so large that service providers still make good money with smaller-than-normal percentage slices. Emerging talent tends to pay the full rate because career revenue isn't large enough to merit a discount, and emerging talent still requires costly services.

As with all contracts, it's important to agree on the scope of services to be provided (and thus understand what is *not* included), whether the contract covers international

Left: Singer Celine Dion (R) and manager René Angélil at the 83rd Annual Academy Awards.

Photo © Jason Merritt/Getty Images.

services, the status of fees in the event third parties don't pay or income is significantly below expectations, and the length of the agreement (such as a specific end date or conclusion of a range of activities such as covering multiple albums or tours for performers). Representation deals can be finalized by long-form contract, a short **deal memo** containing key financial points, or a handshake with no paperwork.

In this chapter, the roles of agents, managers, and attorneys are defined and discussed as they relate to the arts and entertainment industry. In the music industry, performers, musicians, label executives, labels, producers, composers, lyricists, music supervisors, and top recording engineers might seek one or all of these services. Figures 8.1a–c illustrate possible configurations of an artist's team of professional assistants.

Figure 8.1a   **The Team**

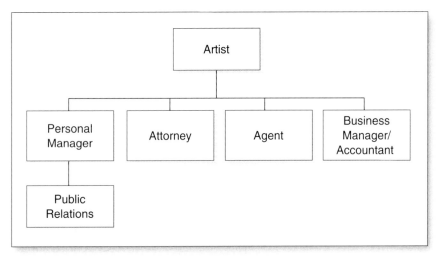

Figure 8.1b   **The Team in the Studio**

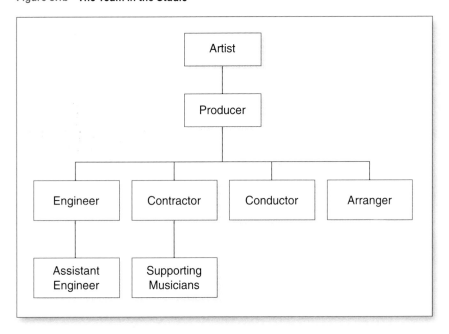

Figure 8.1c   The Touring Team

Agents

An agent represents clients by seeking employment for them, and as an employment agent, this person is subject to state laws.

Agents go by various names. Many people refer to them as *booking* agents, which most of them are. In California, they are known as *talent* agents. Sometimes people in and out of the business use the term *manager* or *artist's manager* interchangeably with *agent,* although these roles are separated by some state laws. A high percentage of agency work is conducted in California, so the word *agent* is used here the way California statutes define talent agent—that person who is in the full-time business of procuring employment primarily for performers, writers, producers, and directors. In the music industry, talent agents work primarily in booking live performances of artists, whether at clubs or concerts, and product endorsements that can involve TV and radio commercials. Their fees are typically 10% of artist income from concert tours and product endorsements. Music talent agents generally do not negotiate recording contracts (there are some exceptions), songwriting activities, and licensed merchandise and are not particularly involved in overall career guidance (as are film and TV agents).

The talent agent has two kinds of clients in the concert segment. The first is a roster of performing artists. The other kind of client is the buyer of such talent—such as TV producers, concert promoters, and club owners. The talent agent's job is to deliver artists to talent buyers, to serve as the middleman, the negotiator who knows, or should know, what an artist is worth and what the buyer is willing and able to pay. The agents who are most successful over the long run have earned the respect and confidence of both buyers and sellers. It is the agent's task to obtain the highest possible fees for clients and to work closely with an artist's manager.

Regional and Boutique Agencies

An agent often starts out in a medium-sized city working alone, quickly discovers it is hard to be very effective that way, and connects with one or two other local agents. Perhaps three of them can afford to rent a modest office and hire a secretary. Agencies of this size handle most local bookings, attempting to persuade local club owners to try live music instead of recorded music. One of their greatest challenges is locating acts attractive enough to pull dancers and drinkers into local clubs. Most of the acts sending them demos are, at best, semiprofessional—clearly not strong enough to justify the club owner's paying them even union **scale**. So the agent keeps searching for buyers and qualified talent.

Until the agent can discover acts with some drawing power, there will rarely be a chance to build the booking business above a minimum survival level. But now and then, local acts create a following and start to command fees high enough to earn the agent a respectable income.

Agents with ambitions transcending the city limits search out contacts and joint bookings with national, and even international, agencies. Such deals ordinarily involve commission splits.

Another type of talent agency in this classification is the boutique, which is relatively small and specialized. Boutiques usually can be found in Los Angeles and New York and confine themselves to just one aspect of entertainment—such as only booking music acts at live events (so no TV, film, etc.). For example, the Gorfaine/ Schwartz Agency just focuses on composers, songwriters, music supervisors, producers, and editors.

National Full-Service Agencies

National booking agencies—often called full-service agencies—employ hundreds of people and often operate with offices in the major cities of the world. Agencies such as William Morris Endeavor Entertainment (WME), International Creative Management (ICM), Creative Artists Agency (CAA), Paradigm, and United Talent Agency (UTA) handle hundreds of artists and gross hundreds of millions of dollars a year.

Such booking agencies generally take commissions of 10% (and occasionally up to 15%) of the music artist's gross income from work generated by the agency or otherwise eligible for commission. These same full-service agencies also represent film and TV's biggest stars and major behind-the-camera talent. The big talent agencies try to represent artists in all fields of entertainment, including concerts, television, recordings, films, commercials, video games, publishing, licensed products, and product endorsements. A music artist signing with a national talent agency may negotiate for **carve outs,** such as excluding music publishing, composing, and TV acting from the contract.

Major agencies rarely sign unknown talent; they are preoccupied booking their stars. Unknown acts must struggle along with local agents, usually until they achieve some success as recording artists.

In the process of signing an artist, a large agency may submit a package of 10 or more contracts for the signature of the new client. Some of these agreements are form contracts used by that particular agency. Of the many contracts submitted to prospective new clients, only a few are frequently used for contemporary recording artists or performing groups:

1. American Federation of Musicians (AFM) Exclusive Agent-Musician Agreement

2. American Federation of Television and Radio Artists (AFTRA) Standard Exclusive Agency Contract

3. The talent agency's own general services and materials agreement. This is a comprehensive agreement that covers creative materials, services, TV and movie packages, and other kinds of entertainment deals.

Altogether, the agreements generally provide that the agency serves as the artist's adviser and representative in respect to the artist's activity and participation in fields such as merchandising, testimonials, and commercial tie-ins. The standard contracts often used by talent agencies in California incorporate language of the union contracts stipulating that the artist's approval is required prior to the agency committing the artist. The parties also agree that the contract can be terminated if the agency can't find work for the artist for a specified number of consecutive months, that any disputes are to be referred to the Labor Commissioner of the State of California or binding arbitration, that the agreement shall not conflict with any union contracts involving the artist, and under what circumstances the agency has the right to assign the contract to a third party.

It is also possible for an artist to work with an agency on a nonexclusive basis or even with no written agreement at all—a so-called handshake agreement. An agency might be hired to work with an artist in a limited or specific territory or kind of performance. An example of this kind of limited representation would be an artist who retains an agency to book live performance tours in a certain territory or for a specific tour but who does not use that agency for deals involving other territories, movie companies, or commercials. For pop/rock tours, large agencies sometimes join forces with other agencies to jointly administer the tour.

Changing Representation. Artists frequently change agents and agencies in the hope that new representation will further their careers. Often lesser names feel they get lost in the shuffle of a big company attempting to find work for its big earners. The major agencies are aware of these negative views of their operations and attempt to offer each of their clients the personal attention of at least one particular agent on their staff who is assigned to keep the artist working and happy. The AFM agency agreement, for example, requires that the firm name the specific individual agents who are to handle the affairs of the musician under contract.

On occasions when agents change companies or break off and set up their own firms, it is particularly disruptive to their artist clients. Often, personal relationships and confidences are built up between agent and artist. When the agent leaves, it is a common occurrence for those artists to seek relief from their contracts with the company, declaring their intention of following that agent. A court battle may ensue. In general, in these kinds of altercations, the courts have tended to find for the artist, recognizing that in the employment field, the element of personal relationships is entitled to special consideration. Many artists insist on inserting **key man clauses** into their agency agreements, giving the artist the right to terminate the agreement if the specific agent or "key man" is no longer with the agency. While the key man's importance to the agency is cemented in such agreements, the agency as an institution may object to this clause.

Regulation of Agents

Some of the colorful characterizations of booking agents depicted in old movies might lead one to believe that the only qualifications needed by an agent are a tolerance for cigar smoke and a pair of alligator shoes. Although such images of unscrupulous agents may be interesting movie fiction, the modern talent agent is a professional whose success is measured, in large part, by the success of the talent or business entity represented.

Statutory Regulation. Agents and artist managers proliferated early in the last century with the rapid growth of the movie industry. In the early days of agents' abuses of performers, wages would be skimmed or never paid; collusion between agents and employers would occur. Artists would be dispatched long distances to jobs that never existed. Because agents became particularly active in the early days of the film industry, California was early to grapple with abuses. Following first attempts in 1913 to regulate employment agencies, California enacted its Labor Code in 1937. This code made a distinction between "motion picture employment agencies" and agents active primarily in booking vaudeville acts, circus performers, and actors for the legitimate stage.

In 1943, California added a new category, "artist's manager." In 1967, California repealed substantial portions of its Labor Code. "Theatrical employment agencies" and "motion picture employment agencies" were eliminated as separate categories. But the "artist's manager" category was retained and placed under the jurisdiction of the Labor Commissioner of the Department of Industrial Relations. "Employment agency" provisions were shifted to the jurisdiction of what is now the Department of Consumer Affairs.

In 1978, California altered its artist's manager statute, the principal change being one of nomenclature: Artist's managers were to be known as "talent agents." Because of widespread abuse of artists by agents in the past, California laws today severely limit the activities of all persons involved in artist representation. Procurement of employment for artists and entertainers in California is closely regulated by two state statutes: the Talent Agencies Act of 1978 and the Employment Agency Act. Simply stated, all persons engaged in the procurement, or attempted procurement, of employment for an artist must be licensed by the state to do so. Any contract can be canceled by either party or the state where an individual engaged in procuring employment lacks the required state license.

Union Regulation. In addition to state laws governing persons engaged in agency activity, talent agents representing union musicians are restricted severely on a national basis by the various performers' unions and guilds. The organizations most involved are the AFM for instrumentalists, SAG-AFTRA for singers, and the American Guild of Variety Artists (AGVA) and the American Guild of Musical Artists (AGMA) for opera/dance.

Artists' guilds and unions vary in what they require when they **franchise** or license a talent agent, but the following requirements are typical of most agreements:

1. Maximum allowable commissions are stipulated. For example, AFTRA and SAG historically have applied a 10% ceiling on commissions applied to the artist's gross compensation. The AFM allows a 20% commission on one-night gigs and 15% if the job runs 2 or more days per week for the same employer. In cases where AFM agents have a Federation Personal Management Agreement with AFM musicians, the AFM will allow an additional 5% commission.

2. SAG-AFTRA generally franchises only those agents who agree to limit their professional activity to procurement of employment for artists. This constraint is designed to protect the artist from paying superfluous or excessive commissions for other nonagent services. The disadvantage of this restriction is that some professionals are barred from acting as agents because they also participate in other entertainment industry enterprises such as management, production, publishing, and recording.

3. Lengths of contracts are limited, usually to 1 or 3 years depending on the union.

Getting Started. Individuals wanting to get a career started in the talent agency field often find it daunting. Sometimes, students can enter a talent agency as apprentices. Perhaps, after a stint in the mail room or a short training period, they may be put on as assistant agents. Artists' unions license all owners of each franchised agency and then permit subagents to work under an individual owner's license.

Managers

The arts and entertainment industry engages a number of different kinds of managers. The most influential among them is the artist's personal manager. Personal managers are expected to perform tasks ranging from negotiating multi-million-dollar contracts to checking on the star's wardrobe. Fees typically range from 10% to 25% of artists' deals. Managers of less famous stars may earn a higher percentage than otherwise, as they invest more effort in building a career at a time when the artist's earnings are low.

Regulation of personal managers is loose, and professional competence varies between managers. This segment is rife with complaints of manager malfeasance, particularly when young artists have family or friends as managers. Once the artists become stars, they often battle managers' pay claims—which usually assert a portion of future earnings—when moving to better-connected handlers. This can happen if first contracts were not well crafted and thus subject to various interpretations.

This chapter limits the discussion of personal managers to how they are regulated by state statutes and artists' unions. Personal managers have their own trade groups, including the National Conference of Personal Managers for the United States and the multinational International Music Managers Forum. The manner in which management contracts are negotiated and how managers advance the careers of their clients is treated in Chapter 9.

Regulation of Managers

California regulates artists' personal managers quite strictly. Because many management contracts are negotiated with these professionals, an understanding of California's regulations is most useful.

Statutory Regulation. As mentioned above, in California, only licensed talent agents are allowed to procure employment for an artist. Personal managers are supposed to be principally concerned with advising and counseling their clients about their overall careers and longer-term objectives. But booking gigs is important to clients, so it is difficult for personal managers to completely separate themselves from that activity.

If the personal manager in California wants to stay within the law, book gigs, and remain in the management profession, he or she needs to obtain a talent agent's license. But then the individual would have to function under the constraints imposed by artists' unions on talent agents. If the manager decides against becoming a licensed talent agent, there are other options:

1. The manager may voluntarily forgo commissions on all employment procured by a talent agent. However, in various rulings, California's Labor Commission has frowned on this practice.

2. The manager may go into partnership with the artist. Both parties may find this unattractive, however, in that they are exposed to liability for their partner's actions.

3. The manager may employ the artist exclusively and supply the artist's services to third parties. This might serve the manager's interests, but it will seriously disadvantage the artist by imposing restrictions on the artist's activities that could go well beyond the terms normally encountered in a regular management agreement.

4. The personal manager might set up a corporation that would deliver the artist's services to third parties, although this potentially adds tax liability for the artist. Some lawyers believe this may offer the best insulation available from the constraints of talent agent licensing requirements.

Next to California, New York hosts the greatest number of personal management contract negotiations. That state offers a less restrictive regulatory framework than California. New York avoids the issue of licensing personal managers in that it defines theatrical agencies (booking agencies) as those that procure employment other than incidental to the manager-artist relationship. This would appear to exclude personal managers because most of their procurement activity is incidental.

Union Regulation. Personal managers of good reputation could obtain a franchise from an artists' union, but they would then fall under close regulation. The unions would impose a ceiling on their commissions, the term of their contracts with clients would be shorter, and they would probably be required by the franchise agreement to engage in employment procurement activity full-time and not engage in other business activities concurrently. Few managers could function under these restrictions; it is the very nature of the business for them to be involved at any given time in a number of entertainment business activities, particularly publishing, licensed merchandise, and recording. Generally, managers in New York are not union affiliated.

The personal manager in California has one other option: to take out a union franchise, then ignore the union's restraints. This is a temptation because unions have rarely enforced these rules. But ignoring union rules can be risky: No one can predict when the union might start enforcing its franchising agreements. Also, clients could later cite the absence of a union franchise as justification for refusal to pay a manager's commission. The end result of statutory and union constraints on personal managers is that, in California at least, many established and respectable personal managers opt against both state licensing and union franchising.

Disputes With Clients

The various prohibitions on managers directly soliciting and booking work for clients—which is the heavily regulated role of agents—is the catalyst for many disputes between managers and talent. In a landmark case, the agent regulations were cited by TV actress Rosa Blasi as justification to quit paying commissions to her management firm. She asserted that her entire management contract was voided because the firm illegally served as an agent on some of her acting jobs.

Hollywood labor unions sided with Blasi. In the other corner, managers around Hollywood backed her manager, Marathon Management, saying an ungrateful client was trying to stiff the organization that engineered her career success. In 2008, the California Supreme Court ruled that Marathon's contract was not entirely nullified because of Marathon's limited violations of the Talent Agencies Act and that "an isolated instance of procurement does not automatically bar a manager from collecting commissions." This was a partial victory for personal managers everywhere since only fees connected to direct bookings were disallowed. The decision cooled interest of artists to invoke this justification when attempting to break contracts, but the issue continues to flare up. For example, in 2010, pop singer Ke$ha responded to a lawsuit of over $14 million in claims for management fees by alleging that her personal management company crossed the line into agenting. The two parties agreed to an undisclosed settlement in 2012. Other artists have asserted their claims regarding this issue directly with the California Labor Commission.

Steely Dan (circa 1973). Artists, producer, publicist, booking agent, and managers show off the evidence of their collective success.
Photo © Tim Mosenfelder/Getty Images.

Assistants to Management

Most managers will try to accompany their artists to all performances or events that are important for the artist's career—the start of a long run in the main room of a Las Vegas casino, big city stops of national concert tours, and star performances on TV shows. Few artists' managers attempt to travel regularly with their clients, however, and assign such duties to a road manager. **Road managers** handle all logistics of the artist's touring—the transportation of people and equipment, meals and lodging, ensure that adequate security is provided, supervise the crew (i.e., sound reinforcement and lighting and even wardrobe personnel), check box office receipts, and collect performance income. Road managers who learn the business and know how to hustle often graduate to artist management jobs. Some have become producers.

Many young people break into show business by signing on as *roadies,* the word often used to describe persons hired to move and help set up the performance. Even though some roadies have previous training in areas such as lighting or sound, others seem to learn what is expected of them on the job.

The people hired on as road crew members for lesser known acts usually earn minimum salaries plus their travel expenses; such acts have little difficulty locating individuals willing to work for low wages and high adventure. In contrast, today's top acts tour with highly disciplined, well-paid crews.

Whether the individual is a recording artist or some other kind of professional in the field, when income reaches a respectable level, other support personnel will be required to advance that performer's career. This is treated in Chapter 9, "Artist Management."

Attorneys

Entertainment business attorneys are greatly important due to the constant stream of transactions inherent in the music business. With the continuing transformation of existing entertainment companies and the shifting ground rules of new forms of media, the role of the entertainment attorney is more crucial today than ever before.

Law practices are often roughly divided into litigation services and transactional services. In litigation, attorneys press the rights of their clients in court cases (or threatened court cases) over copyright, contract issues, disputes over rights to names, and rights to music. Relatively few disputes, of course, escalate to the point where litigation is required. The bulk of day-to-day legal work is performed by transactional attorneys who negotiate and draft contracts, register copyrights, research suspected copyright infringement, assist in vetting client work to ensure originality, and sort out co-ownership issues when artists collaborate. Although some firms specialize in entertainment litigation, most entertainment practice falls into the transactional category. For the glamour fields of music, theater, movies, and TV, law schools are turning out more interested graduates than are needed. Despite the unemployment (or underemployment) among graduates now emerging from law schools, there is an actual shortage of lawyers fully qualified and experienced to practice in the entertainment field.

Entertainment attorneys tend to specialize in chosen subareas of the business. Some work primarily with issues of **intellectual property**, including copyright and trademark. Some negotiate with recording and publishing companies; others work with clients who are involved with the theater or TV or movies. Law firms frequently employ a number of attorneys with different entertainment specialties and thus can move a given music client's business to specialists within the same law firm. Specialized attorneys have the advantage of drawing on past experience and thus understand what deal points the other party may concede and what may be a line in the sand that can't be crossed. In fact, most attorneys would prefer to battle a knowledgeable adversary rather than a naïve newcomer.

The most experienced lawyers in copyright are found in Washington, D.C., New York City, Nashville, Chicago, and the state of California. The best-qualified lawyers in general music business practice are found in the three recording centers in the United States. In Canada, entertainment lawyers practice mainly in Toronto and Montreal.

Retaining Legal Counsel

How can someone go about finding a qualified attorney? A good starting point is to check with colleagues in the business or do online research through a professional social networking site. Attorney organizations also provide one-stop information. For example, the Beverly Hills Bar Association has a specialized entertainment section. Local and state bar associations and the American Bar Association's Forum on the Entertainment & Sports Industries, a national organization, are another starting point.

These questions might be asked:

1. What is the prospective attorney's reputation, and how reliable is the source of your information? Is it objective? The fact that a lawyer has passed the state bar examination and offers all the appearances of respectability is insufficient reason for complete trust. Read the music trade news to see who is active in the field, check online listings, and view individual law firm websites. Find out which attorneys already represent successful artists, managers, and companies in the business, since their preexisting contacts can open doors.

2. Is the prospective lawyer sufficiently experienced in the music field to look out for the musician's interests in publishing, recording, live performance, and foreign rights?

3. Is the prospective lawyer savvy about the nuances of copyright protection?

Although a licensed music attorney could offer other legal services (such as real estate or tax advice), most music lawyers stick to their branch of specialization—which is challenging enough to master. For nonmusic issues, the client may be referred to another lawyer in the same firm or another firm altogether.

As the role of the music attorney has significantly expanded over the decades, some clients retain attorneys primarily for their inside-industry connections. It is now common for lawyers to perform tasks that seem more appropriately handled by managers, such as circulating demos to labels: Established lawyers are highly respected by A&R (artist and repertoire) executives. Some law firms even have separate artist management departments, and some of the most successful managers are or were lawyers. Before employing an attorney, be sure to know precisely what services may be provided.

Payment Options. One of the universal complaints about lawyers is their cost. Attorney fees can easily exceed thousands of dollars per transaction, which might be greater than the revenue of a deal for a client at the bottom of the music industry ladder. But when legal services are imperative and the transaction involves enough revenue to justify professional fees, the client has a number of payment options.

The usual arrangement is paying an hourly fee. Before running up a bill, the prospective client should simply ask the lawyer, in an exploratory meeting, about the charges. If ongoing legal services are needed, the client may place the lawyer on a monthly retainer so that expenses are predicable.

Another payment option is a fixed fee to complete a specific transaction, doing away with hourly billing. The third alternative is a contingent payment plan that is pegged to a percentage—typically 5% but sometimes higher—on specified aspects of the deal. For example, the percentage could be applied to the recording budget or artist advance. Such contingency arrangements may include a minimum fee specified by language such as "but, in no event, less than X dollars." All **contingent fee** agreements must be in writing. When the client is a production company or film producer, the lawyer might *participate,* a term used in the industry to describe sharing in an investment in a project or a company. A participating attorney might charge no legal fee but "take **points**" instead—receive a small percentage of specified deal elements being negotiated. The lawyer may have a central role in finding a deal for the artist by shopping the artist's demo to record and publishing companies. If that is the case, the lawyer deserves compensation for legal services that are contributing to the artist's success.

How much is a lawyer entitled to charge for services? State bar associations publish guidelines for their members.[1] Professional canons of ethics call for lawyers to follow them.

Form of Organization. When an attorney accepts a client, one of the first tasks in many entertainment industry situations is to determine the client's legal status. In business and legal relationships, will the client be best served by being self-employed, a partner, proprietor, or independent contractor—or would interests be better served by forming a corporation or taking part in joint ventures? The client (who may be a group of persons) will need the lawyer to explain the advantages and disadvantages of these options.

Contract Negotiations. As pointed out, nearly all significant events in the entertainment industry involve the negotiation of contracts. And that is the business of lawyers. The number and kinds of contracts commonly used in the industry are extensive. Typical agreements include the following:

Composer with a publisher, coauthor, or employer

Music supervisor, arranger, producer, and others involved in music recording services with employers

Performer with employer, agent, promoter, producer, performing group, lawyer, broadcaster, merchandiser, advertising agency, recording company, or publisher

Producer with a recording company, performer, recording studio, production company, publisher, distributor, merchandiser, or lawyer

Talent agent with a performer, promoter, club owner, producer, production company, recording company, or film company

Artist's personal manager with an artist, recording company, broadcaster, accountant, auditor, or road manager

The Adversarial Relationship. Individuals entering into contract negotiations are, by definition, adversaries. They may be the best of friends, but once they start negotiating a legal agreement, the parties should seek every legitimate advantage available. Contract negotiations need not be unfriendly encounters, but the parties are advised by their attorneys, as a rule, to go for whatever they can rightly get. Having worked on many previous deals, knowledgeable attorneys representing each party start out with an idea of what all parties will get in the end—even if they don't immediately volunteer this in back-and-forth negotiations.

Each party entering into contract negotiations should have separate legal counsel. When one lawyer attempts to represent both parties, there may be difficulty serving them impartially. The American Bar Association's Code of Professional Responsibility and most state bar associations' codes of ethics assert that in the absence of full disclosure and an agreement signed by all parties, lawyers should not represent adversaries and should urge prospective clients to retain their own attorneys.

Independent legal counsel is particularly important in situations where collateral contracts are entered into simultaneously—for example, an artist-manager contract and an artist-manager-publisher deal. If an attorney is involved in two or more of the collateral contracts, then that attorney faces the quandary of representing more than one side of interconnected deals and potential exposure to conflicts of interest. Disputes can arise about the legitimacy of transactions where conflict of interest by negotiating attorneys exists. Often, these conflicts are inadvertent. When conflicts occur, courts have sometimes found that a lawyer had taken advantage of the client's ignorance and subsequently determined that one or more of the contracts is unenforceable.

Extralegal Services. While clients may ask their attorneys to recommend agents and managers, frequently the attorney offers some of the same services. It is not unusual for a lawyer to agree to administer the client's publishing company, for example. In general, a lawyer attempting to provide a client with two different kinds of professional services is exposed to potential conflicts of interest, but this can be handled if discussed in depth in advance and the client provides a waiver. Some of the sharpest critics of conflicts of interest have been lawyers themselves.

Bar associations state that lawyers shall not enter into a business transaction with a client or knowingly acquire a financial interest in an artist's enterprise potentially adverse to the client unless the transaction

> is fair and reasonable to the client and fully disclosed and transmitted in writing to the client in a manner which should have reasonably been understood by the client . . . and the client is advised in writing that the client may seek advice of an independent lawyer of the client's choice . . . and the client thereafter consents in writing to the terms of the transaction.[2]

If a lawyer provides extralegal services and enters into business or investment deals with a client, legal ethics demand that all conduct be in accordance with the ethical and legal constraints imposed on a licensed attorney-at-law.

Termination. The law provides that a client can **discharge** a lawyer at any time.[3] But some courts have held that the discharge of a lawyer does not necessarily discharge a former client's liability. For example, dismissing an attorney where a contingent fee arrangement is in place can become sticky for the client. In this kind of situation, the former client will probably have to continue paying the attorney, after disengagement, on earnings flowing from contracts negotiated before the parties went separate ways.

Whether or not a contingent fee is involved, a client who discharges a lawyer should send written notice of termination. Where the artist is retaining a new attorney, the former attorney should be asked, in the notice of termination, to forward all material in the client's file to the new lawyer. Bar associations view this kind of procedure as a matter of professional courtesy.

Notes

1. Language in the California Bar's *Rules of Professional Conduct* is typical: "A member of the State Bar shall not enter into an agreement for, charge or collect an illegal or unconscionable fee."
2. Quoted from p. 15 of "Ethical Constraints on Contingent Fee Arrangements" in *Rules of Professional Conduct*. Sacramento: California Bar Association.
3. Code of Civil Procedure, Section 284.

Chapter Takeaways

- Talent agents seek employment for music artists, primarily in the field of live performance.

- Managers guide careers and, depending on the jurisdiction and contractual obligations, are often restricted in negotiating specific employment for clients. This restriction is most prevalent in California because

of historical abuses in the motion picture industry.

- Road managers oversee the complexities of touring operations.

- Attorneys negotiate the many contracts that undergird the business. Some attorneys are engaged as much for their "street credibility" and networking skills as they are for their legal knowledge.

Key Terms

- boutique agencies   (p. 148)
- carve out   (p. 148)
- collateral contracts   (p. 157)
- conflict of interest   (p. 157)
- contingent fee   (p. 156)
- franchise   (p. 150)
- full-service agencies   (p. 148)
- guilds and unions   (p. 150)
- key man clause   (p. 150)
- participate   (p. 156)
- points   (p. 156)

Discussion Questions

1. Who does a professional artist need on his or her team? Why is each of these roles important?

2. What different functions do agents and personal managers serve, and which position is the most heavily regulated?

3. Attorneys draft contracts and litigate (i.e., represent artists in court for legal disputes). Discuss why law firms often offer a team of attorneys with different specialties to music clients.

4. Discuss reasons contract negotiations, even between the best of friends, should be handled by independent legal counsel.

CHAPTER 9

Artist Management

In Chapter 8, personal management was discussed only from the standpoint of regulation by state statutes and artists' unions. This chapter examines financial relationships and the manager's functions in advancing the artist's career.[1]

"Management, too, is an art."

—Mozart's father (and manager)

How important is a good manager? Ask a record company. Labels today prefer an artist who has good management. They believe it is not cost-effective to invest time and money in an artist whose career is not thoughtfully planned. Good management is so important, in fact, that some labels will actually help certain artists find a good manager.

At what point do artists need a manager? About the time they discover they can earn more than union **scale**, suddenly they are in need of someone to handle their business affairs and develop their careers. This can be a difficult time, because many established managers are unwilling to take on a new, unproven act.

Discovering Each Other

An artist searching for a personal manager should look for a person who

- Is well organized, systematic
- Is straightforward and honest, and has a reputation to prove it
- Is an effective communicator, writes well, and is an articulate, persuasive speaker

---

Left: Robert Plant and Alison Krauss perform in Oregon.

Photo © Chris Ryan/Corbis.

- Won't try to fake expertise if lacking competence in certain fields; will hire outside experts when needed
- Has good industry contacts; if not, is busy developing them
- Believes in the talent of the artist
- Shares the artist's long-term vision and career goals

Some managers have a strong creative side as well as good business skills. A manager might help to put an act together by advising about choice of artistic personnel. The manager may also help to make decisions regarding production of an album and choice of material to be included on the album.

Some managers are closely involved with the negotiation of business contracts. Some handle an artist's finances. Whatever the manager's innate skills, each artist-manager relationship should be structured to best serve the client.

Successful personal managers have one other kind of expertise: They know how to spot a potential star. They cannot afford to invest their time and money in anyone who lacks what the manager views as the potential talent to reach the top. And until a manager's clients develop strong earnings, there won't be many dollars available to produce commissionable income—the manager's livelihood.

Experienced managers and artists all agree on one issue: The relationship depends on strong personal ties of friendship and trust. Although sometimes it may appear to be the other way around, the manager works for the artist, not vice versa. The manager is the extension of the artist and should act in ways appropriate to that artist. Behavior of the manager, both positive and negative, reflects on the artist and is ultimately the artist's responsibility. Good managers must strike the delicate balance between passivity and aggressiveness; they should motivate without stepping on toes and be congenial without being a pushover.

When a manager and artist are considering joining forces, they might well enter into a short-term "trial" or "honeymoon" agreement, usually 6 months to 1 year. If the manager achieves the objectives outlined in the trial agreement, the contract is generally extended to full **term**—3 or more years. A word of caution to the artist: Be sure that the management agreement is nontransferable—that is, the contract cannot be bought or sold.

The Financial Relationship

Established personal managers usually insist that the artist agrees in writing that the manager be authorized to handle the artist's money—what comes in and what goes out. If an artist is fearful of granting the manager complete control over the money, the artist should not sign with that person.

As an alternative arrangement, a business manager who provides financial and accounting services is selected by both parties and is responsible for tracking artist income and paying artist expenses. When an act generates large sums of money, this is often a preferable arrangement because the business manager is responsible for the interests of the artist, not the personal manager.

A major recording star requires a financial adviser who understands international tax treaties and the exchange of foreign currencies and fluctuating money markets. When accountants lack specialized knowledge, an act of international stature can have little confidence that the worldwide movement of royalties is sufficiently protected.

Although the personal manager should recruit a qualified accountant, the artist should approve the selection of that individual or firm. A major act may also need independent auditors to conduct periodic examinations of the books—not only those of the manager but of the publisher and recording company as well. Contracts with these parties must specify under what conditions audits can be performed and precisely who will be liable for the auditing expense.[2]

Controlling Expense

Because the "successful" artist has to pay 10% to 25% of the gross to a manager, another 10% or so to a booking agency for concert tours, and perhaps additional fees to a business manager, attorney, or accountant, the best hope of realizing a profit on what is left is to exert stringent control over all other expenses. Although a manager may make recommendations for expenditures, the artist's attorney should include spending constraints when the management contract is negotiated.[3]

However, many artists (and managers) have only a dim view of the realities of the rational business world. Many artists throw their money around, hoping that those earnings are going to keep rolling in forever. In such a case, a seasoned manager might persuade the artist to accept a weekly allowance and/or a tax savings plan. Show business stories abound of how former stars went through millions only to end up financially destitute. Submitting to a modest weekly expense account increases an artist's chances of surviving the late lean years when fame and income have faded.

Many personal managers also find it necessary to loan money to keep an act alive, at least in its developing stage. However, the manager is usually under no contractual obligation to loan money or advance money to the artist, no matter how serious the crisis may be.

Manager's Commission

It is standard practice in the industry for personal managers to earn compensation for their services through commissions on the artist's gross income. Managers will rarely accept any other arrangement. Their argument is a simple one—and persuasive: The manager may be the person principally responsible for the rise and fall of the client's income. The manager invests time (and often personal funds) in getting a career off the ground and is entitled to participate in the artist's prosperity, should it ever come.

The informed artist's point of view on this issue is set forth in the draft contract at the end of this chapter.

Going Rates

In recent years, certain "going rates" have become recognized in the industry for personal managers' commissions. They range from a low of 10% to a high of 25%. Factors influencing these rates include the following:

1. The stature and track record of the manager. A manager with powerful contacts in the industry—and who usually comes with a team and infrastructure that has its own overhead—may be worth 25% to a novice or moderately successful artist by increasing the artist's income. A manager with little or no track record may earn a lower commission.

2. The income of the artist. If the artist has a high income, the manager will come out well even at a relatively low commission rate.

3. The extent of the manager's services. For example, if the manager farms out all business management, accounting services, and promotion services, top commission rates may not be appropriate.

An Argument for Reasonableness. A powerful manager can often get a very high commission even from an act that may be struggling to pay its rent. But if that artist later develops a high income, the artist often pushes to renegotiate the manager's commission to lower the percentage. Wise managers often volunteer to reduce or eliminate commissions on specific projects or concert dates. Such gestures go a long way in establishing long-term trust and goodwill between manager and artist.

Commission Base. Personal managers' commissions are usually based on the artist's gross income from all activity relating to the entertainment industry. In this context, "income" includes not only wages but also whatever is of value that comes to the artist from the entertainment industry, directly or indirectly, including sources such as royalties; an interest in, or ownership of, a production company, TV package, film, publishing, or recording company; stock in a corporation; interest in a partnership; bonuses; licensed merchandise; product endorsements; tour sponsorship; commercials; video sales; and even gifts.

The commission *base* can be more important than the commission *level*. If the artist has a competent, aggressive attorney, and if the personal manager lacks the clout of the artist, the commission base can sometimes be limited to what can be called the adjusted gross income. An artist negotiating from strength should be able to convince the manager to accept a commission based on the artist's actual piece of the pie, not on all the money simply passing through the accounts to support other persons and other activities. The artist will probably seek to exclude from commission items such as recording costs and **negative tour support** or tour shortfall (money the label has advanced to make up for deficits the artist incurred while on tour). The pros and cons of this fundamental issue are set forth in the draft contract later in this chapter.

The Money Flow

Like marriage, an artist-manager relationship is easier to enter into than to leave. When the artist and manager get divorced, not only will they suffer the wrenching experience of ending a close personal relationship, but they will also have to negotiate some kind of "property settlement." A divorcing couple can eventually agree on "who gets the house, who gets the car," and so forth, but the artist and manager have a much more complicated set of financial issues.

The essential difficulty here is that an established act has money flowing in from contracts the manager negotiated, and when the couple disengage (for whatever reason), that money continues to flow. Should the departing manager continue to receive commissions on income from the contracts he or she has negotiated? Some lawyers make the argument that, unless negotiated otherwise, such commissions continue in perpetuity.

The richest source of these funds usually comes from publishing and recording contracts probably worked out during the period of service of the departing manager. Nearly all personal management contracts state that the manager is entitled to full commissions on this money, without diminution, for the full term of those contracts. Part of the problem this creates for the artist is encountered during the search for new management. If the artist's major source of income is already tapped for years hence by the old manager, what has a new manager to gain by signing on with an act so encumbered with prior commitments?

A Possible Compromise

If it is assumed the parties possess about equal bargaining strength, one of the simplest compromises available is an across-the-board de-escalation of commissions over a year or two following termination of the working relationship. This arrangement between artist and manager is often called the **sunset clause.** Figure 9.1 shows how this might work: The old manager continues to enjoy 100% of commissions for the first 6 months following disengagement from the artist. Then follows a 50% reduction for the next 6 months. At the start of the second year following disengagement, the artist pays the former manager only 25% of what would have otherwise been earned. After 12 months at this rate, all commissions to the former manager end.

If the manager is negotiating from greater strength than the artist, the same de-escalation formula might still be used, but the percentages could be set higher and stretched out over a longer time—up to 7 years. For instance, the old manager might earn a 100% commission indefinitely for deals he or she negotiated. The new manager might earn a 100% commission on all new deals set up for the artist. The new manager will also earn 100% commission on a holdover deal that is significantly revised during his tenure.

One final advantage of a de-escalation formula: If the second manager accepts the plan suggested here, the parties should have little difficulty negotiating a similar de-escalation plan for the second manager as well when that relationship ends.

The Manager's Role

Producing the Act

Once the artist and manager have negotiated their agreement, one of the first tasks they face is polishing the act—creating the presentation of the artist to the public. Many artists owe a big part of their success to how attractively they are presented.

Figure 9.1 Artist's Money Flow to Managers in Transition

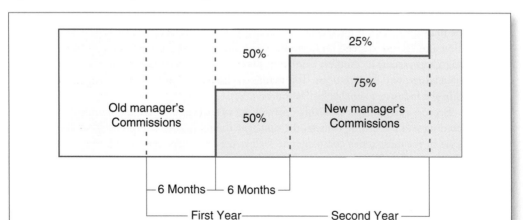

Note: Under this possible scenario, a new manager receives 100% commission from the outset on new business that the new manager generates.

An objective appraisal must be made at the outset on these basic questions: (a) Just what kind of performer or act do we have? (b) To what audience does the artist appeal? (c) Can that audience be expanded? (d) What must we do for the artist to fully exploit all the potential?

In addition to engaging voice coaches, choreographers, wardrobe consultants, and more, the manager who takes the long view of the client's career will probably want to provide dramatic training, too. Nearly all musical performers who reach national prominence eventually receive opportunities to play dramatic roles in TV, movies, and live stage.

Some managers provide important assistance when they have the ability to identify good musical material. Few artists—including those who write much of their own material—ever seem to have a sufficient supply of high-quality songs. The manager may have to take time listening to demos and helping search out usable songs. The act may also need **special material**—songs, patter, and routines created exclusively for that artist. Practically all stars booked into major venues such as in Las Vegas consider using special material that is essential to a big-time presentation.

Once the act has been fully prepared, the next move is to place it on stage, under flattering lighting, in an appropriate setting. If the manager can't handle this task, someone should be engaged who can. Major acts often tour with their own stage directors who supervise lighting, staging, and sound.

Programming

Experienced managers representing powerful acts control the selection of opening and supporting acts, making sure that the headliner comes on at the best possible time and under the most advantageous circumstances. From the early days of vaudeville, headliners insisted on warm-up acts to preheat the audience. This sequencing of acts is called programming, and the manager must control it when possible. If the manager's client is to be introduced by a master of ceremonies (**MC**) or some other person, the manager must make sure the introducer says the right things and says them briefly.

Advancing the Career

The manager's main responsibility is advancing the career of the artist, whose reputation and income depend on how effectively this is done. A first-rate manager will design and execute a complete campaign for each artist, starting with people—with personalities, not organizations. Top managers develop extensive lists of key personnel in the industry to enable fast action on tasks.

Because the manager probably operates out of, or regularly travels to, one of the recording and publishing centers, the manager should know who the decision makers are in the most active companies, as well as the important agents, promoters, and industry lawyers. The music industry is a giant, but only a few hundred individuals have positions of real power. When a manager is negotiating with one record company, the competing record companies for that contract have probably heard, privately, about what each side is offering. So the experienced manager knows vital competitive information that is not published in regular media outlets. The inner circle of powerful people knows who is a con artist, who will keep an agreement, who can deliver.

How does a new manager develop a network of contacts? By demonstrating credibility and competence.

The artist's manager must also develop good contacts wherever clients perform—the top music directors and programmers, retailers, distributors of recordings, merchandise licensees, media personnel, influential bloggers, the important promoters, and agents. Given time, a network can be developed of key personnel in branch offices of record labels with whom clients are under contract.

Keep in mind, however, that the relationships between individuals are often not as significant as the relationship between corporations. Aspiring managers must not just cultivate relationships with individuals but must also keep abreast of corporate relations between labels and artists. A good manager will be on top of trends that influence the contracting, packaging, and sales of musical artists and how the corporate climate may affect business decisions.

Gaining Traction as an Aspiring Talent

There are numerous ways that young talent with little income but big ambitions can land an experienced personal manager, although none is easy or surefire. A necessary eventual step is an in-person meeting, which comes after talent has demonstrated a voice, dexterity with a musical instrument, or other relevant music industry skill that impresses the prospective personal manager.

But how do you get to that face-to-face meeting? One way, the manager may find you. Personal managers are themselves keen judges of talent, so they will attend performances at night clubs, concerts at big and small venues, artist showcases, and music school recitals. For performers, recommendations from teachers, music coaches, and other professionals with contacts can smooth the path to meeting a personal manager.

The process of building recognition has evolved somewhat over the years. Performers from earlier eras might acquire a national following through media such as network radio, television, the movies, Broadway, and even vaudeville. Today, aspiring talent can post music videos and audio, offer fan pages that attract followers, showcase music reviews, and generate a measurable online buzz that can turn the heads of industry pros. Even a local or regional following is significant because it suggests the potential for a national breakout.

Personal managers offer the following advice for fledging talent looking to attract (and also evaluate) a possible future manager. Always check out references of prospective personal managers, because some are actually just modeling agencies and photography studios pretending to manage careers. The personal manager field is lightly regulated, so anyone can claim competency. Also, the search for a manager requires focus, because a very personal relationship is at stake. Sending generalized email blasts will probably just annoy the manager who is being wooed. Do the necessary homework. Conduct extensive online searches to size up managers, so any letters and emails sent later are peppered with reasons why the talent is a good fit with the manager.

Landing the Record Deal

Keep in mind the ultimate objective of the process: Landing a recording contract is often the primary goal for an artist teaming up with a manager. Occasionally, the artist's attorney will recommend that a personal manager be engaged only if the manager can, indeed, secure a recording deal. No recording contract, no personal management agreement. To many aspiring performers, a personal manager has little to offer without delivering at this level.

Prospects for the manager's success in landing a record contract for a client will probably be determined by the answers to these kinds of questions:

How strong are the manager's contacts in the industry?

How strong is the manager's team (lawyer, accountant, support staff, etc.)?

How strong, how unique is the artist's talent? Is there star potential there?

Is the manager's approach timely? Is a prospective label signing anyone at this time?

Does the recording company believe in the manager? The label may love the artist but lack confidence in the manager's ability to deliver.

The Process. Here is the sequence of events that might lead to the securing of a record contract:

1. The manager makes a frontal attack on the label itself, almost always starting with the A&R (artist and repertoire) department. If unable to gain the attention of the top decision makers, the manager works on the next level down. Recording companies are populated with employees trying to score points with the boss by pointing out new musical talent. Among the lower-level contacts the manager might pursue are promotion people and field personnel for the label. The alert ones are on the lookout for new talent. Even lowly A&R assistants can be valuable contacts.

2. The manager will try to work with the songwriter-client's publisher. If the client doesn't have a publishing deal, the manager will aggressively shop for one. Major publishing executives have excellent contacts with label executives and independent producers. It is, however, rare for an artist to get an attractive publishing deal without a recording deal.

3. The manager fails to reach the attention of record companies and focuses on independent producers and production companies. The best of these have direct contact with record labels. The manager may determine that an offer from a record production company looks more attractive than signing directly with a label; the production company may be able to present its services and the artist's services as a package to some label.

4. The manager arranges for third parties to catch the artist in a showcase performance or watch a video demo. If some respected individual in the industry tells a friend (who tells a friend . . .) about a great new talent, the word may get back to a decision maker at some recording company. Word of mouth may turn out to be as effective as knocking on doors.

The Result. If the manager should fail to get the client a recording contract after 1 or 2 years' effort, the artist may need to search for a place in some other sector of the entertainment industry. But let's assume the manager succeeds in persuading a recording company to negotiate a contract. What is a "good" contract? How much dare be asked? Is the label excited and ready to get behind the new act with strong promotion and lots of money?

Let's assume the next step: The contract is signed; everyone is happy. At the moment, that is. Now the manager must keep nudging—assertively, without being a pest—the label to promote the recordings. If the effort is halfhearted, the artist's recordings may never gain sufficient exposure. At this moment, the manager's greatest service will be prodding the label to perform on the contract, to deliver what was agreed. The manager must keep the artist a priority by talking to the label, the radio promo people, and the marketing department. Efforts in this direction can never stop.

Let's make one more assumption in this scenario: The record label fulfills its promises of promotion and the recordings sell very well. Now the artist has so much money rolling in, it seems time to say to the manager, "My friends tell me your commission is out of line. I want to renegotiate our contract. Your new rate is now 10%, not 25%. If that is unacceptable, I will sign with this other management company that will probably do more for me—and for a lower commission than I've been paying you." This kind of scenario is common. Personal managers may struggle for years establishing an act. Their biggest problem may turn out to be success. When their clients start coming into really big money, they may defect to a manager who had nothing to do with building the act to high-income status. A lawsuit could result if a contract is in place and the artist tries to break it.

Why do bright people go into the personal management field? Probably because the really competent managers continue to be in high demand, and they often seem able to develop sufficient loyalty among their clients to be in on the receiving end when careers prosper. These kinds of managers can easily become millionaires.

Care and Feeding of the Media

In executing a campaign to exploit an artist, the manager must develop contacts (and friends) with those who influence the audience through mass media as well as highly targeted information platforms. This includes influential music bloggers, video channels (e.g., MTV, Fuse, Gospel Music Channel), networks, radio stations, wire service reporters, feature writers, syndicated columnists, syndicated radio programs, specialty websites, and the music press—the opinion-shapers focusing on personalities in the music and entertainment fields. They are not difficult to contact: They look to artists, managers, and publicists to feed them information.

Materials. When contact is made, the manager must feed these sources with appropriate material. This is usually done with electronic press kits (**EPKs**). Depending on budget and circumstances, press kits often include press releases, the artist's biography, news clips, previous media reviews, digital artwork, and photos. Sample CDs or DVDs may also be provided. If a recording company is involved, a major promotion will often include a material object (a novelty of some kind, sometimes called **swag**) that ties in with a new recording's release. The manager or the artist's publicist will help in getting these kits and trinkets to the press, disc jockeys, radio program directors, and perhaps to the employees of record distributors and retail outlets.

Interviews. Managers have learned that one of the most economical techniques to generate strong publicity for a touring artist is to set up audio interviews in advance of the artist's arrival.

As the artist travels across the country, the label's publicity staff will set up news conferences. Most reporters and camera people are dispatched to these events by their assignment editors; they will appear where they are assigned to cover a story. But freelancers and stringers can often be persuaded to cover a press conference if free food and drink are available. When the budget allows, some press conferences are planned as press parties. Enterprising publicists can often induce the press to show up for these happy hours even when the artist is relatively unknown.

In addition to news conferences, a manager or publicist can arrange for exclusive interviews. One interview or guest shot with a syndicated columnist or network TV program can yield more good **PR** than many open press conferences.

Artists' managers rarely attempt to handle all the PR for their clients; instead, they often try to convince the record label to handle public relations, either in-house or through a third-party firm. Services of these companies can run up to $6,000 a month or more, depending on the services required and the track record of the supplier. Competition among publicists is keen. In their effort to produce maximum attention, **flacks** will sometimes resort to outrageous publicity stunts. The media and the public may actually enjoy a crazy hype for a while. But it is the personal manager's responsibility to rein in PR types when they try too often to substitute promotion gimmicks for campaigns based on something approximating reality.

Billing. From the early days of the entertainment industry, it has been standard practice for managers and promoters to control what professionals call *billing.* Billing has to do with the size, emphasis, and position of artists' names in print ads and screen credits. If an artist ranks as a "star," the name might be set above the name of the production—in large, bold type.[4] If the artist is a "costar," the name will appear below the name of the production and in type smaller than that used for the star. If the artist is a "featured" player, the billing will be much less prominent and relegated to an inferior position in the layout.

As the manager's client gains prestige, attention must be given to the possibilities of negotiating for increasingly prominent billing. An astute manager will occasionally accept a lower fee for the client if the billing is strong.[5] In rock shows, the second act is often called "special guest star" and may receive 75% of the billing (size of artist names in marketing materials) that the main act receives for the show, depending on the contract.

Controlling Performances

One of the personal manager's most useful services is controlling the client's performance opportunities. Once a career gains momentum, the artist often receives more offers to perform than can be accepted. Both the agent and the manager are tempted to maximize income and accept every gig in sight. But it is the manager's responsibility to limit the frequency of performances to avoid exhausting the artist's energies and to avoid overexposure of the act. The manager will be particularly concerned with travel times between engagements.

As important as determining the frequency of performances is the selection of the kinds of engagement offers. The sharp manager understands the artist's unique identity and the nature of the artist's audience. Insensitive talent agents and promoters will offer the manager job opportunities from time to time that are totally unsuitable. The money might appear attractive, but placing an artist on a bill where the audience might have different tastes can do more harm than good for a career. In considering potential concert dates for a pop performer, the manager will consider the importance of the market—for instance, record sales in that market, the artist's product presence in local record retail outlets, and whether local radio stations are playing the client's music.

In addition to controlling the frequency and types of engagements, the manager must determine when the client is "ready." For example, if the performer is primarily a singer and the job opportunity also requires acting, the manager, in consultation with the client, should try to determine before they sign whether the artist can handle the role, whether the script is "right," and whether the production will be of respectable quality. The process of choosing particular opportunities can be a bit sticky because although the manager plots a strategic course for the artist's career, the manager must rely on a separate party, a licensed talent agent, to arrange talent engagements for specific gigs. This process is further explained in Chapter 16.

In summary, it becomes evident that the personal manager is a key professional in the entertainment industry, often wielding more power and influence than any one person should be expected (or entitled) to handle. All that is asked of the manager is omniscience.

Personal Management Agreement

Once the artist and manager decide they want to tie their fates to each other, they should both engage their own independent legal counselors and proceed to negotiate a contract. If their attorneys are well informed and aggressive, the artist and manager should negotiate for all they can get for themselves. Normal procedure is for one side to express demands—from a position, quite naturally, of maximum self-interest. The second party then counters with a position—similarly biased in that party's favor. At this juncture, the parties will need to negotiate compromises, with results being as satisfactory as possible to both parties.

To start negotiations, the manager will often issue a **deal memo** (a summary document that covers term, commission, and other major points of the potential contract).

The draft contract that follows assumes that the parties start their negotiations in the sequence just described. Where issues are particularly controversial, we articulate the opening position of each party. Then follows an articulation of a compromise position—what might be a fair resolution and balance of interests if the parties had equal bargaining strength.

The compromise positions expressed here are a consensus of opinion prevailing among a number of distinguished entertainment industry attorneys.

• • • Draft Agreement

This draft agreement is for study purposes only. Its language should not necessarily be used verbatim in an actual contract. Each party involved in negotiations is urged to retain independent legal counsel to draft the actual language of a contract.

The body of the draft contract uses the pronouns *he* and *his* rather than *he/she* and *his/hers*. This usage is for simplicity and is meant to include both men and women.

AGREEMENT made (date) _____ by and between _____, the Artist, and _____, the Personal Manager (hereinafter called Manager).

WITNESSETH

Whereas the Artist wishes to obtain advice and direction in the advancement of his professional career, and

(Continued)

(Continued)

Whereas the Manager, by reason of his knowledge and experience, is qualified to render such advice and direction,

NOW THEREFORE, in consideration of the mutual promises set forth here, the Artist and Manager do agree:

DEFINITIONS

The "Artist"—the first party to this agreement—appoints the second party, the Personal Manager. The Artist may be one or more individuals comprising the professional performing group. If more than one individual signs this agreement as an Artist member of the performing group, then this Agreement shall be binding upon all such persons, individually and severally, and all of the representations, warranties, agreements, and obligations contained herein shall be deemed to be individual, joint, and several.[6]

This agreement covers all of the professional talents, activities, and services of the Artist in all sectors and media of the arts and entertainment industry, as an instrumentalist, singer, actor, entertainer, composer, writer, editor, arranger, **orchestrator**, publisher, executive, producer, manager, audio technician, promoter, and packager.

"Personal Manager" is used here to describe the individual who advises and counsels and directs the Artist's career and manages the Artist's business affairs.

"Third Party" is any individual, company, or corporation with whom the Artist and/or Manager do business relating to the agreement, such as talent agent, producer, publisher, record company, production company, promoter, business manager, accountant, auditor, union or guild, broadcaster, merchant, advertiser.

"Entertainment Industry" is used here, not only in its generally understood meaning, but also including all related aspects of literary activity, publishing, broadcasting, filming, telecommunications, online, promotion, merchandising, advertising, through all media of communication now known or later developed, of the arts and entertainment industry.

1.0. APPOINTMENT

Artist's Position: It is in the artist's interest to place strong language in the agreement setting forth precisely what the personal manager is obligated to do. To offer "advice and counsel" is ambiguous. The artist will seek a specific list of services to be rendered and require the manager to use the manager's "best efforts" to meet his responsibilities.

Manager's Position: The manager will seek only a general statement regarding his appointment. He may not accept the language committing him to his "best efforts," in that his commissions under such language might not be automatic.[7] The manager may prefer the expression "reasonable efforts."

Compromise Position:

The Artist appoints the Manager as his exclusive personal manager throughout the world in all fields related to the arts and entertainment industry. The Manager will offer the Artist advice and counsel and will use his best efforts to advance the Artist's career.

The Manager accepts the appointment as set forth here and agrees that, in fulfilling the appointment, he will (1) make himself available to the Artist at reasonable times and places; (2) devote his best efforts to the Artist's affairs; and (3) maintain an office and staff adequate to fulfill the appointment and his responsibilities thereunder.

1.1. Exclusivity. The Artist appoints the Manager as his exclusive personal manager and will engage no other personal manager during the term of this agreement. The Manager's services to the Artist are nonexclusive; he may manage other artists concurrently and carry on other business activities, at his sole discretion.[8]

1.2. Business Management. The Manager shall be in charge of the Artist's business affairs personally or, with the consent of the Artist, engage a Third Party as business manager.

1.3. Representation. The Manager shall represent the Artist's best interests with Third Parties and supervise agreements with them.

2.0. EMPLOYMENT

Artist's Position: Despite the language in most contracts of this kind, the artist expects the manager to actively procure employment in the form of a recording agreement. This is the very reason most artists sign on with a particular manager.

Manager's Position: The manager will insist that the agreement specifically excuse him from any obligation to procure employment for the artist. If the agreement is negotiated and "performed" in the state of California, the strict state regulations will prompt the manager to require extra-strong language here disavowing any hint of attempting to procure employment, even indirectly.

Compromise Position:

The procurement of employment, or the attempt to procure employment, for the Artist is not an obligation of the Manager, and the Manager is not authorized, licensed, or expected to perform such services. But the Manager recognizes that the obtaining of employment is of the essence in advancing the Artist's career and that the Manager shall, after consultation with the Artist, engage, direct, and/or discharge persons such as talent agents, employment agents, as well as other persons and firms who may be retained for the purpose of securing engagement contracts for the Artist.

3.0. ASSIGNMENT

Artist's Position: The artist will attempt to deny the manager the right to transfer or assign the contract to another party. The artist enters into the agreement

(Continued)

(Continued)

largely because of his feeling of confidence and trust in this particular manager. The artist could not be assured this same confidence and trust could be found in some other party who was allowed to take over the contract. To protect himself, the artist will seek a key man clause (below).

Manager's Position: The manager will seek to avoid inclusion of a key man clause, arguing that he may become disabled or otherwise unable to perform. He may develop different interests and want to be free to assign the contract. If the manager is employed by a management company, his company will probably insist it retain the right to assign the agreement.

Compromise Position:

The Manager is the key man in this agreement and is denied the option to assign this agreement without the prior written consent of the Artist. Any other party under consideration in this context shall agree to assume all the responsibilities assigned to the first Manager and be fully qualified, in the opinion of the Artist, to perform in a manner and at a level comparable to the first Manager.

4.0. TERM, TERMINATION

Artist's Position: Unless the artist is in an inferior negotiating position, he will seek an initial term of 1 to 2 years. He will try to avoid a longer first term on the possibility that the manager may do an inadequate job and it may become necessary to free up the commission for a new manager; or alternatively, the artist may want to negotiate more favorable terms at the end of the first term—or seek to terminate his manager and engage a new one willing to serve for a lower commission.

Manager's Position: It is in the manager's best interests to negotiate a maximum term allowed by state statute for personal services contracts. He seeks maximum assurance that he has the artist tied up and can enjoy high income for years to come. He wants to recover his investment made during the lean years of the artist's career.

Compromise Position:

The initial term of the Agreement shall be for 2 years, provided the parties satisfactorily fulfill their mutual obligations. If either party has substantial cause to claim the other party has failed to perform under this Agreement, the claimant must send a written notice by registered mail, return receipt requested, citing specific reasons for the complaint, allowing the recipient of the written notice 30 days to cure and reasonably satisfy the complaint. If the aggrieved party does not receive a response that is reasonably satisfactory to the claimant, the claimant may then terminate this Agreement by sending written notice 10 days in advance to the other party.[9]

The Manager may be given the right to exercise options to continue the Agreement beyond the initial term for additional 1-year periods, provided that certain performance criteria have been met, such as securing a recording agreement or generating a minimum amount of income as described below. The number of options should probably not exceed three.

4.1. Options. The Artist grants the Manager options to extend the initial term of this Agreement to a maximum aggregate total of _____ years,[10] provided the Artist has been offered opportunities for employment so that the Artist's gross income from the entertainment industry during the preceding year(s) aggregates these totals:

(A) First term:

$ _____

(B) First Optional Extension Period of One Year (total of (A) and (B)):

$ _____

(C) Second Optional Extension Period of One Year (total of (A) through (C)):

$ _____

(D) Third Optional Extension Period of One Year (total of (A) through (D)):

$ _____

The foregoing notwithstanding, the Artist grants these extension options only on the condition that the Manager fulfills, in the initial term and optional extensions thereof, all his responsibilities and obligations set forth herein.[11]

5.0. Power of Attorney

Manager's Position:
The manager will attempt to get general **power of attorney**, including, among other powers, the complete and unrestricted right to (1) collect and disburse all the artist's money; (2) negotiate and sign contracts on behalf of the artist; (3) engage and discharge personnel; (4) exploit the artist's personality, name, likeness, photographs, which would include commitment of the artist to product endorsements and commercial announcements; and (5) exert "creative control," including the selection or rejection of musical and literary materials, record producers, staging, and costuming.

Artist's Position: An artist will seek to limit a grant of power of attorney. Grant of general power of attorney is all encompassing and affords exposure to conflicts of interest and abuse. The artist will probably be most resistant to extending power of attorney to creative control. Unless the manager is fully qualified to make artistic judgments, for example, the manager could impose poor decisions in sensitive areas such as selection of music to be recorded, the manner and style of presentation, and the selection of record producers. Whatever resolution the parties make in regard to creative control and constraints on decision making, the artist will probably demand that power of attorney be cancelable by the artist at any time.

Compromise Position:

The Artist agrees the Manager may need limited power of attorney from time to time for his convenience. Accordingly, the Artist grants limited power of

(Continued)

(Continued)

attorney to the Manager to serve as the Artist's agent and **attorney-in-fact** in emergency situations only and denies the Manager this power without the prior written consent of the Artist (1) to accept any performing engagement on behalf of the Artist exceeding one week in duration; (2) to sign checks drawn upon the Artist-Manager's Trust Account with a face value greater than $1,000 and of an aggregate monthly amount in excess of $5,000 for all such draws; (3) to sign any agreement on behalf of the Artist that is of more than incidental importance or having a term longer than 1 month; (4) to engage or discharge support personnel; (5) to accept on the Artist's behalf any product or service endorsement; and (6) to limit the Artist's creative control over matters such as the selection of musical and literary material, and determination of the manner and style of performance, including staging and costuming. The Artist may terminate this power of attorney at any time, without notice, in the event that the Manager misuses, in the sole opinion of the Artist, this power.

The manager usually insists on the right to collect the artist's income early on in the artist's career to ensure reimbursement, payment of expenses, and the receipt of his commission. The artist should, however, make provision for a third-party business manager to handle all the money once income reaches a certain level, since abuses of artists' finances by personal managers are legendary in the music business.

6.0. ARTIST'S RESPONSIBILITIES, WARRANTIES

6.1. Encumbrance. The Artist warrants that he is under no restriction, disability, or prohibition in respect to the Artist's right to execute this Agreement and perform its terms and conditions. The Artist warrants that no act or omission by the Artist will violate, to the best of his knowledge, any right or interest of any person or firm or will subject the Manager to any liability or claim to any person.

6.2. Commitment. The Artist will devote his full time and attention to the advancement of his career.

6.3. Ownership. The Artist warrants that, to the best of his knowledge, he is the sole owner of his professional name,[12] _____, and that this warranty is restricted to adjudicated breaches.

6.4. Advice. The Artist will accept in good faith the advice and counsel of the Manager, in recognition of the Manager's special knowledge and experience in the entertainment industry.

6.5. Income. The Artist shall encourage all agents and employers to make payments of all monies due the Artist to the Manager, or to a Third Party approved by the Artist and Manager.

6.6. Employment. The Artist shall refer all offers of employment to the Manager, and the Artist shall not accept offers of employment without the consent of the Manager.

7.0. MANAGER'S COMPENSATION

Artist's Position: The artist will seek to sign the manager for a 10% to 15% commission. If this is unacceptable to the manager, the artist may offer to increase the rate as gross income rises.

Manager's Position: If the manager is new at the game and anxious to get into the field, he might accept a commission as low as 10%. An unknown manager will probably be able to attract only relatively unknown artists, so the parties must agree to struggle together in the early stages of their relationship. The astute manager who accepts a low starting income will seek commission increases when he can manage to grow his client's income substantially.

Compromise Position:

The Artist shall pay the Manager 15% of the Artist's gross income for the first year of this Agreement. "Gross income" shall include, without limitation, all fees, earnings, salaries, royalties, bonuses, shares of profit, stock, partnership interests, percentages, gifts of value, received directly or indirectly, by the Artist or his heirs, executors, administrators, or assigns, or by any other person, corporation, or firm on the Artist's behalf, from the arts and entertainment industry. The commission shall be 20% in the second year of this Agreement, provided the Artist's gross income for this second year increases _____ % over the first year. If this Agreement is extended to a third year, the commission shall rise to 25%, provided the Artist's gross income increases _____ % over the prior year.

In other circumstances, the parties may choose to decrease the percentage as income rises, thereby acknowledging that the Manager may be contributing less significantly to the generation of income but still resulting in more money for the Manager because the income is higher.

8.0. COMMISSION BASE

Artist's Position: An unknown artist may have to pay an established manager on the artist's unadjusted gross income. But an established artist with an aggressive lawyer may be able to obtain certain exclusions from that gross, such as those listed in the Compromise Position that follows.

Manager's Position: The manager will fight for the broadest possible commission base and seek to calculate his percentage on the artist's unadjusted gross income. But if the artist has any bargaining power, "gross income" will probably become an adjusted gross income.

Compromise Position:

The foregoing definition of the Artist's "gross income" notwithstanding, the following sums shall be deducted from the gross income for purposes of calculating the Manager's commission: (1) the first $25,000 aggregated income in any single year derived from the entertainment industry or $500 per calendar week, whichever is

(Continued)

(Continued)

greater; (2) recording production expense where a Third Party provides same to the Artist; (3) record producers' fees, points, and percentages where a Third Party pays the Artist for same; (4) performance, production, and travel expense including salaries of support personnel connected thereto where a Third Party pays the Artist for same (often called "negative tour support"); (5) legal fees incurred by the Artist in dealings with the Manager and Third Parties in the negotiation and performance of agreements; and (6) passive income where the Artist receives money or other things of value from sources outside the entertainment industry or the Artist's income from investments inside or outside the entertainment industry.[13]

In any circumstances where the Manager has a financial interest with a Third Party or company with whom the Artist has any kind of business relationship, the Manager shall receive no commissions on any monies the Artist receives from such sources.[14]

When this Agreement and all extensions thereof terminate, the Artist shall pay the Manager 100% of his commissions for a period of 1 year from all income generated by contracts and agreements set up by the Manager during the term of the agreement. For the following 6 months, the Manager's commission is limited to 50% of the Artist's commissionable income. For the subsequent 6 months, the Manager's commission is limited to 25% of the Artist's commissionable income. Thereafter, all Manager's commissions on the Artist's commissionable income cease. The Manager is not entitled to any commissions on albums released after his tenure has expired.[15]

9.0. FINANCIAL ACCOUNTING

Within 30 days following the execution of this Agreement, the parties shall select, by mutual consent, a certified public accountant to provide accounting services for the Artist.

9.1. Records. The parties shall exchange informal financial records of all monies flowing through their hands that relate to this Agreement. The Manager's financial records shall account for all receipts, disbursements, commissions withheld, advances, loans, and investments, if any. Copies of the parties' financial reports shall be forwarded monthly to the accountant.

9.2. Audits. The Manager shall engage independent auditors, with the consent of the Artist, to conduct periodic audits of the Artist's publisher and record company to determine if these firms are fully paying royalties due the Artist and paying in a timely manner.

9.3. Limitations. The Manager may not incur any expense on behalf of the Artist in an amount larger than $ _____ for any one expense, without the consent of the Artist. The Manager may not incur monthly expenses on behalf of the Artist that exceed $ _____ without the consent of the Artist.

9.4. Loans. The Manager is not expected or required to make loans to the Artist or advance the Artist money. The Manager shall not make loans of the Artist's money to any other person or invest the Artist's money without the prior consent of the Artist.

If the Artist asks the Manager to loan him money, and if the Manager voluntarily agrees to do so, the Manager shall be entitled to recover when due such loaned money together with reasonable interest. If such repayments to the Manager are not made when due, the Manager may recover the amount outstanding from the Artist's current earnings from the entertainment industry.

9.5. Overhead. The Manager's office overhead is not recoupable from the Artist, nor is the Manager's travel expense within a 50-mile radius of his office. The Artist shall pay the Manager's travel expense outside this radius when the Manager is requested by the Artist to travel.

9.6. Liability. Neither party is liable to the other for debts and obligations they may incur that are not covered by the Agreement.

10.0. GENERAL ISSUES

The present Agreement constitutes the entire understanding between the parties, and no other agreement or commitment, oral or written, prevails between the parties. Neither party may change or modify any part of the present Agreement without the prior written consent of the other party.

If one or more parts of this Agreement are found to be illegal or unenforceable, for any reason or by any person, the same shall not affect the validity or enforceability of the remaining provisions of this Agreement.

10.1. Incorporation. If the Artist incorporates, he agrees to cause said corporation to sign an agreement with the Manager that provides no less favorable terms than the first agreement.

10.2. Default and Cure. If either party claims that the other is in default or breach of this agreement, the aggrieved party shall provide written notice setting forth the nature of the dispute. The accused party is then allowed 30 days to cure the alleged default, during which period no default or other grievances shall be deemed incurable.

10.3. Arbitration. The parties agree to submit all disputes to the American Arbitration Association and be bound by and perform any award rendered in such arbitration.[16]

10.4. This Agreement is made under the laws of the state of _____.

IN WITNESS WHEREOF, the parties hereto have executed this Agreement as of the day and year first indicated above.

_____

Artist

_____

Personal Manager

Notes

1. In this chapter, the terms *artists* and *stars* refer not only to performers but also to other professionals who, from time to time, engage personal managers, such as writers, producers, directors, and choreographers.

2. When a major act audits a recording company, the expense can run from $30,000 to $100,000 or more.

3. Suppliers often try to overcharge entertainment business personalities, apparently assuming that such customers are not concerned enough to examine their bills critically.

4. Similar billings are used for producers, writers, directors, and others. In complex productions such as theatrical motion pictures, these participants may all joust for good billing, further complicated by union rules. Some participants are so prestigious (or have invested so much money) that they receive star billing—their names positioned above the title of the production.

5. Contracts often specify billings in terms of relative percentages. For example, it might be required that an artist's name never be printed less than 50% as large as the production title—or that an artist's musical director's name appear 25% as large as the artist's name. These kinds of billings can be readily observed on Las Vegas hotel billboards.

6. The manager may require here that the members of the performing group are individually and severally liable for any claims against any other member of the group or the manager.

7. Joseph Taubman, *In Tune With the Music Business* (p. 80). New York: Law-Arts Publishers, 1980.

8. The artist may seek to limit the manager's freedom here by requiring a listing of current clients and agreement to limit future activity to those clients. This may help assure the artist that the manager will have sufficient time to serve the artist's best interests.

9. The parties may prefer that this option to terminate not be allowed and that all serious claims of failure to perform be referred to arbitration. But a powerful act may demand the right to terminate at any time, making the claim that the manager serves at the pleasure of the artist. But no prestigious manager would accept this, arguing possible vulnerability to a capriciously behaving artist.

10. States have statutes of limitation on contracts involving "personal services."

11. Whatever the circumstances of termination or disengagement, the lawyers will need to exchange notices of release. These releases may include **executory provisions**—requirements for performance, payments, and so forth following termination of the agreement.

12. Courts have held that the legal ownership of a trade name ultimately resides not with the person first using it but with the person or persons identified with the name when it acquires a "secondary meaning."

13. A manager with a strong track record and powerful contacts will probably not accept these commission exclusions—or not without a higher commission rate. The author's rationale for suggesting these exclusions is simple: Most of these exclusions are not the artist's income; they are his overhead. The manager is entitled to commissions on income but not outflow.

14. The attorneys need to negotiate how commissions, if any, are to be paid where a corporation provides the artist's services. The commission will be adjusted to reflect whether the artist, in this circumstance, has a financial interest in the corporation, is only an employee, or both.

15. This compromise of entirely eliminating the manager's commission after a relatively short period of time may be unacceptable to a manager. If the manager is responsible for securing a beneficial recording agreement for the artist, it may be that even a successful artist has little or no commissionable income during the first few years of the agreement. For this reason, managers may justifiably seek to receive some reduced commission in perpetuity for every album produced under the contract they arranged or, at the very least, for every album produced during their tenure.

16. Many contracts include a compulsory **arbitration clause** calling for the parties to submit disputes to the American Arbitration Association or similar body. Although rulings can be prompt through arbitration proceedings, their implementation may still result in lawsuits; if, for instance, one party refuses to abide by the decision of the arbitrator, the other party would file suit for **breach of contract.**

Chapter Takeaways

- A manager typically earns a commission of 10% to 25% of the artist's gross income, one of several major expenses for an artist.

- Managers may guide an on-stage persona for the performing artist in addition to overseeing the business of maximizing artist income throughout the entertainment industry.

- The music industry is a giant, but only a few hundred people have sustained positions of real power. A good manager knows how to tap the power network.

- Although a traditional record deal may not be as crucial to success as in earlier eras, a manager's main task often is to get and maintain a good label contract on behalf of the artist.

- Artist and manager should each engage experienced lawyers to negotiate a comprehensive artist management agreement.

Key Terms

- A&R (artist and repertoire) (p. 168)
- deal memo (p. 171)
- EPK (electronic press kit) (p. 169)
- executory provisions (p. 180)
- flack (p. 170)
- master of ceremonies (MC) (p. 166)
- negative tour support (p. 164)
- special material (p. 166)
- sunset clause (p. 165)
- swag (p. 169)
- term (p. 162)

Discussion Questions

1. What is the economic overhang when changing personal managers? Discuss what financial obligations talent may have to an ex-manager under long-term deals.

2. Outline the process of how aspiring artists should approach searching for a personal manager.

3. What does a personal manager look for in an aspiring artist?

4. Discuss the manager's role in working with a new artist. How might that role change over time? How does it stay the same?

CHAPTER 10

Unions and Guilds

Workers involved in the music and entertainment fields have developed numerous organizations to represent their interests,[1] and that sometimes makes the labor landscape tricky to navigate. Worker organizations are structured in a variety of ways. Some, such as the American Federation of Musicians (AFM) and SAG-AFTRA, are trade unions focused on bargaining with employers for pay and work rules and are connected with the giant American Federation of Labor and Congress of Industrial Organizations (AFL-CIO). Others are more accurately described as **guilds**, which unite artisans from a single craft and attempt to maintain or celebrate industry standards but do not negotiate wages with employers. Still others are simply associations of **independent contractors**. If this is not complicated enough, the list includes entertainment industry guilds (e.g., the Dramatists Guild), whose members may own the company (a **loan-out corporation** that provides services of a person) with whom they are supposed to negotiate for their services.

> "No member shall render any services or make an agreement to perform services for any employer who has not executed a basic minimum agreement with the union. . . . This provision applies worldwide."
>
> —Global Rule One of the SAG-AFTRA union

Discussed below are the AFM, SAG-AFTRA, the American Guild of Musical Artists (AGMA), the American Guild of Variety Artists (AGVA), and the Actors' Equity Association. Other unions and guilds are described at the end of the chapter.

When young artists start their careers, they are often reluctant to join the unions for their respective crafts because enlisting seems expensive and restrictive. But if a demand develops for the artist's services, opportunities will arise for which union affiliation is not only advantageous but imperative. Most employment available to artists above the small-time level is "union," meaning that if an individual wants to be a professional performer (or arranger, **copyist,** director, conductor, actor, dancer, etc.), those services will most likely be under the jurisdiction and control of a union contract. Indeed, bigger Hollywood productions sign contracts agreeing to only hire union workers for many job categories.

The arts organizations and industries employing artists have recognized, often reluctantly, the bargaining rights of AFM, SAG-AFTRA, and the other unions. But artists' labor organizations have experienced, in recent years, the same problems affecting the labor movement as a whole: decreased bargaining power and loss of jobs through foreign competition and developing technologies.

American Federation of Musicians

The full name of the AFM is American Federation of Musicians of the United States and Canada. It is the oldest union in the United States representing individuals professionally active in the fields of entertainment and the arts, its history dating from the 19th century. AFM has always been one of the largest artists' labor organizations and today has around 80,000 members. Through the decades, however, the AFM has been losing members and some of its power. Why? A number of reasons have been advanced: (a) difficulty in attracting many of the new, young professionals; (b) state and national laws restricting certain kinds of **collective bargaining** agreements; (c) continuing displacement of live performances with recorded music; (d) increasing displacement of live musicians by electronic instruments; (e) importation of music recorded abroad; and (f) increasing prevalence of nonunion performances, live and recorded. In recent years, in at least some local branches, the trend toward lower AFM membership has started to reverse itself, and membership numbers have begun to rise.

AFM membership includes professional instrumentalists, conductors, arrangers, **orchestrators,** copyists, music librarians, orchestra **contractors,** and proofreaders, as well as some related fields, such as **cartage** people (or roadies) and, when there are no jurisdictional disputes, engineers. The union maintains no jurisdiction over the professional services of composers (although practically all composers professionally active in film, television, radio, commercials, and **syndication** are AFM members by virtue of their services as conductors, instrumentalists, arrangers, or copyists).

If a musician sings professionally, it is not necessary to be an AFM member unless the musician also works professionally in one of the capacities listed for regular AFM membership.

Unlike a number of guilds and professional associations in the arts, the AFM is a bona fide labor union: Its members are employees, and the AFM represents the interests of its members to employers.

The AFM functions on two levels—**local** and federation (United States and Canada). The local offices of the union have jurisdiction over all union work for musicians that is not covered by federation-wide contracts. AFM federation contracts embrace all services of musicians in the fields of recording, network broadcasting, theatrical film, television film and tape, **live-on-tape** network television, home video, online video, syndicated programs and services, subscription TV, commercial announcements, and contracts covering prerecorded music for certain traveling productions, such as circuses and ice shows.

National federation contracts are mostly administered by the union's Electronic Media Services Division (EMSD), which is under the direct supervision of the AFM president. This unit covers music labels, motion pictures, TV programs, national radio, industrial films, and commercials. EMSD has resident representatives in New York City and Los Angeles.

AFM contracts, whether local or federation, generally include agreements on issues such as wages, hours, overtime, working conditions, instrument **doubling,** instrument cartage, type of venue (meaning different performance platforms such as a night club, symphony hall, or TV show), rehearsal fees, pay for leader and contractor, **tracking scale, reuse,** and new use of recorded material.

The AFM manages to negotiate reasonably satisfactory contracts, at least from the union's point of view, at the national level. But at the local level, union control over wages and benefits varies. This is largely because certain states invoke their **right-to-work laws** and, more significantly, because of the constraints on union jurisdictions imposed by the Taft-Hartley Act (1947). Under a National Labor Relations Board interpretation of this law, absent a collective bargaining agreement (CBA), musicians are considered independent contractors. As such, they are prohibited from compelling purchasers of musicians' services to recognize the AFM as the musicians' collective bargaining agent. As a consequence, these purchasers of musicians' services (such as club owners, hotels) are not required to contribute to employee benefits such as unemployment insurance, payroll taxes, and pension funds. Under these circumstances, however, a bandleader may be considered the employer and therefore compelled to make benefit payments. Over many years, the AFM has urged Congress to curtail Taft-Hartley's impact of classifying musicians as independent contractors and has won labor regulatory rulings extending the employee designation that brings some worker benefits.

AFM Local 47 building, an industry landmark on Vine Street in Hollywood.
Photo by Gordon Carmadelle courtesy of Professional Musicians, Local 47.

Union Finance

The union finances its activities with new members' initiation fees, annual dues, and work dues. The amount assessed as work dues varies from local to local. Generally, mandatory union fees are several hundred dollars per year plus 2% to 5% of wages earned on union jobs.[2]

A share of these monies collected by the locals is forwarded to AFM's international headquarters in New York City to finance the union's activities throughout the United States and Canada.

Other Services

The AFM attempts to license and control booking agents through franchising them. This process is described in Chapter 8. The union also seeks to protect its members from employers who don't pay union musicians what they are due. Slow-paying or nonpaying employers are sometimes sued by the union. AFM locals notify members to steer clear of potential employers who have not signed AFM contracts or who are under AFM jurisdiction but are delinquent in their obligations.

AFM contracts covering the record industry are described in Chapter 12. With respect to AFM employment in film scoring, see Chapter 21.

SAG-AFTRA ▆▆▆▆▆▆▆▆▆▆▆▆▆▆▆▆▆▆▆

SAG-AFTRA, which was created in a 2012 merger, has 160,000 members, and its representation in music stems mainly from the pre-merger union of the American Federation of Television and Radio Artists (AFTRA). Prior to the merger, AFTRA alone handled 70,000 professional singers and other vocalists, actors, news broadcasters, dancers, talk show hosts, disc jockeys, announcers, and other television and radio personalities.[3]

SAG-AFTRA's main business is working out labor agreements with employers, often through its regional offices, called locals, scattered across the United States. As with most national labor unions, SAG-AFTRA's leadership negotiates its national and local contracts with industry associations representative of the major sectors of the entertainment industry—record companies, music video and audio book producers, movie producers, TV and radio networks and stations, TV program producers, producers of commercial **spots,** and producers of content made for new media.

When a singer gets an opportunity to perform for the first time in a field where SAG-AFTRA has jurisdiction, the gig may be accepted without joining the union, because the Taft-Hartley Act initially excuses the performer from this obligation. But the artist typically must join the union within 30 days thereafter to continue accepting jobs where SAG-AFTRA has organized workers at an employer. As is generally true with trade unions, members' dues vary widely and are determined by the individual's applicable annual earnings on SAG-AFTRA jobs.

With respect to SAG-AFTRA's jurisdiction over professional singers, the union's contracts classify nonroyalty artists as soloists, duos, or group singers. Scales are highest for soloists and duos; soloists who step out of an ensemble momentarily for a featured segment earn second-highest wages. Background singers are paid at a sliding scale in accordance with the size of the group. A group of three to eight singers is paid more than members of larger choral ensembles.

For years, performers in music videos mostly worked on a nonunion basis. In 2012, SAG-AFTRA hammered out a landmark agreement with five major companies covering dancers and background singers. The contract sets minimum pay rates, establishes work rules to enhance safety, and contributes to worker health/retirement funds. Music videos produced by nonsignatory companies remain mostly nonunion.

Of all the artists' performing unions, SAG-AFTRA has the most complicated schedule of wages. Particularly in the commercial spot field, **union stewards** tell a producer what the costs will be for singers relative to the intended market for the spots, whether they are for local, regional, or national broadcast. For commercials, wages are calibrated to the size of the market, meaning population area. So a commercial that runs in a big city generates a bigger fee for talent than if the same commercial runs in a small city. In the commercial production industry, it is not unusual for large production companies and advertising agencies to have at least one full-time employee helping spot producers figure out the correct wage scales. Smaller producers outsource this complex union payment calculation work to specialist payroll companies, which have expertise in sorting out fees.

One of the most important components of SAG-AFTRA contracts is the provision for new use or **extended use.** As with most other artists' union contracts, when a union member performs on a recording intended for one medium, additional money is earned if that recording is later used in a different medium, such as when a commercial recording might be licensed for use in a movie or a television show. SAG-AFTRA artists also earn additional wages when the use of a broadcast commercial extends beyond the initial 13-week term (additional 13-week cycles trigger additional payments for up to a 21-month maximum). Because many spot campaigns are broadcast for long periods of time, even years after the initial use, earnings of union members from this source can become very large.

As with the AFM, SAG-AFTRA requires a union steward on the job if there are three or more background singers, to make sure the producer meets all the obligations to the performers under contract. Usually, the union steward is one of the singers, unless the steward is an adult with a children's chorus. SAG-AFTRA is almost exclusively concerned with negotiating and implementing singers' activities covered by national contracts, particularly the recording, radio, and TV industries. The performers' union has minimal control over singers performing on local shows and commercials outside the recording centers of New York, Los Angeles, and Nashville.

The Screen Actors Guild (SAG) is probably the most widely known artists' union in that some of its members are world-famous movie stars. For decades, SAG's jurisdiction covered filmed entertainment—both movies and TV programs. Established in 1933 and merged with AFTRA in 2012, creating SAG-AFTRA, SAG has a rich history in the American labor movement, from negotiating with studios in Hollywood's "golden era" to asserting artists' rights amid the digital revolution of the 21st century. Even before the merger, SAG divided jurisdiction with AFTRA over all actors, singers, and on-screen instrumentalists who act or appear in scripted TV, commercials, music videos, and industrial films. For a discussion of SAG-AFTRA's involvement in the recording industry, see Chapter 12.

The 4As

SAG-AFTRA is a member of a loose alliance known in the industry as "the 4As." The term stands for Associated Actors and Artistes of America; all unions under this banner are affiliated with the AFL-CIO. This group includes the Actors' Equity

Association, SAG-AFTRA, AGVA, AGMA, and the Guild of Italian-American Actors (GIAA). The 4As have helped reduce jurisdictional disputes among performers' unions, although each 4A member organization requires performers to belong to its particular union when jurisdictions appear to overlap. The AFM also zealously guards its own turf. For example, a singer who also plays an instrument on a network TV show must belong to both the AFM and SAG-AFTRA.

American Guild of Musical Artists

The American Guild of Musical Artists (AGMA) is one of the 4A AFL-CIO unions (despite the word *guild* in its title). AGMA was organized in the 1930s to serve the interests of singers and dancers working in the opera, dance, concert, and recital fields. AGMA employment agreements are always negotiated for a particular employer, such as the New York Grand Opera and the San Francisco Symphony Chorus. Only performers working at that employer vote on the contract; there are no national contracts or master agreements. Most AGMA contract negotiations are with nonprofit arts organizations such as the American Ballet Theatre.

American Guild of Variety Artists

The American Guild of Variety Artists (AGVA) represents singers, dancers, comedians, ice skaters, jugglers, magicians, stand-up comics, and others who perform live, primarily in venues such as theaters, theme parks, clubs, casinos, resorts, circuses, and fairgrounds. AGVA includes in its membership not only the struggling regional performer but also world-famous artists drawing huge fees, performing live on Broadway, at the Radio City Music Hall, in Las Vegas, and elsewhere. AGVA negotiates national agreements with venues in which its members perform.

Actors' Equity Association

Some 50,000 professional actors, chorus members, and stage managers on the legitimate stage in the United States are represented by the Actors' Equity Association, which theater people refer to simply as "Equity." **Equity** is the oldest of the major actors' unions, founded in 1913.

For many years, Equity membership was made up mostly of personnel working in New York City. Today, Equity has members all over the country. This has come about with the growth of regional theaters, stock and dinner and small professional theaters, and acting companies in residence on college campuses.

There are more than 40 national and regional contracts, which Equity either negotiates with collective bargaining partners or promulgates on its own. Actors and stage managers employed on Broadway work under the Production Contract that Equity negotiates with the Broadway League (formerly known as League of American Theatres and Producers, Inc.). Other negotiated contracts include the **Off-Broadway** Contract, and the LORT (League of Resident Theatres) Contract, which governs employment in regional theaters.

Of all the artists' unions, Equity enjoys the best reputation with producers for its awareness of the economic variables within the theater industry: It knows that there are more members out of work than there are jobs for them to fill. While Equity will not permit the reduction of minimum salaries for Equity actors and stage managers, it may make other alterations (known as "concessions") in its agreement with a theater that can assist that theater in achieving financial stability. However, any such easements usually have an expiration date, requiring a return to the higher rates unless renegotiated.

One of Equity's primary benefits to its members is to require a bond, which protects the minimum guarantee of employment (usually 2 weeks), should a producer default on an obligation before or during rehearsal or during the performance period.

Equity also permits limited talent "showcases," called *Codes,* in New York, Chicago, and Los Angeles. These Codes are developed by and for members for the opportunity to gain experience, recognition, and, it is hoped, employment. The word *codes* comes from "code of conduct" because the showcases are not covered in union contracts. A recurring controversy within the union is whether regularized wages and benefits should be extended to this netherworld of performances that are creatively fulfilling but not really capable of providing a living wage through ticket sales.

International Alliance of Theatrical Stage Employees

The International Alliance of Theatrical Stage Employees, Moving Picture Technicians, Artists and Allied Crafts of the United States, Its Territories and Canada (IATSE) is the craft workers union for the United States and Canada having jurisdiction over stagehands in the legitimate theater and in the majority of motion picture and (filmed) television productions. Among the many jobs under IATSE jurisdiction are sound technicians, wardrobe, camera, postproduction services, and animators. In legitimate theater, jobs range from stage hands to ticket sellers.

Organizations with which IATSE has agreements include the following:

- All the major motion picture studios
- All the networks as well as some local broadcasters in radio and television
- Most major opera, symphony, and ballet companies
- Most major arenas, outdoor concert venues, and civic centers
- Major producers of traveling theatrical productions

Other Unions and Guilds

National Association of Broadcast Employees and Technicians– Communications Workers of America

The National Association of Broadcast Employees and Technicians–Communications Workers of America (NABET-CWA) is another union that represents audio engineers and technicians and other workers in radio and TV, including makeup artists and some on-air talent. NABET, as it was known, was historically the union with jurisdiction for crew jobs at broadcasters. It is now linked to the larger Communications Workers of America and is an AFL-CIO affiliate.

Dramatists Guild of America, Inc.

The Dramatists Guild is a trade association that could be considered a traditional guild of artisans and thus not a labor union. It represents 6,000 composers, lyricists, and book writers active in the theater. The guild also includes, as members, playwrights who write plays without music or plays that use music only incidentally.

Royalty payments, maintenance of subsidiary rights, artistic control, and ownership of copyright have remained of paramount importance since the guild was established in 1919. The guild helps ensure that the ownership and control of the music, lyrics, and book of a show remain in the hands of its authors and composers—not the producers. Guild members retain copyright in their material, including the licensing of performances of dramatic rights (grand rights). The guild also helps its members preserve the integrity of their works, in that producers and directors are not allowed to alter music, lyrics, or the book to a show without the composers' and authors' consent.

Related Unions and Guilds

Other unions and guilds related to the music and/or entertainment fields are the Writers Guild of America (West and East), the Directors Guild of America, the Producers Guild of America, the National Conference of Personal Managers, and the Society of Stage Directors and Choreographers.

With respect to audio technicians working in recording studios, no one union has managed to organize the majority of workers in this segment. Many employers of these kinds of technicians have been able to avoid **union shop** status, in large part because fast-changing technology constantly reshapes the industry. The rise of home recording is also a factor.

Open Shop Agreements

Some situations have both union and nonunion employees. Often in such a case an open shop agreement is established. Open shop agreements generally stipulate that individuals employed in such a situation are subject to the collective bargaining agreement in effect between the pertinent union and the employer, even if all employees are not union members. In the event of a dispute, the terms of the collective bargaining agreement govern the employment of the nonunion employee.

Other Issues

Additional concerns relating to unions and guilds have to do with the employment of minors and the issues of immigration and work permits, where one country seeks to limit foreign artists from displacing its own citizens from job opportunities. Individuals needing definitive information on these kinds of issues are advised to search online for current regulations and contact attorneys experienced in labor or immigration law.

Notes

1. The following kinds of professionals are among those represented in some kind of organization: composers, arrangers, lyricists, instrumentalists, singers, playwrights, theatrical producers, directors, stage actors, screen actors, choreographers, dancers, scenic designers, scenery builders, stagehands, electricians, personal managers, record producers, audio technicians, and educators specializing in the fields of music management, merchandising, and recording technology.

2. As is frequently true in many entertainment job categories, employers of AFM musicians will often pay musicians through an artists' payroll service company. AFM

contractors sometimes use this kind of company to handle wages, tax accounting, and benefit payments.

3. In Canada, the comparable union is the Association of Canadian Television and Radio Artists (ACTRA).

Chapter Takeaways

- The two labor unions with the most influence in the music field are the American Federation of Musicians (AFM), mostly covering instrumentalists, and SAG-AFTRA, representing singers and dancers. They and other unions with smaller involvement in the sector have collective bargaining agreements with employers.

- A large proportion of work in the music industry is nonunion, often by what are deemed as independent contractors. This is particularly the case outside of the media centers of Los Angeles, New York, and Nashville.

- Unions generally prohibit members from working for nonunion employers, which creates an incentive for the employers to become union shops. For workers, wages and benefits in union jobs are typically higher than comparable nonunion work.

- Guilds are organizations for a specific class of artists with similar creative interests and thus are different from unions that are focused on employer-labor relations. However, note that some true unions may have "guild" in their names.

Key Terms

- Codes (showcases)   (p. 189)
- collective bargaining agreement (CBA)   (p. 184)
- Equity (union)   (p. 188)
- extended use   (p. 187)
- loan-out corporation   (p. 183)
- open shop   (p. 190)
- right-to-work laws   (p. 185)
- tracking scale   (p. 185)
- union stewards   (p. 187)

Discussion Questions

1. What are some benefits of union membership? Which union or guild best represents the area of the music business you are interested in?

2. What are some reasons to attempt to join a union before being required to do so? Why might you delay joining a union?

3. Discuss the pros and cons of unions competing among themselves for jurisdiction over workers and, in other instances, cooperating as with the loose confederation of the Associated Actors and Artistes of America (4As).

The Recorded
Music Industry

PART 4

Record Labels

Recorded music overwhelmingly dominates the art and business of music. Once a piece of music is composed, not much of importance can happen to it in the marketplace until it is recorded. The lives and fortunes of composers, performers, publishers, agents, and merchants rise and fall with the sale and licensing of recorded music. If recordings can be successfully monetized, by whatever means, all other sectors of the business prosper. When they flop, other sectors struggle to fill the financial black hole.

And although the business has shifted dramatically in recent years, it is still true that record labels are a vital link in the nexus of the industry overall. For an understanding of how the recording industry evolved to its current state, see Table 11.1 for recorded music's historical background.

"I have learned from experience that it is easier to make a businessman out of a musician than a musician out of a businessman."

—Goddard Lieberson

Perspective

Even outside the crowded DIY realm, a huge number of recognized record companies operate in the United States, with releases on thousands of different labels. Probably the best way to gain a true picture of the traditional record business is to analyze it in terms of *major* versus *independent* labels. It is probably best to define a major label as any label that is owned and/or distributed by one of the handful of

---

Left: The Capitol Records building in Hollywood, California.

Table 11.1 **Development of Recorded Music**

1877	Edison invents the cylinder phonograph.
1894	The first commercial disc recordings appear in the U.S. market.
1900s	The Victor Talking Machine Co. is incorporated in 1901, develops 10,000 dealers. At first, opera repertoire dominates. Then dance music begins to sell well (on Victor and Columbia labels).
1917	The first jazz record is released.
1920s	By 1921, 100 million records are produced in the United States. Large impetus from "commercial" jazz. Bell Laboratories develops an electrical process for recording in 1924, increasing audible range over the earlier acoustical recordings to 100–5,000 Hz. Bass instruments can be heard for the first time. Over $100 million in total retail sales in 1927, then meteoric rise of radio puts recording industry into a tailspin.
1930s	The Great Depression hurts all business, particularly the record industry. Sales of discs and phonographs plummet. Jukebox industry grows large, helping to salvage the record business. By the late 1930s, the jukebox operators were buying 13 million discs to serve their machines. Decca starts marketing low-cost ($0.35) singles featuring artists such as Bing Crosby, the Mills Brothers, the Dorsey Brothers, and Guy Lombardo; sells 19 million records in 1939. First albums appear by mid-1930s, each individual 78-rpm disc within the binder sells for $0.50. Department stores introduce record and phonograph departments.
1940s	Weekly volume of new records released in the early 1940s: 10 to 20 singles (78 rpm); by the end of the decade, 40 to 100 per week, depending on the season. American Federation of Musicians (AFM) strike against record companies paralyzes the industry 1942–1945 and damages popularity of big band recordings, which, in turn, accelerates sales of records featuring pop singers. Airplay not yet a major promotion factor except big band remote broadcasts. Jukeboxes help break new hits, particularly in "race music" (as it was then called) and country genres. Late 1940s: One-stops (distributors handling all labels) come into being, mainly to accommodate jukebox operators. Rise of independent record labels, which begin to dominate the rhythm-and-blues (R&B) field. Proliferation of distributors into smaller markets. Average dealer markup: 38%. In 1948, Columbia introduces the 33⅓-rpm LP, retailing for $5.79. This becomes the playback standard for decades. "Race records," country and western (C&W) diverge from pop records.
1950s	Television rises rapidly, grabs a large share of the radio audience. To economize, radio stations drop most live music and turn to recorded music. Increasing popularity of TV also sharply reduces record sales from 1949 to 1954. R&B and C&W markets become dominated by independent labels. Interest in high-fidelity sound increases buyers of middle-of-the-road records. Rock and roll craze begins in the mid-1950s. "Cover record" concept initiated.
1955	Mail-order record clubs begin. Columbia starts, soon followed by RCA and Capitol.
1957	Rack jobbing begins.
1958	Stereo is introduced. Record retailing changes. Proliferation of labels and products burdens retailers with huge inventories. Space demands force abandonment of listening booths. Record supermarkets begin concurrently with proliferation of the small-rack setups.
1959	Classical music's first million-record seller: Van Cliburn's performance of Tchaikovsky's Piano Concerto No. 1.

1960s	Social turmoil of the decade finds its "voice" in popular music, influences large sales increases of rock, R&B, soul, country records. Rock becomes the catalyst for Woodstock-type mass concerts. National Association of Recording Merchandisers (NARM) formed in early 1960s by record wholesalers (later called the Music Business Association). "Mom-and-pop" retailers lose market share to rack jobbers, record supermarkets, and chains. Beatles craze accelerates worldwide interest in pop-rock music; sales boom ensues. Major labels recapture some markets lost earlier to independents.
1970s	Independent record producers rise to greater importance. Singer-songwriters become the superstars. Crossover records become superhits. Sophistication of technology increases: 16- and 24-channel consoles, synthesizers, computer-assisted mixing, digital recording. Sophistication of music increases: Rock softens due to classical influences on polyphony, texture, instrumentation, form.
1980s	Technological change advances sophistication of recording/reproducing equipment. Inexpensive keyboards and samplers enable a new generation of young producers to make records. Compact discs (CDs) gain market share. Video clips change record promotion methods, break new acts. Long-form videos develop as take-home consumer software.
1990s	New technologies make high-quality home recording possible. Sophisticated in-store sampling units provide new vehicles for exposure and trial. DAT (digital audiotape) hardware is approved for consumer use in the United States. Electronic delivery of music arrives, in addition to traditional sales at record stores.
2000s	Government clamps down on label co-op ad business practices, lowering CD prices. Consumer broadband growth spurs unauthorized peer-to-peer exchange of music files, reducing sales of cash-cow CDs. MP3s and Napster scare labels with threat of piracy, eventually triggering new online label distribution approaches. As the rise of legal downloads only partly compensates for the fall-off of CD sales, the industry realigns to produce more revenue from sources such as publishing, licensing, concerts, and merchandise.
2010s	Well-financed independent labels use 360 deals to infringe on major labels' turf. DIY labels take root, operating without big-label infrastructure. Vinyl undergoes resurgence as a boutique format even as CD sales continue a long decline. Streaming gains momentum over both physical formats and downloads.

major distribution companies. Conversely, an independent ("indie") label is any label lacking an affiliation with a major.

An understanding of this structure is important because the majors dominate the sales of records in the United States. Even though independents account for the overwhelming majority of the many thousands of different records released each year by non-DIY sources, majors account for a hefty majority of the records sold. Major labels are well funded, giving them the economic heft to sign top artists, which leaves independents scrambling to fill niches and work with artists that don't immediately interest the major labels.

Major Labels

Although the economics have shifted over the years, the mass-market record business still requires a tremendous investment in the areas of production, distribution, and marketing. A commonly quoted industry statistic is that only one of five records earns its money back. By being well financed, the major labels can ride out the frequent losses and wait for the big scores. Moreover, artists are attracted to the large advances and the prestige of being associated with a label such as Sony or Island Def Jam, the security of knowing there are sufficient funds for marketing, and the stability of an established company in a business where one of the greatest difficulties is getting paid. The major labels can also afford to fund more elaborate recordings with the best producers, musicians, and studios. Prominent artists are attracted to major labels primarily because of their powerful promotion departments and well-organized distribution networks.

The advantages in economies of scale are also profound. When a big firm releases a new recording, it can assign much of its field force and merchandising personnel to that particular project. They can bring to bear 200 or more individuals actively working a particular release. Although major labels rarely assign their full energies to just one release, they can shift their field personnel whenever they find it necessary to push particular products. Because they sell more records, they can put much greater pressure on retailers to accept a lot of titles, particularly from new artists. And major labels offer stability and longevity. This can mean that they are more likely to maintain inventories and continue distribution of recordings long after their first release. Smaller labels may find it impossible to offer such ongoing service.

Again, the structure of the majors allows a large staff to work together on distribution and marketing. Radio promotion can cost $100,000 or more per single. Video production costs range from $50,000 to $500,000 for one song. Retail placement and promotion can easily run into seven figures for a single album release. Add to this amount the cost of advertising, **tour support,** publicity, and the overhead for staff and it becomes obvious that the majors have a clear advantage in the costly marketing of records.

All this clout means that a major-label sales force can push to sales success even a weak recording. This issue is strongly disputed, with some arguing that even heavily concentrated promotion cannot persuade the public to buy music that doesn't actually have it "in the grooves." But certainly, the powerful promotional forces of the major labels have much greater success with weak material than the smaller firms.

Independent Labels

Fortunately for the independents, the sheer size of the majors has built-in disadvantages. First, they are conservative companies that tend to be slow to catch up with changes in musical tastes. Most important developments in music have started at the independent level: rock and roll in the '50s and '60s, punk and modern rock in the '70s and '80s, and alternative and "grunge" rock as well as rap and hip hop in the '80s and '90s. Knowledgeable music industry professionals have described independent labels as the "lifeblood of the business." To discover "the next big thing" in music, you need only look to the indies.

Of course, the natural evolution and goal of some independents is to become so successful that they are ultimately bought out and absorbed by the majors for many millions of dollars. Many of today's biggest major labels started out as independents, having lived through high-risk periods to develop into large companies.

Three English labels that started very small and grew very rich before being bought out by major labels are Island, Chrysalis, and Virgin. Three U.S. labels that did the same thing are Arista, Geffen, and Sire. From the outset, these companies exhibited creative leadership and determination—a winning combination.

However, developments in technology lessen the scale advantage of the majors. The affordability of recording equipment and the proliferation of home studios have brought the cost of recording down considerably. The refinements of CD replication and the number of competing factories have brought manufacturing costs down. Low-cost equipment facilitating do-it-yourself recording, together with online distribution, has made it possible for almost anyone to promote and distribute music to the entire world.

One company offering help to indie labels in the realm of distribution is the Alternative Distribution Alliance (ADA). ADA offers many of the functions that the majors have long relied on, including marketing, product tie-ins, worldwide distribution, and music licensing services. This means that indies are no longer forced to stitch together a patchwork of different distributors and wholesalers to cover the entire market.

With their historic advantages in productivity and efficiency now blunted, majors now rely more heavily on their other differentiating characteristic—financial heft. More so than before, the majors concentrate their efforts on the most popular music with the best sales potential. This leaves many of the more modest-selling genres and artists to the independents or left to fend for themselves in the world of DIY.

Independent labels can develop brand-name awareness and consumer loyalty that is rare among the majors. Music fans will often purchase records from labels such as Alligator, Rounder, and Sub Pop Records ("We're not the best, but we're pretty good") on the basis of their trust in that label's taste.

Another fertile area for an independent label is at the local or regional level. An independent can make necessary connections with the radio stations, publicity outlets, and retailers in a limited geographical area. Relationships are the backbone of this industry, and if a group can earn the good favor of a few regional program directors, editors, and store managers, a modest success can begin and grow from there, especially if the acts can play in the area.

Specialty Labels

Some of the most successful independents are specialty labels, and a number of these, including Nonesuch, Deutsche Grammophon, and Odyssey are in the classical music field. The classics have been and are still being recorded by the world's greatest artists, and classical labels are largely concerned with selling known masterworks. From time to time, larger classical labels such as Columbia will record and market the works of contemporary composers.

Some specialty labels, particularly in the field of contemporary classical music, release their records "privately." They bypass more conventional distribution channels and seek to locate buyers of their sometimes-esoteric products, usually selling to colleges, universities, and others through specialty markets or the Web.

Other specialty labels limit their activities to certain demographic markets. They find ways to reach cultural enclaves or ethnic groups and work directly with retail outlets in those communities. Another specialty label, Folkways (now administered by an affiliate of the Smithsonian Institute), offers a variety of folk, blues, ethnic, and jazz music and sells mostly to schools and libraries.

One of the most successful types of specialty label sells gospel music. Among the most effective promotional methods used by gospel record companies are the many personal appearances of their contract artists. Touring gospel singers draw large audiences and sell lots of music.

Once again, these labels are successful because they do not compete directly with the mainstream music concentrated on by the majors and because they do not rely as heavily on traditional and expensive forms of promotion, such as radio and video. Of course, a DIY label is an extreme example of the trend—where the distribution brand and the artist are essentially one in the same. See Chapter 26.

Record Company Structure

Record companies range in size from the multinational major to the modest, one-person DIY operation, and their structures vary accordingly. But whatever their structure, they must handle the kinds of tasks described in the following sections, and certain generalizations can be made about how production, distribution, and marketing are organized and administered. Figure 11.1 gives an illustration of how a major record company (that is, a global distribution company with multiple affiliated labels) might be organized.

Executive Officers (CEO, COO, CFO, General Manager)

The CEO or president is often a strong entrepreneur who started the label and who had the vision it reflects. CEOs come from a variety of backgrounds, but two stand out. Lawyers often assume this position because the record business relies in large part on contracts and copyrights. Producers are also quite often in charge of labels because they know the music. This is particularly true in country music and urban music. Whether or not CEOs are lawyers or producers, they must have their respective abilities: They must know the "art of the deal" to negotiate favorable business arrangements, and they must have good "ears" to evaluate commercial recordings. They are often strong leaders, like David Geffen, Clive Davis, and Ahmet Ertegun.

Artist and Repertoire (A&R)

A&R executives are concerned first and foremost with finding and signing new talent. The A&R staff needs to keep informed—through a network of contacts, by evaluating demos, tracking the independent music scene, reading industry publications, and going to clubs to hear new music. After an act has been signed, the A&R professional remains involved on a number of different levels, including assisting artists in developing a particular project and/or their careers; administering the many production, budgetary, and other details of a product release; or just acting as liaison between the artist and the label. If the label is large enough, separate departments may be established to handle these specific tasks, such as Artist Development, A&R Administration, Artist Relations, and Production on both the audio and video side. A major company incorporating multiple labels may house A&R executives under a particular label rather than under an all-encompassing A&R department, as illustrated in Figure 11.1.

Distribution/Sales

Whether a record company is a major or independent, it must have personnel who either oversee or are directly involved with convincing retailers to order and showcase its physical product in stores and also get prominent "shelf space" at online stores. For CDs, ordering sufficient quantities is a science, because the label does not want excessive "returns" from retailers later and at the same time doesn't want retail shelves to go bare while consumer interest is strongest.

Figure 11.1   **Major Record Company Structure**

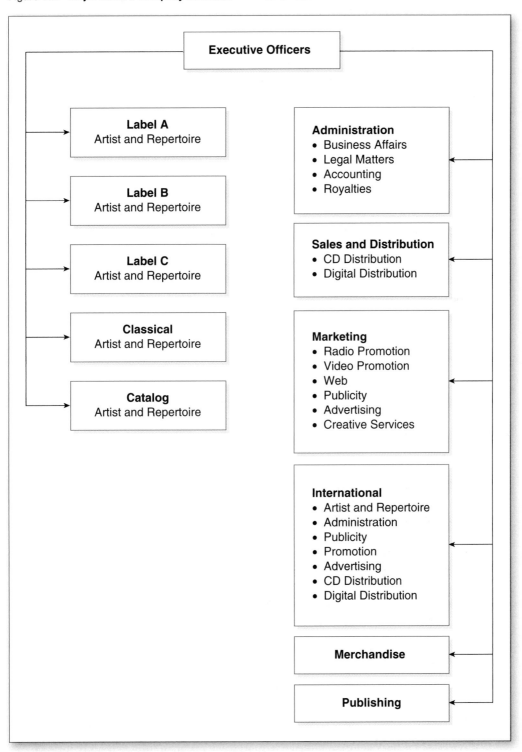

Marketing

While sales and marketing are often linked, the marketing role is so distinct that it usually functions separately and is divided into several areas of specialization.

Product Management. Found in most medium and large record companies, **product managers** coordinate and oversee all aspects of a current release, including packaging, advertising, tours, publicity, promotion, and sales activities.

Radio Promotion. This is the very heart of most record marketing in many genres. The radio promotion department is in charge of getting radio airplay and charting. Some large labels subdivide this department by genre of music. In addition to crafting a strategy to gain airplay and chart position, the radio department works with stations to arrange promotional appearances, interviews, giveaways, and contests.

Video Promotion. This department attempts to get video airplay on TV and video streaming on the Web.

Publicity. In-house publicists manage media exposure through TV appearances, magazine and website articles, online social network promotions, email campaigns, newspaper reviews, syndicated radio programs, and the like. Many labels are concentrating more and more on publicity because it is so much less expensive than promotion.

Advertising. This department arranges the advertising for a label and may be part of or work closely with the distribution and sales department since much of the consumer advertising cost is shared between label and retailer (co-op advertising). Ad departments also book trade publication ads that promote things such as the label's brand (and its relationship with artists) to distributors and retailers.

Creative Services. The creative services department is responsible for designing and producing any materials necessary to execute a marketing campaign such as posters, point-of-purchase materials, ads, website graphics, album artwork, and window displays.

Special Products (Catalog)

The special products department, sometimes called *catalog,* has two core responsibilities: (a) handling incoming requests to license masters of older product and (b) finding new ways to redesign or repackage the music that the company has previously released. Special products executives usually create "best of" packages, themed multi-artist compilations, or other reissue techniques, such as box sets or rereleases of a record, sometimes with new packaging, **mastering,** or unreleased recordings.

International Department

The global nature of the record business is such that most large companies have international departments to oversee foreign sales and ensure effective communication between domestic and foreign affiliates. The major labels often generate at least half their total revenue from local offices in the biggest 40 to 50 non-U.S. territories. Typically, a major's significant foreign territories will maintain their own A&R operations to sign local talent (such as a French act for the French and Canadian market). (See Chapter 30 for a discussion of the international business.)

Business and Legal Affairs

Since this industry revolves around contracts and copyrights, record companies usually have legal departments to negotiate and draft agreements. These range from artist recording agreements to licenses issued by and to the record company for the use of copyrighted works. This department must also do its best to minimize litigation. Some larger companies have a separate department for business and legal affairs or smaller departments to handle specific tasks, such as licensing or copyright departments. These functions may all reside under a broad administration department, along with centralized functions such as accounting, purchasing, finance, and facilities.

Accounting

Record companies can require large and sophisticated accounting operations to handle a host of financial functions. Professionals with financial skills are involved in the development and administration of recording budgets, inventory, and manufacturing, with separate departments designed for each, such as operations and finance departments. Royalties are frequently handled in a separate department dedicated to that function. At very small labels, all these tasks might be performed in a single, integrated department.

Merchandise

Some labels historically maintained departments to support concert tours of their artists. Nowadays, a critical function is handling artist-related merchandise, much of it distributed under license at concert venues. This function is particularly critical if the label has a 360 deal with an artist, which gives it a direct stake in merchandise revenue.

Publishing Affiliates

Labels generally own or control at least two publishing companies—one connected with the American Society of Composers, Authors and Publishers (ASCAP) and one signed with Broadcast Music Inc. (BMI). Labels often seek to persuade their contract artists to grant them publishing rights to music recorded for the label. Although a publishing company may be owned by the same parent company as its affiliated record company, the publishing company is expected to show profit from its own operations and may sign artists who are not on the record company's roster. An exception may be found with publishing companies that are affiliated with very small labels. These companies may exist solely to handle the publishing of that label.

Trade Associations

A large number of associations represent individuals and companies in the recorded music business. Among the two more prominent groups are the Recording Industry Association of America (RIAA) and The Recording Academy.

Recording Industry Association of America

The trade group representing the labels, major and minor, that account for the lion's share of sales is the Recording Industry Association of America (RIAA). RIAA is well known for certifying best-selling records. In addition, the organization lobbies government for label-friendly regulations, represents industry to consumers, collects industry statistics, and battles online piracy and CD counterfeiting. RIAA is the most prominent force in the big music labels' drive to curb piracy.

The Recording Academy

What was once The National Academy of Recording Arts & Sciences (NARAS) is nowadays generally referred to as The Recording Academy. The organization is best known to the public through annual telecasts of its Grammy Awards. Voting membership is limited to persons professionally active in the creative or technical side of the industry (composers, performers, producers, engineers, etc.). Associate membership is open to music industry professionals whose business activity is directly related to the recording, live performance, or music video industries or to creative and technical music professionals who do not have the required documentation in order to be voting members. Applications are accepted online at www.grammypro.com.

A student membership program is also available. Grammy U is a community of full-time college students who are pursuing a career in the recording industry. Events and educational programs touch on all aspects of the music industry. More information about the program is available at www.grammyu.com.

Receipt of a Grammy Award is prized not only for the prestige but because the attendant national publicity often helps boost record sales.

The Recording Academy sponsors several charitable endeavors, including a community outreach program called "Grammy in the Schools," a program to help musicians in need called "MusiCares," and various other grant and assistance programs to help further music and its preservation.

Chapter Takeaways

- Record labels are primarily in the distribution business. They also serve as music financiers when they advance funds to artists to create music.

- Record distribution tends to go through an upheaval with each subsequent invention of playback technologies—from vinyl disc albums of the prior century to today's streaming.

- Although major labels command the bigger share of recorded music revenue, independent labels fill valuable niches and historically have been on the leading edge of creative trends.

- The segments of a label enterprise include marketing focused on consumers, distribution that places product in retail outlets, artist and repertoire that oversees creative affairs, business affairs/accounting, music publishing (through an affiliate), and, in some cases, licensed merchandise.

Key Terms

- Grammy   (p. 204)
- independent labels   (p. 198)
- major labels   (p. 198)
- special products (catalog) (p. 202)
- specialty labels (classical music, gospel, jazz, etc.) (p. 199)

Discussion Questions

1. What are the advantages a major recording label has over independent labels? What advantages do independent labels have?

2. What are the pros and cons of recording with an independent label as compared to a DIY career?

3. How do you distinguish the difference between independent labels and specialty labels?

4. Discuss the different tasks a label (major, independent or specialty) needs to cover. How might each type of label be structured to accomplish these tasks? How might a DIY operation handle these tasks?

CHAPTER 12

Artists' Recording Contracts

To produce and distribute recorded music, a label must negotiate the acquisition of a variety of goods and services, all of which become part of the finished product. Among the most essential elements of this package are, of course, the services of musicians who perform on the recording. Some recorded works are by **self-contained groups**. Others use a mix of **sidemusicians** (instrumentalists employed for the session), background (or backup) vocalists, and a featured vocalist or vocal group. The services of backup performers are often controlled exclusively by the terms of the applicable union agreements. The featured artist may also be a union member and, as such, is also subject to the union agreements. However, contracts for featured artists go beyond the issues covered by union contracts; these artists negotiate separate agreements adding, among other terms, a **royalty** based on record sales. This chapter addresses both the standard union and **royalty artist** agreements.

"I don't know anything about music. In my line you don't have to."

—Elvis Presley

SAG-AFTRA Agreements

The major labels and many independents are among hundreds of signatory companies with labor contracts for the services of singers with the SAG-AFTRA labor union. This agreement, known as the SAG-AFTRA National Code of Fair Practice for Sound Recordings, covers all singers on a recording—from featured artists to backup vocalists, soloists, to full choirs. The contract addresses wage scales, **overdubbing,** working conditions, reuse payments, and labels' contributions to AFTRA's Health & Retirement Funds.

Left: Elvis Presley singing and playing the piano during a recording session for RCA.

Photo © by Hulton Archive/Getty Images.

Vocal Contractors

Where recording involves three or more SAG-AFTRA-covered singers, SAG-AFTRA requires the designation of a union contractor, who must be a singing member of the group. Contractors are defined as "those artists who perform any additional services, such as contracting singers, prerehearsing, coaching singers, arranging for sessions or rehearsals, or any other similar or supervisory duties, including assisting with and preparation of production memoranda." SAG-AFTRA makes no distinction in this respect between a vocal contractor and a vocal director. The contractor must be present at all recording sessions to supervise the adherence of the record producer to the terms of the SAG-AFTRA code. A contractor is also required when the recording of a Broadway show involves three or more singers. In addition to compensation as a group singer, the contractor receives a fee per hour or per song, whichever is higher.

One of the contractor's important responsibilities is to keep track of overdubbing, or reuse of a recorded performance of voices. Voices are overdubbed either by mixing a live performance with a recording or through electronic means, such as mixing various recorded performances. These techniques are sometimes used to change the timbre, resonance, or intensity of voices. Sometimes, through a process called tracking, a mixing engineer can cause one to four voices to sound as if many more singers are performing.

Because most tracking results in a net loss of employment for singers and more work for the singers on any particular project, SAG-AFTRA endeavors to control its use through assessing extra charges for such services. It is the task of the contractor to log these events, then charge the producer for them. When singers record additional tracks, they are paid for the session as if each overtracking were an additional song. Producers sometimes find that extensive overdubbing can cost more than hiring additional singers in the first place.

An additional source of income for performers is a share in the fees paid by users of the sound recording copyright, a revenue stream that began as a trickle in the United States with the passage of the Digital Millennium Copyright Act of 1998 and has grown more significant in recent years. The version of the code implemented in 2015 incorporated payments for non-U.S. streaming on platforms such as Spotify, Tidal, and Rdio (the latter subsequently acquired by Pandora for its global footprint), extending a benefit that had applied only to U.S. revenues.

For all sessions involving union-covered singing groups, the contractors, the producers, or the singers must render SAG-AFTRA's Sound Recording Sessions Report, which cites the record producer's name, hours of recording, the names of singers involved, and wages due them. The contractor has the producer sign this form, then turns it in to the SAG-AFTRA office.

Scale

The SAG-AFTRA code sets forth in detail its requirements regarding minimum wages. There are several common classifications of employment and wages, including the following:

1. Soloists or duos

2. Group singers

3. Classic recordings

4. Soloists who "step out" of a group

5. Actors, comedians, narrators, and announcers

6. Singers who record original cast albums (Broadway shows, etc.)

7. Sound effects artists

A royalty artist may be given a recording fund or other advance to cover production costs and will then earn royalties based on unit sales after production costs have been recouped. If the album is released by a record company signatory to a SAG-AFTRA or AFM (American Federation of Musicians) agreement, the company may be required to pay the royalty artist up to three times minimum scale per recorded side (regardless of the number of sessions required to make the recording).

It wasn't until 1974 that predecessor union AFTRA managed to negotiate a contract incorporating the minimum royalty concept—a significant breakthrough in how extra wages were calculated for session singers. AFTRA singers who previously did not receive a royalty started receiving additional wages based on recordings sold. These extra payments became known as **contingent scale payments.** For example, when an album reaches 157,500 in sales, nonroyalty SAG-AFTRA singers on that album receive a payment equal to 50% of their original scale for those particular sessions. There are 15 such contingent scale plateaus, up to as high as 3 million in sales, totaling an additional 1,005% of scale. Other payment schedules apply to single recordings and original cast albums.

A recording generates these payments for a period of 10 years following its initial release, and payments are limited to sales in the United States that occur through normal retail channels (so, for example, albums distributed for promotional purposes are excluded). SAG-AFTRA nonroyalty singers also receive extra payments for the sale of digital downloads, ringtones, and music video downloads. Digital downloads earn for singers a percentage of record label revenue. Music videos are also paid as a percentage of wholesale, with one rate for the first 10 years from release and a different percentage for an additional 5 years. Singer payments are processed through the AFM & SAG-AFTRA Fund.

With respect to the AFTRA Health & Retirement (H&R) Funds, record companies are required to pay on behalf of SAG-AFTRA artists (royalty and nonroyalty) about 12.75% (the rate may vary) of their gross compensation for the recording. The term *gross compensation* is defined by the SAG-AFTRA code in this respect as including total compensation paid to SAG-AFTRA-covered artists by the record company. Payment into the fund is limited to the first $140,000 of gross compensation paid to the artist and $180,000 paid to an artist group of three or more by the record company in any calendar year. The payment into these funds is also required with respect to the contingent scale payments described above.

The SAG-AFTRA code also requires that H&R contributions be made on royalties earned, even if those royalties are unrecouped by the label due to low sales. Therefore, if the artist has royalties earned and credited, even if unpaid because of recoupment, the artist receives his or her SAG-AFTRA H&R eligibility. Importantly, record labels are required to make a contribution on behalf of every royalty artist under contract to entitle that artist to a minimum of individual health insurance, regardless of earnings, if the artist enrolls in the SAG-AFTRA benefits plan.

Acquired Masters

When a singer records for an SAG-AFTRA signatory label, SAG-AFTRA has little difficulty controlling minimum wages and working conditions. But in a widespread practice, many recordings are made by very small companies and by independent record producers who later attempt to sell or lease their masters to a third party. Here full union control is difficult—often impossible—although SAG-AFTRA and the AFM do what they can to protect their members.

The SAG-AFTRA code requires that if a signatory record company acquires a master from a nonsignatory producer, that producer must retroactively pay up to meet the SAG-AFTRA code in effect at the time the recording was made. The purpose here is to ensure that no producer will be economically motivated to create a master for a nonsignatory as a way of avoiding minimum union payments.

When a signatory third party acquires interest in or ownership of a master recording that uses SAG-AFTRA members, it must comply with the obligations under the code, including the making of H&R and contingent payments. The SAG-AFTRA code specifies that the original owner must require any successor to accept the terms and obligations of the code.

Artists' unions also endeavor to protect the interests of their members when masters recorded for one medium are licensed for use in another medium. Perhaps the most common occurrence of this kind involves a master prepared for a commercial sound recording and then transferred for use on television, a theatrical film, or a video game. Whatever kind of secondary use is made of a recording (called a conversion, new use, or reuse), SAG-AFTRA requires the record company to get a warranty from the new user guaranteeing that the singers will receive no less than the appropriate scale payment for the new use. With respect to the music video field, SAG-AFTRA has a separate agreement with the producers.

Nonunion Recording

Even though SAG-AFTRA has agreements with all the major labels, the practice of nonunion recording is widespread. Aspiring young performers, who are eager to jumpstart their careers, often are only offered nonunion work by low-budget producers. It is important to remember that there is typically a pronounced disparity of bargaining power between any one artist and an entertainment conglomerate. Unions, therefore, remain key players in the entertainment business, providing an important source of artists' rights protection.

Changing technologies provide more opportunity than ever before for artists who can't—or don't want to—sign with existing record labels. Performers can inexpensively produce their own masters at home, then market their wares via their own websites, iTunes, social networking sites, and Internet sales aggregators like CD Baby. Rarely do such entrepreneurs adhere to SAG-AFTRA or AFM regulations or scales for themselves or supporting personnel. Some DIY operators manage later to sell or lease their masters to an established label with national distribution. At that point, either the original entrepreneur or the lessee must meet the SAG-AFTRA obligations described above.

AFM Agreements

Sound Recording Labor Agreement

Many labels that have agreements with SAG-AFTRA also have agreements with the AFM for the services of instrumentalists, conductors, arrangers, orchestrators, and copyists. Approximately every 3 years, the AFM negotiates a successor agreement with recording industry representatives. The current contract is known as the AFM Sound Recording Labor Agreement. It governs wages, benefits, and working conditions for the services of musicians working in the recording industry in the United States and Canada. The agreement provides for the production of music videos, online video, and concert DVDs.

In addition to wages paid for musicians' services, the contract also requires the employer to pay into the AFM Health and Welfare Fund (AFM **H&W**) to locals that have established them or directly to musicians, absent such a plan, and up to 11.99% of gross (scale) wages into the AFM-**EP**, the AFM Employers Pension Fund.

The contract provides 200% of sidemusicians' pay for the leader (musical director). Where a session calls for 12 or more musicians, an AFM contractor is required and receives two times the sidemusician's wages. Musicians doubling on a second instrument are paid, with some exceptions, 20% extra for the first **double,** then 15% for each additional double. The agreement contains many other provisions covering rest periods, meal breaks, and surcharges for work performed after midnight and on holidays, as well as special rates and conditions for work performed on electronic instruments. Even cartage fees for heavy instruments are stipulated.

As with SAG-AFTRA, AFM contracts control wages and working conditions for backup artists. But the acts whose names and sounds are used to sell records negotiate their own contracts, although the union contracts do set a floor for the individual agreements, along with many of the nonwage benefits. The AFM defines such royalty artists as individuals or self-contained groups contracted to receive a record royalty of at least 3% of the suggested retail list price or a substantially equivalent royalty.

The AFM Sound Recording Labor Agreement provides that royalty artists receive one session payment for each song recorded on an album. The session payment may be part of recording costs that are recouped from artist royalties.

The agreement also requires that all music "prepared" for recording must be handled exclusively by arrangers, orchestrators, and copyists who are AFM members. Because the AFM claims no jurisdiction over the work of songwriters and other kinds of composers, the agreement does not cover their services.

Enforcement of union scales and working conditions generally goes smoothly with well-established, recognized labels when they produce their own masters. But as noted above, record companies frequently lease or buy "outside" masters. The agreement deals with this scenario in detail, but policing of these transactions is difficult, sometimes impossible. Labels under union contract are prohibited from using acquired masters unless the music was recorded under the AFM contract and scale wages were paid, or the musicians have been paid equivalent wages and the record company makes its required contribution to the AFM Pension Fund. The company may satisfy its obligation by securing a "representation of warranty" from the seller or licensor of the acquired master that the requirements of the AFM have been met.

Sound Recording Special Payments Fund

Sound Recordings. When a recording company becomes a signatory to the AFM Sound Recording Labor Agreement, it must simultaneously execute a Sound Recording Special Payments Fund Agreement.

Record companies make payments into the Sound Recording Special Payments Fund twice each year, based on the aggregate sale of recordings in the company's catalog. The royalty due the fund has changed over the years, but as of 2015, the record company payments averaged about $0.03 per CD sold and $0.004 per song downloaded.

Record labels pay all these royalties to the administrator of the fund. After administrative expenses are deducted, all funds are then paid to the musicians who, during the preceding 5-year period, performed on any of the recordings covered by the Special Payments Fund Agreement. Musicians who earn the same scale payments from work on sound recordings will receive the same amount from the Special Payments Fund, even if one musician worked on a multiplatinum album and the other worked on an album that sold only 5,000 copies.

The Sound Recording Special Payments Fund Agreement recognizes that during the 10-year royalty payment period, the ownership and control of a recording may change. The agreement requires any such purchaser, assignee, lessee, licensee, transferee, or user to assume the original master or record producer's obligations to the AFM. Because of the frequent changes in the recording industry—companies and ownership come and go—the control and collection of these funds by the AFM is not foolproof.

Motion Pictures. The Film Musicians Secondary Markets Fund is collected from film companies and paid to musicians who have worked on soundtracks of films. Unlike the Sound Recording Special Payments Fund, payments to the Film Musicians Secondary Markets Fund reflect the relative success of each project. A musician who worked on a picture that made a lot of money will receive more than a musician who spent the same amount of time working on a commercially unsuccessful film. In both cases, musicians are also paid for the hours they actually work in the studio.

Music Performance Trust Fund

The Music Performance Trust Fund was established in 1948 as a nonprofit public service organization to help keep live music available to the public. From the beginning, the AFM recognized that the increasing impact of recording technology was devastating to the music profession except perhaps for the AFM members who earn at least part of their livelihood from recording. The AFM managed to negotiate agreements with record companies that return to union musicians at least a fraction of the income lost through the displacement of live performances by recordings. Signatory recording companies must enter into a Music Performance Trust Fund Agreement with the AFM. Payments are made to the fund's trustee and are based on record sales.

The agreement requires the trustee to use all monies collected, minus operational expenses, to schedule live music performances by AFM members. In actual practice, administration of these monies is shared by each of the AFM locals that parcel out jobs to their members, irrespective of whether they are recording musicians, and calls for prevailing local union scales. AFM locals may use some of the money to hire halls, finance publicity, print tickets, and so on. Cosponsors of concerts are generally required. The fund's purpose is to foster public understanding of and appreciation for live music. Most performances are for schools, hospitals, religious organizations, cultural events, and patriotic celebrations. If no admission is charged, the live performances may be broadcast. Established cultural organizations, such as symphony orchestras, opera, and ballet companies, often call on the fund to finance or partially finance live music performances.

Nonunion Recording

AFM and SAG-AFTRA have tried for decades to maintain **union shops**—requiring all employees on a job to be union members—with uneven results. Following enactment of the Taft-Hartley Act and right-to-work laws in various states, which allow employers wide latitude in setting wages and working conditions, the establishment and maintenance of a strict union shop concept has been difficult. The AFM oversees all professional symphony orchestra recording in the United States, along with most popular music recording in the major recording centers. Union control is less strong in the gospel, Christian, jazz, and country fields. The AFM, from time to time, implements a PR campaign to attract young players ("Young Sounds of the AFM") with reduced fees and dues. As young musicians gain professional experience, they usually discover that working under the protection of AFM membership offers financial advantages over participating in nonunion gigs.

Another kind of nonunion recording is the **spec** session. Producers will hire some musicians at below-union rates with the promise to make full payment later, "when the recording sells," in an amount equal to AFM scale. Still other producers pay the musicians (union or nonunion) nothing upfront, promising to pay full union scale later when the producer can raise the money. Both these kinds of spec recording are disapproved of by the AFM, although the union contract does provide for a lower "demo" scale than its regular recording rates.

For more information about how the AFM helps musicians with record deals and recording contracts, go to www.afm.org/departments/electronic-media-services-division.

Royalty Artist Contracts

Many performers think the way to prosperity—the big money, the international reputation—largely depends on obtaining a recording contract. Until a performer becomes recognized as a recording artist, according to this outlook, it is almost impossible to attract enough notice to get gigs from concert promoters, major booking agencies, television, and film producers. Of course, an artist can develop a satisfactory career in one area—for example, on Broadway—without selling records. But most performers, particularly those in mainstream genres that benefit from radio airplay and big-box retail exposure, seek the prestige and potential income gained through recording with a label.

Types of Deals

In earlier times, it was simple: A record company signed an artist, instructed one of its house A&R (artist and repertoire) people to produce the record, and that was that. And that formula sometimes still applies. More often, though, the record company and the artist have a number of other options when they negotiate a contract. These options have come into play partly because of the decline in the clout of record companies, as well as the economic ascendance of other key industry participants, among them the independent producer.

Today, deals placing an artist under contract include the following:

1. The label signs the artist, then has one of its producers handle the project **in-house**. The artist gets royalties; the staff producer receives a salary and perhaps a royalty override—a modest royalty since the producer is already on salary at the label. The label pays all costs pursuant to a budget and may or may not pay advances to the artist. This deal is less common than in the past.

2. The label already has the artist under contract. It retains an independent producer (or production company) to deliver a **master**. The record company assigns a production budget to the producer and may pay a production fee upfront, usually an advance on royalties. The producer also gets a royalty of 2% to 6%, based on the wholesale price of records sold and on the prior success and negotiating strength of the producer.

3. The independent producer and an independent artist strike a deal, create a master, and then try to induce a record company to acquire it. The label accepting the master pays the parties royalties based on units sold (the artist and the producer had previously arranged how they would share these royalties).

4. In a master lease deal, the artist or production company pays all recording costs and leases the master to the label in exchange for a royalty. The label may or may not pay an advance in the form of reimbursement of recording costs. Since the artist or production company as licensor assumes the risk of recording, the record company normally does not obtain ownership but merely distribution rights limited by time and geographic territory.

5. An artist forms a production company to deliver a master to a label. The producer on the project might be on the production company's payroll or might be engaged freelance just for this project. The label pays the artist's company a royalty, and the artist then pays the producer a share of those royalties.

Negotiations

Currently, most record companies choose their talent more selectively than ever. Today's more conservative signing policies result largely from the prohibitive costs of "breaking" new pop artists, which can start at $500,000 to $1 million for production and initial marketing expenses for a major-label artist.

The negotiation process begins when the label executive sits down to discuss the terms of a contract with the artist's manager or lawyer. The terms of the deal are determined, and then lawyers meet to hammer out the fine print. This scenario typically develops after an artist with savvy management has created a "buzz" among industry insiders. In the most desirable situation for an artist, several companies bid competitively to sign the artist.

If the artist lacks management and legal counsel, labels will insist that an attorney represent the artist. This is smart for both sides. Courts have set onerous contracts aside when it was learned that the artist did not have an independent attorney.

Both parties see these negotiations as an opportunity to maximize self-interests. It stands to reason that the party getting more favorable terms is the one with greater clout. Compromise, however, is usually the key to an enduring, long-term relationship. Take, for example, one chief negotiating point—the advance payment. A large signing advance or recording budget is a win for the artist in terms of both personal enrichment and imposing a financial incentive on the label to push the project to recoup the label's investment. Naturally, labels will seek to limit their risk in contract negotiations. An effective negotiation might satisfy both parties by providing royalty rate adjustments or bonuses as certain sales levels, sometimes called plateaus, are reached.

The Issues

Well-drawn recording contracts will cover the following issues:

Term. In the past, the standard length of an artist's recording contract was 1 year, with a specified number of 1-year options (usually three to five options) for the company to extend. It then became more common, at least with established artists, to have the contract duration tied to delivery of one or more albums and a period of evaluation by the record company. Experienced artists' lawyers would attempt to negotiate contracts on a multiple-album basis—for example, a "firm" three-album contract. If the first album does not sell well, the parties are still bound to each other for two follow-up releases. On the other hand, the record company preferred the commitment to be for an initial album with options for one or two more albums, which it will exercise based on the success of prior albums.

In a "firm" three-album contract, should the label decline to release all three albums, the artist's attorney often tries to stipulate that the contract provides a sizable penalty (a "kill fee"), normally a sum of money ("liquidated damages") payable to the artist. The label, however, prefers the penalty to be only the minimum union scale payment for the unrecorded album. Many deals can be viewed as one-sided in that they may bind an artist for as many as seven albums if the label exercises a series of options. But the artist does not have any corresponding right to opt out or obligate the label to release and promote a recording. Fairly drawn contracts provide guarantees of an artist's delivery by a certain date and the company's release of the recordings. Lawyers representing artists try to get the label to guarantee release within months following delivery of the master to the company. The number-of-albums contract structure that was the hallmark of the late 20th century is in some ways archaic, in that the industry overall is not as dependent on the album as the basic consumer product.

Exclusivity. Almost all recording contracts require the artist to record, during the term of the contract, only for the label that has the artist under contract. But if the artist also records from time to time in a capacity other than as a solo artist or featured group—for instance, as a session musician or sidemusician on a jazz recording—the artist's lawyer will push for the contract to permit such outside services.

Royalties, Advances. Depending on the relative leverage of the record company and the artist, the royalty offer will generally be in the range of 13% to 17% of the wholesale price. Major stars have been known to get as high as 18% to 22% of wholesale. (Occasionally, the percentages or points are expressed as a percentage of retail, in which case the numbers will be lower.) Sometimes a label will try to hold the initial royalty below 10% and then escalate the rate as sales rise. For example, the artist might receive 9% on the first 250,000 unit sales, 10% on the next 250,000, and 12% if the recording "goes platinum" by selling over 1 million copies. In this scenario, the artist might persuade a label to compromise by upping the royalty rate on the second album, should sales of the first album turn out to be satisfactory. If an artist's royalty deal is **all-in,** the cost of paying the producer's royalty will be deducted from the artist's royalty—a substantial bite out of the artist's share.

There is no standard policy among record companies on royalty advances. An advance is really a prepayment of royalties, so the amount of an advance is based on an estimate of future sales. Any subsequent payments occur only after the label recoups the advance fee. If an artist has a history of sales of approximately 100,000 albums and an average royalty is in the area of $1.00 per album, then an advance of somewhat less than $100,000 might seem reasonable.

Production Budget Minimums. Major recording artists can negotiate big-budget commitments from a label to cover recording production costs, while less prominent artists generally cannot extract such benefits. But a promising new artist is well advised, if negotiating with a label of limited resources, to demand a minimum budget commitment or risk being caught in a low-quality project that could hurt a developing career.

A recording budget is an estimate of the cost of the album production. If actual production or recording expenses come in under budget, the record company generally doesn't pay any more than actual recording expenses unless the contract provides for a recording *fund* rather than a recording *budget*. In that case, an agreed-on sum is set aside for a fund, with one third to perhaps one half of the amount being released to the artist (or the producer) at the commencement of recording. The balance is released from the fund following completion and satisfactory delivery of the master. Should the production expense total an amount smaller than the recording fund, some contracts allow the artist (or producer) to keep the difference, with the understanding that the entire sum is recoupable by the label from royalties earned by the artist on sales of the record.

Creative Control. The artist's track record and bargaining power will determine the amount of control an artist has over issues such as song selection, choice of producer, and style of album graphic art. Stars get lots of control, while less established artists generally have to accept the judgments of the record company. The parties usually decide together on selecting the producer or producers. Labels usually want new artists to collaborate with producers having proven track records. As for the selection of songs, record companies rarely give up the final decision on which tracks to record, but few labels force their artists to record specific pieces of material.

Commitment to Promote. Disagreement over promotion is one of the chief causes of artist-label tensions. If the music doesn't sell, the label blames the artist; the artist insists sales would have been just fine if the label had done its job promoting and marketing the release. Artists and their managers ideally seek label commitment for **tour support**, press coverage, interviews, independent radio promotion, retail in-store promotion, and ads. (Often, half the money spent on promotion is recouped from the artist's royalty earnings, providing a disincentive for artists to go crazy with spending demands.)

Chargebacks. Royalty contracts routinely stipulate that the label does not have to pay the artist any royalties beyond whatever advances are negotiated, until the label has recovered, through a recoupment from the artist's royalties, its out-of-pocket production costs and advances. Production expenses that are considered legitimate to **chargeback** include studio rentals, union wages to AFM and SAG-AFTRA members, music arranging and copying expense, producer costs, and any other expense directly or indirectly related to production of the album. Such costs can easily total hundreds of thousands of dollars for a pop music album. Once the advance money is used up, no more money comes to the artist until the label has recouped.

If album sales are not sufficient to recoup the advance through artist royalties, the artist is usually not obligated to return any of the advance money, which in any case has probably been spent.

Obviously, recoupment of an artist's recording account is not always necessary for the label to realize a satisfactory return on an artist's recordings. For example, although it is true that it would take 100,000 unit sales to generate royalties of $100,000 if the rate were $1 per unit, at a wholesale price of $10.00, the label would generate $1 million in gross income. Of course, there are additional costs involved with those sales (such as salaries of label executives, office expenses, etc.), but it's likely that the record company in this situation sees profits long before the artist's royalty account is recouped.

It is not unusual for an artist to have fulfilled all recording obligations under a contract, have some recordings that sold well, and still not receive any royalties beyond the advance. A simple fact bears emphasis: The vast majority of recorded music never recoups. And, to further reduce the potential artist payoff, almost all record companies include a clause in the contract making costs accrued on every recording recoupable out of royalties on all recordings (see the Royalty Discounts section, below). For example, if an artist makes three albums with each having recoupable costs of $100,000 and the albums sell very few copies but the artist makes a fourth album for $100,000, then the artist will not receive any royalties until the label has recouped $400,000. This concept, called **cross-collateralization,** makes it difficult for the artist's royalty account to ever be recouped or "in the black" because any album that underperforms eats into the income of other hit albums.

Ownership of Masters. Initially, the recording company owns all rights to the masters. But when a contract is terminated, artists' attorneys often try to negotiate transfer of ownership to their clients. Record companies vigorously resist giving up ownership and distribution control of an artist's old masters, since old recordings of successful artists can have considerable residual value, particularly in the form of repackages and/or reissues.

Reissues of old recordings in new formats have contributed significantly to album sales over the decades. Most major record companies now have separate departments dedicated solely to "vaults," or reissues of their back catalogs. True superstars might, in some cases, be able to negotiate eventual return of their masters, but in general, if a label pays to record a master, the label will control it for as long as it can retain the copyright.

Publishing Rights, Controlled Compositions. When a performing artist composes or cowrites original songs, the label will usually try to persuade him or her to place them with a publishing company owned by or affiliated with the label. When this happens, the artist-writer may receive additional advances. If the label's publishing wing cannot obtain full publishing rights, it will probably offer to share the publishing revenue with the composer-performer in what is known as a **copublishing** arrangement. If the label or production company cannot share "in the publishing," it will almost always demand a reduced mechanical rate, commonly 75% of the current **statutory rate,** for all works owned or controlled by the recording artist. Such language is called controlled composition language, and the artist refusing to accept this language may not get signed.

Controlled composition language usually specifies that the label won't pay more than 7.5 times the single-composition statutory rate for all cuts combined on an album no matter how many are actually included. This could lead to disastrous results when the artist records both controlled and noncontrolled compositions. The publishers of the noncontrolled compositions are, of course, not required to abide by the 75% language and may demand the full 100% rate, which, in the case of longer works such as jazz recordings, could exceed the minimum rate applicable to works of 5 minutes or less. Since there is that total album cap of 10 × 75% of the minimum statutory rate, the artist's own mechanical royalties could be reduced below 75% in some instances if the label must pay the full statutory rate for noncontrolled songs. The statutory rate used in such calculations is the minimum rate in effect at the time the album was delivered or supposed to have been delivered. These contract provisions can rarely be avoided except by major stars.

Video Rights. Many labels demand the exclusive services of their contract artists for any and all performances on videos and DVDs (clips, compilations, and long forms such as concerts), offering to share the potential income from distributors. They also charge to the artist's recording royalty account all or part of video production costs.

A typical recording contract includes agreement on the following issues relating to videos:

1. Videos, depending primarily on how they are used, are categorized as either "promotional" or "commercial."

2. The label generally pays for production costs of the video. Video costs are recouped first from royalties on video sales. To the extent that video sales are insufficient for the recoupment of these costs, most recording contracts provide for recoupment of the balance of those costs from the artist's general audio royalty account, typically at a rate of 50%.

3. If the artist owns or controls any of the music used on a video, the artist will be expected to waive licensing fees and royalties on that material, provided the video is for promotional purposes only. If the video is nonpromotional in nature, the artist-composer can argue for synchronization fees and mechanical royalties.

4. The artist should seek reasonable control over the selection of video directors, other production personnel, the budget, and storyline.

5. If the label refuses to produce a video, the artist may try to reserve the right to produce the video at the artist's own expense.

Foreign Releases. The artist's lawyer should try to persuade the recording company to specify the foreign territories in which the recording will be released. In addition, the attorney should try to get the label to effect these releases simultaneously with or shortly after the American release, to maximize the effectiveness of a promotion campaign and minimize the damage of both Internet piracy and imports into territories where cheaper records imported from Europe and the United States compete with the expensive domestic version. All major labels have their own foreign operations, but smaller labels work through licensees—third-party labels in overseas territories.

It is important for the artist to negotiate carefully how royalties are earned on sales in foreign territories. Many labels pay only 50% of the domestic rate for foreign sales, especially for territories handled by licensees that take a cut of music sales, but this can often be increased through negotiation. When a sale takes place outside the United States, the artist is entitled to an accounting only after the licensee accounts to the U.S. label.

Overseas, recordings are rarely sold on consignment. Once a record has been purchased by a retailer, it cannot generally be returned. This makes accounting simpler and obviates the need for the foreign licensee to hold back royalty reserves. The U.S. label might still take a reserve on foreign sales, though, because it would not differentiate these sales in terms of general reserve policies.

Assignment. Contracts normally specify the terms under which a label may assign a contract to another entity. When a contract is assigned, the new label owns all the recordings and artist services signed to the previous label. Record companies, especially smaller ones, often change ownership, leadership, or direction, and such circumstances may result in the label assigning its contract rights.

In negotiating an artist's contract, the artist's attorney should try to limit the label's right to assignment to the sale of the company's total business or assets. Generally speaking, the right to sell existing masters is permitted, while the right to require the artist to record for another company can be restricted to an affiliated entity.

Right to Audit. Royalty statements are rendered semiannually. The parties usually agree that the artist may, after proper written notice, audit the books of the label. In most states, a right to audit would be inferred by a court even if it weren't in the contract; therefore, labels write in a very restricted audit clause to avoid a much broader one being imposed later by a court.

Because most experienced auditors work by the hour rather than for a percentage of the recovery, audits for major stars are expensive. The artist's lawyer should seek a provision in the recording contract that requires the recording company to pay the entire cost of the examination if the amount found to be owed exceeds 10% of the amount actually paid. Although audits rarely reveal that the company has deliberately cheated an artist, discovery of royalties owed is a regular occurrence.

Default, Cure. If the parties have a fundamental disagreement, certain remedies are available to either side. If, for instance, the artist is scheduled to deliver an album but decides to take a 6-month vacation, the label may argue that the artist is not meeting contractual obligations. It can then either suspend the term of the agreement and its obligation to pay royalties, or terminate the agreement and possibly sue for damages.

Because recording contracts involve personal services, few courts will tell an artist to perform such services against the artist's will. If the label enjoins the artist from recording for a competitor during a dispute, the artist has three options: (a) not record at all, (b) attempt to renegotiate the contract, or (c) continue recording for the first company.

Sometimes a label agrees to renegotiate rather than pursuing legal remedies. Neither party wins, and good music rarely results, when a contract is viewed as inequitable or unfair.

Royalty Discounts. Record companies try to reduce what they pay artists through a variety of techniques. In addition to discount factors that we've already mentioned, such as cross-collateralization, here are some possible limitations on the royalty base, some of which are receding in importance as physical goods continue to become less of a factor:

1. *Breakage allowance.* Some labels still offer royalties based on 85% or 90% of sales, a practice justified decades ago by the fact that about 10% of the old 78-rpm records were damaged in transit. Although damages are nowhere near that percentage today, the practice of paying royalties on less than 100% of sales hasn't disappeared.

2. *Packaging discount.* Labels may deduct a fee to cover the cost of packaging materials. These materials don't approach the historical cost levels anymore, but the charge may be assessed anyway and can be as high as 25% of retail on CDs.

3. *Free goods.* Labels don't pay royalties for free goods given to distributors and retailers as incentives and quantity discounts (e.g., "Buy 10 and we'll give you 12").

4. *CD rate discounts.* Artist royalty rates may be reduced 15% to 20% for CDs (as opposed to tape formats), payable on a reduced number of royalty-bearing units. In this instance, an artist royalty rate in a contract of 10% effectively becomes a net artist royalty rate of 7.5% to 8%.

5. *Merchandising.* Some record companies acquire these rights and make merchandising deals on behalf of the artist. Artists' attorneys should seek to retain rights in this area unless the label is in the merchandising business, which may or may not be the case.

In most cases of contract negotiation with new artists, the record company bargains from a position of strength, creating a contract that is essentially one-sided and most likely will not yield significant royalties to the artist. As an artist's success grows, advances, recording budgets, and royalties go up and the balance of power begins to even out. When superstardom is achieved, the record company sometimes becomes more of a distributor, working for a relatively small "participation" to recoup an enormous investment.

360 Deals

The widespread phenomenon of the 360 deal illustrates the shifting dynamics between artists and record companies. With the sale of physical copies of recordings no longer the industry's growth engine, labels want agreements under which they can earn income from a wide range of an artist's activities.

There are two basic types of 360 deals, also known as "artist brand" agreements. In the first, the record company receives traditional revenues from sales of the product and simply gets a percentage of the artist's other income streams. These may include merchandise sales, endorsements, touring, ticketing, and, in a favored legalism, revenues coming from anywhere "now known or hereafter developed." When they meet resistance from artists, the labels argue that 360 deals are good for artists because these deals incentivize the labels to spend significant development and marketing resources on the artist's behalf—including dispersing free goods—so that everyone comes out ahead in the end.

The second kind of 360 deal goes beyond basic revenue sharing and finds the record company in a true partnership with the artist. The label directly handles many nonrecording activities, and both parties have to agree on major decisions. In a typical deal of this kind, the label's share of nonrecord fees would average upward of 10%. In some cases, where the label has leverage due to the artist's lack of a successful track record, the label's share has gone as high as 50%. Another variable is under what circumstances the percentage that goes to the label is calculated from the artist's gross or net receipts. These seemingly arcane distinctions can have a huge impact on who gets what when payday comes around.

A 360 deal can also be structured as a traditional recording contract but give the label an option to convert to a 360 arrangement based on certain criteria such as gross sales.

Trading on an artist's brand can be profitable for record labels, but the new environment is a double-edged sword. Artists who can afford it, or who want to take a chance, are increasingly abandoning their labels and exploiting themselves through the very same activities record labels are seeking to cash in on. If a label wants a piece of all the action, an artist with leverage has to ask if it's really a deal worth making. And traditional labels aren't the only potential partners. This deal structure has also lured other firms, with heritages ranging from artist management to concert promotion, to enter into 360 deals that otherwise might be signed by traditional labels.

New Use and Legacy Royalty Rates

Over the decades, the recording industry has absorbed dramatic changes in technology, and its standard recording artist's agreement has been adjusted accordingly, although not always quickly. Deals incorporating the long-playing album, the 45-rpm single, various configurations of tapes (including reel-to-reel, cassette, and 8-track), and the CD all evolved out of contracts addressing the original 78-rpm, 10-inch shellac record. This herky-jerky evolution has led to numerous anomalies, such as a lower percentage royalty for CDs than for the cassette format they displaced. And for many years, most royalties were calculated on something close to the suggested retail list price (SRLP), but nowadays the calculation typically uses the wholesale price as the benchmark. All these changes mean that comparing a royalty rate in two different contracts, particularly ones drafted in two different eras, is an apples-and-oranges challenge.

The standard recording artist agreement provides for payment to the artist at different rates depending on whether the record is sold, licensed, given away, or used as promotion. Direct sales by the label, as we have seen, provide a royalty payment to the artist that varies according to the type of sale. Licenses of masters for motion pictures, commercials, or television generate a license fee, either in the form of a percentage royalty or a flat payment, which is usually shared with the artist on a 50–50 basis after deduction of out-of-pocket or third-party costs.

For royalty artists, digital downloads are basically treated as a record sale or license.[1] It is a sale or license depending on whether the download is from the label's own site or whether it is licensed to a third-party site. Since the license rate is generally higher than the sale rate, labels will seek contract language to discount the license rate in those circumstances. Promotional downloads are free of royalty even though the label may receive some compensation.

If a master is licensed for a ringtone, the label would treat it either as a license and pay the artist a percentage of that fee or as a sale and pay a reduced royalty. If only the underlying composition is used, and not the master, then the artist would only be compensated if the performer is also the composer.

■ Note

1. In 2010, rapper Eminem won just such an argument before a federal appeals court, which declared that downloads by third parties should earn him the higher 50% royalty rate. However, the principle isn't automatically applicable to others because it always depends on the particular language in a specific artist's contract.

Chapter Takeaways

- Although many performers of recorded music are represented by unions, it is through separately negotiated "royalty artist" contracts that truly lucrative deals are struck.

- Nonunion recording sessions are commonplace. A union signatory label wishing to release a recording acquired from a nonsignatory party must pay union scale to participants retroactively.

- Terms of royalty artist contracts vary significantly. Lacking negotiating clout, an unknown artist often ends up accepting unfavorable terms; a superstar may be able to dictate many key contract provisions.

- Most recording deals are unrecouped—meaning the artist frequently sees no royalties beyond the upfront advance payment.

- Although more lucrative for labels, 360 deals are actually a sign of the declining role of labels in powering the music industry economic engine.

Key Terms

- chargeback   (p. 216)
- contingent scale payments   (p. 209)
- controlled composition rate   (p. 217)
- double/doubling   (p. 211)
- gross compensation   (p. 209)
- new use   (p. 221)
- overtracking   (p. 208)
- recording fund   (p. 216)
- reuse   (p. 207)
- royalty artist   (p. 207)
- scale (wage)   (p. 208)
- sidemusicians   (p. 207)
- spec session   (p. 213)
- Taft-Hartley Act/right-to-work   (p. 213)
- tracking   (p. 208)
- union shop   (p. 212)

Discussion Questions

1. Discuss how union rules in general squeeze extra compensation out of multiple uses of music from the same artist in a single recording.

2. Discuss the different types of deals record companies and artists might make. What are the advantages and disadvantages of each one?

3. Is a 360 deal better for the label or the artist? Why?

4. How can an artist mitigate the impact of controlled composition language in a recording contract?

CHAPTER 13

Record Production

J ust as it is said that movie making is "the director's art," so one may say that creating sound recordings is "the producer's art." It is rare to hear a successful recording today that does not reveal the sure hand of a competent producer, backed by talented engineers who have worked their own brand of electronic artistry—whether in million-dollar suites in lush commercial studios or at low-cost computer-based workstations in cozy home setups. Even if the song is great and the performance outstanding, these elements must be brought together and presented to the ear as one artistic whole.

> *"I can't record in the morning because I sound like Barry White."*
>
> —Toni Braxton

The record producer's number-one challenge is matching artist to repertoire, seeking a union of the performer and the material. An imaginative producer goes beyond this to devise ways of producing a good master even with material that is less than great, with an artist who may not always shake the earth. Under a savvy producer's capable control, the musical sum will always be greater than the parts. When the magic happens, it adds up to a hit.

Record Producers

What is a record producer? The details of the role vary depending on the needs of a particular project, the artist's individual strengths and weaknesses, and the producer's official job title. Some are big-picture organizers (**executive producers**),

Left: Producer Quincy Jones speaks with producers and musicians during rehearsals on stage at Circus Maximus in Rome, Italy.

while others are detail people (engineer-producers), creative voices (artist-producers), or jacks-of-all-trades (producer). Different musical genres, too, present differing demands and challenges for a producer, from the beat-driven dance sector to vocals-focused pop to instrumental rock. Some productions—of jazz and classical recordings, for instance—emphasize skill in capturing live work in concert or in the studio, while others test a producer's technical artistry in the stitching of individual beats and tracks into a seamless whole. All producers, however, must be the objective, independent voice in the studio, the one who bridges the gap between commercial viability and artistic expression. He or she must analyze what is working (and, more delicately, what is not) and inspire the very best performances. The bottom line is that a music producer is responsible for doing whatever is needed to keep the recording session moving forward toward the desired outcome: a commercially viable, marketable master.

Whether a producer will have **creative control**—the right to make artistic judgments—is another variable in the contemporary workday equation. Occasionally, the artist may have such high stature that creative control is relinquished to no one. In this case, the producer is charged with implementing the artist's ideas. More likely, the producer and the featured artist share in the making of creative decisions, with plenty of spirited give-and-take along the way.

Probably the most contentious creative call is in the selection of material to be recorded. Ideally, the producer and artist work together to winnow the choices down to the strongest songs. This process can be more difficult when the act composes its own songs, about which it surely feels possessive and protective. The producer has the tough task of selecting the best material and rejecting the weakest without offending the writers.

Matching Producer to Artist

Before song selection becomes an issue, of course, the producer and recording artist must first choose *one another*. A bad fit is in no one's best interest, and unless the producer is new to the field and hard up for work, selectivity in assignments is crucial. An experienced producer will meet with the act before signing up for the project. Preliminary meetings are particularly critical when working with a new artist or group; the artists probably have only a dim view of what lies ahead and are fearful of the outcome, but all jobs should include this step to ensure that producer and artist are compatible in working styles, expectations, and personalities.

Although you likely won't see it on the course list at music schools, most working producers will tell aspiring students they must develop a talent for "people skills." Producers say they find that at least half their time must be spent as resident psychologists, appraising the personality traits of the individuals, diplomatically delivering artistic criticism, learning whom they can pressure when necessary and who withdraws for hours when reproached.

Production Deals

How a producer and an artist come to work together, and under what terms, will vary depending on the production deal in effect. Over the years, employment practices concerning producers have varied widely. Until the advent of rock and roll, recording companies maintained a staff of full-time house producers, who had strong control over who was recorded and precisely what material the chosen few were to record. This setup began to shift in the 1960s with the rise of a new breed of rock acts that typically composed their own songs and wanted to control the selection of material. They achieved this either by sheer weight of their influence or by insisting they obtain creative control and hire their own producers. Since that time, most record companies, large and small, have used a mix of **in-house** and independent producers.

For the most frequent working arrangements for producers, see Table 13.1.

Royalties, Fees

Except perhaps on work turned out by a label's staff producers, virtually all independent production agreements today provide a **royalty** for the producer. In this sector of the business, people often refer to a producer's **points,** a term synonymous in this context with percentages. One point equals 1% (e.g., 1 point may equal 1% of retail or wholesale price of albums and singles). A point may also equal a percentage of a

Table 13.1 Types of Producers

Producer as label employee	A record company engages a producer as a full-time employee, provides a weekly salary, perhaps a royalty override. The label's head of A&R (artists and repertoire) assigns projects to the producer, who may have little to say about which artists or what music is recorded for the company.
Independent producer under label contract	The producer works as an independent contractor—as an entrepreneur or for a production company. Labels that employ the producer assign a budget, "deliver" the artist, and expect completion of a master. The producer will receive a portion of the recording advance and artist royalty.
Independent producer under artist contract	The producer's services are delivered by the artist, who has the producer under contract. This is sometimes called an "all-in" deal: Artist's representatives negotiate a package with a record company that involves a royalty and an advance on royalties. The artist then shares the advance and the royalties with the producer.
Independent producer/"spec" deal	The producer delivers the artist and a master. The producer and artist invest their time and money in the project and then try to sell the master to an established label. If they succeed, the parties negotiate a master purchase agreement that will provide the recoupment of all or part of the production costs, as well as a royalty that is shared by the producer and the artist. In some cases, the producer alone may pay for the cost of production of the master recording, which will then be shopped to record companies. This is known as a spec deal (short for speculation deal) and will generally occur when a producer believes very strongly in the potential of an artist. Although taking on all the risk, the producer also stands to gain more should such an arrangement lead to a contract with a label; the producer will get a larger portion of the advance and, in some cases, a promise to produce future projects with the artist.
Producer/label entrepreneur	Although the label-creation route has traditionally been the option of last resort for artists and producers when no buyer can be found for a finished master—"I'll show the big shots. I'll set up my own label!"—a growing number of producers, engineers, and studio owners explore the opportunities presented by releasing records on their own labels. The required investment, and thus the financial risk, has decreased significantly with the ever-expanding availability of low-cost, high-quality recording and replication equipment and the inexpensive avenues of promotion and sales offered via the Web. Of course, a producer hoping to establish a full-scale independent label will still need sufficient funds for promotion, distribution, placing music on digital platforms and manufacture of physical CDs, and the knowledge to operate such a diverse enterprise. An established producer may have the track record and industry clout to line up investors and attract strong acts, raising the odds of success.

percentage (e.g., 1 point may equal 1% of retail of 90% of recordings sold). How many points can a producer earn? The party with clout prevails. A young producer just breaking in may get only 1 point. Most producers receive 2 to 4 points. A few superstar producers ask for and receive 5% or 6% on sales.

Some contracts treat the producer better than the featured artist, who must wait for royalties until the label has recouped its production costs. (Many releases fail to recoup their costs.) The artist will normally receive a royalty two to five times higher than the producer's, but the producer will generally have a contract that requires royalties from sale Number 1 (sometimes called "record one royalties"). This means that if an album sells poorly, the producer might get a small royalty payment while the artist receives no royalties at all (considered fair because the artist presumably received a big advance payment).

For top producers with negotiating clout, contracts may have escalators if their albums become best-sellers. The labels agree to such escalators because their upfront direct costs, such as recording expenses, will have been recouped when albums pass the contractually defined sales levels (such as 500,000 or 1 million unit sales). Of course, producers of lesser reputations are unable to negotiate such contingent bonuses.

In addition to royalties, it is standard practice for the label to pay a production fee. Some producers are fortunate to get a few thousand dollars upfront as their fee, half of which is normally paid before the first session begins and the other half upon delivery of the master. Some fees are not extra payments but may be minor advances deducted from the producer's royalties. Major producers can get tens of thousands of dollars or more in production fees, usually nonrecoupable by the label from royalties.

In exchange for the "privilege" of choosing their producer, recording artists often pay the producer's points out of their own record royalty. The paperwork required between the producer, artist, and **record label** will be a few short pages and is referred to as a *letter of direction*. Typically, a letter of direction informs the record company of the fee that the artist will assign the record producer out of his or her advance or future royalties and how many of the artist's royalty points the producer is to receive. In addition, the artist also grants permission to the record company to handle the accounting and pay the producer directly, which relieves the producer of worries that the artist may be hard to find and collect from in future years.

The Recording Studio: Operation and Selection

Once a producer has aligned with an artist and struck a deal with the artist, a label, or both, another key early decision to be made is a basic one: Where will the music be recorded? The rise of the high-quality home or project studio, the contraction of the U.S. music market, and a resultant tightening of recording budgets by labels have combined in recent years to put a squeeze on the commercial studio sector. Although this can work to the advantage of a producer and recording artist in potentially driving down fees and opening up slots, it makes it harder for the studios to make money and stay in business. To compete, commercial studios are stressing those factors that make them unique—from spacious room size to specialized staff and support, from properly designed acoustic environments to luxurious amenities.

Studio Operation

Except to industry insiders, the recording studio sector is largely a hidden business—most of the best of them remain unknown to the public. Thousands of people are employed full-time in this unique industry, which requires cooperation between entrepreneurs, technicians, **engineers,** designers, acousticians, managers, and musicians. Here, art and technology must find accommodation. And while producers and engineers may never opt to open their own commercial studio operations, they can count on spending plenty of time in them over the courses of their careers. Having at least a general knowledge of the operations of the studio sector thus makes good sense for anyone interested in being a part of the music industry.

Although staffing levels fluctuate with the ebb and flow of business, label-owned studios and the larger independent studios traditionally maintain a full-time staff of between 10 and 40 members, a smaller number than in the heyday of prior decades. The technology revolution has crimped the big multiroom studios by enabling medium- and small-sized recording businesses to proliferate. These smaller studios, often operating as a family business, may be equipped with semi-professional recording equipment that nevertheless delivers good audio quality. Modern recording equipment is compact and mobile. Small recording studios can offer remote recording services with high quality and low prices that would have been unthinkable a few decades ago.

One human impact from the cheap recording technology revolution is that the skill of engineering and production staff is now of paramount importance. Because the equipment provides so many options, the human decisions on which avenues to pursue—rather than the expense of the recording equipment—are larger factors in final product quality.

A studio's staff also includes traffic managers, who book studio time and must sometimes contend with the feast-or-famine scenario of producers desperate for specific times, usually all at the *same* time. Traffic managers must sometimes schedule weeklong sessions months in advance, booking time for acts, for example, who will be coming off the road and who are determined to lay down an album at a specific time of the year. Besides these long-range booking problems, the studio traffic department must be adept at estimating when a session may run overtime.

Studio profit depends on how closely contiguous hours can be booked. When sessions fail to begin and end on schedule, both the studio and producer may experience serious financial losses. Major accounts planning to record an album often "block book" studio time. The producer estimates how many days or weeks are needed to lay down 10 or more songs and then requests the studio to reserve a particular room exclusively for that project. In block booking, the artists can leave equipment and microphones in place and not waste time trying to reinvent the setup that worked so well the previous day. Also, studios that block off a room for several days or weeks will offer the producer a much lower total price for the project than would have been charged on a per-hour basis.

In addition to the traffic manager, the staff of a full-line studio includes a chief engineer, a staff of house engineers, mixers, editors, **mastering** engineers/technicians, perhaps a video/film projectionist/technician, maintenance personnel, and people handling setups and the equipment movement. A business manager is responsible for collecting delinquent accounts and determining to whom credit should be extended. An office crew completes the staff of a full-line studio.

Few recording studios have sales departments or promotion people. Management finds that business comes or goes based largely on the word-of-mouth reputation of a studio. Ads generally do not help much. With the tougher recording environment of the past few years, however, savvy studio operators are working harder than ever to network in the industry, to help spark that all-important positive chatter.

Students working in the University of the Incarnate Word recording studio.
Photo © Doug Ensley.

Studio Design

A studio with even the latest hardware is in trouble if it lacks good acoustics in two critical areas: the control rooms and the studios themselves. Qualified engineers can predict how sounds will behave in a given space. But modern control rooms are difficult to design because the proper balance of stereo depends largely on where the **mixer** sits in the room; the producer, perhaps only 3 feet away from the mixer, hears a different balance. The interest in 5.1 surround sound compounds this problem, because sound is derived from six locations rather than two, putting a different spin on the entire process.

One essential acoustical requirement for orchestras and ensembles is sound diffusion, which allows performers to hear a fair amount of the sounds occurring around them. However, the precise opposite occurs in **tracking**: Performers want very short reverberation times when using earphones, because they want to hear only themselves and the program coming over the earphones. The latest bells and whistles aside, though, studios ultimately sink or swim on whether the performing musicians feel comfortable in them.

Selecting a Studio

A number of factors will play into a producer's selection of a studio, but the first filter will likely be cost: How much can the act spend to make its record? Those on extremely limited budgets will not have the luxury of even considering the highest-end studios, whose state-of-the-art equipment, top-tier staff, and luxurious accommodations come with an equally high-ticket price tag.

The next factor is where the act will be comfortable: Is a big city desirable? A small town where everyone can hang out after hours at a local bar? Although the industry is primarily based in New York, Los Angeles, Nashville, and, to some extent, Chicago, professional studios can be found in countless other areas of the country, with affiliates around the world and creative resources everywhere. That a label bigwig is less likely to wander in during the sessions "just to see how things are going" is an added bonus to heading off the beaten path, some musicians say.

The available equipment, the level of service, and the staffing provided will also be factored into the equation. The producer wants to select a studio in which a good sound can be achieved and where the hardware maintenance is reliable. One of a producer's biggest problems is **downtime** in the studio. When equipment is not working properly, the loss is not only in dollars but also in momentum. If a particular studio has a staff engineer who can keep the equipment working, that facility may be favored over one with more sophisticated equipment.

The producer who brings in a freelance engineer can expect an experienced mixer to adapt quickly to a new console. A producer who is particular about equalization (**EQ**) and **timbre** will usually go into a studio with the engineer prior to the sessions to check out the console, the monitoring system, and the acoustics. One who goes to this effort (not uncommon among pros) brings in a familiar recording. If the playback does not sound exactly as it should, the producer spends time with the engineer and a house engineer to adjust equalization of speakers and amplifiers. It is important to know precisely what sounds are coming over the monitors.

Another consideration for the producer is the range of equipment on offer. Some want **digital recording;** others insist on **analog** equipment. This, of course, presents a monetary challenge to already stretched studios: Only heavily capitalized operations can keep up with every innovation. Studios often start out by leasing leading-edge gear because of the lower capital outlay—and because they want to trade in outdated equipment as more sophisticated hardware becomes available. Some so-called digital recordings are not wholly digital; the recording machine may employ digital technology, but it can be hooked up to analog microphones and consoles. Studios use "automated" consoles **interfaced** with computers, and these consoles are used as a mixing and remixing aid. The computers "remember" previous sound settings, leaving the engineer free to perform other tasks.

Finally, a producer and the recording artist will consider intangibles such as a studio's hit-making reputation and overall "vibe." Many refuse to book time in a studio that has not produced successful or great-sounding records.

Types of Studios

With a checklist of desired attributes in hand and a budget in mind, the producer can consider the available options. Keep in mind that projects often encompass more than one studio. Rehearsals and **demos** may be done in one facility, for instance, while backing tracks could be laid down in another environment, and mixing and final mastering could occur in a third type of studio. The choices include the following:

Home/Project Studios. These are not the "converted garages" of old, where shaggy-haired guitarists rolled tape (among other things). Although hard-disc recording has existed in commercial products since the early 1980s, recent developments have made digital audio workstations (**DAW**) that combine recording, editing, mixing, and mastering functions in a single software/hardware package much more user-friendly and, equally important, much more affordable to a wide range of users. Leading the DAW revolution is the Pro Tools system, which in its basic form comprises hardware and sound cards connected to a computer on which digital music recording software is installed. Such systems now give even amateurs the means to achieve professional-sounding recordings in their own homes. These studios still serve their traditional role as a training ground for aspiring producers, engineers, and musicians, who can set up a versatile entry-level studio for around $1,000, but they are now also the professional playgrounds for established producing, engineering, and recording talents, who can choose among a significantly higher-end selection of professional-quality workstations and software. These types of studios are thus a viable, and increasingly popular, option to use for at least part of the recording process.

Preproduction/Demo Studios. The traditional entry-level commercial studio for musicians is one that specializes in rehearsal space and/or demo recordings. Nearly all of them offer 4- to 8-track tape equipment or some basic digital recording device and room enough for a small ensemble. Because demo studios can offer hourly rates far lower than full commercial studios, they service the bulk of demo recording needs of writers and publishers and are an efficient and cost-effective place for an act to work on its material for an upcoming recording. Well-managed demo studios can make a profit; however, financial difficulties may occur as the small operator attempts to keep up by purchasing all the latest equipment. Some demo studios live long and prosper by becoming headquarters for small production companies, small labels, beginning publishers, and even artists' managers and agents trying to get established. Another kind of recording operation, which might be called the in-house studio, has become increasingly popular with publishers and advertising agencies. These are private operations, rarely open to the public, and intended to serve the host company and its business associates. They range in size from 8- to 16-track and provide in-house production for everything from simple demos to sophisticated masters for commercial CDs.

Independent Studios. A big step above the demo studio is the full-line independent studio, which has at least 24-track tape recorders with multi-input consoles and other **outboard equipment** sufficient to compete with plants operated by the major record labels. Digital equipment offers the capacity for even more audio tracks. A full-service independent studio will normally have one or two rooms capable of handling a studio orchestra or smaller groups, mixdown and editing, full Musical Instrument Digital Interface (**MIDI**) capabilities, equipment rack rooms, and possibly a maintenance shop, traffic control office, and lockers for equipment storage. Although these studios can pretty much be counted on to have the array of digital tools so pervasive in the recording business, they are also where producers and artists can usually find large-format analog tape recorders and consoles.

Label-Owned Studios. A carryover from the days when the major recording companies controlled all the links in the record-making chain, the label-owned studio still exists in large cities such as Los Angeles, Nashville, New York, and Miami. And although major-label consolidation has winnowed the list of music-business heavyweights down to a precious few behemoths, all still have a stable of studios—some of which are simply small, private setups—available to their various labels' artists, producers, and publishing groups. Many also operate as commercial recording studios, open to outside acts and producers, although label acts are usually given priority. Physical facilities and equipment are generally equal or superior to those found in major independent studios.

The Five Stages of Record Production

Studio selection comes during the preproduction or planning stage of record production, when budgets are also being mapped out and set. The other four phases are basic tracking, overdubbing, mixing, and mastering (see Table 13.2). Each is a critical link in the music-making process.

Table 13.2   The Five Phases of Record Production

The following is a representative rundown of the many steps required along the route to a successful album production. The exact order may vary, particularly in the preproduction stage. This list presumes that a producer initiates the project, as opposed to being assigned to it by a label or recording artist.

1. Preproduction: Budgeting and Planning

   - Create the concept
   - Prepare a budget, raise the money (or negotiate the budget with the label)
   - Locate and sign an artist (or sign on to an existing project with a label, artist)
   - Select the songs
   - Negotiate mechanical licenses
   - Lay out how each song is to be treated, engage arrangers to score the charts
   - Engage the musical director, union contractors
   - Book time in a studio
   - Engage an engineer, test studio equipment, acoustics
   - Confirm availability of any special equipment and instruments needed
   - Make sure all performers sign contracts, including friends of the artist who drop-in unexpectedly and contribute
   - Reconfirm all of the above
   - Rehearse the music

2. In the Studio: Basics and Tracking

   - Record the basic/backing tracks for each song
   - Maintain a tracking sheet, detailing what is laid down on each track
   - Execute punch-ins as needed to fix/alter basic tracks

3. In the Studio: Overdubbing

   - Identify performances that still need to be fixed or fine-tuned
   - Add sweetener tracks
   - Record the vocals

4. In the Studio: Mixing and Final Preparations

   - Make decisions about levels, EQ
   - Prepare final mixdown to two-track stereo or a multichannel format
   - Sequence album tracks
   - Pull out possible singles and edit for length
   - Make copies as needed
   - If songs are composed during recording, settle on composer credits immediately at end of session
   - Prepare union contracts for instrumentalists and vocalists

5. Postproduction: Mastering and Delivery to Label

   - Locate a mastering studio
   - Supervise mastering
   - Obtain clearances from graphic artist, photographer, liner notes writer
   - Turn over signed mechanical licenses to the record company
   - Obtain W-4 and I-9 wages and work eligibility forms, and copies of identification from all employees
   - Deliver W-4 and I-9 forms, copies of identification, and union contracts to the company
   - Deliver lyric sheets and technical credit sheets to the company
   - Identify samples/interpolations and hire a sample clearinghouse
   - Deliver information on any samples/**interpolations** to the company
   - Confirm that all bills have been paid
   - Reconfirm everything
   - Deliver final master

Preproduction: Budgeting and Planning

The responsibility of developing and controlling budgets is a key part of the producer's job, whether the work is being done for a label or on a freelance basis. Preparing a production budget with precision is difficult because many of the expenses can be only roughly estimated. At budget-writing time, the producer may not even know in which city the recording will take place. Perhaps a rhythm section must be flown in from Nashville. Will some of the songs on the album require an expensive complement of string players? All the budget maker can do at the outset is identify expense parameters. After assembling all available data, costs must be specified in detail.

Budget Control. Well-organized producers work up budgets on some kind of summary sheet. Table 13.3 shows one kind of budget sheet, which may be used as is or tailored to a specific situation.

A budget control sheet must reflect careful research of current studio costs and the latest union wage scales and surcharges. Experienced producers often call in their American Federation of Musicians (AFM) and SAG-AFTRA contractors to help them pull together accurate figures, especially when they need to hire **session musicians.** These superb artists sight-read the charts and are able to perform an acceptable **take** on the second or third reading.

In calculating the expense of recording an album, the producer potentially enters an arena of high finance and equally lofty risk. In some cases, the expense of recording a quality master for an album will start in the six-figure range. Other major-label budgets will be in the five figures, whereas still others for smaller independent companies or fledgling bands won't go far into four. Although the smaller budgets demand a much larger degree of creativity and flexibility in approach, all producers are charged with the task of turning in a quality master from the investment allotted, whatever its size.

Producers of rock albums often budget 10 to 20 hours of studio time per song. Some rock albums may clock 300 hours or more, including mixing, editing, and mastering. Producers and other recording executives worried about exorbitant recording costs might want to compare their figures with the studio time required by artists in other genres. Jazz album producers, for instance, may let the machines roll and catch great performances the first time, entirely unrehearsed—improvised. An even more impressive comparison of recording time for rock can be made with the classical field. A professional symphony orchestra of the second or third rank can record a 15- to 25-minute work, such as Stravinsky's *Rite of Spring,* in 6 to 9 hours! Of course, the orchestra would have learned the piece a few seasons back, but such an achievement is still remarkable.

Among the reasons that recording costs can exceed their budgets are these:

1. The group is poorly prepared; it uses the recording studio for rehearsal, even for composition.

2. The performers can't read music, can't mesh their performances, or can't come up with the right style.

3. The producer can't decide what is needed.

4. The engineer can't come up with the right sounds.

5. One or more of the participants is not qualified for the job, lacking the talent or the experience to compete professionally.

Table 13.3 **Recording Budget**

Artist/Group _____   Date _____
Producer _____   Studio _____
Label/Client _____   Project No. _____
Contact _____   Engineer _____

	Cost per Unit	No. of Units	Total Unit Cost	Subtotal	Extension
STUDIO					
Studio					
Basic Rate					
Outboard Equipment					
Setup/Strike					
Basic Tracks					
Overdubs					
Vocals					
Mixing/Editing					
Tax					
ENGINEERS					
First Engineer					
Second Engineer					
ARRANGING/COPYING					

Music Title		Arranging	Copying			
1.						
2.						
3.						
4.						
5.						
6.						
7.						
8.						
9.						
10.						
Union surcharges						

ARTISTS	Instrumentalists	Singers	Soloists			
Rehearsals						
Basic Tracks						
Sweetening						
Union Surcharges						
EQUIPMENT						
Rentals						
Cartage						
Tax						

MISCELLANEOUS (payroll tax, etc.)

UNFORESEEN EXPENSE (15% of total)

TOTAL PRODUCTION COST
_____

With these possible problems in mind, the experienced producer will "pad" the estimated recording budget so as to have access to additional funds without upsetting the record label; in effect, he or she "budgets" for budget overrides. A savvy producer will also attempt to head off as many potential budget-busting scenarios as possible; he or she may raise the subject of hiring a session musician or two to "ghost" some of the musician's parts that aren't coming out right, for instance, or ask the chief studio engineer or owner to be on hand for the first day or two to assist should there be any problems or questions about the equipment.

Recording expenses paid for by the record label are considered an advance against future earnings. As explained in Chapter 12, if the master is produced for an amount less than the fund, some contracts provide that the balance can be retained (by the artist or the producer, depending on their contract with each other) as an advance from the label against royalties.

Not surprisingly, recording funds and budgets are more often overspent than underspent. Most record labels keep a sharp eye on the progress of the recording. They assign a budget monitor to keep track of the money flow on a day-to-day basis, and the producer will be asked to keep this individual informed whenever expense is incurred. When a project is nearing completion and has developed momentum, many labels permit reasonable budget overruns of around 10% or less. But a label might also include the equivalent of a "stop loss" order in its contract with a producer or artist, giving it the right to halt the recording process at any point if it believes the project is careening toward severe budget overrun.

Arrangements and Rehearsals. After having set a budget and selected the songs to be recorded—a tough process, as discussed earlier—the producer and act must lay out how each song is to be treated. Does this need strings or horns? Is some of the material going to be most effective when presented with complete simplicity? When these kinds of decisions have been made, the producer engages arrangers to score the charts. Producers with strong musical backgrounds will probably work with arrangers in sketching out the arrangements, to increase the likelihood that the producer's conception will be implemented.

If the act and the producer have reached a working understanding on how the material is to be treated, preproduction rehearsals will follow, to make sure the music is prepared before going into the studio. Organized groups rehearse for free, of course. But if the charts call for added instruments such as horns and strings, established session musicians expect to be paid for rehearsals, often at straight recording scale.

If the charts call for outside session singers, the producer needs to know which AFTRA union contractors can deliver them.

Basics and Tracking

Now that the producer and the artist have begun recording, the second stage of the production process focuses on capturing the basic elements of each song, or the backing tracks. In most cases, this is when the rhythm section is recorded or, in the case of dance and hip-hop music, when the beat is built. For some genres, almost everything that appears on the record is captured live. The producer will be looking for a steady rhythm that is appropriate for the song and has a good "feel" or "groove."

Practices vary, but most producers keep a written record of what is laid down on each track; this record is referred to as a tracking sheet. Tracking sheets cite the artist, the date, the studio, song titles, take numbers, timings, and footage counts for the start and end of takes. Of course, if the recording process is digital with search-and-find capability, location and level settings are readily recalled with the push of a button.

As the recording process goes forward through this stage, the producer can expect to be challenged from all sides. Although the first concern will be the music, the producer is supposed to know enough about recording technology to work effectively with the engineer. The self-confident producer will encourage the engineer to contribute creatively to the recording process. When the producer cannot come up with a solution to a problem, perhaps the engineer can save the day. Usually, the most successful producers will welcome and carefully weigh all the creative input they can find, whatever the source.

The rise of user-friendly digital recording technology has added a new challenge to producers during the recording process: the lure of having endless options. It is now all too easy to postpone a decision on the "best take" because a producer can record as many as desired—and retain them all. Likewise, some producers hear the siren call of the "undo" button, which allows experimentation without risk—and sometimes without end. An ability to know when they have got *the* take or achieved the best sound—and a willingness to commit to it—remains a big part of producers' jobs, whatever the technology being used.

Overdubbing

With the basic elements of the recording in the can, it is time to focus on those performances that need to be fixed or fine-tuned, to record the vocals, and to get creative and add any other instruments or effects to help **sweeten** the track. This process is known as overdubbing. Some producers may do some of the overdubbing while laying down the basic tracks—for example, it is more efficient to fix the bass player's mistakes right away than to try to remember to do it later and have to find a time when the musician may be available. These fixes are called **punch-ins.** In other instances, a separate track is immediately recorded instead.

The most important part of the overdubbing process for noninstrumental productions is the recording of the lead vocals, which will be the centerpiece of the recording. Vocals can be as hard to capture as they are critical to success, and the process will likely be equal parts trade craft (the right mike and correct placement) and skillful cajolery (knowing the ways in which to somehow elicit the best possible performance from the singer).

The producer must gauge the psychological and physical makeup of the lead vocalist: Does the vocalist need the session to be closed to nonessential people, for instance, or does he perform better with an audience on hand? Will several hours of singing push her voice too far, or is that much warm-up required before she hits her full vocal stride? Editing software, of course, provides plenty of opportunities to manipulate the vocals after the fact, from basic pitch correction or doubling to the more radical stitching together of pieces from multiple recording sessions.

Mixing

This stage in the recording process is when the decisions are made about what instruments should be at what level, which performances make the final **mix** from the sessions, what the tonal qualities and EQ should be, and where to place the instruments in the stereo mix. That last decision has been getting more interesting with the number of recordings mixed or remixed in multichannel sound as opposed to traditional two-channel stereo. Mixers have the option of creating various virtual experiences via the multiple channels, such as re-creating a live concert experience by placing the music upfront, as on a stage, and positioning audience ambience in the rear channels, for instance.

Whatever the technology, the human element—the mixer, or "mixing engineer"—will be the most important factor in success at this stage of production. Studios and record labels have had difficulty finding mixers and engineers who are thoroughly qualified and sufficiently versatile because obtaining adequate preparation is challenging: This group of professionals is expected to be fully educated in two different disciplines—electrical engineering and music. The aforementioned shrinkage of big multiroom recording studios with large staffs has even reduced the opportunities for newcomers to intern or serve as **gofers** at the hands of masters.

The mixers most in demand are those with "magic ears" for the current hot sound. They may not understand how to trace a short in an amp or adjust the azimuth on a recording **head,** but they do know how to piece together all of the tracks into a winning mix. They ride those **faders** with a sure touch, pulling from the console much more interesting sounds than what originally went into the microphones. In short, the top mixers are sensitive to sound and music, and they work their electronic wizardry like sound sorcerers—which they are. They have a good feel for the impact that a sound or musical sequence will have on the listener.

Besides the ability to ride a console with sensitivity and creativity, these artists have one additional attribute without which they would run screaming from the control room: Their temperament seems immune to high stress and tension. The mixer bears great responsibility for the final result. The top mixers feel the pressure, but they can handle it.

Although the industry is saturated with mixers, those who have "the ears" and a cool temperament are the individuals most likely to find regular employment and a high income. But however talented the mixer and however good the mix sounds when piped through the studio's professional monitors and top-quality speakers, most producers won't OK it just yet. First, they want to hear how it sounds in a *real-world* environment, over the various types of low-end speakers, iPods, basic radio receivers, and car stereos that most music fans actually use.

Master Delivery Requirements. Even when the producer has survived the production and mixing of the master, the job is far from over. If a recording company has retained the producer, the firm now imposes specific delivery requirements that need to be completed prior to the company's acceptance of the master. For example:

1. The master tape must be mixed down to two-channel stereo or multichannel sound, as appropriate, on half-inch or quarter-inch tape, high-quality CD-R, or hard disk. The preferred delivery requirement will likely include "flattened" Broadcast Wave Files as well as backups/safeties to protect the long-term value of the recording as an asset. The label will probably also expect the producer to pull out several tracks for possible release as singles. If so, the singles must be edited to appropriate lengths (usually under 4 minutes).

2. The producer must deliver letters of consent that were obtained earlier from all individuals involved in the project, allowing the label to use their names and photographs in promoting the music. Release letters must also state that the artists, musicians, and other creative personnel are unencumbered by conflicting recording agreements with any other firm. Should an artist on the recording be signed to an exclusive recording contract with another label, the

producer must obtain permission in writing and alert the label as to any specific demands (i.e., the recording company must receive a courtesy credit in the liner notes, the artist's name cannot appear on the cover of the recording, among many other requirements).

3. The producer must deliver letters of consent from all photographers and graphic artists for the use of their works.

4. The producer must furnish evidence that all copyrights are clear and the owners have granted mechanical licenses for each cut on the album.

5. Lyric sheets must be submitted. Labels want to determine whether the song texts are acceptable for radio broadcast and the standards of some mass-merchant chains, although presumably the label knows in advance whether to expect objectionable language. A decision must also be made as to whether the release will carry a parental-advisory label.

6. A technical credits summary sheet is required setting forth details such as the names of the engineers, sidemusicians, and background vocalists; where the master was recorded; who the arrangers and musical director were; the names of the union contractors; who mastered the tapes; and identities of artists' personal managers and booking agents.

7. A sign-off statement is required from the producer providing evidence that the bills have been paid and that there are no liens or encumbrances that might prevent the label from releasing the recording.

8. The producer must collect W-4 forms, I-9 forms, and union contracts for every individual involved on the project to whom wages were paid.

The smart producer won't mail in the master but will make an appointment with the person who set up the job, then walk in with the master and present it personally. At the same time, at least two or three CD transfer copies should be delivered so that the A&R people and other executives in the firm can hear the producer's work.

Assuming that the label accepts the master, the producer will then be paid the other half of the production fee or advance on royalties.

Mastering

Once the record is mixed and approved, it is sent to a mastering studio to prepare it for mass production. It is customary for the record company to pay for mastering and all subsequent steps leading to manufacture of the recordings; some companies seek to have mastering charged to the artist and producer's royalties, however. Although it is generally not part of the production agreement's requirements, a seasoned producer will be involved in the mastering process; decisions can be made at this point that will affect the sound of the final product.

The mastering engineer might do basic preparation work such as sequencing the album, adding the space between each song, and making sure that the track starts at the correct moment with regard to the corresponding track number. But this is also the last opportunity to make any sonic corrections to the recording. For example, the master might be too bass heavy, so the mastering engineer will "roll off" some lower EQ frequencies. The mastering engineer might also add some compression to the recording to make it sound fuller and more radio friendly. Once this process is finished, the producer's job is really, truly done, right? Well, almost. Some conscientious producers continue their postproduction services up to and including the checking of test pressings, to make sure all the effort invested in the project will be reflected in the ultimate sound of the music.

Getting Started in the Business

So you have now studied the sector, assessed the challenges and opportunities, and decided that you do want to be an engineer or producer. How does one get started? The answer is simple: Start working. Set up a studio at home or start going into a nearby studio and record your music, record your friend's music, or offer to help a local artist.

Starting as an Engineer

Aspiring engineers, of course, need to be technologically adept to work in today's studios. Increasingly complicated multitimbral synthesizers as well as digital and multimedia techniques challenge recording studio personnel. Take advantage of every opportunity to use and learn more about these! Keyboard players who play several electronic instruments simultaneously will expect the engineer to accommodate their recording needs. Engineers must also understand how to properly record synthesized percussion, various portable keyboards, and experimental instruments that defy classification.

Starting as a Producer

Many producers come from one of three entry points. Some start as a musician in a band that is recording. They find that they gravitate more toward the control room than the live room. They begin to take a leadership role in the recording session and become actively involved in all phases of the project. Some move from the engineer's chair into the producer's. They find that not only do they have the skills necessary to capture sound and make the band sound fantastic, but they also have an ear for which takes sound good and which ones should be done again. The third group begins its journey as passionate students of recordings. These people are usually critics, audiophiles, or both. They listen to a lot of music and can explain what makes one recording better than others.

Whatever the starting point, all young and ambitious producers will listen to, analyze, and critique many recordings, both current and classic. It would be wise to pay close attention to the works of legendary and successful producers such as John Hammond, George Martin, Teo Macero, Sam Phillips, Jerry Wexler, Quincy Jones, Dr. Dre, and Rick Rubin, to name just a few.

Key Requirements of a Producer

Before you get too far along with your pursuit, also ask these hard questions:

1. Have you got the will and the passion to succeed in a competitive, demanding discipline? Can you hang in there in the face of inevitable challenges and setbacks?

2. Are you gifted in locating artists with star potential? Neither you nor your acts will make a dime unless that potential is there. Can you persuade strong acts to work with you?

3. Do you have a talent for picking quality songs? Do you recognize commercial potential?

4. Can you evaluate the combined impact of the material, artist's delivery, and production sound?

5. Do you have access to money? Do you know how to present a convincing plan to potential investors?

6. Do you know how to present your artists to potential buyers of master tapes? You have three ways to do this: present live showcases, present demos (audio, perhaps video), or present masters.

If you lack any of these abilities, you must locate collaborators who are strong in areas where you may be deficient. Translation: Form an independent production company. Few individuals are talented or fortunate enough to go it alone.

You may also wonder whether you need to be a technical wizard to make it as a producer. Although many producers have come up through the engineering route, the answer, as proven by the number of highly successful producers who have *not*, is no. But you will need to be able to communicate effectively with someone who does know the equipment. Particularly in an age in which it is rare for a commercial recording project to be untouched at some point by Pro Tools or another software-based platform, a producer at the very least should have a basic understanding of the terminology of both digital and analog recording and editing systems, as well as their options and functions.

The Do-It-Yourself Artist

For the musician or vocalist wanting to produce, the audio technology revolution has unshackled artists from the studio, allowing recordings to take place in spare bedrooms or even on rolling tour buses. There are many advantages to the do-it-yourself (DIY) ethic: the ability to record when inspiration hits, the artist's control of sound, the ability to be productive during in-between moments of life, and the opportunity to experiment with unusual sounds. But DIY also comes with some disadvantages.

Acoustics of the impromptu sound room are usually not ideal, for which the solution is to **close-mike** the audio source. Still, **slap** and invasion of external low-frequency noise, like the rumble of trucks on the street, can creep in. Another complaint is that low-cost digital equipment can produce a harsh, literal sound for tracks and overdubbing—prime activities of DIY recordings. Of course, a hard sound can often be softened in mixing when done on professional-grade equipment with pro engineers, but only if the budget allows.

DIY also means working in a world with less than the traditional level of collaboration. The DIY artist cannot benefit from the insights and ideas of experienced, trained engineers and staff at a professional studio. Another drawback for artists intent on video recording their studio sessions for later promotion is the often bland and inappropriate visual setting of the DIY environment.

Experienced recording professionals say self-recording sounds easy, but when an artist gets stuck on a problem, lack of experience can make it maddening to resolve. Indeed, good engineering skills require education and experience, difficult to acquire in a DIY-only environment. But recognizing that DIY is here to stay, some professional studios offer fee-based services to fulfill backend needs of the self-recording semi-pro artist. Besides mixing the artists' DIY tracks, these services can include on-site tech support, equipment repair, and CD mastering, duplication, and artwork design.

Professional Associations

Individuals who are serious about getting into sound recording may also want to become acquainted with the professional associations serving this sector of the industry, many of which offer educational workshops and forums.

The Audio Engineering Society (AES) holds annual conventions that feature seminars, technical paper presentations, and workshops on new recording technologies and displays of equipment manufacturers' latest audio products. AES has a committee dealing with the educational aspects of recording technology and career opportunities in audio.

The Society of Professional Audio Recording Services (SPARS) also concerns itself with educational standards for training audio technicians. Its programs include intern placement, business conferences, educational seminars, mentoring, networking, and consulting. SPARS membership includes postproduction recording studios, individual engineers and producers, production houses, postproduction facilities, manufacturers of professional audio recording equipment, schools, colleges, studio designers, leasing companies, and those who serve the audio recording industry. It increasingly offers services to members with small operations; such services may include advice on complying with local zoning regulations and formulating financial business plans.

The Recording Academy is probably best known as the organization that administers the coveted Grammy Awards each year. Previously known as the National Academy of Recording Arts and Sciences (NARAS), it is also home to the Producers & Engineers Wing, which boasts thousands of producers, engineers, remixers, and other top audio professionals as members. Among the Wing's activities are occasional professional education events, forums, and seminars.

Individuals believing they may want to work in the audio departments of TV and film studios can learn more about this field from SMPTE, the Society of Motion Picture and Television Engineers (see Chapter 21).

Chapter Takeaways

- The record producer's core role is creating great music by meshing the talents of the lead artist, songs, accompanying instrumentalists and singers, and audio engineering.

- Besides getting creativity on track, the producer is typically responsible for scheduling all aspects of recording and keeping the project on budget.

- Top recording producers negotiate compensation that includes a percentage of music sales, which are called royalties and result in big payouts for hit records.

- With digital technology, relatively inexpensive home recording equipment can achieve high-quality rendering of basic tracks. This tool is a big enabler of the DIY production.

- While some artists like to record tracks outside a studio with inexpensive mobile gear, the final mix for top records with a polished sound is mostly done in studios with professional equipment.

- Producers often play back mixes on an assortment of consumer devices—such as car stereos and iPods—to test how the music sounds on equipment music buyers will actually use.

Key Terms

- "all-in" deal   (p. 227)
- close-mike   (p. 241)
- creative control   (p. 226)
- DAW   (p. 231)
- demos   (p. 231)
- EQ   (p. 231)

- interpolations   (p. 233)
- master purchase agreement   (p. 227)
- master tapes   (p. 238)
- mastering   (p. 229)
- MIDI   (p. 232)

- mixer   (p. 230)
- overdubbing   (p. 237)
- punch-ins   (p. 237)
- session musicians   (p. 234)
- timbre   (p. 231)
- tracks   (p. 226)

Discussion Questions

1. Can education and training help producers better identify good takes from bad ones, or is this an innate ability? Explain your answer.

2. What are the most important characteristics of a good producer? Which of these characteristics fit you? Which might you need to develop in order to become a successful producer?

3. Discuss the types of music producers. As an artist, which type of music producer would you want to work with? Why?

4. What are the pros and cons of DIY music production?

Record Label Marketing and Distribution

The Marketing Plan

To paraphrase an old adage: If you make a great record and no one hears it, was it really great? Every participant from the largest label to the self-released independent artist will benefit by knowing the market, identifying the target audience, and planning an effective marketing and promotion strategy. After all, everyone goes to extreme lengths to record the best possible sounds.

"The music business is dead, but there's lots of interesting life forms crawling out of the corpse."

—Peter Gabriel

Today, legitimate recorded music is offered to the public in multiple ways, from streaming to downloads to CDs to retro vinyl LPs. In any given week, there are many thousands of recordings (both new releases and not-so-new) fighting for attention. To successfully promote recorded music in this turbulent environment, it is as important as ever to understand the elements of a marketing plan. Whatever the distribution medium, demand must be developed, not only nationally but also all over the world. Especially for a mainstream release, a label usually has to sell a lot of records—quickly—to be successful.

SWOT

An important early step in devising an effective plan of attack for marketing is to do a basic **SWOT analysis.** SWOT stands for "strengths, weaknesses, opportunities, and threats." This analysis gives a good perspective on what marketing concepts may be employed, what hurdles may be faced, and how those hurdles can be overcome.

Left: The Black Keys performing live in Milan, Italy, in 2012.

Photo © Henry Ruggeri/Corbis.

Strengths. What does this project have working well in its favor? For example, if the artist has a successful history of radio airplay, it will be easier to get this artist's new single added to radio **playlists.** Perhaps the artist has built a loyal fan base through continuous touring, generated an online buzz with fans by dating another celebrity, or cut a tremendous new track that will be groundbreaking creatively.

Weaknesses. Part of efficient marketing is avoiding tactics that aren't going to pay off. For example, if the artist will not be able to tour for health reasons, alternatives to personal appearances must be formulated.

Opportunities. Touring, TV appearances, and tie-ups with third parties (including other musical artists) are all potential avenues to exploit. If an artist has good relations with the media, fruitful TV appearances and journalist interviews can be expected.

Threats. It is equally important to identify possible forces that may be working against marketing efforts. Such conditions might include a crowded month of high-profile releases that will be competing for airplay and press attention or the release of a big video game or movie that drains the wallets of teenagers who are the target demographic. By identifying threats, marketers can chart a course that will both address these threats and find other ways to achieve exposure.

The Concept

Crafting an effective marketing plan can mean the difference between a hit and a flop. Sometimes the target market is obvious—such as selling a record in the young children's category to parents and teachers. In less obvious cases, labels may enlist market research to help understand and identify the target groups most likely to buy. Narrowing the marketing aim to a target audience means marketing sources are focused on the demographic most likely to respond, which results in less wastage of resources on unresponsive consumers.

At this early stage, the company's marketing executives try to come up with a hook that will bait potential audiences, which market research may later explore in greater detail. Those invited to help formulate the hook and the resulting marketing plan might include the artist's manager, the producer of the album, the head of marketing at the record label, the art director, the heads of promotion and publicity, and the A&R (artist and repertoire) representative.

The Marketing Team

Although marketing concepts may be similar whatever the label size, the number of people involved in a marketing project varies substantially with the scope of the overall organization. Larger labels may include in their marketing departments the following personnel:

- Marketing executives. Responsible for conception and execution of multimedia campaigns, providing sales aids to retailers and igniting fan interest online
- Radio promoters. Responsible for gaining exposure on the radio
- Publicists. Responsible for getting stories, reviews, and news releases to online, print, and broadcast media
- Advertising managers. Responsible for the conception, production, and placement of paid ads

Campaign Management. Most labels assign one individual—the **product manager**—to manage a marketing campaign. These managers receive a budget from the company and are expected to oversee a promotion strategy, coordinate the various departments (marketing, radio promotion, publicity, and advertising), and execute the marketing plan. They may also have the responsibility of assigning promotion personnel to certain geographic areas and coordinating the efforts of staff promoters working out of the label's branch offices. Product managers designate timing of the campaign and how much attention and emphasis it receives.

To the extent broadcast exposure for the project is key, product managers also keep track of which radio and TV outlets are adding or dropping the new release. If they observe good airplay developing in a particular geographic area, they may double efforts there in an attempt to develop a regional hit. They then alert the marketing and distribution departments of the new regional radio acceptance to ensure that sufficient product is in retail channels to meet the possible demand caused by the airplay. The sales team documents airplay popularity that is in turn presented to retailers to convince them to showcase the music product.

Product managers follow the progress of a new release on the trade charts and collect point-of-sale (**POS**) reports for CDs and sales of digital downloads. Information on the entry, rise, and fall of a recording via these metrics provides guidance on how to spend (or withdraw) the money available for a campaign.

The Elements of a Marketing Plan

The Strategy

A marketing plan is a broad strategy to convince a target audience to buy. It can contain many elements, depending on the concept, the nature of the target market, and the budget. One element is promotions, which are one-time special efforts that communicate marketing messages, typically mounted in conjunction with other parties. For example, in 2015, 50,000 CDs of Bob Dylan's *Shadows in the Night* album from Columbia Records were randomly bundled with the high-circulation print magazine of AARP, a nonprofit organization for senior citizens. Since Dylan's photograph was also on the cover of the AARP magazine that was mailed to millions of households (some containing CDs, although most not), his new album got a big promotional bang. Promotions can include temporary in-store displays marking an album's release; events mounted with media outlets such as a music magazine, retailer, soft drink company, or cellular phone provider; getting a celebrity to plug the release to Twitter followers; and "street teams" of hired staff creating awareness in public places of urban areas.

Another element is publicity, aimed at nudging journalists in radio, TV, magazines, newspapers, and websites to create editorial content discussing artists and their music. A third element is paid advertising, which tends to be a relatively small effort for music since the industry relies on cheaper publicity and promotions.

Once the label crafts the marketing concept, certain basic steps follow, regardless of budget: The art (or **creative services**) department renders sketches for cover art and one-sheet promotion pieces, a photographer or other artist is engaged, the copy is written, and the graphic design is created for packaging. But that's just the beginning.

Radio Promotion

Although radio's importance for record sales is eroding, it is still the single biggest catalyst. Digital media play and fan buzz are growing and substantial but still secondary to radio. Music might first get attention with a niche audience online, which traditional radio notices and then adds the music.

It's the later radio play, if it occurs, that is the catalyst necessary for huge success. "Radio remains the top method of music discovery, and its local nature makes it an integral part of the daily lives of hundreds of millions of consumers in markets large and small," said market researcher Nielsen in 2014. "Fifty-one percent of consumers use radio to discover new music." Every day radio exposes millions of potential music buyers to countless musical experiences. But radio is no easy challenge for promoters. Fearful that unfamiliar artists and their music will turn listeners away, broadcast radio outlets restrict their playlists and are cautious about new and untested sounds.

Large record companies employ a staff of full-time people to handle promotion in-house. Outside (independent) promoters may also be used; however, this type of promotion is so expensive that record companies may negotiate recoupment of some or all independent promotion expenses against artist royalties.

Promoters must decide on the station musical styles or formats that would be most appropriate in promoting the recording. Station formats are either singles based or album based. For example, a singles-based format such as Top 40 radio requires the label to choose a specific song from the album to promote to the panel of stations in that format. If the format is album based, such as for college radio, the panel of stations wants the whole album delivered, and each station chooses the track or tracks it prefers to program.

Reporting Stations. Promoters focus nearly all their attention on reporting stations—that is, outlets that the trade papers, electronic song-tracking services, and tip sheets monitor to learn which songs have been programmed. Note: Although all reporting radio stations are monitored, not all monitored stations are considered reporting stations, mostly because the music they play is not considered current enough to be useful for charts (e.g., "oldies" stations, **adult contemporary** stations, some country stations). Tip sheets are regular commentaries of interest to programmers from independent analysts about trends and specific songs. Years ago, some tip sheets were highly influential, but as available music research data improved (see Chapter 15), the value of such third-party analysis declined.

If an unheralded new release lands in the midrange of a national chart ranking popularity of songs, the promotion people more often than not have a hit on their hands. At this point, most record companies accelerate their efforts, instructing their label's regional promotion staff to intensify their campaigns for airplay. The promotion staff is now in a position to prove the claim that the new release, which is starting to break nationally, has strong hit potential. At this point, radio station programmers who were too timid weeks ago to take a chance on the new release may now be persuaded to jump on this potential hit. Sometimes there is a catch to this. Occasionally, the broadcast successes don't have desired impact: A recording manages to get good airplay, but audiences just don't buy it.

To gain the confidence of radio program directors (**PDs**), promoters must establish a reputation for credibility. What the PD needs most is useful information—research, not fast talk. The station needs to know whether a new release fits its programming and whether it is gaining airplay elsewhere. It also wants to know a release's overall ranking with the rest of the records getting researched; it wants to know the release's "burn factor"—do people really want to hear it more?

If a promoter cannot provide these assurances to the station, there is one other hope: The music might appeal to the personal tastes of the PD or musical director. Occasionally, these decision makers will program a new release just because they like it, but few outlets permit personal tastes to have too much influence on these important decisions. That influence is now even more limited with the advent of the group PD—a single PD responsible for a group of stations in a format or clustered geographically.

Mailings, Telephone, Email Follow-Ups. Because only a small number of stations can be reached by in-person contacts, promoters implore in phone calls, mail, and email free promotional copies to influential outlets. Of course, PDs are inundated with such airplay requests but give close looks to communications from promoters with track records of suggesting hits.

The success of this kind of follow-up also depends not only on the suitability of the record but also on the rapport between the caller and the station programmer.

Payola. The correlation between record sales and radio play has led to many eras of abuse. The first well-known cases of employees of a radio station taking money or favors in exchange for airplay or chart position surfaced in the 1950s. Although there was a very public trial and condemnation of the practice of "pay for play," new ways of corrupting the air ensued. In a modern grey area, music promotion executives target curators of online music streaming services to play select songs and elevate those titles on digital hit lists. Online is not covered by federal regulations banning payola that apply to terrestrial radio, so promoters are free to pay digital taste-makers consultancy fees and offer other inducements for favorable treatment.

Using a third-party independent promoter has tended to insulate the client record label from direct involvement in seamy practices, and third parties might presumably be more willing to stretch the rules than staff employees of labels. But using such third parties hasn't always protected labels from liability. For example, in 2005 and 2006, three major record companies agreed to pay penalties of $27 million to resolve **payola** charges. Some of the abuses involved individuals who portrayed themselves as music consultants to radio stations but in fact were also getting consideration from record labels for programming their product. Unfortunately, the practice muddies the waters for honest radio consultants who operate without conflicts of interest.

Beyond Terrestrial Radio

As **AM** and **FM radio** have become more difficult to break into in recent decades, other media have emerged as promotion platforms for new music. Satellite radio—typically a monthly subscription service with relatively deep playlists—boasts many genre-specific channels that must be filled with music. Digital cable music channels and Internet radio also add promotional punch. Cable video music channels are another key target for promotion, where an attention-grabbing video can support a new audio release. Record companies work particularly hard to get songs played on digital streaming platforms, given their vast capacity for music with multiple channels, although with smaller-than-radio audiences for any one channel.

Sometimes dance clubs have been effective places to test or showcase new recordings. Prior to commercial release, labels may remix a single into a longer version favored by dancers and then get it into clubs to test patrons' reactions. If the clubs report a strong response, the label will be encouraged to launch a general commercial release and tell radio executives the music was a hit in clubs.

Promotions

Music sellers, whether online or brick-and-mortar, are eager to give an extra marketing push to recorded music when they get a window of exclusivity and the artist plugs the retailer. Typically, the exclusivity period is 2 or a few weeks, after which the same music goes on sale everywhere. Retailers usually commit to delivering minimum sales in exchange for their early window and give the record lots of promotion.

But there can be a downside of exclusivity—other retailers will penalize a recording in stocking and for in-store visibility because of being excluded from early release. The other drawback is the risk of deterring the music-buying consumer by not having music available on a broad array of retail platforms from the start. An even more expansive exclusive, U2's *Songs of Innocence* album was a "free" download for a limited time to iTunes users. Apple paid an undisclosed fee for every album activated on its iTunes platform. "In the next 24 hours, over a half a billion people are going to have *Songs of Innocence* . . . should they choose to check it out," frontman Bono wrote on U2's website. "People who haven't heard our music, or weren't remotely interested, might play us for the first time because we're in their [iTunes] library." However, retailers were particularly standoffish when the *Songs of Innocence* freebie ran out, saying there is nothing left to sell for an album that is given away free initially.

In other wrinkles to exclusivity, labels try to bolster second-stage release by adding bonus material to the recorded music being sold, reflecting ongoing experimentation to improve the downstream sales for music titles launched initially as exclusives. Compilers of music charts typically reduce or don't count music distributed for free or deeply discounted, which is another drawback because it penalizes chart rankings that influence airplay and consumer perception. Music chart handicaps were also suffered in album promotions involving Jay-Z (Samsung mobile) and Guns N' Roses (Best Buy).

Publicity

Many record companies handle their publicity activities in-house; others have only a small resident staff and engage publicists and public relations (PR) firms to help out. A small label may depend totally on an outside firm or independent publicist for PR.

The publicity campaign attempts to create a buzz that convinces magazines, newspapers, and online outlets to publish content on a record release, a process that may begin when the artist gives an interview. The campaign also includes booking personal appearances on TV, radio, and webcasts. In a technique known as the "satellite tour," the artist conducts a series of interviews with different media outlets back to back over several hours while in a single studio. The name harkens back to the era when a satellite uplink was necessary to connect to media. Among the more desired media outlets are the traditional media—the print magazines—and their associated websites. Monthly print magazines have a lead time of 3 months, so any hope of securing a cover or feature story starts well before an album hits stores and download platforms.

Dailies and weeklies (newspapers and the weekly arts publications) are other types of publications available. These publications tend to focus on local artists and artists playing concerts in the area.

Fanzines are publications with a relatively small consumer base, usually written and published by a fan of an artist or style of music. Although not as widely circulated, the readership includes more proactive consumers.

Advertising

While publicity is desirable because the cost to the label is relatively low, paid advertising has the potential advantage of yielding a large number of controlled **impressions.** Large labels find it profitable, from time to time, to place ads in digital media, magazines, and specialty newspapers. But in general, the music industry has not found multi-million-dollar ad campaigns to be cost-effective. So while movie distributors buy ads in TV's most expensive platform—the Super Bowl telecast— music labels do not (although top acts may get free exposure in the Super Bowl half-time show).

Most consumer advertising either is paid for by the label (and doesn't mention a specific retailer carrying the release) or is **cooperative,** in which case the "co-op" retailer is listed in the ad and pays part of the ad cost directly with cash or indirectly by meeting certain inventory ordering requirements.

Another type of advertising is trade advertising. The label places an ad in publications and websites aimed at companies within the industry—not consumers. It could be as all-encompassing of the music industry as *Billboard* or as specific as *Pollstar* for the live entertainment industry. These ads help in both promoting the release and confirming to the music industry community the label's commitment to its artist. Marketers use the expression *pull-through* to describe advertising or promotion that induces consumers to buy and *push-through* to describe advertising that induces retailers or distributors to order merchandise to put on sale.

Digital Marketing

Promotion, publicity, and advertising efforts are typically also handled by specialists in *digital marketing.* All significant labels have digital marketing teams, whose efforts are augmented by outside agencies given specific assignments to promote releases and artists online. Editorial outlets are barraged with press releases, photos, audio content, and videos hoping for material to get posted and generating a buzz online. Marketing campaigns are anchored on a timeline to unleash initiatives in waves, with each successive wave larger as a recording's release date approaches.

A favorite starting point for recorded music campaigns is usually the artist- or label-controlled media techniques, such as Twitter followings of artists and band websites. Here, the marketing messages are under complete control, and the devoted fan base that receives the message is expected to enthusiastically tell others. When Beyoncé released her eponymously titled album, fans who "liked" her Facebook page were in the first wave (Facebook had a formal partnership deal). Artist-owned media have the most loyal fan base, which is ideal to gradually ignite interest that news and social media outlets then pick up. With artist-owned media and then later other outlets, artists can dribble out content such as interview snippets, pieces of new music, and behind-the-scenes material, either widely or in exclusives with media outlets that agree to aggressively promote the new music.

Music videos and video clips of famous artists are particularly valued by digital outlets, which partner in promotions because star power helps stand out amid the cluttered media landscape. So labels sometimes have revenue-sharing deals for ads placed in and around their content, which means they earn a trickle of revenue even as the content publicizes a new release. In another prong, labels might buy some digital media ads on platforms with which they have formal, but noncash, promotional tie-ins. All the options to mix editorial with advertising or negotiated placement illustrates that the line between advertising and editorial is fuzzier online than in traditional media, which traditionally doesn't guarantee editorial coverage on the condition of a related purchase of advertising.

The publicity, promotion, and paid ads are usually part of a grand plan, and this deliberate interlocking of elements is called *marketing integration*. The belief is that interconnected efforts will drive traffic to digital media placements that might otherwise be ignored, and this integration—elements feeding off each other—is far better than a broadly focused, scattershot approach. Integration can combine traditional and digital media—for example, a paid ad placement in a print magazine that directs readers to a website, which has vast content that gives users an immersive experience.

Another of the plan's goals is to make digital media interactive. The media may be seeded with content that users can customize through modification: Consumers may email to friends music content that they've altered, which serves as a form of viral media. Since the activity of website and email users can often be counted, labels and artists can measure the popularity of individual elements, such as various types of content. Another type of interaction is the forum in which consumers post comments.

Labels and DIY artists are constantly coming up with new digital marketing approaches. Table 14.1 summarizes a few common techniques. For a fuller description of social media resources, see Chapter 26, "The DIY Toolkit."

International Marketing

Multinational recording companies may spend more money and effort promoting releases abroad than they do domestically because the foreign market is a patchwork of territories, each requiring individualized—and often costly—attention. A multinational label must determine whether to have a foreign release occur simultaneously with the U.S. release or whether to test the audience response in the United States (or in another territory) before rolling it out globally. With pervasive record **piracy**, the trend for some time has been to release simultaneously so that legitimate music is available as an alternative to unauthorized versions. In fact, the artist's recording contract may specify the countries where the label is to make recordings available simultaneously with domestic release.

Foreign promotions cannot be handled like those in the United States. The big record companies have staffed affiliates in 40 to 50 foreign territories that have the responsibility of releasing and promoting the firm's product. In all these territories, differences in the radio landscape, satellite and cable availability, law, language, culture, and buying power require different approaches. Among the strongest foreign markets for breaking new U.S. recordings are Japan, Germany, the United Kingdom, France, the Netherlands, and Australia (see Chapter 30).

Record Distribution

In 1999, at the peak of the CD era, recorded music trade group the RIAA reported 45% of recorded music retail sales came from record stores and 53% from other channels for physical product such as mass merchants, Amazon.com, and mail order. Legitimate digital downloads weren't yet a real factor. Years later, the distribution landscape has been dramatically reordered by the shift in delivery formats.

U.S. recorded music revenue from digital downloads surpassed physical sales such as CDs a few years ago. Today, specialty brick-and-mortar record stores are mostly a memory, and the remaining CD sales are concentrated at mail order from online or mass-merchant stores such as Walmart and Best Buy electronics. Product travels

Table 14.1   **Selected Digital Marketing Opportunities**

Email lists assembled by label. Emails are most useful if the label's music is focused by genre, because the audience is then potentially predisposed to all the music offered. Emails usually contain multiple hyperlinks to third-party pages related to the label's acts. To spur consumer interest to actually open the email, contests and prizes are often offered.

Email lists assembled by the artist. Because they are associated with the talent, these are opened far more often than emails from labels or corporate entities and are less likely to get caught in users' spam filters. Artist emails can be a jumping-off point for powerful viral buzz if forwarded to a user's acquaintances because the endorsement comes from a personal friend. These emails can carry photos, touring news, snippets of songs, and links to radio stations where fans can ask for songs to be added to playlists. Artists often let labels step in to manage and market to these lists because labels may have greater expertise and resources.

Label websites. These tend to present brief explanations of albums and bands in a brochure-like format. Links to related third-party websites are essential to get users more deeply immersed.

Artist websites. Fans demand to voice their views, so an essential element is the capability to host discussions where users can post comments and band members provide blog commentaries. Content such as news and photos should be more personal than that found on a label or third-party website. Websites for new artists launch with little traffic, and there is no assurance traffic will ever become sizable. Convincing other reputable websites to link to and embedding popular keywords lifts search rankings.

Retailer websites. Online commerce destinations communicate with signage and overt recommendation messages such as "we think you'll like this." Labels and artists sometimes negotiate deals offering to direct traffic to online retailers in exchange for promotional support. The goal is to get recorded music displayed beyond the simple alphabetical listing.

Third-party websites. These are crucial because they already have substantial traffic, and music videos are easiest to place because platforms crave music and flashy visuals. Vevo, YouTube, Yahoo!Music, MTV Networks, music fan websites, and music news websites are leading destinations. Videos need precise artist, song, genre, and message keyword labeling (meta-tagging) to lift rankings in consumer searches. Well-known artists and their labels want to strike promotion partnerships with high-traffic websites, which allow them to broaden their Web circulation, since label and artist websites have limited audiences. The ad-revenue sharing deals offered by hosts help shape label decisions about where to concentrate promotion for label videos.

Blogs. Many music bloggers have established Web traffic that makes them useful for publicity and promotions. Journalists and DJs tend to be prolific bloggers.

Online music stores. Many download retailers such as iTunes closely manage their environment, so few opportunities exist to barge in with ad hoc publicity. The only real publicity options come through formal joint promotion deals. Emerging bands can make headway with The Orchard, Tune Core, SirGroovy, and others, which usually work with up-and-coming bands and independent labels lacking significant in-house digital operations to circulate music in cyberspace.

Social media. Most artists have an official presence on Facebook, Twitter, and MySpace, which are prized because they have huge built-in audiences to support new album releases and concert dates. The ability to feed a stream of personal comments gives Twitter a blog-like capability. Content is usually a mixture of professional and personal news that fits the social atmosphere.

Hashtag conversations. A component of social marketing, hashtags (#TheBigRelease) initiate long-running online conversations, mainly via Twitter and Instagram. This is a tactic to engage and rally an already dedicated base of fans.

Celebrity endorsements. Artists are treasured by their followers, so a first wave of sketchy announcements often starts with Twitter and Facebook to "reward" fans with early news. Marketers preplan timelines for several waves of messages, each more detailed and urgent than the previous.

Talent tie-in promotions. Artists engage in online discussions with fans, sit for interviews, concoct online "events" like reunions or concert kickoff parties, and post content of a personal nature in promotions with digital destinations. In exchange for artist involvement, the platforms agree to highlight recorded music for longer time periods and deliver specified audiences. Online platforms in music commerce and platforms attracting the music's target audience demographic make ideal tie-in partners.

Search engine marketing (SEO). Labels optimize websites to pull traffic and will buy keywords if a new release has potential to attract a new audience. All traffic should be funneled to one URL address to maximize ranking in search results. It's expensive to buy keywords, so this advertising is used sparingly.

three avenues to the marketplace: physical (largely CDs), digital downloads where users retain copies, and streams where music is consumed online but not retained. Physical CDs get stocked in brick-and-mortar stores via mass merchants, a dwindling lineup of music specialty retailers, general entertainment specialty stores, supermarkets, and discounters. In the albums category, new releases, which require expensive marketing, account for 60% of unit sales. Older catalog product requires little marketing support and accounts for the remaining 40%. Besides singles and albums, the product mix includes other configurations (such as ringtones and ringbacks) that are purchased by the consumer. In summary, the distribution picture is a jumbled mix of competing approaches, with the ascendancy of digital over physical the major theme.

Digital Distribution

Once perceived as only a threat to the legitimate business, online music has evolved to become a key channel for legitimate distribution since labels began licensing their music to online platforms. Apple's iTunes online store, which launched in 2003, gave a big lift to digital music with its simple pricing of $0.99 for many singles, a closed ecosystem so music could not easily be pirated, and a vast base of iPod portable players. By 2014, iTunes confirmed that it sold its 35th billion song worldwide, which by then had a catalog numbering 26 million music tracks, establishing iTunes as the world's most important music "store." However, the music industry grumbled that iTunes' success gave Apple too much power in pricing and packaging of digital music.

Within a few years, nonphysical formats grew to command the majority of U.S. recorded music revenue whether downloaded or streamed, sold by subscription or by track or by album equivalent, or experienced through a handheld device or a desktop computer. Subscriptions offer unlimited access to a specified pool of music for a flat monthly fee. In another variation on the business model, the access may be free to the user, with the labels receiving a share of the advertising revenue generated by the online platform hosting the service.

Warner Music, one of the big three recorded music giants, said in an annual report to shareholders,

> We have integrated the sale of digital content into all aspects of our business, including A&R, marketing, promotion and distribution. Our business development executives work closely with A&R departments to ensure that while a record is being produced, digital assets are also created with all distribution channels in mind, including streaming services, social networking sites, online portals and music-centered destinations. We also work side-by-side with our online and mobile partners to test new concepts. . . . We also continue to experiment with ways to promote our artists through digital channels with initiatives such as windowing of content and creating product bundles by combining our existing album assets with other assets, such as bonus tracks and music videos. Digital distribution channels create greater marketing flexibility that can be more cost effective.

A drawback to labels from the digital revolution is the "unbundling" of music-purchasing behavior. Consumers tend to buy individual songs priced at $0.69 to $1.29 online as downloads, which are far less costly than $15 albums with nine or more songs that dominated purchases in the CD era. One benefit to the record labels of digital downloads is that labels get a higher percentage of the consumer spending than with physical product. When record labels or bands deliver downloads from their own websites, they don't pay a fee to a middleman or music retailer.

Some digital media outlets also sell physical CDs and thus follow in the steps of yesteryear's mail order (when orders were made by phone or mail instead of via a website). Digital media outlets for music sales include iTunes, Amazon.com, Walmart.com, BarnesandNoble.com, Google Play, and fye.com. Traditional brick-and-mortar retailers, including mass merchants, are in the mix by offering an online service to complement their stores. All the online retailers replaced the "music clubs" that started in the 1950s and used printed catalogs to sell physical music products at low prices to members who committed to buying a certain quantity. Often, the member's first LPs, audiocassettes, or CDs were bought for just pennies, but consumers also committed to purchasing full-priced products later. The most famous music club—Columbia House Records—launched in 1955 and flourished for years. Its successor company filed for bankruptcy in 2015 due to a steady decline since a peak in 1996.

If online downloads and streaming were the first wave of the digital revolution and subscription music a second, then digital 3.0 is consumers storing their legally purchased media content of all kinds—music, movies, and electronic books—in remote online digital "lockers." We wait, as we always do, to see what new technologies will do to shift the dynamics of nonphysical distribution.

Physical Distribution

For physical product, the challenges to labels of manufacturing, shipping, and managing inventory add substantial layers of cost. As physical product has declined in market share, the large-run CD replication facilities have become a less ubiquitous link in the chain to deliver music to consumers. As a result, for nonhit product, *manufacturing on demand* emerged, where CDs are manufactured in small quantities as they are ordered, such as with Amazon-owned CreateSpace.

In physical distribution efforts, labels distribute CDs and other offline products in specialty record/DVD/game stores, supermarkets, mass merchants, and discount stores. Such distribution is a challenging business because a great deal of capital can be tied up in massive inventory, profit margins tend to be slim, and there are many thousands of unique products (called stock-keeping units, or **SKUs**) that must be provided to retailers quickly and efficiently. Several kinds of distribution and wholesaling organizations may serve as intermediaries to get merchandise to those who actually sell the product to consumers. (Figure 14.1 illustrates several pathways for major-label SKUs to reach the end user.)

Types of Distributors

Majors. A handful of major multinational distributors are integrated with the biggest record companies (as outlined in Chapter 11). These behemoths serve as umbrella organizations for a large number of labels, collectively accounting for the lion's share of records sold in the United States. These majors offer merchandise through their own far-flung distribution organizations, historically characterized by large staffs located in branch offices. Major distributor branch offices traditionally have two divisions. One handles regional promotion; the other concerns itself with distribution and sales. The distributor's promotion staff coordinates with the promotion staff of each affiliated label.

Figure 14.1   Record Distribution and Retailing

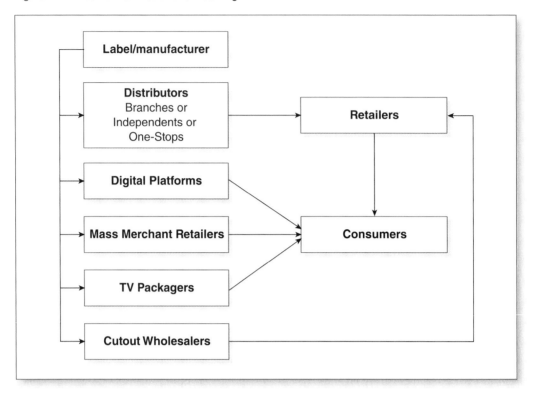

Independents. The majors don't do it all. A small but significant share of the business is in the hands of independent distributors who provide services for hundreds of independent labels and artists who release their own recordings. Independents, who don't handle product sourced from the majors, usually provide promotion services as well. Most have a staff that calls or visits retailers, delivers merchandise, sets up store displays, makes deals with websites for music downloads, and operates online music sales operations—much like the major label branch offices do.

One-Stops. In the 1940s, distributors called **one-stops** formed to offer a full music product line to jukebox operators and small retailers that could not get the attention of the big labels or big wholesalers. They handled merchandise delivery and setup of in-store promotions to mom-and-pop stores. One-stops typically sold product (sourced from major labels and some independents) in low volume at high unit prices. In recent years, they have declined along with the rest of physical distribution.

Rack Jobbers. This is a service business that places shelves ("racks") in retail outlets such as car washes and convenience stores and is responsible for selecting product and restocking displays. Consumers patronizing the stores don't realize that the music racks are the property and responsibility of an unseen third party that is either subleasing the space or otherwise splitting the revenue with the host merchant. Today rack jobbers are common only in specialized niches, such as offering Latin product to retailers catering to Hispanic clientele.

Retail Merchandising

From the distributor or label warehouse, the physical goods flow to retailers. Retail competition is bruising, particularly as sales of physical CDs dwindle. For online commerce, cyberspace retailers have unlimited "shelves," so there's no running out of stock with digital copies. For physical goods, nimble retail managers are constantly juggling the dollars set aside to buy inventory (called **open to buy**), scrambling to advertise and build excitement in the aisles, and setting prices that will allow them to protect market share (by being low enough) and profit margins (by being high enough). Winning is by no means guaranteed. The categories of retailers that dominate the business have shifted dramatically over the years.

Mass-Merchant Chain Stores

The same "big-box" transformation in retail exemplified by Wal-Mart that has swept over many kinds of merchandise has remade the landscape of music retailing. As recently as the 1990s, the majority of CDs and recorded cassettes were purchased at independent or chain music-only record stores. Since then, mass merchants such as Target have commanded the biggest slice of the business in physical product.

The mass merchants—which are now the masters of retailing in the brick-and-mortar arena—have amassed such clout that in many cases, they can dictate prices. They can even demand changes in the music itself to meet the objections of their core middle-market audience, such as revised versions of CDs that don't contain crude lyrics. The major labels tend to sell direct to these big-box merchants, thereby eliminating the expense of a middleman wholesaler.

Reflecting this transfer of marketplace clout, some big acts agree to release their CDs only through a single mass merchant or to give the mass merchant an exclusive early window. In exchange, the mass merchant agrees to accept a large quantity of CDs with no or limited returns of unsold merchandise.

From time to time, labels have tried special tie-ups with other kinds of retailers, such as restaurant and coffee chains. In a sign of dwindling physical sales, Starbucks stopped highlighting CDs at its stores in 2015, after offering a limited selection of CD music for years. In the same year, Starbucks made Spotify the music supplier for its company-owned stores in the United States, Canada, and the United Kingdom, reflecting the ascendency of digital streamed music. Their tie-up includes providing Spotify reward points with Starbucks purchases and having special Spotify playlist music in its stores.

Entertainment Retailers

The type of retailer that once fueled the recorded music business—the record store—has been on a long slide toward obsolescence. Iconic record retail brands such as Tower Records, Sam Goody, and Virgin Megastore shriveled away. The surviving specialty record stores of yore have largely evolved into mass merchants of another stripe—broader-based entertainment software chains with DVD, game, and music product on their shelves. This kind of retailer may be categorized by some as a record store, but recorded music might not constitute the majority of its sales.

Parent Advisory Label

Labeling music to identify crude content is an on-and-off hot-button issue for the music industry. The Recording Industry Association of America (RIAA) created the Parent Advisory Label (PAL) as "a notice to consumers that recordings identified by this logo may contain strong language or depictions of violence, sex or substance abuse. Parental discretion is advised."

Photo by Robert Marich.

When lyrics are flagged, the RIAA's PAL logo is typically applied prominently to the outside of the permanent packaging and in advertising. For digital versions, RIAA instructs the presentation "shall clearly and conspicuously communicate the presence of PAL content," and RIAA recommends those warnings be incorporated "at all stages of the purchasing process" from browsing to shopping cart checkout.

The website of RIAA states that, in some instances, record companies recommend that an artist re-record certain songs or modify lyrics, creating an "edited" version that does not require the PAL warning notice.

Labeling to advise parents began in 1985 under pressure from a consumer group and U.S. Senate hearings on songs with crude lyrics. These days, a very small proportion of albums carry PAL warnings. While the music industry addressed the issue, in general the music industry exerts less self-restraint than the movie/DVD and video game industries. Indeed, while labels work out content problems with acts after albums are recorded, film director employment contracts routinely specify that directors deliver a movie that will achieve a specified audience classification. In addition, the movie industry goes to great lengths to "grade" all its releases with multilevel audience classification ratings.

One type of relatively small record store may prosper when it is well managed and situated where retail rents are cheap: the proprietor who earns the confidence of a small but loyal clientele and stocks the particular kind of music that appeals to that community—such as blues, urban, Asian, or classical. Even vinyl clings to life. Some such battles for retail survival are being won, but the war to preserve the traditional neighborhood record retailer is largely lost.

Cutouts and Repackaging

Consumers are always looking for bargains, and so there is a lively niche market selling deeply discounted music. This merchandise has long been known as **cutouts,** although that term is slowly slipping into disuse. But the bulk purchase of slow-moving CDs to be resold at sharply reduced prices remains a significant business.

These can include excess CDs from current titles and also familiar oldies with low or no royalties payable to the artists (thereby facilitating the low pricing). The retail outlets include discount dollar stores, regular convenience stores, restaurants, car washes, and truck stops.

For years, cutout merchants and repackagers have been able to sell "re-releases" or "new" releases of the big-name band hits of the 1940s and genre **compilations** such as *Now That's What I Call Music.* Perennial repertoire also comes from early rock-and-roll hits and reissues of country music. Direct response marketers buy relatively cheap ad inventory and typically acquire merchandise at a discount from normal wholesale pricing. The resulting commercials are well known to TV viewers who suffer from insomnia.

Retail Terms and Inducements

The recorded music industry has generally offered retailers generous returns policies on physical media such as CDs and the revived vinyl LP records, allowing the return of a substantial portion of purchases for credit if the goods don't sell (this was up to 100% in music's boom years when labels wanted their products to dominate store shelves). By federal law, distributors cannot give individual direct accounts special discounts. All must get the same discount offer, although the value of that discount will vary depending mostly on volume. Labels can, however, offer more co-op advertising or prerelease exclusivity to selected retailers.

Record companies, of course, always want eye-catching placement within the store. Once a recording is out of a routine location such as alphabetical bins, labels believe a consumer is more apt to make an impulse purchase—the same principle that leads to a candy display at the supermarket checkout counter. Many retailers offer a variety of opportunities for a label to purchase what is referred to as "price and positioning." Most of these programs include having CDs both on sale and in a special location, and highlighted in "listening stations" where consumers can play select music in store. Examples of special treatment include **end caps,** or racks at the end of aisles or in prominent locations in the store where a SKU will be on display at a sale price. Sometimes these end caps promote multiple SKUs and have a theme, such as "music of the holidays" or "June is blues month."

In addition to price and positioning, record companies may try to have point-of-purchase (**POP**) displays set up in the retail store, announcing the availability of product. POP displays might include one-sheet posters, banners, cardboard stand-ups, special display racks, window displays, flags and streamers, and perhaps swag that the merchant can give away. POP displays can be costly to distribute, and thus the technique isn't universally employed. Some retailers view POP displays as a distraction and won't accept them from manufacturers even if they are free.

Sometimes a retailer gives a release better positioning in exchange for free or discounted CDs to sell. These CDs are referred to as "cleans" because they are "clean" of any of the markings they would have if they were for promotional use only. "Promos" are altered or labeled in some other way, indicating that they are not for sale to the public. The wide distribution of free goods can be problematic for artists, because free goods may depress an artist's royalty income.

A hidden force in the marketplace is MAP (minimum advertised pricing) where retailers agree not to market music lower than a specified floor price. MAP is tricky to implement because it borders on price fixing, which is not legal. Music labels and their distribution affiliates have used MAP to prevent retailers from price wars, which debase the perceived value of recorded music. MAP most affects large discount retailers from undercutting smaller merchants by threatening those outlets that violate MAP policies (such as price floors) with a temporary suspension of co-op advertising funds and other promotion support.

Music Business Association

The Music Business Association (formerly known as National Association of Recording Merchandisers, or NARM) is the nonprofit trade association that represents commerce of recorded music in all channels: physical media, online, and mobile. It serves as an exchange for business information for its members, mounts marketing initiatives to interest consumers in buying music, and organizes industry events.

Chapter Takeaways

- When planning a launch campaign, label marketers should employ a SWOT analysis—examining strengths, weaknesses, opportunities, and threats.

- In some genres, promoters spend considerable effort to convince radio stations and streaming platforms to add new records to playlists, hoping to alert music lovers to a new title's availability.

- Successful publicity campaigns, prized because they can be inexpensive to execute, often hinge on getting artist interviews in print and electronic media.

- Paid advertising can augment a marketing campaign but often is secondary to promotion and publicity.

- Multinational record companies dominate distribution of music, but independent distributors and other wholesalers fill vital roles in feeding product to retailers.

- For physical product, over the years, "big-box" mass merchants and entertainment software chains have eclipsed the role of the once-common neighborhood record store.

Key Terms

- co-op   (p. 251)
- cutouts   (p. 258)
- digital marketing (p. 251)
- end cap   (p. 259)
- MAP (minimum advertised pricing)   (p. 259)
- marketing integration   (p. 252)
- mass merchant   (p. 257)

- Music Business Association (p. 260)
- Parent Advisory Label (PAL) (p. 258)
- payola   (p. 249)
- playlist   (p. 246)
- price and positioning   (p. 259)
- product manager   (p. 247)

- Recording Industry Association of America (RIAA)   (p. 258)
- returns   (p. 257)
- satellite tour   (p. 250)
- SKU (stock-keeping units) (p. 255)
- station formats   (p. 248)
- SWOT   (p. 245)

Discussion Questions

1. How would you design a marketing plan for an artist's new album if you had a limited marketing budget? What would you add to the plan if you had a larger budget?

2. What are some creative promotions and marketing plans you have heard of? What made that plan successful?

3. What are the advantages to giving one retail outlet a limited-time exclusivity to sell a specific recording and what are the drawbacks?

4. What are the promotional trade-offs between uncensored lyrics that are true to an artist's vision and having that music labeled with the Parental Advisory Label for explicit content?

5. What are some techniques for selling music in brick-and-mortar stores?

CHAPTER 15

Marketplace Research

Understanding the Consumer

For decades, recorded music was strictly a creative-driven business built on the song, artist, and gut intuition of executives. The philosophy was if those forces aligned, music sales would surely follow. Labels treated radio stations as their most relevant customer, with little interest or understanding of the identity of music buyers—the folks who actually plunked down the money to purchase their products.

"Music critics get their records for free so their opinions usually don't matter."

—Marilyn Manson

Technology has changed all that, for two reasons. First, the art and science of consumer research became more sophisticated, enabling stakeholders to receive better answers to questions about consumer behavior and attitudes. And second, new distribution technology threatened the business model of selling physical media, forcing labels especially to fight harder, and smarter, for every dollar.

Until the 1990s, research of record "sales" data was generally imprecise and too often failed to make clear the distinctions between the figures for merchandise actually sold and the huge amounts of unsold stock returned by retailers. Whole genres and stylistic trends were underreported (such as country music) or overreported (hard rock), questionable "hits" climbed the charts in mysterious ways, and misleading manipulation of the crude methodology was commonplace. Part of the problem was that the estimates were projected from a retail sample that was neither randomized nor big enough.

Left: Grammy Award ®© NARAS.

But research tools and sample bases improved steadily. In the first decade of the 21st century, labels under financial pressure were forced to better understand music consumers because online piracy cut into sales of recorded music. In recent years, there has been a pronounced rise in the use of statistical analysis to solve business problems of all kinds, employing a tactic that has risen in sophistication to become a discipline in itself—**analytics.**

In the industry today, analytics researchers and product managers collect and crunch data to solve the problem of how to entice both discovery and sales of music. These professionals measure the impact from advertising, publicity such as artist interviews, radio play, promotions with third parties, and even "accidental" leaks of artist music done on purpose to generate attention. What impact? It's in buzz online, news media coverage, radio play, concert ticket sales, sales of recorded music, and licensed merchandise transactions. Analysis of cause and impacts helps guide decisions on how to allocate marketing resources. Analytics can also spot music trends and thus also influence concert bookings, airplay decisions, signings of acts by labels, and outsiders contemplating contracting with music interests, such as for licensed merchandise.

In addition, analytics can point to niches where new demand could be spurred by a combination of delivery of the right kind of music to specific kinds of fans, pricing, promotion, and retailing. All this is done by a mix of on-staff label executives, artist management staff, and outside analytics vendors with a broad revenue base from multiple clients to support extensive data gathering. Collected data and analysis are often crammed onto single-screen displays called *dashboards,* which executives can scan when formulating plans and allocating money and personnel. All the major labels assemble compact data displays on their acts to help guide decision making—Warner Music's is called Artist Dashboard, while the Universal Music platform is Artist Portal.

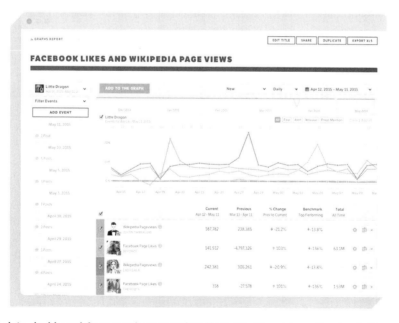

A data dashboard from music researcher Next Big Sound logs Facebook likes and Wikipedia page views for four artists in a line chart.

Photo used with permission of Next Big Sound.

Data always need human interpretation and insights from past experience. For instance, the youth audience practically lives online while senior citizens often don't, so it's statistically less likely that a social media-centric effort will appeal to mature adults. Experience matching data with music sales provides insights about instances when marketplace buzz doesn't translate into music sales. The dilemma is similar to the experience in another era when radio airplay didn't always translate to success at the cash register.

Music research can also go into nonmarketplace areas such as monitoring airplay for music royalty collections, assembling lists of music for business searches, breaking down songs to analyze audience appeal based on their audio characteristics, and corporate credit/investment analysis of industry companies. The Web experience, whether as part of a sales transaction or simply as a tool to spur engagement, is increasingly shaped through the continuing refinement of the sources and tools.

Reflecting a newfound thirst for actionable intelligence, the music industry's big companies bought or joined forces with a slew of analytics data outfits: In 2015, Universal Music Group formed joint venture Global Music Data Alliance (GMDA) with advertising giant Havas Group, and separately trade group the Music Business Association (successor to the trade group NARM) partnered with Audiomonitor to receive ongoing insights on music consumption. Internet streamer Spotify bought music data/app outfit The Echo Nest in 2014. Apple, which owns iTunes, bought social media analytics startup Topsy Labs in 2013. Concert juggernaut Live Nation bought analytics compiler BigChampagne in 2011. Performance rights organization ASCAP cofounded monitoring service Mediaguide in 2002, although it later closed.

Most consumer research in music falls into three general categories:

- Periodic surveys measure unit sales (such as a count of albums or singles) and track consumers' online activities when pursuing music. This information is typically delivered at set times on a corporate subscription basis so a large number of industry players receive a steady stream of data.

- Consumer attitude research reports may be **one-off** or infrequent (such as quarterly), which typically mesh findings from consumer interviews with sales data. The surveys are sold and used widely in industry.

- Then there is "custom research," where an entity such as a trade group, artist manager, or record label hires a research company to report on a desired topic. The full report won't be sold to others. The custom research report doesn't fit any specific format.

Techniques include tracking transactions at the point of sale (POS)—such as scanning a barcode at a cash register or counting an iTunes download—interviewing consumers individually in shopping malls, gathering several consumers in one place for small and intimate focus groups, begging consumers to fill out online surveys, or interrupting the evening meal with intrusive telephone calls.

Some of the more exotic online data present values for consumer engagement and also return on investment (cost of extra sales generated from specific marketing initiatives). Users of consumer research include record labels, music wholesalers, music distributors, performing artists, personal managers, booking agents, retail stores, new media commerce outfits, concert promoters, concert venue operators, and the investment community. A key point of contention is who sets the research agenda and who owns and controls the data.

Research Topics

The Charts

The growing music industry interest in consumer research replaces a fixation for decades on measuring music popularity solely by the **charts**, which are lists of most popular music typically associated with trade publications. Music trade newspaper *Billboard* publishes the most widely quoted charts in part because they are posted for free online. Such music rankings are now ubiquitous since online sellers such as iTunes post lists of top sellers, while other music trade publications post various hit lists. In some cases, online platforms will provide specific unit sales and play data for each song, in addition to its overall ranking. Nearly every category of music has its own chart, some more than one.

New charts emerge in response to turns in the marketplace. When the popularity of pay-per-download services such as Apple's iTunes and Napster 2.0 helped revive the single in 2003, *Billboard* introduced the Hot Digital Songs chart to monitor sales of downloads. In 2012, *Billboard* added online streaming play by services such as Spotify and Rhapsody to its broadcast radio data to calculate the flagship Hot 100 songs. In 2014, the *Billboard 200* album chart added streaming (1,500 streams count as one album transaction) and single digital song sales (12-track purchases equal an album) to its ranking criteria.

Demographics

An important yardstick for analyzing the marketplace is the characteristics of consumers—age, gender, ethnicity, income, geographical location, and so on. This is called **demographic** information, referred to in research as "demos" (and is in no way related to "demos" that are demonstration recordings shopped to labels by acts seeking recording contracts!). For example, see Figure 15.1, which reports that for 2014, those ages 18 to 50 were above average ("over-indexed") in terms of buying recorded music while those older underperformed. The same simple bar chart can reveal multiple insights. For example, in that year of transition to a streaming model, a majority of all CDs were purchased by those older than 35, while a majority of all downloads were purchased by those who were younger.

By putting a microscope on the different demographic segments, marketers glean insights into slices of music buyers to target them efficiently. This represents a major mind shift from the music industry's traditional mass-market approach. If labels can identify and sell effectively to the consumer segments (such as early teen girls or men ages 18–24), then those segments can be piled up on a brick-by-brick basis to increase overall music sales. It sounds simple to target consumer segments. But the trick is to understand consumers and their behavior in order to minimize marketing and distribution waste when selling music; otherwise, a big expensive marketing blast reaches too many consumers in the wrong demos (who are unlikely to be buyers).

Record Categorization

It's easier to describe something, and thus to sell it, if it fits into a neat category. The reality in music, however, is that categories constantly morph as new trends emerge and old styles fade. An album seemingly belonging to one genre may "cross over" to one or more other genres. It may appear in more than one genre chart or play on two radio stations in the same city with seemingly different formats.

For many years, the record-buying public has repeatedly demonstrated that it is attracted by the sound of the music, not its type. Table 15.1 illustrates the impact of

Figure 15.1   U.S. Recorded Music Unit Sales Share by Consumer Age in 2014

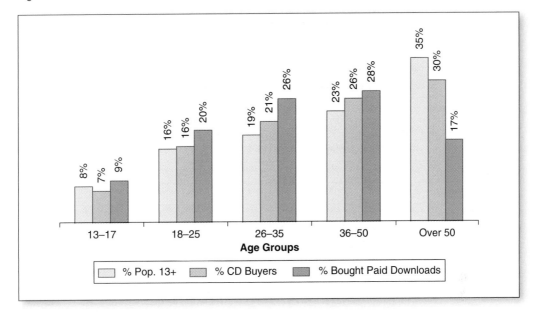

Source: MusicWatch.

Note: The far-left bar "Population Ages 13+" in each age group cluster is the baseline for a demographic; when "CD Buyers" and "Bought Paid Downloads" bars are higher, the age group outperforms other cohorts in legitimate consumption of recorded music; if those bars are lower than the baseline, the age group underperforms.

this dilemma on research results. It reports album sales by genre, but albums perceived as belonging to multiple genres are counted here in multiple categories.

Stylistic Preferences

Because music is in a state of constant development and change, acts—particularly in the pop, rock, and hip-hop fields—can go from star to has-been status, sometimes within the same year. Artists who attach themselves to musical trends (or who are marketed that way by their record companies) are often washed up once the public tires of the trend. Those artists who show the ability to transcend trends tend to have the longest and most successful careers.

Sometimes, however, shifts in the musical climate are too dramatic for artists to successfully navigate. For example, when Beatlemania hit America in the mid-1960s, pop crooners such as Bobby Darin and the Four Seasons saw their fan base virtually disappear overnight. Similarly in the early 1990s, Nirvana's punk-influenced grunge sound made the slick pop-metal of bands like Poison and Warrant immediately passé. Some genres perceived at the time as fads have surprised the "experts" with their longevity. Despite what some assumed to be a narrow cultural appeal, rap music has skyrocketed in popularity around the world, today rivaling rock for social relevance and becoming one of the top-selling music genres.

Research Revolution

Today, charts, demographics, and stylistic preferences are only a small part of the research story. A big area of research is music consumption of nonphysical media, a field that allows companies to determine where to make music available in the digital world

Table 15.1   Online Consumer Buzz by Music Genre

Genre	% Mentions and Plays
Pop/rock[a]	24%
Rap	11%
R&B	9%
Electronic	9%
Pop	8%
Rock	8%
Indie rock	7%
Country	7%
Classical	6%
World	4%
Latin	2%
Reggae	2%
Metal	1%
Other	2%
Total	**100%**

Source: Next Big Sound.

Note: Quantifies average distribution of mentions and plays on Spotify, YouTube, Vevo, Facebook, Twitter, Wikipedia, SoundCloud, and Instagram.

[a] Pop/rock is commercial-oriented rock; note pure pop and pure rock are ranked separately.

and how to price it to maximize revenue and profit. Advances in technology allow many actions of a Web surfer to be monitored so, in the online area at least, it is possible to build a vast historical record of detailed consumer activity. DIY artists can monitor the use of their music and their fan activities online with readily available digital media tools, as explored in Chapter 26. One drawback is that identities of Web surfers might not be known, so activity can't always be matched up with consumer demographics. (Of course, for privacy advocates, this drawback is a safeguard against abuse.)

College students make up an audience segment of particular interest. They are big consumers of music and have a propensity to use the latest media technology, which makes them trendsetters. Yet, they are a difficult audience to research as access to university emails is restricted and students are often just seasonal residents at their schools.

Pricing and what consumers value in terms of product offers form another field of keen study. In the digital era, a lot can be bundled in a music product purchase: coupons for ringtones, coupons for free or discounted digital music downloads, online fan club subscriptions tied to artists, online commerce selling band and album merchandise, discounts to concert tickets, and, of course, CDs.

Data Sources

In the analog era, researchers could at best collect small amounts of data from a small base of activity that would hopefully represent the entire marketplace. In the digital era, vast amounts of consumer activity can be tracked, which means research more completely represents the music-consuming population. It's a vast landscape because consumers operate billions of Internet devices globally. To easily aggregate many kinds of data on behavior, preferences, and demographics, audience tracking firms set up big consumer samples—which are larger than ever possible in the analog era. Just one vendor, for example, may have millions of media users in its global consumer panel. Research suppliers, of course, come in all sizes and with many specializations, ranging from music analytics, to consulting, to music exposure tracking. The long list of vendors includes BigChampagne, comScore, Edison Research, The Echo Nest, Forrester Research, Gracenote, Harris Interactive, Ipsos MediaCT, Mediabase, Mark Mulligan's MIDiA Consulting, Music Ally, MusicWatch, Music Xray, Next Big Sound, Nielsen, NetBase Live Pulse, and Shazam.

Digital platforms control a wealth of data on their listeners' music consumption, and many display counters showing traffic numbers. Much more information is collected behind the scenes. When consumers load mobile apps to their devices, their app activity can be precisely monitored and the identity of the consumer is known (which provides demographic information). Some music platforms give audience listening data to artists and their managers for their own music, but of course that provides no insights into the broader marketplace. Further, comprehensive market research is conducted (or commissioned) by the labels' trade group, the Recording Industry Association of America (RIAA), and its global counterpart, the International Federation of the Phonographic Industry (IFPI). Here is a representative sampling of research sources:

Nielsen

The sprawling Nielsen research conglomerate tracks music sales, airplay, and streaming within its Nielsen Music unit, whose services range from syndicated data reports issued periodically to custom research focused on music consumers. Another division collects consumer data on mobile devices involving music such as ringtones/ringbacks. In late 2013, Nielsen acquired rival research outfit Arbitron, which measured radio audiences. The Arbitron name has been phased out, and its service is now called Nielsen Audio.

Nielsen Broadcast Data Systems

Nielsen's Broadcast Data Systems (Nielsen BDS) electronically logs music played on selected radio stations and TV channels 24 hours a day in the United States, Canada, and Mexico (and has historical airplay data for numerous European countries). The Nielsen BDS service "listens" to broadcasts and recognizes songs and commercials by the "fingerprint" from encoded audio. Nielsen BDS tracks music on terrestrial radio, satellite radio, and TV channels devoted to music videos.

This methodology is far more accurate than having human researchers listen and log music manually or relying on playlists supplied by outlets that aren't necessarily eager for the outside world to dissect their programming moves. By detecting actual airplay, Nielsen BDS's computer-based technology prevents programmers from giving false airplay reports. However, even Nielsen BDS is not beyond manipulation. In 2003 and 2004, several labels attempted to influence chart positions by buying cheap overnight radio advertising in small and medium markets, where the songs in ads could be misidentified as regular airplay. Nielsen now requires a minimum of 1 minute of song play before music is logged.

Nielsen SoundScan

SoundScan—which like BDS is owned by research giant Nielsen—tabulates unit sales of recorded music in a number of countries. It tracks both physical product (such as CDs) and digital downloads, and its data are used to help compile some *Billboard* music charts. In the United States, the SoundScan sales trackers are linked to download platforms and barcodes from brick-and-mortar retail outlets representing more than 90% of the nation's record sales. Walmart and Target are among store chains reporting. SoundScan uses that big base to project unit sales estimates for the full marketplace. Labels and artists report sales of recorded music at qualifying concerts and music events. They pay a SoundScan registration fee. Deeply discounted recorded music is not eligible for such self-reporting, as are sales at certain types of venues like concerts at libraries and churches.

SoundScan's sales tabulations are offered to the music industry on a subscription basis. Many media outlets reprint the SoundScan lists, and thus the service has visibility in the consumer market. Founded in 1991, SoundScan was acquired a few years later by what is now Nielsen.

Before SoundScan, record companies lacked current sales data to forecast record sales, which guided manufacturing decisions. Even approximate net sales figures were not available until the retailer had shipped unsold product back to the label, which is known as *returns*. Some retailers neglected to include country, rhythm-and-blues, and other genre product in their lists of the top 200 albums sold, relegating those releases to specialty charts, even though they might have been outselling more mainstream titles. What's more, the old system was subject to manipulation by recording companies that targeted certain stores for extra promotion and by bribable store managers and radio programmers. SoundScan eliminated much of the potential for inaccuracies in reporting by tracking barcoded POS activity.

Mediabase

Radio airplay/programming is also monitored across the United States and Canada by Mediabase, a unit of radio group broadcaster iHeartMedia (formerly Clear Channel). Besides logging airplay, the service originates charts ranking music popularity and provides subscribers with analytic tools. Mediabase also provides monitoring of a host of other programming elements—promotions, contests, and morning-show components, for example—that go beyond the identification capabilities of computer-based-only airplay monitoring. Mediabase also operates the consumer music-testing website, www.ratethemusic.com.

MusicWatch

MusicWatch analyzes purchasing patterns, consumption of recorded music in physical and digital formats, music listening habits, and demographics of the music audience. The researcher publishes syndicated reports and also conducts custom analysis. Its website is www.musicwatchinc.com.

Music Xray

By harnessing computer power to analyze acoustic characteristics of music and amass human feedback from listeners online, some researchers combine analytics, music, and digital media. One such independent service is Music Xray, which is an online music discovery community that includes fans and also industry professionals. The feedback identifies strengths and weaknesses of music by comparing to other songs in the Xray community, and Music Xray also says its high-ranked tunes come to the attention of industry pros that peruse its website.

Next Big Sound

Next Big Sound, which in 2015 was bought by Internet radio outfit Pandora, was founded by college grads in 2008 and funded by venture capitalists. It mines online data regarding consumer activity and buzz for music and sales. Page visits, likes, and followers are among the 200 online metrics tracked. Next Big Sound helps identify strengths, weaknesses, shifts in the marketplace, comparisons to peers and *benchmarks* (meaning the standard against which peers in a group are judged), and areas of opportunity for music products and artists. See Chapter 27 for a profile of the company.

Pandora AMP

A digital radio music streamer shares its audience analytics data with artists and their managers for their own songs in a formalized initiative known as Pandora AMP (for Artist Marketing Platform). The Pandora data are not available to the general public and only report each artist's own music. Reports include the listening audience for individual songs, number of fans that created a station for the artist's tunes, an interactive "heat map" locating listeners geographically, and demographics of fans. Pandora said the AMP program, which started in 2014, "eliminates the guesswork" for artists in connecting with their audience.

Chapter Takeaways

- Market research is much more sophisticated than in earlier eras, when the only question was whether a record was climbing "the charts."

- Today's research includes point-of-sale transaction censuses, consumer attitude surveys, plus custom research on purchase preferences, behavior, and/or demography.

- A goal of analytics is to measure the effectiveness of marketing efforts such as promotion efforts with third parties and paid advertising, which will guide allocation of resources for future marketing programs. An array of independent research organizations is in the field, constantly churning out torrents of data that influence music industry decision makers.

Key Terms

- airplay reports   (p. 269)
- analytics   (p. 264)
- charts   (p. 266)
- dashboards   (p. 264)
- demographics   (p. 266)
- fingerprint (audio)   (p. 269)
- point of sale (POS)   (p. 265)
- SoundScan   (p. 269)

Discussion Questions

1. Beyond sales of prerecorded music, what other music activities can research illuminate?

2. What would be the advantage in hiring an outside company to perform analytical services, as opposed to doing the work internally?

3. How should an industry professional rate the importance of buzz versus physical sales versus downloads versus streaming plays? Defend your view.

Live Performance

PART 5

CHAPTER 16

Concert Production

While the sale of recorded music has struggled mightily for years, it's a different story for live concerts. Although hardly immune to the vagaries of the greater economy, live music has an enormous economic advantage over recorded music. A fan must generally pay hard dollars to enjoy a live performance by a favored act, while an unauthorized shared download or a free stream puts little or nothing in the artist's pocket. Music concerts generate over $6 billion in ticket sales in North America, according to the trade magazine *Pollstar,* not including the value of resale of tickets on the secondary market and many acts not touring nationally. Add to that sum other ticket resales, corporate sponsorships, and the economic spillover for supporting vendors and restaurants, and the vast economic footprint of live music becomes obvious.

"An artist, in giving a concert, should not demand an entrance fee but should ask the public to pay, just before leaving, as much as they like. From the sum he would be able to judge what the world thinks of him—and we would have fewer mediocre concerts."

—Kit Coleman

Besides generating substantial revenue from ticket sales, live concerts boost record sales. Live concerts also increase demand for artist-related spinoffs, such as T-shirts, posters, jewelry, keychains, and books. Concerts and the sale of ancillary products are so critical that major recording companies are reluctant to sign an act that doesn't also have a compelling stage presence. And if the label does sign the act, there's a good chance it's part of a broad **360 deal** that yields the label a healthy piece of the box office.

Three key players move and shake the concert promotion industry: the event promoter, the artist's manager, and the tour-booking agent.

In Chapter 8, we detail the manager, agent, and attorney's roles; this chapter focuses on the **promoters,** the people and their organizations that oversee tours and are key to whipping up fan interest.

Concert Promotion

Concert promoters take the risks, pay the acts, market the shows, and sell the tickets. They risk not making more money from ticket sales and other revenue sources than they will pay out in expenses. A half-century ago, the industry was characterized by a patchwork of local and regional promoters. But by the mid-1990s—and even more so in the new millennium—consolidation and centralization became the story. As is true with many industries, economies of scale and the ability to diversify risk can provide an operating advantage to large, sophisticated players. Among the best-known concert promoters are Anschutz Entertainment Group (that includes AEG, Concerts West, Goldenvoice, and Messina Group), Another Planet Entertainment, C3 Presents, I. M. P., Jam Productions, Palace Sports & Entertainment, and SFX Entertainment. The giant is Live Nation Entertainment, which is a $7 billion-revenue music/live entertainment conglomerate that books 23,000 events a year at over 150 venues. Live Nation also owns ticketing juggernaut Ticketmaster, which handles ticketing transactions at company-owned and third-party facilities. With that clout, it books $300 million a year in event sponsorships and advertising. In recent years, Live Nation has become more integrated within the concert business by buying artist management firms, which sit on the other side of the table when venues are booking performers. With the big promoters operating at such massive scale, nowadays major music stars expect **national promoters** (NPs) to coordinate their tours—it just makes sense for continuity and effective organization.

But NPs need local promoters with expertise to recommend appropriate venues, help determine seat prices, and arrange local promotional tie-ins with radio stations and retailers. National promoters quickly become aware of local promoters with good reputations.

National promoters usually negotiate a share of the net receipts—box office income minus expenses. Out of this, they pay the local promoter. Contracts between NPs, local promoters, and artists must be precisely drawn to make sure the expenses charged against gross income are allowable and accurate.

Key responsibilities of promoters include orchestrating ticket sales, organizing sale of artist merchandise at the event, assisting in securing sponsorship deals to support a tour, arranging the stage setup, providing some of the event staff, financial accounting, and complying with a myriad of live-event safety regulations. All this is done by either the NP or local promoter in conjunction with the performing artist and **venue** operator.

Besides the big acts that are handled by the leading promoters, there are thousands of events mounted independently by smaller operators who make up an important part of the live-entertainment ecosystem. Small-scale concerts have low-entry barriers because venues are plentiful and up-and-coming acts constantly seek bookings. In some cases, venues themselves also serve as the promoter of some concerts in their facilities.

■ Getting Started

Despite the industry consolidation, there is still room for the small startup promotion venture on the regional and local level. How do aspiring concert promoters get their start? Some have acts of their own that they book before established promoters take an interest in them. Others break into the business as students by serving on their college campus's entertainment committee. Still others begin by putting together a performance to raise funds for a charity or other organization in need.

The Cost of Doing Business

Few startup businesses run without an initial investment of cash, and concert promotion is no different. Promoters need cash to cover their expenses before the first ticket may be sold, and expenses start with renting a concert hall, advertising performances, producing tickets, securing liability insurance, and making advance deposit payments to talent. Is the act a big name? If so, the performers may demand a luxury trailer and six bottles of Dom Perignon before setting foot on stage. Is the act known to attract rowdy crowds? If so, the promoter may need cash for a hefty damage deposit before the hall can be booked.

Depending on the state or country in which the promoter does business, there may be fees associated with establishing a concert promotion company. Does the county need a business registration? Has a business bank account been opened? For a general discussion of these kinds of challenges, see Chapter 27, "Starting Your Own Business."

■ Booking the Artist

Finding the Artist

Who do people want to hear in a live concert? Preferably a big name, of course. Promoters are responsible for booking the full lineup of artists, which can include an opening act of lesser fame. The music of opening acts should be suitable for the headliner's audience, and the opening act should not overshadow the main talent in terms of intensity or flair; if so, the promoter will then have an angry top-billed star.

Contracts are quite specific in spelling out how headliners and opening acts are presented in advertising and promotion materials, such as requiring that type size for opening acts must be 50% or less than the size of the headliner's name. Promoters also use the secondary act's booking to establish relationships with up-and-coming talent that could flower into headliners down the road.

Promoters who take risks with acts early on hope they are the same promoters who reap the benefits of the acts' eventual successes. The promoter that handled an artist's most recent concert in a given area is referred to as the **promoter of record,** although such relationships are in decline as NPs and record labels with 360 deals try to exert more control over who works with whom.

■ Making an Offer

Booking the act is critical to the concert promotion process. There can't be a concert without a headliner. How do promoters book the artists? If the acts are just starting out, promoters may deal directly with the artists themselves. More likely, however, promoters begin with the artists' agents.

The Agent

As one of the three key players in the concert promotion industry, artists' agents negotiate on behalf of music talent. Because agents work on commission, their job is to present the offers that reap the greatest possible fees. Promoters may find themselves dealing with a small talent agency or with one of the more prominent Hollywood agencies, such as William Morris Endeavor Entertainment (WME), Creative Artists Agency (CAA), or ICM Partners.

Who Represents Whom? The simplest way to find out which agents represent which acts is through the Internet, where artist websites can list contacts. If an act has a recording contract, the record company will put promoters in touch with artists' agents. Trade publications such as *Pollstar* and *Billboard* also print talent and booking directories.

   Promoters and agents often come together through conferences and meetings of performing arts administrators and university groups. Two examples of these opportunities to make agent contacts include the Association of Performing Arts Presenters (APAP) and the National Association of Campus Activities (NACA). At annual NACA conventions, college representatives, talent agents, performing artists, and labels gather for educational and showcasing opportunities.

Preliminaries

What Are the Artists' Fees and Available Dates? Once promoters have connected with the act's agent, they may make preliminary inquiries about the artists' usual fees and available dates. These inquiries can set in motion the preparatory steps necessary for a successful concert promotion, such as placing a "hold" on a particular concert hall for a particular date in anticipation of a formal booking.

What Are the Possible Venues? Securing open dates can be difficult, and open dates are useless without the coincidental availability of the featured acts. In selecting venues, promoters can usually rent the facility for a flat fee or a flat fee plus a percentage of the gross ticket sales. For national tours, there's usually 2 to 9 months' lapse between the first booking inquiry and the artist's first concert at a venue.

What Does the Venue Offer? Venue management generally furnishes the stage manager, box office manager, maintenance crew, and ushers. A facility may also provide security, or the city may require promoters to hire security personnel based on the reputation of the act's audiences. A venue may also offer promoters an option called **four-walling.** In four-walling, the promoter takes all the ticket sales money and assumes full financial risk if ticket sales are insufficient to cover some of the operating costs that would otherwise be absorbed by the venue. Under that arrangement, the venue has guaranteed revenue but no upside.

What Is the Venue's Potential? Here, promoters must be cautious to estimate costs accurately. For example, a facility that seats 1,000 for a show with tickets at $20 each will obviously gross $20,000 if the show is a sellout. But few shows actually sell out, and even if every seat is sold, expenses that aren't anticipated may gobble up any profit. Promoters may more often come out ahead when they locate a 5,000-seat arena, book a headliner, and pull together enough money to finance an extensive promotional campaign. Regardless of a venue's potential number of ticket sales, experienced promoters don't budget for a concert that's standing room only (**SRO**) but for a *60% house,* meaning that 40% of the tickets just won't sell. Projecting SRO sell-outs would prompt a promoter to stretch financially, which is risky. Theater managers have used this 60% house figure since the 1800s in planning their concert promotion budgets.

After the promoter has worked out a preliminary budget based on all the information gathered, it's time to contact the artist's agent and make an offer.

The Offer

Very few acts will perform for a flat fee if they tour nationally. Most of the agents who represent these acts begin fee negotiations on the premise that the show will sell out. Most of the promoters, on the other hand, want a protective cushion. If the show doesn't sell out, promoters want to know that they will, at the very least, earn back their expenses—including production, rent, and marketing costs—and that they will take home a profit before the main attraction and its agent get most of the money.

How these two deal makers come together is the subject of the next section.

The Art of the Deal

Negotiating Artists' Fees

Discussions usually begin with agents expecting for their clients a guaranteed fee plus a percentage of the ticket sales. If the event is free, or if tickets are subsidized by a charity or student activities fund, both parties expect to negotiate only a flat fee.

Promoters will want to negotiate a **split point,** which is a number based on ticket sales and at which point the act and the promoter divide the balance. See Table 16.1 for an example of a split point as well as an expense detail for performance at a moderate-sized venue.

Deal Points. Agents will want to see all the estimated expenses associated with the event, including the artist's guaranteed fee, rent of the hall, labor for setting up and breaking down the stage, production costs (sound, lights, catering, etc.), and any other related expenses. Multiply the total expenses by a percentage—usually 15%— and this is the sum that agents traditionally allow the promoters as profit. Deduct the expenses and the promoters' allowed profit from the gross ticket sales, and this back end—or the balance of the revenue after the split point—is what the promoters and the artists typically split. Custom dictates that this percentage be divided in an 85% to 15% split, with the larger number going to the artists (although the trend for superstar acts is to take even more). Promoters are free to argue for a higher percentage split than 15%, and deal variations exist.

With the lion's share of ticket sales going to the top stars, promoters and larger venues such as stadiums make their money from ancillaries such as car parking, food/ beverage, and licensed merchandise sales, which can easily run into the hundreds of thousands of dollars from an audience of tens of thousands of people. In smaller venues with lesser acts that draw hundreds or just a few thousand attendees, there's no big windfall from ancillaries, so artists typically get a somewhat smaller share of the back end.

Table 16.1   Sample of Expense Sheet

Artist: Venue: Date: Expense Item	Estimated Cost		
Advertising	$20,000.00		
ASCAP/BMI	485.00		
Box office	100.00		
Catering	2,000.00		
Insurance	1,200.00		
Instrument rental	750.00		
Loaders	400.00		
Phones	100.00		
Rent	17,500.00		
Risers	600.00		
Runner	200.00		
Security	1,375.00		
Sound/lights	3,000.00		
Spotlights (2)	400.00		
Stage manager	500.00		
Stagehands (union)	4,800.00		
Piano tuning	125.00		
		Capacity: 3,000	
		Tickets	Income
Total production	$53,535.00	1,200 @ $50	$60,000.00
Headliner fee	15,000.00	900 @ $40	36,000.00
Support act fee	5,000.00	900 @ $30	27,000.00
		Gross potential	123,000.00
Total cost	$73,535.00	Comp tix 100	$5,000.00
Promoter profit (15%)	11,030.25	(100 @ $50)	
Split point	84,565.25		
Split: 85%–15%		Net potential	$118,000.00
		Split point	84,565.25
		Overage	33,434.75
		Headliner share	$28,419.54
		Promoter share	5,015.21
Offer based on 3-hour maximum show, 150-mile radius exclusivity, and local sound and lights; 8 a.m. load-in, stage dark 5 p.m. to 7 p.m.			

Deals with venues vary based on how much competition there is among facilities in an area, assumed fan base in the region, and whether a venue is lightly or heavily booked already. One alternate compensation plan calls for the promoter to promise a guaranteed minimum to the artist, with escalators in the form of revenue sharing for ticket sales that exceed predetermined benchmarks. Another type of deal is putting all revenue from tickets, parking fees, sales of merchandise, and sponsorships in one pot, then subtracting all expenses and dividing the remainder through a percentage formula. Sometimes, venues have deal sweeteners with contracts specifying they get a few dollars per ticket on a sliding scale for tickets sold priced at a specified face value, such as $25. This is often called a **facilities fee.**

In general, it is the promoter that is on the hook if concert revenue is disappointing, but the promoter usually has a window to cancel the date if early advance ticket sales are dismal. Into the 1970s, touring was not a big moneymaker for most artists, who used concerts to promote their recordings. Artists often received **tour support** from labels to subsidize the cost of concerts to create buzz that would drive fans into record stores. Today, it is often profits from live shows that keep the ecosystem working, rather than the other way around.

Of course, concerts don't always make money. Another key point of negotiation between artist and promoter is addressing whether the promoter can deduct shortfalls from concerts that sold poorly from other tour dates that sold briskly. Such **cross-collateralization** can occur when the same concert tour has a multicity schedule. Usually there is a limit on how many low-selling dates in a single tour can be used to deduct from overall artist pay.

Potential Versus Reality

The capacity of the venue (the number of seats that can be sold) multiplied by the value of an average ticket equals the *gross potential* of the event. A theater with 2,000 reserved seats with a uniform ticket price of $25 has a gross potential of $50,000. Some of the tickets will be designated for the artists' guests, and some will be given to the press or to radio stations for giveaways that help promote the concert. Deduct the value of these tickets from the gross potential, and the resulting number is the *net potential.*

Before the act can take the stage, concert promoters must enter into a number of written agreements. Among others, promoters sign contracts with venue management, talent agents, merchandisers, lighting and sound suppliers, insurance companies, transportation firms, and caterers. Insurance includes specified payments to cover losses in the event the act is unable to perform as scheduled. The insurance policy usually specifies specific circumstances that are covered, such as hospitalization and not just calling in sick. Policies also name persons close to a performer (spouse, children, parents, etc.) whose death or hospitalization is eligible for cancellation coverage. Contracts must also put in place clear agreements with the city's police and fire departments with respect to security arrangements. The costs of these contracts must be considered during the negotiation process or the promoter will end up with unexpected leaks in cash flow.

Contracts

Once agent and promoter agree on the broader points of the offer, it is time for a contract. Agents issue contracts, and contracts consist of two parts: the face page and the rider.

The face page defines the basic information: time, date, place, length of show, how the artists' names will be billed (how they will appear in advertising), the agreed-upon fees, and payment schedules.

The rider (or **technical rider**) is a more-detailed document attached to the face page that details the artists' requirements. Riders may include the following: (a) travel arrangements; (b) hotels; (c) food and beverage catering; (d) technical needs, such as band gear, sound, and light systems; (e) size and number of dressing rooms; and (f) any other detail the artist finds critical for performance.

Most promoters will ask to see the rider prior to making an offer. They understand that there are sometimes rider requirements that can kill a deal. For example, if the artist needs the promoter to supply a backup string section of 20 musicians, this might add $5,000 or more to the promoter's expenses and can be the **deal breaker.**

The finer points of the rider can be open to negotiation and may depend on the star power of the act, whether there are multiple acts that must share in the billing and promotional campaign, and what sort of technical requirements the bigger names have requested and the smaller names will accept.

Riders usually start out with a standard contractual text, which parties will then alter by mutual agreement in negotiation. In many cases, changes to the standard text are cross-outs and insertions literally written by hand. The more ticket-selling clout of the artist, the more the artist can negotiate in terms of money, control, and hospitality benefits. The sample provisions outlined below are just that and shouldn't be interpreted as always applicable. In an individual negotiation, the relative leverage of each party controls the outcome. In that sense, there is no "right" or "fair" answer.

Technical Rider

This is a condensed version of a Technical Rider, which is routinely added to a basic contract for a concert performance:

ARTIST RIDER AND ADDENDA ATTACHED HERETO HEREBY MADE PART OF CONTRACT

This agreement is concluded on the date of _____ between _____ (hereafter referred to as "the Promoter") and furnishing the services of _____ (hereafter referred to as "the Artist") and _____ Venue (hereafter referred to as "the Purchaser"). The Purchaser agrees to engage the Promoter for the services of the Artist upon all terms and conditions set forth herein.

1) INDIVIDUAL RESPONSIBILITIES: basic obligation of each party

   a. Signatories to this Rider represent that they are legally authorized to enter into this agreement.

   b. All parties agree to keep terms of this contract and the contract itself secret to the extent permitted by law.

   c. Each party shall be liable for its own negligent acts and omissions. The Purchaser's tort liabilities are limited to the laws of its domicile.

2) DATES/TIME: engagement schedule

   a. Specify the number of shows, day, and date.

   b. The Purchaser agrees to have stage staffing in place one hour before venue doors open to the audience for sound and lighting checks to be conducted by the Artist and its representatives.

   c. Specify the time that venue doors open on engagement days.

   d. State the time for opening act to start performance(s) on stage and minimum length of stage performance.

e. State the time for the Artist/headliner to start performance(s) on stage.

f. Specify a minimum time the Artist must perform to fulfill its obligation to deliver a full concert on stage in front of the audience.

3) EVENT PUBLICITY: publicity, advertising, and promotions

a. Specify billing requirements for the Artist in promotional and advertising material, usually stating 100% of standard headline presentation in marketing materials.

b. The Purchaser agrees that the Artist will be sole billed headliner for each engagement, unless the Promoter agrees in writing to alternative billing.

c. The Purchaser may only use audio/music, artist voice, logos images, art graphics, still photos, and videos of the Artist in consumer marketing that are approved by the Promoter. Usage is limited to advance promotion of the engagement(s).

d. The Purchaser agrees to use tour marketing materials provided by the Promoter that are localized with date and venue insertions.

e. The Promoter agrees to make two email blasts promoting the engagement(s) to members of the fan club of the Artist that are geo-identified as located within _____ miles of the venue. The first blast shall be at least three weeks before the first engagement date and the second blast shall be no later than one week prior.

f. The Artist's content and identification shall not be used in combination with any other product, service, or sponsor in publicizing the engagement, absent the Promoter's prior written approval for each usage.

4) CREATIVE AFFAIRS: who is in charge of concert

a. The opening act must be approved by the Promoter.

b. The Promoter is the ultimate authority for the presentation of the stage show.

c. The Promoter determines what announcements will be made from the stage during the performance, except for safety announcements mandated by law.

d. The Purchaser agrees to promptly make changes in the staged presentation as ordered by the Promoter, as long as such changes do not conflict with government health and safety regulations, contractual union rules, venue insurance rules, or posted venue safety regulations.

5) COMPENSATION: pay for the artist

a. The Purchaser agrees to pay a guaranteed minimum of $ _____ to the Promoter or the booking agent, or __% *(perhaps 85% or 90%)* of the ticket gross after applicable taxes and approved expenses are deducted—whichever figure is higher.

b. The Purchaser will make advanced deposit payment in the amount of $_____ to the Promoter or booking agent by a specified date to a specified bank account.

(Continued)

(Continued)

    c. The Purchaser shall make payment in full to the Promoter or the booking agent of all payments due/final settlement no later than 30 days after the final engagement.

6) TRANSPORATION:

    a. If air travel is provided by the Purchaser, specify the number of tickets provided, class of service, dates of travel, and departure/arrival airports for the Artist *(usually not provided by the Purchaser)*.

    b. Specify air freight and excess baggage allowance *(usually not provided by Purchaser)*.

    c. Specify local hotel accommodations to be provided by the Purchaser to the Artist, including class of hotel, type of rooms, number of rooms, and dates rooms are provided *(usually not provided by Purchaser)*.

    d. The Artist travels with ___ tour buses and the Purchaser agrees to provide reasonable parking and maintain reasonable external bus security during the engagement.

    e. For ground transport, the Purchaser agrees to provide one 15-person passenger van with driver and one professionally chauffeured large black SUV with tinted glass (Cadillac Escalade, Lincoln Navigator, or equivalent). All dome lights in the SUV must be blacked out or disabled so they never illuminate, including when doors open. This chauffeured SUV is on call for the Promoter's tour manager for **load-in to load-out,** starting from one full day before the first performance. Exact times and locations for pickup and drop-off for van and SUV for performances will be provided to the Purchaser by the tour manager at least one day before each pickup *(ground transport is usually provided by the Purchaser)*.

7) SPECIAL PROVISIONS: accommodations at the venue

    a. No visible signage for advertisers and/or sponsors shall be on or near the stage during the engagement. The engagement shall be conducted without any direct or implied endorsement by the Artist of advertisers or sponsors of the Purchaser/venue, including no audio "presents" announcements made in connection with the Artist's concert.

    b. The Purchaser will provide a private dressing room and VIP area for guests of the Artist and the Promoter. The dressing room shall be clean, dry, ventilated and odor free. *Specify minimum dimensions, furnishings, lavatory and, if necessary, showers.*

    c. The Purchaser agrees to provide secure encrypted Wi-Fi wireless access to the Artist, its staff and affiliates of the Promoter.

    d. The Artist's dressing room shall be private, secure, and not be shared with any other performers during the engagement.

    e. There will be no Meet & Greets or press interview for the Artist set up by the Purchaser or its affiliates without prior written approval of the Promoter. The Purchaser may not sell any VIP ticket packages with backstage access without advanced written permission of the Promoter.

f. The Purchaser agrees that its security staff will aggressively prohibit the use of unsanctioned personal audio or visual recording of the Artist backstage and in the Artist private areas by any persons at any time.

g. No audio, video or webcasts recordings or transmission of any part of the concert is permitted and the Purchaser agrees to instruct its staff to take aggressive action to enforce.

h. The Purchaser agrees to provide food/beverage for the Artist as mutually agreed upon. *The hospitality requirement is usually so detailed and lengthy, it requires a separate document attachment (some venues prohibit alcoholic beverages and specify the ban applies to hospitality provided to the Artist).*

i. The Artist travels with touring party of _____ persons and back-stage accommodations shall be sufficient size for the touring party.

j. A large private room to accommodate __ *(number of)* touring crew members shall be provided with a buffet food spread, beverages, lounge furnishings, lavatory, and shower facilities.

8) LICENSED MERCHANDISE: sale at venue of Artist-related merchandise

a. No licensed merchandise containing the likeness or personal identification of the Artist and its affiliates may be sold in connection with the engagement without the advanced written permission of the Promoter.

b. The Promoter shall have the exclusive rights to commission and sell souvenir tour-specific items such as event programs, clothing, and posters on the premises of the venue, getting 100% of net proceeds (after a specified concessionaire expense and applicable taxes are deducted throughout).

c. The Artist shall receive 100% of all net proceeds of CDs and DVDs of recordings by the Artist sold in connection with the engagement.

d. The Artist shall receive 85% of net proceeds of other Artist licensed merchandise carrying the likeness, images, or audio of the artist.

9) TICKET SALES:

a. The Purchaser may not announce, advertise, promote, or sell tickets to the engagement(s) without a signed binding contract or written authorization by the Promoter.

b. All tickets shall be numbered in consecutive order and ticket prices shall not be priced more than agreed upon by the Promoter, exclusive of taxes and other mandatory third-party charges. If the Purchaser sells tickets at less than face value because of discount programs or other special arrangements such as group sales made by the Purchaser, those transactions will be entered as if the ticket sold at full price for purposes of Artist compensation, unless the Promoter allows discounting in writing.

c. For venues with private VIP boxes with unticketed seats, determine if a ticket allocation will be made for unticketed seats for accounting purposes *(although the Purchaser may oppose)*.

(Continued)

(Continued)

    d. The Purchaser agrees to make available to the Promoter or its representative the complete ticket manifest of the venue covering all seats and prices of seats.

    e. The Promoter's representative shall be allowed to inspect ticketing records at any time and any place, and shall be supplied with requested sales information in a timely manner. The Purchaser agrees to the reasonable right to audit by the Promoter and its designated representative.

    f. The Artist is to receive 20 complimentary tickets to each performance for use at the Artist's discretion.

    g. The Promoter is to receive 20 complimentary tickets to each performance for use at the Promoter's discretion.

10) FACILITIES:

    a. The Purchaser agrees to furnish on the engagement dates a suitable venue that is heated or cooled for the season, ventilated, well lighted and in good working order, and with a stage equipped with high-quality curtains, electrical outlets, loud speakers, and lighting. The Purchaser agrees to give technicians and workers hired by the Promoter and the Artist necessary access.

    b. The Purchaser agrees to provide reasonable security for the Artist and its representatives while in the venue in preparation for the engagement, during the engagement, and in the equipment load out after the engagement.

    c. The Purchaser may not assign or transfer this agreement or ultimate responsibility for any elements of the Purchaser's enumerated responsibilities and obligations.

    d. No party to this contract shall violate or cause any affiliates to violate standard work rules in any union contracts that other parties to this rider are signatory.

    e. Nothing in this agreement shall suggest a continuing joint venture, partnership, or ongoing business relationship between the Artist, Promoter, and the Purchaser.

    f. The Purchaser is solely responsible for security, venue insurance, music publishing clearances, and access to the venue.

    g. The Artist and Promoter agree not to bring visibly branded products or services to the engagement that conflict with preexisting branded sponsorships of the venue made by the Purchaser. *(The Purchaser then lists its sponsors with exclusivity.)*

11) EXPENSES:

    a. List all expenses paid for by the Promoter *(short list)*.

    b. List all expenses paid for by the Purchaser *(long list including food/drink for the Artist, electricians, security staff, equipment rentals, insurance expense, etc.)*.

    c. Specify which of the above expenses that the Purchaser may claim as deductions (including amount).

12) EXCUSED PERFORMANCES: cancellations

    a. In the event of inclement weather, the engagement(s) shall be rescheduled on similar terms at mutually agreed dates, with no payments or penalties for the cancelled engagement(s).

    b. If as a result of a Force Majeure Event, the Artist and/or the Promoter are unable to or are prevented from performing as contracted for the engagement(s), the Purchaser fully bears the cost of the cancellation and shall not make claims to the Artist or Promoter.

    c. If as a result of a Force Majeure Event, the Purchaser is unable to provide the venue at the time of the engagement(s) and the Artist and Promoter are ready, willing, and able to fulfill the contract requirements, the Purchaser shall still pay the Promoter ___% of the minimum guarantee. If both the Artist and Promoter are not ready because of a Force Majeure event, then the Purchaser is excused from financial payment obligations but not the personal accommodations that follow. Regardless of any circumstances, the Purchaser remains responsible for any preexisting departure transportation and local accommodations/transportation obligations, even if the engagement is allowably cancelled due to Force Majeure.

    d. A Force Majeure event is defined as any one of the following in the vicinity of the venue or adjacent to engagement dates: severe weather that visibly disrupts civil society on a mass scale; acts or threats of terrorism officially recognized by law enforcement; riots that visibly disrupt civil society on a mass scale; any advisory issued by a controlling government authority curtailing normal civilian activity; shortages of essentials such as fuel, water, and basic municipal services; labor disputes (strikes, lockouts, and boycotts) that directly impact engagement(s); incapacity of one or more members of the Artist; and other occurrences beyond the control of the Artist, the Promoter, and the Purchaser that make the engagement(s) unfeasible or clearly unsafe. All parties have the obligation to notify other parties immediately when claiming a Force Majeure event.

    e. The Promoter has the right to cancel within 30 days of the engagement with written notice with no penalty, unless otherwise specified. Any advance deposit paid by the Purchaser shall be refunded within three business days of event cancellation. Upon such cancellation and repayment of any advance deposit, the parties have no further legal obligations to each other.

13) BOOKING AGENT:

    a. The booking agent assumes no responsibilities other than representing the Promoter and the Artist, and responsibly handling financial affairs. The booking agent has no direct responsibilities or liabilities in staging matters at the venue.

14) DISPUTES AND INCONSISTENCIES:

    a. In the event of contractual disputes, the parties agree to rapid nonbinding arbitration to be administered by _____ whose expense shall be shared equally by parties involved. After arbitration, the parties are free to pursue other remedies.

Production Planning

As preparations for a performance unfold, promoters can find it daunting to make sure all the many required tasks are performed correctly and in the right sequence. A key step that falls off the to-do list can lead to disaster. As an example of how to approach this organizational challenge for a college concert, Table 16.2 lists the many tasks that must be *back-timed* so that preparations for a performance can unfold in orderly fashion. Anyone involved in the management of a production on a college campus should find this form helpful.

Table 16.2   College Production Planning

Lead Time	Control Number	Responsibility
6–12 months	1.	Research history of college promotions in your area. What has worked well in the past?
3–6 months	2.	Formulate budget for forthcoming school year; appeal for funding.
	3.	Place tentative holds on performance facilities.
	4.	Make preliminary contact with talent agents to learn of tentative costs, available artists, and dates.
3 months	5.	Get school's approval of your plans. Submit bid for artist, specifying date and price.
	6.	Get acceptance, rejection, or counteroffer from agents.
	7.	Negotiate contracts with agents. Pending formal execution of contracts, exchange written confirmation.
	8.	Confirm your hold dates on facility, then formulate a written agreement with the facility management.
2 months	9.	Execute contracts with agencies, including technical riders. Add the booking to the calendar on the venue's website and other marketing materials.
	10.	Contact artists' record companies for help with promotion. Ask for press kits, promotional materials, money for block-ticket purchases, cooperative ads, templates for advertising, and even services of promotion personnel.
	11.	Formulate promotion budget and campaign. Calculate ad costs (a local media-buying ad agency can provide estimates).
	12.	Contract for outside suppliers, as needed, for sound reinforcement, lighting, security, caterers, etc.
6 weeks	13.	Place printing orders for tickets, posters, banners, etc.
	14.	Line up cooperative ads with record stores, radio stations, etc.
4 weeks	15.	Contract for ticket-selling outlets.
	16.	Seek store displays of posters, albums, etc.
3 weeks	17.	Deliver printed tickets to outlets. Set strict controls for accounting.
	18.	Line up student volunteers for ushering, ticket takers, setting up/ striking stage, publicity, gofers, box office, etc.

Lead Time	Control Number	Responsibility
	19.	Clear plans with fire department: size of crowd, control of aisles, exits, etc.
	20.	Clear security plans with police, sheriff, rent-a-cop firm, and campus police. Discuss liabilities with school's legal counsel.
	21.	Distribute promotional materials to print and broadcast media. Schedule press conference, interviews. Mount banners and posters.
2 weeks	22.	Reconfirm arrangements with outside suppliers (sound, lighting, transport, caterers, etc.).
	23.	Check ticket sales. Adjust promotion budget accordingly.
1 week	24.	Call a production planning meeting with facility manager, stage manager, production director, and student volunteers. Issue written instructions to everybody concerning their responsibilities, schedule, and contingency plans.
3 days	25.	Reconfirm everything! a. With artists' road managers regarding any changes in time of arrival of personnel, equipment b. With outside suppliers c. With facility stage manager d. With student crew chairpersons e. With ticket sellers (If sales are lagging, execute preconceived last-minute promotion campaign.)
Performance day	26.	Call production meeting 1 hour prior to scheduled arrival of equipment and roadies. Everyone charged with responsibilities relating to the production and performance attends this meeting and takes notes. Last-minute changes in plans discussed.
	27.	Set up. Confirm that all personnel and equipment are arriving per plan.
	28.	Pick up money and unsold tickets from outlets. Deposit money in bank, deliver unsold tickets to facility box office for sale there.
	29.	Welcome the performing artists and their entourage. Control issuing of backstage and auditorium passes. Save the best (free) seats for unexpected important guests.
Postproduction	30.	If agreed contractually, join the road manager for a count of receipts and unsold tickets shortly after the box office closes.
	31.	Make agreed payment, then arrange for secure place to store cash overnight.
	32.	Feed your people after the show, at least your volunteers. They've earned it!
	33.	Confirm facility cleanup is proceeding per plan. Did the place experience more-than-normal wear and tear? If so, discharge your contractual responsibilities.
	34.	Write a summary report, following a short meeting with your key personnel: What went wrong, what went well?
	35.	Thank the participants by telephone, email, or letter for their cooperation, particularly those who worked as volunteers.

Marketing

How does the ticket-buying public know that tickets for an upcoming concert are on sale? Through marketing, or bringing all this pertinent information to the **market**.

Marketing can be divided into two categories: that which is paid and that which is not.

Online and Mobile. The online world offers an amazing confluence of forces to promote concerts. Artists market through their fan club websites, and venues use their own websites to reach potential concertgoers. Each maintains a list of fans that made contact for use in pushing events and merchandise sales. A unique characteristic of online is that these platforms facilitate direct interaction with consumers—there is no media middleman such as a newspaper or radio station, for example—and the platforms can execute online ticket sales directly to the consumer.

Display ads can be placed on third-party music, entertainment, and local media websites, and those sites can be enlisted to give extra promotional visibility in exchange for concert ticket and band merchandise giveaways. Mobile devices—such as smartphones and tablets—are increasingly favored by consumers and are also able to facilitate purchases.

Radio and Television. Broadcast television advertising can be useful if the goal is to reach a broad audience within a station's geographic area, but the expense is often not justified depending on the nature of the act and the size of the venue. With radio, there is some segmentation based on music format and a narrower demographic focus, a combination that often makes the medium a good advertising vehicle.

Radio stations sell air time in 30- or 60-second units, with fees based on the station's **rate card,** a list price based on estimates of how many listeners (in what demographic categories) tune in and at what times of day.

Local cable television systems offer city and regional commercials on basic **cable networks** such as the MTV channel cluster, Great American Country, Revolt, and BET Gospel. The viewing audience on any single cable network is typically smaller compared to a broadcast TV station. But a cable interconnect (a cluster of adjacent cable systems) typically offers the advantage of placement by selected geographic areas, which in theory leads to less waste in advertising expenditures.

Direct Mail and Email. Targeting a specific audience can be effective through direct-mail advertising and promotional emails, but using the right mailing list is vital.

Mailing lists assembled by artists, promoters, and venues are valuable because they typically aggregate the most promising prospects to buy concert tickets. But such lists tend to be small—typically just a couple hundred or thousand contacts for a geographic area close to the concert venue. To cast a wider net, promoters can buy syndicated mailing lists with thousands or tens of thousands of consumers, or mount tie-ins with third-party organizations to gain access to mailing lists.

Emailing is attractive because there are no postage and paper costs, but blasting unsolicited emails is problematic. Consumers are weary of promotional barrages, so they punch up their spam filters to intercept messages, which makes emailing a hit-or-miss proposition.

Deals to piggyback on third-party mailing lists can involve purchasing ads for cash or bartering in exchange for concert tickets. For example, concert ads can be placed on email lists from radio stations, which would use the tickets as prizes in on-air promotion. Such tie-ins are often negotiated as part of paid advertising campaigns.

Print Media. Mainstream publications such as daily newspapers are often avoided because their audience is broad and much of the readership may be off target. Typically, the main print buy is the "alternative" print media of free weekly newspapers, which have less expensive ad rates than the mainstream daily city newspaper but lower circulation. These weeklies often list cultural events in their cities and cater to young audiences oriented to out-of-home entertainment, most famously by the *Village Voice* in New York City and *LA Weekly* in Los Angeles.

Promoters who present ethnic music may find print media that cater to a slice of the ticket-buying public eager to support such music. Irish performances, for example, may sell more tickets through Irish publications than through the mainstream print sources.

Advertising Production

Once promoters decide their media mixes—how much they want to spend on newspaper, radio, mail, online, and television ads—they need to produce the ads they want to run.

More and more, major artists themselves control production of the commercials and print advertising that announce their performances. (When rock star Prince wanted to be billed as "The Artist Formerly Known as Prince," promoters complied.) Artists and promoters typically specify using template advertising materials that they prepare that leave spaces for insertion of venue name and engagement date. In display materials, size is often stated as a percentage proportion, such as the name of the supporting act should be no more than 40% the type size used for the headliner. If the performance is sponsored, ads will feature the sponsors' names and will mention the acts' latest recordings.

Nationally touring acts typically employ one set of advertising materials that can be used for all their concerts with minor customizing for a local venue and date. For local bands just getting started, radio stations and local cable interconnect ad networks can create satisfactory ads, if provided with audio and video tracks. Promoters can also call on the services of professional production companies. Although these companies require a fee, the higher quality of the commercials may outweigh the cost worries by ultimately being a catalyst for higher ticket sales. ■

Publicity and Public Relations

Cheaper than advertising—and perhaps even free—publicity and public relations help promote live performances. Publicity is a nonpaid marketing function that includes issuing press releases, providing news outlets with video and audio clips, and generating favorable news coverage by making artists available for press interviews.

Recipients of publicity materials include all traditional and new media outlets that cover entertainment. The payoff is unpredictable because it's up to media outlets whether to publish or post anything. When a report is published that's favorable or informational, it's highly influential because consumers view such news and informational editorial content as unbiased.

It may be worthwhile to hire professional publicists. A PR specialist has contacts in the press, knows who to work with in the editorial process, and devotes time when promoters cannot. Fees are usually negotiable, and a major feature story could be worth many dollars that promoters would otherwise pay to advertise.

Postering/Street Teams

The digital revolution is the trend setter for media these days, but old-fashioned boots-on-the-ground still proves to be highly effective for publicizing concerts. This involves placing posters in prominent locations with heavy foot traffic such as restaurants, taverns, night clubs, shopping malls, and so on. Sometimes the distribution is via *street teams* of temporary hires wearing identical clothing—such as T-shirts with artist logos—placing posters and passing out fliers to pedestrians in an attempt to draw attention to the concert.

Johnny Lloyd of rock four-piece Tribes perform at the London 2012 Olympic Torch Relay Special City Celebration at Leeds Temple Newsam Park, presented by Coca-Cola in Leeds, United Kingdom.
Photo by Shirlaine Forrest/Getty Images for Coca-Cola.

Sponsorships

Many promoters find that the most efficient and profitable concert promotions are those with one or more sponsors backing the project. Although sponsors may indeed pay hard dollars for the privilege, much of the benefit to artists and promoters comes from the promotional clout that the sponsors and their marketing engines provide.

Record Company Sponsorship

Recording industry executives know that the successful promotion of a new album may depend on coordination with a concert tour. Record companies that help underwrite the costs of the concert production provide promotion materials, such as flyers, posters, and banners. Some will buy blocks of tickets and then give them away to people they believe might influence the ticket-buying public, such as disc jockeys or local media celebrities.

Recording companies may lend their own publicists or product managers to ensure a concert's success. Sometimes recording companies will organize and produce national tours for new acts, and there may be room for local promoters to work with labels as part of these national efforts. Labels have always been at least indirect benefi-ciaries of a tour's success. With the rise of 360 deals (see Chapter 12), labels often have an even stronger incentive to ensure the money from live performances keeps flowing.

Radio Station Sponsorship

Radio stations frequently sponsor or cosponsor concerts in their listening area that fit their audience profile. Radio outlets negotiate for tickets to give away to their listen-ers in exchange for free or reduced-rate radio advertising for the promoter. Concert promoters welcome radio sponsors because the people who listen to radio are pre-sumably the same who will come to the concert.

Venue and Corporate Sponsorship

Venues themselves cosponsor live events, especially when the venue is smaller and perhaps less known than the big arenas with frequent bookings. A smaller, more intimate venue can adapt quite well to major artists, and promoters expect the trend of venue sponsorship to increase.

From Microsoft Theater in Los Angeles to the Barclays Center arena in Brooklyn to the Pepsi Center in Denver, major corporations want to tie in to the concert busi-ness, through links to venues or artists. Each year, hundreds of concert tours are supported by corporate sponsors. Electronics manufacturers, communication giants, computer companies, automakers, financial services, and beverage companies spon-sor artists' tours, because big business knows these events reach their target audiences.

Corporate sponsors provide cash and/or services in exchange for signage at con-certs and corporate identification in concert materials ranging from advertising to souvenir programs. The services provided by sponsors include promoting concerts in their own corporate marketing materials, which reduces marketing expenses directly borne by the tour and venue. For example, credit card outfits promote concerts in client communications, such as "bill stuffers" that accompany monthly statements whether mailed or online. Sponsors of all types may run sweepstakes and ticket give-aways, which directly promote concert dates in marketing materials not paid for by the promoter. As part of the deal, sponsors may get to distribute free tickets, dis-counted tickets, special access "VIP" seating, and other enticements, such as free parking and co-branded artist merchandise.

Ultimately, the sponsor is seeking a subtle rub-off of the performer's popularity, along with a memorable concert experience, to benefit the company and its products. Sponsoring hotels promote their hosting of touring performers (leaving the audience to dream of running into Mick Jagger in the lobby of their local Hilton hotel). With local merchants, Live Nation lines up promotions where, for example, convenience stores near its venues provide a free drink with purchase to patrons showing concert ticket stubs.

Contracts always specify exclusivity in a category, such as only one women's cloth-ing brand or one soft drink. Defining categories can create a tug-of-war in negotia-tions. For example, a consumer electronics sponsor might seek broad exclusivity while promoters will seek a narrow definition, like just TV sets. Settling on just "TV sets" lets the promoter seek additional sponsors for other consumer electronics categories such as personal computers, smartphones, tablets, music players, video games, and digital video recorders. The computer and video game categories can be further sub-divided into hardware and software. Promoters who attach sponsors to concerts must keep in mind that the artists may have the right to reject the sponsor or limit the sponsors' exposure. Artists may also ask for additional fees if products are to be identified with their shows or their personas.

Promoters should also watch for conflicts in corporate sponsorships. If Toyota sponsors a tour, and the venue has an arrangement with Honda requiring that only Honda gets signage at that venue, the promoter may need to book a different location.

College Sponsorship

Colleges and universities sponsor a large percentage of the live concerts in the United States. Student-run committees handle the school's annual budget for campus-sponsored entertainment, but because college students generally lack sufficient experience to promote or book on their own, schools often bring in professional promoters to assist. From this exposure, the promoters of tomorrow may be born.

Regional college promoters often band together and offer artists block booking, whereby the promoters take care of tour dates, venues, production, and promotion for a series of area concerts. Agents and artists appreciate this initiative to do much of the work for them, and the college block can also benefit through negotiating strength.

The Future of Live

Private Concerts

Not all concerts involve selling tickets to the general public. There is a little-publicized but thriving business for private concerts. Over the years, financial tycoons have hired the likes of Guns N' Roses, Elton John, Paul McCartney, Rod Stewart, and Rolling Stones to serenade hundreds of their by-invitation-only party guests on the front lawn of their mansions or at Las Vegas casino theaters. Asking prices for top performers is $1 million and includes personally meeting the 60-something birthday boy and, on a limited basis, the guests. Usually, contracts specify "surprise" performances with little or no advance publicity. Headliners don't want their fans to know they're at the disposal of the filthy rich, and no publicity is an attraction because it means no marketing expenses.

Further down the popularity scale, other performers with charted music are available for private affairs for $3,000 to $150,000 per concert. Talent representatives will book performers for birthday, graduation, anniversary, and holiday parties, if the price is right. Talent ends up performing at the local wedding halls or even in the backyards of middle-class homes. Because of the staging limitations of venues, many performances are cut down from tour-scope and sometimes can involve just a piano or guitar. Travel expenses are usually paid on top of performance fees.

Live Virtual Reality

In a new wrinkle that eliminates multicity tours, some concerts by popular musicians are "live" events transmitted as cable pay-per-view, to movie theaters via closed circuit, or via online video—all with fans paying premium prices to view and hear. With one performance, the artist reaches a wide audience and sidesteps the rigors of going on the road. In another development, 3D hologram performances of iconic but dead artists are presented in venues as "live" concerts.

There is little fear, though, that in-person performances will generally fade away in place of electronic substitutes. An artist in a live venue reaching out and touching someone—figuratively at least and perhaps even literally—is just too powerful a force.

Chapter Takeaways

- Artists receive varying slices of the box office pie, depending on their own clout and the revenue-generating capability of the venue.

- A handful of competitive national promoters handle big acts making national tours. Local promoters with lesser known acts account for the rest of the concert ecosystem.

- Concerts drum up ticket sales through a combination of publicity-generating news stories, paid advertising, short-term promotions where third parties such as radio stations get the word out, and long-term sponsorships with partners such as cell phone carriers.

- Concert tours mounting tie-ins with corporate sponsors get the sponsors to pay for some of the marketing costs, in exchange for allowing sponsors to associate with the tour and artist.

- College students interested in the field can gain valuable experience organizing and promoting campus performances.

Key Terms

- back-timed   (p. 288)

- block booking   (p. 294)

- four-walling   (p. 278)

- load-in/load-out (p. 284)

- national promoters (NPs) (p. 276)

- paid advertising   (p. 290)

- publicity   (p. 291)

- split point   (p. 279)

- sponsorships   (p. 292)

- standing room only (SRO) (p. 279)

- technical riders   (p. 281)

Discussion Questions

1. What are a promoter's options for filling up a venue when ticket sales are weak?

2. Describe the various marketing methods that employ either paid advertising or publicity to promote a concert.

3. Discuss various types of digital media that can be used to promote concerts and their strengths.

4. Has the massive consolidation in the concert industry made life better or worse for artists? Record companies? Fans?

CHAPTER 17

Concert Venues

V enues come in all sizes and types, from giant, sprawling sports stadiums to mid-sized arenas to recital halls to roadhouses with 12 × 8 plywood stages. At one time or another in a career, an artist might be found playing dates at state fairs, outdoor festivals, amusement parks, casino ballrooms, municipal auditoriums, night clubs, or college multipurpose rooms (see Table 17.1).

> "The play was a great success, but the audience was a disaster."
>
> —Oscar Wilde

The venue industry's scale and dynamism is enormous. Think opera houses and traditional concert halls are a stagnant, no-growth part of the economy? How's this for a factoid: For the past two decades in the United States alone, an average of more than one opera house or concert hall a month has opened either for the first time or after extensive remodeling, with some projects costing hundreds of millions of dollars apiece. Add to that the countless smaller venues that house artists of every level and every genre, and the opportunity is obvious.

Venue Contracts

As we've seen in other parts of the music business, contracts are the glue that sets the rules for relationships between parties working together to achieve mutual success. And how the rules are written largely depends on the clout of the various parties. A **promoter** and booking agent representing a top-tier act bring clout to a negotiation with a venue that has plenty of open dates and a mortgage to pay. But often the balance of power is different. Most artists are just passing through town with no permanent roots in the local community, so venues don't expect to be able to sort out issues after performances. Because of this lack of clout postevent, venue operators typically

The concert venue business carries the important responsibility of public safety. Seven people died in a 2011 outdoor stage collapse amid gusting winds at the Indiana State Fair. The contractor that built the stage, the Indiana State Fair Commission, and a stagehands' union were blamed in a subsequent state safety agency investigation. Among other safety concerns are drug overdoses and, as evidenced by the mass shooting at a Paris venue in 2015, the risk of terrorism.

Photo © Steve C. Mitchell/epa/Corbis.

Table 17.1   Seven Types of Concert Venues

Stadiums. The largest facilities for concerts, these multipurpose venues offer seating of 30,000+ and typically are configured for sports events. Since such facilities are not designed for live concerts, they require extensive setup/tear-down of concert stages.
Amphitheaters. Outdoor venues typically seat between 5,000 and 30,000 and are used primarily in good weather/summer seasons. These are specifically designed for concerts, with permanent stages.
Festival Sites. Outdoor locations used seasonally typically accommodate between 10,000 and 130,000 patrons for daylong or multiday concerts. For operators, these venues are attractive because of low overhead costs, resulting in some of the industry's highest profit margins.
Arenas. Smaller than stadiums, these indoor venues typically seat between 5,000 and 20,000. Arenas often have luxury private suites—premium-priced seating areas that amphitheaters lack. Because they are multipurpose facilities, they typically require extensive modification to install stages.
Theaters. Venues designed for legitimate theater can be easily adapted for concerts and typically have seating for 1,000 to 6,000.
Mid-Sized Music Venues. Designed for concerts, these indoor facilities have ready-built stages and typically have capacity for between 1,000 and 6,500 persons. With this low-capacity seating, however, they don't offer potential for outsized profits, as do the larger venues, even in a sellout.
Small-Sized Music Venues/Clubs. Music and comedy clubs dominate this category of indoor venue, which sometimes provide beverage and/or meal service for patrons at their seats. Because seating is typically less than 1,000, capacity limits revenue potential and seats are sometimes moveable chairs. But these facilities have built-in stages, which reduces costs.

take a hard line on facility rentals. Full-length contracts must be signed by responsible parties. It's common for venue operators to refuse to do business with acts that advertise concerts before a contract is signed, figuring if early ticket sales are weak, the artist will walk away, leaving the venue with a hole in its booking schedule.

Venues generally offer a limited spectrum of stage-related equipment and staff-supplied technical service, so it's rare for an artist to perform on a stage with everything supplied by the venue. Venues have found that because stage equipment is a personal choice, it is difficult to fulfill all equipment requests from the stream of artists passing through, and portable on-stage equipment can get damaged or disappear. When stage equipment is supplied, it is often subject to extra fees beyond basic facility use. Typically, off-stage equipment such as loudspeakers built into walls and standard lighting are part of the basic facility rental. Contracts also specify what parts of a facility artists can take over temporarily for their use, beyond the performing stage.

If venue staff is responsible for stage setup and supplying musical instruments, it can be blamed for technical problems by the artist or promoter, so venue staff duties are typically limited. However, the smaller the venue, the more on-stage service needs to be offered because semi-pro and little-known professional acts tend not to have the money for extensive touring equipment and roadies.

Well-paid stars tend to bring their own stage equipment and staff, so their stage equipment is always the same at every stop on a multicity tour, and their own workers are familiar with setup. If a venue is signatory to a union contract—such as the International Alliance of Theatrical Stage Employees (IATSE)—renters have to comply with union rules for facility staff—which typically include the union workers operating curtains, sound amplification, and lighting. The leading venue operators such as AEG and Live Nation Entertainment each manage multiple facilities in different cities. But there are many standalone operations of various sizes and organizational structures, including nonprofits.

Venue fees can be fixed-price rentals, a percentage cut of box office, or combination of those two elements. Whatever the formula, venue prices vary by season and day of the week—with in-demand weekends usually priced at a premium. Payments are usually made in installments, with the first money deposit due upon signing a contract that is weeks or months before a scheduled rental. Venues typically negotiate for limited circumstances for giving full or partial refunds if performances are cancelled or dates moved.

Another crucial point of negotiation is an arena's geographic exclusivity for star acts. Contracts will usually state that an artist cannot play a venue within a certain distance of the hosting facility for a specified time period. Otherwise, the audience in a geographic zone will be diminished if an artist is playing more than one gig in an area around the same time period.

Performance Rights in Concerts

A public performance of a copyrighted song triggers an obligation to pay composers, lyricists, and publishers a fee collected by a performance rights organization (PRO). With some exceptions, venues are responsible for securing the performance rights license (and not the artist or tour promoter). But in cases where music is not regularly presented at a venue, the promoter and not the venue may be responsible for paying the PRO. The fee is typically a small slice of gross ticket revenue, so the payment is a sliding scale. And the fee is due even if the performing artist is the sole composer of the performed works. This practice may defy common sense but is reasonable since a venue manager is hardly in a position to parse the details of co-publishing arrangements that determine royalty allocations.

• • • Case Study: Climbing the Job Ladder to Make a Career That Lasts

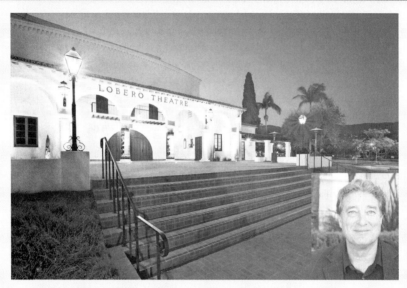

David Asbell of Lobero Theatre.
Photos © Patrick Price and David Asbell.

Having staying power in the music business often requires climbing the job ladder even if one enjoys the simple life of working on the crew. David Asbell was quite happy doing scenic stage work at nonprofit theaters, except for the moderate pay and lack of health insurance and retirement benefits.

A college graduate with a degree in economics, he advanced to lighting manager, production manager, and operations manager—each with a better pay package. Eventually, he parlayed his theater experience to management and is executive director of the foundation running the 604-seat Lobero Theatre in Santa Barbara, California, which is not far from where he grew up.

"When you are young working in theater, it's long hours but you like it," he says. "But I didn't want to be the guy doing the load-out for a show at 3 or 4 in morning when I'm in my 50s. And you can only make so much money as a stage manager."

At the Lobero, he oversees a historic theater built in 1924 that is a cultural hub of an affluent community outside of Los Angeles. About 70% of its performances have substantial musical content. Lobero books local community musical groups of all stripes, plus touring jazz, classical, Americana folk, blue grass, pop, rock, and lots of dance for 180 performances a year before an audience. Its crew is unionized with the International Alliance of Theatrical Stage Employees (IATSE). The Lobero has 12 full-time employees and a half dozen part-timers and fills union crew jobs from a pool of 25 IATSE workers.

Asbell says the theater's goal is for tickets and related sales to cover 60% of revenues, leaving donations to the nonprofit to pay the remaining 40%. In other ways, economics of a nonprofit are much the same as a for-profit theater. Paying touring performers is the biggest expense and trying to keep the load-in/loud-out efficient so that it doesn't get excessively expensive—issues that are the same at both for-profit and nonprofit theaters.

Asbell worked for nonprofit theaters in Colorado, Georgia, and California, remembering in another job at another theater a particularly gratifying stretch when the money rolled in, facilitating a string of inspired productions. "But there also was a 5- to 6-year stretch where there were big deficits," he recalls. "People had to take pay cuts and we didn't do as many exciting productions."

Venue work has always been fun because he had a knack for it and loved the artistic atmosphere. But even with the compensation benefits of being a high-up desk jockey now, Asbell adds, "You are still working long hours, weekends and evenings."

Asbell says that he's not an artist, but he relishes being surrounded by them. "It's great working with so many people passing through such as choreographers, musicians and designers, and tour managers," he says. "You are dealing with people with big personalities, and that has its rewards and pitfalls."

Ticketing

The venue is booked, the artist is signed, the sponsors are on board, and the promotion strategy is in place. All that's left now is to sell those tickets. Promoters, as their name implies, are responsible for encouraging people to buy tickets. But online ticket sellers typically contract with venues, not promoters.

Ticket Purchasing

Centralized online ticket purchasing is a far cry from the long lines outside box offices that buyers had to face decades earlier. Now fans typically purchase their tickets online and arrange for pickup at the event, or simply print out a machine-readable barcode or QR code, or else save the code on their smartphones to have it scanned at the event. Artists often reserve part of a venue's tickets for members of their online fan clubs.

Online ticket purchasing has itself become a big business. A leading online ticket seller is Ticketmaster, which Live Nation Entertainment acquired in 2010 and whose platform issues about 300 million tickets per year. For slow-selling concerts, some or all of the unsold tickets get sold via discount services like Groupon, since a cut-rate seat generates more revenue than an empty one.

Ticket prices vary based on the caliber of artist, prestige of the venue, and economic heft of the city. Midsized arenas with music talent that has radio play but is short of big-star talent often price tickets $15 to $75. When superstar talent plays in major cities where there's a big section of wealthy residents, ticket prices can range from $25 to $350. Some superstars offer front-row seats with backstage access for even more money in big cities where affluent patrons are concentrated and can afford VIP treatment. A top act might take the most expensive seats in the house and bundle them as "meet-and-greets" only available for purchase through the artist fan club.

Fan customs vary by city, with some fans buying tickets within just a few days of the event or even making walk-up purchases on the very day that a concert is held. Transactions for tickets sold for cash are difficult to trace later, so there is always a possibility of undercounting an audience. In such cases, the venue could shortchange the promoter or the promoter could shortchange the artist. Some promoters place their own people at venue entrances to count the audience as it streams in or photograph the crowd in their seats, in order to generate their own independent estimate of crowd size.

Ticket Terms

The term that promoters hate to hear most is *deadwood,* which refers to unsold tickets. Promoters who ask, "How much deadwood did we have tonight?" clearly want this number to be low or, better yet, zero.

If it's obvious that ticket sales are slow and there will be a lot of deadwood, promoters might choose to **paper the house,** where they give away tickets (or sell at rock-bottom prices) so the audience doesn't seem embarrassingly small. One technique to boost sales is to sharply cut prices of the least desirable seats to spur sales to bargain hunters.

Deciding how many of which type of seats will be sold at what price is called **scaling the house.** Seats in the first few rows of each section are generally priced higher, although there may be venues in which the better seats are midsection, near the wings, or just outside the orchestra section. Another concept used by some big acts is **dynamic pricing,** where ticket prices can be changed instantly based on online demand, a practice pioneered by airlines. Promoters are attracted to the concept as a way to capture more of the value of their tickets that might otherwise get resold for more money.

Tickets for reserved seats guarantee their bearers a specified seat in a specified location. General admission (GA) tickets mean that whoever arrives first has the choice of seats. GA concerts generally require more security concerns due to ticket holders pushing their way to the better seats.

Secondary Ticket Market

Some websites, such as StubHub, specialize in reselling tickets at prices higher than face value for in-demand acts or closer to original value if a concert suffers slow sales. Reselling occurs in what is called the **secondary market.** Fans and the music industry gripe about huge markups and blame speculators, called *scalpers,* but sometimes it is the artists and their associates who are confidentially making their allotment of tickets available to third-party resellers.

The ticket scalping problem is driven by basic supply and demand, but such ticket scalping is problematic for the artist, agent, and promoter. They usually share in none of the profits, and the scalper has taken advantage of a paying customer. The markups irk fans and have brought criticism from artists like Bruce Springsteen. Scalping is illegal in many areas, but the practice continues because ticket resellers have found legal work-arounds. The nontransferability of some tickets purchased online tends to take a bite out of the secondary market, but such controls also can annoy fans.

• • • Digital Venue Infrastructure

Since audiences love their mobile devices like smartphones, venues push wireless interaction with electronic devices bought by the audience. The ambition is to present a multimedia experience where the concert medium drives users to wireless online content, especially at moments when there's no active stage

Photo © Eloi_Omella/iStock

performance. While there's a desire to install enablers like Wi-Fi to connect audiences, there are no industry standards, and what is implemented is patchy because arena ownership is so diverse. Arenas can be owned by local governments, schools, nonprofit arts organizations, and very for-profit outfits, each with different philosophies toward infrastructure investment.

Connecting audiences is not a snap. Wireless networks can get overloaded when thousands of concertgoers simultaneously upload their I'm-at-the-concert-now selfies. A technology fix are distributed antenna systems (DAT), which are wireless signal repeaters that serve high-traffic areas and fill dead spots in buildings.

Despite the obstacles, venues tap audience devices by presenting digital access codes on arena signage, in printed programs, in Short Message Service (SMS) messaging, and with tie-ins with third parties ranging from fan clubs to corporate sponsors. The audience sees the code and then inputs it in their devices. Once engaged, users are entertained on their personal devices with concert-specific content, contests, and promotions for commerce ranging from future concerts to fan merchandise. Another objective is to continue the engagement after the event, so interactive content may ask users to opt in to mailing lists for future communications. Arena interactive is most advanced with sports teams because of their frequent use of venues, easy-to-target localized fan bases, and fan base consistency (concert audience demographics vary for each genre such as jazz, rap, rock, and classical).

Music events lag in wireless audience interaction because of this disconnect: the venue hosts the wireless Wi-Fi, and thus controls the audience connection, yet it's the traveling promoter that is most responsible for advertising ticket sales and managing fan bases nationally and it's to the artists that the audience is most attached. The promoter and artist are in a position to connect to the audience if in-venue messaging points to destinations like the artist's fan website, which typically collects personal data on visitors. So the promoter and artist can push commerce, market, and harvest personal data if the audience is herded to their online affiliates.

Licensed Merchandise

Both as an extension of the venue ecosystem and as a revenue stream in its own right, music-related licensed-merchandise generates $2.5 billion in annual consumer spending in the United States and Canada, according to *The Licensing Letter*. That store-level sales covers popular images and brands emblazoned on posters, T-shirts, coffee mugs, and the like but excludes recorded music and concert tickets. From that consumer spending on merchandise, it is estimated that over $120 million in royalties is directly pocketed by artists, tour promotors, and venues. Growth in this merchandise (**merch**) market has come from innovations that go beyond the sale of traditional T-shirts and posters. Now, music stars promote leading fashion brands and license their persona for fragrances.

Merchandise Contracts

In general retail distribution, royalties—a payment for the right to use creative property such as artist names and images—received by music entities (whether headed by artists or artist managers) range from 8% to 14% of the wholesale price of merchandise—sometimes referred to as manufacturer's net revenue. Other deals are based on the artist and the merchandise outfit dividing net profits (revenue minus direct expenses). Artists can take 75% or more of net profits, but the merchandiser first gets all its expenses covered. The royalties based on retail or wholesale price are more straightforward for the artist, because using the alternative net profit approach leaves the door open for the merchandise company to pile on every conceivable expense that will shrink the shared revenue pool. For a multiperson act, deals usually include the name of the band as well as individual band members in a single transaction.

Each category of product typically gets an exclusive licensee, meaning for example that only one company manufactures coffee mugs. In some cases, a master licensee

Vendors selling souvenirs at a concert.
Photo © Neal Preston/CORBIS.

handles all or broad categories, keeping some for itself and sublicensing to others to cover a wide array of products. The artist's manager may be in charge of the relationship with the merchandiser. Particularly if the record label has a 360 deal that covers merchandising, the label may guide the relationship.

For big stars, the licensed merchandise company typically makes an advance payment upon signing a contract, although such advances are partly returnable if merchandise sales fall short. If there is an advance payment, the artist usually doesn't get further pay until calculated royalties exceed the sum of that upfront pay. Another key point of negotiation is the length of a merchandise contract, which can run across a multicity tour or one or more album releases.

Another issue contracts need to address is artist obligation for unsold merchandise when any deal expires, because the merchandise company doesn't want to be stuck with goods and the artist doesn't want the overhang of excess old merchandise hampering future deals. The ways leftover merchandise is handled vary. The artist may have no responsibility, might have to suffer a royalty offset, or might be required to purchase unsold goods at or slightly above cost (for the artist to sell online, sell in bulk to a liquidator, or hand over to the next merchandise licensee).

Artist Merchandise at Concerts

For merchandise sold at concerts, royalty rates to artists are boosted to 15% to 22%, since artists create foot traffic for vendors. The venues themselves typically negotiate a 25% to 40% cut of merchandise revenue from concert dates, which is why prices are boosted for T-shirts, posters, and other items sold on-site in conjunction with tours. It's a negotiating point whether the venue's take—sometimes called **hall fee**— is excluded or included in calculating royalties going to the artist.

The typical arrangement has the concert venue staff selling merchandise that has been delivered by the master licensee, using display racks and booths owned by the venue. The total sale at the venue is calculated by subtracting the face value of merchandise that was unsold and carted away. When venues provide the labor for merchandise sales, venues get a variable return based on their percentage of total sales (the hall fee) and risk losing money if their cut of sales doesn't cover labor and other direct costs.

Generally speaking, the smaller the seating capacity of a venue, the higher the expectations are for merchandise sale on a per capita (each person) basis. The thinking is that the most loyal fans will account for most of a small audience. Conversely, per capita sales expectations are lower for the biggest venues—such as stadiums— because the throng is usually a mix of light and die-hard fans.

Another issue sometimes addressed in contracts is specifying a venue's responsibility to crack down on sale of unauthorized artist merchandise—which is illegally made and marketed—that might spring up around a venue on concert day and diminish sales of artist-sanctioned merchandise. Finally, concerts with many artists performing, such as festivals, are the least lucrative because fans buy "event" merchandise such as souvenir programs that do not generate royalties for any one artist.

Venue Trade Association

The venue business trade group, the International Association of Venue Managers (IAVM; www.iavm.org), helps industry professionals navigate in a changing field. IAVM members manage stadiums, arenas, concert halls, amphitheaters, convention centers, and arts centers. The nonprofit organization advocates for the industry and also promotes education in booking, ticketing, crowd management, and building security.

Chapter Takeaways

- Concerts venues come in an array of configurations ranging from cavernous stadiums seating tens of thousands to intimate settings that can hold only hundreds of spectators.

- Venues can be hard-nosed negotiators with promoters and performers, because they don't want to be left with unexpected liabilities when everyone else leaves town.

- Ticket sales remain a contentious issue, with artists, promoters, venues, and secondary distributors tussling over slices of an enormous revenue pie.

- Venues increasingly install wireless communications infrastructure in arenas to connect to audience smartphones and other mobile devices. Such multimedia interactions increase audience satisfaction and create a link with concertgoers that can be used for later marketing.

- Music artist-themed licensed merchandise is a multi-billion-dollar business in itself.

Key Terms

- deadwood   (p. 302)
- dynamic pricing   (p. 302)
- geographic exclusivity (p. 299)
- hall fee   (p. 305)
- merchandise   (p. 304)
- papering the house   (p. 302)
- royalties   (p. 304)
- scaling the house   (p. 302)
- secondary market   (p. 302)
- ticket scalping   (p. 302)

Discussion Questions

1. What are the advantages and disadvantages of securing a larger or smaller venue?

2. What are some challenges presented by secondary market ticket sales? Why might some artists and promoters encourage these?

3. Why are the concert promoter and artist disadvantaged in collecting audience personal information from in-venue wireless communications with the audience? What can they do about it?

4. Describe how the split of sales of licensed merchandise at concerts is particularly beneficial to the performing artist and the concert promoter.

CHAPTER 18

Arts Administration

Precise definitions for general terms such as *popular, classical,* **art music,** and *serious music* can get slippery. Confusion prevailed long before the 1924 premiere of George Gershwin's symphonic jazz composition *Rhapsody in Blue,* and disputes about the correct way to classify music will continue. But to provide a framework for this chapter, the terms *classical music* and *art music* are used interchangeably to discuss the repertoire generally associated with the symphony orchestra, opera, ballet, recital, modern dance, choral music, chamber music, and church music.

> "Life can't be all bad when for ten dollars you can buy all the Beethoven sonatas and listen to them for ten years."
>
> —William F. Buckley Jr.

Even though pop music gets most of the publicity, a great many people are involved in the classical music field, and its production and consumption are big business involving thousands of jobs and many millions of dollars per year.

The production and purveyance of serious music has traditionally been separate from pop. Although the artists and administrators often come from different backgrounds, they are, more often than not, engaged in very similar kinds of work. "Crossing the line" is an everyday occurrence. Individuals qualified to function in the world of "art music" often end up in "commercial music"; some who start their careers in one of the pop fields may find themselves working for a symphony orchestra or perhaps promoting classical artists.

It is customary to distinguish between pop and art music by describing the former as commercial or profit oriented and the latter as primarily nonprofit, since large performing groups such as orchestras, ballet companies, and the like are legally formed as not-for-profit **501(c)3 organizations.** But in actuality, profit and nonprofit segments intersect, because many in the serious music business make a fine living from performing or producing **classical music.** For example, it isn't unheard of for starting wages of a major symphony orchestra musician to be in the neighborhood of $80,000 to $100,000 per year. However, for the sake of clarity, this chapter uses the customary terms *nonprofit* or *not-for-profit* in discussing arts administration where accumulation of wealth is not the underlying purpose of the organization.

Perspective

Fueled in part by a healthy economy, the quarter century from the early 1960s to the mid-1980s saw an unprecedented growth in the arts in America. The number of professional symphony orchestras and opera or music theater companies nearly doubled, and ballet and modern dance companies burgeoned from 30 to more than 150. Those years also saw a dramatic increase in arts performances, employment of artists and arts administrators, and attendance at arts events. That encouraging picture, however, was changing by the end of the 1980s. In subsequent years, economic shocks and other upheavals stunted the growth of the arts generally and music specifically. Arts organizations, especially orchestras, began aggressive marketing campaigns to increase audiences.

The exposure afforded by televised viewing of the arts, particularly through the Public Broadcasting Service (PBS) and the Corporation for Public Broadcasting (**CPB**), as well as a number of cable channels, accelerated interest in the symphony, opera, and dance. There have been sponsored weekly radio broadcasts of the Metropolitan Opera since 1931 (the longest running radio show to date), as well as of symphony orchestras (San Francisco, Seattle, Los Angeles, and Chicago, among others). Telecasts of the Boston Pops and Boston Symphony have drawn audiences of millions. Imaginative producers such as Emmy Award winner Allan Miller have found ways to make symphonic music look interesting on film and TV.

Despite these successes, a daunting fact remains: Only a small portion of the public has a serious interest in serious music. Classical music recordings have rarely sold in large quantities. In the 1960s, Stravinsky complained that sales of records of works he had written after 1920 rarely exceeded 5,000 copies. These pieces—even by the world-famous composer—lost money for record labels. However, record companies and arts organizations have worked together to create innovative ways to promote and package releases appealing to buyers who formerly limited their purchases to pop music.

The **crossover recording** in the classical field now reaches expanded markets worldwide, as evidenced by the success of artists such as Yo-Yo Ma, Josh Groban, and Sara Brightman. Another tactic was used in the case of *Chant* in the mid-1990s, a recording of traditional Gregorian chant brilliantly marketed to the pop audience. And, there was Jackie Evancho, the young opera singer/overnight sensation who became popular as a result of her time on *America's Got Talent*. As pointed out in coverage of the recording industry, one of the strongest markets for crossover records is with movie music; soundtrack music appeals to both classical and pop music fans here and abroad.

Some serious music recordings, particularly the repertoire called *contemporary serious music,* often have difficulty making a profit. An important group of recordings of this repertoire is found on the CRI (Composers Recordings Inc.) label, now owned by New World Records, another nonprofit group whose mission is recording and distributing the music of contemporary American composers that might not otherwise be available for purchase.

How serious music organizations will weather the downturns of this or future eras remains to be seen, but if history is a predictor, they will be around for the next century and beyond. Arts organizations, especially orchestras, will always need to keep an eye to growing audiences both in terms of numbers and demographic composition.

With hardship, creativity is often born, and there are signs of creative health in the arts. Following are a few examples:

- Some orchestras that have had trouble in recent years attracting and/or making profits from recording deals have created their own record companies and produced their own products. The London Symphony has led the way with LSO Live recordings—offering conductors and musicians a stake in the profits as opposed to **upfront payments.** The Chicago Symphony's CSO Resound is another example of an orchestra-controlled record company. This independent venture has been quite successful with various recordings available in both CD and Super Audio CD (SACD)—high-quality audio—versions. As with DIY popular artists, the orchestras retain the rights to these recordings for use in future projects.

- Other arts organizations, particularly smaller ones, are able to make limited releases of recordings not to make a profit but as a marketing tool—to increase the exposure and stature of the organization—often asking conductors and musicians to work gratis or to settle for a share of the profits rather than for an upfront fee.

- The Metropolitan Opera has been notably aggressive in embracing technologies of the 21st century with initiatives such as its own media player available through a subscription service, partnerships with Rhapsody and Sirius XM, and a content-rich website. The Met also successfully presents live **HD** performances throughout the world in selected theaters—and even offers some performances live on the Web.

Representative Organizations

The world of classical music and arts administration includes a number of important organizations that represent the special interests of professionals in the field (see Chapter 10 on the unions and guilds representing artists in the classical field). A number of other important groups—not necessarily "guilds," despite some of their names—are listed below.

- The special interests of composers in the classical field have been served, since 1937, by the American Composers Alliance (ACA). Its American Composers Edition serves as a music publisher for its members, making scores and parts available through loans, rentals, and sales. One of ACA's member services is registering works with Broadcast Music Inc. (BMI). For many years, American composers have been active in the U.S. Section of the International Society for Contemporary Music (ISCM), founded in 1922 and formerly called the League of Composers. Founded by Aaron Copland and other distinguished American composers, this group has fostered public acceptance of contemporary serious music by offering concerts, goodwill, and publicity. The ISCM is active in 50 countries and sponsors the annual World New Music Days.

- Another organization devoted to the promotion of contemporary music is New Music USA (formerly the American Music Center), which provides composers and performers with assistance and information on funding, performance, and study opportunities. It maintains a library of scores and recordings available for circulation worldwide.

- The professional organization most representative of opera is Opera America. Its mission is to promote the creation, preservation, and enjoyment of opera in the United States. Through the Opera Fund, technical and financial support is provided to opera companies; the organization also provides consulting services on a wide range of topics for general directors of opera companies.

- Professional music critics have formed the Music Critics' Association of North America, which includes a large number of major critics in its membership.

- The organization Americans for the Arts (formerly Associated Councils for the Arts and the American Council for the Arts) forms a useful clearinghouse for information and ideas relating to state and regional arts council activities. It also provides extensive arts industry research, information, and professional development opportunities for community arts leaders nationwide, through a variety of programs and services.

- Arts presenters have organized the Association of Performing Arts Presenters (formerly Association of College, University and Community Arts Administrators). The Association of Arts Administration Educators represents educators in that field.

- International Society for the Performing Arts (ISPA) is an international network of performing arts professionals from more than 40 countries whose goal is to advance the performing arts on a global scale.

- An umbrella organization of broad scope is the National Music Council (NMC), chartered by Congress in 1956 to serve the interests of commercial and noncommercial music associations throughout the United States. It has some 45 member organizations that represent, in turn, an aggregate membership of more than 1 million. A partial list of its member organizations indicates the breadth of NMC: AFM, AGMA, AMC, ASCAP, BMI, CMA, MENC, MPA, NARAS, NMPA, RIAA, SAI, and SESAC. The National Music Council has been designated the official U.S. representative to the International Music Council, a UNESCO-sponsored organization of national and international music committees. It holds a biennial general assembly and World Congress to discuss issues of musical importance, and it initiates a research into new media and technologies.

- Almost every instrument represented in the orchestra has developed an association to develop performance, networking, and research presentation opportunities for their members. Examples include the American Guild of Organists, International Double Reed Society, International Trombone Association, and the International Trumpet Guild.

Symphonic Music

Although classical music has a much smaller market than popular music, a lot of money is generated by musical organizations performing this repertoire. The largest audience in this field is for symphonic music. There are about 2,000 symphony orchestras in the United States, with more than 50 of them claiming an annual budget of over a million dollars. These orchestras typically file with the IRS as 501(c)3 nonprofit organizations and are run by boards of directors in the community. These symphonies collectively employ thousands of musicians and require varying support positions, including managers, booking agents, librarians, and venue management personnel.

League of American Orchestras

Founded in 1942 and chartered by Congress in 1962, the League of American Orchestras (formerly the American Symphony Orchestra League) is the national nonprofit service and educational organization dedicated to strengthening symphony

Table 18.1 Symphony Orchestras in the United States With Budgets Over $15 Million

Los Angeles Philharmonic	Indianapolis Symphony
Boston Symphony Orchestra	Baltimore Symphony
San Francisco Symphony	St. Louis Symphony Orchestra
New York Philharmonic	Houston Symphony Orchestra
Chicago Symphony Orchestra	Dallas Symphony Orchestra
Philadelphia Orchestra	Seattle Symphony
Atlanta Symphony	San Diego Symphony
Cleveland Orchestra	Metropolitan Opera Orchestra
Cincinnati Symphony	Detroit Symphony Orchestra
Pittsburgh Symphony	Milwaukee Symphony Orchestra
National Symphony Orchestra	Utah Symphony & Opera
Minnesota Orchestra	

Source: Compiled by Jeffrey Clymer from information released by the American Symphony Orchestra League and International Conference of Symphony and Opera Musicians (ICSOM).

and chamber orchestras. The League's annual conventions draw enthusiastic delegates from all over the country. Its professional staff provides artistic, organizational, and financial leadership and service to the music directors, musicians, direct-service and governance volunteers, managers, and staff who make up its member orchestras. Its work is made possible by grants from private and public institutions, contributions from individuals, and members' dues; for member orchestras, these dues are scaled according to the size of the orchestra's annual budget. The League is research oriented and serves as a source of data for its members, who are interested in arts administration, audience building, and fundraising.

Education is one of the most useful services provided by the League. Each year, the League staffs and sponsors regional workshops. Professional managers, symphony board members, conductors, and volunteer workers attend these meetings to learn from experts how to function more effectively in their own communities. The League offers annual workshops and symposia with leading orchestra conductors. Its Resource Center provides updated literature on governance. It also sponsors orchestra management seminars where current and aspiring orchestra managers attend classes for several days of intensive study. The League receives partial support of its educational activities from the National Endowment for the Arts.

Funding the Arts

Arts organizations garner two kinds of revenue: (1) "earned" income, which includes ticket sales, music download receipts, and other direct payments for what they do, and (2) "contributed" income, which includes donations and grants. The hard fact is that even the best-managed arts organization cannot expect to break even at the box office. All symphonies and opera and ballet companies, no matter how efficiently run, are unable to earn sufficient income from performances to cover their expenses. Simply stated, all arts

Vancouver Symphony Orchestra with Bramwell Tovey.
Photo © The City of Vancouver.

organizations are dependent on outside funding for survival. This has been through-out history. Among the earliest patrons of the arts in the Western world were the church and the nobility. Concurrent with patronage of this kind, artists occasionally earned part of their livelihood from municipal and national governments. When public theaters and concert halls increased in number in the 17th and 18th centuries, money generated by ticket sales to the middle class helped support musicians, as did persons with private wealth. In modern times, "arts societies" were formed by patrons to organize financial backing for orchestras and opera companies. For generations, U.S. arts organizations enjoyed large gifts from wealthy individuals. Even today, individuals account for the bulk of money that is contributed. But in recent decades, changes in federal tax laws have made it more difficult for arts organizations to depend on large gifts from wealthy individuals.

Ticket Sales

Performing arts organizations typically earn anywhere between 30% and 65% of their costs of operation by ticket sales. If ticket prices were raised to cover all expenses, the resulting cost would be out of the range of all but the wealthiest patrons. Knowing this, arts organizations are always looking for strategies to maximize the revenue that does come in from this source. Tickets may sometimes be more easily sold for individual performances, but most major symphonies and opera and dance companies prefer that their energies are spent seeking sales of a full series of performances. Income from subscription sales and season tickets allows arts organizations to plan their budgets and fundraising activities for the year, rather than simply from concert to concert.

Subscriptions

Enthusiasts who buy season tickets not only commit themselves to more money but also are much more loyal and enthusiastic than those who attend only occasionally. The subscriber feels like a patron of the arts, a supporter of the performing group who takes pride in its health and progress. But selling subscriptions can be challenging, as audience members want flexibility to pick and choose. Successful organizations are redefining what subscription packages are and how to promote them.

Foundations, Corporate Giving

Foundations have long been a major arts funding source; they still are, but their significance has diminished. When difficult times periodically hit organizations, as they invariably do, generous organizations such as the Ford and Rockefeller Foundations may find that their assets have dropped in value and will need to cut grants accordingly. Nonetheless, hundreds of foundations still make important grants to the arts as they are able. Everyone in the field knows this, and these organizations spend much of their time receiving and processing pleas for money.

The Foundation Center is a clearinghouse for information about foundations and the grants they award. The organization publishes *Foundation Fundamentals: A Guide for Grantseekers,* which includes recommended procedures for locating information on foundations in specific areas and identifying their particular interests. Among its many targeted publications, the Foundation Center produces *The Grants for Arts, Culture and the Humanities.* (Most of the Foundation Center's research tools can be found online.)

Many businesses are interested in and eager to support their local arts organizations. When arts groups complain about their lack of support from big corporations, the problem may not be lack of interest from the corporations as much as the absence of proper solicitation. Some of the big companies have never been asked—or asked correctly. And most will not give money until someone steps forth and helps them understand why they should. Companies want to know about audience demographics—are the people coming to the event the same people who are buying our goods and services? Many businesses are more likely to fund arts groups that have a direct impact on their own communities.

The Business Committee for the Arts (BCA), a division of Americans for the Arts, founded in 1967 by David Rockefeller and other prominent business leaders, is a national, not-for-profit organization that encourages businesses to support the arts and provides the resources necessary to develop effective business-arts alliances. BCA's more than 100 member companies have long-term commitments to developing partnerships with the arts that benefit business, the arts, and society.

Government Subsidy

In Europe, symphonies and opera companies have long enjoyed governmental subsidies. This is such a strong tradition that music lovers there have some assurance that their symphonies and opera companies will survive from year to year. In contrast, governmental support of the arts in the United States has been near zero throughout most of its history, but in the late 1960s, it increased measurably and continued to rise through the 1970s. In the early 1980s, federal funding for the arts was reduced, but there was an upswing in state funding in the mid-1990s only to fall again in the early part of the 21st century. It is likely that governmental support for the arts, either directly through grants or indirectly through tax benefits for donors, will continue to ebb and flow. While these funds are an important revenue source for many arts organizations, they can't rely on government money as a reliable long-term subsidy.

National Endowment for the Arts

In 1965, Congress established the National Foundation for the Arts and Humanities. Within the foundation, two agencies were formed: the National Endowment for the Arts (NEA) and the National Endowment for the Humanities (NEH). In 1966, Congress appropriated $5 million for these agencies to "foster the arts." The appropriation for 2015 was approximately $140 million. The enabling legislation provided that NEA funds were to be allocated upon the advice of the National Council on the Arts, a group of 18 private citizens appointed by the president and six (nonvoting) members of Congress to oversee the affairs of the NEA and NEH. Currently, the NEA receives several thousand applications a year, with nearly half of the music requests receiving grants. To be eligible, an organization must be not-for-profit and have had at least 3 years of programming. On average, applications take 7 to 12 months to process.

State Arts Councils

According to the NEA, the number of community, regional, and state arts councils has been on the increase. Federal law requires the NEA to assign 40% of its programming funds to state and regional arts agencies.

Some state legislatures began support of the arts with great reluctance, but pressure on politicians from their constituents has often changed that. Many states assign tax dollars to help support artists and arts organizations beyond the monies from the NEA. For example, New York began to appropriate far more (total) dollars for the arts than any other state years ago, after a wide-scale study of the cultural and economic impact of the arts on the state reported that the great majority of the electorate favored generous support of cultural enterprises from tax money and that money spent in these ways benefits the state's economy.

Arts enthusiasts in other states have used similar evidence to demonstrate the favorable economic impact of dollars paid out for symphonies, opera, and ballet companies. For example, the millions spent each year for the Boston Symphony Orchestra exert a strong influence on the economy of the Boston area. About one half of that huge budget will be spent around Boston through the wages paid the orchestra's artists and staff people. Other millions of that budget will be fed back into the local economy for transportation, utilities, advertising, and equipment. And hundreds of thousands of concertgoers further feed the Boston-area economy for things such as dinners out and taxicabs. The NEA estimates that the arts (both for-profit and non-profit sectors) contribute about $700 billion to the U.S. economy, more than 4% of gross domestic product (GDP). Another national estimate of the full economic impact of nonprofit arts and culture is offered in Table 18.2.

Volunteer Support

There are many opportunities to seek funding, but grant writing and soliciting donations take a great deal of time and energy. Financially vibrant performing arts groups often have experienced **development officers** who know how to solicit the support of savvy volunteers who know how to ask for money. Boards of directors comprise individuals who have been asked to join the organization for a variety of reasons, but almost always some seats are reserved for individuals from the community who have connections to wealthy community members. These individuals are expected to capitalize on their influence and connections to convince people of means to share their wealth with the organization. Arts organizations typically hope to enlist large numbers of socially conscious citizens to get out in the community and seek donations, large and small. Symphony, dance, and opera companies that can organize several dozen committees to get on the telephone and follow up with mail and email solicitations generally find that this group of people becomes an irresistible force. The most effective campaigns of this kind are not only carefully timed and organized, but each solicitor undergoes training—how to talk to people, what to say, how to "close the sale."

Table 18.2   Economic Impact of U.S. Arts and Culture Industry

Nationally, the nonprofit arts and culture industry generates an estimated $135.2 billion in economic activity annually—$61.1 billion in spending by organizations and an additional $74.1 billion in event-related spending by their audiences. The $135.2 billion in total economic activity has a significant national impact, generating the following:
• $86.68 billion in household income • $6.07 billion in local government tax revenues • $6.67 billion in state government tax revenues • $9.5 billion in federal income tax revenues

Source: Arts and Economic Prosperity IV Study from Americans for the Arts, 2010.

In addition to selling subscriptions, volunteer committees take on a variety of other fundraising projects, including gala events such as fashion shows, antique sales, and auctions. These projects raise millions for the arts. And to hear the volunteer workers tell it, taking part can be great fun. No arts enterprise could function without the generous and enthusiastic efforts of its volunteer workers.

No account of subsidies for the arts would be complete without recognizing the generous contributions of the artists themselves—composers, conductors, and performers. In every community, these individuals subsidize the arts by working without a fee or for fees significantly below professional levels. They donate their artistry to the cause because their love for music exceeds their desire for financial reward. Without their gifts of time and talent, the production and performance of the arts would suffer greatly.

Classical Artist Management

Just as popular musicians look for managers and talent agencies, the most well-known and sought-after artists need help finding and negotiating performances and scheduling tours. Many agencies specialize in classical artists, such as IMG Artists and Opus 3. One of the oldest and best known is Columbia Artist Management Inc. (CAMI). Formed in the 1930s, CAMI assists artists with career development and concert touring. It boasts a roster of international artists from a broad range of genres, including instrumental soloists, opera singers, conductors, classical music ensembles, orchestras, dance companies, popular and theatrical attractions, and fine arts media productions. These artists play hundreds of gigs per year, and some command impressive fees for their performances.

Administration

The Need

Training. Leading U.S. arts administrators define their work as "the art of losing money gracefully." Until recent decades, their profession was unknown. The people who had the responsibility of managing an orchestra or opera company learned on the job and muddled through. This pattern still prevails too often today in hundreds of smaller arts organizations, which may be one reason many of them experience serious financial trouble.

Today, many quality educational programs in colleges and universities—from Claremont Graduate University in California to Florida State University—offer graduate degrees in arts administration or allied disciplines. The Association of Arts Administration Educators keeps updated information available on current programs and how to contact them (www.artsadministration.org).

Although a few thousand graduates of various arts management training programs are currently employed in the field, there still is a shortage of fully qualified candidates to manage the affairs of arts groups, many of which have operating budgets in the millions. The League of American Orchestras states that there is an acute shortage of persons qualified to fill the job openings in this country for symphony orchestra management. William Dawson, former executive director of the Association of Performing Arts Presenters, has said that jobs await individuals possessing "professional skills" in the field. And fortunately, more and more resources are becoming available to hone the skills needed for success.

One way to gain a perspective on the need for professional arts administrators is to look at the staff of a major symphony orchestra. An organization with an annual budget in the range of $5 million to $10 million will have these professionals at work 50 weeks a year:

• General Manager or Executive Director	• Personnel Director
○ Assistant Manager	• Road Manager or Stage Director
• Director of Development	○ Assistant Stage Director
○ Assistant Director of Development	• Property Manager
○ Development Manager	• Head Librarian
• Special Projects Coordinator	○ Assistant Librarian
○ Two to four additional professional money raisers	• Controller or Accountant
• Publications Director • Director of Public Relations or Director of Press Relations	○ Two to four assistants to the Controller (bookkeepers, etc.)
○ Assistant Public Relations Director	• Ticket Sales Manager
• Art Director	○ Assistant Ticket Manager
• Advertising Manager	• Office Manager
• Volunteer Activities Coordinator	○ Secretaries, Assistants

Responsibilities. The general manager ensures that the other individuals understand their responsibilities and discharge them properly. If the manager's associates function properly, the manager has time to operate at a strategic level—thinking, planning, budgeting, promoting, following directives from the board, raising money, handling finances, and creating an environment for the symphony that makes possible ever-finer artistic achievements, the reason this effort is expended in the first place.

Management, too, is an art, as Mozart's father once said. First and foremost, it is the art of working with people effectively. Arts organizations are remarkable in that they involve professionals and volunteers working side by side. The smooth cooperation of professionals and amateurs is not achieved easily, and some arts administrators never really get the hang of it. When people work for free, they must be treated with respect by their managers. The armies of volunteers essential to all arts organizations just won't work unless they believe wholeheartedly in the artistic goals and the management of the ensembles and know they are appreciated and crucial to the success of their organizations.

In addition to possessing the ability to organize and motivate large numbers of volunteer committees, the arts administrator must be responsive to the policies of and instructions from the board of directors. The League's Ralph Black was fond of saying that the number one problem of professional symphony orchestras is not money but weak boards. Helen M. Thompson, former staff head of the League, directed a study some years ago that showed that truly successful symphony orchestras enjoy the support of board members who really work at it. The second finding of the League's research demonstrated that really well-run orchestras "had etched out a sound basic philosophy of the value of the orchestra as a permanent institution in the life of the community."

Assuming the manager and the board see eye to eye, the administrative head may have any or all of these responsibilities:

1. Supervise the work of the staff. Hire and fire.

2. Organize and supervise volunteers.

3. Direct long-range planning.

4. Raise money. This is a large part of the board's responsibility, but it needs direction and a lot of help.

5. Prepare budgets, including debt management, endowment funds, retirement plans, campaign funds, and operations budgets.

6. Work with the artistic director in the conception and implementation of programs—including casting and scheduling.

7. Negotiate contracts for professional services. The most difficult may be with the AFM, whose contracts normally run for 2 to 3 years. Dozens of contracts must also be negotiated with guest conductors and guest soloists. The manager who spends too much leads the organization deeper into debt. If too little is spent, artistic standards may drop.

8. Supervise technical matters relative to performances, the daily moving of artists and equipment, staging and lighting, and booking transportation, hotels, and meals for more than 100 artists. (Other staff members will generally handle many of these duties, but the director carries the ultimate responsibility for them.)

9. Handle press relations and public relations; keep the volunteers happy, the press happy, the politicians happy, the schoolchildren and their teachers happy, the National Endowment for the Arts happy, the board happy, and, above all, keep the audience happy.

Because no one individual knows how or has the time and energy to accomplish all these things directly, it might be more instructive to list the specific skills and attributes required of a successful arts administrator.

The ideal administrator:

- Doesn't just like music but *loves* it
- Has great energy and enthusiasm—the kind that inspires others to want to work, too
- Uses energy and time efficiently and knows how to organize the energies of others
- Knows how to run a meeting: starts on time, announces a specific agenda, manages the flow of conversation, prohibits digressions, encourages all points of view, summarizes decisions made, and adjourns on time
- Keeps in mind long-range goals but knows the most important thing to do on Monday morning
- Can prepare a sensible budget, present it clearly, and stay within it; although not a CPA, can count and is careful with other people's money
- Interacts successfully with artists and their representatives

- Recruits effective professionals and helps them to work together toward a common goal
- Understands the need for cultural diplomacy and diversity

Financial Management

Management of arts organizations is difficult because there will never be enough money, so administrators may limp along, improvising each day some kind of quick fix against impending disaster. Arts groups that survive must manage their finances astutely, starting with a well-conceived financial plan. This is a minimum requirement in avoiding serious fiscal difficulties but not an easy one. An arts organization's financial plan is not like a plan for a commercial business operation, because a symphony, opera, or dance company has no easy way of calculating what accountants like to call cost-benefit ratios. This is a way of asking, "If we spend $1,000 here, what benefits will that money produce?" Because arts groups are generally not-for-profit, the decision about that $1,000 outlay must be calculated not on what profit it might yield but by what it might produce artistically—and artistic achievements cannot be listed on profit-and-loss statements. So the arts administrator must make many important financial decisions intuitively.

In many communities, experts in financial management, insurance, advertising, printing, graphic arts, and public relations volunteer their assistance without cost to arts organizations. These are significant contributions and help keep costs low. CPAs often tell arts administrators that their money problems don't particularly stem from a need for more frugality. Indeed, many arts groups can teach commercial concerns how to get things done at minimum cost. Rather, the financial experts observe that lack of financial planning by boards and arts administrators for income, expense, and debt management is at the heart of many arts administration problems.

Audience Development

Between the "graying of America" and the decline of arts education in school systems, arts organizations are struggling to engage younger audiences (see Table 18.3). Consequently, audience development has become a major focus for arts administrators, especially in the classical music field. "We have to create our own audience, just like with any industry," explains Michael Millar, an educator and veteran arts administrator in California. Arts organizations of all kinds have undertaken myriad initiatives to build audiences and attract younger audiences. Notable among these efforts are special-interest concert and opera events, informal preconcert lectures, and performances incorporating film and other visual and electronic media. The now-common use of English supertitles for operas has made that art form more accessible to audiences of all ages. Programs undertaken by local symphony and chamber orchestras, such as active outreach to schools and instrument classes offered by orchestra musicians under the sponsorship of the orchestra, have made the organizations more visible in their communities, building broader bases of support. The decline of arts education in school systems over the years has affected all arts organizations. But some organizations are fighting back with innovative programs, such as cut-rate tickets for the under-40 age group. Many varieties of community engagement—which require listening to the community as well as simply evangelizing for its support—are planting seeds that arts organizations hope to harvest over time.

If an arts organization can learn good financial management and has a knack for audience development, the other essential component leading to success is a passion for the cause. Money and passion: a powerful combination.

Table 18.3   Attendance Rates for Arts Activities by Age

Of people who reported attending live arts activities at least once during the year 2012, the chart below shows the percentage of people in each age group who attended live jazz, classical, and opera concerts.

Age	% Attending Live Jazz Music	% Attending Live Classical Music	% Attending Live Opera
18–24	12%	11%	2.2%
25–34	12.5%	13.5%	3.7%
35–44	15.8%	15.6%	3.8%
45–54	16.8%	16.7%	4.7%
55–64	21.8%	23.0%	5.9%
65–74	19.1%	31.3%	9.7%
75+	14.1%	36.5%	9.7%

Source: "A Decade of Arts Engagement," NEA Research Report #58, 2015.

Chapter Takeaways

- The production and consumption of "serious" music is big business involving thousands of jobs and many millions of dollars.

- A wide variety of organizations promote the art and dissemination of classical music, including the League of American Orchestras, Opera America, Americans for the Arts, and the National Music Council.

- Even well-managed symphonies and opera and ballet companies require subsidies to cover all their expenses. Ticket sales,

particularly subscriptions, are vital but not sufficient.

- Financial support for arts organizations comes from foundations, corporations, and various levels of government. But the largest source of contributed revenue comes from individuals.

- Management of arts organizations—a key for success—has been improved in recent decades by a variety of education and training resources.

Key Terms

- 501(c)3 organizations   (p. 309)
- art music   (p. 309)
- classical music   (p. 309)
- crossover recording   (p. 310)
- development officers   (p. 316)
- National Endowment for the Arts   (p. 315)
- supertitles   (p. 320)

Discussion Questions

1. What are some ways art music has crossed over into the popular music arena?

2. As government significantly reduces funding for the arts, how can nonprofit arts organizations maintain excellence?

3. Discuss the skills successful arts administrators need to have.

4. What can arts administrators and others in the art music field do to develop and engage younger audiences?

Music in the Marketplace

PART 6

CHAPTER 19

Music in Radio

For decades, record labels aggressively pursued radio airplay because it was the surest path to increased retail music sales. There was no doubt radio was the best medium to introduce new songs to vast audiences. However, the dawn of the digital media explosion in the early 1990s diminished the supremacy of broadcast radio. Over the years, a succession of digital music platforms carved out slices of the music-consuming market—portable CD players made popular by the Sony Walkman, Apple's iPod and iTunes, MTV: Music Television and other music TV channels, Internet radio, satellite radio, and the mushrooming streaming revolution.

Yet it all started with broadcast radio. The early radio broadcasts were all live, of course, often featuring opera stars and other artists in the classical field. The audio quality was poor, and the broadcast signals were filled with static, but audiences loved the novelty of radio and rushed out to buy the new crystal sets[1] to receive the broadcasts in their homes.

The first commercially licensed station went on the air in 1920. Entrepreneurs saw the potential of the medium, and within 3 years, more than 500 stations were licensed and the first radio network had been formed. Radio grew, as did the popularity of phonograph records, and these two industries formed the first mass media for sound. In the early 1940s, the *Make Believe Ballroom* made its appearance and attracted a big following—it was the first radio show to use only recorded music.

> "For a long time I wasn't listening to music, to the rock and roll stuff on the radio, because it would cause me to get sweaty. . . . If it was good, I hated it 'cause I wasn't doing it. And if it was bad, I was furious 'cause I could've done it better."
>
> —John Lennon

Stations throughout the country quickly followed suit, spurred by the realization that they didn't need live orchestras to attract listeners.

It seemed radio was headed for near extinction in the late 1940s, as the emergence of television not only siphoned audiences but also drained radio of its **programming**, which at the time consisted of scripted comedies, dramas, and variety shows, in addition to music. Radio stars such as comedian Jack Benny, baritone narrator and drama actor William Conrad, and comedian/actor George Burns departed for TV. A legendary Texas broadcaster, Gordon McLendon, perfected radio's salvation in the early 1950s with a then-revolutionary concept of broadcasting genre-specific programming instead of a broad mix of general entertainment. His most famous creation was Top 40 radio on Dallas radio station KLIF. The format called for a tight **playlist** of hit songs, on-air contests, goofy promotions, and banter from "personality" disc jockeys. Although derided over the years for slavish conformity to current hit songs, Top 40 was an innovation at the time.

In 2003, the broadcast radio sector introduced HD Radio™[2] technology, allowing AM and FM stations to **simulcast** their main signals in a digital format, offering improved audio quality. In addition, FM stations are able to squeeze more audio channels in their allocated spectrum via HD Radio™ technology through what is called **multicasting**. (AM stations cannot insert multicast channels because of their spectrum limitations.) FM multicasting helps close the gap with satellite radio's vast channel offerings, although HD Radio™ is only slowly making inroads.

Today, as digital media capture consumer fancy, radio is struggling as an advertisement-supported medium. Yet, although no longer dominant, radio is still potent. An estimated 242 million persons ages 12 and older in the United States tune in to radio each week, which translates to 91.3% of that population. A typical listener tunes into 2 hours and 32 minutes of radio each day, and that is significant media consumption. That's for broadcast radio, HD, and streaming of radio stations measured by Nielsen Audio. There is also limited reporting of satellite radio listening. To get a picture of how the phenomenon has developed historically, see Table 19.1.

Types of Broadcast Radio Stations

One way to classify stations that broadcast from terrestrial transmission towers is by their carrier waves. AM stands for amplitude modulation, where the power or amplitude of the carrier wave varies but the wave frequency remains constant. FM stands for frequency modulation, where the carrier wave frequency varies but its amplitude remains constant. In the beginning, AM stations dominated radio broadcasting. Although FM stations have been around since the 1940s, in the early 1970s, they increased their share of the audience dramatically. Today, FM stations generally are music stations, and AM is the home of news, talk, and sports.

Another way to classify stations is by their call letters. The earliest U.S. radio stations selected their own three- or four-letter call letters beginning with either a W or a K. Stations in Mexico and Canada were required to use an X and C, respectively. In the 1920s, the Federal Radio Commission devised a system requiring new stations east of the Mississippi River to adopt call letters beginning with a W and stations in the West to start with a K, which is opposite the designation for ship radio stations in the Atlantic and Pacific Oceans.

Table 19.1   Historical Development of Music in Radio

1864	The basic theory of electromagnetism is set down by British scientist James C. Maxwell.
1865	Italian inventor Guglielmo Marconi develops the first radio.
1920	The first commercially licensed radio station goes on the air (KDKA, Pittsburgh), broadcasting the presidential election returns (Harding vs. Cox).
1922	The novelty of radio quickly attracts larger audiences. Sixty stations are on the air.
1923	Radio broadcasting booms. AT&T inaugurates the first radio network.
1926	Radio rapidly becomes "show business." Stars of the Metropolitan Opera and other classical artists are featured. Vaudeville headliners begin to be programmed.
1930s	Over 600 stations are on the air by 1931. In 1934, the Federal Communications Commission (FCC) is set up by the Federal Communications Act. Broadcasting is turned over to "free enterprise" with minimum federal control. During the Great Depression, when people cannot afford to buy records or tickets to the movies, radio offers "free" entertainment to mass audiences. Network shows feature vaudeville headliners, movie stars, and name bands. Advertising revenue soars.
1940s	Soon after the FCC authorizes commercial FM stations, the onset of World War II delays marketplace development until peacetime.
1950s	The rapid growth of television nearly kills network radio, quickly wiping out most live music and radio staff orchestras. Radio stations narrow their programming to one genre of recorded music, pulling impressive audiences. The personality-oriented disc jockey begins to dominate. **Payola** scandals bring national attention to the way music is selected for airplay.
1960s	The FCC authorizes **multiplex** broadcasting. The record business booms, largely due to the promotional medium of radio. FM stations increase in number and begin to attract specialized audiences.
1970s	FM stations turn more toward the "middle" audience in quest of a larger market share. Most AM and FM programming becomes predictable, with few programmers risking innovation. The medium continues to earn good money.
1980s	The FCC relaxes controls over programming. FM stations gain larger audiences. Radio's once-dominant power to influence record sales is now shared by music video.
1990s	Formats split into tighter niches. Digital audio reaches radio stations in the form of digital workstations in production rooms and control rooms. Number of stations individual owners can hold increases, radically changing management and staffing patterns and greatly speeding up the spread of successful formats.
2000s	Traditional radio stations face new competition from commercial-free, newly launched, subscription-based satellite radio and streaming Internet audio stations. Spanish-language outlets pull in large ratings and are among the most popular stations in certain U.S. markets. Cable TV and digital media siphon audiences and advertising dollars with their segmented programming, bringing financial strain to station groups and program syndicators. The birth of HD Radio™ brings improved audio quality as traditional radio stations simulcast their main signals in the digital format.
2010s	Broadcast (terrestrial) radio continues to fight for listening share with Webcasters, which in turn struggle financially because of higher performance royalty expenses than rivals. Media giant Walt Disney takes a financial write-off on the value of its owned radio stations after finding less than one fifth of listening for its Radio Disney audio network comes from over-the-air broadcasting.

Audience Identification and Market Research ▰▰▰

Most radio stations adopt a supremely simple programming philosophy: To attract a particular segment of the radio audience, broadcast its favorite music. As an advertisement-supported medium, radio station managers start by identifying audience segments in a given metropolitan area that have appeal to advertisers. They then select a program format expected to attract that audience after assessing whether there is room for them to compete in that segment.

Demography. Audience research is based on **demographic** studies, which deal with the distribution, density, and vital statistics of populations. Stations and their advertisers are interested in the location, ages, gender, education, economic status, and other characteristics of their potential audience—and above all, how many people listen to the station at various times during the day.

Research Methods. Radio market research largely depends on polling samples of its audience or potential audience. Companies sampling broadcast audiences assert that their figures are in the 3% to 5% accuracy range. But not all market research is this good or this useful to broadcasters and their advertisers. Research methods range from casual to scientific. The most trustworthy, systematic methods used for broadcasters attempt to determine three basic sets of statistics:

- Station rating. This is determined by counting the percentage of the potential audience that is listening to a particular station at a particular time. For example, if a station has a rating of 5.2 at noon on weekdays, that means that of every 1,000 households surveyed, 52 were listening to that station at noon on a weekday.
- Sets in use. This is a count of the actual number of homes with radios turned on. If the market had 100,000 households and 62.4% of the sampled homes had radios turned on, then sets in use would be projected at 62,400.
- **Audience share.** This is a statistic indicating the comparative popularity of a program being broadcast at a particular time. For example, if a show has a 10.1 share, that means that, of the homes that had their sets turned on, 10.1% were listening to that particular program at that particular time.

Radio operators conduct their own music popularity research in addition to buying *syndicated* research (identical reports and data sold to multiple clients). To estimate the audience size that drives the placement of billions of dollars annually in radio advertising, Nielsen measures listening in the top 48 radio metropolitan markets using its Portable People Meter (PPM) electronic survey system, and the remaining 200+ markets are measured using the less-sophisticated audio diary method. PPMs are small electronic listening devices worn by consumers that detect and identify radio station audio. National radio listening data are reported quarterly. Separately, Nielsen Music electronically recognizes and counts over 1 million songs per day on 2,000+ radio stations and cable networks in the United States, Canada, Mexico, and Puerto Rico. Nielsen Music also receives reports from some music-streaming services in the United States and Canada. This kind of airplay information provides insights to radio operators on trends around the country as well as local competitors' programming. Prior to this kind of automated electronic measurement, airplay lists were largely compiled by asking radios stations what music they played, a methodology subject to manipulation since stations were under no obligation to provide accurate answers. (For a further discussion of market research, see Chapter 15.)

■ Spectrum of Formats

Commercial radio stations programming music tend to devote themselves to one type of music, which makes the station a destination for the audience segment devoted to that genre. In an age of **narrowcasting,** formats constantly emerge, evolve, and recede.

Table 19.2 **America's Top Radio Formats**

% Ranked by Share of Total Listening	Format
15.2	Country
10.6	News/talk
8.0	Pop contemporary hit radio (CHR)
7.6	Adult contemporary (AC)
5.6	Classic rock
5.5	Classic hits
5.3	Hot adult contemporary (AC)
4.3	Urban adult contemporary (AC)
3.5	Contemporary Christian
3.3	All sports
3.2	Urban contemporary
3.0	Rhythmic contemporary hit radio (CHR)
2.6	Mexican regional
2.0	Active rock
1.9	Adult hits + '80s hits
1.8	Alternative
1.7	Album oriented rock (AOR) + mainstream rock
1.5	Classical
1.3	Spanish contemporary + Spanish hot AC
1.3	Religious
1.3	All news
9.5	30 other miscellaneous formats
100.0	Total

Source: Nielsen ranking average quarter-hour (AQH) share among listeners ages 12+ in spring 2014.

National Public Radio. The **FCC** sets aside a segment of the FM broadcast band (88–92 megahertz) for schools, colleges, civic entities, and others who devote all or part of their programming to education, the arts, and other kinds of nonprofit enterprise. Most public radio stations are low powered, 10 watts or less, although most simulcast on Internet channels that enable listeners to bypass their weak over-the-air signals. They do not accept most forms of commercial advertising, and their audiences are generally smaller than those of commercial stations.

Stations located on college campuses are often connected with one or more campus departments, such as music, broadcasting, or theater. Programming tends to lean to the personal tastes of the current group of station managers. Alternative music and lesser-known recording artists are sometimes featured. Promoters and agents for the artists are well received by campus stations, and promoters from recording companies say that pushing alternative releases to college radio stations has had an impact on sales. Most public radio stations are receptive to special programming that might include chamber music, opera, electronic music, avant-garde, ethnic and world music, campus recitals, and concerts featuring faculty and students. These stations also sometimes broadcast educational music programs, such as "Music Appreciation" or "Understanding Jazz." Noncommercial programs like "Morning Becomes Eclectic" on KCRW in Santa Monica, California, are legendary as a platform for promoting new music through both in-studio performances and nonmainstream recordings.

Many public radio stations are affiliated with National Public Radio (**NPR**), which was incorporated in 1970. The network and its affiliates receive financial support from the federally funded Corporation for Public Broadcasting, the federally funded National Endowment for the Arts, cities, state arts councils, and private donations. Some public radio stations receive support from American Federation of Musicians (AFM) locals, which use this medium to foster "live" broadcasts of music and musicians. NPR has a longstanding agreement with the AFM to pay union wages and to protect AFM members from unauthorized new uses of music originally cleared only for NPR broadcasts.

NBC Radio, 1949.
Photo courtesy of Roberta Baskerville archive.

Live Music Then and Now: In the Golden Age of network radio, live music predominated, such as on this 1949 musical quiz show broadcast nationally from NBC studios in Hollywood (above). Today, live radio music is a rarity but still exists. This NPR station (opposite) features live music from bands seeking to promote themselves and their local club dates.

Band performing on "Morning Becomes Eclectic," KCRW Studio, Santa Monica College.
Photo courtesy of KCRW.

How Commercial Radio Stations Work

Staffing

As a result of the 1996 Telecommunications Act and the resulting consolidation of ownership of stations, the management structure of the majority of commercial stations has shifted over the years. Where it had once been common to see one general manager, program director, and marketing and promotions director for one or two radio stations, it soon became clear that a company that owned or managed eight stations in one market could administer them all with one manager. It's now common to find one market manager running six stations in a given city, a promotions manager in charge of those six, and one sales manager selling their advertising, either individually or in combination. Radio stations in the same market but with different ownerships can contract for such local clustering agreements. Program directors (PDs) and **engineers** often perform their functions for several sister stations, as well. (For a description of music-related careers in radio, see Chapter 28, "Career Options.")

Programming

Once a station has settled on a format, there's the ongoing work of putting together the week's playlist and the day-to-day programming, including which new songs to fold into the current playlist and which older ones to drop. The consolidation of radio stations has made it more difficult for songs to make it on the air, because the decisions about what gets aired rest in the hands of fewer people. For many years, songs landed on a station's playlist based on three criteria: local sales figures, requests, and the music director's gut instinct. Today, music selections often come from a radio group's corporate brass—which typically is in a distant city. Still, many stations, particularly contemporary hit-music outlets, like to play up the audience's perceived participation in shaping the playlist.

Until the late 1950s, most of the records that got on the air were selected by the disc jockeys, who were prime targets for the blandishments and bribes of music business promoters, which led to payola scandals that hit the national news. Since then, there have been occasional scandals involving independent recording promoters, but for the most part, stations have kept a careful eye out to prevent them happening again. However, controversy still exists over some stations' allegedly strong-arming artists to play station-sponsored events in exchange for airplay. In a typical week, perhaps 10 to 15 songs are "adds" of new music for a playlist (and a commensurate number of songs are dropped). However, usually only a handful of songs will be chosen for the choice spots, called heavy rotation, which means lots of exposure.

Song Clustering, Pacing. Whatever the dominant type of music programmed, stations often cluster their songs, then cluster their commercials. Some studies show that this pattern of grouping tends to hold an audience more effectively than a pattern of announcement-song-commercial, announcement-song-commercial, and so on. A typical example of clustering is the playing of sets, such as six songs in a row or 30 minutes of nonstop music.

There are different views on how to pace recordings. Some believe that in a three-song cluster, audiences will favor a sequence of tempos, say, slow-medium-fast. Others prefer to alternate solo artists with groups. Over the years, radio varied the **commercial load** in response to swings in advertising demand, sometimes reducing music. In 2005, the radio industry began reducing commercial load after listeners and advertisers complained of oversaturation. Radio was forced to accommodate listeners, who increasingly have alternatives with handheld audio devices such as smartphones, satellite radio, Internet radio, and music on-demand online.

Stations using **cluster programming** and **back-announcing** allow a span of airtime for the disc jockey to speak, thus affording the station an opportunity to invest some personality into an otherwise canned program.

Networks and Syndication

The original concept of a radio network as defined by the Federal Communications Act—linked stations broadcasting the same programs simultaneously—dominated the industry until about 1950. At that time, the national networks were NBC, CBS, ABC, and MBS (Mutual Broadcasting System).

Today, networks and independent production companies package complete programs, then license them to stations. Such programs are said to be in **syndication**; their packagers are called syndicators. A key difference between networks and syndication is that syndicated programs run at different times on their station lineup. The producer of syndicated programs determines a format for a show or series of shows, engages the announcers, then lays in the elements—music tracks, interviews, whatever is to go into the programs.

Syndicated program material can range in length from 30 seconds to a full **day part** or more. It can be an individual, one-time program or a series. For example, Westwood One places programs on thousands of radio stations ranging from talk shows of a few hours daily to round-the-clock music formats like Hot Country that emphasizes hit country-genre songs from the 1990s and 2000s.

For many years, syndicated programs were mainly once-a-week countdown programs, say, of the Top 40 pop or country songs, and talk shows. One of the consequences of syndication has been that the air talent displaced by syndicated shows has grown in number, and opportunities have greatly diminished for up-and-coming talent to land positions in smaller markets and hone their skill before moving up to the larger markets—the traditional route of disc jockeys in the past.

Satellite Subscription Radio

Satellite radio, offering a subscription service, was launched in 2001 and became a $3 billion-revenue business in the United States within a decade. It is dominated by Sirius XM Radio, which was created in a 2008 merger and offers 175 audio channels. The business model is primarily built around offering unlimited consumption of commercial-free broadcast music and audio content for a fixed subscription fee, including on-demand content that consumers personally select (there are also separate, smaller travel information and limited video services too). Although Sirius XM Radio is received on a wide assortment of consumer listening devices, most of its customers subscribe to use on their car radios while driving. As automobile manufacturers add Internet access capabilities and docking slots that connect smartphones to in-car entertainment systems, satellite radio is increasingly competing with Internet radio and a wide range of mobile devices that store/playback music in automobiles. Satellite radio came into conflict with the music industry after introducing portable receiver/recorders dubbed XM+MP3. Music labels filed a lawsuit against XM, which reached settlements in 2007 and 2008 by agreeing to an expanded music **royalty** deal covering subscriber recording.

Satellite radio offers an abundance of niche music channels focused on specific music groups or eras as well as mainstream music formats such as hip-hop, blues, country, Latin, and classical. However, music is considered the "bulk" of the satellite radio program offer and is not a vital point of differentiation with terrestrial radio (AM and FM). Rather, it is exclusively the talk formats—such as shock jock Howard Stern and play-by-play sports event coverage—that historically have driven significant sales of satellite radio subscriptions.

Internet Radio

Once an oddity on the fringe of the media revolution, Internet radio has morphed into a big business. Streaming audio programming, which marked the beginning of Internet radio, started in the early 1990s as a novelty. Internet radio—also called **webcasting**—benefited from the arrival of broadband Internet connections that replaced the often-erratic signals of dial-up narrowband connections.

Traditional radio stations usually simulcast their signals via the Internet, thus serving out-of-town audiences and achieving global reach at a low cost. Measuring listenership can be superior to broadcast measurement because each consumer's listening device can be identified when it hooks into an Internet server and the length of connection is known. Over-the-air radio stations routinely place a link to their Internet radio stream on their stations' websites, which carry advertising, content, and promotion.

Internet radio also includes original linear audio channels, which enables a greater degree of specialization than in broadcast radio. Channels range from free, usually with advertising, to ad-free programming for listeners paying subscription fees. Internet radio reception has broadened from personal computers to hundreds of consumer devices, including smartphones and car radios, and this has significantly increased Internet radio's popularity. For example, channel originator Pandora, a fledging Internet radio startup, reached a milestone in mid-2011 when, despite being unprofitable, its initial public stock offering gave the company a $2.56 billion stock market capitalization because of its growth potential.

In the early days of Internet radio, music performance royalties were small, so music rights organizations pushed for bigger payments. Internet radio performance royalties for sound recordings were set in 2007 by the Copyright Royalty Board (**CRB**), a federal government agency created by Congress, and the Webcasters Settlement Acts of 2008 and 2009 then set lower **statutory license** rates. However, only recordings made after February 15, 1972, are covered by these federal actions, leaving pre-1972 recordings governed by a murky patchwork of state and common-law regulations.[3] CRB designated nonprofit SoundExchange as the entity to administer royalty collections and payments. Internet radio stations complain they are forced to pay higher fees for sound recording performance royalties than rivals, but Internet radio outlets remain free to try to negotiate better deals directly with music rights holders. The radio broadcaster now known as iHeart Communications agreed to pay radio performance royalties for both broadcast and online in a groundbreaking 2012 deal negotiated directly with Big Machine Label Group, whose artists include Taylor Swift and Tim McGraw. Such direct agreements bypass SoundExchange for online.

Notes

1. Early consumer radios, called crystal sets, were popular because they worked without electricity from a wall plug-in, although the audio signal the sets provided was weak.
2. HD Radio™ is a proprietary trademark of iBiquity Digital Corp.
3. As explained in Chapter 7, in 2015 Sirius XM bowed to legal pressure and agreed to pay royalties on pre-1972 recordings. Prior to that, it had only paid royalties on the compositions copyrighted in that era, not the recordings of those compositions made during the period. Since inception, it has paid royalties on post-1972 recordings.

Chapter Takeaways

- Commercial radio stations orient their programming toward a specific audience demographic. This concentration on audience types is attractive to advertisers.

- Music delivery platforms ranging from the portable iTunes to music audio channels in subscription entertainment have siphoned audiences from broadcast radio.

- Due to easing of ownership rules, much of the radio industry has consolidated, frequently leading to multiple stations in a market being run by the same management team. Among the effects: tight playlists.

- Regular ("terrestrial") radio stations, which broadcast in analog, offer digital programming via HD Radio™.

- Satellite radio, which launched in 2001 and is heavily geared to the car radio market, is offered as a subscription service for a monthly fee.

- Internet radio, which is also called webcasting, streams continuous audio that potentially is available around the globe.

Key Terms

- back-announcing   (p. 332)
- cluster programming   (p. 332)
- day part   (p. 332)
- HD Radio™   (p. 326)

- Internet radio   (p. 333)
- multicasting   (p. 326)
- narrowcasting   (p. 329)
- network   (p. 332)

- rating   (p. 327)
- satellite radio   (p. 333)
- share   (p. 326)
- syndication   (p. 332)

Discussion Questions

1. How does the need of advertisers to reach specific demographics drive radio programming?

2. How has the dispersion of radio programming across platforms such as the Internet, satellite, and terrestrial radio affected access to niche music?

3. What are the ethical issues in accepting payments in secret to program certain music?

4. As broadcast radio stations simulcast their signals on the Internet, what are the potential benefits for stations reaching listeners outside the range of their over-the-air signals?

Music in Television and Video

For a full understanding of the present chapter, refer to Chapters 4 and 7 (video copyright and licensing), Chapter 12 (video issues in recording contracts), Chapter 14 (promotion and distribution), and Chapter 21 (dramatic scoring).

> " *"The sound and music are 50% of the entertainment in a movie."*
>
> —Filmmaker George Lucas "

Long before MTV made "music television" into a corporate brand and pop-culture catchphrase, the two entertainment industry sectors were deeply intertwined. From *The Ed Sullivan Show* piped into a 13-inch black-and-white console to *Soul Train* strutting through a 27-inch color set to *American Idol* blasting out of an expansive 55-inch LCD HDTV screen, music has always been part of the broadcasting picture, however fuzzy the image or sharp the sound. It's sometimes the star of the show (on music specials and variety shows, for instance) and often a bit player (piped softly into the background during a dramatic scene, perhaps), but it's always there, *somewhere,* occupying a vital role. Any full discussion of the music business, therefore, must include a look at TV.

Why is it so important? Because for the music industry, the broadcast TV networks, cable networks, and online video services represent the following:

- A key income source (via licensing for performance rights and commercial uses)
- A prime marketing vehicle (via spotlight placement in specials, series, and online discovery)
- A national stage for exposure (via band bookings on talk shows and other entertainment programs)

Left: Ne-Yo's video shoot for "Closer."

Photo © Matthew Simmons/WireImage.

- A means of selling music directly to a targeted audience (via promotional programming or commercials bought by labels or direct-response marketers)

In recent years, the broadcasting arena has also become a populist **A&R** mechanism—letting TV audiences select the next **record label** signings through reality show talent competitions in genres including pop, country, and hip-hop. New technology, meanwhile, is opening doors to interactive music programming and direct impulse purchases by viewers, enhanced by the popularity of handheld devices such as iPods and smartphones as well as by high-definition big screens.

Although important to both sides, the music industry/TV pairing has not always been without static, and this too is something as old as the broadcast medium itself. Janet Jackson's infamous "wardrobe malfunction" during the 2004 Super Bowl halftime show may have sent shockwaves through the halls of the FCC, but Elvis Presley, The Beatles, and the Rolling Stones long before her had caused headaches for TV programmers worried about breaching the broadcast standards of the time.

Table 20.1 provides a timeline of some of the significant moments in the evolution of music on television from its early history to the rise of online video.

Variety and Talk Shows

The music variety show was one of the most popular types of programming in the first two decades of TV, especially during the 1950s "Golden Age of Television," after

The Voice finalists at BBC Breakfast Studios, Media City, Salford Quays, Manchester, United Kingdom. Pictured here: Jermain Jackman.
Photo © Infukima-02/INFphoto.com/Corbis.

the American Federation of Musicians (AFM) negotiated a system of new payments from TV producers to musicians. Variety shows employed live orchestras, backup singers and dancers, arrangers, and the leading stars of the day. "High-culture"

Table 20.1 **Historical Development of Music in Television**

1930s	First television broadcasts available in London in 1936.
	The 1939 New York City's World's Fair demonstrates the first TV broadcast to the American public, although World War II delays its rollout.
1940s	The AFM tightens control of the music industry by banning live music on TV and prohibiting members from recording for television programs until 1950.
	Kraft Television Theatre brings Broadway-quality live theater to TV.
	The Ed Sullivan Show debuts on CBS and becomes TV's longest running and most successful variety show (1948–1971).
	Bandleader Lawrence Welk begins broadcasting performances of "champagne music" that appeals to traditional tastes.
1950s	TV set penetration balloons from fewer than 4 million U.S. households in 1950 to over 40 million by decade's end.
	Variety shows, amateur talent shows, and classical performances dominate the "Golden Age of Television."
	Omnibus, hosted by Alistair Cooke, launches to become a revered cultural series and provides inspiration for American public television.
	Classics birthed: *Name That Tune, So You Want to Lead a Band, The Tonight Show, Musical Chairs.*
	ABC's *Rock 'n' Roll Show,* hosted by Alan Freed, is the first prime-time network special devoted to rock music.
1960s	ABC's *Hootenanny* is the first regularly scheduled folk music program on network television, followed by CBS's country music and comedy series, *Hee Haw.*
	73 million viewers watch The Beatles perform on *The Ed Sullivan Show,* which translate to 40% of the population.
	ABC airs the youth musical comedy series *The Monkees* as an American answer to The Beatles.
1970s	A Coca-Cola commercial makes the ad's song "I'd Like to Teach the World to Sing" into a worldwide hit.
	Soul Train debuts and is syndicated in 1971.
	TV shows based on musical personalities abound: *The Partridge Family, The Sonny & Cher Comedy Hour, The Captain & Tennille Show, Donny & Marie Show,* and *The Jacksons.*
	The late-night slot becomes a showcase for musical performers with *Midnight Special, In Concert, Don Kirshner's Rock Concert,* and *Saturday Night Live.*
	PBS's Great Performances series debuts.
1980s	The Black Entertainment Television and Country Music Television networks debut.
	Chart-based music show *Solid Gold* debuts in syndication.
	MTV signs on cable TV, introducing the concept of a 24-hour music channel.
	Pepsi fuels the trend of high-profile music marketing by hiring Michael Jackson as pitchman; his hair famously catches fire during the commercial's production.
	Viacom targets older music fans with VH1 and then launches the European version of MTV.
	The growth of prerecorded videocassettes creates a new market for long-form music video.
1990s	MTV spreads its music channel programming formula abroad, becoming a global cultural force.
	MTV diversifies by moving beyond compilations of video clips into program production that introduces an MTV lifestyle with *The Real World,* spawning a cultural fascination with reality TV.
	Enter *Beavis & Butthead,* an animated show about two heavy-metal music fans doing stupid things, designed to keep young male viewers from channel hopping.

(Continued)

Table 20.1   (Continued)

2000s	Nearly 3 billion people worldwide tune in to TV or Internet telecasts of the 2005 "Live 8" global poverty benefit concert series with 1,000 musicians performing in nine countries.
	American Idol, which is a format adaption of the U.K. show *Pop Idol*, debuts on Fox Broadcasting, eventually making recording stars of many of the winners and runners-up who were selected by viewers.
	The popularity of DVDs with their high audio and visual quality expands the allure of music videos.
	Music videos get posted on the Internet, allowing consumers with broadband connections to select titles at will, ending decades of viewing being dictated by TV schedules.
2010s	Viewers begin to consume TV with on-demand video, which puts them in control of selecting shows and threatens subscription TV's economic model.
	Video piracy sparks industry fears that rights holders will lose control of distribution, just as they did with audio P2P file sharing.
	Music videos on the Internet begin to resemble the selectivity of jukeboxes of the past by offering songs on-demand from websites such as YouTube and Vevo.

performances of classical music, opera, and theater were showcased on all three networks throughout the 1950s and into the 1960s, but high production costs and poor ratings killed these series with high aspirations.

By the early 1960s, another type of show had begun to emerge. Aimed at a youth audience, it often took its cues from the Top 40 charts in terms of popular artists and featured a throng of dancing teenagers. *American Bandstand* is the best known, but others included *Hullabaloo, Where the Action Is,* and the long-standing syndicated favorite, *Soul Train*. In the 1970s, *In Concert* offered a live rock concert every weekend and set the stage for later series such as *Austin City Limits.*

In terms of sheer significance, however, no music variety program can match the prime-time weekly series *The Ed Sullivan Show* for breaking new ground. It presented Elvis to the American mainstream (while censoring his gyrating hips), first televised the Rolling Stones and the Doors, and launched the British Invasion with its historic showcase of The Beatles in 1964.

Taking up the live-music showcase mantle for established acts, in large part, are an expanding slate of morning, daytime, and late-night news/entertainment/talk shows that regularly feature performances by the hottest bands from that week's charts. Particularly coveted by the labels for their promotional power are bookings on the major late-night shows and morning programs. Daytime talk shows are less likely to feature musical performances on a regular basis, but when they do, they can offer an opening for artists outside the pop music mainstream, including classical and show music performers. The long-running comedy sketch show *Saturday Night Live* has remained for many years the most sought-after TV series booking, guaranteeing a buzz infusion.

Music Specials/Events/Awards Shows

Although "music variety shows" have faded out as a series format on mainstream English-language TV, the prime-time live-music special or event on TV has continued to thrive. Just as it once wasn't Christmas until crooners Bing Crosby or Andy Williams sang about the season with other sweater-clad stars on TV, the holidays today still inevitably bring forth a range of special musical programming, in multiple genres and various show formats. Particularly high-profile concerts (such as "fare-well" performances or lavishly staged spectacles) also find their way onto television, as do "mini" concerts keyed to other events, such as halftime at the Super Bowl. A small number of stars still get their own telecast specials on occasion.

The most abundant source of music event programming comes from an array of music awards shows, which now cover the gamut from pop to country to hip-hop to Latin music to "people's choice" picks across the musical spectrum. The main music awards shows are The Grammys, the MTV Video Music Awards (VMAs), the CMA Awards (from the Country Music Association), the Rock and Roll Hall of Fame Induction Ceremony, and American Music Awards. Even nonmusic shows such as the Emmy Awards, the Oscars, and theater's Tony Awards have carved out airtime for musical performances of nomi-nated show songs or musicals. Performing slots on the highest profile of these shows are valued as much as, or more than, the trophies themselves. The power of an award to boost a winner's album sales can vary from greatly to hardly, but sales upticks are easily measured in the catalogs of acts that performed live during the shows.

As one might expect, music specials are major productions to pull off and are eco-nomically feasible for producers only when generating fees as network shows and cable TV specials. It is probable that part of the cost of such productions is borne through exploitation of **aftermarkets**— home videos, online streaming, and licensing over-seas, for instance. On the plus side, these programs offer employment opportunities for a wide array of creative individuals, from **studio musicians** to background singers to art directors who create the visual look that accompanies music (see Figure 20.1). The many steps required to put together a music special are outlined in Table 20.2.

Theme Songs

Many TV theme songs (e.g., the country whistling tune of *The Andy Griffith Show,* the organ-heavy *The Addams Family* theme, the hopeful piano lilt of *Hill Street Blues,* the techno-sound throb from *Miami Vice,* and the plaintive electronic piano-clarinet over-ture of *Law and Order*) have claimed a place in American popular music history. A select few, such as the *Miami Vice* theme and the Rembrandts' rendition of the *Friends* theme ("I'll Be There for You"), have even taken up residence for a time on the pop music charts. Today, fewer shows have full-scale opening theme songs (networks fear viewers will channel-surf away during a long introduction), and others use existing pop songs in place of original material. Still, the TV theme song remains a vital part of the TV scene.

Background Music and Foreground Spotlights

Like film music (see Chapter 21), the majority of TV music serves as "background," added during editing to create mood, to fill gaps, and to provide cultural context. Although the use of background music for TV shows has been a constant since the medium debuted, the prominence given to that music has been on the rise over the years. Background music, in effect, has come increasingly to the *foreground* in some shows. Teen-targeted programs have led this trend, using large excerpts of new songs during each episode in what is called a "back sell": telling viewers at the end of the show what music was featured, displaying the album cover, and sending viewers to the network's website to buy the album.

Another innovation is the "club" set added into the regular environment for some TV shows, into which bands are booked to perform in the background while the TV

Figure 20.1   TV and Video Production

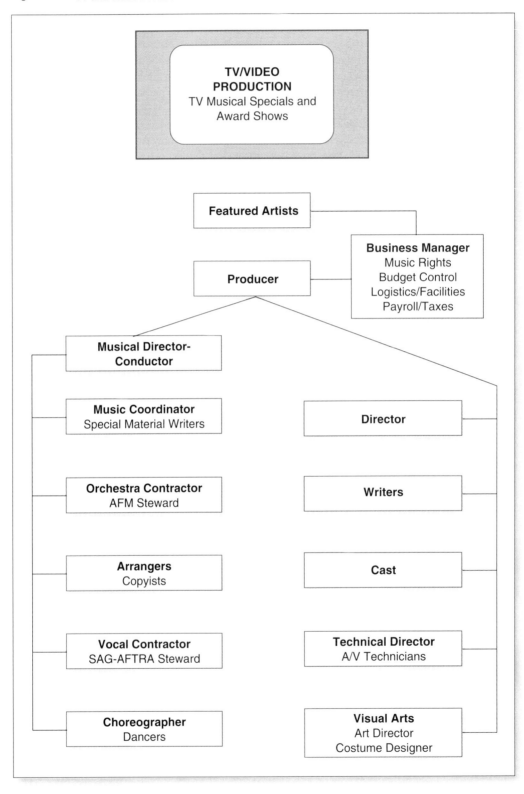

Table 20.2 Production of a TV Music Special

A program of this kind requires the services of a large number of talented artists and businesspeople. The following is a typical sequence of activity.
1. The producer contracts with the director, writers, and performers. Supporting talent is identified and then booked to complement headliners and/or the theme of the show.
2. The producer schedules a series of meetings to decide what music is to be programmed (original or preexisting; live or prerecorded) and who is to perform it. Star performers' personal musical directors and/or personal managers may also provide input.
3. The musical director meets with the "special material" writers, music coordinator, and featured artists to set music routines—style, key, sequence, and so on. The music is sketched for full scoring later.
4. More decision making by the director, writers, the content creative team (producers of videos that play behind artists), choreographer, featured performers, and art director.
5. The musical director hires arrangers to score the music for the orchestra, if a full orchestra is used (rare these days).
6. If live background singers are used, they rehearse. But in most cases, the band and vocalists are one preexisting package whose performance has already been mapped out by Pro Tools computer software.
7. For big productions pulling together lots of musicians who haven't worked together before, individual parts for the instrumentalists and singers are run off copies as needed.
8. Meanwhile, the musical director has hired an AFM contractor to engage the individual musicians, if there will be a studio orchestra. The contractor and supervising copyist develop a list of doublers—the musicians in the orchestra required to play more than one instrument. The contractor notifies the doublers what additional instruments to bring to the sessions.
9. Prerecording sessions are conducted. Featured singers might prerecord their voices if they are called upon to dance while singing. If a full orchestra is used, much of its music is prerecorded.
10. In one session, the background singers record their tracks. Meanwhile, the audio engineers have been busy recording the best possible live performances that eventually are combined with prerecorded tracks. The engineers are assisted by music editors in assembling a master containing all the video and audio of the completed program.

characters carry on the plotline in the foreground, making a point to mention the band's name once or twice.

The Evolving TV Picture

Why has TV become such a vital medium for the music industry, as outlined above? Just consider the numbers: 97% of American households have at least one TV set, making television's potential programming reach enticing. More than that, however, is the opportunity that TV programs present to connect with audiences who might not otherwise be exposed to music.[1]

Although station affiliates of NBC, CBS, and ABC claimed 80% of the viewing audience in 1980, network-affiliated TV stations—the leading purveyors of "free TV"—have seen their share of the overall audience pie steadily slip to 32% in prime time, according to researcher Nielsen. This has posed challenges to the traditional business model for TV networks, although broadcast TV remains powerful by virtue of each channel's still sizable audience (compared to the diffuse cable TV audience) and its reach to nonbroadband households.

Claiming more and more of those viewer eyeballs are the huge slate of cable channels, which offer "narrowcast" programming centered on everything from food to sports to gardening to soap operas to game shows to science fiction to, of course, music (more on this segment—and the pioneering MTV—a little later on). The revenue model for a basic cable network has typically been a dual-revenue stream, including both ad sales and subscriber fees paid by cable operator systems, satellite TV, and other multichannel platforms. Faced with this new environment, the networks/cable distinction is blurring into a new "conglomerate" model, with networks, cable companies, and/or program producers being brought under single corporate umbrellas.

Besides traditional linear TV channels, consumers now have TV options that they can call up whenever they desire, which puts consumers "in charge" in the digital media revolution:

- Pay-per-view (PPV): PPV delivers events such as concerts, movies, and sports at a scheduled time.
- Video-on-demand (**VOD**) programming: Unlike PPV, where viewers cannot control when they view movies or programs, on-demand programming allows the user to choose precise viewing times, as well as to rewind and pause programming. On-demand choices are offered for a one-time fee, free with preroll advertisement, or as part of a subscription service.
- Interactive programming: This form of programming exists primarily as a so-called two-screen experience, where viewers use their PCs and tablets with Internet access to interact with a program via quizzes, contests, or voting; the aim is to increase the amount of time that a viewer "sticks" with a program and thus make it more appealing to advertisers.

Innovative interactive platforms have been great for viewers, but their popularity strains the economic fabric of the entertainment industry. On-demand programming and digital video recorders (**DVRs**) put pressure on advertisers to develop commercials or promotional programming that viewers might *choose* to watch, since hard-sell and abrasive commercials will lead to tune-out now that viewers have plenty of options. And video programs served directly over broadband connections without the cable TV middleman (called **over-the-top** video or OTT) give heartburn to distribution entities that depend on subscriber fees paid to legacy cable channels. OTT started as special-interest video channels, but increasingly, media companies offer mainstream cable TV and broadcast TV channels in low-cost subscription packages that bypass cable delivery.

MTV and the Rise of the Music Video

Any exploration of the role of music on TV must include some discussion of MTV, the pioneer and champion of "music television." Although not the first to air music videos—the broadcast of minimovies of The Beatles' "Strawberry Fields Forever" and "Penny Lane" in the 1960s first broke this ground, and other clips shows followed over the years—MTV *was* the first to build an entire commercial channel around the concept. It signed on August 1, 1981, with a clip of the Buggles' "Video Killed the Radio Star," and although that prophecy did not come to pass, the music video channel did permanently alter the promotion and marketing equation for record labels and bands, putting a new premium on presentation and visual image. In the years since its debut, MTV has shifted its programming

Photo © Anatolli Babli/iStock.

focus to include fewer videos and more original shows while also spinning off a host of new channels and subchannels focused on music segments, including music for baby boomers and college students as well as **alternative music.** Competition has also arisen from Country Music Television, Black Entertainment Television, and others.[2]

The rise of MTV also sparked the growth of a relatively new industry: the music video production business. Video quickly became a standard promotional tool for major-label acts in the 1980s and 1990s after marketing executives realized the power of the TV medium to captivate fans—and motivate album buyers.

Producing Short-Form Videos

The production of music videos, or short-form videos, demands many of the same sets of skills and cast of professionals needed to make long-form projects: directors, producers, editors, special-effects experts, and so on. Many of the directors working in the field, therefore, have backgrounds directing films or commercials. Unique to the video clip process is the role of the record company, which most often produces the music videos (either sharing costs or charging all of the costs to the artists' royalty account).

Most recording companies do not have in-house video directors; instead, they generally have someone in charge of overseeing video assignments for the label's acts. This person is commonly called a "video commissioner."

In a typical scenario, the artist and/or label executives overseeing music videos will approach a number of directors; generally, they will do this by going through the **executive producer** or director's rep at one of the many video production companies, which often boast rosters of 5 to 20 directors. Sometimes, they may also consider someone unaffiliated with a production company who has made a strong impression via a music video reel sent in to the label, unsolicited.

Each of the selected candidate directors will then come up with a concept for the video, incorporating into it any style/thematic preferences that the artist or label has put forth (oftentimes, they leave the creative end entirely to the director; other times, they have a specific idea in mind). In most situations, directors come up with their own concepts and thus perform double duty as writers as well, although a few do work with third-party writers.

In pitching the director's concepts to the label/artist, the production company's producer will hand over the director's treatment (typically a one- to three-page script of how the director sees the video), design aids (photos or scenes from movies or other things to explain or demonstrate the vision), and a budget based on the elements of the treatment. This budget should fit within the monetary guidelines originally put forth by the commissioner. (For a sample music video budget worksheet, see Table 20.3.)

The commissioner will then narrow down the pitches and go to the artist and the rest of the management and creative team at the label to choose the one that best fits their needs. At this stage, a few of the directors may be asked to fine-tune certain parts of their treatment, before they choose the one they want to go with.

Once a video director has been selected, he or she will want to engage, early on, a production designer and possibly a choreographer. A video **storyboard** or visual references presentation is sometimes created, when the budget is sufficient, similar to the storyboards created for TV commercials (see Chapter 22). A visual references presentation amalgamates elements that convey an atmosphere and hopefully gets everyone focused on a single vision. Once a consensus is reached, a shooting schedule is set. Many music videos are now shot on location because it is less expensive than building sets (and budgets have been decreasing). Table 20.4 shows the three phases characterizing most short-form video production.

During production, differences may arise over "artistic control." The director may want one thing, the featured artist something else. The artist's recording contract, when properly drawn, will articulate who decides how the videos are to be handled, particularly in respect to style, content, and choice of director. Smart artists will usually defer to the judgments of directors of proven ability. It should be noted,

••• Case Study for Music Videos: Close-up of a Video Commissioner

While Emmanuelle Cuny-Diop has her own office at Atlantic Records, she spends most days away juggling the 20 music video projects that she has on her plate at any given time. With the title vice president of video production, she's what's known as a "video commissioner" who represents the record label in the planning, budgeting, producing, and editing of music videos.

In her career, she's worked on music videos for Kanye West, Flo Rida, Travie McCoy, Janelle Monae, Cam'ron, and Wiz Khalifa. "No matter how much you prep and how much experience you have, there's always something that doesn't quite go as planned," Cuny-Diop says. "You constantly have to be thinking on your feet for solutions." She finds the steady stream of unexpected challenges one of the charms of her job, along with helping artists realize their creative visions.

She makes sure productions remain on track and serves as a liaison with the artist, the artist's management, the video production company, and the label's management and the marketing department. Over the years, this work has taken her to Argentina, Brazil, the Czech Republic, and cities across the United States.

Although a mid-career executive, Cuny-Diop has already witnessed considerable transformation in the music business. Early in her career, she worked on some $1 million-budget music videos—like Jay-Z's *Big Pimpin'*—but these days music economics mandate much lower budgets.

Falling budgets do have a silver lining because Cuny-Diop says music video makers are more open to hiring young talent since not as much money is on the line as in the past. The new blood has a knack for creativity to make modest budgets seem large on the screen.

Emmanuelle Cuny-Diop.
Photo by Robert Marich.

Another new wrinkle is that artists and labels issue video content in multiple ways as the online landscape expands and no longer are just thinking a traditional song in a 4-minute linear format for conventional broadcast and cable TV channels. "The music business is going in a whole lot of different directions at once," says Cuny-Diop.

Growing up on the lower east side of Manhattan to Indian and French immigrant parents, Cuny-Diop first cracked the music business while in college studying business via an avenue that she still recommends today—the internship. She was interviewed for an internship at a fledgling record label through a contact she made on the production set while working as an extra at a movie shoot. "I started the next day," she recalls.

She progressed to receptionist at the label, was promoted to assistant in radio promotions, and then moved to assistant in video production and marketing. As luck would have it, that label was the famed rap and R&B house Roc-A-Fella Records that was cofounded by Jay-Z. Later, Cuny-Diop later became a freelance consultant on music video productions, eventually landing her full-time job at client Atlantic Records.

Her philosophy toward work and music? "You have to do what you love so it never seems like work," she says. "That doesn't mean I don't ever get frustrated at times or have some bad days. But every day is a new adventure."

however, that the final product belongs to the record label and that it retains the final approval on edits. Occasionally, directors who are highly respected will be awarded "final cut," but such occurrences are rare.

The organization representing short-form video producers is the Music Video Production Association (MVPA). The nonprofit trade group MVPA provides a forum for examining industry issues.

Table 20.3   **Music Video Budget Summary Worksheet**

Production/song title _____ Date _____	
Video commissioner/label _____	
Director _____	
Principal photography begins _____ No. of days _____	
Above-the-Line Expenses	
Production	**Cost**
Director	
Producer	
Above-the-line subtotal	
Below-the-Line Expenses	
Production assistants	
Extra talent	
Set operations	
Property	
Wardrobe	
Makeup and hair	
Electrical	
Camera	
Crane rental	
Sound (playback, sound package, walkie-talkies)	
Transportation	
Hotel (out-of-town talent)	
Helicopter rental	
Location (rental, permits, catering)	
Set security/police	
Animals, wranglers	
Film, tape, and lab	
Other	
Subtotal production	
Postproduction	
Offline editing	
Online editing	
Stock, dubs, transfers	
Subtotal postproduction	
General and administrative	
Photographer/still photos	
Insurance	
Office and miscellaneous	
Contingency	
Subtotal general and administrative	
Below-the-line subtotal	
Grand Total	

Note: Production budgets for music videos range all the way from a few hundred dollars ("let's grab a camera and shoot in the park") to several hundred thousand dollars ("Madonna wants another 50 medieval extras for the night banquet scene at the castle"). The bigger variables include size of the crew and number of shooting days.

Table 20.4 Short-Form Video Production: The Three Phases

Preproduction phase
1. Audio master tape is completed. Record company negotiates a synchronization license with the music publisher for the video.
2. Label determines a production budget, negotiates with the artist for possible sharing of costs.
3. Budget is set, and label engages a freelance video director.
4. Director, label, and artist develop a concept for the video.
5. Director engages a producer, possibly a choreographer, supporting cast, director of photography.
6. Director and production designer lay out a storyboard.
7. Sets are designed, then constructed or rented; locations are scouted and secured.
8. Costumes are designed, then executed or rented.
9. Soundstage is booked; production manager engages production personnel (gaffers, stagehands, etc.).
10. Producer rents equipment as needed (cameras, lights, dollies).
11. Director orders audio click tracks to aid rehearsals.
12. Producer arranges accident, health, and liability insurance.
13. All of the foregoing are reconfirmed.
Shooting phase
1. Director rehearses the performers' lip-synching, stage movements. Choreographer rehearses dancers.
2. Director rehearses camera movements, approves lighting, and plans special effects.
3. The production is shot.
4. Producer orders return of all rented equipment, sets, costumes; orders sets struck, soundstage cleared, locations cleaned up.
Postproduction phase
1. Director supervises all postproduction work, including editing, processing of visual effects, computer graphics, opticals; edits final master, orders copies made.
2. Producer (a) obtains releases from all performers, artists, and creative personnel; (b) gets signed W-4 forms from all personnel; (c) satisfies all union contracts; and (d) authorizes payments to all personnel.
3. Director delivers video master to the record company.
4. Record company seeks airplay for promotional purposes and hopes to recoup production costs through other revenue streams, including advertising revenue from online streaming.

Music Video Economics and Distribution ▬▬▬▬▬▬

Today's video budgets—perhaps tens of thousands of dollars up to low six figures—are down sharply from the heyday in the 1980s and 1990s when video budgets well into six figures, and occasionally past the $1 million mark, were common for top artists. In the glory days of video, a milestone occurred in 1983 with the 14-minute, zombie-themed music video for the song "Thriller" by Michael Jackson, which reportedly cost $1 million to make and created a global sensation. Consumers bought over 9 million units of a 60-minute video *The Making of Michael Jackson's Thriller,* which was a staggering sales figure for the videocassette era (actually, a staggering figure for any era). The music industry hoped *Thriller* would herald an ongoing business of consumers buying packaged music videos, much like the economic model for records at the time, but music videos became only a minor and inconsistent retail sales business.

Today with falling production budgets, it's a tough financial environment for production companies. Some multimedia producers maintain a foothold in music videos simply to nurture young producing talent that eventually segues to more lucrative TV commercials and other media.

Music Videos Online

Labels have increasingly sought to monetize video projects by capturing online advertising connected to video streaming. To that end, Universal Music and Sony Music Entertainment launched the advertising-supported website Vevo in 2009 as a platform for music video playback and the placement of music videos on third-party platforms such as YouTube. Vevo's music video placement contract with YouTube helps YouTube keep away content from its rivals such as Facebook. Through that placement arrangement, called syndication, Vevo controls advertising around its videos on other platforms, and much of the revenue Vevo collects flows back to the record labels. It's estimated that a popular music video provided in a streaming format can generate tens of thousands of dollars in advertising revenue in the United States. In some cases, labels assign third parties other than Vevo to handle syndication. In other cases, labels line up one-time alliances with digital media outlets, such as picture messaging app Snapchat premiering Madonna's *Rebel Heart* music video. Deals vary, but digital partners typically agree to deliver a big marketing push that will help an artist's recording and concert business, a big cut of ad revenue associated with video play, and—in some cases—cash in exchange for a short-term exclusive window.

The music video concept is increasingly being revamped from emphasis on a single polished music video to an array of content pieces that spring from one foundation music video. Fans crave personal behind-the-scenes content and interactive video offering more than one storyline, which can be produced in parallel while making traditional music videos. So the vast appetite of today's online landscape creates a need for more video content, even if much of the content isn't highly polished. The side content pieces can be posted on artist platforms, fan websites, and general entertainment outlets. One casualty of the trend to quantity over quality is the "making of" mini-documentary, also called the behind-the-scenes (BTS) video, which historically were short but highly polished documentaries on the making of big-budget music videos. Now the money previously budgeted for that single mini-documentary video gets spread around, generating more varied music video content.

Music consumption online is driven by consumer preferences for particular artists and genres, so music company brands in themselves are not a big draw. But record labels plant their flags in cyberspace anyway since it's inexpensive to fill online video with already produced content. For example, major recording companies have their own multichannel networks (MCNs) on YouTube such as The Live Room Powered By Warner Music, Universal Music Group, and Warner Music Group—which are three separate video "channels." An advantage of MCNs is their owners control the environment, which means they dictate presentation of their brands (and bands). Another online-only effort is the YouTube Music Awards (YTMA) show that launched in 2013 and is streamed live.

For amateur musicians, YouTube posts instructional videos and do-it-yourself toolboxes to encourage posting of original music. The YouTube instructional package includes tips on how to label music so it pops up high on searches and cautions about copyright infringement, and there's even a tab labeled "Build A Career." And the industry is watching because record labels sign musical talent with proven audience appeal based on the size of their online audience and buzz metrics in social media. For music rights owners, YouTube offers its Content ID program to participating rights holders that polices unauthorized posts of their content.

Another small but growing source of monetization is the collection of fees for showing branded products in videos, which is known as product placement. It's estimated that music video owners are collecting over $20 million a year by plugging products in music videos. A related revenue stream comes from corporate sponsors tied to tours, acts, and labels in exchange for associating themselves with videos.

Despite mushrooming online, the biggest audience for music videos remains cable and broadcast TV channels, where labels mostly grant rights for such telecasts at no charge to promote music (composers and lyricists do get standard performance royalties). For select superstar videos, TV outlets like MTV quietly pay labels fees for limited exclusivity, after which the music videos are widely available to other TV outlets at no cost. Over the years, labels have tried from time to time to wring money from music TV channels as a standard distribution practice, but such initiatives did not gain traction in the United States. Some overseas TV channels, however, do consistently make payments to labels.

Notes

1. Consider the case of Ken Burns's *JAZZ*, a 10-part PBS documentary series that ran in 2001 and created an immediate surge of sales for jazz titles both directly tied to the broadcast and others simply featuring acts showcased in the series. There are many other examples throughout the years of sales spikes for music in genres with few other wide means of exposure.
2. Both CMT and BET were later acquired by MTV parent company Viacom.

Chapter Takeaways

- Music was prominent in TV's early days with regularly scheduled music-oriented series and variety shows.

- The first 24-hour music TV channel launched in 1981 and spurred demand for promotional videos made by artists to market their songs.

- Handheld devices with video capability have expanded the realm of music TV.

- Televised music awards shows that have proliferated are useful promotion platforms for selling songs and artists.

- To monetize music videos, which TV channels mostly get for free, music labels attempt to capture advertising dollars from online streaming.

- Record labels generally outsource production of music videos to specialist producers.

- The strategy for music videos increasingly emphasizes creation of a larger quantity of content instead of a single highly polished title.

Key Terms

- affiliates (network TV) (p. 343)

- aftermarkets   (p. 341)

- back sell (of music titles) (p. 341)

- foreground   (p. 341)

- MTV   (p. 337)

- multichannel networks (MCNs) (p. 351)

- short-form video   (p. 345)

- storyboard   (p. 346)

- streaming   (p. 341)

- theme songs   (p. 341)

- treatment   (p. 346)

- video commissioner (p. 345)

Discussion Questions

1. Has television made a significant impact in the launching of successful musicians and bands? Explain why or why not.

2. Describe the process for selection when major labels seek an outside producer to make a music video.

3. What needs to be considered and budgeted for in creating a music video?

4. What are different ways music videos can earn money?

CHAPTER 21

Dramatic Scoring for Movies, TV, and Games

Many musicians have a common ambition on their multifaceted career "to-do" lists—to score the music for a movie, TV show, or video game. Others in the industry make a good living by crafting such creative works as their only pursuit.

Although scoring is most often associated with music for the blockbuster theatrical release or the hit TV series, much of the work in the field is performed with other markets in mind. Video games, along with business, educational, training, and documentary films and videos, offer potential employment opportunities because they, too, require scoring. Under the term *scoring*, we include composition, orchestration, copying, and recording. Professionals use the expression *film scoring* in reference to the preparation and recording of **dramatic music** intended to synchronize with and augment the action on the screen.

It's been said that the musical score is the glue that holds much of a movie together. The action on screen can be intensified, made humorous, or relaxed (or trivialized) by what happens in the score. Sometimes, it functions as background; other times, the music is definitely in the conscious foreground. Film composers have saved many a weak scene. The artistic contributions of our best movie composers often match those of the actors observed on the screen. As for public acceptance, on occasion a movie soundtrack album can turn a profit rivaling the film itself, and some of the music scored for TV dramas will probably be remembered longer than the programs.

>
>
> *"[An intellectual] is someone who can listen to the 'William Tell Overture' without thinking of the Lone Ranger."*
>
> —John Chesson

Left: Actress Jodie Foster on a scoring stage.

Photo © Michael Tighe/Getty Images.

Background

From the very first days, music has been an integral part of the movie experience. Silent films were accompanied by small orchestras or, if that was too expensive, by piano players or, in the big movie palaces, organists, who improvised to suit the action (at least, the first time they saw a film).

The first music heard by the public on a movie soundtrack occurred in 1927, when vaudevillian Al Jolson broke into song in the middle of a film titled *The Jazz Singer*. The public loved it, and very quickly producers began adding music and audible dialogue to their movies. At first, they simply borrowed music from other sources—Broadway, Beethoven, Liszt, **Tin Pan Alley**, just what the musicians for silent films had done. But soon, producers turned to classical composers to score original music. These included many prestigious composers of the early 20th century: Satie, Stravinsky, Schoenberg, Toch, and Copland. These composers scored films only sporadically; composers who work in the field full-time have scored most movies.

The period of the 1930s and 1940s is known to film music buffs as the Golden Age. All the then-major studios in Hollywood—MGM, 20th Century Fox, Paramount, Columbia, Universal, Disney, Warner Bros., and RKO—had composers on salary full-time. Each major studio had a staff orchestra of almost symphonic proportions, required because the preferred musical style was **neo-romantic.** Producers would explain that they wanted music that sounded like Tchaikovsky, Rachmaninoff, or Debussy. Leaders in the neo-romantic style were Alfred Newman, Franz Waxman, Bronislau Kaper, and Miklós Rózsa (although Rózsa broke 19th-century bonds with period pictures such as *Ben Hur*). These scores sounded European because most of these composers were either from Europe or trained in European styles.

Changing Styles

Tastes began to change after World War II. In the 1950s, a number of first-rate film composers began to abandon the musical clichés to experiment with more contemporary American sounds (jazz, big bands, etc.). Those breaking away from European romanticism included Hugo Friedhofer and John Williams.

Composers were influenced, until the 1960s, by techniques used for movie cartoons, such as Popeye the Sailor and Mortimer (later changed to Mickey) Mouse. Producers wanted their composers to **catch the action:** If Mickey Mouse slipped on a banana peel, the composer was expected to **underscore** the action with a trombone **glissando.** When the Good Guy discovered the Bad Guy lurking in the shadows, the orchestra was expected to play what is still known in the business as a **stinger,** a **sforzando** chord. Remnants of the old Mickey Mouse style remain here and there, but a film score using it today can sound silly, because audiences have long since memorized these clichés from watching old programming on TV.

In many of the early comedies, the entire movie was underscored with a popular song droning in the background, even under dialogue. Of a higher artistic order was the practice in the 1930s of hiring Broadway and Tin Pan Alley composers to write songs for feature films. Some of these early Hollywood musicals spawned a fair share of the standards we know today such as "(Somewhere) Over the Rainbow."

The discovery by film producers of the value of a good popular song occurred in 1949, when the main theme from *The Third Man* film, featuring a zither, hit the pop record charts. The message was not lost on other film producers, who searched for film composers who could turn out hits that could be incorporated into their features. By the 1950s, movie composers could be classified into one of two categories: (a) those able to underscore drama on film and (b) the pop songwriters, most of whom were unfamiliar with techniques for writing for soundtracks or background music but could create hit songs. By the 1960s, a third group had emerged, artists who could not only underscore film drama appropriately but who could also invent attractive melodies that could be pulled from a soundtrack to fuel hit records and sell sheet music.

Jazz found its place in the movie-scoring business, too, and was given further impetus from television. In 1959, film composer Henry Mancini wrote the score for the television mystery series *Peter Gunn.* It was agreed that Mancini would use a "big band" playing driving jazz. It was particularly appropriate for this series, because the big-city chase scenes seemed to call for the frenetic energy of jazz. It worked so well it became one of the great classics of TV scoring.

A new generation of film composers emerged who could do both dramatic, classical-based underscoring and contemporary jazz. Some left concert touring with name bands and found new homes (big ones!) in Hollywood. Lalo Schifrin, European trained but very creative in jazz styles, not only handled dramatic underscoring but would occasionally score an entire visual work using improvised jazz, such as in the National Geographic TV series, *The Hidden World of Insects.* For this series, he brought to the scoring stage just some sketches, tone clusters, and 12-tone rows, then instructed his small chamber orchestra to improvise freely on these fragments.

After some experimentation with synthesizers when they first hit the scene, the industry turned again to late 19th-century neo-romantic music with full orchestra as the basic foundation for film music, even the thrillers. Into this, themes, styles, and instrumentation from the whole world of music are integrated, in the service of enhancing the films. For films with a strong ethnic element, native instruments are folded into more standard orchestration, and musical clichés and phony ethnic music are carefully avoided. Moviegoers (and directors) have developed sophisticated ears.

Emergence of Soundtracks

Including potential hit songs in soundtracks has evolved to the point where **song scores** are now quite prominent. Many of these songs and soundtrack albums have been gigantic hits, netting tremendous profits for the films' producers and the composers (see Table 21.1 for a hypothetical example).

The Craft

Those who underscore films use many of the techniques employed for centuries by opera composers, and some film composers are classically trained and fluent in many musical dialects. But the unique time-lapse illusions in cinema art challenge the creative powers of film composers well beyond the more familiar techniques of scoring music for the theater.

The Process

The film is first shot completely and taken through at least one edit, often more. At this point, a *temp score,* a mock-up of the score to come, is put together by a music editor (also called a **cutter**), gleaning from existing music. Sometimes, the temp score is so appropriate that the director prefers it to the finished score. There have been many cases where the temp score was used in the final movie and an original score thrown out, such as in *2001: A Space Odyssey* and *The Exorcist.*

Table 21.1   **Hypothetical Revenue Streams to a Songwriter and Music Publisher for a Successful Original Movie Song[a]**

Synchronization and video buyout	$32,000
U.S. radio and TV performances	640,000
U.S. album sales (CDs and downloads)	120,000
U.S. single sales (CDs and downloads)	62,000
Academy Awards telecast	1,300
Grammy telecast	1,300
Sheet music and folios	14,500
Ringtones and ringbacks	42,000
Foreign performances: radio, TV, and theatrical	240,000
Foreign album sales (CDs and downloads)	90,000
Foreign single sales (CD and downloads)	26,000
Miscellaneous royalties	24,000
TV and radio commercials	28,000
Video games	0
Total combined songwriter and publisher receipts	$1,321,100

[a]Revenue presented is best-case scenario for a major hit.

Spotting the Film

The first time the composer views the movie, it is usually in the company of the producer, director, film editor, and music editor. The director and composer watch the film roll by and *spot the film,* identifying the turning points, the changes in mood. Just as important, they also discuss where music should not be used. The music editor listens to this conversation and makes notes and comments on what the other two have decided. The music editor gives the composer **spotting notes,** which specify where each cue will happen when in the movie. When this spotting process is complete, the composer generally receives the first part of the agreed-on fee.

Scene Breakdowns. For several decades, music editors have used video/SMPTE (Society of Motion Picture and Television Engineers) time code standards to gather the timing information needed to write scene breakdowns for each reel, which is a file of 5 to 10 minutes of video. The word *reel* is still in use, although this dates to the analog film era, when it referred to a 1,000-foot roll of film or **magnetic stock.** In mapping out scores, composers make notes for indication of **click tracks.** The "click" is simply a steady beat that can be made to go faster or slower, depending on the needs of the scene. The click track enables the composer to sync music to film with mathematical precision.

Theatrical film moves through the projector at a rate of 24 frames per second, or 1,440 frames per minute; video flashes on screen at 30 frames per second. For film music, *beats per minute* (BPM) is the measure. To create a film music *tempo,* meaning speed of the music, the editor or composer divides the tempo into 1,440 (frames in a minute of film); the result is known as a *frame-click tempo.* Let's say the tempo is 144 BPM (a chase scene); dividing 1,440 by 144 gives 10. In past years before computers entered the process, the music editor prepared a 10-frame loop with 35-mm film and punched a hole in every 10 frames. These holes produced a flash and "click" sound when read by an optical film reader. That click sound was fed to headsets of the conductor and orchestra so the music that was written to match the film is then played in perfect synchronization to the visuals. Headsets for listening to clicks are still used in recording sessions.

Today, click tracks are generated by a computer, which is precisely locked to video without a chance of "drift" as in the past when a number of mechanical elements were "locked" together with film. When click tracks are generated by computer, it's easy to determine clicks for *rubato* (speeding up/slowing down) passages while staying in perfect sync with the visuals. This is called a *variable click track,* and it can identify those split-second timings in the score when the music must catch the action precisely. The most widely used film timing program in the score creation process is Auricle, which received an Academy Award and an Emmy for technical achievement.

Composers on major films will usually view a picture several times before starting to score it, and they use video to do so. The use of actual film work prints in this process is a rarity today. The picture is played back using computer-based recording and editing systems such as Pro Tools. The digital copy of the edited image sequence will have a SMPTE time code that appears on the screen such as "00:10:23:18," which translates to 0 hours, 10 minutes, 23 seconds, and 18 frames. Sometimes the "hour" reference is the reel number instead of the running time of the not-yet-completed work. In features, 10 reels are common if a movie is originally shot in 35-mm film.

Sometimes the film composer receives the film transferred to a DVD. When opened, the video can be **slaved** while running a computer sequencer program. The composer then may play the score to the visuals, compose detailed phrases in the sequencer, or write the score by hand, although it will need to be transferred to the sequencer. What method is used is driven by personal preference.

Composition

Having become familiar with the film, the composer writes the new score. When the score is complete, another installment of the salary fee is paid. Composer fees are typically paid in three installments, and the total can range from tens of thousands of dollars for a movie to over $1 million for "A" list composers. The composition fee for a major studio film is normally in the low to mid-hundreds of thousands of dollars. One quirk of film composition is that producers might opt to license hit music at the last minute and thus discard big chunks of original score. To counter financial losses from this decision, composer contracts may require the producer to guarantee a minimum performance royalty regardless of whether the composed music is shelved.

Because the scoring needs to match on-screen action, a composer starts serious work only when editing of visuals is finished. Many contracts for full-length feature films provide that the composer shall write the music and have it recorded in 10 weeks. In actual practice, the producer is more likely to give the composer 3 to 4 weeks to complete the job. Some composers work under 6-week deadlines, which may or may not include recording.

In Europe, the composer has traditionally been expected to present a completed score to the **copyists**. In the United States, film composers may compose orchestral sketches, perhaps three to eight **staves** per system (system being a grouping of staves), then give the sketch, with indications for instrumentation, to an **orchestrator** to render the full score. This practice developed because producers were always in a hurry—and still are. They have been willing to pay the extra costs of dividing the writing of movie scores between two persons. A few unschooled but highly gifted composers also hire orchestrators to write out their scores.

Recording to Film

Then it's time to record the music. If the score is an expensive orchestral work, an electronic mock-up is usually prepared for approval prior to recording with the actual orchestra. Whether a film composer uses a computerized or optical click-track method, it should be pointed out that many composers prefer to conduct to a film's more emotional scenes by free timing, using a system of "streamers and punches" as timing guideposts. A streamer is a straight line that takes 2 seconds to traverse the screen from left to right. A "flutter punch" is the flash of light produced by punching a hole in the film, usually every three frames for free conducting. Such composer-conductors leave precise cueing to the ingenuity of their **music cutters** and their computer software.

Many films combine synthesizers, samplers, and orchestra, as well as require **multitrack** recording and **mixing**. Feature films are commonly recorded all at once, "live," with the full orchestra present, often including an extensive arsenal of electronic (MIDI, or musical instrument digital interface) instruments as a significant section of the big studio orchestra. Most feature films are recorded on movie "scoring stages." These facilities are huge. Soundstages are attended during recording sessions not only by a half-acre of musicians but also by scoring **mixers,** a music librarian, the music editor, the composer's agent, and the head copyist.

Occasionally, a film director will throw out a complete score, fire the composer, and engage another one to redo the job. But these instances are rare, especially since scoring occurs late in the filmmaking process. However, producers and/or directors often require music changes on the scoring stage, placing everyone under tremendous pressure. Usually, this high-tension environment proceeds with efficiency—because the stage is inhabited by pros.

The Final Mix

Following the music recording sessions, which last for several days on major films, the music is combined with dialogue and sound effects in dubbing sessions. This final phase of sound synchronization, called *rerecording,* is mostly concerned with setting relative sound levels and making final choices regarding the music and sound, including whether some segments need to be recut. The composer, music cutter, sound effects person, and one to three engineers or mixers attend these dubbing sessions. At elaborate dubbing facilities, the remixing setup may call for up to seven mixers at a huge console. Film directors sometimes attend these sessions to make sure the sounds they require are sufficiently prominent. Not infrequently, the composer approaches despair when music gets lost behind shouting dialogue or screaming sirens.

Music Scoring for TV

Television programs employ the same stylistic approach as for feature films, but the time frame is faster, and the person who makes the music decisions is often the producer of the show, not the director. Composers often work in both media.

TV drama series (including soap operas and sitcoms) also use original music along with **production music libraries** (see Chapter 25) of prerecorded themes and melodic fragments. Composers for shows often compose 2 or 3 weeks' worth of new material to establish the "feel"; for later shows, the music editors cut the bits they want from the show's library, which has been created from the new music.

Styles incorporate the same wide range as feature films; one multiple Emmy Award winner, for instance, orchestrated a Beethoven string quartet to underscore a chase scene! It has been the task of the music cutter over the years to lay in the various musical sources as appropriately as possible in subsequent shows in a series, trying to make them fit not only new timings but also different dramatic situations. There is no standard way that TV series composers work. Some assemble and command big workforces. Others work almost as a one-person band—composing, conducting, and playing the music, perhaps joined by a few other instrumentalists. In general, the composer has one or two assistants, along with a music engineer, and occasionally may assign orchestration to freelance personnel.

Rates for composing and delivering music for episodic TV vary, particularly based on how heavily reliant the TV series is on low-cost, off-the-shelf production music library tunes. One vital score for TV is the original theme music, for which composers are typically paid tens of thousands of dollars. Fees run a wide range and can be extremely low for new talent just breaking into TV scoring. There's usually a big battle over whether the composer or TV company retains the publishing rights, which may become quite valuable because the theme is part of every episode and is used for TV show branding with the public.

• • • Case Study: Composer Takes Indirect Route to Hollywood Scoring Fame

You never know what avenue in music will lead to a desired career destination, as Emmy-winning composer Jeff Beal can attest.

Beal grew up in Northern California, where his early interest was jazz. Composing was always his ambition, but Beal gained initial career traction as a jazz trumpeter after graduating from the Eastman School of Music in Rochester, New York. Eventually relocating to Los Angeles, he worked on recording and live gigs, networking with fellow musicians who recommended him for some of his earliest composing work in Hollywood.

"Anybody who is successful in this business can tell you at least half the work you get should be through your own networking and contacts," says Beal. "You need to see what's out there. You can't just rely on your agent and manager."

An early gambit that paid off was renting recording studio time for a 3-hour session with an orchestra to make demos of his original compositions set to popular Hollywood visuals. His agent was playing one of those demos in her office when a film editor passing in the hall took an interest, leading to Beal landing a scoring gig for a sword-fighting B movie. Beal got his important *House of Cards* assignment after impressing the hit series' director David Fincher when they worked together on a cellphone commercial.

(Continued)

(Continued)

Jeff Beal.
Photo © Fritz Meyers.

Beal's career thrived scoring TV series such HBO drama *Carnivale* and off-beat mystery *Monk*, whose theme song got Beal one of his three Emmy Awards. His movie scoring credits include modern artist biography *Pollock* and documentary *Blackfish*.

As an established TV composer, his external professional support team consists of an agent to land scoring gigs, a manager for his concert work, BMI to collect publishing income, a music editor who can interact with the production, and an AFM contractor who books musicians for his recording sessions.

Beal typically writes, records, mixes, and delivers all music for projects for a single fee, which makes him responsible for the whole process in creating tunes. Known as a "package" fee, this one price for a finished product arrangement is common for composers working in TV programs and independent films. He does most of the work at his studio-equipped home, which has an annex room where he composes and also a large tracking room that has held up to 26 musicians for recording sessions. Sometimes his wife, opera singer Joan Beal, does voice work.

Composer Beal is comfortable with the home studio arrangement because he prefers working in solitude and it saves time, which is precious with the bang-bang pace of TV scoring. He says the composers of TV series are often required to finish 20 to 30 minutes of music in a week or less that is "fully composed, recorded and mixed. When you are on that kind of work-flow pace, every hour counts." The reason for tight deadlines is that music can't be written until there's a final cut of video, since the score needs to fit the pacing of the visuals.

In quieter moments, Beal plans to combine Hollywood music with large screen projection images in live performances, which fuses his passions of live performances and Hollywood soundtracks.

■ Music Scoring for Video Games

The process of scoring for video games is very similar to film and TV. Indeed, a number of renowned film and TV composers have lent their talents to video games, among them Bill Conti, Mark Mothersbaugh, and Hans Zimmer.

The composer's objective is to capture a game's personality and emotional heart in music. Games are interactive—the screen action appears unpredictable. Despite that difference from linear content, game composers say there is no special twist to scoring video games other than to be true to the title's spirit. Games are electronic products, so it helps if composers are game aficionados and have a tech orientation, but this is not mandatory.

Much of the audio content of video games is original since signature music further embeds the "brand" of the game in the minds of consumers. Branding is important to game companies because game content passes through various media; games can be played on consoles, portable handheld players, and mobile devices and can be adapted into movies and TV programs.

Composers are hired on a freelance basis, although game companies have staff music supervisors to manage each project. With hit video games out-grossing some movies, a game's creative content can be quite valuable. Composing fees have escalated from the earliest days in part because of licensing of game music to other media such as soundtracks. Some music has been created specifically for release through video games: the *Grand Theft Auto* series hooks up with various hip-hop recording artists and producers, Rise Again's 2009 track "Death Blossoms" was written for *Guitar Hero: World Tour,* and Motley Crüe released the single, "Saints of Los Angeles," in 2008 as a download through *Rock Band.*

Not all game music is originally written for the medium, of course. When popular music is used, labels, artists, composers, and publishers would, in theory, derive a stream of royalty payments from licenses negotiated by game developers. However, developers typically insist on a fixed-sum **buyout** that is paid to cap their music rights expense, which of course requires that rights holders agree. Typically, the fee is far smaller than the budget for a major feature film. When a video game has music at the heart of the game, it provides another profitable avenue for game licensing. Music-based games have been aggregators of music, such as *Guitar Hero: Greatest Hits,* which featured tracks from Alice in Chains, Queen, Poison, Rage Against the Machine, Twisted Sister, and Heart.

■ Production Music Libraries

Beyond the glitter of Hollywood, thousands of educational films, documentaries, and movies are produced for business and industry every year, and many of them use only tracks from production music libraries. The reason is simple: low cost. Licensing of prerecorded music from a library includes all necessary clearances and licenses for use of the music. A producer can underscore complete productions with cues (or **bridges**) lifted from the music library.

Production music libraries license a whole catalog or individual **needle drops.** Even "neutral" bridges are available. The lengths of these fragments are rarely critical. The director can instruct the mixer to fade out the music whenever necessary. Library-type material is often prepared by composers with MIDI studios. See Chapter 25 for more information about production music libraries.

Synch Fees

The "synch" fee has become a significant source of revenue for a growing number of independent music artists. The term is short for "synchronization," which refers to the pairing of music and picture, mainly in the form of film and television, but which increasingly encompasses multimedia. The licensing of original songs in films, television shows, and commercials has always been a significant business for some in the music industry, but for decades, it was dominated by major music labels as content developers sought to license songs that were already hits to put into movies and other audiovisual works.

However, the huge expansion in the number of outlets for original programming, from hundreds of new cable channels to online channels and professional productions for online, coupled with a sharp drop in production budgets as the audience continues to fragment, has led producers to increasingly tap the vast pool of independent artists in the search for original music.

A few years back, teen-oriented programming became a big user of indie music tracks; shows such as *Buffy the Vampire Slayer* and *DeGrassi* looked for indie music to help convey a message of coolness and discovery. Over the years, series like *True Blood, Dexter,* and *House* have had soundtracks made up largely of music from unknown or periphery artists, as have commercials from companies like Apple and T-Mobile. The Black Keys are one of the best-known success stories in the music-licensing realm; in addition to placement in feature films, their music has appeared in commercials for Nissan, Sony Ericsson, Victoria's Secret, American Express, and Zales.

However, while more artists than ever have received exposure through synch deals, a high level of financial success has become increasingly rare. The five- and even six-figure licensing deals of the 20th century have given way to synch fees as low as a few thousand dollars. But even those lower payouts have to be considered in the context of longer term artist strategies for exposure. As one music supervisor interviewed for Grammy.com pointed out, artists including Paramour, Natasha Beddingfield, All Time Low, and The Academy all agreed to relatively low synch license buyouts early on for *DeGrassi,* and all benefited when the series became a teen tastemaker. In addition, artists can also make step deals—one amount for the initial broadcast and additional payments for new uses as the series catches fire.

Not surprisingly, these kinds of placements have attracted a huge assortment of brokers, including conventional music industry professionals such as A&R staffers, publishers, and record producers. There is also an array of online companies that specialize in making the connection between music and picture. Many consider synchronized music placement to be the "new radio" for independent artists who are all but shut out of terrestrial hit radio rotation. It has definitely added one more dimension to the toolkit.

Hiring Practices

The pathway to underscoring jobs is often a connection to the film's director or TV show's producer, who oversee hiring of all creative workers. Professionals recommend that scorers have a competent attorney and music publisher to negotiate deals that leave composers with some rights to their music, instead of signing away everything to the producer. Also useful are a good agent to draw up contracts and a manager to guide careers (and help manage personal finances of self-employed talent).

AFM Contracts

The musicians' union does not set **scales** for composition, leaving that issue to be negotiated between the composer and the producer. But the American Federation of Musicians (AFM) does set minimums for other persons engaged in **music preparation**—arrangers, orchestrators, copyists, proofreaders, and librarians. Union musicians earn premium rates for services performed after 12 a.m. and on holidays, and music preparation workers earn the same fringe benefits as instrumentalists. Recognizing that some independent pictures are produced for a total cost that's less than the music budget for a blockbuster, the AFM has come up with a multitier scale for motion picture work. Producers of music for low-budget films are allowed to hire musicians at a significantly lower scale than that required for a high-budget film.

Musicians working in film and television receive additional income once a year, in the form of **residuals** from the Film Musicians Secondary Markets Fund, a nonprofit entity established for collecting and distributing fees. The residuals are derived from revenues that movie and television producers, distributors, and movie studios receive from licensing rights to their movies and television programs in secondary media.

Package Deals

In the film-scoring field, producers and directors require the services of composers, orchestrators, arrangers, music editors, supervisors, copyists, librarians, and instrumentalists, as well as recording and mixing engineers. At one time, all these services could be provided by the major film studios, which retained these artists and technicians on staff, most of them full-time. But after 1957, when the staff musicians were let go by the film studios, producers had to engage all their musicians on a freelance basis. To make this situation manageable, producers would often negotiate **package deals** with independent contractors paying a prenegotiated flat fee for all music service, especially for TV shows. Some composers of electronic scores agree to package deals because their compositional skills combined with their computer skills allow them to function as the composer, orchestrator, copyist, instrumentalist, and scoring mixer.

Producers like package deals because the system transfers their financial risk to the independent contractor, meaning the composer. If this approach is used, the production company usually budgets a set figure for music. That money must cover all music production costs—composition, orchestration, arranging, copying, proofreading, library services, conducting, instrumentalists, instrument cartage, studio or soundstage rental, recording media, mixing, and editing.

Composers

Well-known composers say they get their picture assignments because of their reputations, although they also have agents to find them jobs and assist in drawing up contracts with producers. A composer has a better chance of securing an agent and influential music lawyers after achieving several scoring credits. Some composers rely on building and maintaining good relationships with particular filmmakers to land their projects and use the services of attorneys for the contract negotiation rather than agents.

Top film composers sometimes get so busy they find it necessary to call in helpers to meet deadlines. These assistants include not only arrangers, orchestrators, and copyists but composers as well. Under pressure of time, or possibly because the producer has provided funds to pay for orchestration in addition to composition, studio composers will entrust completion of their sketches to arrangers and orchestrators who understand how the composer wants the music to sound. The composer, not the producer or director, selects all arrangers and orchestrators used in these secondary capacities.

The use of orchestrators is much more common in feature film work than in television. They are paid by the musician whose name goes on the screen credits. Purists may be bothered by the **ghostwriting** phenomenon, but this is the route many hopefuls have found for breaking into TV and film scoring. Yet another way of cracking these high-paying media is to be an advanced student of a busy composer. Teachers often farm out some of their work to their best students, who later begin to locate scoring jobs in their own names. Sometimes, composers take on composer assistants, a form of apprenticeship of benefit to both parties.

Original movie and TV program scores are recorded around the world, with the most popular locations in Los Angeles and New York. In what perennially irks American musicians, European symphonies and other musicians overseas get Hollywood film work because of lower cost, particularly in London and Eastern European cities such as Prague. Their basic pay is less as well as residual payments producers pay to musicians when works run in secondary media. In recent years, the biggest gainers recently have been smaller American cities, which offer lower cost and a well-qualified talent pool.

Music Supervisors

The job of curation of music in movies, TV programs, and video games goes to music supervisors. They have become behind-the-scenes rock stars in Hollywood because those with an ear to select inspired music—whether original or already recorded—can significantly lift the audience appeal of visual products. Once a mid-level job for feature films and television shows, the music supervisor today is often on the same level as the record producer, A&R (artist and repertoire) person, and publisher. These professionals should know popular music, be acquainted with production music libraries, and also be aware of off-the-beaten-path independent music, which is professionally recorded but not widely known. In some situations, this individual finds songs and music to support and enhance the video or film image. An example is selecting bouncy 1974 pop hit "Hooked on a Feeling" that was recorded by Blue Swede for a starring role in 2014 blockbuster movie *Guardians of the Galaxy*. The oldie song with its memorable "oogachaka" chant was incorporated in the movie's prerelease trailer where it practically branded the film—a huge success for a decades-old kitschy tune. Such selection responsibilities of the music supervisor are much like those of a record producer or an A&R executive with a recording company, as explained in Chapter 13. Sometimes, the music supervisor is responsible for putting together only the songs used in the soundtrack but in other instances is in charge of every facet of the score, including hiring a composer for dramatic scoring.

Music supervisors may have various duties, depending on the type of production and the size of budget. A music supervisor may be asked to

1. Make up a budget, make deals, and act as a music department for an independent film company.

2. Place existing songs, whether established hits or the creation of emerging independent talent, in appropriate spots of the movie.

3. Oversee a musical movie, picking songs from a certain period or place to match the action and plot of the movie.

4. Be in the studio when a performer from the movie is recording a song that will be used in the movie.

5. Prepare people for the set, deciding on those who can do their own vocals and those who will need to lip-synch over someone else's singing voice.

6. Assist the director and choreographer in designing shots that will work with the music.

7. Explain "score design" to investors and other interested parties. Producers and project investors often want to see evidence of progress during the movie-making process, so music supervisors make the temp tracks available for a showing of a movie preview.

The music supervisor may also help make the transition from the temp track to the music track that is eventually composed for the movie. This can involve hiring a person who can take a MIDI file—a score or cue that does not exist on paper but instead has been created in a computer sequencing program—and translate it into a conventional sketch that then goes to the orchestrator.

Copyists

Copyists are engaged by the composer or sometimes by the orchestrator to convert rough handwritten music manuscripts into a neat score used in recording sessions. In the film and TV fields, it has been traditional to schedule composition and recording sessions within a time frame calculated to produce a maximum level of panic in all concerned. Last-minute recording sessions are the rule. Also standard in the business is the tendency for composers to begin their assignments several hours beyond the last possible minute. Thus, the copyists consistently work under intolerable time pressures.

Because an individual cannot copy many scores in the time available, it is common practice for head copyists to turn over some or all of the work to a music preparation service. Although some copyists still manually write notes in musical parts, others are adept at using the various computer programs that exist for this purpose, such as Finale. Most computer music programs allow the copyist or arranger to make instant changes of key and time signature if such changes are required to suit the picture.

When television shows or films are being recorded, the supervising copyist is expected to attend the sessions to serve as music librarian and, more important, to be available to correct errors in the extracted parts during the recording.

Orchestra Musicians

Instrumentalists hired to play film and video scores produced in the United States are most often members of the AFM. Despite this dominance, the number of movies produced in the United States that are scored and recorded by nonunion musicians has increased through the application of MIDI studios and computer one-person bands. When large groups of union musicians are called for, they are engaged by the orchestra contractor. The contractor and the composer together prepare a **first-call** list of players, with a supplemental list of second- and third-choice players, should their favorite musicians not be available. Many composers conduct as well, but some prefer to hire conductors so they themselves can oversee in the sound booth, conferring with the mixer and the film's producer or director.

In New York and Los Angeles since the 1930s, the instrumentalists getting this high-paying work have been selected from a relatively small pool of musicians. These musicians have earned reputations over the years for being able to play almost anything placed before them perfectly at sight, and they often make the music sound better than it is on paper.

Musicians who play in major symphony orchestras have successfully completed a series of demanding and highly competitive auditions, but musicians who work in recording studios rarely audition for those jobs. Instead, they prove their worth and bring themselves to the favorable attention of music contractors by word-of-mouth recommendations and strong resumes. Musicians who want to break into the studios are rarely accepted before they've spent the time necessary to prove their abilities to the inside pool of players.

Another pipeline to the inside is through players who are also teachers. Musicians too busy to accept all the offers they receive may recommend their most advanced students for studio and symphony jobs.

Often, string players are current members or alumni of symphony orchestras. In this group, a high percentage are former **concertmasters** or **first-desk** players. Besides competence in standard orchestral playing, these string players must understand jazz phrasing and the kind of style sometimes called "the Hollywood sound"—beautiful tone, romantically expressive, perfect intonation, entirely relaxed. As for double bass, many studio players have, in addition to extensive traditional backgrounds, the ability to play jazz—and often the electric bass. But when a really hot bass line is required, specialists in the rock or rhythm-and-blues fields are added.

In the 1940 to 1960 period, many brass players came off the road from name bands. In more recent decades, some brass players have come from the nation's leading university concert bands. All brass players, whatever their backgrounds, are expected to handle not only **legit** music but any other style, from country to rock. When brass players take their chairs in the studio or on the scoring stage, they already know who is expected to play lead; which chair, if any, is "the jazz chair"; and what horn player will play the lyrical solos. Many studio woodwind players have backgrounds in professional symphony orchestras, and many are graduates of university concert bands and orchestras. It is generally known that woodwind and saxophone players are expected to be competent doublers on clarinet and flute, perhaps even **double** reeds. But this demand for doubling is less common for feature films and TV movies, where the composers may prefer to engage specialists on each instrument.

Many woodwind and brass players now double on MIDI controllers. Composers ask for these instruments because of their versatility and the seemingly infinite number of colors and effects that are possible. They are particularly popular in TV scoring.

Studio percussionists usually come from wide backgrounds that would include extensive study and experience in styles ranging from jazz and Latin to symphonic and rock. When a particularly authentic rock or "urban" sound is wanted, sometimes specialists are brought in. The use of electronic drum sets and MIDI percussion has become widespread, and most working commercial drummers own electronic setups.

If the timpani work is extensive, many contractors will engage a player with solid experience in symphony work. Even though nearly all studio percussionists play mallet instruments, contractors will sometimes hire special artists to handle elaborate solos.

Keyboard players are expected to be able to play traditional and current styles, sight-read, and improvise. The use of MIDI keyboard controllers has become so prevalent that it is now rare to find a working studio keyboard player who does not own an extensive collection of synthesizers, samplers, and related gear.

Guitarists must be competent in several musical styles. Not only are they expected to be excellent sight-readers, but they must also be able to improvise, to play music by ear, or even to compose music on the spot, to suit the style of music being recorded.

Music Editors

Music editing can make or break a film's score. The editor often must make copies of cues in order to use pieces of them again in the film and cut down existing cues when the picture is recut after it has been scored. Many low-budget films provide no budget at all for music cutters and expect composers to deliver a fully synchronous score, whatever system is used for timing music to picture. Composers just breaking into the profession must often function as the music editor on their projects.

The job of the music editor is to make sure the music is cued to exactly the right spots in the action. An understanding of SMPTE code and click tracks is essential, as is familiarity with editing software such as Pro Tools. Years ago, music editors were required to be completely literate and fluent in music. Now, many editors with good technical skills but without academic credentials in music are at the top of the field.

Although some schools have emerged with good training programs, film music editors often acquire their skills on the job. Some start out as film editors who then turn to music cutting. Others are composers or orchestrators, then switch to music editing. The best music cutters are amazingly versatile, possessing great musical sensitivity, a keen ear for balance, and an awareness of how music can make or break a scene, all combined with knowledge of the special technology used in synchronizing music tracks.

Organizations

For composers, an organization to be aware of is the Society of Composers and Lyricists, whose members work in TV and films.

Professionals seeking greater knowledge about recording techniques in film and TV may participate in the Society of Motion Picture and Television Engineers (SMPTE). In addition to serving as an information exchange, SMPTE attempts to standardize recording and synchronization techniques to enable its members to move comfortably to jobs in either medium. SMPTE has its headquarters in White Plains, New York.

Chapter Takeaways

- Although not as celebrated as the visuals, music in movies, TV programs, and video games is crucial in creating an atmosphere that advances the overall creative objective for the project.

- Into the 1960s, composers often emulated cartoon techniques of exaggerating music to conspicuously punctuate visual action on the screen.

- Scoring increasingly requires computer software skills in addition to the traditional attributes of creativity, ability to work under severe time pressure, and ease in collaborating with other professionals.

- Production music library content—available for easy licensing with usage rights already cleared—is financially attractive content for producers of film, TV, and video game productions.

- Decades ago in movie work, composers needed to be fluent in classical music and musicians needed a background in symphonic orchestras, but in recent years, movie music has become increasingly diverse and music talent increasingly comes from an assortment of backgrounds.

Key Terms

- click tracks   (p. 358)
- cues   (p. 363)
- music supervisor   (p. 366)
- package deals   (p. 365)

- residuals   (p.365)
- rubato   (p. 359)
- SMPTE code/Society of Motion Picture and Television Engineers   (p. 369)

- spotting notes   (p. 358)
- supervising copyist (p. 367)
- temp score   (p. 357)
- underscore   (p. 356)

Discussion Questions

1. Why have computer skills become essential for the scoring process, while in the past the emphasis was mostly on artistic music credentials?

2. Aside from original music, what are the other sources that music supervisors tap to assemble scores for a movie, TV program, video game, or industrial film?

3. Prenegotiated fees in packaged deals provide what comfort to producers and what pressure on composers?

CHAPTER 22

Music in Advertising

One of the first memorable uses of "commercial music" was the radio **jingle**, "Pepsi-Cola hits the spot/Twelve full ounces/That's a lot." The early jingles jangled, and the "jingle" label stayed on long after the maturation of the first-generation advertisers who created the monotonous promotions in the early days of broadcasting. The public simply calls them commercials, of course. Advertising agencies and broadcasters call them **spots**. As the media world expanded, campaigns also spread across TV, the Internet, cellphones, and even in video games. The unique vocals and orchestration of the music in a given advertising campaign remains constant across media types, keeping ads on message and reinforcing a brand in the consumer's mind.

"Give me a laundry list and I'll set it to music."

— Gioacchino Antonio Rossini

As pointed out in the chapters on radio and television, it would be difficult to exaggerate the importance of broadcast commercials in the field of advertising. With radio, it is sounds, creating a "theater of the mind," that sell. In TV, it is pictures and sounds together that move the goods and services, and musical sounds can often be more effective sellers than strictly verbal ones. With online video, music can become the signature for an interactive media experience.

Although music without lyrics can be effective, it's often true that ad copy that is sung is easier to remember than copy that is spoken. Music also enhances the pictures and acts as a "**clutter**-breaker" to sort out the jumble of spots. Advertisers continue to pay for music in commercials, knowing that it is money well spent.

Left: A 1950s print ad for Coca-Cola features guitar-playing teenagers at a party.

Photo © Genevieve Naylor/CORBIS.

Influences on Style

Ad agencies and their clients expect the musicians they hire to be capable of performing in current styles. The most effective spots often copy the music trend that is receiving a lot of airplay and appeals to the target demographic. However, the decision to use a certain type of music should spring, ideally, from the concept that shapes the particular spot. Many television commercials employ the visual effects pioneered by music videos. These high-energy, fast-paced, audacious production styles hold viewers' attention. However, a slower paced spot sometimes makes a very effective contrast, with the added benefit of still being visually coherent when fast-forwarded on digital video recorders, unlike quick-cut ads.

One advertising agency executive said that his clients are searching for unusual sounds to put in their spots that will "rivet the ear and stop the zap." To concoct attention-grabbing audio, the line between music and sound effects has blurred so that sounds made by musical instruments are now being combined with those from many other sources. In response to this new emphasis on unusual sounds, "sound design" and "sound specialists" have sprung up in creative centers across the country for advertisers who want a distinctive sound to go with their pictures and words. Today, to capture the public's attention, sound must go beyond reality, merging organic and synthetic elements.

Jobs

Writing music and lyrics for commercials is an exciting combination of composition and commerce and, in the larger markets, is one of the most lucrative forms of music employment available; the competition for jobs is therefore ferocious. At the national level, advertisers and agencies are willing to pay fees large enough to attract hit songwriters and alumni from Broadway. Commercials were a starting point for successful musicians such as Barry Manilow, Paul Williams, and punk rocker Iggy Pop. In addition, the advertising field at the local level affords good opportunities for talented but unknown writers to break into the business.

Music Uses

In the musical commercial, the composer's goal is to form in the listener's mind a memorable association of the music with the product. A good musical theme and underscoring will establish immediate identity with the product; if it includes words identifying the product name, it is even more memorable, often inseparable in the listener's mind.

Another use of music with commercials involves underscoring dramatic action in a manner similar to the way films are **scored**. Many commercials are conceived as little plays, and music is used to help create the appropriate mood or perhaps to **punch up** action. If the minidrama is comedic, the music may be scored in a style associated with movie cartoons or television situation comedies, because the thematic treatments from these shows are already familiar to the audience.

Sometimes commercials will simply borrow music from another source. The melody may already be familiar to the listener, but the original words are discarded and new language is written to convey the advertising message. If the producer wants to borrow a copyrighted melody, permission must be obtained from the copyright owner to alter the material and use it for advertising purposes.

Another type of musical commercial might be called "star based." A well-known person offers, by acting or singing or dancing, a "testimonial" for the advertiser. The advertiser assumes the audience will be persuaded to buy the same product the star "uses." Original music is composed for the star, but if the artist has a pop, rock, or country hit, that recognizable tune might be sung with modified lyrics, as mentioned above.

■ Budgets

Music budgets range from several thousand dollars for a local spot to the high six figures and sometimes even seven with **licensing** and **performance rights** included (for well-known celebrity music) for an elaborate national campaign with a multiple-year contract. Microsoft reportedly paid millions of dollars to use the Rolling Stones tune "Start Me Up" in the multispot Windows 95 ad campaign, and Ford later licensed the same song for vehicle ads. These days, the most expensive individual TV commercials rarely reach $2 million for 30 seconds.

One of the reasons the spot business is so good for musicians is that even hometown, local advertisers like to promote their products by purchasing their own theme music or aural product **logo.** Many composer-directors of limited experience break into the music spot business through low-budget advertising jobs financed by the local furniture store or car dealership.

The small-budget TV advertiser may try to save money by using music from a **production music library** that supplies radio, TV, and films with original off-the-shelf music. If an advertiser also uses local radio spots, portions of the audio tracks may be **lifted** and transferred to video use, thus drawing extra mileage from the money originally invested in custom music for the radio campaign.

■ Station Branding Logos

One of the most widely used types of musical commercial is the **station logo** or **ID,** which gives an outlet a "brand" image or identity to stand out as the media landscape fragments. Most radio and television stations hire an independent production company to create a musical "trademark" or fragment of sound that is used whenever the station announces (or shows on the screen) its call letters. Many station logos feature a small vocal ensemble. Electronically synthesized sounds are primarily used (at a cost far less than a full orchestra) and are often supplemented by "real" or **acoustic instruments** (live drums, guitar, flute, saxophone, or strings). In some cases, a production music library is used; when signature music is used, it is usually licensed exclusively to specific geographic markets. Logos vary in length from a few seconds to thematic types of extended duration. The latter, sometimes called "image-type" logos, function more as theme songs and can be broadcast full-up or in the background for announcements. Wealthy TV, radio, and new media outlets often use a whole series of musical IDs, played frequently enough for the listener to learn to associate the music with the outlet.

■ The Agency Role

Most advertising is handled through advertising agencies. These firms range in size from one-person, office-in-your-hat operations to global supergiants such as Havas, Interpublic Group, Omnicom, and WPP, whose **annual billings** in broadcast and production media alone total in the billions of dollars. Most advertisers prefer to place their radio and TV spots through ad agencies for two reasons: The agencies negotiate low ad rates by aggregating buying for many clients, and, as large centralized media buying entities, they can better support overhead costs such as personnel salaries and office space leasing.

Compensation for ad agencies used to be a simple 15% of the media advertising space—the amount charged by broadcasters that air the spots. These days, ad agency fees can vary from an hourly billing for work performed to a negotiated flat fee for specific services over a specific time frame, to having escalators based on higher product sales or other performance metrics. The production cost itself, including music, may be charged back to the advertiser or be covered by the commission—it's all negotiable. The straight 15% commission fell out of favor when advertisers began hiring different agencies to buy media and create ads and as the landscape fragmented to include new media such as smartphones and video games.

The larger agencies tend to offer their wide array of services on an à la carte basis. This allows an advertiser to engage an ad agency for its media buying, consumer research, publicity, and/or promotional marketing services but perhaps to use commercials created somewhere else. Some small and specialized agencies, called creative boutiques, offer single services, such as only creating ads. Such creative boutiques are particularly common in the movie business for theatrical campaigns.

Advertisers retain ad agencies on the theory that companies specializing in marketing know more about how to sell things than the advertisers. Some big- and medium-sized advertisers maintain **in-house** "advertising agencies" where their own employees conceive, produce, and place the company's advertising. But even such **house agencies** will often retain an external agency to assist it in spot production and media buying.

An advertiser determines what can be spent in 1 year for advertising, then retains an ad agency to offer advice on what part of that ad pie should be allocated for various media buys—print, TV, search marketing, and so on. Once the budget for TV, radio, and new media ads (such as Web banners) is agreed on, the agency implements the campaign. If the ad agency is very large, it will have on its staff a production department and its own in-house staff of writers. Large agencies also often have their own small recording studios in-house. Although it is rare for even the largest agencies to attempt to record masters involving music in-house, they will often use their own facilities to produce demos and voice tracks.

The ad agency's next task is to farm out what it cannot handle in-house. This would normally include rental of production studios, set design, acting, music composition and performing, and editing. Even the largest agencies will normally go outside their own shops for music. Many agencies do retain individuals on their creative staffs with some competence in music, particularly in the composition of lyrics and other kinds of copy intended for the musical setting.

The ability to send production content over the Internet has sped up and smoothed out the process enormously. And it has broken down barriers to working with artists worldwide. A composer in London can post music securely on the Web, the agency in Chicago that has requested it can hear it within minutes, and a technician in Los Angeles can be mixing it, practically simultaneously.

After the production work is completed, the agency has the responsibility of recommending to its client how and when the spots should be placed. Once the client and the agency agree on these matters, the agency instructs its **media buyer** to purchase advertising, and the campaign launches. If the campaign appears to be selling effectively, the advertiser will stay with what is working. If the results of the campaign are disappointing, the advertiser may change the creative message—or it may fire the agency. Alliances in advertising survive only as long as the advertiser is satisfied with the results.

In addition to serving their advertising clients in traditional ways, some large agencies are involved in outside work—for example, the production of music videos for record companies. Not only do music videos offer a fertile field for ad agencies' creative talent to get really inventive, but the fees paid by music clients also help cover ad agency overhead. Increasingly, ad agencies create long-form content for the clients, which can include "infomercials" up to 1 hour in length, entertainment content that subtly pitches advertisers, sponsored online content, and websites promoting client products or services. The expanding media world provides vast potential for such sponsored content.

Spot Production

All advertising is concerned with persuasion. Because most TV spots are now 30 seconds or less in length, skill is required to make the "sale"—fast!

Writing Copy

Top writers make these recommendations:

1. Mention the advertiser's name as often as you dare.

2. Be economical with words. In radio, let the music say it; in TV, let the pictures "talk."

3. Use simple language.

4. Express one or two ideas—again and again.

Another school of thought, born of this age of clutter, is that the body of the commercial should interest the viewer and pique curiosity, but the name of the advertiser is shown or mentioned only once at the end of the spot. Sometimes less is more.

One of the things done least well by advertising agencies is writing copy to be set to music. It is astonishing how often even **national accounts** will accept music that is almost halted in its flow by the awkwardness of the words being sung. In preparing ad copy or lyrics for singers, the minimum requirement is to come up with language that permits a natural rhythm.

• • • Advertising, Music, and the Age of Social Networking

For years, advertisers and agencies have been vexed by the declining impact of traditional broadcast spots in a world increasingly dominated by more interactive media such as online video. A months-long promotion from Sprite soft drink was a fitting example of how a multinational brand can become a willing partner with even an unknown musical artist—who got a global stage out of the association.

(Continued)

(Continued)

Aspiring British songwriter and singer Katie Vogel (also known as Katie Waissel) was showcased in a series of 5-minute videos that were subtly sponsored by the soft drink on YouTube and had a tie-in with Facebook. A marketing team from Sprite selected Vogel—who then lived with her parents in London—from an open audition to relocate to New York in her pursuit of pop music stardom as cameras tagged along. The online video series was called "Green Eyed World" in a nod to Vogel playing a green guitar and Sprite being a lemon-lime drink.

"I was told they were looking for someone who was ready to have their whole life recorded, rewound, and remixed," Vogel said in a Web video that aimed to be compelling reality TV for a youth audience. Sprite, a Coca-Cola brand, drove traffic to the videos via online promotions, TV spots, special packaging on Sprite cans in some countries, and live events featuring Vogel.

Vogel got to keep rights to her songs. Unlike in a typical label deal, the financial support from Coca-Cola in this case was designed to produce marketing fizz, not back-end royalties for the advertiser. The limits of a viral marketing campaign—and Sprite provided lots of muscle—are evident because Vogel's career didn't take off immediately, although she did subsequently record and make TV appearances.

Katie Vogel.
Photo © C Brandon/Redferns/Getty Images.

Scoring Music

Clients are not always articulate when it comes to musical sounds. The smart composer will arrive for a briefing session armed with examples, usually actual sample **tracks**, either original or taken from current on-air notables.

Instrumentation was once determined largely by budget constraints. Synthesizers changed that somewhat, but the amount of instrumentation is still determined by budget. Synthesized music is more economical, but as always, more tracks cost more money. Unlike much popular music making, just about everything for commercials is written out. Improvisation is limited to appropriate liberties taken by the rhythm section. The arranger's main goal is to have the **front line** stay out of the way of the singers or speakers.

The advertiser wants to hear the text, not the background. The cardinal rule for all arrangers scoring backgrounds is, *stay out of the way of the words*. Modern technology helps, because each vocal line is often recorded on a different track. During mixing, when the final sounds are selected, the main track is mixed farther forward (made to sound more prominent) than the background music, allowing the listener to hear the words. The important rule for arrangers is to score backgrounds in a range different from the main vocal line.

Production Companies

Although commercial production companies once specialized in either radio or television, a common practice these days is to put TV and radio under one roof, separate from online advertising. The TV/radio production firms are typically staffed by a producer (or producer-director), a director (or director-cameraperson), office personnel, and sales staff. The production company will sometimes contract for audio and video technicians through a technical production house. An art director and perhaps a graphic artist will be engaged freelance, as will musicians.

Television production companies lease or own their own studios, which must provide room for at least single-camera film, sophisticated lighting, scenery/prop/graphics production, and film- and tape-recording facilities. Almost all commercials today are edited at a video postproduction facility because they can afford the most sophisticated editing equipment. Wages and rental of facilities run to hundreds, sometimes thousands, of dollars per day, depending on the extent to which the production company farms out part of the work.

Companies outside the major production centers are typically smaller operations that serve local, regional, and, occasionally, national accounts. They usually have an in-house staff of two to five persons. Companies with small staffs may have modest TV shooting studios, or more likely, they will rent shooting stages. Audio is usually recorded in recording studios and, later, synchronized with tape or film.

Small production companies offering radio commercial services have studios big enough to handle small choral/instrumental sessions. When an advertiser wants something on a grander scale, producers rent independent recording studios. In smaller markets, there is often a close relationship between the local radio stations and production companies. In fact, very often the local radio station *is* the production studio for local producers.

Going beyond basic commercial spots, firms involved in production often offer their clients complete programming services in whatever musical format the station wants—CHR (contemporary hit radio), adult contemporary, country, rap, and so on. They write original music tracks for the client. In addition, full-production houses also offer their clients music library services that include "**commercial beds.**" These are 30- or 60-second music tracks arranged for use with whatever ad copy the station or advertiser wants. For example, the library may contain solid, dignified-sounding music for sponsors such as banks and insurance companies. When a station needs music background for a store advertising clothing for teenagers, it can select any number of CHR-type beds from the library.

Library services also include a selection of "neutral" tracks for advertisers not seeking a particular musical trademark or association. These commercial beds are often arranged in three segments: A 60-second bed might open with a 20-second front that establishes the tone of the commercial. A bridge follows, where the music is less full in orchestration and less active in texture. This provides a musical background (bed) that makes it easier for the listener to understand the ad copy. This copy can be read live by the disc jockey or it can be prerecorded. Following this middle section, the remaining time, perhaps 10 seconds, is where the bed rises up, so to speak, offering a musical reprise of the front. This end section is often called the *tag,* a term borrowed from vaudeville. Tags return to the **up full** sound of the front.

Production companies can be engaged to add singers and custom copy to the front and tag sections of **canned tracks** of this kind. This radio commercial format was widely used in the 1950s and beyond. Because the format became so predictable, more imaginative producers and advertisers now prefer a less pat format and have experimented with a variety of sequences of copy, music, reprises, **cold** copy, and musical trademarks.

Commercial producers, whether supplying custom spots or tapping outside production music library services, regularly offer their clients *lifts*. These are usually 10-second extrapolations from 60-second spots that were initially scored in anticipation of a short section being lifted from the full-length commercial. These lifts provide the sponsor with the option of buying 10-second time segments and having available spots of the appropriate length—with minimal additional production cost.

Artists and Fees

Advertisers and agencies are accustomed to paying **creative fees** for music and texts. Although some composers charge no creative fee—only for their arranging, copying, and conducting—it is not uncommon for a spot composer to get paid a creative fee (for one piece of material) of $500 or more for a local campaign. At the national level, creative fees vary widely, from thousands to tens of thousands (or even more) if using a "star" composer.

Composers generally work for ad agencies on a buyout basis: As employees performing "work for hire," they give up all copyrights in their work. For a while, many advertising agencies agreed to contracts that allowed the composer to retain copyright in the music and assigned rights for use into perpetuity to the agency or the advertiser for advertising purposes only. This kind of contract left the composer free to seek exploitation of the material in other media, particularly the pop song field. But agencies worried signature music would lose its exclusivity and also began to realize that there is gold in music publishing rights, so they seek to control the publishing rights, too. The composer with clout doesn't let them do that. The lesser-known composer has no choice. Some ad agencies that "buy out" a composer's copyright may still allow the composer to collect the writer's share of performance income.

Fees are paid in a number of ways. There is usually a partial payment when the contract is signed and final payment when the material is completed. Sometimes, however, the creative fee is paid upfront; then the commercial is written. If the client approves the spot, the rest of the fee is then paid upon the completion of the project after everything (orchestration, recording, etc.) is finished.

In small markets, advertisers will often seek package deals. A composer-arranger discovers a prospective client who has, say, $7,500 for a musical spot. The musician agrees to take on the complete package for that fee and composes the music and perhaps also the text, scores the arrangement, extracts the parts, rents the studio, engages the performers—and delivers the finished master to the client. If this packager could get away with using just one singer and a three-piece band or, better yet, one synthesist who sounds like a three-piece band, there might be a few hundred dollars left for the 2 weeks of labor. Or if the job was budgeted carelessly and ran overtime in the studio, the packager could end up in the hole.

In national campaigns, package deals are less common. But here, instead of one individual taking on the whole project, an ad agency will engage a music production house for a flat fee. This kind of company often figures its budgets on two levels: **above-the-line** costs (creative fees, "talent") and **below-the-line** costs (expenses such as studio rentals, scale payments to union artists, music copying, and recording incidentals).

Some music production firms are owned or partly owned by the composer. Such houses will offer a client, for one lump fee, composition, text, arranging, orchestration, and musical direction. Such fees for national accounts are in the tens of thousands of dollars.

A producer or agency may locate a naturally gifted songwriter to do the creative work for a campaign. Some of these individuals may have attracted the attention of producers through their songwriting success on pop records. Some are musical illiterates and are helpless without the aid of competent arrangers. They will often sing their tunes into an audio recording device so an arranger can render it in correct music notation. The **leadsheet** thus produced is then turned over to the arranger-orchestrator-director who is hired to score the music for the recording session.

Artists' Contracts

Singers, instrumentalists, arrangers, and copyists employed on national spots are members of their respective unions. The total dollars earned by American Federation of Musicians (AFM) members working in the spot field rivals the amount earned by union musicians scoring TV movies and theatrical motion pictures. The national contract covering AFM members in this field covers employment in radio and TV commercials, as well as their use on commercials for in-store videos, movie theaters, and online.

The contract also governs the employment of AFM instrumentalists, leaders, contractors, orchestrators, music librarians, and copyists—but not composers. As with certain other AFM contracts, "leaders" generally receive double scale. A leader may be a conductor or an instrumentalist who has some extra responsibility during a recording session. Instrument **doublers** make extra wages of varying percentages for the first double, then in many cases extra fees for additional doubles. If the orchestra contractor is an individual other than the leader, the contractor earns double scale.

The use of synthesizers is treated not as instrument doubling but as **overdubbing**: The musician charges scale for each of the different parts that are played, although the number of parts for which a synthesist will be paid will probably be negotiated upfront, before the session begins.

If the employer is a signatory to the AFM contract, the employer agrees to abide by the terms of that contract, which includes using AFM musicians and music preparation employees paid at contract scale. The employer (who may be the advertising agency or the spot producer) must also pay into the AFM-EP (Employers Pension Fund). The AFM contract stipulates that the employer is responsible for additional payments to the musicians for uses of the music following the initial 13-week period covered by the basic fees for national spots. For such extended use (starting with the 14th week) or for each spot dubbed into a new commercial or used in a new medium, each AFM member who was employed on the original project receives an additional payment per 13-week cycle. National advertising agencies and their clients are accustomed to paying these extended-use (or new-use) payments, as well as side-line payments for any appearances on camera. Musicians who perform on national spot sessions can sometimes earn big money over the years, if their spots have long runs. However, spots usually just run one or two cycles.

Local spots under union jurisdiction are paid at a lower wage scale than national spots. At the local and regional levels, circumvention of extended-use and reuse payments is common. Many local spots are produced for straight buyouts by the advertiser or the ad agency for all services creative and artistic. Many are nonunion.

Historically, the American Federation of Television and Radio Artists (AFTRA) claimed jurisdiction over professional singers on radio and most of television, and the Screen Actors Guild (SAG) claimed jurisdiction for some television. Now these unions have merged to form SAG-AFTRA. Signatory agencies and advertisers are obligated to adhere to union scales for national campaigns and most regional campaigns. As with standard recordings prepared for commercial release to the public, in the spot business, SAG-AFTRA has set special scales for solo, duo, and group (three or more) singers.

One of SAG-AFTRA's important tasks is obtaining payments for each use of its members' recorded work. On one hand, rates for singers are per use of the singer's recorded work: Each use requires a new payment. On the other hand, AFM members are paid per 13-week cycle for all use, not for each use. (To be clear, "use" means the type of exploitation. Each individual airing of a spot does not count as a separate "use.") Responsibility for payment of fees may rest with different entities or their successors, depending on the terms of the initial contract for the union artists. As with the AFM, SAG-AFTRA artists may well receive more income via reuse payments than they do from the initial recording sessions. When singers receive conflicting calls for jobs, they will opt for the work that appears most likely to stay on the air the longest. Top jingle singers in the major production centers can earn huge incomes through extended-use payments across multiple commercials just at SAG-AFTRA scale.

The singers who get hired to record national spots are usually drawn from a select pool of vocal artists. In addition to being able to sing almost any style and sight-read like demons, spot singers must excel at clear diction. The advertiser's first concern is not an "operatic" voice quality—**bel canto**—but clarity of language. The composer may have scored music comparable to the "Hallelujah Chorus," but the ad agency's **account executive** may demand it be discarded in favor of a **voiceover** if the listener can't make out the words.

Production Sequence

The process of producing a broadcast commercial is very involved. Here is how the events might fall in place for a **network** television commercial where the budget for music is large. In this hypothetical case, the advertiser instructs its advertising agency to come up with a TV campaign for a new soap product. Also, we will assume the advertising agency retains a production company to assist. Events might occur in a different order than the sequence listed here.

1. The agency, through its **creative director,** decides on a concept and calls a production meeting. Agency staff members attending are the creative director (chairperson), writers, TV producer, art director, and account executive.

2. The creative department creates a storyboard for the advertiser's approval. A TV storyboard is a visual representation, either rough drawings of the sequence of events scheduled to occur on the screen or in some cases crude animation. If the storyboard is presented as still frames, the aural components (dialogue, music) are indicated below each picture as captions, enabling the stakeholders to perceive an approximation of how the eyes and ears are engaged in the 30-second spot (see Figure 22.1). The advertiser accepts the advertising concept for the campaign.

3. The agency develops a detailed budget to cover the cost of production.

4. The agency's creative director or **house producer** contacts two or three **music houses** (production companies) and/or recognized commercial music composers and invites them to submit appropriate music, from which it will make its selection. Composers and houses will compose soap-selling music—good,

clean sounds—as a demo, on spec. Some ad agencies will pay for costs of demo production, typically passing on the cost to the advertiser. The agency creative group selects its favorite from the spec demos submitted.

5. The agency contacts a casting agent or casting director, who may issue what is known in the trade as a **cattle call** for actors, according to the specifications that the agency supplies. Or the agent may simply select from casting books half a dozen pictures or videos of actors who might look right for the cast. If a casting session is held, it is usually videorecorded. The advertiser approves the casting.

6. The producer notifies the music house/composer of which track on the demo the advertiser and agency people liked best, and they settle on a creative fee for music. The music house/composer accepts the fee and asks to retain all publishing rights exclusive of the advertiser's uses of the music. The agency, well aware of the value of holding on to music publishing rights, balks on this point, and further negotiations ensue, resulting in a contract price high enough to convince the composer to give up the publishing rights.

7. The producer tells the music director or business manager of the music house that there is a production budget for a 20-piece orchestra and five singers, and a recording date is set.

8. The composer reserves a studio for the recording and is guaranteed a favorite engineer.

9. The business manager/musical director calls up an AFM and a SAG-AFTRA contractor to engage the performers, telling the AFM contractor that the musicians will be expected to bring an array of musical instruments.

10. Before the recording date, the music director instructs the music preparation service to deliver copies of the score to Studio A for the orchestral recording session at 9 a.m. and the vocal recording session at 10 a.m. in Studio B.

11. The morning of the date, the orchestra reads through the chart and records Take 1. Takes continue for the hour budgeted.

12. As the orchestra is finishing the final takes, the singers arrive. The SAG-AFTRA contractor-vocal director rehearses the singers. For the rest of the hour budgeted, the artists record takes with the prerecorded orchestral music.

13. The final mix, attended by the producer and the music director, may be done that day or another day.

14. The musical director, producer, and account executive select the best take and instruct the studio to deliver a finished file to the agency by 5 p.m. that same day.

15. The producer meanwhile has filmed all the visuals, created a final edit, and proceeded to lip-synch the actors with the musical track. Following adjustments in the picture transfer, the complete commercial is ready for duplication and distribution to broadcasters.

16. The agency files work reports with all the unions representing the singers and musicians. The agency, working through a talent payroll service familiar with all the current rates, issues the payroll checks for distribution.

Figure 22.1   Storyboard Excerpts From Honda 2012 Super Bowl Spot.

Postscript. In rare instances, the wise and/or powerful composer who has been able to retain publishing rights to the music (limiting the advertiser's music rights to use in advertising) finds a lyricist to set new words to the music, then submits it to a publisher. A publisher accepts the song in the hope that it can get a free ride based on the current popularity of the music generated by the broadcast campaign. Everyone is happy, even the advertiser, who now enjoys additional identity through the popularity of the pop song version of the theme music.

Chapter Takeaways

- Advertising music can be lucrative, particularly with national or big-market campaigns.

- Agencies are often engaged by advertisers to both create spots and buy media advertising time to run them.

- Independent production companies are frequently subcontracted to produce an entire spot or just the music for the spot.

- Online technology allows some professionals in the advertising-music production chain to work remotely—uploading their parts of the work product to others for approval or mixing.

- Composers generally write advertising music for a flat fee or "buy out" of all rights. In some cases, they retain publishing rights to benefit from later exploitation of the work.

Key Terms

- above-the-line   (p. 380)
- account executive   (p. 382)
- below-the-line   (p. 380)
- commercial bed   (p. 379)
- creative boutique   (p. 380)

- lifts   (p. 375)
- media buyer   (p. 376)
- overdubbing   (p. 381)
- spot   (p. 373)
- station logo   (p. 375)

- tag   (p. 379)
- testimonial   (p. 375)
- voiceover   (p. 382)

Discussion Questions

1. Why does the advertising industry prefer clearly sung commercial lyrics that feature simple language?

2. What is the composer's goal in a musical commercial? Discuss appropriate music for a comedic commercial as opposed to a dramatic commercial.

3. Why are local commercials more likely to be recorded on a nonunion basis than national commercials produced for big advertisers?

4. Discuss the production sequence for a large-budget commercial. How might the production sequence differ for a commercial with a small budget?

CHAPTER 23

Music and Theater

Music has played an integral part in the theater for centuries. Many of the master composers experienced their greatest success in the theater: Wagner, Stravinsky, Gershwin. In Western civilization, musical theater can be said to have started in the Jewish synagogue and the Roman Catholic Church; most religious ceremony would be unthinkable without music. Much religious pageantry, of itself, is choreographed music.

> "Extraordinary how potent cheap music is."
>
> —Noel Coward

Musical theater's earliest patronage, in addition to organized religion, came from the aristocracy who built and operated theaters right on their own premises. Later, men of wealth—for example, the merchants of Venice, the Medici family of Florence—became enthusiastic patrons of the arts. By the 17th century, public opera houses began operating, selling tickets (at the current equivalent of about 50 cents each) to cover production costs. In the 18th century, years before he scored his biggest hit with *Messiah,* Handel was hustling around London, buying and managing theaters, booking talent, scoring, producing, conducting operas, even doubling as a **pit** musician (keyboards) in his own theater. Competing musical shows, particularly *The Beggar's Opera,* eventually drove impresario Handel out of the musical theater business, while other producers, whose ears were more in tune with current taste, established a musical theater tradition in London that flourishes to this day.

By the 19th century, musical theater in Europe and this country, including everything from grand opera to minstrel shows, was prospering, selling tickets, and turning a profit. Early in the 20th century, opera and ballet production costs began to exceed

---

Left: A Large *Les Misérables* Banner on the Outside of the Queens Theatre in London.

Photo © Gordon Scammell/LOOP IMAGES/Loop Images/Corbis.

box office income, and the musical patron, the big giver, reappeared to keep these art forms alive. Meanwhile, imported European operetta was being transformed in this country into forms such as the musical revue, musical comedy, light opera, and, since *Show Boat* (1927), the musical play. In our own time, it is musical theater that keeps Broadway and most regional theater going. Giving more recent momentum to musicals, Hollywood movie studios have set up divisions to mount Broadway musicals and touring versions based on their film properties, after Disney Theatrical Productions created a hit with the stage version of film *Beauty and the Beast*.

Types of Musical Theater

Broadway Musicals

That piece of territory in New York known as Broadway has seen the production of contemporary musical theater's most treasured repertoire; it has been the working place for dozens of America's most gifted composers, lyricists, playwrights, producers, directors, and performers. Broadway would have collapsed had it not been for the musicals that kept it alive after 1945. Some Broadway musicals have produced more profit through recorded music sales and publishing income than they ever generated through ticket sales. Royalties from successful Broadway musicals have earned substantial sums of money for the composers, lyricists, and book writers (the term *book* is used in the musical theater to describe the scenario and dialogue of the musical drama; it excludes music and lyrics).

Broadway musicals have always been the most expensive kind of production to mount. In 1950, a sumptuous production cost $200,000. Today, a producer may have to raise $10 million or more to mount a first-class Broadway musical; the star-crossed *Spider-Man: Turn Off the Dark* reportedly cost an over-the-top $75 million to stage and lost a staggering $60 million before it closed in 2014. Many musical plays do not start turning a profit until they have successfully run 2 or even 3 years.

Costs are now daunting because of theater rental expenses and high wages for Broadway's heavily unionized skilled workers. No matter how carefully a show is budgeted, a producer cannot increase the "efficiency" of live singers, dancers, and musicians. The live audience may total only 1,000 per performance, not the millions available on television. Investors have risked their money partly in anticipation that the Broadway run is but a preliminary phase of the potential profitable life of a musical through original cast recordings, performance licensing, national tours, and perhaps even movie rights. Broadway producers with track records (such as Andrew Lloyd Webber, Cameron Mackintosh, Scott Rudin, and the husband-and-wife team of Barry and Fran Weissler) can raise money more easily than others. Some of them have a consortium of investors waiting to risk their money.

The death of Broadway has been predicted since the 1930s, but this lively tradition refuses to attend its own funeral. Encouraged by the amount of money to be made by a hit and the glamour, investors have been more than willing to take risks.

Off-Broadway Theater

As rising costs began to reduce the number of shows mounted on Broadway, producers in the 1950s began to develop a theatrical movement that came to be known as **off-Broadway**. This movement away from New York's 10-block theater district centered on drama, particularly experimental theater. It had minimal impact on musical theater until 1967, when the late Joe Papp, noted producer of the New York Shakespeare Festival, purchased an about-to-be-demolished library and reopened it as the Public Theater. Dedicated to the production of new plays by American writers, the Public's first presentation was *Hair,* which became the first successful rock musical and moved to Broadway after its premiere. Going the same route some years later was *Two Gentlemen of Verona.*

Unquestionably, the Public's most spectacular success came with *A Chorus Line,* which opened in 1975 and became one of Broadway's longest running musicals ever. The income from *A Chorus Line* was undoubtedly the single most significant factor in keeping the New York Shakespeare Festival running. Because of the rising costs of musical theater production, even off-Broadway has become financially prohibitive for many small shows in New York City and elsewhere. For this reason, some shows are first presented in small theaters that are known as off-off Broadway productions.

School Productions

Concurrent with the off-Broadway movement, American universities began to increase their musical show production. Before a musical show can be legally performed at a school, the school must first get a license from an amateur performance licensing agent, typically a publishing house such as Samuel French, Inc. As described in Chapter 7, such an agent will license the right to present the show and will also rent the script and the musical parts. The agent traditionally gets 10% of the license fee. The other 90% of the license fee goes to the authors and their overall agent.

Regional Theater

Also around the same time as the off-Broadway movement, indigenous theater began to develop and became known as regional theater. At last, Broadway lost its monopoly on professional musical production. Regional theater includes amateur, semiprofessional, and fully professional productions, often functioning in that gray area between the fully professional and the semiprofessional worlds. Labor union Actors' Equity regularly negotiates agreements with regional and community theaters that permit Equity members to perform in the same cast with non-Equity members. Actors, singers, and dancers now use university and regional theaters to learn their craft. These establishments help fill the void left by the death of live-stage national variety circuit vaudeville in the 1930s where, as the show business expression has it, performers found "a place to be bad" while practicing their craft.

Regional theaters find particularly strong public acceptance for plays, dances, and shows designed for children. Some children's theaters will break even at the box office. Regional theaters that focus on the classics or on experimental, noncommercial productions may receive financial support from the National Endowment for the Arts to help them stay alive and well. They also depend on grants and funding from private donors and foundations, city governments, light opera associations, and regional arts councils. Earned income through the sale of tickets is often insufficient for survival.

A particular kind of regional theater—dinner theater—finds that its biggest draws are productions of hit Broadway musicals. The public does not seem to tire of yet another production of *Camelot* or *Carousel.* Only very rarely do dinner theaters invest in the production of original musical plays, which is a common policy with many non–dinner theaters as well. Many dinner theaters cast leading roles with established performers, stars of lesser stature, or talented college students. But the students get paid, and in this sense, dinner theaters can be considered part of the professional theater as well as a valuable training venue. These establishments rarely have a **proscenium** stage; they mount their productions in the round, use **blackouts** instead of curtains, employ a minimum number of dancers on their small stages, and make do with duo-piano accompaniment or a tiny pit band. Despite these limitations, some dinner theaters turn out attractive shows.

Summer Theater

Another component of musical theater is summer theater, which is popular across the country. Cities with particularly successful summer theaters are Chicago, Kansas City, Houston, Sacramento, New York, and Dallas, as well as the Berkshires region in Massachusetts. They mount proven Broadway musicals almost exclusively. Many of these productions are quite good. They usually hire name artists for the leads, support them with the best local talent (professional and semiprofessional singers, actors, and dancers), and employ a pit orchestra of AFM (American Federation of Musicians) musicians. Many summer theaters break even, perhaps even turn a profit, at the box office during their seasons, which may run from 2 to 6 weeks. Productions are mounted in old movie houses, community arts centers, parks, theaters, and even tents. These productions offer short-term professional employment, and some of their performing alumni go on to careers on Broadway, television, music, and film.

National Tours

An important part of musical theater is touring shows. Most Broadway hit musicals develop at least one road company that begins touring as soon as the investors believe the public has heard about its New York success. Major hits have more than one New York–mounted road company that not only prosper on national tour but also produce a lot of employment for singers, dancers, and musicians.

Road companies generally tour with their own musical conductor, perhaps a percussionist, and one or two lead players, then fill in the pit orchestras with a dozen to three dozen local AFM members. The producer or musical director uses local AFM contractors, perhaps through the local promoter, to engage the pit musicians. These "casual" jobs provide considerable supplemental income for musicians across the country, many of whom are otherwise employed as music educators, members of local symphony orchestras, or studio musicians. There are "first-class tours" in so-called first-class cities, which are defined by tradition rather than other characteristics, such as size of the city or venue. There are also so-called bus-and-truck tours that go into the smaller venues.

Classical and modern dance are a part of American musical theater. Resident and touring companies offer at least seasonal employment for dancers and the musicians who are engaged to accompany them. Many dance companies perform to recorded music, which limits live employment of union musicians despite the AFM's efforts to reduce this practice. But the bottom line is as important for theaters as it is for any business, and recorded music is much less expensive than hiring an orchestra or even a small combo.

Las Vegas and Other Entertainment Centers

A significant part of musical theater in this country is found in Las Vegas and other entertainment centers, such as Atlantic City, New Jersey, and Branson, Missouri.

The quality of the arrangers and players working in Las Vegas ranks with the best anywhere. A number of them were first drawn westward in search of work in Hollywood, then moved to Las Vegas and accepted steady employment there in preference to intermittent jobs in the Los Angeles area.

Revues are popular in Vegas, although headliners also continue to perform with their own music directors and nucleus of musicians, augmented by local instrumentalists.

Industrial Shows

Another component of American musical theater is the industrial show. When new products are introduced or national sales campaigns are being organized, companies such as Toyota and IBM hire a producer or a production company to create commercial entertainment packages designed to motivate and instruct their sales staffs and to show appreciation to customers. These kinds of shows are not open to the public and are scheduled in major cities where the corporation might pull in its regional sales force. Industrial shows often have big budgets and offer seasonal employment for composers, arrangers, copyists, singers, dancers, and instrumentalists. Writers and producers of industrial shows are usually found among the group that also produces broadcast commercials. Several major cities—including Detroit, Chicago, Los Angeles, New York, and Philadelphia—have production companies set up to turn out the kind of shows major corporations want.

Amusement Parks and Cruise Ships

Many amusement parks around the country present musical stage revues, particularly during the peak summer and holiday seasons. These are usually original shows themed to each individual setting but can also feature Broadway or contemporary hit songs. Cruise ships also offer original musicals and abridged versions of Broadway shows.

Theater Associations

The League of Resident Theatres (LORT) is a multiemployer bargaining association representing individual, not-for-profit theaters. LORT represents member theaters in negotiation with three **collective bargaining** units: Actors' Equity Association (AEA), Stage Directors and Choreographers Society (SDC), and the United Scenic Artists (USA). Member benefits include centralized collective bargaining and legal advice.

The Broadway League (formerly known as The League of American Theatres and Producers) is the national trade association for the Broadway industry. Its 700-plus members include theater owners and operators, producers, presenters, and general managers. The League supports its members through an array of programs and events designed to promote Broadway as a vibrant national entertainment medium. Other key services include overseeing government regulations for the Broadway industry, maintaining research archives and databases, and investing in audience development programs. Due to the costs of employing live orchestras, the Broadway League negotiated reductions over the years in the minimum number of musicians to 3 to 19 persons, depending on the size of the theater.

An organization that produces new works as well as the "standard" musicals both on- and off-Broadway is the Nederlander Producing Company of America, Inc. Nederlander, based in New York City, operates about two dozen theaters throughout the United States, as well as several theaters in London.

Also interested in the creation of new musicals is the National Alliance for Musical Theatre, an association of about 160 producing organizations that present theater on a cooperative basis. Any number of member companies pool their artistic and financial resources for one production of a show rather than stage several separate productions of that same show.

Production Components

The Producer

For almost every theatrical production, everything begins and ends with one individual: the producer. Usually, all employment and all income are initially generated through the producer's vision and resources. In musical theater, the producer's work begins with acquisition of a property. Broadway's musicals are either original or based on an underlying property, such as a novel or dramatic play. The producer enters into an option agreement with the owner of the property (usually the playwright), providing that the producer will pay a nonreturnable advance against royalties to have the right for a period of time to develop and subsequently present the play. Sometimes, subsequent option periods are conditioned on certain additional requirements, such as the producer's engaging a composer, a book writer, lyricist, or well-known director. If option conditions are met, the option period can be extended with the payment of additional money. The same concept is applied in the producer's contracts with the show's composer, lyricist, and book writer: The producer gets the exclusive right to create and present the show, which must happen during the option period(s) or the producer loses all such rights.

Producers are not always the only individuals seeking musical show properties. An influential director or aggressive agent can also put together a package and then seek out a producer to assume the overall responsibility of pulling the production together and mounting the show. Composers afflicted by the Broadway itch continually search various sources—novels, plays, even movies—for properties that they believe might form the basis for musical treatment. If they are successful in securing an option on a property, they can then take it to a producer.

Sometimes the authors put the shows together without a producer. In that instance, a collaboration agreement is first entered into among the authors that spells out the parties' respective rights and obligations and contains options and elements, similar to the ones in the agreement between the producer and the authors described earlier.

If the musical is heading for Broadway, the producer must negotiate contracts with the book writer, the composer, and lyricist. The Dramatists Guild of America has developed standards and procedures contained in the document known as the **Approved Production Contract (APC)** for first-class productions. Its membership includes numerous playwrights and musical show book writers, composers, and lyricists active on Broadway.

Subsidiary Rights

The producer negotiates contracts with the show's book writer, composer, and lyricist that specify what these authors are to receive in advances, royalties, and credit and what the producer will receive from the authors' **exploitation** of **subsidiary rights**. Once the show has completed its first run, the authors have the right to exploit the valuable subsidiary rights; the producer may receive a part of the income but has no control over the exploitation or disposition of these rights. Examples of subsidiary rights include movie rights, stock and amateur rights, touring rights (to the extent that the producer doesn't exercise the producer's option with respect to them), and rights to do different productions and derivative works (e.g., the right to have a dramatic play turned into a musical or vice versa). The book publishing rights of a play are usually retained by the book writer and not shared by the producer or the other authors. Separate rights to the music and lyrics are normally carved out by contract and retained only by the composer and lyricist and/or their music publisher.

Original Cast Album

The original cast album right is neither an author's subsidiary right nor exclusively a producer's right but a hybrid right involving both. Generally, the producer negotiates for the right to make the cast album deal, providing certain conditions favorable to the author, such as a minimum **royalty**. Conditions might typically include an agreement about the division of recording company royalties that will be payable to the producer and to the author. An author might agree, for example, to allow the producer to make the cast album deal with a record company if the label pays a royalty of at least 14% of the retail price of the album.

Option and Royalty Payments

The typical producer-writer contract provides for the writer to receive an option payment during the period the show is being created, with an additional advance payment to be made during rehearsals. With the APC contract, the writer gets significant advances, but the "royalty pool" concept also has been added; so after the advance payment, the writer may not receive a significant amount of money beyond a guarantee in the early days of a show while the pool is in effect.

Approvals

These contracts also provide that when the show's director, cast, conductor, dance director, and designers for costumes, scenery, lighting, and sound are engaged, approval for these artists must first be obtained from the book writer, composer, and lyricist (such approval is either by unanimous or majority vote, depending on the arrangement made by the particular individuals involved). Furthermore, the producer cannot delete or add a song without the approval of the authors. The producer cannot make any changes at all to the authors' work without their approval, and the author involved owns all the changes. This is different from the movie industry, where the writer usually has no ultimate control.

Costs

Concurrent with the effort to raise money for the show and sign the writers, the producer employs a general manager who prepares a preliminary budget and negotiates many of the creative contracts. One of the largest components of weekly running costs will be a combination of theater rental and labor-related expenses. Rent is generally a flat amount, but theater owners frequently negotiate a percentage of the adjusted gross box office receipts. There is no standard percentage amount on this revenue sharing.

A producer schedules production time after estimating the date for opening on Broadway and then tries to locate a suitable theater that will be available. Most Broadway theaters are relatively small; the producer of a Broadway musical must locate a house that provides more than 1,000 seats in order to have sufficient capacity to generate adequate weekly box office revenue to be able to recoup the large costs of mounting and running a musical.

Broadway theater owners know from long experience that the life expectancy of a new musical ranges from one performance to several years. They, too, must gamble with the show. A theater owner is reluctant to sign a rental agreement with any but a reliable producer and will be more willing to risk tying up the theater if the producer has a good track record, if the show's writers are well known, or if the cast includes a star. The rental agreement calls for the producer to reimburse the theater owner for all the theater's operating expenses—fixed costs, such as utilities, heat, and air conditioning, and the salaries of ushers, box office staff, and other personnel—plus a rental fee that may be a percentage of the weekly gross box office receipts. All theater rental agreements have a "stop" clause that gives the theater owner and the producer the right to terminate, in the event that the show receipts fall below a certain negotiated amount. It is evident that a costly Broadway musical must do near-capacity business to stay alive.

The investors have a contract with the producer that says if there is any money left after the producer has paid the costs of mounting and running the show, the investors will next receive all the money that's left until they've recouped their investments. After recoupment has been achieved, the investors split the show's receipts, normally 50–50 with the producer, depending on the producer's share as outlined in the investment contract. The production company's receipts include the net receipts from the production company's presentation of the show and any portion of the subsidiary rights income to which the production company becomes entitled.

Typical weekly running costs of a full-line musical show will include most, possibly all, of the following:

1. Royalty payments of from 6% to 9% of the box office gross, divided among the writer, composer, lyricist, director, choreographer, and designers, drawn from a *royalty pool*. This pool is a complicated formula for allocating a certain number of percentage points to each individual involved, with a minimum guarantee per point plus an allotment of the profits.

2. Salary (plus a possible weekly royalty) for the star.

3. Salaries for leading players (actors, singers, dancers).

4. Salaries for the stage manager and assistant stage manager.

5. Salaries (based on Actors' Equity scale) for supporting actors, dancers, and singers.

6. AFM scale for the pit musicians and any musicians who might appear on stage.

7. Salaries for union stagehands, electricians (including audio technicians), carpenters, wardrobe personnel, hair and wig stylists, and other theater personnel, such as treasurers.

8. Producer expenses. The producer's "cash office charge" (usually a fixed amount per week) is provided in the agreement that defines the producer's rights in relation to the investors' rights. This agreement, although negotiable, often says that in addition to the cash office charge, the producer (who

raised the money) will receive a producer's royalty each week equal to 1.5% to 2% of the gross weekly box office receipts before the investors get their money back and before the promoter-producer or the investors share net profits. The producer may also receive income for providing electrical, sound, or other equipment for the production. There is usually a fee to the general manager of the show as well. This is normally a weekly dollar amount commencing a few weeks prior to rehearsals and ending a couple of weeks after the closing of the show. The general manager is the person who is knowledgeable about budgets and about how to negotiate an appropriate lease with the theater owner. A good general manager is crucial if the producer is good at raising money but doesn't know the nuts and bolts of producing.

9. Salaries for production assistants, retainers to public relations personnel, and fees (or percentages) to theater party promoters who are part of the public relations efforts.

10. The rental payments under the theater lease.

Obviously, these financial commitments add up to an expensive, risky undertaking. One of the reasons investors continue to put their money into this high-risk field is that income from subsidiary rights sometimes will not only help cover production costs but might even exceed box office revenue.

Grand and Small Rights

After the initial run, subsequent producers wishing to reproduce musical plays and operas are required to pay royalties to the copyright owners for performance of the show. When such producers license the rights to an existing show from the authors' agents, the producer has to negotiate for these **grand rights**. These kinds of performance licenses (see Chapter 7) are required for both amateur and professional productions.

If a song from a musical is performed separately (not as a part of the musical show), on radio, on TV, or in live performance, the rights to nondramatic performance become part of the **small rights** that are licensed by the performing rights organizations, which collect a performance royalty from the music user and distribute that royalty to the composer, the lyricist, and the publisher of that song.

Chapter Takeaways

- Elaborately staged musicals enjoy enduring popularity in live theater. The famed Broadway circuit in New York would likely have suffered economic collapse in the television era without loyal audiences that support music-oriented stage productions.

- Music in theater is more diverse than what plays under the bright lights of Broadway. It encompasses song-oriented performances in regional theater, dinner theater, Las Vegas and other entertainment centers, summer theater, industrial shows, amusement parks, and cruise ships.

- Obtaining the right to and making rights payments for musicals in theater requires navigating a complex contractual thicket. Producers, lyricists, composers, stage-play authors, performers, and directors make varying proportional claims to revenue streams generated by stage performances, original cast record albums, and touring versions.

Key Terms

- Approved Production Contract (APC)   (p. 394)
- blackouts (stage)   (p. 392)
- book writer   (p. 390)
- collective bargaining   (p. 393)
- first-class tour/production (p. 392)
- national tour   (p. 392)
- off-Broadway   (p. 390)
- pit   (p. 389)
- proscenium   (p. 392)
- royalty pool   (p. 396)
- subsidiary rights   (p. 394)

Discussion Questions

1. Besides on Broadway, what are the employment opportunities for talent in musical stage productions?

2. Describe the responsibilities of the producer of a musical theater production.

3. Describe what's included in "subsidiary rights."

4. What costs need to be considered in running a full-time musical show? Why might investors be willing to take the risk of these costs?

CHAPTER 24

Music Products

The music products industry is a major player in the overall U.S. music business, generating revenue of $6.8 billion annually in retail sales for new products through music stores and related websites. In the United States, there are tens of millions of amateur musicians in addition to the sizable number of professionals. These performers all need music, equipment, and accessories, and the music products industry sees to their needs.

> "Playing this instrument brings out my soul."
>
> —Toots Thielemans

For our purposes, the music products industry includes all musical hard goods and printed music. Musical hard goods have traditionally included acoustic and electronic keyboard equipment; wind, brass, percussion, and string instruments; and amplification and recording gear. With improvements in manufacturing technology and competition from off-shore factories, musical instruments are selling at lower prices than in the past, yet they offer higher quality. There is also a growth of electronic and personal computer-based products producing a wide array of synthesized sounds, and playback equipment for electronic dance music is also rising. Meanwhile, once-hot-sellers *Guitar Hero* and *Rock Band* video games (that are bundled with rudimentary connected instruments) have cooled. The industry also encompasses the services needed for customers to enjoy the products they purchase, such as repairs and lessons, and the merchandising and retailing of these products. (Chapter 14 covers merchandising of recorded music.)

Especially at the retail level, musicians often enter this field as a fallback option to performing full-time but discover that careers in the music products industry become their most realistic choice for making a living.

Photo © George Doyle/Thinkstock.

Music Retailers

Full Line

Music stores come in all sizes, carry thousands of products from guitar picks to booming drum sets, and will gross anywhere from hundreds of thousands of dollars to $10 million annually. The trade newspaper *Musical Merchandise Review* counts 7,650 musical instrument stores in the United States. The big retailers, all with stores and mail order, include Guitar Center, Sam Ash Music, Schmitt Music, Brook Mays Music, and Quinlan & Fabish Music. Available products may include traditional and electronic instruments for rent, purchase, or lease; accessories such as cables; fretted instruments; electronic and recording equipment; DJ gear; recorded music; printed music scores; and publications from books to magazines. These stores serve as a one-stop service center for musicians and can be small "mom-and-pop" operations or the megabox stores that emerged in the 1990s.

It is often smart, and sometimes critical, for full-line music retail stores to give lessons to help their customers enjoy their instruments. For pianos and organs, it's customary for 6 months of lessons to be included in a **rent-to-own** contract. Along with teaching the customers to enjoy their purchases and creating a sense of community, the music school generates foot traffic, a vital ingredient for any retail store to keep its doors open. Parents who are unsure of their child's commitment to music will often gravitate to used instruments, which are less expensive than new products. The ability to personally examine a used product is a crucial in-store advantage over online instrument sellers, who are mostly confined to new products. However, emergence of eBay and CraigsList as convenient marketplaces for easily selling used equipment has eroded this segment for brick-and-mortar stores.

A service frequently offered by full-line stores is instrument and equipment repair. These services can be hard to find and very time-consuming and costly if instruments need to be shipped out of town. Although it is becoming increasingly difficult for music storeowners to find and hire qualified repair technicians (and thus a good career opportunity!), this can be an important part of a store's offerings. Efficient, well-run repair departments help stores develop customer loyalty and, again, add to foot traffic as instruments are dropped off and picked up.

As in many fields of retailing, independent music retailers in the United States have been challenged by the "**big-box**" operations—the musical equivalent of Wal-Mart. But the 2003 bankruptcy of MARS, the initial leader in the big-box concept for music retail, gave investors second thoughts about too-rapid expansion in this retail category.

The Combo Store

Narrower in scope than the traditional full-line store, combo stores generally deal with drums, guitars, amplifiers, speaker systems, audio mixing panels, public address systems, and lighting equipment—and the accessory items that go with them all, such as microphones and stands, cabling, drumsticks, snares, and the like. Recording equipment can also be found in this group, and it has become very saleable, with the vast improvement in technology, the significant drop in price, and the advent of the home recording studio. Bands and individuals are now able to produce their own good-quality demos or **DIY** releases. It's a boon for music retailers, not to mention the increased opportunities for creative musicians, amateur and pro, to let their imaginations roam.

Attendees visit a music products booth at a NAMM trade show.
Photo courtesy of NAMM.

School Music

The **market** for band and orchestra instruments and equipment is made up of three groups of customers, the smallest being professional musicians. The next largest group includes amateurs, the individual music hobbyists—children and adults. The largest part—at least 75%—involves schools and colleges, which host multiple musical ensembles. These ensembles have an aggregate membership of several million young musicians (it has been estimated that 1 in 10 elementary school students joins a school band or orchestra). Their instruments, equipment, and music are acquired by individual musicians' families and by the schools themselves. The success of school music merchants depends on developing strong and loyal business relationships with the school band and orchestra directors in the area.

The instruments normally purchased or rented by students and families include flutes, clarinets, trumpets, alto and tenor saxes, trombones, violins, and violas. Often, retailers offer a rent-to-own (or lease-to-own) option where the rent or lease money can be used toward purchase, in whole or part. Merchants serving this community sometimes build up a large, lucrative rental business.

Many of these instruments are manufactured in three levels of quality and price that roughly correspond to the three groups of purchasers: student, step-up (i.e., midlevel), and professional musicians. The least expensive models are often recommended to beginners and their parents, since it's uncertain whether the youngsters will continue their musical activities. These instruments are ruggedly constructed, provide acceptable intonation, and are the type normally used for rentals. Some firms manufacture instruments and equipment "privately labeled," as well as their own name brands. This has become prevalent with the influx of instruments made in China and Taiwan. The Conn-Selmer Company, for example, has offered two lower level instrument lines, the Prelude and the Aristocrat, that are made in Asia to the company's specifications.

Frequently, schools own background instruments (tuba, string bass, cello, bari-tone sax, French horn, euphonium, English horn, bassoon, oboe, piccolo, and lower-voiced clarinets) and the entire percussion section. These are obtained through a purchase order or bidding process with a local or national retailer. Also, many schools have discovered the advantages of a corporate or store lease as a way to obtain much-needed musical equipment immediately, with annual payments locked into a specific figure they can afford over a 3- to 5-year period.

To service schools, store reps pick up and return instruments for repair and carry along a good stock of accessory items such as reeds, mouthpieces, **ligatures,** valve oil, cork grease, and the like. Competent repair service for all customers, school based or otherwise, is critical. Free or discounted repair loaners are often available. And anyone working in the music products industry must know instrument nomenclature for all instruments they sell, such as "undercut tone holes" and "diaphragmatic soundboards."

Specialty Shops

As students make progress, some trade in their beginning instruments for step-up or professional instruments. These two levels of instruments cost at least twice as much as the economy student model. Some of the high-end professional instruments and gear have such a small market that most retailers cannot afford to carry them, and they are available only in stores that specialize in this very small niche market or by special order.

These mini "meccas" often attract customers from around the country who travel great distances with checkbooks in hand to take advantage of merchandise available only through these shops. Other entrepreneurs have taken advantage of online commerce to market their offerings to customers at a greater distance. Still, for many professionals, the tactile experience of testing an instrument before it is purchased cannot be replaced.

• • • Case Study: Drum Shop Oozes With Hollywood History

In the heart of Hollywood, Pro Drum Shop is a combination museum, musicians' social center, music book publisher, and musical instrument mecca that embodies that famous real estate adage to emphasize "location, location, location."

The percussion instrument store opened in 1959 across the street from union Local 47 of the American Federation of Musicians—and both haven't budged in over a half century. Stan Keyawa, whose family owns Pro Drum Shop, estimates any one-instrument store also requires at least a 4 million population to be economically viable, and the Hollywood location in the heart of Los Angeles provides that population support.

Stan, his brother Jerry Keyawa, and their mother Dolores Yeager are the proprietors of Pro Drum Shop whose walls are filled with signed photos of drummers; an early 1970s vintage Slingerland-brand drum set used by the late drum legend Buddy Rich is prominently displayed in store (his signature "BR" logo is on the base drum). The store's Facebook page overflows with still photo nostalgia, and there's even a 2010 TV documentary on Pro Drum Shop. Milking heritage in one product line, Pro Shop introduced 55 Zildjian-brand cymbals commemorating the store's 55th anniversary, each consecutively labeled with years stamped on from 1959 to 2014. The $600 per cymbal line sold out quickly.

Stan Keyawa and Jerry Keyawa, owners of the Pro Drum Shop.
Photo © Pro Drum Shop.

But the Keyawas say what's crucial is friendly service to every drummer whether a famous pro or amateur, fast equipment repairs that the big chain stores don't match, and accessories sales. Stan says it's the "cymbals, sticks, bags, heads and accessories that are the money makers. That's what keeps us alive."

Pro Drum Shop occupied a front-row seat for recent musical instrument history. Rock musicians in the 1960s drove manufacturers to make drum sets bigger, but now Jerry sees tastes shifted back to smaller equipment that is more easily transported. The store is working with Yamaha to downsize drum hardware to 25-inch sections that fit into existing cases that Pro Drum Shop sells.

Jerry notes that today, clamp accessories are becoming quite diverse and in demand as drummers attach all kinds of gadgets for unusual audio, and drummers today are infatuated with technology to meticulously fine-tune their sound. Stan observes even local customers have embraced the shop-at-home mania by increasingly ordering online from the store's website, which expands the Pro Drum's sales territory through Internet commerce but is no game-changer. "It's a rough part of the business because everyone is competing on price," Stan notes of online.

Going back to the late 1960s, the store staff fashioned a hand-crafted consolette with a rail that held seven concert tom-tom drums, which enlarged setups to 11 drums. After the consolette rail was seen nationally on network TV, demand soared and manufacturers mass-produced imitations of what Pro Drum Shop pioneered.

Jerry says that the craze for electronic drum sets with electronic pads in the late 1970s and early 1980s was "a little bit of a scare" because electronic drums required rapid turnover as new models are quickly introduced, which played into the hands of big-box music stores. However, customer interest faded, and Pro Drum remains focused on acoustic percussion products.

The Keyawa brothers are the second generation manning the counters, starting in the late 1960s working for their stepfather Bob Yeager, who co-founded Pro Drum Shop with friend Chuck Molinari.

"We're kind of hands on," says Jerry. "I think that's why we have been successful over the years."

Consumer Audio Equipment

There are three levels of audio equipment: professional, semiprofessional, and home use. Most audio equipment purchased for the home is sold through electronics retailing giants who stock the great variety of products on the market. Home-use music products can also be found in some electronics retailers. Stereo stores rarely sell professional audio equipment, the kind required for theaters and arenas. Professional systems of this kind are typically sold, installed, and serviced by sound companies specializing in this kind of business. An online search for "professional audio equipment" will provide a list of specialized sound companies.

Keyboards

A well-rounded keyboard department or store offers a full line of vertical and grand acoustic pianos, to accommodate the full gamut of musicians, from the professional who needs a 9-foot concert grand to the student first learning to play. These stores also make vertical, student-grade pianos available through rent-to-own arrangements or other forms of financing. The entry-level product for this marketplace is the electronic keyboard, which comes in a range of models from grand piano configuration to small, easily portable instruments. They offer a wide variety of sound combinations to the player. The standardization of **MIDI,** developed in the 1980s, allows different electronic musical instruments (usually keyboards) to communicate with each other. A simple patching job makes equipment **interface** easy and inexpensive. Several synthesizers can be played at once from a single keyboard, providing **multitrack** layers of sound. The principle behind the General MIDI is simply that any sequence should sound the same no matter what General MIDI instrument is used.

The development of the electronic organ has made it possible for the music merchant to be the major player in the church organ market. Pipe organs have priced themselves out of all but the top end of the market, and they are fragile and require constant maintenance. The Allen Organ and Rodgers Instruments electronic organs have become very acceptable instruments for serious concert and church performances. Competent repair service and technicians are a must in supporting pipe organ sales and acoustic pianos, while the more widely used electronic organs are low maintenance. Electronic church organs must be ready for church services; to meet this need, organ companies promise quick emergency response.

Print Music

Two types of retail outlets generally sell print. One is the music store that concentrates on instrument sales and stocks print as a service to its customers. A full-line store stocks pop folios, piano music to support serious piano study, and pedagogical vocal music, such as the Schirmer Library editions. This kind of retailer usually doesn't delve into the school and church music market.

The second type is the **institutional print** dealer. Institutional print music is purchased by schools, churches, and community groups for performance by choirs, bands, orchestras, and small (chamber) ensembles. The leader in this institutional sector is family-owned J. W. Pepper & Son, headquartered in Exton, Pennsylvania. Although founded back in 1876, J. W. Pepper is a 21st-century company offering **sheet music** via digital e-Print, which recipients print out on their own computer printers.

J. W. Pepper has two large music distribution centers and 11 retail store locations across the country. When shopping online, customers can hear and see the music offered for sale. The online store has broadened its customer base to include students, hobbyists, and musicians. Besides its main mail-order website, the company created a website exclusively for pianists at PianoAtPepper.com.

The profit margins for selling printed music are comparable to other parts of the industry, but it takes a lot more $25 and $50 sales to net the kind of profit generated by the sale of one Steinway piano. The biggest challenge for the institutional print retailer is how to make the buyers aware of new music—a lure that encourages school music directors and music teachers to visit their stores. This is done in a number of ways: J. W. Pepper mails printed catalogs and sends out emails to 40 different lists focused on different kinds of music, new-materials reading sessions arranged through retail stores, and direct-mail efforts of recordings of new material.

Books, Magazines, and Trade Journals

Music Books. The biggest market for books on music is in the elementary education field of school music. Perhaps the next biggest sellers are the popular accounts of the life and times of rock stars, followed by the next largest market share in music appreciation and music theory books. Jazz history books also sell well. The increase in record industry technology courses has generated a sizable market for textbooks in that field. Another popular type targets the amateur songwriter. Interest in textbooks in the music business is also growing. There are also certain scholarly books on music, of interest to musicologists and college students working on graduate degrees. W. W. Norton is the leading publisher in this field.

The merchandising of these products covers a broad range of outlets. Textbooks are naturally marketed through the bookstores of colleges offering pertinent courses. Some instrument stores carry books that might be interesting to their customers (e.g., some drum shops carry biographies of famous drummers and histories of particular kinds of drums). Bookstores market the more general-interest titles if their communities respond, and the Internet provides access to practically any title, no matter how esoteric.

Music Magazines and Trade Journals. The publication and sale of music-related magazines and trade journals are important facets of the music business, although print publications have declined as information moves to the Web.

There are two basic categories of music magazines: popular (for music fans) and professional (for those who earn a living in music or aspire to do so). In the professional realm, *Music & Sound Retailer, Music Inc., Music Trades, Musical Merchandise Review, PLAYback,* and *Canadian Music Trade* are the primary journals for music product sellers. *Billboard, Variety,* and *HITS Daily Double* are leading notable industry publications, offered at select retailers, by individual subscription, or on newsstands in major recording centers.

Outside the professional trades are the "popular" music magazines such as *Rolling Stone* and *Down Beat.* But in recent years, other consumer-focused magazines have discontinued print publication to exist only online. Established professional musicians receive *International Musician* each month if they are members of the American Federation of Musicians (AFM). Arts administrators value the League of American Orchestras' *Symphony* magazine. Another publication, *Campus Activities Programming,* is the journal for college concert promoters and talent agents. Scholarly music journals should be mentioned: *Notes,* read by music librarians; *MEIEA Journal,* serving music industry scholars; and the *Journal of the American Musicological Society.*

For a more complete listing of the leading music magazines, see Selected Readings at the end of this book.

Sales Leaders

While each store proprietor needs to decide what type of store he or she is interested in—and what will work best in a given community—it is wise for these owners to keep track of current buying trends. According to NAMM,[1] the following categories of instruments top the best-seller chart in the U.S. music products industry. As shown in the following list, fretted products are the top leaders in sales (based on dollar volume), with the guitar proving once again to be the most popular instrument.

1. Fretted products
2. Sound reinforcement products
3. Wind instruments
4. Printed music
5. General accessories
6. Microphones
7. Percussion
8. Computer music products
9. Acoustic pianos
10. Signal processing
11. Instrument amplifiers
12. Portable keyboards

Sales data on the music products industry do not include figures on the used-instrument market, which is substantial but difficult to measure.

Growth Areas. Sales of computer-controlled and electronic instruments with synthesized sounds are booming. Instruments personalized for females have become popular, such as Daisy Rock guitars, which come in appealing colors and are designed to fit female body contours. Disc jockey gear and also sound reinforcement products, such as power amps, speaker enclosures, and powered mixers, continue to make sizable gains.

Promotion of Musical Products

The proprietor who has invested money in a music store is not really alone financially. The investment is backed up by the far larger resources of manufacturers of the lines sold.

One sales promotion device is the cooperative ad: The manufacturer and the merchant share the cost of online display ads, emailing, and radio, local cable TV, and print advertisements. Another cooperative effort develops when the manufacturer supplies point-of-sale items for the merchant to display, such as signs, banners, streamers, show cards, special display racks, and window dressings. Stores festoon their premises with these point-of-sale stimuli.

To pull floor traffic in slow periods, retailers may temporarily lower prices on some items in heavily advertised promotions that occur like clockwork at the same time each year. One major retailer schedules a Green Tag Sale every March, an Anniversary Sale in August, and Black Friday sale in November.

Since school and college musical directors are among the biggest buyers of background instruments and equipment, manufacturers display these wares at professional educators' meetings and conventions. Manufacturers often employ well-known professional performers as goodwill ambassadors to attend conventions and music clinics, representing themselves as enthusiastic users of the firm's instruments. Some firms supply the services of these professionals to schools for benefit concerts and clinics with school bands or orchestras, further developing goodwill for the firm and its products.

Blending distribution and promotion, acoustic and electronic piano manufacturers have linked up with retailers to offer instrument loaner programs for colleges and universities. The retailer buys the instruments, loans them to the school (usually for the school year), offers them at sale prices at the end of the year, and then pays the manufacturer for them. In this kind of creative alliance, everyone benefits: The school has enough instruments for its students, the students have good instruments to learn and practice on, and the manufacturer and retailer have good opportunities to sell the instruments and, again, build name recognition.

Even more direct contact with potential customers occurs on the floor of the store when a family walks into the shop. The youngster of the family may have dropped in to get something repaired and left with a new Selmer alto sax. Many large sales develop through a store's offering music accessories, including instrument cases, straps, replacement strings, and equipment designed to enhance the performance of the musical instrument. Accessories offer high markup, draw a variety of customers into the store, and then cause them to return, since most accessories wear out and need replacement.

Although many merchants cater to young musicians and schools, retailers also seek the business of professional musicians where feasible. They not only buy the higher priced professional instruments and equipment but also can be an effective sales force for the store—nearly all professionals, even semiprofessionals, have pupils who need recommendations on where to shop. Professionals who frequent music stores also use them for communication centers ("I need a drummer for Saturday night. Know anyone who can do the gig?").

■ A Changing Industry

Mail Order and Online Sales

Not long ago, the brick-and-mortar music retail industry joined the rest of the retail world in fighting mail-order sales that came with the Internet explosion. However, no single Web juggernaut has emerged for the music industry (as Amazon is to booksellers), because mail-order Web commerce of music products is fragmented. The market is served by multiple specialists as well as by the online divisions of several large retail chains.

Musical instrument stores typically carry several thousand different products and accessories, while mail-order outlets stock tens of thousands. Benefiting from centralized warehousing, mail order tends to experience fewer out-of-stock items than stores whose capacities are limited to on-site storerooms, and it also escapes the burden of financing a broad inventory to support only a local market.

Mail order has boomed with the advent of broadband connections that bring full-featured **catalog** information via websites with audio, video, and multiple images, a big improvement from the static printed catalogs of the pre-Internet era. Music product sellers report that consumers tend to buy from both local stores and online mail-order suppliers. It is common for a consumer's online supplier to be the website of their favorite local store.

Product Manufacturing: A New World

Economic globalization has spurred increasing cross-border trade, and musical instruments are now manufactured around the world for sale globally. The United States imports about $5 billion worth of musical instruments a year—mostly from Asia, Mexico, and Canada—but also exports $2 billion in music products around the world.

Asia has become a hub of manufacturing because of low labor costs, which results in lower prices for consumers and stiff competition between Asian countries. In many cases, musical instruments produced in China and Indonesia now undercut the prices of products made in Japan, just as decades earlier, Japanese manufacturers undercut the prices of products made in the United States. One example of this competition is a sprawling 1 million-square-foot musical instruments factory in the north China city of Quingdao. South Korean–owned Sejung Musical Instrument Manufacturing established the manufacturing hub in 2001. Today, the plant is owned by Chinese company Parsons Music and employs several thousand workers with a capacity of making hundreds of thousands of guitars and tens of thousands of pianos annually.

U.S. manufacturers are also taking advantage of expanding global trade by bringing in raw materials from international sources. For example, cross-border shipment of unfinished high-quality exotic wood prompted a U.S. Justice Department raid on U.S. manufacturer Gibson Guitar in 2009 and again in 2011. Gibson asserted that it complies with regulations for its importation of wood from Madagascar and India,

A technician works on a wind instrument.
Photo © Annett Vauteck.

and India raised no objections to Gibson's practices. The imported wood was used to manufacture guitars in Tennessee.

Trade Associations

The music retail business has a number of trade associations that are active, vital, and dedicated to members of the industry. The leading associations in this segment are the National Association of Music Merchants (NAMM), the National Association of Professional Band Instrument Repair Technicians (NAPBIRT), and the Guitar and Accessories Marketing Association (GAMA).

The most representative trade association for people selling instruments, equipment, and accessories is NAMM. It is composed worldwide of more than 9,200 music retailers, manufacturers, and their representatives, wholesalers, and distributors. NAMM helps its members increase their business by providing training programs, supporting private and public music education, and generally promoting the benefits of music making.

The NAMM trade shows, held twice yearly and not open to the general public, showcase musical instruments, professional audio equipment, and the latest in music electronics and software. NAMM provides educational sessions, sales and management seminars, and market research studies to its members. NAMM's annual statistical review of the music products industry, *The NAMM Global Report,* is a useful summary of market sales and trends in the musical instrument field.

To develop the next generation, NAMM created the NAMM Young Professionals group, which is open to professionals under age 40 at NAMM member businesses. Members can apply for scholarships, participate in music trade events, learn from industry leaders, and make connections that can lead to jobs.

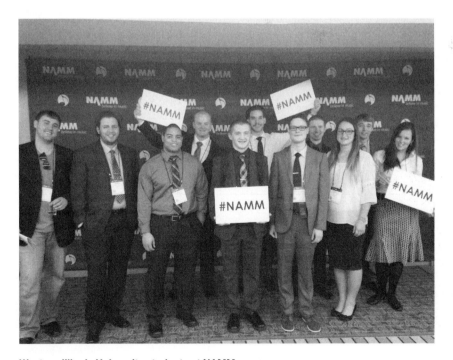

Western Illinois University students at NAMM.
Photo © Courtney C. Blankenship.

Opportunities for Employment

The music products industry is a dynamic field where music students often work part-time. It can become a full-time career by design or occasionally a career fall-back for graduates struggling to find other jobs. Illustrating the field's size, the national retailing and mail-order chain Guitar Center employs about 11,000 persons on both a part-time and a full-time salary basis. Opportunities in the music products sector range from entry-level retail positions to finance, marketing, or management for retailers, distributors, or manufacturers of musical instruments and accessories.

Music business curricula have been developed at the college and university level to train young people for careers in this industry. These degrees combine training in music and business since a solid background in both areas is beneficial. A degree in this field, combined with real-world experience, has led many individuals to fulfilling careers.

Note

1. As per The NAMM 2014 Global Report.

Chapter Takeaways

- The musical products industry is dominated by specialty music stores. A few popular items such as guitars, amplifiers, and drums are stocked by mass merchants, but their product lines are limited.

- Brick-and-mortar specialty stores generally operate websites, extending their reach into the online sales market.

- Specialty stores rely on their knowledgeable sales help that mass merchants don't match, instrument repair services (as well as providing loaners), stocking niche accessories such as reeds and valve oil, and instructional lessons on-site.

- Sale of sheet music, to both individuals and institutions, is a steady business.

- Specialty stores are a source of employment opportunities, perhaps for students seeking part-time work in areas where they can be close to music.

- Some musical instruments are manufactured in the United States and Canada, while imported equipment comes mainly from Asia and Mexico.

Key Terms

- accessories   (p. 401)
- combo stores   (p. 402)
- full-line music retail stores (p. 402)
- institutional print dealer (p. 406)
- mail order   (p. 402)
- music magazines/trade journals   (p. 407)
- NAMM   (p. 411)
- rent-to-own   (p. 402)

Discussion Questions

1. How have globalization and online storefronts changed the way brick-and-mortar stores are run?

2. What are some factors that contribute to successful music product retailing?

3. What are music product needs in your community? How are these needs being met through local and online retailers and service providers? In your view, what is missing?

4. What are the arguments for and against importing environmentally sensitive raw wood in order to manufacture instruments in the United States, especially if exporting the wood is legal in its country of origin?

CHAPTER 25

Business Music and Production Libraries

Foreground and Background Music

A substantial portion of music produced today is not really meant for active listening. Rather, it is intended to remain on the edge of consciousness, providing an "extramusical" service, affecting people's moods and energy levels. Background music murmurs on, as we all know, just about everywhere people can be found: in many places of business—including restaurants, malls, supermarkets, airports, elevators, sometimes even in restrooms—and during "hold" time on the phone.

> "I worry that the person who thought up Muzak may be thinking up something else."
>
> —Lily Tomlin

Considering the sheer frequency of exposure to music, the "business music" audience is by far the largest in the world. For years, business owners have looked to music as a means to attract more customers, motivate employees, and sell more. Over time, business music users have put more focus on music's direct impact on the customer's experience and its support of marketing objectives for businesses' brands.

Traditionally, business music has been separated into two basic categories: foreground and background. **Foreground music** is usually described as music designed specifically for the business in which it is used and played for very particular purposes, such as drawing in targeted customers and keeping them in stores, entertaining telephone callers on hold so that they will be less likely to hang up, or helping airline passengers stay calm and relaxed. Foreground music tends to be played at a higher volume than background music.

Left: Photo © Comstock/Thinkstock.

Although as carefully designed for its particular setting, **background music** is intended to go largely unnoticed in a conscious way, an unobtrusive accompaniment to work, shopping, conversation, dining, and relaxation. In health care, it's used to reduce stress and even to make the hearers more likely to stay healthy.

The lines between foreground and background music have become blurred with the greater emphasis on music as a design and branding medium. Using traditional definitions, businesses have moved toward foreground music and have begun meshing sight, such as video billboards, and scents with business music audio in a designed multimedia environment.

Research has demonstrated that the controlled application of music can modify mood, energy level, and behavior. Studies of manufacturing plants, for example, show that workers exposed to music are more productive and happier than when working in silence or with nothing but the drone of machines in the background. Psychologists and music therapists consult with companies offering music services so that the selections heard are programmed to fit specific environments. Hospitals use it to help doctors as well as patients. Many studies have shown that music has an unusual power to help patients' recovery from physical or mental trauma.

Business Music

Although Muzak is probably the most iconic name in this specialized field, the name itself was officially retired in 2014 by parent company Mood Media. But Lily Tomlin's comic jab, quoted at the opening of this chapter, has proven prophetic. The company of today produces many strands of multimedia ranging from digital signage to "broadcast" scents to tickle people's noses. Although Mood Media and associated brand DMX are diversifying their services, music remains an important business with millions of songs in their production library. Repertoire runs the full gamut. Another business music company is PlayNetwork.

These service companies not only offer the music but also create proprietary product platforms that deliver the music. They also design, install, and service the sound systems. The companies contract with businesses nationwide through an extensive integrated network of sales and service offices or through in-house project management and field technician teams and a wide network of affiliates.

Transmission. Service companies use delivery transmission systems that include streaming via satellite, Internet protocol (IP) store-and-forward, and disk delivery, depending on individual clients' needs. The IP and satellite transmissions enable large numbers of locations to be served with an economical amount of bandwidth. Most of the satellite receivers used can be controlled remotely, which allows companies to control which music program is playing and which advertisements (if used) are aired. These systems are designed to protect the music assets by encrypting the source.

Musical Production. In its early days, pioneer service Muzak used to face copyright and licensing restrictions that limited its access to original artists' music, so it produced its own versions. For many years, this music did not incorporate vocals, and the instrumental music became ingrained in the American pop culture lexicon as boring "elevator music." Material was drawn from music already published, ranging from standards to current hits, and musicians were hired to record it. Although some of these recordings were made in the United States, others were made in Europe, where musician pay rates were lower rates than union AFM (American Federation of Musicians) **scale** in the United States.

Licensing and Copy Protection. In the early 1980s, companies gained access to music by original artists—the same music heard on the radio. They addressed the licensing and copy protection laws that previously limited access to original music by establishing new-use licensing agreements with performing rights societies. Business music libraries now mostly contain music by original artists, including tunes uploaded by DIY composer-musicians.

Airline Music. One specialized field within this already specialized field is supplying music to airlines for the in-flight entertainment of travelers. More than a dozen companies compete for this market nationally and internationally. For example, Spafax, founded in 1985, services over 60 international airline clients worldwide, providing audio- and video-on-demand (AVOD) channels, custom publications, and original content such as boarding and safety videos. Airlines choose music from several genres. Airlines can also select preprogrammed audio channels, featuring hosted music shows, stand-up comedy, interviews, magazine shows, and information such as documentaries. The music is delivered by several methods, depending on the needs of the airlines. The vast majority of music transmits from hard drives on each airplane.

Each airline also chooses how often to refresh content with additions and deletions. As a rule of thumb, 30% of content is replaced each month. Given the vast on-plane audio library, some music may remain in inventory for up to a year. As with other business music, the programs are designed to enhance the airline's image—and also to ensure that the passengers recognize a majority of the selections on their chosen channels. Sometimes, there's turbulence in the air from litigation about in-flight music rights. In one recurring issue, music rights holders sue airlines and their entertainment suppliers alleging they source music in countries with low music royalty rates.

Production Music Libraries

Production music libraries—previously referred to as "stock music"—offer music and sound effects that are original rather than covers of already existing songs and music. Musicians record original music that is then sold or licensed for specific use, such as theme music for a news broadcast, parts of radio and TV commercials when signature theme music isn't playing, moody background music in TV programs, and industrial videos. Buyers are not the general public but businesses looking for short pieces of music as foreground or background in audiovisual works. Content is often delivered online from authorized websites, streamlining the customer's search for just the right cut.

Before 1980, the AFM and AFTRA (American Federation of Television and Radio Artists) required that musicians who recorded production music be paid each time the music was used, so recordings were done mostly in Great Britain, Germany, and France, where such reuse payments were not required. In recent decades, AFTRA and AFM have been unable to control work in this aspect of the music industry, and recordings made in North America are often nonunion.

As the library business increased, the quality of their original music improved to such a point that production music is even sprinkled in big-budget theatrical films and pricey TV commercials. Production music is also used extensively in theatrical film trailers, because original music from the film is usually not yet finished when the marketing starts. Also, hit music in films requires an additional rights payment if used in the trailer for the same film, so producers often turn to production music to hold down trailer costs.

Typically, executives for library companies are also accomplished musicians, composers, and producers, and these skills enable the executive to create content with collaborators and also commission works by third parties that fill gaps in the production music library's offering. Many production companies, which are mainly located in Los Angeles, Nashville, and New York, are members of the Production Music Association, a trade group established in 1997 that has hundreds of member companies.

Killer Tracks, a production music library that opened its doors in 1989, serves as a good example of a modern music production company. Its catalog, available in the form of 2,500 digital albums, has been a source for music licensed in feature films, commercials, corporate productions, TV shows, networks, cable TV outlets, DVDs, and online content such as YouTube videos. Killer Tracks is owned by music giant Universal Music Group.

Material is licensed in perpetuity for a fee based on the type and scope of the clearance required for a specific project. Each use of music, referred to as a **needle drop** or cue, requires licensing. For instance, if a music user licensed a piece of music for a 30-second use as background music in a newscast, a separate license would be required if the licensee wanted to use that same music in a 30-second ad spot for television. The exception to the rule would be the **production blanket,** which allows an unlimited use of music in one production for a capped or flat fee. This fee is based on the length of the total production and the clearance category required.

Production music companies offer libraries of albums in diverse categories and musical styles. Some albums feature compositions in 30- and 60-second lengths. Others contain full-length **cuts,** in addition to 30-, 60-, and a variety of 10- and 15-second lengths. Each cut may feature a variety of mixes, such as "full," "underscore," and "alternate." The underscore version deletes the lead or melody instrument so as not to compete with a narrator's voice. The alternate version may offer additional instrumentation, a "lite" rhythm mix, or something unexpected. Also, many compositions feature live vocal effects. Software is available that allows the user to retrieve, sort, cross-reference, and log use of the music that has been chosen. Digitally recorded libraries of thousands of sound effects are also available. Production music libraries offer employment for veteran musicians as well as newer composers, who can use this experience as a springboard for work in films and television.

Royalty-free music libraries, which also offer hundreds or even thousands of hours of original music and audio, are another source of off-the-shelf music. Such music is promoted as "free" to producers of movies (typically those skipping theatrical release), TV shows, commercials, Internet content, and corporate videos. Among the players in this space is the YouTube Audio Library, which made its debut in 2013. Its tunes are provided to users posting original video content who want to avoid label take-down notices, which happens when amateur video makers misappropriate copyrighted music.

For the royalty-free category, users don't have to pay royalties to publishers, composers, and for reuse of music, hence the word *free* that is emphasized in promotion. But most charge a nominal upfront payment—$30 to $100 is common—for access online or for CD/DVDs with shipping. So the original business model for royalty-free music libraries was unlimited use of music by the original acquirer after payment of a one-time fee. Now, some libraries push low-priced monthly or annual subscriptions with promises of new audio content constantly being added to the available pool.

While the word *free* is employed because users don't pay publishing royalties and reuse fees, these libraries make money in other ways. They aim to collect **performance royalties** from third parties when content runs in media such as TV and radio and **mechanical licenses** if the content is mass duplicated as physical media for sale to consumers. Producers are asked to supply libraries with cue sheets—so libraries know exactly where their music is used—and report when and where content runs in media so performance royalty income can be claimed. Royalty-free libraries are something of a backwater because their minimal economics rely primarily on performance royalties, while production music libraries generate meaningful upfront revenue from deals with producers, which funds creating higher quality content.

Chapter Takeaways

- Business music helps businesses improve the productivity of workers and relax customers, and it is selected by institutions to positively influence the attitudes of their patrons.

- Production music libraries offer musical snippets and full-length songs that business users can put to use for specific production purposes, such as a station identification jingle for a radio station, TV commercials, corporate videos, and even parts of theatrical movies.

- Royalty-free music libraries provide prerecorded music and sounds to producers at a nominal one-time upfront fee. The libraries make most of their money by claiming performance royalties when the content runs on TV and other media or mechanical royalties if content is mass duplicated.

- Production music libraries and royalty-free music libraries buy from musicians of all skill levels and thus are prospects for employment by those seeking their first professional work.

Key Terms

- background music   (p. 416)
- business music   (p. 416)
- foreground music   (p. 415)

- needle drop   (p. 418)
- production blanket   (p. 418)

- production music libraries (p. 417)
- royalty-free music libraries (p. 418)

Discussion Questions

1. Is it healthy for the industry overall to encourage a greater use of production libraries? Why or why not?

2. How do royalty-free music libraries make money, and are they really "free"?

3. What do you think characterizes quality foreground music for a coffee shop? For an outdoor mall?

4. What would be important to consider in choosing or creating background music for a medical waiting room area?

The Entrepreneurial Musician

CHAPTER 26

The DIY Toolkit

The Economics of Indie

As we've discussed, the revenue equations of the legacy music industry were once fairly straight-forward: composer-performers signed to labels could expect to receive mechanical royalties, publishing royalties, and other payments such as synchronization fees. Today, the new music business landscape has far more configurations and opportunities, but it has become so diffuse that it presents almost too many possibilities to the do-it-yourself (**DIY**) artist. As our inside front cover shows, lobbying organization The Future of Music Coalition surveyed working musicians about their actual income and came up with a list of 45 revenue categories! They included publishing and record label advances, mechanical and airplay royalties, **sheet music** sales, ringtone revenues, live and recording session work, litigation settlements with labels and publishers, merchandise sales, speaking fees, fan funding, interactive service payments, ad sales revenue sharing from outlets such as YouTube, teaching, endorsements, acting, corporate sponsorship, and funding from government grants. Perhaps no one musician taps into all 45 sources, and many sources on the list offer little in the way of predictable recurring revenue. But taken together, they form the new music industry's economic mosaic.

> "It just seems like musicians want to sell a few records and put out a perfume line, and I think it's so sad that there are so many musicians who don't want to change the world. . . . Music has been so much more."
>
> —Moby

Left: Moby in his home studio.

Photo © Redferns.

The Direct-to-Fan Era

Twenty-five years ago, recording artists might have incurred a debt to their record label of $1 million or more for a first album, video, and related costs like **tour support** before the first record could be sold. To show for it, they would have had the record and the video, but the copyrights to both would be retained by the label.

Years later, that same artist or band might invest a fraction of that amount in recording equipment and have not only the same creative output but also the means of production for the next album and video—and the next and the next. Instead of paying over $100,000 of fully recoupable dollars for 2 months in a traditional recording studio, they can pay less than $20,000 for a comprehensive computer-based recording system. Instead of over $250,000 for a music video, they can purchase affordable video editing software and a high-definition video camera for well under $2,000. Instead of the high-overhead workings of major corporation publicity and marketing materials for the record release, they can use powerful graphics/word processing/website creation software suites costing only several hundred dollars. They can choose from any number of Internet-based services that provide promotional services for independent artists and record labels. At the end of the day, the independent artists not only own the equipment but can also retain the rights to their recordings and are thus able to repurpose and remonetize them for years to come.

Just as independent labels saw their market share rise somewhat versus the majors as physical formats receded, so too have DIY artists gained momentum as the old production and business models loosened their grip. With little or no fan base initially, independent artists can introduce new music through streaming and online services to showcase their talents, build a following, and create a promotional and monetization opportunity. Tim Westergreen, founder of Pandora, told the *New York*

The ability to purchase software and equipment to produce high-quality video and audio recordings has opened the door to many DIY musicians.
Photo © Ihsan Eroglu/Thinkstock.

Post, "There are artists who were invisible in the music business who now get exposed to an audience that is big enough to support them. There's an opportunity for a really well-run band to take control of their careers."

Doing the Math

The lower capital costs of this new economic order enable artists to sell their music for less, yet retain a higher percentage of the revenues. For instance, an artist signed to a major label might, with its more sophisticated promotion and distribution capability, sell 200,000 units of an album at a wholesale price of $12 each for gross sales to the label of $2,400,000. Under a typical split with a major label, the artist's share of that might be 15%, or $360,000 (some or all of which would be applied to any advance the artist had already received). An independent artist could approximate that same level of income with sales of only a quarter of that at an even lower unit cost—50,000 units at $10 per album. If 60% of the sales were through iTunes (grossing $300,000), the indie artist would net the 70% iTunes usually pays to the label, a net of $210,000; assuming the remaining 20,000 units were sold direct-to-fan (D2F) via gigs or through the artist's own website, the artist could expect another $200,000 in gross revenue.

This is a highly simplified example and doesn't reflect the percentage of sales the artist would have to pay to management and attorneys or the **points** due a record producer. Nor is it meant to suggest that independent music artists routinely achieve those kinds of numbers—the vast majority will not. But it does graphically illustrate how the economics of independent recorded music can, under the right circumstances, achieve respectable numbers. This, combined with revenue from live performances, from which an increasing number of artists derive the majority of their income, indicates that even in today's challenging music business landscape, making a decent living is possible when artists can effectively leverage the recording, promotional, and distribution tools to which they now have access.

Making Money With "Free"

There are numerous revenue model permutations in the music business today. One of the more radical models is called "freemium," where artists literally give away recorded music or allow consumers to decide how much they are willing to pay for it. This model was applied most famously by Radiohead in 2008, when the band, which had ended its deal with EMI Records, offered its new LP, *In Rainbows,* via the band's website. According to ComScore data at the time, approximately 60% of downloaders paid nothing while the average price among those who did pay was about $6 per unit. However, when all other sources of sales were combined, including CDs, vinyl, boxed sets, and digital downloads through paid portals such as iTunes and Amazon, the band's publisher and administrator, Warner Chappell Music, reported that *In Rainbows* had sold over 3 million units.

The freemium experiment, while not inherently profitable, had created significant consumer awareness that helped promote the record for sales through other venues and, in the process, validated the idea that music pricing could be dynamic. The approach has been widely applied and adapted since then, even with video games and other content. One of the most highly cited examples was the 2011 release of comedian Louis CK's television special as a download from his website. This program

Radiohead live in Berkeley, California.
Photo © Matthew Hickey.

generated $1 million in sales at an asking price of just $5 each, against reported production costs of $250,000. The Louis CK example suggests that consumers are willing to pay for recorded content rather than try to get it for free as long as they perceive they are receiving good value for their money.

The testing of new business models illustrates how far the industry has come in a very short time. Not that many years ago, the question about touring was how much a label would spend to subsidize money-losing live concerts in order to create buzz that might get fans into a record store. Today, it might be the recorded music that's the means to an end, not the other way around. Free sites and streaming services like Apple Music, YouTube, Spotify, and Pandora make digital music available to millions of listeners. For the artist, recorded music can be an effective marketing tool, driving sales of merchandise and concert tickets, providing a means to access a broader following, and converting some to paying fans.

Success, of course, is far from assured. A big source of tension in the business today is that the freemium offerings of some services aren't translating into a living for seemingly "popular" artists, measured by how much they are "heard" in the ecosystem. The reality is that in instances where discovery models only lead to awareness, and the artist can't sufficiently monetize the benefits of the buzz, then the new paradigm fails to lead to a sustainable income.

Tools of the Trade

Music artists can be forgiven if they pine for the business models of the legacy record industry. For all of its excesses and financial tenuousness, it at least seemed comprehensible: Success usually required money and an array of industry specialists, hence the vital role of big labels that had both capital and a multifaceted workforce. Labels still scramble for market share, of course, but the intriguing story in the new century is DIY. Compared to the good ol' days, today there are fewer consumer dollars to fight over, more releases vying for prominence, and a kaleidoscope of technologies and services offering to assist those trying to promote or merchandise music.

Independent artists are confronted by a plethora of companies offering them various combinations of assistance with names seemingly drawn from a Dr. Seuss book—Bandzoogle, Mobile Roadie, Snapchat, Tunecore, Reverb Nation, Topspin, Sonicbids, D2Mondo, and scores more. Some of these tools could be used by labels as well, but they're generally of more value to DIY musicians who use them as a substitute for resources that a larger label should already have in place. (Elsewhere in the book, we outline how the industry traditionally addresses some of the needs these tools are designed to meet.)

The DIY services of today can be interfaced with and support the growing array of social media outlets that increasingly ally themselves with commercial music companies, such as Facebook's alliance with streaming music giant Spotify. Increasingly, musicians can also turn to Internet-based companies to help them coordinate and promote their live performances, which in recent years have become the main source of revenue for independent artists. Finally, the proliferation of media content channels on television and online has created a growing demand for more music. Songs from independent artists now often constitute the entire soundtrack for motion pictures, television programs, and broadcast commercials.

Web-based tools for independent music artists can be broken down into four broad clusters: sales/promotion, financing, live touring, and licensing. What follows is a brief discussion of each category.

Sales/Promotion

Sales and promotion tools help artists decide how to connect online with fans and potential fans, as well as provide various types of distribution formats, including file downloads, streaming, and physical media. This is the most populous category of Web-based tools. Some examples include the following:

- Topspin (established 2007) offers tools to help artists create online sales and distribution strategies, gather **analytics** on their sales, and leverage those to boost sales. Like many such services, Topsin charges a modest monthly fee that provides a hosted website and online sales portal with social media integration widgets and targeted emails to up to 2,000 fans. Topspin also offers a premium membership, which adds subscription membership sales, preorders, third-party fulfillment partners, and targeted emails to up to 20,000 recipients. The Topspin Enterprise version offers sales reporting to data tracking company SoundScan, as well as other specialized features such as extensive email marketing capabilities.

- Bandcamp (2007) is another sales and promotion portal based on the direct-to-fan (D2F) concept. Bandcamp does not charge a monthly or annual fee but instead takes a 15% cut of sales up to $5,000 and 10% for sales above that. That's not a bad deal for artists compared to regular-label royalty rates, except of course for the big difference: Under this model, it's incumbent on artists to finance, produce, and market their own work; all of these types of online toolsets add leverage to the artists' own sweat-equity investments in themselves.

- CD Baby (1998) might be considered the grandfather of all online toolsets for music artists and it's one that, via its relationship with parent company Discmakers, offers CD replication (mass production generally requiring minimum runs of 500 or more units) and duplication (per-piece manufac-turing of CD-R discs with virtually no unit-run minimums) integrated into online sales portals/website and promotional tools. Its rights management service, CD Baby Pro, allows independent artists to tap into mechanical royal-ties from streaming services both in and outside of the United States.

Other companies offering services along these lines include Tunecore (2005), RecordUnion (2008), and ReverbNation (2008).

Financing

The traditional way of financing a music career via investment by a record label is no longer the only way, and given the 12% to 15% minority stake artists often receive in label contracts, this is not necessarily the best deal for the artist. Self-financing alter-natives, also known as "crowdfunding," allow artists to develop funding sources for music from the public at large by offering a premium, such as copies of a finished prod-uct financed by small donations or buy-ins.[1] The drastically reduced cost of recording technology and diversity of affordable distribution and promotion methods make this approach a viable option for some. Companies in this category include the following:

- Kickstarter (2008), a Brooklyn company that serves as a conduit for artists, musicians, industrial designers, and others to solicit donations to capitalize artistic projects. (While Kickstarter is used by a wide range of people seeking to fund a wide range of artistic and other types of projects, music projects were the largest category of all project types. In 2014 the service dispensed far more in arts funding than the government-backed National Endowment for the Arts.) Those seeking funding pitch their project via a post or video on the Kickstarter website and ask for a specific amount of money over a certain number of days. Once the pledge deadline has been reached, the artists collect the funds via Amazon payments, the project moves forward, and contribu-tors are rewarded with promised results; usually in the case of music projects, donors receive a CD or a file download of the project, but contributions can be tiered. For instance, small contributors might receive a CD; donors who gave slightly larger amounts will get an autographed CD; larger amounts still can result in anything from a prominent thank-you credit on the record to a private performance at the contributor's home. Kickstarter takes 5% of the amount raised for the project as its fee plus 3% to 5% of money raised through Amazon Payments. Musician Amanda Palmer famously raised $1.2 million on Kickstarter in 2012 for an album, book, and tour.

Other companies offering similar crowd-sourced financing services include Patreon (2013), RocketHub (2010), ArtistShare (2003), and PledgeMusic (2009). It's worth noting that both ArtistShare and PledgeMusic are among the crowdfunding portals that focus almost exclusively on music.

Touring

Over the years as revenue from physical formats continued to shrink, live concert performances have emerged as the single largest source of revenue for the vast major-ity of music artists. Many of the sales/promotion websites also have some tools to help artists promote their live appearances, both as ways to increase revenue through ticket sales and as a venue for additional record and merchandise sales. However, as live music takes on even more importance in the revenue mix for music, more companies are offering dedicated toolsets for this aspect of the music industry.

- Indie on the Move (2008) allows users to announce and promote their live shows via press, radio, and Internet, look for and apply for club and other **venue** bookings, and share reviews of not only their shows but also their experiences with various clubs and promoters.
- SonicBids (2000) connects touring musicians with venues and bookers as well as fans. Like many Internet-based service companies, it has tiered membership with monthly fees varying depending on the level of services required.

Other companies that emphasize live performances include BandsInTown (2007), which relies heavily on social media to connect artists with fans for their live shows. Gigwell (2013) enables talent buyers to book gigs and pay fees negotiated by agents. Eventful (2004) connects live performers, including touring music artists, with consumers. Ourstage (2007) helps artist members advance their careers by allowing consumers to rank Ourstage-client songs appearing on the platform.

Licensing

The "synch" fee has become a significant source of revenue for a growing number of independent music artists. As we explain elsewhere, the term is short for "synchronization," which refers to the pairing of music and picture, mainly in the form of film and television, but which increasingly encompasses multimedia.

However, while more artists than ever have received exposure through synch deals, a high level of financial success has become increasingly rare. The five- and even six-figure licensing deals of the 20th century have given way to synch fees as low as a few thousand dollars. Fees may be lower, but the exposure can be valuable enough to justify granting the license. Not surprisingly, these kinds of placements have attracted a huge assortment of brokers, including conventional music industry professionals such as A&R staffers, publishers, and record producers. There is also an array of online companies that specialize in making the connection between music and picture. They include Audiosocket (2008), Jingle Punks (2008), Pump Audio (2001), Rumblefish (1996), and Broadjam (1999). For a discussion of the role of music supervisors in facilitating these placements, see Chapter 21.

Many consider synchronized music placement to be the new radio for independent artists who are all but shut out of terrestrial hit radio rotation. It has definitely added one more dimension to the toolkit.

• • • Music in Social Networking

Social networking is perhaps the most significant digital phenomenon of recent years. Websites like Facebook, Instagram, Snapchat, Tumblr, Foursquare, Rockbot, and Twitter create a pervasive connection between millions of users every day. Music is an integral part of this social interaction. At the very least, a Facebook page is considered critical to marketing music by new and established artists alike, as well as record labels, music venues, and other business entities. In only a few years, an entirely new universe of online tools has emerged to help music artists cut through the "noise"

(Continued)

(Continued)

of so much music on the market. These include FanRX, Beetailer, ReverbNation, Pagemodo, and many others, all of which have dedicated Facebook interfaces. Others, like Tweepi and Tweetdeck, are designed around the Twitter platform. Mobile app introductions from Twitter's Periscope (2015) and Meerkat (2015) assist fans eager to share live streaming videos to their social network. Snapchat (2011) gained attention as a social platform for independent artists to promote themselves and engage with fans through photos, short videos, stories, contests, and exclusives.

Shares and likes.
Photo © twinsterphoto/iStock.

Filtering the Noise

Many tools now exist to do battle against obscurity. Websites like Taxi.com, which seeks to connect its membership with an array of placement possibilities for their music, and AirPlay Direct, which offers online promotional materials, purport to help music artists differentiate themselves in an increasingly crowded market.

Listeners, too, can be overwhelmed, and they turn to a slew of music blogs, review websites, and taste-making enterprises, such as Pitchfork.com, that apply collaborative filtering techniques to steer consumers toward more music they might enjoy based on what they already know they like. For instance, at Pandora.com, music is deconstructed, song by song, bit by bit, reduced to elements that can be matched by Pandora's algorithms to similar elements in other songs that the service then recommends to users. Major digital distributors, such as Amazon.com, have integrated collaborative filtering into their customer interfaces. Apple's iTunes includes a feature that suggests new songs from the iTunes online store that complement what the user is playing from a personal song library, with the added benefit of not recommending any song the user already owns.

Through social media, fans expect more from their artists than ever. They want to interact with artists as individuals. Simply consuming the music is not enough.

Communities for Musicians

Musicians themselves have their own specialized networked communities that have become so plentiful and diverse that they can be categorized by location (www.bandmix.com), belief (www.christianmusicnetwork.com/), gender (www.femmuse.com), genre (www.folkjam.org), and ethnicity, as the Vietnamese Musicians Network (www.vmnusa.blogspot.com) illustrates. Musicians made seemingly redundant by developments such as sequencing, sampling synthesizers, and drum machines might find some comfort in www.musicianscollaboration.com, which allows musicians to exchange multitrack music files, then add overdubs or mix them. Novice songwriters looking for mentors, online forums, and local member communities may find connections through www.justplainfolks.org.

Online social networking has taken the last of the levers from the hands of the traditional music business by eliminating the engineered smoke and mirrors of conventional music marketing. It's connected artists to their fans in an immersive manner and allowed fans to determine their own level of engagement. If social networking is the manner in which people connect, what music has done with digital technology has provided the soundtrack for those lives.

■ Online Platforms: Now You See It, Now You Don't

Like the music itself, these tools for independent musicians can be ephemeral. One of the most notable examples of how online tools can become quickly popular and ubiquitous and just as rapidly fall out of favor is Myspace. Founded in 2003 as a social networking site with an emphasis on music as a shared experience, by 2008 it was considered the leading social media website, drawing more unique visitors at the time than Facebook, and along the way eliciting a $580 million purchase by global media giant News Corp. However, by 2011, Myspace had been overtaken by Facebook's growing number of more specific tools that more precisely targeted musicians' and recording artists' needs. Underscoring this loss of popularity, News Corp. sold Myspace in 2011 for $35 million, an embarrassing collapse in value. The next year, Facebook's market capitalization hit $104 billion the moment its shares were offered to the public.

The surviving incarnation of Myspace fell far short of its early successes, but the need that it tried to address remained very real. Within a year of the sale of Myspace, television music channel MTV launched Artists.MTV, an online hub for known and unknown music artists, which industry observers viewed as an updated version of Myspace's original aspirations. If the motto of the digital age is "Everything changes," the digital music industry's version of that is "Everything changes very quickly."

■ Conclusion

The DIY model for music remains a work in progress. New tools appear constantly that purport to help independent music artists further their careers, and revenue can come from an ever-greater number of sources. But the individual revenue sources themselves can be minimal. Several surveys in recent years reveal embarrassingly meager financial returns to artists—even those regarded as otherwise successful—from services such as Spotify, Rhapsody, and Pandora. Independent musicians can make their careers economically viable, but only if they continuously cultivate multiple sources of revenue. And of course, the other ingredients for success haven't disappeared in this brave new world—things like talent, hard work, and luck.

■ Note

1. The crowdfunding concept has gone well beyond individual artists seeking capital. In 2012, the Jump-start Our Business Start-ups (JOBS) Act created a new category of "emerging growth" companies that can raise up to $1 million in public funds through stock offerings while remaining exempt from most financial disclosure and Securities & Exchange Commission requirements for up to 5 years.

Chapter Takeaways

- Low operating expenses mean DIY artists can sell their music for less, yet retain a higher percentage of the revenue than is possible through a traditional label deal.

- Many companies out there offer DIY artists various combinations of assistance with sales/promotion, financing, live touring, and alternative revenue sources.

- DIY artists must continuously cultivate multiple sources of income in order to be successful.

Key Terms

- crowdfunding   (p. 428)
- D2F   (p. 425)
- DIY   (p. 423)
- freemium   (p. 425)
- social networking (p. 429)

Discussion Questions

1. Which one of the four Web-based tool categories—sales/promotion, financing, live touring, and licensing—is most crucial for an independent musician to focus on?

2. What are the pros and cons of using the freemium pricing model? Do you think offering free music reduces music piracy?

3. Based on your own experience as a user, discuss which factors you think influence the success or failure of competing online services.

4. Let's say you're an artist who has a record deal coming to an end that never yielded more than 200,000 album sales per release. Should your goal be to sign another label deal or become strictly a DIY entrepreneur? Defend your reasoning.

Starting Your Own Business

"Hell is full of musical amateurs."

—George Bernard Shaw

In the United States, more than 20 million people are in business for themselves, and many more operate as small partnerships or corporations. Examples in music are everywhere: Classical musicians are redefining performance careers by working as **independent contractors** for a variety of small orchestras or starting their own ensembles, playing the music they want to play with the musicians they want to work with. Composers are contracting to create and perform complex **underscores**—the kind of work that in another era was performed by union workers employed by studios or networks. And inventors of innovative musical products and services aren't waiting for a large company to employ them or license their creations. All across the music industry, people have broken away from the traditional mold, running businesses the way they want.

Technology has had a huge influence. Because of the availability of high-capacity digital technology, unprecedented opportunities have opened up for small businesses. Artists can now record and promote their own work using ever-cheaper recording equipment and the far reach of the Internet. Some may choose to stay independent throughout their careers; others will leverage their successes from self-promotion into signing that first major record deal.

Self-employment requires energy, enthusiasm, motivation, and an approach beyond the average 40-hour week. On top of this, no matter how great an idea is, if it is not accompanied by skills in diverse disciplines such as accounting, marketing, operations, and salesmanship, the enterprise quite possibly won't survive. Still, the means are available to help entrepreneurs succeed.

Left: Weeks Technology Center, Frost School of Music, University of Miami.

Photo by Elaine Maltezos, used by permission. Photo courtesy University of Miami.

Getting the Process Started ▰▰▰▰▰▰▰

Getting a business started is often the hardest part for many would-be entrepreneurs. Fortunately, there are some good resources available, including the Small Business Administration (SBA) government program, as well as a significant number of Internet resources full of practical information. (Table 27.1 outlines a step-by-step approach for starting a music publishing business.)

The first thing any aspiring entrepreneur needs is a business plan. This plan can be a few pages long or a lengthy document, depending on the scope and scale of the ambition. Whatever the format used, the business plan should answer the following questions:

What is the planned product or service?

Who will own/run the company?

What resources will be needed?

Who are the customers and how will they be reached?

What is the size of the target market and how fast is it growing?

How will the product or service be distributed?

What is the competitive and regulatory landscape?

When will the company be cash positive? Produce returns for investors?

If the company raises more capital, how will existing investors be affected?

What might go wrong, and what is the contingency plan if it does?

Table 27.1   **Starting a Music Publishing Company**

Publishing is one of the easiest music businesses to get started and can be the least expensive to finance. Hundreds of new publishing firms are started every year, usually by frustrated songwriters.
Here is a step-by-step approach to setting up a publishing company in the popular music field.
1. **Research.** Study this book and publications concerning business management found in most libraries.
2. **Acquisitions.** You have to acquire copyrights (property interests in musical compositions) before you can start publishing. The easiest way to acquire copyrights is to write your own original music. In addition to your own copyrights, search out other qualified writers to gain their confidence and assistance in your publishing plans. Retain a lawyer to assist in drawing up contracts. Use the guidelines listed in Chapter 6.
3. **Structure your financing and business entity.** Once you have a business plan and decided whether the enterprise will be organized as a sole proprietorship, partnership, or corporation, you can estimate and solicit the working capital you will need.
4. **Search ASCAP, BMI, and SESAC.** Tentatively choose a company name and ascertain if it is (or isn't!) already registered at any of these three **performance rights organizations** (PROs). It's wise to have ready backup choices for your firm name. An optional additional step would be conducting a trademark search to see whether your prospective name is used anywhere else in the United States. If any similar names are already in the music business, pick another designation to avoid confusion because the first in has the legal high ground. Affiliate with one of these PRO organizations after deciding on a name that is not in use by another company (see Chapter 7).

5. **Register your firm name.** If your company is a sole proprietorship or partnership, check with your county clerk and recorder's office and search the records to learn if your choice of firm name has been previously registered in the county. Duplications will not be accepted. Unless you identify the company with your own full, legal name, you will be required to register a fictitious firm name (some counties use the term *trade name*). For example, if your name is John Doe, the county will record your firm as "John Doe dba Hit Publishing Company" ("dba" is the abbreviation for "doing business as"). Procedures and applicable fees vary from county to county.

6. **Establish your company bank account.** It's wise to establish a bank account to segregate company funds and avoid comingling with personal funds, especially if there are multiple company owners. Banks typically won't open a business account until the name has been cleared, as stated above.

7. **Business license.** If you limit your firm's activities just to publishing, you may not need a business license. But if your company should branch out into artists' agency work, most states would consider that as a kind of employment agency, and nearly all states license and regulate employment agencies.

8. **Arrange outside services.** Because most new publishing companies start very small, proprietors generally do not attempt, at the outset, to directly administer everything themselves. Vendors are available to handle just about any service a business needs—information technology, visual design, administration, bookkeeping, accounting, and more.

9. **Prepare your materials.** A songwriter sometimes manages with leadsheets and demos prepared by amateurs. But now that you are a publisher trying to exploit your properties, prepare everything professionally that you present to impress producers and artists considering business ties.

10. **Your first success.** The essence of the publishing business in the pop field is getting material recorded and released. The first release of any recording requires the manufacturer to receive a mechanical license from the publisher. Many publishers use their own mechanical license forms and negotiate directly with the recording companies, settling on mutually agreeable terms. When a recorded song hits, you may want to publish it in printed form. You will probably license a music print company to handle this for you (see Chapter 6). Also, reread in Chapter 6 how to set up subpublishing deals abroad through licensing agreements with firms active internationally.

11. **Forms, contracts.** Copyright forms are readily available, without cost, from the U.S. Copyright Office (www.copyright.gov). When you negotiate writers' publishing contracts, retain a qualified music business attorney—or use the draft contract discussed in Chapter 6 as a basis for your discussions with an attorney less experienced in the music field.

12. **Your second company.** PROs won't accept a publisher imprint already affiliated with their competitor. Just as soon as your first company gets under way, establish a second one at another PRO so that you can accommodate properties from writers affiliated with ASCAP, BMI, or SESAC. Except for the preliminaries outlined here, the procedures for setting up a second firm are the same as for your first venture.

13. **Persistence and continued success.** Once your new firm starts to get its copyrights licensed, don't sit waiting for royalty checks. Real profitability comes along when a firm can achieve continuity year to year, building catalogs of hundreds, eventually thousands, of songs and exploiting those copyrights. So the search for new writers and new properties goes on and on. That is the publishing business.

Choosing a Name

When choosing a name for a new company, both aesthetic and practical considerations are important. First, the name should fit with the company's offerings, as well as the image the company wants to put forward and what the company may grow into. Second, the name should appeal to the target customer. A memorable name is necessary to stand out in the cluttered marketplace. Once an investment has been made to market the name—building brand recognition and loyalty—it will be hard to change. It also might be a good idea to trademark the name of the company and its unique products. The application can be found at the U.S. Patent and Trademark Office website (see Appendix A). Hiring an attorney specializing in **intellectual property**, although expensive, is a good insurance policy to fend off or lessen future problems.

Forms of Ownership

In the United States, a business enterprise is generally organized in one of three basic ways: sole proprietorship, partnership, or corporation. Each form of ownership has certain advantages and disadvantages.

Sole Proprietorship

The principal advantage of a sole proprietorship is that it is easy to set up and get under way. All the entrepreneur needs is some money (personal or borrowed funds), a great amount of energy—and a lot of nerve. The sole proprietor who wants to fold the venture can do that, too; there is no need to call a meeting of the board to make decisions.

That's the good news. The bad news is that the sole proprietor is personally responsible for all financial losses the business may experience. If the company cannot pay the bills, the creditors can press to take possession of personal property, including musical instruments, office equipment, pet parakeet—whatever is of value. The sole proprietorship has the challenge of limited capital. Even if the business is going well, the single operator may find it difficult to raise enough money to move the business forward. A proprietor may employ many others, although typically, the team is small.

Partnership

The Uniform Partnership Act defines partnerships as "associations of two or more persons who operate a business as co-owners by voluntary legal agreement." General partnerships are established when all partners involved carry on the business as co-owners. Limited partnerships (although restricted in some states) are composed of one or more general partners and one or more limited partners. A limited partner is one whose liability to the company is restricted to the amount that person has invested in it. **Joint ventures** are a third type of partnership and are popular with investors who come together temporarily to undertake a business enterprise with a specific focus, such as producing a show.

Partnerships offer certain advantages of ownership. First, they are easy to form. All that is required is a written agreement that defines shares of ownership and spells out each partner's responsibilities. Second, partnerships can tap more pockets for **working capital** than sole proprietorships. Third, a firm where two or more individuals are active in management will probably have people with complementary skills (for example, one partner may be tops in sales and another may be adept at accounting).

The principal disadvantage of this form of organization is that the partners may disagree on how to run the business, how outstanding debts will be paid, and selection of products offered. There is also the possibility that the partners may develop personality conflicts. And if an impasse is reached, it may be difficult for the company to be dissolved.

Corporation

To investors, the most obvious advantage of a corporation is that their liability is usually limited to the value they contribute, even if the losses of the company exceed that capital. If the corporation eventually goes public, meaning its ownership shares are sold through a wide offering via the stock market, corporate management will be able to raise even more capital. On the downside, the corporate structure is the most difficult to set up and the slowest and most expensive to get into operation. Each state charters corporations according to its own laws, and state and federal regulatory agencies can burden management with costly paperwork and legal fees.

Another disadvantage for investors in corporations is that some forms of corporations experience double taxation: Not only does the enterprise pay corporate taxes, but the investors also pay personal income taxes on dividends received from the corporation.

A comparison of advantages and disadvantages of the different forms of ownership is shown in Table 27.2.

Permits and Legal Issues

The legal preparation required to start a business varies widely from state to state and town to town and depends on the type of service offered. Once the enterprise exists as a legal entity, the next usual step is to obtain a business license from the city or county.

A number of other permits may also be required, such as health department permits, professional licenses, and so on. The best place to get advice on what exactly is needed is the local Small Business Development Center. Appointments with counselors there are usually free of charge, and they offer invaluable assistance.

Even a small, part-time operation must charge (and remit) sales tax for taxable products or services. To do this, a business tax identification number must be obtained, and filing must be done on a periodic basis, usually quarterly. Historically, products sold over the Internet out of state have not been taxable, but tax laws and rules constantly shift. Failure to collect, file, and pay quarterly tax returns could result in significant fines and penalties.

Some people are tempted to think this paperwork step is too complicated and expensive and that they can bypass it and stay under the radar. Don't do it. The music industry is particularly fussy about copyright issues, and working through all the legalities of using prerecorded music is not for the faint of heart. The Internet is particularly visible—open to any browsing eyes—so extra care must be taken to avoid

Table 27.2 Types of Business Ownership

Sole Proprietorship	Partnership	Corporation
Typical Advantages		
1. You are the boss 2. Easy to form, easy to dissolve 3. You retain all profits	1. Simple to organize 2. Complementary management skills	1. Limited personal liability 2. Perhaps more capital
Typical Disadvantages		
1. Unlimited financial liability 2. Management deficiencies 3. Limited working capital 4. Potential lack of continuity of operation	1. Unlimited financial responsibility 2. Strategy conflicts 3. Personality conflicts	1. Expensive, complicated 2. Legal restrictions 3. Double taxation

any improper use of copyrighted material—visual or aural—in website promotions. Keep in mind that many people have had great ideas and put a good deal of effort into starting something, only to be shut down—sometimes permanently—because they failed to obtain the right permits and permissions.

Raising Funds

Some small businesses do not require much start-up capital. Many *service* offerings—where the customer is paying primarily for human labor as opposed to a tangible product—fall into this category. However, the majority of companies will need some working capital, often more than the owners themselves can provide.

There is a lot of hype on the Internet about free money and grants to start small businesses. For very speculative businesses, there is *venture capital,* which may inject seed money in startup companies or growth capital in larger startups. Venture capitalists are pure financial entities that may focus on specific business sectors to exploit the investors' particular expertise. Most of the recipient businesses fizzle, and venture capitalists expect this. So they choose investments based on very high growth or profit potential, figuring the few investments that succeed will be financial gushers covering the losers.

Another type of funding comes from *strategic investors,* which are entities already embedded in an industry. For example, the big musical instrument companies will consider strategic investment in smaller enterprises developing promising new instrument products. Radio companies or record labels might invest in online music streaming businesses to extend their reach to emerging digital media. In those examples, music-related companies are strategic investors that either consolidate strength in their core music business or expand into an adjacent field that is a goal of their corporate strategy. The strategic investor may condition the investment on being the first in line to buy out the recipient if the startup company is sold down the road.

Strategic investments can be big or small. Strategic investors tend to look for less speculative opportunities than homerun-seeking venture capitalists and, because of their allegiance to their industry, strategic investors are willing to stick with investments longer.

Unfortunately, the money doesn't always materialize from these sources. This leaves the time-honored tradition of going to the bank to seek a loan. Banks are difficult to tap because they likely will insist on a history of profitability or collateral—assets pledged to cover any shortfall in repayment—to secure the loan. Although not commonplace, an SBA loan guarantee may be available for some music-related businesses. For some ventures, crowdfunding (discussed in Chapter 26) can be an effective way to raise money from fans and other nonprofessional investors. The stark reality is that the most common sources of funding for a small business are the pockets of the entrepreneur, or perhaps the contribution of friends and family.

Marketing

Contrary to popular belief, marketing and advertising are two very different things. Advertising is just paid media exposure. Marketing is broader, covering every aspect of getting people interested in a business and its services. One of the simplest ways to get an overview of this concept is through the four Ps of marketing model developed by William D. Perreault Jr. and E. Jerome McCarthy[1]: *product, price, place,* and *promotion.*

Product

The first step in the marketing process is to examine the products or services being offered. Will the offering satisfy an important need or desire? Why will customers part with their hard-earned cash? By answering these questions, an offering can be designed that customers are looking for—not one that will need to be pushed on them.

Price

What is the service worth? Many entrepreneurs initially think of a markup strategy that simply tacks a percentage on over the cost of production. However, this is rarely the best strategy, because there are too many other factors to consider when setting a price. Although many theoretical models are involved in price setting, one of the most practical is to decide what the customer is willing to pay. Then, working backward, consider the cost of production. Can a sufficient profit be made at that price? If not, both service and business goals should be reconsidered.

Place

This is also known as distribution and is a tricky part of the marketing plan. The Internet has rewritten most of the traditional rules about distribution, and one company, eBay, has made it possible for almost anyone to sell almost anything for a very small charge. Although large companies take advantage of the Web to varying degrees, the real benefit has been to the small entrepreneur. With the click of a mouse, customers from thousands of miles away can reach a virtual storefront more easily than they could drive downtown. This is particularly helpful for entrepreneurs who have chosen a specialty niche. The important thing is to match the channels of distribution with the product and the audience, and that matching requires careful analysis and a dash of intuition.

Promotion

This term is often used interchangeably with marketing; it means getting the word out about a company and its services. There are many ways to do this, and these ways are often split into two categories: advertising and publicity. Advertising is media coverage that one pays for. This may involve ads in local newspapers, on TV, on radio, by direct mail, and banners on the Internet. Publicity, on the other hand, involves getting local or specialty media interested in the company's "story," without having to pay them to print it. The music industry, of course, is famous for taking advantage of this. Any news that gets an artist on a cover—good or bad—can equal money for the company. Clever entrepreneurs will make friends with media outlets and provide them with material to secure that "free" press.

Mushrooming digital media is a good promotional tool for new businesses—especially for companies that specialize in a niche market and need to reach a wide geographic area. To attract and keep online customers, a site must offer something (usually entertainment or information) for nothing. The most successful websites offer their customers dynamic, ever-changing content. In addition, a site could provide special offers, content and messaging pushed out to a growing list of recipients, and customer support—anything to keep its users satisfied and eager to return.

• • • Case Study on Starting a Business: From Intern to Entrepreneur

When Alex White was a college student in 2008, he noticed a disconnect between the priorities of two giant music labels—where he worked summers as an intern—and the music consumption habits of his classmates back at the dorm. The labels were focused on selling CDs by supporting retail stores and artists while touring, while fellow students were consuming all their tunes via the then flowering online landscape.

That observation germinated Next Big Sound, a music data analytics company that White co-founded with two class-mates at Northwestern University. The company began by tracking online music activity on Facebook, Twitter, Last.fm, and even nonmusic platforms like Wikipedia (where lookups of artist profiles are tracked). The information is licensed to industry players: major and independent labels, artist man-agement companies, and indie bands (the general public is not a buyer of Next Big Sound data).

Alex White

Thanks to the label summer internships, White got to know music executives who volunteered to be sounding boards for the business plan for Next Big Sound. The plan was honed through feedback received from numerous informal pitches. White's intern work itself was fairly mundane: making sure local stores had plenty of CDs in stock when the labels' bands came to town on tour and also being a local legman for the tour. Using data to understand music played off White's college major of Organizational Change, which studies how institutions learn and transfer knowledge; his minor in business; and finally a concentration in music, for which Evanston, Illinois-based Northwestern is renowned.

Upon graduation, White and his partners moved themselves and the company to Boulder, Colorado, to further refine their plan at an incubator for startups funded by venture capitalists (VCs) and **angel** investors. That resulted in even more pitching, but this time to VCs who were open to bankrolling high-risk ventures. The process: "We tell a 'story' of what we thought Next Big Sound could become, and also communicate our excitement and passion," says White, who became CEO of Next Big Sound. "It's never easy getting grilled by prospective investors, but over time the story got tighter and I became more confident because there was no question that I hadn't answered before."

Next Big Sound was built around analytics—using statistical data to solve business problems—applied to the music business. "We deliver insights on the activities and interactions of the fan base like connecting a spike in YouTube plays to higher download sales on iTunes," says White. "We're providing greater understanding of cause and effect, greater accuracy for forecasting, and helping setting realistic expectations for artists' album releases." Another key insight provided by analytics is comparing the fan activity of one artist to that of peer artists. Comparisons help identify promising avenues used by rivals as well as seeing where an artist is underperforming. By 2015, the thriving Next Big Sound was acquired by Internet radio giant Pandora and landed on Fast Company's list of most innovative companies.

Once music consumption moved from physical to digital, a treasure trove of data became available tracking online actions of music consumers. White recalls when first pitching Next Big Sound data—which are sold on a subscription basis—industry executives initially responded that they didn't care about music consumer behavior online. "Why do I care how many Myspace plays I got last week?! I'm just trying to sell records and T-shirts," White remembers being told. But that reluctance gave way as the industry saw the impact of a fast-changing environment on the traditional ways of the business. Sometimes, at least, the industry learns as much from an intern as the other way around.

Accounting and Finance

Although accounting software can do calculations, there are some decisions where the manager (and perhaps the accountant) will need a human touch to decide how to keep track of the money. Among the key decisions is how to record the "when" and "how" of an individual transaction.

When to Record a Transaction

There are two basic methods of recording a transaction. The "cash" method involves entering the record of a transaction when the money is received (or disbursed). The other way to record a transaction is called the "accrual" method, which is the most commonly used accounting method. In the accrual method, money is listed in the accounts receivable so the business can better see what funds are "in the pipeline" and revenue is matched with corresponding expenses to better determine profitability. In cash accounting, a bill that is owed (say, a credit card bill) does not exist in the books until the check is written. In an accrual system, the expense is recognized in the books when it is due—even if the check isn't paid on time.

Keeping Track of the Money

Three financial statements can be done quite easily and should provide useful information to even the smallest of operations.

Balance Sheet

The balance sheet is particularly valuable in understanding exactly what a company is worth at a specific, given point in time. The balance sheet always includes three categories—assets, liabilities, and equity.

Assets: Among other things, will always include cash, accounts receivable (money owed to a company by its clients), and value of inventory

Liabilities: Includes accounts payable (bills owed), interest charges, taxes due, and loans

Equity: The sum of invested capital and retained earnings

This "snapshot" of the business is labeled the balance sheet because of the well-known accountant's formula: assets = liabilities + equity. This formula is used to create a trial balance that helps accountants make sure that all money has been "accounted" for. A little algebraic contortion may help put this formula into a more understandable format.

Assets (what a company has) – **Liabilities** (what a company owes) = **Equity** (what a company is worth)

Income Statement

This statement shows (in a simplified format) where the money came from, what was spent, and what was left over after all expenses were paid. Unlike the balance sheet, the income statement always applies to a period of time, such as a month or a year. A typical income statement might look like the following:

Acme Musical Products

Income Statement (for the period 01/01/2015–12/31/2015)

Sales revenues	30,000
Cost of goods sold	10,000
Gross margin/subtotal	**20,000**
Sales, administration, and general expenses	5,000
Depreciation expenses	2,000
Earnings before interest and taxes (EBIT)/subtotal	**13,000**
Interest expenses	600
Earnings before income tax/subtotal	**12,400**
Income tax expense	4,000
Net income/the bottom line	**8,400**

Cash Flow Statement

A cash flow statement, derived from the income statement and balance sheet, shows the cash and cash equivalent entering and leaving a company over a specific period of time. The money coming into the business is called cash inflow, and the money going out from the business is called cash outflow. Cash can come from three avenues: core operations (sale of products or services), equity investment received, and financing such as borrowings that have to be repaid. The cash flow statement is different from the balance sheet and income statement in that it does not include the amount of future incoming and outgoing cash that has been recorded on credit. The cash flow statement is useful in determining the short-term viability of a company—particularly its ability to pay bills—and how much cash it generates, particularly from its core operations. This would be of particular interest to investors.

Pop Sounds Musical Products

Cash Flow Statement (for the period 01/01/2015–12/31/2015)

Cash flow from operations	40,000
Cash flow from investments	(20,000)
Cash flow from financing	5,000
Cash Flow for fiscal year ending 12/31/2015	**25,000**

With or without such statements, an independent businessperson will need to know how much money is being made. This may seem like a simple task, but seasoned professionals will tell you it is sometimes difficult to know where and how the money travels through a business. Once this information is acquired, the best decisions can be made—and that can make the difference between a healthy business and an unexpected bankruptcy.

Operations Management

Many people get into a business because they are already giving a service away and see the potential to sell it for a profit. If this is the case, it is relatively easy to expand the service and begin to charge for it. Although the business is small, it will be easy for a single person—or a small team of individuals—to provide the service. However, as the business grows, it may get harder to meet demand—especially in the time each person has to give to the company. Although this problem is the sign of a healthy, growing company, it can create logistical difficulties. The academic subject of operations management offers many ways in which a business can overcome these problems and effectively meet demand. A few of these concepts can be particularly helpful for small companies facing production issues.

Gantt Charts

Organization is a key component for people in business, whether in a one-person operation or a larger company. Planning is also important. One simple aid used frequently in business is the Gantt chart. The idea behind this organizational tool is to provide a clear outline of the steps needed to complete a project within a given time frame. These charts can be set up in fancy formats using computer programs, with standard word-processing programs, or even done by hand. It might look something like Figure 27.1.

The example in Figure 27.1 highlights each event and gives it a corresponding date. Taking the time to do this makes the project manager consider all steps in the process and provides everyone involved with realistic, well-defined goals.

Management

Authoritative studies have shown time and time again that some 90% of business failures result from poor management. Individuals planning careers in the music

Figure 27.1   **Gantt Chart**

business as, for instance, agents, managers, attorneys, or entrepreneurs will probably increase their chances of success by studying business management.

Dozens of books and hundreds of college courses treat the subject. Although they differ in approach, the most respected writers and teachers on the subject generally agree with this summary of what good management entails: planning, organizing, staffing, leading, and controlling.

Any discussion involving management should probably start with the boss. Effective leaders come with lots of different attributes. Some are authoritarian—making all the decisions themselves—whereas others prefer to involve employees in the decision-making process. Some lead by making expectations known and clearly outlining tasks for employees to accomplish. Another kind of leader, a transformational leader, is one who inspires employees through enthusiasm and vision. These leaders can, and do, really make a difference for their companies and employees—just as long as their creativity does not totally eclipse the need for taking care of details.

Where to From Here?

Research suggests that people entering the workforce today will have, on average, seven different careers. It just goes to show that planning for the unexpected is always a good idea (think about this if you are just starting college). Landing a job right out of school and spending 40 years there (the stereotype of earlier generations) is just not conceivable in today's world. Workers must be ready to adjust to change. Many opportunities will be presented during a career, one of which may very well be to escape the corporate world and make a go of it on one's own. Entrepreneurship is certainly not for everyone, but for those individuals who crave freedom and creativity over everything else, it can be a healthy alternative. In fact, for some, it may be the only way to go.

Note

1. From *Basic Marketing: A Marketing Strategy Planning Approach* (New York: McGraw-Hill, 2013).

Chapter Takeaways

- Many songwriters establish their own publishing companies, a type of business typically requiring less capital than most.

- A business plan outlining strategy, resources, and financial requirements is essential.

- In the initial stage, the entrepreneur must decide whether to establish a sole proprietorship, partnership, or corporation.

- Investigate and acquire all the necessary licenses and permits, saving headaches later.

- Venture capitalists are purely financial players that invest in risky startups that have potential for huge profits.

- Strategic investors are entities already in a sector, such as the music industry, that invest in complementary businesses to support their core mission.

- To finance a small business, often the most realistic source of funds is friends and family.

- Financial statements (balance sheet, income statement, and cash flow statement) are important to monitoring performance and staying out of financial hot water.

Key Terms

- DBA   (p. 437)
- fictitious firm name   (p. 437)
- Gantt chart   (p. 445)
- general partner   (p. 438)

- performance rights organizations (PROs)   (p. 436)
- product, price, place, promotion   (p. 440)

- Small Business Administration (SBA) (p. 436)
- strategic investment (p. 440)
- venture capital   (p. 440)

Discussion Questions

1. What are the differences between venture capital and strategic investment?

2. What are the four main aspects of marketing and why is each one important?

3. Why are accurate accounting records vital to the health of a company?

4. Why do you think Alex White and his co-founders succeeded in attracting venture capital backing for their startup company, while many other entrepreneurs have failed to do so?

PART 8

Career Planning
and Development

CHAPTER 28

Career Options

Tell people that you intend to work in the music industry and they will probably imagine that you have one of two goals in mind: rock star or record label mogul. While those are two potential options, the reality is that music-related occupations run an extremely wide gamut. When you consider the many points at which music intersects with the wider entertainment industry—from films to TV shows to radio to video games to the Internet—the potential opportunities expand still further. There are careers to be made both onstage and backstage, in the spotlight and behind the scenes, in big-city offices and small-town schools. Some offer steady paychecks and structured workweeks, while others hold out the promise of rich rewards without providing any guarantees of making next month's rent.

"You could be dumb as a rope and be in the music business."

—Dinah Shore (1956)[1]

The U.S. Bureau of Labor Statistics' *Occupational Outlook Handbook* forecasts that overall employment in the category of musicians, singers, and related workers will grow slower than the general economy through 2022. It also notes that many musicians and singers will find only part-time or intermittent work. But there is always room in *any* field, however, for new talent and well-qualified candidates.

Reflecting the border-crossing nature of the entertainment industry, many jobs (such as songwriter, **music supervisor,** or composer) will have value in multiple industry sectors. To provide a perspective of the various career options, however, we group them broadly as follows:

Broadcasting/Film/Video Game Careers

Concert Venue/Touring Careers

Left: Singer-actress Dinah Shore, a major star in the 1950s and 1960s.

Photo © Corbis.

Creative Careers

Directing/Producing Careers

Entrepreneurs/Starting Your Own Business

Instruments/Equipment Careers

Music Management/Legal Services Careers

Performing Careers

Teaching Careers

Choosing the right career can be one of the most important decisions in a person's life. Before proceeding to examine the options available, look at the summary in Table 28.1, which outlines the stages the prudent individual could go through in planning and developing a career.

Creative Careers

- Professional Songwriter
- Lyricist
- Composer of Show Music
- Composer of Educational Materials
- Composer of Children's Music
- Composer of Classical Music
- Arranger-Orchestrator
- Music Editor
- Music Copyist

Professional Songwriter

Career Description. Typically, the professional songwriter spends about half of his or her time composing, focusing creative energy on one market—the record industry. (Writers will also find work in the advertising, broadcasting, and video game sectors, which are addressed later in this chapter.) The other half of the songwriter's workweek is usually spent promoting—trying to persuade performers and producers to actually record the material. This is a highly competitive field, and thus most beginning songwriters find it necessary to support themselves with other kinds of employment that may or may not relate to music. Once genuinely talented songwriters gain an initial degree of success, they may be able to discontinue moonlighting and devote their full attention to writing and promoting their songs. When this happens, they often find themselves increasingly involved in related activities such as music publishing, record production, and even artist management or show production. The real pros write not just dozens of songs but hundreds, knowing that prolific activity is required to sustain a full-time songwriter career.

Professional songwriters generally find it helpful to live and work in a major recording center, where they can make direct personal contacts with publishers, record producers, and recording artists. Working conditions are ideal: The songwriter sets the

Table 28.1 **Career Planning and Development**

Discovering Yourself
Self-appraisal of temperament, talent
Professional assessment of your temperament, talent
Defining Goals
Personal needs, preferences
Investigation of career options
Short-term employment objectives
Long-term career goals
Getting Prepared
Education, training
Apprenticeship, work experience
Diplomas, degrees, licenses, union affiliations
Finding Work
Surveying the job market: current, potential
Predicting entry: time, place, pay, status
Breaking in: auditions, demos, emails, letters, résumés, interviews
Self-employment options
Climbing the Ladder
Planning advancement: status, income, power
Vertical vs. horizontal job change
Quitting vs. hanging on
Attainment of career goals
Realization of personal goals
Periodic reassessment of goals
Retirement
When, how
Estimated financial requirements

hours and vacation periods, usually writes at home, and can limit professional contacts to the kinds of individuals desirable to be around—musicians and show people.

Qualifications and Preparation. Because the publishing/recording business requires hundreds of new songs every week, even untalented, poorly prepared songwriters may sometimes get heard—initially. But those songwriters who hope to build a *lasting career* will need to possess true talent and genuine skills. How can one honestly assess these attributes? It is the marketplace itself that will ultimately offer the most realistic career guide: Aspiring songwriters should offer their songs to as many producers and performers as possible over time; they will then learn, with persistent effort, whether these professionals—the actual song users—judge their work good enough to merit a possible recording.

Assuming that the aspirant has demonstrable creative talent, a second key requirement is to learn the craft. Chapter 5 treats this topic at length. Songwriters who tend to make it have a strong sense of curiosity. They may start out ignorant of both their craft and their profession, but they study, observe, absorb, and ask questions.

Unless the songwriter is so creatively gifted that song users beat a path to the door, certain personal traits will also be required to survive in the field. The essential one is determination. The writer must be strongly motivated to write songs and then more songs, and then push the material unrelentingly, day after day, persevering until gaining acceptance. Even established pros rarely enjoy the luxury of simply entertaining offers that arrive unsolicited.

Employment Prospects. Most songwriters do not hold traditional salaried positions but, rather, earn money based on their creative output; *how much* depends largely on how popular those songs are in the marketplace, since income derives from performance and mechanical royalties.

As in all creative careers, there are no guarantees of success. That said, there is also no reason an aspiring songwriter *can't* succeed if he or she is genuinely talented, is professionally competent, has the right temperament, and is persistent.

Writers traditionally strike deals with music publishers under which the publisher will contract for the writer's services for a year or more on an exclusive basis, meaning that the individual can write only for that particular publisher. These deals typically give the writer monetary advances in return for the publisher's taking a large percentage of the royalties earned from the songs. As explained in Chapter 25, among the other sources for employment are **production music libraries**—which stockpile and syndicate original tunes for movies, commercials, video games, and industrial films.

Lyricist

A subset of the "songwriter" career option is that of the "lyricist," who writes words to songs. The first difficulty in attempting to make it as a lyricist is the same one confronting the pop singer: Almost all of us think we can do it. Employment prospects of lyricists aspiring to full-time careers are not promising for anyone lacking a distinctive creative talent. Unless writers are richly endowed, their careers may continue to support them only if they become active also as composers or in some other music-related work, such as teaching music, publishing, producing, or artist management. A lyricist who is able to team up with a talented musical collaborator to form a strong songwriting team stands better odds. Talented wordsmiths may also find a welcome in the advertising business, which is addressed later in this chapter.

Lyricists who want to write for the musical theater must have a love for what takes place there. They will probably associate themselves with other composers and creative talents of similar tastes and professional goals. This often occurs, as it did with Cole Porter, Richard Rodgers, and others, when the writer is still in college, where student-written shows provide vehicles for novices to learn their craft.

When a writer has a feeling for how a song can contribute to the progress of the drama on stage, the writer will probably take the next step and become involved in collaborating with others in writing the book for shows, a term used on Broadway for the text of a musical play. Among the most distinguished (and wealthy) lyricists who also wrote (or helped write) books for successful Broadway shows were Ira Gershwin, Oscar Hammerstein II, and Alan Jay Lerner. The field of writing for the professional musical theater is very difficult to break into, but the rewards, artistic and financial, can be rich indeed.

Composer of Show Music

Career Description. A small group of professional composers devotes most of its creative efforts to writing music for shows. Years ago, this would have meant only the kind of creative work involved in mounting a Broadway production. Today, additional show-writing opportunities can be found off-Broadway and "off-off-Broadway," as well as in regional theaters, children's theater, and industrial shows throughout the country.

Show music composers work differently than do pop songwriters. The latter are free to invent whatever material they think might appeal to record producers. But show music composers normally start work only after a producer or writer has presented them with a script defining the nature of the show, the scenario, dialogue, and, early on, the book for the production. The composer works sometimes on a daily basis with the show writers and producers, searching for music and lyrics that enhance the show and move it forward. Show music composers often work steadily on a project for several months, even a year or more, shaping and reshaping the music to fit the script—which is also probably undergoing constant rewriting. Show music composers may be handed a lyric and be asked to come up with the music in 2 or 3 days, even overnight. Some great standards that were composed overnight have emerged from Broadway hits; Stephen Sondheim wrote the music and lyrics to *Send in the Clowns* in just one evening! On the other hand, Rodgers and Hammerstein (*Oklahoma!, South Pacific, Carousel, The Sound of Music,* etc.) were known for working and reworking music and lyrics on just a handful of songs for a year or more until they attained their artistic goal.

Composers and lyricists of stature are almost always called on to serve as consultants to the producer in matters such as casting, dialogue, staging, and orchestrations. Some show music composers are occasionally called on to write not just show songs but also instrumental music, dance music, even **dramatic music** to underscore stage action.

Qualifications and Preparation. Show music composers must possess the same qualifications cited for songwriters plus a sense of theater. Show composers are often expected to work well with collaborators, particularly lyricists. Although Broadway has had a few masters who could write words and music—Cole Porter, Irving Berlin, and Stephen Sondheim, for example—most shows are created by a kind of committee involving composers, lyricists, playwrights, and directors. Choreographers and lighting directors also help shape the final composition. The creative artist who is comfortable only when working alone is better off staying away from the theater.

How does a person prepare for this level of composition? Unless gifted with bountiful natural talent and polished with private instruction, such a composer would have to spend at least 4 to 6 years beyond high school studying music, probably in a university. The student might major in composition and minor in theater—getting experience in campus or local productions, as did Stephen Sondheim, Oscar Hammerstein, Cole Porter, Richard Rodgers, and many others. The "complete" show music composer would not only become immersed in the Broadway repertoire but also study the great "show music" composed by earlier masters, such as Mozart and Wagner, not to mention Stravinsky and Copland in the 20th century.

What kind of temperament is required? The show music composer must be able to endure the sudden rejection of material without experiencing collapse of ego. The aspirant must have unlimited patience—be willing to work on one project for a year or two, then see the show fold after one performance and be willing to go through the whole process again. The person must also possess sufficient aggressiveness to search for show backers and producers. Creative musicians working in the theater must hustle their own financial support and convince investors that the project is as good as the composers believe it is. In this aspect of a theater composer's career, there is little room for modesty. Self-confidence and drive are as important to professional success as creative prowess.

Employment Prospects. There is no such thing as an "employer" or a "job" for show music composers. Rather, they work on projects, perhaps for long periods without compensation, in the hope that they can locate a financial backer along the way. Despite the daunting ratio of flops to hits among musical shows, every season, financial benefactors, or **angels**, emerge with money in hand, ready to sink up to several million dollars into an untried, unproved musical dream. A show composer may struggle for years and never find financial backing or a receptive producer. Still, writers new and old continue to make their way in the theater.

Composer of Educational Materials

Career Description. When schools and colleges accelerated their music education programs following World War II, publishers became increasingly involved in attempting to supply the print music needs of school bands, orchestras, and choruses, as well as the requirements of the individual student in search of learning materials. This print music market expanded in the 1960s to involve several hundred composers/arrangers/editors in the publication of music education materials. Today, many composers of educational materials are educators themselves; of those, most are affiliated with a college or university.

The most successful composers of educational materials usually concentrate on the particular medium that they know best: Band directors tend to compose mostly band pieces; choral directors tend mostly to create choral repertoire; orchestral directors compose and arrange orchestral literature. Occasionally, composers of educational material extend their talents beyond grade school and university-level literature and compose works for professional ensembles such as symphony orchestras, ballet and opera companies, and military bands.

Qualifications and Preparation. Most composers and arrangers of educational music have a degree in music; most have an advanced degree in composition and several years of experience with school ensembles.

Employment Prospects. It can be tricky to get a foot into the educational-music door. Composers, arrangers, and transcribers who are not affiliated with a major publishing company but who wish to have their works published should shop their material to a smaller, independent publisher or consider self-publishing their material. Those submitting to a small firm that accepts unsolicited work will help their prospects if they strictly follow submission guidelines. And all aspiring composers should be sure their music addresses a specific market (such as a high school marching band).

Composer of Children's Music

Career Description. Anyone with a child at home can testify to the power, the popularity, and the pervasiveness of children's music, which can be found on albums, TV shows, DVDs, websites, and films. Disney led the way in marketing such specialized music, eventually discovering that soundtracks and videos are extremely lucrative reminders of a pleasant viewing experience, but today numerous record labels and video companies specifically target little eyes and ears with a wide variety of releases.

A composer seeking a professional career writing children's music must understand how to score ideas in a simple style yet avoid the simplistic. Competition in the field is strong, and even the simplest songs should reveal at least a hint of charm, if not originality. Song texts are essential to most music appealing to children—the sing-along factor is often key. If not adept at composing lyrics, the composer will need to locate a strong collaborator. Also, the aspiring composer in this field needs to know how limited in range melodies must be for young voices.

One aspect of composing music for kids spills over into the educational field, particularly through children's television and online programming and educational DVDs. This market includes material that helps young children learn to count, to spell, to recognize the names of animals, and so forth, sometimes correlated to music books with sound recordings. Composers interested in this kind of writing and production are involved not just in entertainment but in education as well.

Qualifications and Preparation. Musicians may find work in this field with the qualifications cited above for writers of popular songs—natural creative gifts. Publishers and record producers, given a choice, will prefer to look at the music submitted by musicians who know how to score what they create. Serious children's writers also need a good grasp of children's age-level characteristics and would be well advised to make themselves knowledgeable about child development and current trends within children's entertainment.

Employment Prospects. Most income in this field derives from recordings and printed music that follow the release of a successful musical film or TV program. Some of this work is rendered by songwriters hired by the film producers. Music publishers and recording companies then follow up the film with special editions. The qualified composer aspiring to work in the children's music field should contact publishers within this market who accept unsolicited work.

Composer of Classical Music

Career Description. Musicians who aspire to professional careers as composers of classical music generally view themselves as functioning outside the music "business," believing they can spare themselves confrontation with the commercial world. But most composers in the field bump up against the rude realities of the marketplace just like their counterparts in popular music. If gifted with both abundant talent and the right temperament for such a career, the serious music composer should become acquainted with the professional lives of Bach, Handel, or Chopin—not to mention Schoenberg and Bartók. Each of these composers discovered that he had to devote much of his time to hustling for jobs, commissions, and students. Nowadays, only a handful of composers devote their full workweek to composing. Either through choice or financial necessity, nearly all composers divide their time among composing, teaching, performing, and job hustling.

Practically all serious music composers find that about the only place they can find steady employment is on the teaching staff of a conservatory or university (in the past century, Schoenberg, Bartók, Harris, Piston, Hindemith, Persichetti, Crumb, Foss, Schuller). Once a composer starts to acquire a good reputation, commissions follow. A composer of national and international reputation could live fully off commissions alone, but the composer aspiring to this high station may have to wait a lifetime to reach these heights.

Composers of even modest reputation enter composing contests. These come along all the time, and an energetic composer can often earn several cash awards a year this way. Certain contests of this kind can lead to a national reputation; through them, composers can receive commission offers, even teaching jobs.

Qualifications and Preparation. To find employment, the composer must be highly motivated and determined, but there is no consensus on how to establish a first-rate reputation as a music composer.

As it turns out, the composers who manage to achieve more than regional reputations are those who attract media and critical attention. Sometimes this attention is generated by using outlandish tricks (quartet for strings and cement mixer)—or "composing" pieces that are silent musically (John Cage). Or a composer may attract attention through tricking critics (garnering rave reviews for a piece that was deliberately performed backward). Other serious music composers get their music played because they appear as soloists or conductors. If they are really good at either, they give the impression of being first-rate at anything musical.

How does a serious music composer prepare for a career? Practically all of them today who get teaching jobs must have an earned terminal degree from an accredited university. Of these, the most useful is the doctor of musical arts (DMA) in composition, the degree now most often awarded to musicians planning professional careers as composer-teachers. Some colleges and universities award the doctor of music, doctor of philosophy, or master of music as the terminal degree, also with a specialization in composition. Most advanced-degree candidates serve as teaching assistants to the faculty under which they are studying or teach music in a school to support themselves financially during the arduous period of graduate study. Whatever the work/study combination the degree candidate can set up, advanced study focuses on developing the student's craft through extensive exercises, performances, and study of master works.

Employment Prospects. The musician aspiring to employment as a composer of serious music cannot expect to earn a living scoring masterpieces. The aspirant will almost certainly find work, early on, primarily as a teacher of theory and composition in a college or university. As a potential pedagogue, the aspirant should know that the supply of qualified, certified teachers has often exceeded demand. Still, those who are sufficiently motivated will continue their quest for employment as serious composer-teachers.

How does the aspiring composer-teacher land the first job? In these ways:

(a)   developing a good reputation with influential musician-teachers;

(b)   joining the College Music Society and following up its job-opening notices;

(c)   registering with the alma mater's placement bureau;

(d)   attending professional meetings and making contacts, setting up performances of new work, seeking publicity;

(e) registering with teacher employment services; and

(f) persevering for at least 5 years.

Arranger-Orchestrator

Career Description. Many creative musicians earn most of their incomes as arrangers. They take music written by someone else and arrange or add voices to suit the needs of the artist or film company. They accomplish this in diverse ways, ranging from writing **leadsheets** to scoring motion pictures. Hundreds of arrangers make their living working for songwriters and publishers, turning out leadsheets and song copies. The American Federation of Musicians (AFM) has pay **scales** covering this kind of work, although the scales only apply to the few jobs offered by employers under union contract.

Publishers engage arrangers to score various editions, particularly for the educational field. Astute publishers hire only specialists for this kind of work—choral arrangers for vocal editions, jazz specialists for jazz charts, and so on.

The largest segment of professional arrangers work for performers. Most professional performers use custom arrangements exclusively. Nearly all arrangers are employed freelance; few are retained on regular salaries. Their services are considered, under copyright law, as **work made for hire;** they receive one flat fee, upfront, and do not receive royalties on copies or recordings sold.

Orchestrators take music that has been written by someone else and write or score the music for instruments. Arrangers and orchestrators usually work under tight deadlines, largely because composers and producers are also working under tight deadlines. It is a high-pressure field. Panic-type time schedules are regularly relieved, however, with intermittent periods of idleness. But musicians attracted to the arranging field appear to love their work and manage to survive careers that are a mix of great artistic satisfaction and trips to the unemployment office.

Many musicians work as part-time arrangers, dividing their professional efforts among related fields such as composition, directing, producing, and performing. Others are working at least part-time in fields such as publishing and management.

Qualifications and Preparation. To qualify as a professional arranger, the individual should have thorough training in music theory, sight singing, and ear training. An arranger's ear must be as finely tuned as that of a composer, and many professional arrangers qualify as composers, too. An arranger is expected to work quickly and be able to knock out a score overnight when necessary.

Besides schooling in music theory, the best training for aspirants is to write—and write and write—then hear the score in rehearsal. Then rewrite. Then rehearse the revision—and on and on over several years of experimentation, trial, and error. All good writers, whether they create prose, poetry, or music, recommend two basic activities: Read a lot and write constantly.

Employment Prospects. The aspiring professional arranger need not starve throughout the learning experience. All arrangers who eventually make it as pros begin to pick up small jobs early on—first for free, then maybe for a few dollars for one of their charts—if they'll copy off the parts and run the rehearsal. Top arrangers working in the recording field for stars or busy record producers earn big money. If they manage to keep abreast of ever-changing musical styles, their careers can last longer than those of the artists for whom they write.

Music Editor

Career Description. There are several kinds of music editors, some of which will be described elsewhere in this chapter. Here we discuss the kind of music editor who prepares music manuscripts for publication.

All publishers of printed music require professional editors, because even skilled composers and arrangers are rarely knowledgeable concerning precisely how scores and parts must be edited before the music is printed. In the popular field, most publishers contract with one of the major print houses to handle their music editing and paper publishing.

Music print publishers of classical music engage editors to rewrite the composers' or arrangers' scores so that they conform in content and style to the standards this country inherited centuries ago from master European engravers and printers. Most modern printed versions of musical notation are produced on computers and then printed in quantity. Prospective music editors are advised to gain substantial knowledge of music-editing traditions as well as computer software skills.

The music editor must first correct and proofread music that has been submitted to the publisher. Part of this work can involve actual rescoring, arranging, and even original composition. The music editors who are most in demand are almost always qualified as composers and arrangers, too. Many editors specialize in just one field, such as choral music or piano music.

Editorial staff often contribute to judgment on acquisitions in respect to musical quality, style, and market suitability. Publishing decisions will be based on those judgments.

Qualifications and Preparation. To qualify for a job as a music editor, the individual should undertake a complete musical education in theory, history, literature, and performance practices. This broad background is most readily available in universities with strong music departments.

Employment Prospects. For many musicians, particularly composers and arrangers with good educational backgrounds, music editing is a fallback position; they enter the field as a second career choice or, more commonly, as one component of a combination career.

Music Copyist

Career Description. Many musicians break into the composing and arranging fields as music copyists, who transcribe musical parts onto **staff paper** from a score. The tasks may include copying various parts for different instruments or voices. Other musicians develop well-paying careers in the copying field itself.

Qualifications and Preparation. Many professional copyists are also arrangers, for the two professions have much in common. Aspiring copyists must be highly skilled in notation and transposition, have music theory training, and be extremely accurate. Professional copyists are expected to make no mistakes, and they are also expected to correct the errors in the scores they work on. The experienced professional copyist may not be able to reach the composer-arranger to answer questions about illegible notes or incomplete sections. The copyist must then have sufficient skill and knowledge to correct and complete the score without guidance. Computer-generated scores and parts are commonplace, and the aspiring music copyist must become proficient in using these tools.

Employment Prospects. There is an actual shortage of fully qualified musicians who have the knowledge and skill required of professional copyists, and copying jobs exist everywhere. Most copyists supplement their income in other branches of music. Combination careers can often yield satisfactory incomes.

Directing/Producing Careers

- Music Director-Conductor
- Record Producer

Music Director-Conductor

Career Description. Most musical performers require musical direction of some sort.

The conductors best known by the public are those engaged as music directors of symphony orchestras and opera companies. Some are called "artistic director." It is customary for musicians holding these posts to assist management in contracting guest conductors and guest soloists, selecting programs, working with orchestra managers in planning operating budgets, and hiring and firing musicians.

Artistic directors also become involved with the major orchestras in negotiating recording contracts for their ensembles. Because of the heavy responsibilities assumed by these kinds of musical directors, they require at least one assistant conductor. Some of the major orchestras have two or more assistant conductors who help the artistic director by conducting performances for schoolchildren and pop concerts.

Musicians who serve time as assistant conductors often graduate to roles of principal conductors and music directors of orchestras and opera companies.

Music directors and assistant directors have such heavy responsibilities that they rarely find time for any other professional employment, save for guest conducting other symphony orchestras. In addition to their directing, they must meet with the various committees charged with raising money for operations. An important part of this aspect of the work is fostering goodwill among the individuals and corporations and foundations that pledge money to support the artistic goals of the ensemble.

Some music directors are engaged by arts centers and community centers as artistic directors. They not only may conduct rehearsals and performances but are also likely to function as organizers and supervisors of artistic and educational programs for these entities.

Thousands of music directors are employed by churches. These professionals may be organists or other performers, many of whom serve double duty as choir directors. Large churches sometimes call their music directors "ministers of music." A person serving in such a capacity may direct choral and other musical groups for the institution. While the largest churches pay their music directors full-time salaries, smaller institutions do not, expecting them to fill out their incomes through other activities.

Music directors for movies and TV can be hired first as composer-arrangers and be expected to conduct their own music when their scores are recorded (more information on the film/TV music sector can be found later in this chapter). This same pattern prevails in the field of production music libraries: Music directors usually serve the producers as triple-threat artists—composers-arrangers-directors.

In the pop field, the individual serving as music director may not be a conductor but simply a performer in the group who assumes a leadership role. Musical direction of groups of this kind is sometimes shared. As for soloists, when an artist reaches star status, he or she usually finds it necessary to employ a music director, at least for appearances on tour. These individuals are almost invariably rehearsal pianists-accompanists who assist the artist by selecting material, arranging it, and conducting rehearsals and live performances. Many of these pianist-conductors are not trained baton twirlers but manage to make sufficient gestures from their position at the piano keyboard to **cue** the musicians.

Some jobs for music directors in the pop field are found in major cities, conducting shows. Other musical directing jobs are available in the field of industrial shows. Broadway, off-Broadway, and regional theaters employ music directors.

Qualifications and Preparation. All successful music directors share a common attribute: a commanding presence. They know how to lead, either intuitively or through training. This leadership quality is not limited to musical matters but extends to relationships with the variety of human personalities they work with in rehearsal and performance.

Nearly all successful music directors have had extensive schooling, often a combination of formal education and private instruction. Because music directors must be well informed on all aspects of music, their education, at least through the baccalaureate degree level, will be broad. Postbaccalaureate study may include emphasis in performance, composition, or conducting.

In the pop field, directors are often performers, and they are usually involved in composition and arranging, perhaps rehearsing and directing performances of the music they themselves have scored.

The best environment for an aspiring music director is a first-rate university with a strong faculty and a variety of performance groups. In addition, most conductors start early, usually while still in college, to direct a church choir or jazz band or pop **chorus** or whatever group they can get their hands on; some major cities, such as Los Angeles and New York, also have youth or training orchestras that can offer the talented novice conductor opportunities to practice the craft.

Employment Prospects. Job prospects for music directors can be compared with those found in other aspects of the arts and business: Work is available for top people. Symphony and opera conductors of repute often hold down at least two conducting posts. Other fine musicians prefer to serve smaller communities where the salaries are lower, but the pressures are too.

Music directors in the popular field rise or fall less on their abilities as conductors or leaders than on their abilities to please their employers as writers. A music director who is a really competent composer and arranger can usually find work—and the ability to rehearse and conduct groups is a minor consideration. Employers may tolerate weak leadership qualities and baton techniques when the music director is a whiz at writing music.

Record Producer

Career Description. The work of the various kinds of record producers is described in more detail in Chapter 13. Some producers are successful largely because they are very good at locating the right musical material, then matching it to the right artists. This is why the old label for these practitioners was "artist and repertoire producers." Some producers are masters of the control room and may have started out as recording engineers. Others know how to raise money, then hire outside experts to arrange the music, mix the sound, and supervise postproduction. Still other producers are master musicians who succeed because they are creative and capture artistic

A control room of a recording studio.
Photo © Comstock/Thinkstock.

performances on disc. No matter the point of entry, the producer must always be the bridge between artistic integrity and commercial potential.

The majority of the work is performed freelance. The nearest thing approaching steady employment is found with major labels, although label jobs have been in decline for decades. The majority of producers float from job to job pretty much like recording artists; they get return engagements when their music sells and their reputations grow. If they produce a string of flops or are difficult to work with, their telephones stop ringing. Income can keep coming in from past hits, though: In addition to upfront fees, producers are paid royalties on the records they produce.

Independent producers often own their own production companies, and some launch their own independent record labels.

Qualifications and Preparation. An individual aspiring to a career in record production should not expect to follow an orderly path; each producer has his or her own unique story to tell. Nearly all producers who make it discover that they must first become recognized in an allied field—such as songwriting, arranging, sound mixing, criticism, musical direction, or other related experience. In addition to competence in one or more of these facets of music, the record producer usually possesses some kind of leadership ability and a temperament that mixes well with artists, technicians, and executives. The producer must remain stable when others on the project are disintegrating through frustration or fatigue.

The producer has the additional worry of staying within budget. So the record producer must be a kind of miracle person—possessing strong musical ability, technological know-how, magic ears, a psychologist's mentality, the stability to remain rational under great pressures, *and* business acumen.

The producer of classical music must possess many of the same qualifications as the pop record producer, plus a few more. This professional has to be as good a score reader as the conductor and know details of the score being recorded. Ideally, the producer in the booth should be the twin of the conductor on the podium, so closely must they understand each other and the musical interpretation the literature requires.

To qualify to produce classical music recordings, the musician must have training identical to the kind described for classical music conductors. In addition, the producer must have knowledge of technology, perhaps even acoustics, sufficient to give direction to the mixing and **mastering** technicians.

Employment Prospects. Because no one possesses all the talents outlined above, those who come close find themselves in high demand. Although record production budgets have been tightening and competition for slots increasing, labels and artists are always searching for those record producers who can pull all the elements together in the studio to create a chart-worthy hit. Producers possessing the essentials of the art *and* craft will work and prosper.

Because of the absence of employment continuity, nearly all record producers have other irons in the fire, just as most musicians do. They may write songs, own part of a publishing company, manage artists, function as agents, write arrangements, produce shows—whatever works.

Performing Careers

- Singer
- Instrumentalist

Singer

Career Description. This is one of the more open-ended career categories, because it can encompass a wide range of professional possibilities. In the field of popular music, singers find careers not only as soloists and recording artists but also as group singers, background vocalists on commercials, and "production" singers, singing actors, or singing dancers. As most singers have already discovered, a career often starts at school, college, or local clubs where the individual can learn quite early whether audiences respond well. In the pop field, these amateur and semiprofessional beginnings are often combined with instrumental performance or songwriting, sometimes both.

Steady employment depends on the performer's skill. Successful singing careers involve a mix of live appearances and recordings. Established recording stars also appear on television and sometimes in commercials and films. Professional singers' lives are filled with almost incessant travel. The longest engagements occur when an artist remains in one location for a month or two to complete recording an album. Stars who play Las Vegas may be booked in for a few weeks, but most other singing jobs in the pop field are strings of one-nighters or weeklong engagements. Few experiences are more exhausting than constant traveling, and a professional singer's first concern, under these strains, is to stay healthy despite the rigors of the road. The second concern is, or should be, finding a competent personal manager. The third priority is the ongoing search for good material.

Even singers who write most of their own songs may need outside material to feed their acts. Nonwriting singers never stop searching for good songs. Writers and publishers know this and follow singers around, leadsheets in hand. Successful singers are also plagued with enthusiastic, even overbearing fans. These multiple pressures can debilitate a performer, and only the hardy can survive. But those attracted to the field seem to sustain themselves on the applause and adulation of their audiences—not to mention the money.

Qualifications and Preparation. To qualify for a successful career as a professional singer, it is helpful to be able to sing. But any audit of the field will reveal that dozens of nonsingers manage to make a living as "singers." Individuals with only modest musical talent sometimes win an audience. This occurs when the public becomes attracted to a performer not for singing ability but because of the individual's personality or acting ability. Those performers who have made a successful career for themselves do, however, share some important characteristics: some musical talent, charisma, self-discipline, physical stamina, versatility, creative ability, and poise.

In classical music, most artists who qualify for work have spent several years studying voice in college or with outside teachers. College music majors often pursue the master's degree, majoring in voice or perhaps choral music. Should the "legitimate" singer aspire to opera, the performer may opt for a music conservatory diploma rather than a university degree. The former provides concentrated training in performance. Opera students must acquire facility in several foreign languages, with French, Italian, and German being the most important.

Employment Prospects. The job outlook for singers ranges from grim to uncertain. Naturally, the fewest opportunities to make a decent-paying career lie in the musical arenas that attract the smallest audiences and, therefore, bring in the least amount of money. These would include the solo recital and concert fields, especially for singers with only classical training. Some employment is available with symphony orchestras and in community concert series, but these engagements are mainly seasonal.

In the field of opera, artist managers arrange some engagements; other artists are in such demand, they book themselves—opera companies outbid each other for their services. Unfortunately, only a few trained singers qualify for leading roles with good companies. Thousands of university graduates aspiring to careers in their fields are disappointed each year and turn to Broadway, regional theater, cruise ship entertainment, theme park troupes, teaching, or voice coaching. Aspiring singers sometimes begin their professional careers as supporting players and then graduate to leading roles.

Churches offer many jobs to trained singers who can also direct choirs. Some singers who are unable to develop the performing careers they had planned turn to teaching, then pick up singing jobs at business events, night clubs, weddings, and funerals. Practically all of this kind of work is nonunion.

Another source of fairly steady employment can be found by crackerjack singers willing to locate near centers of commercial and film and TV music production. These versatile singers need to be expert sight-readers in any musical genre and be able to perform with minimal rehearsal.

When it comes to job prospects for pop singers, there is yet another set of conditions. Here, *image* matters, and record labels likely will be looking for an entire "package"—an appealing personality to market and sell to admiring audiences. Pop singers who write their own songs will find their chances of catching the ears of label executives and audiences alike greatly improved. Since The Beatles in the mid-1960s, the preponderance of new singing artists breaking big in the business has been performing composers. These artists may not be either great singers or top composers, but the combination enchants audiences, and these versatile artists sell a lot of music.

Instrumentalist

Career Description. The working hours of a full-time instrumentalist may average only 3 hours a day, but most musicians are busy at least 40 hours a week. Practically all professional instrumentalists do at least some teaching. These accomplished musicians often have more students waiting for openings than they can accept. Student fees not only offer income to supplement playing jobs, but they can often provide at least minimum sustenance during periods when musicians cannot find playing jobs. Besides setting hours aside for teaching, professionals usually engage in regular daily practice, continuing throughout their careers to polish their skills and expand their repertoire.

In addition to these musical activities, a large percentage of professional instrumentalists are actively employed outside of music. From choice or necessity, many pros moonlight (more often, daylight) at jobs with flexible hours, thus providing release time for them to accept whatever music jobs come along.

Many professional musicians manage a different kind of moonlighting: They accept every attractive playing job that comes along, then fill in the balance of their workweek in music-related employment such as composition, arranging, copying, perhaps artist management or record production. Many professional musicians work fairly regularly as instrumentalists, while filling their daytime hours as music merchants—selling instruments, equipment, and so forth. Many work in "casuals"—club dates, one-night performances—and events such as trade shows, bar mitzvahs, awards banquets, and the like. Others still put together packages of musicians for casuals and work as one part musician, one part producer, and one part talent agent.

An important consideration for those planning careers as performers is the matter of travel. Most musicians must move around a lot—which can be fun when they are young but can become intolerable after several years of the gypsy life. Another important concern is the seasonal aspect of most performing careers. Many symphony, opera, and dance company musicians are laid off in the summer months. Broadway pit musicians know only seasonal employment, which generally means the life of a particular show. Instrumentalists working clubs on so-called steady engagements are delighted when a job extends beyond a few weeks.

Qualifications and Preparation. The young instrumentalist who has ambitions for a full-time, fully professional playing career must be endowed with outstanding musical talent. Instrumental study should begin in childhood and continue throughout the career.

To qualify for the concert and symphonic field, students today will usually complete at least a master's degree, often a doctorate, in performance (some graduates complete a "diploma" program). Whatever amount of formal training the musician might undergo, the working professional must be familiar with performance practices of both classical and popular music. Practically all symphony orchestras have a pops series where traveling artists bring in charts ranging in style from blues to country. And musicians in the theater and recording fields are expected to be able to perform any musical idiom in the correct style. The old days of the sharply delineated "classical" and "jazz" musician are nearly gone. Almost all pros now must cross the line.

The great majority of full-time professional instrumentalists are expected to be musically literate and read at sight what is placed before them. Nonreaders can be financially and artistically successful, but their success is often based more on their personality, composing, or strong natural talent.

Besides having a personality that works well with others, the real pro must be willing to work very hard for long years and persevere during periods of disappointment.

Just "liking music" is not enough. Yet another personal attribute is essential for the instrumentalist who strives for the highest paying fields, particularly symphony and studio work: strong nerves. Young musicians shooting for the big time are generally unaware of the working atmosphere in the recording field particularly, which is one not just of high tension but of sheer terror. Those jobs demand perfection in performance. There is minimum tolerance for error and none whatever for carelessness. A top studio player is allowed an occasional flub but is subject to being quickly displaced, sometimes forever, by a competitor who can demonstrate even greater reliability. Nerves of steel come in handy, but before the faint-of-heart abandon their dreams of the big time, it should be reassuring to remember that artists of international stature—musicians, dancers, actors—have said that controlled tension aids artistic performance.

Employment Prospects. The proliferation of music synthesizers has reduced job opportunities, but even though there are thousands of unemployed and underemployed instrumentalists, the truth is that there is a scarcity in some areas. Employment prospects depend on the particular instrument as well as the musician's talent and training. The best advice is to be around music a lot and get to know successful people in the field who will in turn recommend you for different projects.

Keyboard Players

There is a daunting oversupply of first-rate concert pianists and recitalists. Conservatories and colleges continue to turn out thousands of these artists, but their employment prospects are poor. Most communities have more than enough of restaurant, club, and lounge pianists.

In the theater music field, there is a shortage in most communities of keyboard artists who can sight-read a traveling Broadway show book, handle the written-out parts, and also play **comp style.** In the recording field, there are brilliant keyboard artists but an actual shortage in most cities of musicians who can handle diverse styles such as jazz, pop, and rock. Even scarcer are those pianists who can handle these styles plus Mozart or Chopin or Gershwin's concert pieces. If a keyboard artist seeks work in the recording field (and even in pit orchestras), employability will be increased by facility in performance synthesizers. Many keyboard players specialize in the electronic realm.

Finally, keyboardists can often find employment as accompanists. Some pianists consider accompanying second-class employment, but truly competent performers are often in demand.

Guitarists

There is a huge oversupply of amateur and semiprofessional guitarists who want to become full-time professionals. Many of these individuals do not understand the difference between an amateur and a truly professional performing artist.

But any guitarist who is a good reader and who can perform artistically in the all basic idioms of jazz, blues, rock, and country will probably need help in juggling job offers. This kind of competence and versatility is in demand everywhere.

Percussionists

Even before rock and roll, the world was oversupplied with drummers. Nevertheless, in most communities today, there is an undersupply of fully competent, versatile

A musician playing jazz on saxophone.
Photo © NWphotoguy/iStock.

percussionists. Directors and contractors can rarely find a drummer/percussionist who can really read well and who can handle not only conventional percussion but also mallet instruments and timpani. Many drummers play great jazz or rock or Latin rhythms but don't really know how to play concert or show music.

Few percussionists take the time to study seriously the art of timpani tuning and playing or to learn much about non-Western music. Percussionists who can do most or all the basic musical styles well, and who are good readers, are rare in most areas and in high demand. Percussionists in the next most active group are those who come close to the prowess and versatility of the "complete professional percussionist." Drummers who are unwilling to undertake this level of training will continue to compete with thousands of other drummers of comparable skill. Competition among "average" musicians will always be great.

Wind Instrument Players

The school band programs of recent decades have produced a large supply of good wind instrument performers. There is even an oversupply of fully qualified wind players with master's, even doctoral, degrees. When an opening is advertised by a professional symphony orchestra on, say, clarinet or trumpet, it is not unusual to see several hundred applicants. A respectable percentage of that group would have ability that would qualify them for serious consideration. In recording studios, a great abundance of wind players compete for those high-paying jobs. Extensive woodwind doubling is expected in the show music field and in recording. Because it takes a lifetime to master even one instrument, it is understandable why top doublers are so scarce. Those who come closest to really playing several winds get a lot of work—and when they do, they earn, through their doubling ability, 20% to 100% above basic scale.

In any discussion of career opportunities for wind players, mention must be made of the hundreds of jobs open for them in military bands.

String Players

Hundreds of string players find full- to part-time employment in America's many symphony orchestras. For details, review Chapter 18. Performers heading for careers as soloists in the classical field will find it difficult to break in without the aid of an agent or manager. The most active concert agents and management companies are listed in directory service Musical America, which also includes contact information for symphony orchestras and opera companies here and in Europe.

The most direct route for an instrumentalist in any field to find work is through establishing a reputation for being able to handle whatever opportunities come along—and a reputation for being better qualified than the competition. An instrumentalist of genuine ability becomes known throughout the musical community very quickly. Jobs can be scarce, but when they come along, the really good players are in demand.

A musical reputation can work even more quickly the other way around: Less talented performers, weak readers, and undependable musicians earn overnight reputations too.

Teaching Careers

- Studio Teacher
- College Music Instructor
- School Music Educator
- Music Therapist

Studio Teacher

Career Description. Studio teachers are private instructors who give individualized or group lessons, setting their own fees and developing their own lesson plans. Some teachers are contracted by music stores and may work on-site, while many others operate out of their own homes or offices.

Qualifications and Preparation. The studio teacher most in demand is the professional who is an active performer engaged in teaching as a sideline. However, performers who moonlight as teachers can possibly do more harm than good to their prospective students—if they are not actively engaged in the *teaching* process, the instructor can end up just performing for students and not actually teaching them. To teach, one must be more than just a good musician. The job requires patience and an ability to impart information in a way that can be understood by children and adults. The teacher must be able to relate to the student on his or her age level and level of aptitude. Especially when working with children and adolescents, winning the trust of the student is half the battle. A sense of humor is also invaluable.

Genuinely qualified music teachers have completed 4 to 8 years of college-level music study, are competent performers themselves, possess sound pedagogical techniques, and know how to inspire students. All the schooling in the world will not prepare one for the challenging job of working with, and motivating, sometimes reluctant students.

Employment Prospects. How does a qualified musician build up a student clientele? By building a strong reputation in the community—first as a musician and second as a teacher. Advertising can bring in some students, along with good word of mouth. School music educators can be counted on to make recommendations to their pupils.

Many active professionals teach at least part-time. The best of them fill every vacant hour in 40- to 60-hour workweeks and experience excellent income. Others, unable to stand an unending stream of kids passing through their studios, will accept only a limited number of pupils. Because most studio teachers work for themselves, small business skills are necessary for this career.

School Music Educator

Career Description. Music educators work in public, private, or parochial schools. Duties vary depending on the ages taught and the guidelines often set by state or district supervisors. Music teachers employed in Grades K (kindergarten) through 6 have responsibilities different from those working in junior and senior high schools. Many school districts try to finance a sufficient number of general music teachers for the lower grades to provide at least some music listening and participation for every child: singing, movement to music, and improvised performance on simple rhythm instruments and toys.

Teachers in junior and senior high schools are usually hired for specific duties. One director may be in charge of brass, wind, and string ensembles while another has responsibilities for the choral groups; either of these—or both—may be involved in the production of musical plays. The number of teachers and the division of responsibilities are usually determined by the size and financial commitment of the school.

Bands seem to dominate music education, and most senior high schools have an assortment: concert band, marching band, pep band, and stage band. From August through November, high school band directors' lives are generally consumed by rehearsing for half-time performances at football games. During these frantic weeks, music educators often feel they are not so much musical directors as drill sergeants, arrangers, copyists, and entertainment directors for the school's athletic department. Following football season, these teachers must hastily prepare a holiday program, then come springtime music festivals involving their concert bands and stage bands. When summer vacation finally arrives, they usually spend some of their time off trying to get equipment repaired and shows planned for the fall football season. High school music educators are accustomed to 60-hour workweeks, but many appear to thrive on their heavy loads.

Music Education Supervisor

Most school districts employ at least one **music supervisor** to direct and coordinate activities of all vocal and instrumental music teachers. The role of the supervisor is to guide formulation of educational policy, assist school principals in hiring new teachers, fight for and control music budgets, and offer pedagogical guidance to the music educators employed in their districts. Music supervisors also administer acquisition and circulation of central music lending libraries for their districts. These individuals are also involved in organizing music festivals, reading clinics, and contests. Many also teach. Some supervisors are employed on 12-month contracts.

Voice student and teacher.
Photo © eurobanks/iStock.

Qualifications and Preparation. Except for the field of music therapy, school music teaching is the only kind of employment where applicants are required to have a college degree in music. School music teachers (Grades K–12) in practically all states are also required to have a teaching certificate or teaching credential. Some states will automatically certify a teacher in a particular music teaching field if the teacher holds a baccalaureate degree in music from a state-accredited college or university. Other states require that college graduates in music also successfully pass a state-administered certifying examination. Types of teaching certificates vary from state to state.

In addition to a college degree and teaching license, those who do most of the music teacher hiring (school principals, usually) look for one or more of these qualifications or attributes: a good reputation as a teacher, high grades in college and on the certifying examination, and an outgoing personality.

Employment Prospects. For many years, a reasonably talented college student majoring in music education could expect to find a full-time teaching position after graduation. But more recently, the employment prospects for school music teachers have diminished. Top universities with distinguished track records of turning out fine teachers continue to place most of their graduates. But decreasing employment opportunities for individuals seeking teaching jobs in music and the other arts in most cities will probably continue because of downward pressure on school budgets. Music programs are often the first to be trimmed when money is tight.

College Music Instructor

Career Description. Before describing careers in college and university music teaching, the junior colleges should be discussed. Most junior or community colleges offer courses such as music appreciation, music theory, class piano, perhaps class guitar, band, and stage band. Junior colleges that offer a 2-year associate in arts degree in music may also offer courses such as music arranging, music history, and music business. Individuals aspiring to employment in one of these junior colleges are usually required to teach about 20 hours a week, almost double the teaching load of music instructors in 4-year colleges and universities. Because of this extremely burdensome schedule, few junior college music teachers have adequate time to prepare for their classes as well as for rehearsals, and they are among the most overworked teachers in the music education field.

Quite a different kind of employment is found at 4-year colleges and universities, where full-time music faculty members usually teach between 12 and 16 hours a week. Practically all music instructors at this level specialize in one particular aspect of music, and most, if not all, of their teaching and directing responsibilities relate to that specialty—for example, theory, choral music, instrumental music, applied music instruction, music history, and perhaps jazz education. They may teach only three or four different classes or ensembles a week, but their "off time" is filled with preparation for their hours in the classroom or rehearsal hall. Most university-level music teachers claim to have a workweek that averages well above 48 hours. Teachers who have attained higher academic rank, such as associate or full professor, are normally assigned somewhat lighter teaching loads. But the senior professors may be even busier than their colleagues of lower academic rank—engaged in research and other creative activities such as writing music, articles, and books.

Qualifications and Preparation. Practically all states require that their junior college teachers have not only a master's degree in music from an accredited institution but, in addition, a junior college teaching certificate. Musicians applying for "the choral job" or "the band job" at a particular junior college are expected to have established reputations in their field of specialization. Such reputations are usually acquired first at the high school level before the aspirant is considered for a faculty position in a junior college. Prospective faculty members are normally hired by the junior college president, on recommendation of the resident music faculty.

Four-year colleges and universities normally hire only those individuals who have earned a terminal degree in music—DMA, DM, or PhD, for example. Some prestigious schools occasionally hire faculty members who lack a terminal degree but whose reputations as performers, composers, or scholars are equal in prestige to a doctoral degree. Many colleges and universities will not consider prospective faculty who lack publications; either music compositions/arrangements or writings about music or music-related topics are considered "publications." These same institutions tend to waive this requirement when they are evaluating prospective members for their "applied music" faculty—meaning performance skills over knowledge of theory.

Employment Prospects. In some colleges and universities, funding for new faculty positions has been difficult to find. The number of music majors in American colleges has been influenced by the increasing awareness that many college-level music studies appeared to lead to no job. But the individual aspiring to college-level music teaching would be mistaken to conclude that no career opportunities exist. Although there may be an oversupply of candidates holding even doctoral degrees in theory, history, musicology, piano, and choral directing, some colleges and universities have difficulty finding fully qualified instructors (with terminal degrees) in certain specialties, such as ethnomusicology, music therapy, jazz education, electronic music, pop choral music, improvisation, sound synthesis, recording, and the music business.

Music Therapist

Career Description. Music therapy is the prescribed use of music by a qualified person to effect positive changes in the psychological, physical, cognitive, or social functioning of individuals with health or educational problems. Music therapists assess the emotional well-being, physical health, social functioning, communication abilities, and cognitive skills of their clients through musical responses. They then design therapeutic music sessions using techniques such as music improvisation, receptive music listening, songwriting, lyric discussion, music and imagery, music performance, and learning through music. Interdisciplinary treatment offered by music therapists can be used for a variety of populations, such as people with developmental and learning disabilities, trauma and other mental health needs, Alzheimer's disease and other aging-related conditions, and brain injuries. It can also be of use to those seeking therapy to cope with everyday stressors and for personal growth.

Qualifications and Preparation. To qualify as a professional music therapist, the aspirant must graduate from an approved college degree program—offered at universities around the country—which requires completion of a clinical internship with a

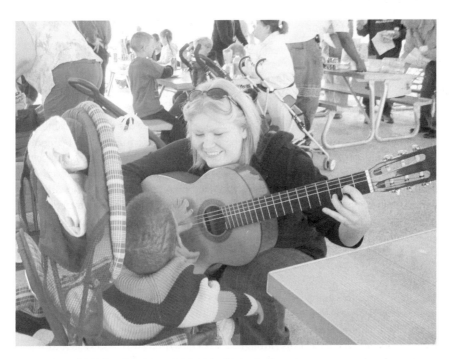

A music therapist works with a child at the Phoenix Zoo.
Photo from Flickr; Creative Commons license.

6-month minimum. These individuals are then eligible to sit for the national examination offered by the Certification Board for Music Therapists. Music therapists who successfully complete the independently administered examination hold the music therapist board-certified credential (MT-BC). The curricula offer a thorough study of music, along with coursework in psychology and the biological, social, and behavioral sciences. Graduate degrees are offered at several universities in music therapy and related disciplines.

Employment Prospects. Music therapists are finding employment in record numbers in psychiatric hospitals, rehabilitative facilities, medical hospitals, outpatient clinics, day care treatment centers, agencies serving developmentally disabled persons, community mental health centers, drug and alcohol programs, senior centers, nursing homes, hospice programs, correctional facilities, mental health residential treatment centers, schools, and private practice. The job outlook is promising, especially in terms of job opportunities related to an aging population and a growing interest in integrative forms of treatment.

Broadcasting/Film/Video Game Careers

- Radio Broadcasting
- Film/TV Broadcasting
- Music Video/Music Special Producer-Director
- Video Game Scorer/Audio Programmer
- Advertising Jingle Writer

Radio Broadcasting

Disc Jockey

Career Description. The individual who masters the ceremony of getting recordings identified and on the air is a key figure in radio broadcasting. In addition to time on the air, the disc jockey (DJ) is usually occupied in a variety of tasks related to the operation of the station. Most station managers try to increase community visibility by encouraging their air personalities to become involved in activities such as being master of ceremonies (MC) for civic affairs such as nonprofit fundraisers, shopping center openings, and judging beauty contests. Many jocks are involved in promoting, even sometimes acting as MC for, rock concerts. DJs in smaller markets are often called on to perform every conceivable task at their stations, from making up **playlists** to sweeping out the studio. A station with a limited budget will also require its DJs to run the audio engineering board concurrently with physically handing the discs and tapes.

Qualifications and Preparation. Some disc jockeys get started with little or no professional training—instead, connecting with employers and audiences by virtue of their outsize personalities and radio-friendly voices. Some self-taught DJs (or on-the-job apprentices) rise to the top of their profession. But the life expectancy of a disc jockey can be short, comparable to that of a professional athlete. Audience tastes change and stations may seek bigger ratings through a new DJ; stations may also switch formats, often necessitating a new group of air personalities; DJs experience burnout from the drain of constantly appearing to be bubbly and entertaining.

Although it is not difficult to get some kind of modest start as a disc jockey, individuals planning a career in broadcasting should take time out to earn a college degree in broadcasting, communication, or an allied field such as music, theater, or media studies. Those who qualify themselves with a good education will almost certainly rise faster in their broadcasting careers than others whose backgrounds may limit their potential for leadership roles.

Employment Prospects. The consolidation of the radio business has put pressure on disc jockey employment. Most jobs are landed through the submission of airchecks accompanied by the individual's résumé. A home tape recording won't do: A station manager wants to hear how the individual sounds on the air during an actual broadcast. Airchecks submitted for audition should have most of the music edited out, retaining only a few seconds to enable the auditor to hear how the performer gets in and out of the music. Those seeking their first job and those changing jobs can learn of available openings by word of mouth and through trade magazines and job boards. Jocks often change jobs as frequently as musicians do. The disc jockey just starting may find opportunities in very small stations whether broadcast, satellite, or online for some kind of tryout, partly because such stations (even some larger ones) pay their inexperienced DJs only minimal wages. By job hopping to bigger markets, DJs can eventually work their way up to big-time **gigs**. Of course, top DJs in major jobs can earn celebrity incomes.

Program Director/Music Director

Career Description. As discussed in Chapter 19, program directors (**PDs**) hold a leadership role at radio stations, including working in consultation with the station's (or station group's) general manager to hire and fire disc jockeys. The PD job also has the responsibility of planning how to best showcase on-air personalities and newscasts. In the past, individual radio stations typically hired a music director (**MD**), who reported to the PD and was solely focused on music issues. However, as radio ownership consolidated, the single-station music director job was often eliminated because program decisions were made at the parent-group level and individual stations followed prescribed formats. Where such a job remains, the MD is responsible for listening to promotional copies of incoming releases, exchanging information with record promoters, analyzing research, and compiling playlists.

Qualifications and Preparation. Some radio PDs gain their background as disc jockeys and may continue as on-the-air personalities with reduced schedules. Radio PDs can perform their jobs well without formal musical backgrounds, depending on their musical intuition. PDs who demonstrate strong leadership qualities may eventually grow into the role of group PD (managing operations at multiple stations) or radio station general manager (GM).

Employment Prospects. As with disc jockeys, competition for PD jobs is most intense in the major radio markets in larger cities. Salaries will rise along with the size of the market in which a PD lands. Within broadcast groups, a station or cluster of stations in the same geography or with similar formats tends to have their own dedicated PDs. There can be another regional layer of program and music executives, and at the top is the centralized headquarters staff.

Film/TV Broadcasting

Composer of Dramatic Music

Career Description. Large numbers of musicians develop full-time careers composing what is generally referred to as "background music" for television and movies but which professionals working in this career prefer to call "the **underscore**." These composers screen the assigned film or other broadcast project and then confer with the film or TV director and/or producer, the **music cutter**, and sometimes the music supervisor (see below) to determine where music should be underscored and just what kind of music would be appropriate for the dramatic situation. Underscoring composers must write at top speed. Producers may demand a score for a 30-minute TV episode, even a 1-hour show, in 1 week or less. Movie producers may require the music score be written and recorded for a feature film within 4 to 6 weeks and sometimes in periods as short as 2 weeks. Even well-established composers in this field experience feast and famine; they live on beans and rice for a while, then suddenly are called on to turn out a 13-week TV series in 3 months and work on a film score concurrently. Hot and cold, rich and poor, that is the pattern.

Generally, TV and film composers must locate in Los Angeles, New York, or a major foreign production center to find work in TV and the movies. Within the field, there is an array of specialization. Some composers specialize in writing musical themes for films and TV series. Others find opportunities writing music for music libraries, which are collections of themes and musical "feels" ranging from **stingers** to longer pieces of a minute or more. These **needle drop** music libraries are used extensively in television in place of original underscoring (see Chapter 25).

Qualifications and Preparation. The musician aspiring to a professional career scoring dramatic music must possess outstanding creative talent. The aspirant must also be highly sensitive to dramatic values, tone painting, and how music can enhance theatrical experience. To have the best competitive edge, film and TV composers should have strong backgrounds in symphonic music and be able to draw from all styles, including hip-hop, ambient, or electronic. Successful film composers today use electronic instruments and computers in all phases of their work, from demos for directors to the final recording itself.

Employment Prospects. The pool of potential TV work has expanded as cable TV shows proliferate. Independent films have also increased, which further creates job opportunities, although many such films don't get theatrical release but instead go direct to DVD, become TV premieres, or surface only online. The most readily employable composers of dramatic music today are those adept at scoring for electronic instruments as well as **acoustic instruments**. One way composers can break into the film world is by first working as orchestrators or apprentices for established composers. For additional kinds of employment prospects in scoring drama, review Chapter 21.

Music Supervisor

Career Description. Starting with the heyday of blockbuster movie soundtracks and continuing through the proliferating channels of cable and satellite TV, music supervision has become an important part of the production process. Album tie-ins are a major marketing item for many movies and television series, and the pressure is on the music supervisor to land promising upcoming artists and established hit makers to pump up the soundtrack and the bottom line. At the other end of the budget world, the music supervisor may have to keep a lid on costs by tapping inexpensive off-the-shelf production music for transition and background uses. A music supervisor's duties for a feature film or television program depend on how the role is viewed by the producers, studio (if applicable), and/or director. In general, the music supervisor is a liaison between the music ("creative") and the business interests on a project.

The music supervisor, who is sometimes called *music director,* may be charged with all, some, or none of the following: preparing a music budget for a project, studio, or production company; hiring a composer, soundtrack producer, music clearance house, and music contractor; clearing recorded music to be used as underscore, source music, or on a soundtrack product; making deals for title songs, end-credit songs, and "special appearances" of current hit bands and artists; overseeing recording sessions; facilitating the composing, prerecording, and technical preparation of source music that will be needed for on-camera use during production ("production music"); securing the services of **sidemusicians** and vocalists for on-camera appearances; and preparing music for DVD and other posttheatrical use. (Music supervisors will also find work in the video game industry; see that section in this chapter for more on this field.)

Qualifications and Preparation. Music supervisors' academic credentials range from bachelor of fine arts in music to no degree at all. Since the job entails a lot of negotiating—for rights and clearances, publishing and performance deals, and so on—many music supervisors have a legal background; some are ex-producers, production assistants, or development personnel who are familiar with the needs of the production process. There are few actual musicians working as music supervisors. Artist-music supervisors (Don Was, David Byrne, T-Bone Burnett) often also function as composers of underscore and/or source music and are usually chosen for the like-minded artists they can attract to a project. There are also ex–rock band sidemusicians, music agents, and managers. Music supervision courses are available in university extension departments (often as part of a music business certificate program), and studios and large music supervision companies often have internships available. Internships lead to assistant positions, which then lead to music supervisor positions. The problem for the musician who seeks to become a music supervisor is that actual musical knowledge—the ability to read, write, perform, and interpret music—is not really needed to do the job, although these abilities certainly can't hurt. Familiarity with popular music styles and artists, knowledge of the production process, extensive contacts in the music and production industries, and the ability to sense a "hit" are all assets.

Employment Prospects. This is one of the few production specialties that has almost unlimited growth potential, because there are no technical qualifications at all and no universally accepted job description. The field remains wide open to people with connections and the ability to get the job done. Virtually every feature film, no matter how low the budget, and every TV series now has a music supervisor on staff (and probably a soundtrack album in production). In addition, most major studios and television networks, as well as large production companies, have staff music supervisors who function as overseers of all the individual projects' music needs. These staff jobs offer more security (in exchange for less money and recognition) because they are not tied to the success of any one hit film or TV series. Staff music supervisors often move into management positions such as music department vice president. Many ex-staffers leave a studio or production company and use the extensive contacts they have built to go into business as independent music supervisors or producers.

Music Editor/Music Cutter

Career Description. Music editors are sometimes called music cutters, referring to the bygone days when an editor's job actually included splicing pieces of audiotape or film together. Music editors are the individuals who are responsible for selection, timing, and synchronization of recorded music to a TV show or a film. Editors also work with music for radio and TV commercials and for music videos. Although many music videos simply present the song as originally recorded, others call for music editors to introduce subtle audio tweaks to mesh with the action in the video script.

Qualifications and Preparation. Those qualified to work as music editor have usually acquired their craft and art as apprentices, working alongside other, more experienced, editors who themselves learned in a master-apprentice relationship over many years. Many good editors are expert musicians. Others are simply very sensitive to how music can enhance dramatic events and do expert work without having acquired formal musical training.

Employment Prospects. The individual seeking a career as a music editor should expect to follow the time-honored apprenticeship training, perhaps getting started on amateur movies or educational or sales films.

Music Video/Music Special Producer-Director

Career Description. The popularity of music videos spiked in the 1980s with the debut of MTV, and they have since become a standard marketing tool for many recording artists. An industry arose around this art form, with teams of directors who specialize in work on music videos. In addition to overseeing the filming, a director's job description can include formulating the "vision" for the video production in consultation with the recording artist. TV music specials are another sector where broadcast-minded music aspirants are employed. Roles here include everything from executive producers and directors to **music coordinators,** audio technicians, arrangers, and copyists.

Qualifications and Preparation. Versatile artists who aspire to direct music videos or other filmed/broadcast musical productions will have spent years in related activities such as songwriting, live musicals, record production, and commercials. Conversely, directors may enter the field from the other direction: They are trained in the production arts first and foremost and pick up what musical knowledge they have as they go along. Both paths are equally valid.

For broadcast newcomers, a good way to learn the craft is directing low-budget videos. Developing a respectable track record in this arena may lead to opportunities for more elaborate projects.

Good preparation can also come from college film/TV programs. Directors sometimes come from the ranks of editors as well as writers. Work on low-budget commercials in local markets could be training for videos, which in turn can lead to longer form work.

Employment Prospects. Although supply exceeds demand, there is always room for a hustling, talented music video director in tune with contemporary tastes. Opportunities to work on music specials are available for qualified aspirants in many different career categories, although the number of such productions is limited.

Video Game Scorer/Audio Programmer

Career Description. This is a career sector for music-minded job aspirants that parallels the film/TV music arena in terms of the need for qualified composers, music supervisors, and sound engineers. Increasingly sophisticated video game platforms have allowed for music on games to move from the "bleeps and blips" of long ago into today's high-quality songs and scores that have been released as popular album soundtracks and performed by major symphony orchestras. Although a good deal of music is simply licensed from record labels for use on the games, there is also a need for composers to create original game music and for audio professionals to provide an array of sound design and sound effects needs. These individuals can work on staff or on a freelance basis for large video game companies and independent game producers.

Qualifications and Preparation. The background required for work in this field will vary widely depending on one's position. Scorers of original game music must possess the creative traits required of all composers and songwriters (see the "Creative Careers" section) but must also be able to write in a style that is based on the need of the game and that reflects the overall setting, emotions, and nonlinear interactivity. Game composers need not be gaming addicts, but it doesn't hurt to enjoy—or at the very least understand—the video game business. In addition to composers/scorers, more technically skewed aspirants can work in this sector as audio programmers and audio directors; these fields usually require a degree in computer science or extensive on-the-job training. Music supervisors and music directors, who may hire composers and supervise programmers, should possess both creative and technical savvy, as well as project management skills.

Employment Prospects. Video game sales have bounced up and down over the years, with corresponding up-and-down appetites for big music budgets. In recent decades, the rise of crossover promotions between record labels, film companies, and big game releases has produced meaningful rewards. The downside in the music industry's heightened interest in video games is the trend toward licensing existing recordings for use on game soundtracks rather than commissioning original music, a maneuver that helps the label if not the composer shut out from a new assignment. Nonetheless, there is an appetite for talented, qualified composers, and those who excel in this field can become stars in their own right. Audio programmers and directors who have a passion for games, a head for technology, and a good feel for music will find themselves with real opportunities.

Advertising Jingle Writer

Career Description. A **jingle** writer is a songwriter/composer/lyricist who specializes in writing music for radio, TV, and online video commercials. These professionals are assigned a product or service and must then craft a composition or song that "fits" with the message/brand identity the client is hoping to convey. Not all jingle writers work exclusively in the field: Some songwriters of popular music write jingles occasionally.

Qualifications and Preparation. Jingle writers must take direction well, since they are responsible for pleasing a client with very specific goals in mind. They should be skilled in many musical styles and be strong arrangers. Needless to say, they must also be able to compose well for a very short form. Lyricists will need to be strong word-smiths with a knack for conveying a message or concept in an accessible, memorable way—and in as few words as possible.

Employment Prospects. There is plenty of work in the advertising field, but there are also plenty of people vying for assignments. Even hit songwriters have competed to compose jingles for major consumer-product brands, such as Coke. The rewards can be lucrative. Smaller ad agencies with smaller businesses for clients provide an opening for newcomers.

Music-Related Careers

- Critic/Journalist/Editor
- Music Librarian
- Science and Technology
- Managerial/Executive
- Sales
- Legal Services
- Visual Arts/Graphics

Some of the careers listed here relate directly to music, others only indirectly (see Table 28.2). Some are open to trained musicians; others offer employment opportunities to nonmusicians. The more prevalent music-related careers are discussed in this section.

Critic/Journalist/Editor

Career Description. Some of history's most distinguished musicians have used their creative energies not just for composing but also to write about music. Although few musicians have managed to perform these two tasks as well as the prolific 19th-century German composer Richard Wagner, today hundreds of creative persons have fashioned careers as music critics, journalists, and editors. Critics will find their work schedules filled with attending concerts and writing up reviews on deadline, and their workdays will be occupied in reviewing endless stacks of new recordings and books on music. Journalists may also act as critics of recordings and shows, but their mandate will probably also include writing news and feature articles about recording artists, industry trends, and events. Editors are often responsible for assigning reviews and articles to other critics and journalists and editing their copy but may also write articles and review music. Those who have both a love of music and a way with words may also find opportunities in other arenas, such as writing liner notes for album releases or music news for broadcast outlets and online music sites.

Qualifications and Preparation. To qualify as a music critic in the classical field, an individual should have a thorough musical education acquired through formalized university-level study or individual effort. Most distinguished critics have grown into their work after long years of observation, study, and publishing commentaries. They not only develop penetrating insights on compositions and performances but manage to write in a style that communicates effectively with a broad general readership.

Table 28.2 A Sampling of Music-Related Careers

Words and Music
Composer
Librettist
Lyricist
Publisher
Writer/Editor
Critic/journalist
Historian
Music services
Music coordinator
Music copyist
Music cutter/editor
Transcriber
Managerial/Executive
Advance person
Artist and repertoire
Administrator/coordinator
Agent (talent agent)
Arts administrator
Artists' union officer
Broadcasting executive
Business manager
Company manager (TV, theater)
Concert promoter
Development director (arts)
Market research director
Nightclub manager
Orchestra manager
Personal manager
Personnel director
Product manager (recordings)

(Continued)

Table 28.2   (Continued)

Production manager
Professional manager
Recording company executive
Recording studio manager
Road manager
Stage manager
Studio manager
Talent coordinator
Tour coordinator
Traffic manager
Broadcasting/Advertising
Disc jockey
Jingle writer
Program director/music director
Promotional staff
Research director
Spot producer/director
Business/Merchandising
Concert promoter
Music merchant
Music wholesaler/distributor
Publicist
Salesperson
Ticket sales manager/agent
Education
Music education supervisor
Music librarian
Music therapist
Teacher-school
Teacher-studio
Arts/Graphics
Commercial artist

Graphic artist
Visual synthesist
Web designer
Music Production (Theater, Film, TV)
Arranger
Audio technician/engineer
Choreographer/dancer
Composer
Conductor
Church music director
Costume designer
Director/supervisor
Floor manager
Instrumentalist
Music coordinator
Orchestra contractor
Producer/executive producer
Singer/actor
Stage director
Stage manager
Studio musician
Synthesis specialist
Talent coordinator
Technical director
Science and Technology
Audio engineer/technician
Computer music programmer
Digital audio editor
Digital remastering engineer
Equipment designer
Equipment maintenance technician
Instrument designer/manufacturer/repairer
Mastering technician

(Continued)

Table 28.2 **(Continued)**

Multimedia developer
Music/rerecording mixer
Piano tuner/technician
Recording engineer
Studio designer/acoustician
Legal Services
Copyright researcher
Copyright lawyer
Entertainment business lawyer
Music rights manager
Paralegal

Not all critics meet these criteria, of course; it is not unusual for a newspaper to ask a general-assignment reporter to cover concerts and review recordings.

Critics in other forms of music, including pop and rock, are less likely to have formal music educations, although most will have a passion for music developed from their earliest years and an endless enthusiasm for hearing new bands and fresh material. Many are at least amateur musicians, although this is not a prerequisite. Nonmusicians who work as critics may tend to focus more on the lyrics of a composition or on the personalities of the performers than on the music itself.

Music journalists need at least basic reporting skills—the ability to conduct interviews with multiple sources, to assemble and check facts, and to write a compelling narrative. Editors should also have those journalistic chops, along with knowledge of the newspaper, magazine, or website production process, and the ability to set and enforce deadlines.

Employment Prospects. Staff jobs for music critics at traditional media have dwindled as more of the work goes to freelancers. There are fewer full-time jobs for music editors as well. TV, radio, and print media find the value of their professional critic reviews diminished as cyberspace is jammed with postings from amateur bloggers. Aspiring freelancers should contact the appropriate editor (e.g., the music editor, reviews editor, entertainment editor) for submission requirements. Cyberspace also presents a host of new outlets for writers and editors, including writing up local concert reviews for online city guides, music-news sites, and other types of websites with dedicated music sections, such as social websites.

Those with little previous writing experience would be advised to start by approaching smaller outlets and publications, such as college and neighborhood newspapers, city guides, local magazines, or even local access television. The pay will be low (or nonexistent), but the work will build up a writer's all-important "clips file" and possibly lead to better paying opportunities.

The great majority of critics and music reporters earn salaries comparable to most other journalists, which are not high, although those who get jobs at major newspapers or magazines can be well compensated. Freelance rates will depend on the size of the publication, ranging from a free CD in exchange for a review (commonplace) all the way up to a few dollars per word for a feature article (a rarity).

Individuals wishing to pursue the various kinds of employment available in writing about music can obtain further information from the Music Critics Association of North America.

Music Librarian

Career Description. Librarians are employed in a variety of settings. The most familiar are individuals working in college and public libraries as music specialists. Some of these jobs involve little more than clerking. At the other end of the scale are the trained music catalogers and researchers who apply knowledgeable judgments and perform sophisticated, occasionally even scholarly tasks.

Qualifications and Preparation. At traditional institutional libraries, all but the smallest employ paraprofessionals and professionals. For the former, college degrees are sometimes required. Individuals aspiring to careers as fully professional music librarians should plan to acquire a baccalaureate degree in music, preferably with a concentration in music history and literature. Then they should plan to go on to a master's degree in library science, preferably from a university with a well-respected curriculum. Few libraries will consider applicants lacking these credentials. Another kind of music librarian is employed by production music libraries. For these jobs, the qualifications are a solid and broad knowledge of musical styles, both contemporary and historical; a terrific musical memory; and an affinity for detail work. No degree is required, but those with degrees in musicology may have an edge.

Employment Prospects. Library work increasingly means navigating electronic archives in addition to paper media, so job descriptions and work opportunities are in flux. Being adept at archival work via online research is key to expanding job prospects as institutions and private industry seek out specialists to navigate humanity's vast repository of musical expression.

Science and Technology

Sound Engineer/Technician

Career Description. Individuals employed in the technical aspects of sound reinforcement, recording, and broadcasting are generally referred to as engineers, which implies a high level of expertise. Many in the field are more properly called *technicians* because their skills are confined to operating equipment. The appellation *audio engineer* is more accurately reserved for university graduates who hold degrees in electrical engineering or, perhaps, physics, audiology, acoustics, or computer science. These engineers engage in work such as research and development of audio equipment, studio and equipment design, record mastering, equipment maintenance, and sound mixing. Most of these engineers are employed full-time by equipment manufacturers, sound reinforcement companies, recording studios, radio and TV stations, and film studios. Some engineers are assigned only one type of work, such as design or maintenance or audio mixing. In smaller firms, audio engineers perform a variety of tasks.

Employers also hire audio technicians, who may or may not have a university-level education. Many audio technicians and mixers are simply talented, self-taught handypersons who, through years of apprenticeship, earn job assignments that involve sophisticated technology. Most engineers and technicians are attracted to these music-related jobs by their love for music, and some of them hold college degrees in music or have studied music informally. The art of sound mixing demands considerable musical knowledge and the ability to make sensitive aural judgments.

Qualifications and Preparation. To qualify for employment as a sound engineer, university degrees in both electrical engineering and music would be ideal, but few professionals are so prepared. With the increasing sophistication of audio equipment, employers more and more require not just audio technicians but sound engineers and computer scientists as well. Engineers believing they may find employment in broadcasting will have to qualify for an **FCC** operator's license. Individuals who want to go to the top in recording technology and sound engineering should not only study as much music as they can but also go on to at least some studies in acoustics. Such persons might be called on to design and build state-of-the-art recording studios. All engineers will be expected to keep up with the latest trends in recording technology.

Employment Prospects. Although there are many people jockeying for engineering positions, those professionals who have demonstrated the qualities outlined above will be in demand and can enjoy good earnings. Those who want to establish long-term careers in this business will also have another qualification not found on any résumé: a high tolerance for stress and tension, required when dealing with unpredictable equipment problems.

Sound engineer in a television gallery.
Photo © antb/iStock.

Instrument Design/Maintenance

Career Description/Qualifications/Prospects. From early times, the inventors and designers of musical instruments have held a distinguished place in the history of the art. Although the basic design of most acoustic musical instruments was set centuries ago, scientists and technicians continue not only to improve instruments but also to invent new ones. Persons interested in the physics of sound, acoustics, and electronics manage to develop music-related careers. It cannot be said that there is a big demand for instrument designers, but positions can be found for qualified persons with manufacturing companies, particularly those involved in developing ever-newer electronic instruments.

As for careers in the field of instrument maintenance, there is a shortage in most communities of competent instrument repair technicians. Qualified repair technicians can just about choose where they want to live, then knock on the door of the nearest instrument repair shop and go to work the same day.

Other jobs await qualified maintenance personnel in school systems, colleges, and universities, not to mention the armed services. Persons aspiring to such careers can acquire their training in some junior colleges and some universities. It is more common, however, for aspirants to learn their craft as apprentices to masters.

Repair technicians often specialize in keyboard instruments. Many communities lack fully qualified piano technicians/tuners. The best of them have been factory trained or learned their craft as apprentices. Fortunately, piano tuners today do not even have to have a true sense of pitch. Tuning can be accurately handled with the use of electronic pitch-measuring machines that are readily available with piano repair kits. Piano technicians are almost always **independent contractors** working out of their homes; they set their own hours and vacation periods. The competent ones are in demand and make a good living.

There is also a shortage of electronic keyboard maintenance personnel. Those who acquire competence in repairing electronic keyboard instruments will be able to find steady employment at good pay. And those with musical backgrounds will, on most jobs, be able to do a better job than just straight technicians.

With the proliferation of lower cost electronic musical equipment of all kinds, it is safe to predict that steady employment at good pay will be available to those who take the time to educate themselves in electronics and music.

Online Music Developer/Operator

Career Description. Those with a love of both music and technology have many career options these days, thanks to the rapid growth of the new-media music business. Companies ranging from global media conglomerates to bootstrap startups are pushing into music-related online businesses. All of these businesses need talented individuals to do everything from setting up and maintaining websites to coding music to designing new site features and promotions, managing content and the user experience, and technical support. In addition, individuals with the requisite abilities in both music and statistics can find positions as analysts in companies of all sizes, while tech-savvy creative types can carve out a business sideline developing sites for fellow artists hoping to promote and sell their music online.

Qualifications and Preparation. Although there are many opportunities for creative people in the online medium, these positions put the emphasis on technical know-how over music industry savvy. Candidates in some cases can be self-taught, but a degree in computer science may be required to open doors for other more technical positions. For software developers particularly, knowledge of multiple computer languages and operating systems is highly desirable. One way to break into the market is to start with exposure through social networking sites and build from there.

Employment Prospects. There is no shortage of people with new media career goals, but candidates with a combination of both advanced technical chops *and* music smarts will find themselves in high demand.

Managerial/Executive

Career Description. Individuals not involved directly in music making can develop successful careers in the business and managerial sectors of the arts and entertainment industry. Many options await them in areas including record labels, artist management firms, public relations companies, music publishers, music video networks, and royalty-collecting societies, among many others. Career patterns are often circuitous. The person who aspires to become an artists' manager may start out in music publishing and end up in record production. The individual who initially wants to run a talent agency may experience greater success as a TV executive. Fast learners who are quick on their feet will seize career opportunities as they develop, but the most creative executives don't wait for job offers; they create their own opportunities.

Qualifications and Preparation. The college or university graduate who has gone through an educational program that integrates music and business and the recording arts has the advantage in breaking into the field. These graduates often have experience with college radio stations or college concert boards. Dozens of colleges and universities in the United States and Canada now offer these kinds of curricula, and their graduates are finding places in the arts and entertainment industry.

Two of the best forms of educational preparation for careers in management are a law degree or a Master of Business Administration (MBA). The higher someone climbs in business, the more valuable those kinds of underpinnings prove.

Of all the music-related career options available, arts administration may present one of the greatest challenges to an individual's versatility and imagination. Educational institutions with degree programs leading to professional employment in that area include Yale University, New York University, and others that can be found via the Association of Arts Administration Educators.

How does one qualify as an arts administrator? A master's degree will probably help. For a fuller answer, review Chapter 18.

Employment Prospects. All music fields, including musical instrument retailers, nonprofit art centers, educational institutions, and concert venues, require management with an affinity for music. And although record labels have been undergoing consolidation and belt-tightening in recent years, they are still large, complicated operations with an ongoing need for new employees and fresh executive-track talent. A clear indication of the need for music business executives is the track record of schools offering music business studies. Those students who take the time to prepare themselves in business and music will be among the most sought-after executives.

Sales

Career Description. No matter how polished the musician or well produced the album, the music business couldn't function without the too-often-unsung talents of another group of individuals: the salespeople. Thousands of careers in the music business are available for individuals who prefer to involve themselves in the marketing or sales of goods and services relating to the industry—the "business" end of the music business equation. Jobs in this sector run the gamut from record store clerks and managers to music merchandisers and distributors to top label sales and marketing executives and everything in between. Whether a product is a physical good, an intangible digital offering, or a live performance, somewhere in the mix is a need for advertising, packaging, and selling by savvy specialists.

Qualifications and Preparation. Until recent years, a music merchant or talented salesperson did not require a university degree to succeed in the music business. Such a person could often make it, at least for a while, just being "street smart." But as the music business has become increasingly dominated by career migration across many branches of a diverse industry, the person who wants to rise to the top may find an edge in a strong academic background. Jobs are now going to the merchants and agents and promoters with expertise in fields such as market research, brand marketing, advertising, accounting, and finance.

Employment Prospects. Individuals who are fully prepared and motivated for work in the sales and marketing side of contemporary business will find good career opportunities. Even in periods of economic downturn, employers will usually take on an employee who can sell—if not on salary, at least on commission. While local retailers offer an entry-level opportunity for music-business job seekers, those with strong university training in music and business will find many more doors opened for them in multiple business sectors. Whatever the educational background, a musician-businessperson's ultimate achievements will probably be governed more by imagination and drive. Armed with these two attributes, the aspirant will create "luck." As more than one person of achievement has expressed it, "The harder I work, the luckier I get."

Legal Services

Career Description. The music business requires the services of legal experts, because nearly every aspect of the industry involves copyright law, the negotiation of contracts, and business dispute resolution. Even though all law schools train their students in contracts, it is often difficult for an attorney in general practice to be sufficiently well informed to handle certain kinds of music business agreements. In the field of copyright, the attorney lacking expertise may be unable to counsel clients adequately.

Qualifications and Preparation. Law students who believe that they will want to practice entertainment law should focus their studies on **intellectual property**, including copyright, patent and trademark, contract, talent agency agreements, unfair competition, privacy, and publicity rights. The individual who is attracted to the law but lacks the means or opportunity to attend law school may be able to carve out a career track as a copyright researcher, music rights agent, or paralegal with more limited professional training.

Employment Prospects. There is an oversupply of attorneys who bring nothing to the dance besides a license to practice and a willing attitude. Attorneys who graduated from top law schools and who have impressive, relevant industry experience often get full-time positions as legal counsel for firms such as publishers, recording companies, and film studios; some may rise up the ranks to senior executive positions in their companies. Others go into artist management. Because the rise of new technologies has created a host of complicated copyright and contracts issues (not to mention lawsuits), attorneys familiar with such new-media issues will be viewed as particularly attractive employment prospects. In addition, those who have already established careers in some aspect of the music industry before attending law school (or who attend concurrently while holding down their day job) may have a leg up on other applicants for music-business legal positions. For an extensive treatment of the role of lawyers in the music business, review Chapter 8.

Visual Arts/Graphics

Career Description. Creative persons in the aural and visual arts have often worked in close alliance. Some have been talented in both fields. For example, Schoenberg and Gershwin were good painters; Stravinsky worked closely with Picasso in stage design and costuming. Today, musical performers must be attractively staged and costumed. Music merchandise must be packaged to sell. These demands create many career opportunities for talented individuals interested in graphics and other visual arts. Job descriptions include designing the covers and packaging for albums and creating promotional posters, advertising layouts, and online marketing materials. In the music video sector, opportunities exist for scenic artists and production designers.

Qualifications and Preparation. Aspirants to positions as art directors or graphic designers should have a good working knowledge of computer graphics and an artistic "eye." Formal training is strongly preferred. Some professionals study commercial art and graphics, whereas others enter the field from a fine arts background. Those specializing in the hot field of user experience (UX) can also benefit from training in statistics and experimental psychology. A sensitivity to music and an ability to bridge the sometimes conflicting demands from the "creative" and "sales" sides of a project are also key to success in serving record labels, concert promoters, retail chains, and the industry's many other sophisticated users of good visual design.

Employment Prospects. As digital business initiatives proliferate, those who can design and operate online platforms are in high demand. Recording companies alone require the services of many graphic artists, whom they employ on staff or on a freelance basis. Commercial art companies contracted to do work for music firms also offer employment opportunities for individuals skilled in creating the striking packaging and displays that are all-important in catching the consumer's eye. Self-employment is a realistic goal for the truly talented who have a "serve the client" mentality.

Entrepreneurs/Starting Your Own Business

Many persons of independent mind choose not to work as an employee, preferring to "go it alone." While the odds of success for any new business are probably the same as they ever were, the monetary risks of failure have often lessened as the required capital investment for a startup has dropped due to cheaper and more versatile technology tools.

Some entrepreneurs choose to launch their own independent businesses in traditional music industry sectors, such as with production firms, concert promotion organizations, management companies, or music-publishing businesses. Others are

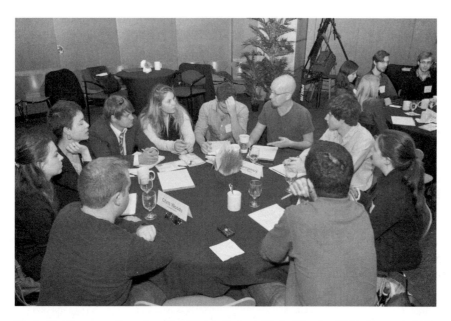

Mark Montgomery, Founder, Flo{Thinkery}, and Chris Woods, COO, Tunesat, both distinguished entrepreneurs with their own startups, advise Berklee Music Business/ Management students during an afternoon session as part of the department's annual Envisioning 21st Century Music Business Models Series.
Photo by Phil Farnsworth.

innovators, seeking out new music market niches to tap and services to offer, either online or offline.

See Chapter 26 about powering up a **DIY** ambition and Chapter 27 for more information about establishing any kind of new company.

▌Note

1. In 1956, star vocalist Dinah Shore advised 19-year-old Barry Freeman to take a job plugging her records with Los Angeles disc jockeys. He questioned whether he could handle the job without a college degree, prompting her to shrug off his concerns with this statement. Freeman went on to a successful 52-year career in the industry.

Chapter Takeaways

- The music industry is populated by far more than a small group of household names hauling down rich paydays.

- Numerous fulfilling music or music-related careers exist in the realms of composing, directing/producing, performing, education, radio, music video, advertising, journalism criticism, library science, merchandising, technology, equipment design or maintenance, management, distribution, and legal affairs.

- To succeed, "liking" music isn't enough. Winning professionals need full preparation, hard work, and luck.

Key Terms

- aircheck   (p. 475)
- angels   (p. 456)
- clips file   (p. 484)

- combination career   (p. 460)
- comp style   (p. 467)
- independent contractor (p. 487)

- master-apprentice (p. 478)
- terminal degree   (p. 458)

Discussion Questions

1. In your opinion, which career path listed in the chapter currently holds the most promise for employment for someone with your goals and abilities?

2. What has had the most impact on the number of open jobs in a given field?

3. Does the "dumb as a rope" view Dinah Shore voiced in 1956 apply today? Defend your opinion with evidence.

4. What are some good combinations of music careers? Why do many people in music end up engaging in more than one music career?

5. Discuss the career path of a successful musician you admire. What different jobs has that person done? How did that person succeed?

Career Development

Defining Goals

Recent studies reveal that one of the most frequently named career goals is involvement in some aspect of music. Millions of young people are drawn to music and dream of becoming part of the profession. But many of these dreams are poorly defined. Aspirants can be attracted by the glamour and big money of the music and entertainment fields but have no clear idea of how to break in.

> "Eighty percent of success is showing up."
>
> —Woody Allen

The world of music and entertainment has always had a certain mystique. The most visible people in these fields seem to be rich and famous. Producing and selling music can be enjoyable and profitable, but there's much more going on backstage, off-camera. In this backstage world, there are thousands of individuals who are employed quite regularly, earning respectable incomes—and enjoying what they are doing.

Landing a Job Versus Building a Career. It is important to distinguish between a "job" and a "career." To borrow from Gertrude Stein, a job is a job (is a job). But a career, properly defined, is an ongoing series of related jobs (or self-employment roles) that add up to a sequence that has continuity and development.

Using Counselors. Although employment counselors may not be able to address everything a person may need, they are probably the most competent people in the community to offer professional help, or what can be called structured intervention. Most counselors have information concerning career options and statistical projections of employment prospects. One of the useful services a qualified counselor can offer is

Left: The Beatles.

Photo © John Launois/Black Star/PNI.

assisting aspirants in finding out who they are. Counselors can offer aptitude tests, interest measurements, and temperament tests. The objectivity and value of these tests and measurements remain in dispute, but they are almost always somewhat helpful, and career seekers should avail themselves of every possible opportunity to find out where they may excel and just what makes them tick.

For people out of high school and college, counselors are available through state employment services. In larger communities, professional career counselors, independent of the government, are available, with payment of a fee. People who are still in high school or college can, of course, seek out their school's advisers and career placement and development staff.

Discovering Yourself. Concurrently with defining career goals, you should try to define *yourself*—analyze not only your interests but also your particular temperament and personality. Along with this personal discovery should come measurement of aptitudes and talents. In addition to doing all you can to discover who and what you are, you should obtain outside appraisals from qualified professionals.

A large part of the workforce is probably miscast. Whole lifetimes can be spent in frustration and failure. Although there are many different reasons for unsuccessful professional growth, very often these workers started off before they knew who they were or considered whether they could meet the competition. Well-planned careers do not always work out, but if you proceed sensibly, using all available information, at the very least you will have reduced the probability of failing in a chosen field.

Many students have used the "Discovering Yourself" form (see Table 29.1), devised particularly for people interested in careers in the arts and the music business. There is no "passing" or "failing" score. Rather, the answers should be interpreted and evaluated in light of the information set forth in these pages concerning music-related careers and the kinds of talents and personalities that have been found appropriate in pursuing certain such careers. For example, if your answers show a dislike for travel and fear of not always having a steady job, you might be unhappy and unsuccessful in attempting to build a career as a performing musician. On the other hand, if your highest priority is being free to create and there is little concern about job security, you might be a strong candidate for building a career as a composer or record producer.

Besides understanding your own interests and value system, it is equally important at this early stage to conduct an inventory of personal strengths, weaknesses, and talents. The accompanying form (Table 29.2) can assist you in these assessments; to be useful, they must be rendered as objectively as possible.

Inaccurate talent appraisals are readily available. For example, a musician who works every Saturday night at the local American Legion Hall can offer a "professional" opinion but may have no idea what level of talent or what type of specific musical skill is required in the major recording studios. The local singing teacher may hold an advanced degree in music but not know what would be expected of voice students seeking work in broadcast commercials. Many of our university professors of music composition do not know the level of talent (and craft) demanded of film composers. Seek the opinion of such people because they have valuable knowledge, but also seek the advice, when possible, of people who have achieved some level of success in the specific career in which you are interested.

If, through systematic appraisal of temperament and talent, the aspiring musician discovers a love of music but no desire to perform, there still are scores of career options in music-related fields. Many musicians are surprised to find that they can be successful in the business world. Many of the same qualities that make a good musician are also important to a music businessperson: perseverance, a willingness to

Table 29.1 Discovering Yourself

Effective career planning should begin with careful self-appraisal. What is important to you? What makes you most effective? What kinds of talents do you have? Place a number from 1 to 10 in the appropriate spaces below. Think of the number 1 as "low," "little," or "poor," depending on the nature of the category. Use the number 5 for "average." Number 10 means "high," "a lot," or "very important." After you have indicated your own appraisals, seek an outside professional opinion to learn if others view you as you see yourself.

My Value System		
	My Estimate	**Outside Estimate**
Need for respect from others		
Need for prestige, status		
Need for audience approval		
Desire for peace of mind		
Need to be liked		
Desire to be loved		
Need for artistic freedom		
Concern for health		
Desire for leisure time		
Desire to have children		
Importance of artistic achievement		
Importance of job security		
Importance of money		
Tolerance for jobs demanding travel		
Desire for personal development		
Desire for artistic development		

work as much time as it takes to get the job done well, and a strong belief in one's own abilities. Of course, it is also helpful to have a "good ear" and to love music.

Climbing the Ladder

No two people hold the same views on just what constitutes success. To many, the professional who earns a good living has achieved success. But in the arts, many individuals place a higher value on personal fulfillment or artistic idealism. They refuse to be seduced by the dollar; they won't "go commercial," preferring to hold to their conception of artistic integrity, whatever the consequences.

Table 29.2 **My Strengths, Weaknesses, Talent**

This form can be revealing for both musicians and people in business. Use the 1–10 numbering system described in Table 29.1				
	Today		When Fully Developed	
	My Estimate	Outside Estimate	My Estimate	Outside Estimate
Motivation, ambition				
Self-confidence				
Creative talent				
Performing ability				
Musical knowledge				
Business sense				
Effectiveness as an oral communicator				
Ability as an organizer				
General leadership ability				
Musical leadership ability				
Capacity to accept direction				
Ability to work with others				
Understanding of the music profession				
Understanding of the music business				
Emotional stability, health				
Intelligence				
Capacity for musical growth				
Capacity for personal growth				
Personal habits				
Ability to adjust to change				
My strongest personal attribute				
My strongest talent				

How many people in the working world are happy with what they do for a living? Many surveys have been conducted; most of them indicate that *more than half* of those interviewed were unhappy with their jobs. Unhappiness over low pay was rarely the number-one concern. Those interviewed have most often complained they felt trapped in their jobs and had little confidence they had a chance to "get ahead."

A majority of those asked stated that, if they had the opportunity, they would change their line of work. Those planning an arts-related career have to know at the outset that they are engaging in a high-risk enterprise. But even though careers in the arts, particularly music, often provide only minimum security, many aspirants would not give up the personal rewards the field offers in exchange for more stable employment.

For those who contemplate climbing the music career ladder, it will be helpful to be aware of the following:

1. Most music-related careers are combination careers. For example, many performers also teach music students in schools or in private studios.

2. Most people experience serial careers; they move from job to job, not necessarily because they quit or get fired but because of the nature of the profession. A typical example is a person who starts out as a gofer; then begins to get a few music copying jobs; may then progress to arranging, composing, perhaps getting into the publishing business; and eventually becomes involved in artist management and record production. Each job helps the individual prepare for the next step.

3. The music business offers decreasing opportunities for the poorly prepared. The jobs offering the best potential for advancement go more and more to well-educated, genuinely competent individuals.

4. Men still dominate the business. Women, with some notable exceptions, are underrecognized, underused, and underpaid at some levels of the business.

5. Young people tend to dominate the creative and performing aspects of popular music. Persons of more mature years tend to dominate the field of serious music, music teaching, and the business and managerial facets of both popular and serious music.

6. All professions within all fields are characterized by rapid change. But in music, career opportunities change every day. New jobs and new opportunities keep coming along.

Finding Work

Career counselors and research experts declare that at any given moment during stable economic times in the United States, there are millions of job openings of all kinds. The person pounding the pavement searching for work scoffs at such a figure when unable to discover even one opening. However, many music and entertainment industry employers complain they cannot find really qualified employees and insist the openings are there for individuals of demonstrated ability. Surveys show that many companies would either offer jobs or create new positions for people who could produce more, sell more, write better, work harder, or manage more efficiently.

Networking. Most career counselors urge job hunters to develop what is often called a "network" of personal and professional contacts. It takes time to develop a strong supportive group of people who will speak well of you, but nothing could be more valuable in building a career. An effective network need not be limited to persons of high influence; the best contact could turn out to be a casual acquaintance in a Laundromat who mentions that so-and-so's band is looking for new people. Social networking sites like LinkedIn and Facebook can become vital tools in your job search.

Most jobs in the music business are never advertised or made known to outsiders. In this field, there is often no need to place ads for help. Applicants line up immediately when word hits the street that some job may be coming up. So who gets the call? As with most fields of endeavor, what really counts in the music business is word of mouth. In short, "Who do you know who could cut it? Who might be ready for this job?" The individual who is prepared has built a good reputation and has a network of supportive contacts—that person wins in the end. Of course, once your network has helped you to get an interview or a job, you also need the specific skills or knowledge required for that job. If you are able to get a job without these skills, you'll have a chance to succeed if you have a good, basic knowledge of the business you're entering so that you can build on the understanding you already have. When you become part of the music business, you'll still need to build on what you've learned through classes and texts like this one, but you'll have a good foundation on which to build.

Internships. Many college music industry programs require or strongly recommend that the student serve an internship as part of the degree requirements. Internships can provide valuable, practical examples of concepts learned in school. They can also help in two other very important ways:

1. They can give you actual experience in the industry. This experience can look very good on your résumé.

2. They can help you build your network of contacts. If you do good work during your internship, the professionals with whom you have worked are more likely to offer you a job or help you find employment after you've graduated. They may also give you permission to use their names as references. A successful intern understands that the internship can act as an audition for a job and will show up early for work and stay late, looking for ways to be useful and things to learn.

Personality, Work Habits. Another major influence on career development is the matter of human personality. Many jobs are won or lost not so much on intelligence and skill as on dependability, flexibility, and congeniality. Research in the field of counseling has revealed that career problems are usually "people problems." Can you be counted on? Can you work effectively with others, or does your network of contacts report back that you are difficult to get along with, that you are not always dependable? People, then—their word about you—can thrust you forward or hold you back.

The Value of Research. If your network of contacts is working for you, not against you, job opportunities are bound to come up. Before trying to get an interview, carefully research your prospective employer. Focus your fact finding on trying to discover what the employer needs most. Present yourself as a solution to the problem. An employer is really searching for an employee who will solve problems. For example, your chances of getting hired might hinge largely on your perceived ability to follow through—filling the shoes of a predecessor whose most annoying shortcoming, perhaps, was never finishing an assignment. Individuals who get hired, get promoted, and earn the most generally appear to have their egos under control and expend their energies trying to make the boss look good.

The Résumé. Job hunters automatically assume that they must send out a lot of résumés to gain the interest of prospective employers. But the usefulness of circulating dozens, perhaps hundreds, of résumés is very limited: Many studies show that only a few jobs are landed through résumé submission. Dozens of books on the subject are readily available; one of the best is Richard Bolles's *What Color Is Your Parachute?* Résumé-writing techniques are covered in other books, so here, information on that subject is limited to what might be especially useful in seeking music business–related employment.

Gaining Interviews. All résumés should be accompanied by a cover letter requesting an interview or audition. Again, you must translate your aspirations to solving your potential employer's perceived needs:

1. Directly address your résumé and letter only to the individual with the authority to hire you.

2. Everything you put in the documents should focus on one thing: helping attain the reader's goals.

3. Keep in mind that all the résumé and letter can really do is describe your past. The reader must guess what your past might indicate for your future and your usefulness to the company tomorrow.

4. Do not use negatives such as "fired" and "didn't like my boss."

5. Use colorful terms to describe jobs you have performed. If you ran errands, don't say you were a "gofer." Try "production assistant."

6. Don't list references, but be sure to state they are available.

7. Emphasize "you," not "I." The first sentence in your letter, or at least one in your first paragraph, should state precisely what you can do to help fulfill the employer's needs.

8. The résumé and letter should be perfectly typed, with correct spelling, grammar, and punctuation.

9. Your résumé and cover letter should each be only one page. The reader is too busy to read your life story.

10. The final sentence should specify just what next step you want the reader to take.

If your résumé and cover letter hit the prospective employer right, you may be invited to interview. In that case, intensify your research on what the company is looking for and what you might expect from the particular interviewer. Don't go in cold. The best books on how to handle yourself in job interviews generally agree on the following:

1. Dress appropriately, in line with other employees at the firm working at levels near the one you might be assigned.

2. Your interviewer may not know how to conduct a job interview properly. Be helpful; raise appropriate questions, if necessary, to deliver useful information about yourself and what you might do for the firm.

3. Don't get too cozy, too breezy—or too formal. Be respectful yet congenial.

4. Learn what the job normally pays, then ask for a little more (not a lot more).

5. Focus on how you believe you can help solve the interviewer's needs.

6. Immediately following the interview—the same day—send a thank-you note to the interviewer for the opportunity provided for you to learn more about the firm. Your thoughtfulness might favorably impress the interviewer.

7. Attend as many job interviews as you can; such experiences often tend to reduce nervousness and increase effectiveness.

Applying these suggestions should be helpful, but successful interviews often depend on intangibles. For example, if the conversation affords you an opportunity to suggest a new idea for the company (usually hard to do), that one contribution might yield a job offer. Or if you and the prospective employer get into discussing a mutual acquaintance, a personal consideration of this kind might help create an atmosphere of trust. A job offer could follow.

It makes little difference in the music business at what level of entry the newcomer breaks into the field. Associates will quickly assess competence, and that person's career will rise or fall accordingly. As has been stressed time and again here, artistic and financial success in the music business is possible, even likely, when you can present this package to the world:

- You have genuine talent.
- You have the right temperament.
- You get the important information.
- You have earned the respect of qualified associates.
- You have the will to win.
- Hang in there.

Chapter Takeaways

- To chart career success, use counselors, self-assessment tests, and other resources to determine strengths and weaknesses, likes and dislikes.

- Choosing the right career path is crucial: More than half the population is unhappy at work.

- Your reputation for competence within a strong network of contacts can be the ticket to getting a good job.

Key Terms

- artistic freedom   (p. 497)
- combination careers   (p. 499)
- job security   (p. 496)
- internship   (p. 500)
- résumé   (p. 500)
- success   (p. 495)

Discussion Questions

1. What do you think is the most important factor in job satisfaction—being well paid or having the chance to be creative? Why?

2. What are employers generally looking for in an employee?

3. What are some important steps in finding work?

4. If your goal is to be self-employed, should your initial career-building steps be the same?

5. Discuss your personal strengths, weaknesses and talents, using Table 29.2.

The Global View

CHAPTER 30

The World Outside The United States

Phil Hardy and Dave Laing

T he international music industry has experienced a sea change as opportunities for global exposure and sales have emerged, opportunities that would have been unimaginable only a few years ago. A confluence of factors—the digital revolution, the Internet, increased globalization, the opening up of huge markets like China and Russia, and the continued consolidation of music companies—have significantly altered the landscape for artists, labels, music publishers, and other music-related entities, from the largest conglomerate with offices around the globe to the lone musician doing it all in the basement. The digital revolution has been a mixed blessing, spawning a new set of challenges, as we'll see later in this chapter.

> "You can never get silence anywhere nowadays, have you noticed?"
>
> —Bryan Ferry

The vital importance of the "global" aspect of the global music business makes it imperative for artists and companies to rethink everything from touring to the myriad means of marketing and sales (including online sales, digital downloads, **streaming,** music subscription services, ringtones, websites, blogs, and social networking). The reduced costs of recording, marketing, and distribution, along with the lightning speed of digital international commerce, have made it possible not only for superstars to brand themselves throughout the world but also for independent and genre artists to develop micro-brands and market their products to specific locales and to dispersed niche audiences.

Left: Panamanian pianist Danilo Perez performs at the 35th International Jazz Festival of Vitoria, in Spain.

Photo © Adrian Ruiz de Hierro/epa/Corbis.

Globalization has wrought many changes in the way music is consumed in various countries, creating more cross-cultural opportunities than ever before. First of all, MTV established networks in many territories, giving exposure to the local music of, say, Israel in the United States and vice versa. Similarly, record companies' and artists' increased reliance on the Internet and the spread of social networking sites, most notably Facebook, have increased the international success of U.S. acts elsewhere in the world and vice versa. The French disc jockey David Guetta accumulated over 60 million likes on his Facebook page, while the first video on YouTube with over two billion views was "Gangnam Style" by the South Korean artist Psy.

The result has been an explosion in the demand for music but not necessarily an increase in the revenues of recorded music companies and artists. To improve the marketing of new releases, the international record industry decided in 2015 to nominate Friday as Global Release Day. The intention was to alleviate the frustration felt by consumers in the globalized market when some music fans can listen to and buy new releases before others. The industry also hoped that synchronizing the online release date would reduce the amount of unauthorized downloading of new tracks.

Live performances in markets outside the United States are more important than ever in developing careers for recording artists. Fans in Europe, Australia, and Japan can be much more open to new artists than those in the United States. Having acts get on the international road to play clubs, concerts, and festivals is perhaps the single most productive way to develop or broaden a fan base, which in turn stimulates revenue for both new and established acts.

The International Scene

Challenges

Because the global economy is so intertwined, key challenges facing the international music business mirror those in the United States. In recent years, the most pressing issues for the recorded music industry worldwide have been a continuing decline in income and the opportunities and threats posed by the Internet and the digital revolution.

The dramatic decline in **soundcarrier** (CDs, tapes) sales has various causes, and it has affected regions around the world in different ways. After years of benefiting from the success of DVD-format concert films and music videos, record companies worldwide have been hurt by the collapse of the overall DVD market as most consumers now access audiovisual product through nonphysical formats.

Despite an improvement in living standards in many parts of Asia, Africa, and Latin America, counterfeiting of CDs and DVDs in those regions remains a problem. In more affluent regions such as Western Europe, Japan, and Australasia, declining spending on soundcarriers principally stems from competition for disposable income from many sources, including legal digital formats, electronic games, mobile telephones, and streaming audio services. Unlawful file sharing via **P2P** networks has also posed significant problems in world markets, but the advent of streaming music sites such as Spotify and Pandora, widespread blocking of P2P websites, and the threat of "three strikes" legislation by governments have reduced P2P's impact. At the same time, **piracy** levels in Russia and China have declined following the demise of the pirate site AllofMP3 in Russia and the licensing of Chinese search engine Baidu by leading international record companies.

In the late 1990s, many experts forecast that online music sales would quickly come to represent a large proportion of global record industry income. These predictions were soon proven premature, in part because the necessary infrastructure was not in place and in part because of only a tentative commitment by the major international record companies, which feared the Internet would reduce their degree of control over their releases. However, within a few years, the digital revolution, which now included mobile as well as online recorded music sales, was firmly established. According to the International Federation of the Phonographic Industry (IFPI), record company revenues from digital recorded music finally reached rough parity with those from physical product in 2014, when digital accounted for a trade value of $6.9 billion, or 46% of total recorded music revenues.

Performance and Performing Rights

Despite global integration, there remain important cultural and legal differences between the music industries of the United States and most other countries. For example, record companies and recording artists outside the United States often enjoy relatively lucrative broadcast **performance rights** for recordings themselves (not just the songs), permitting these stakeholders to collect significant copyright fees from radio and television stations. Historically, the strength of the broadcasting lobby in the United States has led to the United States lagging far behind the rest of the world in generating this kind of income for music makers (see Chapter 4). Outside the United States, record companies collected almost $1 billion from this source in 2014. However, in the United States, performance rights for masters exploited through digital outlets (i.e., not terrestrial broadcasting) grew to become a major revenue stream in just a few years.

Performing rights for songwriters and publishers are also generally a higher priority in Europe, where royalties from broadcasters, concert promoters, and other music users are greater per capita than in the United States. In particular, live music royalties play a much larger role in the revenues of performing right organizations in most European countries, something that benefits touring American musicians who write their own material.

Over recent decades, representatives of U.S. composers and publishers (and those of the United Kingdom) have become increasingly critical of the large deductions made by European copyright societies for spending on cultural activities and welfare payments to their members. Organizations such as ASCAP and BMI retort that a large proportion of these deductions come from royalties earned by American music in Europe but that U.S. songwriters do not benefit from the resulting cultural spending. In response, European societies maintain that it is only because they fund such activities that they have the ear of their governments and are able to ensure that songwriters, including those from the United States, are fairly rewarded for their efforts.

The tension between the Anglo-Saxon (North American and British) and European approaches led to a dispute in the mid-1990s between music publishers, notably those owned by the major international record companies and the European copyright collection societies. The publishers won a reduction in the societies' commission rates on mechanical royalties.

More recently, as **intellectual property** has grown in economic importance, regulators have taken a closer look at the music publishing and recorded music markets. It's all part of a bigger trend. In recent decades, European regulators have been aggressive in trying to blunt what it sees as abuses by companies controlling big-market shares in intellectual property or media, with Microsoft and later Google being big targets for scrutiny. With music, the European Commission (EC) has investigated both aborted and successful mergers of major record companies, challenged the administration of copyrights by the European authors' societies, and recommended new ways of licensing digital rights. The EC made proposals for increased efficiencies in the collection society world and seeking to establish an infrastructure for the development of a commercially viable cross-border digital market in Europe, a process that has been made especially difficult by the fact that while markets are regional and global, copyright laws and authors' societies are national. In response to the last point, a number of leading publishers formed partnerships with individual or groups of societies to more efficiently **exploit** their online rights.

In its role as a competition authority, the EC has authorized or ruled against proposed mergers between major record companies and between large music publishers. For example, it would only permit the acquisition of EMI Records by Universal in 2012 if Universal sold off parts of EMI to other companies. As a result, the Parlophone label catalog of EMI recordings (with the exception of tracks by The Beatles) became part of Warner Music Group.

The independent label sector in Europe has become an influential force in lobbying the EC to curb the market dominance of major companies. Many countries now have strong associations of indies. In turn, some 25 of these national organizations are members of the World Independent Network (WIN). In addition, over 650 indie labels from 40 countries have licensed the Merlin global digital rights agency to negotiate on their behalf with the large online services such as YouTube and Spotify.

These developments are especially important for U.S. rights holders because over the past half-century, foreign markets, especially Europe, have become more significant for the U.S. music industry. There are two reasons for this: Since the 1950s, American pop music has found bigger and bigger audiences around the globe, and since the 1960s, the proportion of world record sales generated in the United States has been slowly declining. In fact, some American artists sell more albums overseas than at home. Similarly, a growing proportion of the royalties collected by ASCAP, BMI, and SESAC, the U.S. performing right organizations, comes from abroad. These organizations receive monies for the use of American music overseas through bilateral contracts with other national PROs.

U.S. copyright owners have also benefited in recent years from the proliferation of foreign music radio and television stations. In many countries, this is the result of the abolition of state-owned broadcasting monopolies, while the spread of satellite and digital technologies has encouraged the launch of regional music channels in Asia, Europe, and Latin America. The increased use of music on the world's airwaves and cables has naturally increased the performance royalties collected by the various copyright societies.

In the 1970s, record sales in the United States accounted for roughly half the world market by value. This share of recorded music has steadily declined and today is about one third of the world value. Nevertheless, with 2014 revenues (all at the trade or wholesale level) of $4.9 billion, the United States remains by far the largest national recorded music market, almost double the size of the second biggest, Japan, where revenues were $2.6 billion. The global trend is consistent: Key world markets have seen a decline in soundcarrier sales and a rise in digital distribution revenue.

In 2014, after the United States and Japan, the other leading markets and their revenues from recorded music were Germany ($1.4 billion), the United Kingdom ($1.3 billion), France ($0.84 billion), Australia ($0.38 billion), Canada ($0.34 billion), South

Korea ($0.27 billion), Brazil ($0.25 billion), and Italy ($0.25 billion). The progress of the market and the growth of digital revenues varied greatly between countries, however. While digital has become the majority source of industry income in the United States, the United Kingdom, and South Korea, sales of physical product still dominated the market in such nations as Japan and Germany.

Although only one South American nation is among the top 10 markets, Latin America has been the fastest growing continental market for recorded music in recent years. In 2014, digital revenues across the region were up by 32%. Nevertheless, the region represented only about 4% of global revenues of the record industry.

Even as recorded music sales have fallen, the revenues of music publishers have risen as new revenue streams emerged, either temporarily or for an extended period. A prime example is ringtones on mobile phones, which, along with mastertones (actual recordings), generated billions of dollars in music publishing revenue in the early years of the 21st century, only to fall later. While the once-dependable growth of music publishers' **mechanical royalties** faltered, publishers have benefited worldwide from the use of music in movies, television, commercials, and video games. This explains why, according to the International Confederation of Societies of Authors and Composers, CISAC, music-related revenues of the societies authorized to collect music royalties on behalf of music publishers, composers, and writers rose by 20% to $7.4 billion in the decade to 2013, whereas in the same period, the trade value of global recorded music sales fell by 33% to $15.0 billion.

New Patterns Around the World

In Europe, the pressure on profits has been mitigated by the blossoming of the long-awaited efficiencies of the European Union's single market. Although most major record companies maintain national offices for A&R (artist and repertoire), promotion, and marketing, in recent years, European manufacturing and production has become more centralized as record companies no longer see such activities as part of their "core business." The major labels also reduce administrative costs by routing much of their mechanical royalty payments through central **licensing** agreements with individual national copyright societies covering several (or all) European nations.

The good news for labels is that the much-predicted death of the soundcarrier has not yet occurred. Despite the global trend for digital revenues to achieve parity with, and overtake, physical sales, in many countries, as we have seen, physical revenues have remained the largest element in record industry finances. Even with record stores closing on a weekly basis and the music racks shrinking, consumers have continued to buy CDs. Increasing numbers are buying an even older format, vinyl discs. In 2014, according to IFPI, revenues from sales of vinyl rose by half, although the format still accounted for only 2% of global music sales by value.

At the same time, the growth rate for digital sales has begun to slow from its initial torrid pace after dramatically changing the patterns of recorded music consumption throughout the world. In Asia, for example, countries previously dominated by cassette sales, such as China and India, have leapfrogged the move to CDs and headed directly to the digital market. In China in 2014, industry revenues from physical sales were less than a quarter of the value of digital sales, which came in at $91 million.

File Sharing and Piracy

The growth of peer-to-peer (P2P) file sharing over the years triggered ongoing battles between Internet service providers (ISPs) and rights owners in many countries. Rights owners have sought to hold ISPs responsible for the actions of their subscribers, while ISPs maintain that how their service is used is not their responsibility. In some countries, including large markets such as the United Kingdom and Germany, there have been attempts to establish agreements between ISPs and rights holders, either voluntarily or by law. Under these agreements, consumers who persist in P2P activities would go through an educative process, followed by warnings that their Internet connection would be terminated or severely limited if they download unauthorized material. In every case, the rights holders' arguments have been strongly resisted, largely on the grounds that users' right of access to the Internet outweighs the infringement of the rights of copyright owners, and it is not the ISP's job to police their customers' activities.

In France, the government established an independent enforcement body, HADOPI, to operate a system of warnings ultimately leading to the termination of Internet subscriptions used for illegal file sharing. Resistance was fierce. French consumer groups attacked the plans as "very harsh, potentially repressive, anti-economic, and against the grain of the digital age." It took until 2012 for the cumbersome enforcement process to reach a "third strike" phase and summon a small number of alleged infringers before a court.

A more effective means to limit unauthorized file sharing has been to act against websites that directly enable such activity. In 2011, the Spanish Congress approved a law that allows the closing down of websites that illegally download copyrighted material. Successful cases involving such sites as The Pirate Bay and Grooveshark were brought in such jurisdictions as the United Kingdom, Denmark, and Finland. Beyond Europe, China and Russia, two countries with the desire to fully enter the mainstream of international trade brought about significant reductions in online piracy. Both countries, which had previously been lax in the supervision of copyrights, chose to be far more responsive to such concerns, as reflected in new antipiracy laws and an increasing number of licensing agreements concluded between companies in these countries and foreign music and film companies.

The market in counterfeit and pirated copies of foreign as well as local recordings is still a major barrier to sales growth throughout much of the world. The United States Trade Representative (USTR) publishes an annual list (known as Special 301) of countries that provide ineffective copyright protection for, or onerous market barriers against, U.S. copyright industries. Such nations may be subject to trade sanctions if they do not improve their commercial and trading practices. The USTR is supported in this work by the International Intellectual Property Association (a U.S.-based lobbying coalition of American copyright-based industry groups).

In recent years, Ukraine has been most cited in Special 301 reports, but each year the list includes more than 30 countries. The piracy problem remained particularly acute in Africa and much of Asia, where meager disposable incomes and political instability in many countries have hampered the development of a legitimate music industry. The situation has become somewhat better in Latin America.

Digital Market Developments

In the longer term, however, the music industry will only secure the digital and online market by encouraging the promising modes of commercial delivery of its products to consumers worldwide. In this process, the industry's partners already include ISPs, cellphone manufacturers, telcos, digital download retailers, and companies dedicated to streaming music. In their early years, often these alliances are uneasy ones, as immature business models lead to fights over what share of the revenue bounty should be retained by which party in the value chain.

Change happens quickly. In the early stages of the digital market, ringtones and ringback tones led the way in monetizing digitized compositions and recordings. These were eventually superseded by digital downloads of albums or individual tracks. Handset manufacturers were among the first to offer large libraries of music recordings, through programs such as Nokia's Comes With Music. But soon, specialist websites took the lead, with the launch of Apple's iTunes in 2004 marking a major turning point. Within a few years, iTunes was the market leader in almost every country where there was a viable digital music market.

Downloads remain an integral part of the global music business, but since 2010, the digital music scene has entered a third phase as streaming has emerged as the most popular means of accessing music in many countries. Outside the United States, the leading players in the streaming market have been Spotify, devised by Swedish entrepreneurs, and the French-owned Deezer. By 2015, Spotify claimed to have 15 million subscribers in 60 countries (about one third of all music fans signed up to streaming deals), while Deezer said its service was available in 150 countries, with subscribers on every continent. Streaming now brings in more revenues than downloads for the music industry in a number of countries.

As well as a new revenue source, streaming brought problems and challenges for copyright holders. There were complaints about the relatively small payments to rights owners even when their songs were streamed many thousands of times, and some music industry experts were concerned about the disparity in take-up between the two tiers of streaming offers. These tiers are the "freemium" level, financed by advertising, and the premium level, without commercials and offered for a monthly

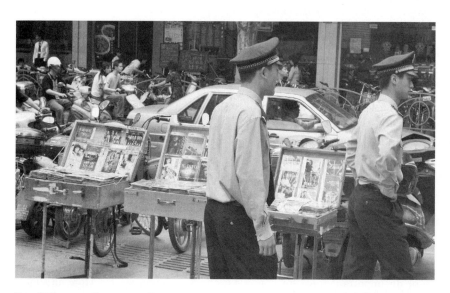

Two Chinese policemen walk past a street stall selling pirated movie DVDs and music CDs in Shanghai.
Photo by MARK RALSTON/AFP/Getty Images.

payment. Many streaming services struggled to persuade significant numbers of freemium subscribers to upgrade to the premium offer.

Breaking Artists

The size of the U.S. music market has made it a prime target for foreign pop and rock acts ever since The Beatles led the "British Invasion" of the 1960s. Although overseas artists account for a small portion of U.S. soundcarrier sales, this dollar value is greater than domestic sales in most other markets around the world. However, only a small percentage of successful acts from abroad achieve success in the United States—due partly to differences in national musical tastes and partly to the different methods of marketing and promotion in North America compared with Europe or Australia. Foreign artists are therefore highly dependent on the local knowledge of their U.S. labels and promoters; it follows that independent labels in Europe and elsewhere prefer to work with partners familiar with the U.S. industry. (Graduates of music business programs in the United States might find it useful to seek employment abroad in this capacity.)

On the other hand, U.S. artists who can't get signed domestically frequently seek deals in other countries or territories. Both recording artists and songwriters sometimes break through in a territory like France and then either make their careers there or eventually also do well in the United States.

Live Performance

Although ticket sales from international performances and tours have grown at a slower rate in recent years, they have remained relatively healthy even as the industry's income from recorded music has stagnated. Superstar acts sell out regularly and command higher ticket prices, while mid-level artists and their managers have had to become more creative in promoting their live appearances, especially at the vastly increased number of music festivals around the world. In some national markets, the gross value of ticket sales and sponsorship has now surpassed the trade value of recorded music sales.

The rapid growth of the secondary ticketing sector has been even more controversial in Europe than in North America. The live music business has been split in its attitude toward the resale of concert tickets, with some promoters forming alliances with secondary ticketing sites but others joining with consumer advocacy bodies and some politicians to lobby governments to control the sector by limiting the markup charged for resold tickets.

For American artists, managers, booking agents, and record labels, international tours are a crucial way to provide exposure to a worldwide audience while capitalizing on one of the few growth areas of the business. Labels entering into **360 deals** with their artists (see Chapter 12) have a particular incentive to pursue lucrative foreign as well as domestic live performances. (U.S. artists frequently engage different booking agents in various foreign territories, rather than using their domestic agents.)

Just as the major world record companies sought to expand their cross-border control in the 20th century, the rise of global promoters for live events promises to be an important force for consolidation in the coming era. More and more domestic and foreign companies are seeking to combine concert promotion with business functions such as artist management, booking shows, and brokering sponsorship deals.

Conferences and Contests

A number of regularly held international conferences and contests provide attendees with the opportunity to make deals, share information, hear some live music, network, and get tips on how to "break" artists in the international market.

MIDEM, held annually in Cannes, is a leading worldwide music business convention, attended by publishers, lawyers, and artists from all over the world. Independent publishers and subpublishers dominate the activities at MIDEM, announcing and making deals to buy or administer catalogs in various territories. In recent years, the 2-day MIDEMNET event, at which digital and music executives mingle and debate, has become a central part of the trade fair.

Other conferences are focused on specific sectors, such as the International Live Music Conference (ILMC), held annually in London since 1989. There are also genre-specific events, including WOMEX for world music and the International Music Summit for the global dance music business, held every year in Ibiza.

There are also numerous song competitions, including the Eurovision and Intervision Song Contests, in which both unknowns and successful writers can break through to international exposure.

Phil Hardy (1945–2014) was the founding editor of *Music & Copyright*. He was the author of *Download! How Digital (Almost) Killed the Record Industry* (Omnibus, 2012) and *Nickles and Dimes* (Omnibus 2013), a study of the music publishing business.

Dave Laing was associate editor of *Music & Copyright*. He is an Honorary Research Fellow at the University of Liverpool.

Chapter Takeaways

- Over the past half-century, the non-U.S. share of the global music business has risen, presenting business opportunities to both local players and the multinational majors.

- Global digital music sales (downloads, streams, subscriptions) accounted for 46% of recorded music sales in 2014, up from 29% in 2010.

- Piracy and counterfeiting of recorded music remain a serious problem in many world territories, stunting legal commerce.

- In China, digital content accounted for more than 75% of record company revenues in 2014.

- Streaming is the main growth sector of the international industry, although many think it brings too little revenue to copyright owners.

- In some countries, ticket sales to live performances now rival recorded music sales.

Key Terms

- MIDEM   (p. 515)
- piracy   (p. 508)
- soundcarrier   (p. 508)
- WIN   (p.510)

Discussion Questions

1. What effects do torrent sites such as The Pirate Bay have on musicians and record companies?

2. Do you think Internet service providers should be required to monitor and prevent illegal downloading of copyrighted content? Why or why not?

3. If you managed a U.S. act without a label deal, why would you or why would you not push to tour in other regions?

4. In your opinion, what are the biggest barriers to combating pirated music globally? What would it take to address these barriers?

CHAPTER 31

International Copyright

Issues of copyright protection and enforcement are complicated on the world stage as each country or regional authority has its own laws and policing methods. In an effort to forge cooperation among nations so that rights holders can be compensated, a number of major international copyright agreements have been reached and modified over the decades.

International copyright agreements fall into two categories. First, there is a series of *copyright conventions* whose membership is open to all nations willing to accept their terms. The conventions (or treaties) are administered by United Nations (UN) organizations, principally the World Intellectual Property Organization (WIPO). Second, there are also *bilateral or multilateral agreements* on levels of copyright protection between trading partners in different countries or groups of countries.

> "Music can change the world because it can change people."
>
> —Bono

Copyright Conventions

Copyright owners are affected by six important international conventions. Three (the Berne Convention, the Universal Copyright Convention, and the WIPO Copyright Convention) concern the rights of authors and composers, and the other three (the Geneva or Phonograms Convention, the Rome Convention, and the WIPO Performances and Phonogram Treaty) deal with the interests of **neighboring rights** owners such as performers, record producers, and broadcasters. The United States is also a member of the Buenos Aires Convention, a regional agreement.

Left: Stevie Wonder at the World Intellectual Property Organization Assemblies.

Berne Convention

The Berne Convention for the Protection of Literary and Artistic Works was signed in 1886 and has been amended six times since. The amendments have endeavored to enable authors' rights to keep pace with new uses of their works brought about by technological change. The Berlin revision of 1908 incorporated references to photography, cinema film, and sound recording. The Rome Act of 1928 extended authors' control of their work to sound broadcasting, and television was brought within the scope of the convention at Brussels in 1948.

The concept of an author's **moral rights** was first included in 1928. Later revisions in Stockholm (1967) and Paris (1971) concentrated on issues such as the *compulsory licensing* of films. The most recent addition to Berne is the WIPO Copyright Treaty of 1996, which provides for copyright protection in relation to the Internet and other digital platforms (see below).

Nine countries signed the original Berne document, seven of them European. Today, there are more than 160 signatories. There are significant limits to the protection a Berne signatory can provide for works of citizens of other Berne states, and nations have to rely on their own national laws for further protection.

A number of Berne's provisions are optional—for example, the granting of moral rights (such as the right of an author to be properly identified and to insist that any editing of a work preserves its integrity). When the United States finally joined the Convention in 1989, pressure from the film industry ensured that it did not accede to the moral rights part of the treaty.

Reciprocal Treatment. The purpose of the Berne Convention is for each country to provide protection for foreign authors within its own copyright laws, and these rights can be adopted into national law in two distinct ways. National treatment for foreign authors means that these copyright owners will receive the same level of protection as domestic authors. But a Berne Convention member can also decide to grant reciprocal treatment, in which case foreign authors will get only the level of protection granted in their own country. The most prominent example of reciprocal treatment for authors concerns the private copying or home-taping levies that exist in a number of European countries. The only foreign composers entitled to share in the distribution of these levies are those from countries that also have a private copying levy in place—thus excluding U.S. authors.

Broadcasting Rights Options. Another "opt-out" written into the Berne Convention's broadcasting clause permits the general rights of authors granted by the convention to include the power to "authorize or prohibit" the use of their work. By the late 1920s, the radio industry had itself become a powerful force in Europe, and music was one of its most important sources of program material.

When the issue of broadcasting rights for composers was considered by the Berne Convention nations, a strong lobby favored substituting a compulsory license for the prohibition right. Under this system, the copyright owner is compelled to allow works to be used, subject to appropriate payment from the user. Rather than codifying this, the Berne Convention signatories provided that each national government could make its own decision. The compulsory license procedure ensured a constant supply of music for radio, even when there was a dispute over royalty payments. What constitutes "equitable remuneration" is determined in most countries by a government-appointed tribunal or special court.

Film Authorship. The definition of *authorship* itself came into question in 1928 when the nature of cinematographic works was under discussion. Prior to this, the Berne Convention had accepted that an author of a book, play, or song was a single individual or a partnership of named individuals. But the collaborative nature of filmmaking made it more difficult to determine an individual author; it was decided that definition of film author(s) should be decided by each member nation of the convention.

Buenos Aires Convention

As noted above, the Berne Convention at its outset was dominated by European countries. Subsequent to its adoption, various countries in both North and South America, including the United States, came together to fashion a similar agreement, the Buenos Aires Convention of 1910. Under this convention, compliance with the copyright law of the country of first publication qualifies the work for protection in the other member countries. Each work must also carry a notice indicating that the property rights in the work are reserved, which is generally satisfied with the inclusion of the words "all rights reserved" in the copyright notice.

Universal Copyright Convention

Although the Buenos Aires Convention governs U.S. copyright relations with most nations in the Americas, it is unlikely to attract additional members because of adoption of the Universal Copyright Convention (UCC) of 1955, of which the United States was a founding member. Over 100 countries are now members of the UCC.

Because the sponsor of the UCC, the UN, wished to attract a maximum number of participants, the exclusive rights granted under this convention are held to a minimum level of "adequate and effective protection." According to the UCC, such protection includes "basic rights ensuring the author's economic interests, including the exclusive right to authorize reproduction by any means, public performance and broadcasting." Formal notification of copyright protections should be indicated by having all relevant copies bear the copyright symbol (©), the name of the **copyright proprietor**, and the year of first publication.

One goal of the UCC was to avoid competition with other prevailing agreements, particularly Berne and Buenos Aires. Where provisions differ, the UCC provides that "the most recently formulated convention" shall prevail.

Rome Convention

The 1961 Rome Convention for the Protection of Performers, Producers of Phonograms, and Broadcasting Organizations put record companies and performers on the international map as rights *owners* as opposed to merely rights *users.*

The Rome Convention confirmed the rights of both performers of music and record companies to control the reproduction and public performance of their work. It set a minimum period of copyright protection at 20 years. Today, most national laws protect sound recordings for 70 years or more, a figure included in the 1996 Performances and Phonograms Treaty agreed to by a committee of WIPO (see below).

Broadcasting Rights. The Rome Convention followed Berne and provided for a compulsory broadcasting license. Both the compulsory license and the 20-year minimum represented concessions to broadcasters who wished to see recordings fall into the **public domain** and become free of copyright royalties as quickly as possible. Signatories to the Rome Convention could also opt out of granting broadcasting rights to producers and performers. Monaco and Luxembourg both exercised this option, and partly as a result, they now have powerful music radio stations broadcasting to neighboring countries. The Rome Convention left it to each nation to determine how broadcasting royalties should be shared between record producers and performers. In the 28 countries of the European Union, these are shared equally.

The relationship between "contracting" and "noncontracting" states is complex when it comes to broadcasting royalties. As with Berne, Rome provides a fundamental national treatment for performers, producers, and broadcasters of other contracting states.

Rights owners from noncontracting states may also share in royalties if the recording in question received "simultaneous publication" in the contracting state. *Simultaneous* is defined here as within 30 days of the recording's release in its country of origin. Any contracting country may, however, drop the criterion of "publication" of a recording and replace it with one of *first fixation,* which refers to the location of the studio where the recording was created.

At the time of this writing, the United States was not one of the 90 signatories to the Rome Convention.

Adopting the criterion of first fixation, as several European countries have done, means that performers and producers of U.S. recordings cannot benefit from airplay of their works in those countries—although under the Berne Convention, royalties must be paid to U.S. songwriters.

Geneva Phonograms Convention

The Rome Convention provided broad protection against copyright infringement, but it was drafted at a time when the piracy of sound recordings was still a relatively minor occurrence. With the arrival of the compact tape cassette in 1963, however, music piracy became big business. By the end of the 1960s, piracy and counterfeiting of prerecorded cassettes were becoming endemic, and the music industry, along with some national governments, saw the need for a new international treaty specifically designed to deal with piracy.

The result was the 1971 Convention for the Protection of Producers of Phonograms Against Unauthorized Duplication of Their Phonograms, known as the Phonograms Convention. This treaty added new import and distribution rights to those in the Rome Convention. Record producers could now stop illegal imports and take action against wholesalers and retailers as well as those who manufactured illegal copies. Almost 80 countries are members of this Convention.

WIPO Copyright Treaty and
Performances and Phonograms Treaty

In 1996, two new international treaties were established to update the Berne and Rome Conventions, principally regarding the use of music on the Internet. The WIPO Copyright Treaty (WCT), which has the status of a "special agreement" under the Berne Convention, provides additional protection for authors when their works are used on the Internet and via other digital services, including downloads and **streaming**.

The WIPO Performances and Phonograms Treaty (WPPT) extended similar protection for neighboring rights owners in relation to the Internet and other digital platforms. The new author's right with respect to downloads and streaming is paralleled by a similar right for performers and record companies.

Other elements of the 1996 treaties include the outlawing of devices designed to circumvent electronic protection systems linked to digital recordings, stronger protection against illegal copying, and confirmation that Berne Convention and Rome Convention provisions on the reproduction of works or recordings apply to the digital domain. Over 90 countries are signatories to each of these treaties.

Multilateral Agreements

The economic importance of the music business and other copyright-based industries has caused the inclusion of copyright protection in many trade agreements between nations. The most far-reaching to date is TRIPS (Trade Related Aspects of Intellectual Property Rights, Including Trade in Counterfeit Goods), which was accepted by more than 120 countries at the conclusion of the Uruguay Round of the General Agreement on Tariffs and Trade (GATT) in 1993. First negotiated in 1948, GATT is an international treaty designed to promote and enforce free trade worldwide. GATT is renegotiated about every 10 years; the 1986 changes incorporated trade in **intellectual property** for the first time.

Many of the TRIPS treaty's provisions echoed the Berne and Rome Conventions in providing fundamental rights for authors, performers, and producers. The treaty makes allowances for developing countries, permitting them to phase in the TRIPS provisions over long periods of time. The treaty has helped Western copyright owners by further opening up Third World markets.

Other multilateral copyright treaties have grown out of free trade issues. Here, the principle is that each country that is a member of a free trade area or "single market" must apply the same standards of copyright protection as its fellow members. The North American Free Trade Agreement (NAFTA) and the European Union treaty are the most important of these accords. Implemented in 1994, NAFTA's intent is to end trade barriers among its members, Mexico, the United States, and Canada. Under NAFTA, the three countries give reciprocal treatment to each other's copyright owners. (But NAFTA hasn't stopped Canada from legally favoring its own nationals through a variety of laws and regulations regarding music.)

The EU single-market program, dating from the 1980s, includes a provision to **harmonize** the copyright laws of its member countries and other countries associated with the European Union. A number of directives were issued to all members, and those affecting the music industry centered on rental; private copying; the transborder aspects of cable and satellite broadcasting; the equalization of the duration of copyright protection for authors and neighboring rights owners; and the enforcement of intellectual property rights. As is often the case, the journey from directive to enactment has never been particularly speedy and often never completed. However, in 2011, the EU agreed to amend Directive 2006/116/EC, thereby granting a copyright term extension for sound recordings throughout the EU from 50 to 70 years and ensuring that performers benefit from the term extension. This change brings

Working at a mixing panel.
Photo © DragonImages/iStock.

Europe's producers and performers more in line with the protection offered to authors and composers, which stands at life plus 70 years. The amendment also narrows the gap between Europe and a number of countries (including the United States) that offer term protection of up to 95 years.

The amended directive included a number of measures to ensure that performers benefit from the additional 20 years of copyright protection. If a record company fails to make commercially available a recording that would be in the public domain without the term extension or refrains from making a recording available to the public, the rights to the performance revert to the performer. The directive also allows for the creation of a fund for session musicians, paid from label revenues in the extended 20-year term. Labels are obliged to set aside 20% of their gross profit (after deducting direct costs) from the recording to make payments solely to nonfeatured performers, such as session musicians, who were paid one-time fees for their performance. Distribution of the paid-in funds to performers will be made by a collection society. For featured performers, the amendment introduced a "clean slate" measure, which writes off any advance payment not fully recouped and ensures that royalties are paid to performers during the new extended period.

Bilateral Treaties

Copyright protection has also been enhanced via bilateral treaties. The United States has made the greatest use of this strategy through the 1988 Omnibus Trade and Competitiveness Act. As explained in Chapter 30, this permits the United States Trade Representative (USTR) to nominate "Priority Foreign Countries" whose trading practices are alleged to be harmful to U.S. industries that are dependent on the protection of intellectual property, including the music industry.

In 1989, the USTR set up a Watch List and a Priority Watch List of countries perceived as unfair trading partners of the United States. Two years later, Thailand, China, and India were the first to become Priority Foreign Countries for their failure to protect U.S. copyright material adequately. China and India eventually agreed to ease restrictions on the operations of foreign companies. Since then, the Priority Foreign Countries list has included a large number of countries.

Table 31.1 lists foreign **affiliates** of the Harry Fox Agency (HFA), which aids clients with **licensing**, collection, and distribution of music. As explained in Chapter 6, HFA, which is now part of SESAC, grants licensees the rights to reproduce and distribute copyrighted musical compositions (songs), including uses on CDs, records, tapes, and certain digital configurations.

Table 31.1   Foreign Affiliates of the Harry Fox Agency, Inc.

Society	Name	Territories of Control
ACUM	Authors, Composers and Music Publishers Assoc., Israel	Israel
AEPI	Hellenic Society for the Protection of Intellectual Property S.A.	Greece
AMCOS	Australasian Mechanical Copyright Owners Society, Ltd.	Australia, Fiji, New Zealand, Pacific Island Territories, Papua New Guinea
ARTISJUS	ARTISJUS Magyar Szerzoi Jogvedo Iroda Egyesulet	Hungary
AUSTRO-MECHANA	Gesellschaft für Musikalische Aufführungs und Mechanische Vervielfältigungsrechte	Austria
CASH	The Composers and Authors Society of Hong Kong, Ltd.	Hong Kong, Macau
COMPASS	Composers and Authors Society of Singapore, Ltd.	Republic of Singapore
COSCAP	Copyright Society of Composers, Authors and Publishers, Inc.	Barbados
COTT	Copyright Organisation of Trinidad and Tobago	Trinidad and Tobago
FILSCAP	Filipino Society of Composers, Authors and Publishers, Inc.	Rep. of the Philippines
GEMA	Gesellschaft für Musikalische Aufführungs und Mechanische Vervielfältigungsrechte	Bulgaria, Germany, Poland, Romania, Turkey
HDS	Croatian Composers' Society	Croatia
ICS	International Copyright Services, Inc.	Republic of Liberia
JACAP	Jamaican Association of Composers, Authors, and Publishers, Ltd.	Jamaica

(Continued)

Table 31.1   **(Continued)**

Society	Name	Territories of Control
JASRAC	Japanese Society for Rights of Authors, Composers and Publishers	Japan
KCI	Yayasan Karya Cipta Indonesia	Republic of Indonesia
KOMCA	Korea Music Copyright Assoc.	Republic of Korea
MACP	Music Authors' Copyright Protection Verhad	Malaysia
MCPS	Mechanical Copyright Protection Society	Bahamas, Bermuda, British Virgin Islands, India, Ireland (Eire), Kenya, Nigeria, Uganda, United Kingdom, Northern Ireland, Zimbabwe
MCSC	Music Copyright Society of China	People's Republic of China
MESAM	Türkiye Musıki Eseri Sahipleri Meslek Birliği	Turkey
NCB	Nordisk Copyright Bureau	Denmark, Estonia, Finland, Iceland, Latvia, Lithuania, Norway, Sweden
OSA	Ochranný Svaz Autorský	Czech Republic
RAO	Russia Authors Society	Russia
SABAM	Société belge des auteurs, compositeurs et éditeurs	Belgium
SADAIC	La Sociedad Argentina de Autores y Compositores de Musica	Argentina
SAMRO	Southern Africa Music Rights Organisation	South Africa
SDRM/SACEM	Societe pour l'Administration du Droit de Reproduction Mecanique des Auteurs, Compositeurs et Editeurs de Musique	Andorra, Luxembourg, Monaco, Republic of France, Algeria, Benin, Burkina Faso, Cameroon, Central African Republic, Chad, Congo, Cote d'Ivoire, Djibouti, Egypt, Gabon, Gambia, Guinea, Lebanon, Madagascar, Mali, Mauritania, Morocco, Niger, Senegal, Togo, Tunisia, Zaire
SGAE	Sociedad General de Autores de Espana	Spain
SIAE	Societa Italiana degli Autori ed Editori	Italy, San Marino, Vatican City
SOZA	Slovenský Ochranný Zväz Autorský	Slovak Republic
SPA	Sociedade Portuguesa de Autores	Azores, Madeira, Portugal
STEMRA	Stichting Stemra	Aruba, Dutch Antilles, Irian Barat, Netherlands, Surinam
SUISA	Schweizerische Gesellschaft für die Rechte der Urheber musikalischer Werke	Liechtenstein, Switzerland
UBC	União Brasileira de Compositores	Brazil

Source: The Harry Fox Agency, 2015.

Intergovernmental Bodies and International Industry Organizations

World Intellectual Property Organization

The World Intellectual Property Organization (WIPO) is an organ of the United Nations, with headquarters in Geneva, Switzerland. WIPO is charged with administering the Berne and Rome Conventions as well as other conventions dealing with non-music-related items. WIPO's meetings facilitate discussions about updating or redrafting of copyright conventions in response to technological developments.

World Trade Organization

The World Trade Organization (WTO) is tasked with implementing and policing the GATT and TRIPS agreements. The similarity between the TRIPS agreement on enforcement and that proposed by WIPO demonstrates the convergence of the international trade organization and the international copyright bodies.

In relation to the TRIPS agreement, the WTO must ensure that developing countries upgrade their copyright laws to TRIPS standards within certain time limits. The WTO is also responsible for resolving bilateral disputes or complaints concerning noncompliance. The United States was adjudged to be guilty in the first copyright dispute dealt with by the WTO. The European Union, supported by several developing countries, was concerned about a provision in U.S. copyright law included in the 1998 Fairness in Music Licensing Act that exempted bars, restaurants, and stores from paying to use copyrighted music when the music was sourced from radio or television programs. In 2001, a WTO disputes panel agreed with the European Union that this was a **breach** of the obligations of the United States as a Berne Convention member. The panel ordered the payment of compensation by the U.S. government, and, with congressional approval, payment was made.

International Confederation of Societies of Authors and Composers

The International Confederation of Societies of Authors and Composers (CISAC) groups together organizations from more than 120 countries. CISAC has a small secretariat based in Paris, and an executive board composed of representatives from many affiliated societies runs the confederation. In addition to convening a world congress every 2 years, CISAC's main role is to encourage cooperation between its members and to help form new authors' societies, particularly in developing countries.

The key issues for CISAC include evolving a common policy for protecting copyright in the face of advancing technologies and the harmonizing of documentation so musical works can be more easily identified worldwide and payments can thus be allocated more efficiently.

To help new societies, CISAC maintains a regional office in Singapore that in recent years has worked closely with composers in Vietnam, Indonesia, and the People's Republic of China. There is also a "twinning" process whereby established authors' societies advise and train officials of new organizations.

The American Society of Composers, Authors and Publishers (ASCAP) and Broadcast Music Inc. (BMI), America's leading performance rights organizations, work with CISAC on issues of international significance and contribute to CISAC events and conferences. Both PROs traditionally have seats on CISAC's Board.

Bureau International des Sociétés Gérant les Droits d'Enregistrement et de Reproduction Mécanique

Founded in 1929, the Bureau International des Sociétés Gérant les Droits d'Enregistrement et de Reproduction Mécanique (BIEM) also represents the interests of composers and music publishers. In regular negotiations with IFPI (International Federation of the Phonographic Industry, the global recording industry body; see below), BIEM sets the standard mechanical royalty rate for most of Europe and Latin America; the BIEM-IFPI rate does not apply in the United States, Canada, Australia, or the United Kingdom.

The BIEM-IFPI contract stipulates a standard rate of 8.7% of the "published price to dealers" of all disc and tape formats. The standard figure is subject to slight variations at national levels, based on local agreements about packaging deductions, including television-advertised albums, the number of tracks on an album, and other factors.

International Federation of the Phonographic Industry

The need to find a common position in relation to BIEM was the major motivation for the 1933 formation of the International Federation of the Phonographic Industry (IFPI), an international organization representing record companies. The federation endeavors to defend in the international domain the interests of its members by preserving their existing rights, statutory or otherwise. IFPI works to safeguard the welfare of its members via representation as a federated body in negotiations with and representations to governments and other interested parties. Over the years, IFPI has become one of the most skilled lobbyists for copyright reform at the international level. It has NGO (nongovernmental organization) status with the International Labour Organization (ILO), UNESCO, and WIPO. IFPI has also established itself as a consultative body with the European Commission.

IFPI has more than 1,300 member companies in over 60 countries. In almost all of these countries, there is a trade organization that constitutes an IFPI National Group. The Recording Industry Association of America (RIAA) is the U.S. affiliate of IFPI.

The policy-making arm of IFPI comprises a main board plus regional boards in Europe, the Pacific Rim, and Latin America. Each board has representatives from the major international record companies as well as leading independent labels. The IFPI Secretariat, based in London, provides the industry's official statistics for soundcarrier sales as well as for global piracy. It also coordinates antipiracy strategy, lobbies for copyright reform, and provides logistical support for negotiations on mechanical royalties with BIEM.

International Federation of Musicians and International Federation of Actors

The two international unions of performers, the International Federation of Musicians (FIM) and the International Federation of Actors (FIA), also have NGO status with WIPO and with the ILO, another UN body. The American Federation of Musicians (AFM) is a member of FIM; Actors' Equity is a member of FIA.

The principal impact of FIM and FIA on the world music business is through their longstanding agreement with IFPI on the distribution of broadcasting royalties between neighboring rights owners. Under this agreement, the two parties agree to divide equally any broadcasting royalties collected on their joint behalf. In most European countries as well as in Japan, there is a single collecting society for performers and producers.

Chapter Takeaways

- A series of international conventions (treaties) governs copyright. Conventions concerning the rights of authors and composers include the Berne Convention, the International Copyright Convention, and the WIPO Copyright Convention.

- Other treaties, focused on issues related to labels, artists, broadcasters, and piracy, include the Geneva or Phonograms Convention, the Rome Convention, and the WIPO Performances and Phonogram Treaty.

- Reciprocal treatment provisions of the Berne Convention block U.S. songwriters from receiving a share of foreign levies on blank media.

Key Terms

- BIEM   (p. 528)
- copyright conventions (p. 519)
- CISAC   (p. 527)
- first fixation   (p. 522)
- harmonize   (p. 523)
- moral rights   (p. 520)
- neighboring rights   (p. 519)
- reciprocal treatment   (p. 520)
- WCT   (p. 522)
- WIPO   (p. 519)
- WPPT   (p. 523)
- WTO   (p. 527)

Discussion Questions

1. How do international copyright laws affect U.S. performers?

2. In your opinion, why has there been a global push to increase the copyright term for rights owners?

3. What challenges are still faced by intergovernmental bodies working for copyright protection? What can be done to resolve some of these issues?

Appendix A

Membership and Copyright Forms

Membership and copyright forms can be downloaded from the Internet at the following websites.

ASCAP

At the American Society of Composers, Authors and Publishers (ASCAP) website, you can download the ASCAP Writer Application, the ASCAP Publisher Application, and the membership agreement form, which appears at the end of both the Writer Application form and the Publisher application form. At the ASCAP home page (www.ascap.com), click on the Join ASCAP link, or go directly to that page using this URL: www.ascap.com/join.

BMI

Go to the Broadcast Music Inc. (BMI) website (www.bmi.com) and click on the "join" link to determine if you are eligible to join BMI as a publisher or writer/composer. To join online, you must meet several requirements: (a) Technical requirements have to do with your computer operating system, ability to read pdf files, and ability to print the application. (b) Professional requirements include having your work commercially recorded and released or having written/cowritten or composed a song that is likely to be performed on radio, TV, the Internet, and the like. (c) Legal requirements have to do with age and affiliation or past affiliation with a performing rights organization.

SESAC

SESAC, as a performance rights organization, is selective about accepting affiliates. At the SESAC website, you can complete an information form to request consideration for an invitation to join SESAC. At the SESAC home page (www.sesac.com), click on the writers/publishers link, or go directly to that page using this URL: www.sesac.com/WritersPublishers/AffiliateForm.aspx.

Copyright Forms

To file a U.S. Copyright Form PA (for a work of the performing arts) or Form SR (for a sound recording) application through the Electronic Copyright Office system, go to www.copyright.gov/eco. There you will also find links to eCO Tips, eCO FAQ, and the eCO Tutorial. Note that Form CO was discontinued in 2012. The current forms, along with Tips, FAQs, and a Tutorial, can be found at www.copyright.gov/forms.

Patent and Trademark Forms

All information and forms relating to patents and trademarks can be accessed at http://www.uspto.gov/products/online-services.jsp.

SoundExchange

In order to receive royalties for sound recordings (not compositions), sound recording copyright owners and featured performers may register on the SoundExchange site at http://www.soundexchange.com/artist-copyright-owner/registration-membership/. You can also view current rates for all categories of statutory licensing at http://www.soundexchange.com/service-provider/rates/.

Other Organizations

Information on other music-related organizations is available through the links listed alphabetically by organization name on the inside back cover.

Appendix B

Selected Readings

Books

2014 NAMM Global Report, Music USA. Carlsbad, CA: NAMM, 2014.

Anderson, Chris. *The Long Tail: Why the Future of Business Is Selling Less of More.* New York: Hyperion, 2006.

Barrow, T. *Inside the Music Business.* New York: Chapman & Hall, 1995.

Black, Henry C., et al. *Black's Law Dictionary.* 9th ed. Garner, Bryan A., ed. Eagan, MN: Thomson West, 2009.

Blume, Jason. *Six Steps to Songwriting Success.* Rev. ed. Watson-Guptill, 2008.

Bolles, Richard Nelson. *What Color Is Your Parachute? 2014: A Practical Manual for Job-Hunters & Career Changers.* New York: Ten Speed, 2013.

Brabec, Jeffrey, and Brabec, Todd. *Music, Money, and Success: The Insider's Guide to Making Money in the Music Business.* 7th ed. New York: Schirmer, 2011.

Christensen, Clayton M. *The Innovator's Dilemma.* New York: HarperCollins, 2003.

Colins, Sarah, ed. *Foundation Fundamentals.* 8th ed. New York: Foundation Center, 2008.

The College Blue Book. 41st ed. Woodbridge, CT: Macmillan Reference USA, 2015.

The College Board. *Book of Majors 2012.* New York: College Board Publications, 2012.

Dannen, Fredric. *Hit Men: Power Brokers & Fast Money Inside the Music Business.* New York: Random House, 1991.

Davies, Ray. *Americana: The Kinks, the Riff, the Road: The Story.* New York: Sterling, 2013.

Denisoff, R. Serge. *Inside MTV.* New Brunswick, NJ: Transaction, 1990.

Eargle, John M. *Handbook of Recording Engineering.* 4th ed. Boston: Kluwer Academic, 2005.

Eargle, John M. *Music, Sound and Technology.* 2nd ed. New York: Van Nostrand Reinhold, 1995.

Elias, Stephen, and the editors of Nolo. *Legal Research: How to Find & Understand the Law.* 16th ed. Berkeley, CA: Nolo, 2012.

Eliot, Marc. *Rockonomics: The Money Behind the Music.* Secaucus, NJ: Carol Publishing Group, 1993.

Fagen, Donald. *Eminent Hipsters.* New York: Viking, 2013.

Faulkner, Robert R. *Hollywood Studio Musicians: Their Work and Careers in the Recording Industry.* Piscataway, NJ: Aldine Transaction, 2013.

Faulkner, Robert R. *Music on Demand: Composers and Careers in the Hollywood Film Industry.* New Brunswick, NJ: Transaction, 2003.

Feist, Leonard. *Popular Music Publishing in America.* New York: National Music Publishers Association, 1980.

Fink, Michael. *Inside the Music Industry: Creativity, Process, and Business.* 2nd ed. New York: Schirmer, 1996.

Friedman, Harry J. *No Thanks, I'm Just Looking: Professional Retail Sales Techniques for Turning Shoppers Into Buyers.* Reprint ed. Dubuque, IA: Kendall/Hunt, 2002.

Gaar, Gillian G. *She's a Rebel: The History of Women in Rock & Roll.* Preface by Yoko Ono. Exp. 2nd ed. Seattle, WA: Seal, 2002.

Gallagher, Mitch, and Mandell, Jim. *The Studio Business Book.* Jewett, Andy, ed. 3rd rev. ed. Milwaukee, WI: Hal Leonard, 2006.

Goldstein, Jeri. *How to Be Your Own Booking Agent: The Musician's & Performing Artist's Guide to a Successful Touring Career.* Estrin, Kari, ed. 3rd rev. ed. Palmyra, VA: New Music Times, 2008.

Greenfield, Robert. *The Last Sultan. The Life and Times of Ahmet Ertegun.* New York: Simon & Schuster, 2011.

Halloran, Mark, ed. and comp. *The Musician's Business and Legal Guide.* 4th rev. ed. Paramus, NJ: Prentice Hall, 2007.

Hilburn, Robert. *Johnny Cash: The Life.* New York: Little, Brown and Company, 2013.

Karlin, Fred. *Listening to Movies: The Film Lover's Guide to Film Music.* New York: Schirmer, 2000.

Karlin, Fred, and Wright, Rayburn. *On the Track: A Guide to Contemporary Film Scoring.* 2nd ed. New York: Routledge, 2004.

Karmen, Steve. *Through the Jingle Jungle.* New York: Billboard Books, 1989.

Kaskowitz, Sheryl. *God Bless America: The Surprising History of an Iconic Song.* New York: Oxford University Press, 2013.

Kaufman, Kenneth M., and Howard Siegel, co-chairs. *Counseling Clients in the Entertainment Industry 2015.* New York: Practising Law Institute, 2015. [Annual]

Knopper, Steve. *Appetite for Self-Destruction.* New York: Free Press, 2009.

Kohn, Al, and Kohn, Bob. *Kohn on Music Licensing.* 4th ed. New York: Aspen Publishers, 2010.

Koontz, Harold D., and Weihrich, Heinz. *Essentials of Management: An International Perspective.* 8th ed. New York: McGraw-Hill, 2009.

Krasilovsky, M. William, and Shemel, Sidney. *This Business of Music.* 10th ed. New York: Watson-Guptill, 2007.

Lathrop, Tad. *This Business of Music Marketing and Promotion.* Rev. ed. New York: Billboard Books, 2005.

Leikin, Molly-Ann. *How to Be a Hit Songwriter: Polishing and Marketing Your Lyrics and Music.* 3rd ed. Milwaukee, WI: Hal Leonard, 2003.

Loewenstein, Prince Rupert. *A Prince Among Stones: That Business with the Rolling Stones and Other Adventures.* New York: Bloomsbury USA, 2013.

Marcone, Stephen. *Managing Your Band: Artist Management: The Ultimate Responsibility.* 5th ed. Wayne, NJ: HiMarks, 2010.

Marich, Robert. *Marketing to Moviegoers: A Handbook of Strategies and Tactics.* 3rd ed. Carbondale, IL: Southern Illinois University Press, 2013.

Martin, George, and Hornsby, Jeremy. *All You Need Is Ears: The Inside Personal Story of the Genius Who Created the Beatles.* New York: St. Martin's, 1994.

Mazor, Barry. *Ralph Peer and the Making of Popular Roots Music.* Chicago: Chicago Review Press, 2014.

McPherson, Brian. *Get It in Writing.* San Diego, CA: Rockpress Publishing Company, 1999.

Miller, Steve. *Detroit Rock City: The Uncensored History of Rock 'n' Roll in America's Loudest City.* Boston: Da Capo Press, 2013.

Milward, John. *How the Blues Shaped Rock 'n' Roll.* Boston: Northeastern University Press, 2013.

Musical America International Directory of the Performing Arts, 2015. New York: Musical America Publications, 2015. [Annual]

Nash, Graham. *Wild Tales: A Rock & Roll Life.* Reprint ed. New York: Three Rivers Press, 2014.

Nimmer, Melville B. *Nimmer on Copyright.* 11 vols. New York: Matthew Bender, 2004.

Passman, Donald S. *All You Need to Know About the Music Business.* 8th ed. New York: Free Press, 2014.

Perreault, William D., Jr., McCarthy, E. Jerome, and Perreault, William D. *Basic Marketing: A Global Managerial Approach.* 17th ed. New York: McGraw Hill, 2009.

Pettigrew, Jim, Jr. *The Billboard Guide to Music Publicity.* New York: Billboard Books, 1997.

Pleasants, Henry. *Serious Music—And All That Jazz.* New York: Simon & Schuster, 1969.

Rapaport, Diane S. *How to Make and Sell Your Own Recording: The Complete Guide to Independent Recording.* 5th ed. Paramus, NJ: Prentice Hall, 1999.

Raugust, Karen. *The Licensing Business Handbook.* 8th ed. New York: EPM Communications, 2008.

Rodgers, Nile. *Le Freak: An Upside Down Story of Family, Disco, and Destiny.* New York: Spiegel & Grau, 2011.

Sanjek, Russell, and Sanjek, David. *Pennies From Heaven: The American Popular Music Business in the Twentieth Century.* New York: Da Capo, 1996.

Schruers, Fred. *Billy Joel.* New York: Crown Archetype, 2014.

Scott, Michael D. *Multimedia: Law & Practice.* Englewood Cliffs, NJ: Prentice Hall Law & Business, 1993.

Shapiro, Carl, and Varian, Hal. *Information Rules: A Strategic Guide to the Network Economy.* Boston: Harvard Business School Press, 1999.

Siegel, Alan H. *Breaking Into the Music Business: Revised and Updated for the 21st Century.* New York: Simon & Schuster, 1991.

Simon, Deke. *Film & Video Budgets.* 5th ed. Studio City, CA: Michael Wiese Productions, 2010.

Stauffer, John. *The Battle Hymn of the Republic: A Biography of the Song That Marches On.* New York: Oxford University Press, 2013.

Steinberg, Irwin, and Greenblatt, Harmon. *Understanding the Music Business: A Comprehensive View.* 5th ed. Needham Heights, MA: National Book Network, 2009.

Stim, Richard. *Music Law: How to Run Your Band's Business.* 7th ed. Berkeley, CA: Nolo, 2012.

Streissguth, Michael. *Outlaw: Waylon, Willie, Kris, and the Renegades of Nashville.* New York: It Books, 2014.

Suisman, David. *Selling Sounds.* Boston: Harvard University Press, 2012.

Voelz, Susan. *The Musician's Guide to the Road.* New York: Billboard Books, 2012.

Vogel, Harold L. *Entertainment Industry Economics: A Guide for Financial Analysts.* 8th ed. New York: Cambridge University Press, 2011.

Wadhams, Wayne. *Sound Advice: The Musician's Guide to the Record Industry.* New York: Schirmer, 1990.

Weissman, Dick. *Making a Living in Your Local Music Market: How to Survive and Prosper.* 4th ed. Milwaukee, WI: Hal Leonard, 2010.

Whitsett, Tim. *The Dictionary of Music Business Terms.* Emeryville, CA: ArtistPro, 1999.

Wilder, Alec. *American Popular Song: The Great Innovators, 1900–1950.* Reprinted. New York: Oxford University Press, 1990.

Winogradsky, Steve. *Music Publishing—The Complete Guide.* Los Angeles: Alfred Music, 2013.

Journals, Magazines, Newspapers, Newsletters

Advertising Age   Biweekly trade publication covering agency, media and advertising, news, and trends. www.adage.com

Billboard   Professional international news weekly for members of music and video and home entertainment industries and related fields. www.billboard.com

Broadcasting & Cable   Weekly business publication for broadcast and cable TV. www.broadcastingcable.com

Campus Activities Programming Magazine   Trade magazine covering college campus programming for the student and professional. www.naca.org/CAP

College Music Symposium   Interdisciplinary quarterly. Symposium.music.org

Columbia Journal of Law & the Arts   Scholarly quarterly with articles concerning timely art law topics. Lawandarts.org

Daily Variety   Daily newspaper of the entertainment industry. Variety.com

DJ Times   Business monthly with the latest technology, trends, music, and business information for disc jockeys. Djtimes.com

Down Beat   Monthly consumer magazine covering contemporary music and aimed at the seriously involved player and listener. Downbeat.com

Electronic Musician   Monthly business magazine covering electronics and computers in the creation and recording of music. www.emusician.com

Film Score Monthly   Online magazine providing film music reviews and composer interviews. www.filmscoremonthly.com

Hollywood Reporter   Daily PDF and weekly print edition of business news and reviews of all phases of the entertainment, theatrical, and new media fields. www.hollywoodreporter.com

The Instrumentalist   Monthly with practical, professional information for school band and orchestra directors. www.theinstrumentalist.com

International Musician   Monthly journal for members of the American Federation of Musicians. Internationalmusician.org

Journal of the American Musicological Society   Scholarly articles on diversified branches of musicology, published three times a year. www.ams-net.org/pubs/jams.php

Journal of the Copyright Society of the U.S.A.   Quarterly dealing with domestic and foreign copyright laws, revisions, and court decisions. www.csusa.org/?page=Journal

Journal of Music Therapy   Research-oriented quarterly for practitioners and others. Jmt.oxfordjournals.org

Licensing Letter   Semimonthly tip sheet offering detailed industry sales data. www.epcm.com/public/department33.cfm

MEIEA Journal   Academic journal of the Music and Entertainment Industry Educators Association. www.meiea.org

Modern Drummer   Monthly for the student, semipro, and pro drummer. www.moderndrummer.com

Music & Copyright   Newsletter providing global reporting on the commercial aspects of the music industry, published semimonthly by Informa Telecoms & Media. www.musicandcopyright.com

Music & Sound Retailer   Monthly serving owners, managers, and sales personnel in retail musical instrument and sound product dealerships. www.msretailer.com

Music Business Journal   A student-produced journal from Berklee College of Music. www.thembj.org

Music Educators Journal   Quarterly dealing with all facets of study and teaching methods at all levels. www.mej.sagepub.com

Music Inc.   Business monthly providing newest trends in product merchandising, new products, industry news, and dealer and manufacturer profiles. www.musicincmag.com

Music Trades   Business monthly for music stores selling instruments, accessories, music, and electronic music and home equipment. www.musictrades.com

Musical Merchandise Review   Monthly trade magazine and weekly eNewsletter for the musical instrument market. Mmrmagazine.com

Notes   Quarterly journal covering developments in music librarianship and activities of the Music Library Association. www.musiclibraryassoc.org/?page=Notes

Pitchfork Review   Quarterly publication for independent music news. www.thepitchforkreview.com

Pollstar   Trade journal tracking the business of live performance. www.pollstar.com

Post   Monthly serving the field of TV, film, and video production and postproduction. www.postmagazine.com

Radio Business Report   Monthly publication covering business issues, inside news on people, and company controversies. www.rbr.com

Recording   Consumer monthly focusing on all aspects of home and small studio recording. www.recordingmag.com

Rolling Stone Magazine   Semi-monthly coverage of American culture. www
.rollingstone.com/subscription

Spin Magazine   Consumer webzine covering trendsetters in music world. www
.spin.com

Sound and Communications   Business monthly for sound contractors, engineers,
consultants, and system managers. www.soundandcommunications.com

Sound & Vision   Monthly service magazine offering guidance to buyers of all
types of audio equipment and the discs and tapes to be played with it. www
.soundandvision.com

Symphony Magazine   Bimonthly publication with news and articles for symphony
orchestra managers, trustees, volunteers, and musicians. www.americanorchestras.
org/symphony-magazine.html

Variety   Business weekly reporting on the entertainment industry worldwide.
www.variety.com

Wall Street Journal   Daily newspaper focusing on the business and investment
communities. www.wsj.com

Glossary

360 deal. A contract in which a record label, which traditionally acquired only recording rights, gains a share of other artist revenue streams such as touring, publishing, and merchandise.

501(c)3 organization. A nongovernmental organization operating under a provision of the United States Internal Revenue Code, which categorizes types of nonprofit organizations exempt from some federal income taxes. Many states reference Section 501(c) for definitions of organizations exempt from state taxation as well.

A&R. For "artist and repertoire"; the role of scouting and nurturing talent as well as matching songs to performers, historically a function performed primarily on behalf of record labels.

Above-the-line (expense). Special production expenses—for example, salaries for featured artists, creative fees, above-scale wages. Contrasts with below-the-line expense.

Access to Music Charge (AMC). A fee paid by Internet service providers to recorded-music rights holders that compensates them for the value of music accessed online by ISP customers.

Accessory. Item, usually relatively inexpensive, used to enhance or support musical instruments, such as case, stand, strap, guitar pick, cleaning tool, and so on.

Account executive. Liaison person between an advertising agency or medium and one of its clients; salesperson.

Acoustic instrument. An instrument that is not electronic and is not amplified.

Adult contemporary. Broad music genre made up of mainstream and modern rock and classic hits from the past.

Affiliate. Broadcasting: A station that airs programming from a specific network.

Aftermarket. Income sources available for exploitation following first exposure. The broadcasting of a theatrical motion picture is an aftermarket of theatrical release.

Airplay. Radio broadcast of a commercially released music recording.

All-in. A royalty deal where the cost of paying the producer's royalty is deducted from the artist's royalty.

Alternative country. Any country music subgenre that tends to differ from mainstream or pop country music. The term is sometimes known as **Alt. country** and has included country music bands that have incorporated influences ranging from American roots music, bluegrass, rock & roll, rockabilly, acoustic music, americana, honky-tonk, and punk rock.

Alternative music. Youth-based, active music incorporating new wave, punk, "grunge," and techno styles.

AM radio. Radio station using an amplitude modulation signal to broadcast over the air.

Analog. An electrical signal or wave form in which the amplitude and/or frequency vary continuously. Frequently contrasted with "digital."

Analytics. The applied science of quantitatively studying and projecting behavior, such as analysis of music and concert ticket buyer behavior and the tracking of consumer awareness of music products or services.

Angel. Individual financial backer of a Broadway show or other business venture.

Annual billing. Amount invoiced time buyers for the calendar year by broadcasters.

Approved Production Contract (APC). Developed by the Dramatists Guild of America, this model contract sets standards and procedures for creative rights in Broadway shows.

AOR. Album-oriented rock.

Arbitration clause. Provision in a contract requiring the parties to submit disputes to an impartial arbiter, often administered through the American Arbitration Association.

Arm's length. Refers to a transaction between parties who act in their own self-interest rather than one party's being under the control or influence of the other or a third party.

Art music. Repertoire associated with opera, ballet, symphony, and chamber music. Often used interchangeably with classical music or serious music.

Assignment. Turning over of a contract or copyright or other asset to another person's control or ownership.

Audience share. Comparative popularity of broadcast program, determined by dividing the program rating (expressed as a percentage) by the percentage of sets in use at a particular time.

Audiovisual work. Work that consists of a series of related images intended to be shown by the use of projectors, viewers, or electronic equipment, together with accompanying sounds, if any.

Back-announce. In radio broadcasting, the accumulation of a group of announcements following several uninterrupted playings of recorded music.

Background music. Music used by businesses that is intended to go largely unnoticed in a conscious way, as an unobtrusive accompaniment to work, shopping, conversation, dining, and relaxation.

Bed. Advertising: Musical background for a commercial announcement.

Bel canto. Fine singing; the Italian tradition of classical vocal production.

Below-the-line (expense). Costs in production budgeting, such as union scale wages for technicians, equipment, and facilities rentals. Contrasts with above-the-line expense.

Best edition. For purposes of copyright: The edition of a work that the Library of Congress determines to be the most suitable for its purposes.

Big-box. A store of substantial size, usually part of a chain, that achieves economies of scale by focusing on large sales volumes, resulting in very competitively priced goods.

Bio. Biography—a written summary of an individual's professional background.

Blackout. A turning off of stage lighting.

Board. Recording or mixing console.

Boilerplate. Time-tested language that may be found in most contracts but does not require a great deal of negotiation.

Book. In a musical play, the scenario and dialogue for a production.

Breach. "The breaking or violating of a law, right, or duty, either by commission or omission" (Black's Law Dictionary).

Breach of contract. "Failure, without legal excuse, to perform any promise which forms the whole or part of a contract" (Black's Law Dictionary).

Bridge. Musical phrase in a song following the hook, sometimes called "release" or "B phrase."

Bundle of rights. The six exclusive rights in copyright ownership vested initially and exclusively in the author of a work.

Buyout. The purchase of rights in a property (usually for a lump sum), rather than the payment of royalties or other variable consideration (usually over time) for the use of the property.

Cable network (channel). A provider of programming on a specific channel, e.g. HBO, ESPN. Compare with MSO.

Canned track. A prerecorded segment of music that has not been written for the particular work for which it may be used.

CARP. Copyright Arbitration Royalty Panel, phased out from 2005 and replaced by the Copyright Royalty Board. (See CRB.)

Cartage. The act of moving heavy or bulky equipment, particularly musical instruments; the union scale reimbursement for same.

Carve outs. Exceptions in legal contracts and other agreements, such as excluding music publishing rights that an artist creates from a broader artist recording contract.

Catalog. A list of songs (or other goods) available for sale or licensing; works that are available but not recently released.

Catch the action. Compose a musical cue to synchronize with specific action on the screen.

Cattle call. Producer's announcement of open auditions.

CATV. Community Antenna Television, or cable television. See MSO.

CD. Compact audio disc.

CD-R. A blank disc that can be loaded with sound recordings by means of a personal computer.

Channel. (1) The frequency of transmission for a broadcaster. (2) A program service feeding programming to one or more stations, cable systems, satellite services, or websites. (3) A mode of product distribution—e.g., cutout channel.

Chargeback. An expense assessment, e.g., a charge by a recording company against an artist's royalties.

Chart. (1) Musical arrangement. (2) Ranking of most popular recordings.

Chorus. (1) The refrain section of a song that includes a phrase repeated at intervals. (2) A group of persons singing or speaking something simultaneously.

Clam. Wrong note in the copied parts or a note performed incorrectly.

Classic jazz. The "pure," traditional jazz sound: predominantly instrumental, rarely vocal, largely improvised rather than arranged, performed primarily on acoustic, not electronic, instruments.

Classic rock. The enduring music of such rock-and-roll trendsetters as Elvis Presley and The Beatles, originating in the 1950s and 1960s.

Classical music. The repertoire associated with symphony, opera, ballet, chamber, and some choral music.

Click path. A report on specific user Web actions that may be aggregated to draw conclusions about consumer behavior.

Click track. Audible guide used by musicians scoring music to aid synchronization with film.

Close-mike. Recording with a microphone close to the sound source.

Cluster programming. Radio broadcast of several recordings uninterrupted by announcements.

Clutter. The airing in rapid succession of many short spots during a television or radio commercial break; the proportion of a program period, such as an hour, consisting of interruptions.

Cold. (1) Advertising copy read without musical introduction or background. (2) A performance without rehearsal.

Collective bargaining. Negotiation between an employer or group of employers and representatives of union employees to reach agreement on terms of employment such as wages, work hours, and conditions.

Collective work. For purposes of copyright: A work, such as a periodical issue, anthology, or encyclopedia, in which a number of contributions, constituting separate and independent works in themselves, are assembled into a collective whole.

Commercial bed. See Bed.

Commercial load. The proportion of a broadcast station's or program's time that is given to spot announcements.

Common law. A body of law, written or unwritten, that originated in England and that derives its authority from tradition or from judgments and decrees of the courts recognizing such tradition.

Comp style. An improvised piano accompaniment often characterized by syncopated, block chords.

Compilation. For purposes of copyright: A work formed by the collection and assembling of preexisting elements that are selected, coordinated, or arranged in such a way that the resulting work as a whole constitutes an original work of authorship. *Compilations* include collective works.

Compressor. Electronic sound device that limits the dynamic response to create a more constant, even dynamic level.

Compulsory license. In copyright law, a right determined by statute rather than negotiation between licensor and licensee. For example, copyright owners of nondramatic music have complete control over recording rights of their properties until they license the material for the first recording. But after this first recording is distributed to the public, they are compelled by law to license any other person to produce and distribute recordings of the copyrighted music in exchange for a fixed statutory royalty.

Concertmaster. Leader of the first violin section of an orchestra who has special authority and consults with the conductor about musical matters more than other musicians do.

Consent decree. A judicial ruling expressing a voluntary agreement between parties to a suit.

Consideration. "The inducement to a contract, the cause, motive, price, or impelling influence which induces a contracting party to enter into a contract. The reason or material cause of a contract" (Black's Law Dictionary).

Contingent fee, contingency fee. A fee that is often a percentage of the money received from a certain contract. An attorney, for example, might charge a fee of 5% of the money received by his or her client as a result of a contract negotiated by the attorney.

Contingent scale payment. Royalties on sales of recordings paid to certain SAG-AFTRA members.

Contractor. In unions, the steward who hires performers, supervises their working conditions, and confirms they are properly paid.

Controlled composition clause. Language in a contract between a recording label and a composer-performer, in which the label demands to pay a reduced mechanical royalty for works owned or controlled by the recording artist.

Cooperative advertising. Form of product-specific advertising or promotion placed by the retailer but funded in whole or in part by the manufacturer.

Copublishing. Act of two or more entities sharing publishing income but not necessarily the publishing responsibilities.

Copyist. A person who copies music or parts of a musical score.

Copyright. The legal right to reproduce, adapt, distribute, perform publicly, and display a work of intellectual property.

Cost-per-thousand (CPM). The fee for delivering a commercial message to each 1,000 readers, listeners, or viewers.

Coterminous. Two or more conditions or contracts that end on the same date.

Country. Music genre traditionally associated with Nashville, now ranging from traditional country/western and bluegrass to pop-flavored styles.

Cover, cover record. Song that has been rerecorded by other artists after a first recording by the artist who introduced it.

CPB. Corporation for Public Broadcasting.

CRB. The Copyright Royalty Board comprises three Copyright Royalty Judges who determine rates and terms for copyright statutory licenses and make determinations on distribution of statutory license royalties collected by the United States Copyright Office of the Library of Congress.

Creative director. (1) In an advertising agency, the individual in charge of creative advertising concepts; supervises writers, graphic artists, and audio-video producers. (2) For a production company or recording label, the person in charge of creative services.

Creative fee. Money paid a composer or copywriter by an advertising agency, producer, or production company.

Creative services. Division of a recording company that provides marketing concepts, graphic art, sales aids, editorial services, and advertising materials.

Cross-collateralization. Shift of royalties earned by one property to the credit or debit of another property, resulting in a net total of royalties earned by all of them. This pooling of royalties may often reduce what would otherwise be the income of an artist-songwriter.

Crossover recording. A recording focused on one market segment that achieves sales in one or more additional markets.

Cue. Labeling a point in a work where an insertion of audio is to be made; short musical passage composed to accompany dramatic screen action or underscore dialogue.

Cure. Satisfy a complaint or resolve a dispute concerning a contract.

Cut. In recorded music, a recording that is part of a whole, as in one cut from an album.

Cut-in. Owner of a property shares ownership or the financial benefits of ownership.

Cutouts. Surplus record inventory sold at bargain prices.

Cutter. An editor, e.g., a film editor of music recorded for synchronization with pictures.

DAT. Digital audiotape.

DAW. Digital audio workstation.

Day parting. Radio programming that divides the broadcast day into segments, such as "morning drive," "midday," and so forth.

Deal breaker. Issue that, if not settled, terminates contract negotiations.

Deal memo. A summary document that covers major points of the contract, often prepared before the full contract is drawn up.

Decay. Diminution of sound pressure (audible volume).

Default. Failure to perform under a legal contract.

Demo. (1) Demonstration recording. (2) Demography, demographic group.

Demography, demographics. The study and measurement of the characteristics of populations, including distribution, density, and vital statistics such as age, income, and gender.

Derivative work. For purposes of copyright: A work based on one or more preexisting works, such as a translation, musical arrangement, dramatization, fictionalization, motion picture version, sound recording, art reproduction, abridgment, condensation, or any other form in which a work may be recast, transformed, or adapted.

Development officers. Professionals who solicit donations to nonprofit causes.

Digital lockers. Remote servers for storing and retrieving music files often operated by third-party companies.

Digital recording. Audio or video recording made with the analog signal converted into a stream of discrete numbers, thus producing an abstract template for the original sound or moving image.

Digital transmission. The transfer of music encoded as digital data. This transfer occurs by means of the Internet,

satellites, cables, phone lines, or other means.

Discharge. To void a contract, cause it to be nonbinding.

Display. To show a copy of a work.

Distributor. A business in an intermediate position in the value chain, such as a wholesaler between a manufacturer and a retailer or satellite operator between a program network and a consumer.

DIY. Do-it-yourself. Recording industry: A label in which one person (or very few persons) performs most functions.

Double. The second (sometimes third) instrument a musician is called on to play. For example, a flute is a common double required of saxophonists.

Doubling. Act of playing more than one instrument in a performance.

Downtime. A period when recording or filming equipment is not functioning properly, thus unusable.

Dramatic music, dramatico-musical. Music closely related to drama or a scenario, particularly opera, a musical play, ballet, narration.

DRM. Digital rights management. DRM protects intellectual property either by encrypting the data so that only authorized users can access is, or by embedding a digital watermark so that the content cannot be freely distributed.

Drop ship. Fulfillment of a customer's order by shipment from an entity other than the one from which the customer ordered.

DVR. Digital video recorder.

Dynamic pricing. Ticket prices that can be changed instantly based on shifting online demand, a practice pioneered by airlines.

Easy listening. Primarily instrumental music genre, gentler in sound than adult contemporary and notably popular in elevators.

EDM. Electronic dance music.

EPK. Electronic press kit that usually includes press releases, the artist's biography, news clips, previous media reviews, digital artwork, and photos.

End cap. Retail display at the end of an aisle.

Engineer. An audio mixer or sound technician.

EP. (1) Employers Pension Fund of the AFM. (2) Extended-play record.

EQ. Equalization.

Equity. Actors' Equity Association.

Executive producer. Top administrator and/or financier of a production.

Executory, executory provision. A requirement of performance to be rendered following disengagement from (termination of) a contract.

Exploit, exploitation. In the entertainment field, to promote, advertise, publicize, display, distribute, license, sell, or advance an artist or a property.

Extended use. A prerecorded tape or film used for a period longer than the one initially paid for.

Facilities fee. A per-ticket fee often paid to concert venues on a sliding scale.

Fader. A recording console control used to effect changes in sound level.

Fair use doctrine. Legal defense to a copyright infringement claim, allowing minimal takings of copyrighted material for purposes such as scholarship, research, and news reporting.

Fake book. A collection of musical leadsheets intended to help a performer quickly learn new songs.

FCC. Federal Communications Commission.

Fiduciary. (1) A person who manages money or other things of value for another person and in whom the second party has a right to place trust. (2) A situation or relationship between persons where one acts for another in a position of trust. Example: a lawyer or agent acting on behalf of an artist.

Find. To decide and declare.

Finding. "The result of the deliberations of a jury or a court" (Black's Law Dictionary).

First-call musician. Performer a contractor prefers to hire above others available.

First desk/first chair. The lead instrumentalist in a section of an orchestra.

Flack. A publicist.

Flat. A natural sound, without coloration or alteration of highs and lows.

FM radio. Radio broadcasting using a frequency modulation signal to transmit over the air.

Foreground music. Music used to draw in targeted customers and keep them in stores, entertain telephone callers on hold so that they will be less likely to hang up, or help airline passengers stay calm and relaxed.

Four-walling. A booking arrangement where the promoter or performer assumes the economic risk for a concert by renting a venue for a flat fee and perhaps by providing some personnel that might otherwise be provided by the venue itself.

Franchised agent. A talent agent or booker licensed by an artists' union.

Front line. Melodic instruments in a band or orchestra, as opposed to the rhythm section.

Gaffer. Lighting technician on a video, television, or motion picture set.

Ghost writer. A writer or composer who does work for hire under the name of another writer or composer.

Genre. A category of musical composition characterized by a particular style, form, or content (e.g., blues, jazz, country, rap, classical, easy listening).

Gig. Job; engagement of a musician or entertainer for a specified time.

Glissando. The musical effect produced by playing a series of instrumental notes in quick succession without performing each individually.

Global Repertoire Database (GRD). A comprehensive database created by the European Commission in order to secure the representation of the global ownership and control of musical works.

Gofer. An assistant who may run errands and "go for" whatever is requested.

Grand right. Performance right in dramatic music.

Graphic equalizer. A sound control that provides adjustment of a signal over a broad range of frequencies.

Guild. An association of professional persons with similar interests (sometimes used synonymously with trade union).

Hall fee. A venue's predetermined portion of the revenue earned for a performance.

Harmonize. Legal: To rewrite or amend statutes or regulations so that they are in agreement or accordance with other statutes, regulations, or treaties.

Harmonizer. A signal-processing device that creates delay effects and changes the pitch of a sound without affecting its tempo.

HD. High definition.

Head. Start of a tape or film reel.

Hook. (1) Song: Memorable melodic (or lyrical) phrase. (2) Advertising: Campaign slogan or concept.

House agency. Advertising department within a company, as distinct from an independent agency.

House producer. One of the company's salaried staff production employees.

H&W. AFM's Health and Welfare Fund.

Hyphenate. Artist providing multiple services—e.g., producer-director, singer-songwriter.

ID. Station: See Station logo.

Impressions. Advertising: The number of perceptions of a message—e.g., 1,000 people viewing a single TV commercial would equal 1,000 impressions.

Independent contractor. An individual or company engaged to perform a role or complete a task not serving in the role of an employee of the client.

In-house. Done within a company itself; not hired out.

Interpolation. An abrupt change of musical elements; unrelated material inserted between two logically succeeding functions; portions of a melody from a previously recorded song, but rerecording it instead of sampling it.

Institutional ad (or spot). Promotion intended to impress the public with a firm's or organization's merit (as opposed to that of a specific product).

Institutional print. Print music used by schools and churches for bands, choruses, choirs, and orchestras.

Intellectual property. Ideas translated from creators' minds to tangible expressions such as songs, writing, and other forms.

Interactive TV. A form of television that permits viewers to change the picture or add to it.

Interface. To connect by means of a machine or specific software protocol.

i.p.s. Inches per second, referring to tape-reel speed.

IPTV. Internet protocol television.

Jingle. Original term for a broadcast commercial (spot) containing music, or the music in the spot.

Joint venture. A business partnership of limited duration set up for a limited purpose.

Key man clause. Artists' contracts: Contractual provision that if an artist's manager, agent, or producer leaves a particular company, the artist may follow that individual without legal or financial reprisals.

Label. A brand of commercial recordings, usually issued under a trademarked name; a record manufacturer-distributor.

Leadsheet. Music manuscript containing a song's melody, text, and chord symbols.

Legal consideration. "One recognized or permitted by the law as valid and lawful; as distinguished from such as are illegal or immoral" (Black's Law Dictionary). The term is sometimes used as equivalent for "good" or "sufficient" consideration.

Legit. Slang for legitimate. Style of music or theatrical performance in the classical, formal tradition.

Library service. A collection of a large quantity and variety of recorded passages available for use in productions not using original or "custom" music. Also known as a production music library.

Licensing. The awarding of rights to perform, reproduce, distribute, or transmit a copyrighted work.

Lift. In broadcast commercials, a short recorded segment drawn from a longer one.

Ligature. (1) A slur indicating a group of notes sung or played as a connected phrase. (2) The group of notes thus indicated. (3) The device on a clarinet or saxophone mouthpiece holding the reed in place.

Limiter. Signal-processing device that reduces peaks but affects overall dynamics less than a compressor.

Live-on-tape. A television production performed live, with TV recording occurring at the same time for later editing prior to broadcast.

Load-in/load-out. In performance venues, delivering and setup up on stage of performance equipment and then later disassembly and removal.

Loan-out corporation. A company an artist sets up as a separate legal entity for legal and tax benefits. The company loans out the artist's services and pays the artist as an employee.

Local. (1) Branch office of a national union or guild. (2) A market or audience contained within one city or area.

Local marketing agreements. Agreement whereby a broadcast station owner may "lease" programming and sales to another station owner.

Logo. A musical or visual symbol used repeatedly in an effort to reinforce public recognition of a product or organization.

Magnetic stock. Motion picture film surfaced with an emulsion of magnetic oxide rather than silver halides.

Market. A particular group of buyers (or a type of audience) that can be identified by demographic research and/or analyses of preferences; a geographically distinct region.

Master. The final version of a recording.

Master use license. A license granting the right to use the recorded master (usually controlled by a record label), not just the underlying song (usually controlled by a publisher).

Master purchase agreement. A contract used by a recording company to obtain exclusive rights in a master recording that has been produced by another person, such as an independent producer.

Mastering. The process by which tracks are equalized and balanced in relation to each other, then transferred to a master storage device (DAT, CD, cassette, or lacquer disc) to be used as a duplicating master for the purpose of manufacturing recordings or otherwise preparing for nonphysical distribution.

Material. "Important; more or less necessarily; having influence or effect; going to the merits; having to do with matter, as distinguished from form" (Black's Law Dictionary).

Merch Licensed celebrity entertainer merchandise.

MC (or Emcee). Master of ceremonies.

MD. Music director.

Mechanical rights/license. Legal permission given by the copyright owner (either through negotiation or a compulsory license) to make and distribute a commercial recording of copyrighted music.

Mechanicals. Royalties paid by a record manufacturer to the owner of a music composition copyright.

Media buyer. Employee who contracts for print ad space or broadcast time buys.

MIDI. Musical Instrument Digital Interface. (1) Technology that allows a composition to be transcribed into musical notation by playing it on the keyboard. MIDI notation prepared for one instrument can be used to reproduce similar performances with other MIDI instruments. (2) Standard for exchanging musical information for musical devices, including instruments.

Mix. To combine and equalize, into one or more channels, a larger number of separate tracks of recorded sounds.

Mixer. (1) Recording technician who operates a console, often referred to as an engineer. (2) Electronic equipment that enables the mixing of sounds.

MOR. Middle-of-the-road type of music, now more commonly referred to as "nostalgia/big band," that favors instrumentals over vocals and is somewhat similar to easy listening music.

Moral rights. The right of an author to be properly identified and to insist that any editing of a work preserves its integrity, without alteration, distortion, or mutilation of the work.

MPEG. The family of digital video compression standards and file formats developed by the Moving Pictures Experts Group.

MSO. Multiple system operator, a cable TV infrastructure company owning more than one system. Compare with Cable Network (channel).

Multicast. System for the simultaneous transmission of two or more signals over the same wire or radio frequency channel. Compare with simulcast.

Multiplex. System for the simultaneous transmission of two or more signals over the same wire or radio frequency channel.

Multitrack. The recording device or tape on which parallel tracks can be recorded. Each track has separate music or information that can be mixed or edited separately.

Music coordinator. Production assistant keeping track of musical elements.

Music cutter. Same as film music editor.

Music house (or music supply house). A company of composers and arrangers offering creative services (and recording) for buyers of "custom" music.

Music preparation. Music manuscript proofreading, extraction of parts from the score, collation, reproduction, score binding, and delivery.

Music supervisor. A person primarily responsible for selecting and licensing music for film, TV, and new media productions.

Music supplier. See Music house.

Narrowcasting. Contrasts with broadcasting: Program material produced and delivered to audiences of special tastes.

National account. Advertising: Customer of an agency or production company that advertises nationwide.

National promoters. Companies (NPs) that work nationally to produce and promote events, often by coordinating with regional or local promotion affiliates or partners.

Needle drop. Brief recorded passage (orchestral or a sound effect) drawn from a transcription library that a producer uses for a dramatic program or broadcast commercial.

Negative cost. Expense of producing a movie or TV show before incurring costs of distribution or promotion.

Negative tour support. The advance a recording company may make to pay the difference between the touring costs and touring income, if an artist's touring does not break even or make a profit.

Negotiated license. In the recording industry, a right to record worked out between a music publisher and a record producer. Contrasts with a statutory or compulsory license.

Neighboring rights (or related rights). The rights in a work that don't belong to the author. There are three general categories of neighboring rights: those of performers, producers, and broadcasters.

Neo-romantic. Any of various movements in the arts considered as representing a return to the artistic styles associated with the romantic period of the 19th century.

Network. Broadcast service usually distributed simultaneously through more than one station or outlet.

New Age music. Mellow, mostly acoustic instrumental music with an ethereal, soothing quality, popularized in the 1980s.

New country music. Music genre that combines elements of country and rock and roll.

New use. Application of recorded music tape or film to a medium different from the one originally intended—e.g., a record album to be used in a film.

Nielsen rating. Percentage of the potential broadcast audience watching a particular program or network, according to Nielsen Media Research. A household rating of 10.0 would indicate 1 in 10 homes watched the program.

Nondramatic music. Musical works, such as pop singles, not incorporated and performed in the context of a story, such as an opera or stage play.

NPR. National Public Radio.

NTSC. Abbreviation for a standard for TV transmission used primarily in North America and Japan.

O&O station. A radio or TV station owned and operated by a commercial broadcasting network.

Off-Broadway. Low-budget, often experimental, professional theater, produced in New York City venues but outside its Times Square theater district.

One-off. Something that is not repeated or reproduced.

One-stop. Record distributor/wholesaler offering a variety of recording companies' merchandise to retailers and jukebox operators.

Open to buy. The budget (such as monthly dollar amounts) for new merchandise purchases by a retailer or distributor.

Opticals. Visual effects created for film or videotape.

Orchestrator. One who takes music written by someone else and writes or scores the music for the various instruments that play it.

Outboard equipment. Recording hardware external to the recording console that is patched into it to enhance the mixer's options of controlling sounds.

Over the top (OTT). Feeding of programming directly to users via broadband connections, bypassing the traditional cable TV distribution economic model.

Overcall album. Recording requested by label but that was not covered by initial contract.

Overdubbing. Adding music or sounds to a previously recorded tape.

Overtracking. (1) Adding sounds to a previously recorded tape. (2) The use of one voice several times or recording one voice several times, then playing them simultaneously on a recording to produce the effect of a larger ensemble.

P2P. Peer-to-peer networks that allow users to freely download content from another user's hard drive without the use of an intermediary server.

Package deal. Combined goods and/or services delivered under one price tag.

Pan pot. Recording console control (fader) used to place a signal to the left, right, or center of the stereo image.

Paper business. Printed-editions sector of a music publishing company.

Papering the house. Concert promotion: Issuing free tickets to ensure a full audience for a performance.

Pass. Make a negative judgment; to turn down, reject.

Pay TV. Television delivery business model for specific channels for which an extra fee is paid, contrasting with basic TV (at a lower cost to the cable viewer) and free TV (no cost to the over-the-air viewer).

Payola. Money or other compensation illicitly given radio station personnel in return for playing particular recordings.

PD. (1) Program director: Job title. (2) Public domain: Content unprotected by copyright.

Performance. A performance occurs any time music is played publicly, whether at a live concert or broadcast over radio, TV, Internet, or other means of transmission.

Performance license. Legal permission granted by the copyright owner or his or her representative for the public performance of copyrighted music in exchange for a fee. These are generally granted in the form of blanket licenses, offering access to a large catalog of copyrights.

Performance right, performing right. Exclusive right given to the creator of copyrighted material to authorize the use of the work in public.

Performance rights organization (PRO). (1) An organization protecting and promoting the rights of songwriters and composers (e.g., ASCAP, BMI, and SESAC). (2) An organization protecting and promoting the rights in recordings of performers and labels (e.g., SoundExchange).

Performance royalty. Payment for the broadcast or performance of a creator's work.

Phonorecord. Any physical object serving as a delivery medium for recorded music, such as a phonograph record, CD, or prerecorded tape. Same as soundcarrier.

Piracy. Illegal duplication and distribution of intellectual property such as sound recordings.

Pit. Area occupied by the orchestra in a theater, often below the floor level of the audience.

Playlist. Radio station's recorded music schedule for broadcast.

Points. Royalties: Synonymous with percentages.

POP. Point-of-purchase (merchandising aids such as signage or posters).

POS. Point-of-sale: (1) Promotional signage. (2) Retail transactional equipment such as a credit card terminal. (3) Data generated by sale transactions.

Power of attorney. "An instrument authorizing another to act as one's agent or attorney; a letter of attorney" (Black's Law Dictionary).

PR. Public relations.

Print. Music published and sold in (1) printed form or (2) in digital form capable of being printed by the user.

PRO. Performing rights organization. An intermediary collecting license fees on behalf of rights owners.

Product manager. Person in charge of a promotional or marketing campaign.

Production blanket. A means of using unlimited amounts of music in one production for a capped or flat fee.

Production manager. Business affairs head for a production.

Production music libraries. Prerecorded music collections with low-cost licensing that offer a broad range of musical styles and genres for purchase for postproduction use in movies, TV, and commercials.

Promoter. The person and/or organization responsible for generating fan interest and ensuring successful turnout at tour destinations.

Promoter of record. Promoter who first produces an artist's or group's public appearances.

Proscenium. Wall arch that separates the stage from the auditorium.

Public domain. The legal status of music or other intellectual property making it available for unrestricted use because there is currently no enforceable copyright or patent right.

Publishing. In the music industry, publishing is the exploitation of rights in musical compositions through printed copies or any other authorized medium of distribution.

Punch-in. Augment taping or filming with insertion of new (or additional) material.

Punch up. Add emphasis to music or script.

Rack jobber. A merchant paying a rental fee or commission to maintain and sell inventory within the retailer's store.

Rack up. TV film and tape presets that may then be called up by a technician for broadcast.

Rap. Lyrics spoken in rhyme to rhythmic music.

Rate card. Summary of advertising rates for a specific medium (radio stations, TV network, etc.) given to ad agencies, clients, and prospective clients.

Record (album, single). Generic term for a commercially distributed recording, e.g., a digital download, compact disc, audiocassette, or vinyl LP.

Record label. The company that coordinates the production, manufacture, distribution, marketing and promotion, and enforcement of copyright protection of sound recordings and music videos; maintains contracts with recording artists and their managers; and manages brands and trademarks associated with the marketing of music recordings and music videos. Also called a record company or recording company.

Release phrase. See Bridge.

Remedy. Solve a problem or cure a default under a contract.

Rent-to-own. A transaction in which the customer rents a product such as an appliance or musical instrument with an option to own the merchandise after a certain number of payments are made.

Residuals. Payments made to performers and other creative personnel when their works are licensed for exploitation in secondary markets.

Reuse. (1) Use of a recorded performance after an initial time period is over. (2) Use of a recorded performance in a medium that is different from the medium for which the performance was first used.

Rhythm-and-blues. Predominantly black music genre featuring a lead vocalist backed with harmonizing singers, piano, bass, and drums, with harmonic structure adapted from popular and blues forms.

Rhythm section. The "motor element" of a band or orchestra, normally composed of piano, bass, drums, and guitar.

Right-to-work law. A state law that makes a closed shop, where union membership is a condition of employment, illegal.

Ring back. The sound made by the phone network to indicate a ringing phone on the other end of the line.

Ringtone. The sound made by a mobile phone when an incoming call is received.

Ripping. The process of copying audio or video content and storing it in a digital format.

Road manager. Handles the transportation of people and equipment, arranges for meals and lodging, ensures that adequate security is provided, hires tour accountants, supervises sound reinforcement and lighting personnel, checks box office receipts, and collects performance income.

Royalty. A fee paid for the use of property such as copyrighted works.

Royalty artist. Union contract: Individuals or self-contained groups contracted to receive a record royalty of at least 3% of the suggested retail price or a substantially equivalent royalty.

Sampling. (1) Music performances: Technique used by music rights organizations to estimate total performances by examining a limited number of performances. (2) Music recording: The digital recording of a sound or series of sounds from already recorded material, for insertion into a new recording so as to enhance that recording's sound; the source sound can be inserted unchanged or transformed by synthesizer or other electronic equipment. For a detailed discussion, see Chapter 6.

Scale. Specified minimum union wage.

Scaling the house. Determining what quantity of available seats in a performance facility are to be priced the least expensive, the next least expensive, and so on.

Score (a film). Compose, perform, and record music to synchronize with a motion picture.

Second engineer. Assistant to the head audio engineer (technician).

Secondary market. (1) Resale of concert tickets, typically via a different platform than the one that handled the initial sale transaction. (2) Exploitation of a work in a distribution medium or geographic territory following the initial form of exploitation.

Self-contained group. (1) Small ensemble that writes its own material. (2) An organized ensemble that performs together regularly without outside members.

Selling agent. Person or firm offering printed music or merchandise for sale at the retail level, under a royalty contract or for commission.

Serialism. The method or practice of composing with tone rows.

Session musician. Instrumentalist employed in recording studios and usually paid union scale.

Sforzando. "Stinger" note or chord that brings special attention to specific dramatic action—e.g., to identify a villain, emphasize the sounds of a fight, or suggest the sounds of a beating heart.

Sheet music. Musical composition printed on unbound sheets of paper.

Shop tapes. Submit audition recordings to potential buyers.

Side. (1) One side of a recording. (2) One song on a recording.

Sidemusician. An instrumentalist other than the leader or contractor.

Simulcast. To transmit the identical programming at the same time on different channels. Compare with multicast.

SKU. Stock-keeping unit. A uniquely configured offering at retail. A vinyl LP of an album would be a different SKU than a CD of the same recording.

Slap. The "tony" or buzzing sound that is produced by plucked/fingered bass when vibrating strings come into contact with the metal frets.

Slate. Chalkboard ID (or visual equivalent) of a filmed or videotaped segment, or a spoken recitation of a description of the take, to aid in identifying the segment during the editing process.

Slaved. To be made directly responsive to another mechanism.

Small right. Performance right in nondramatic music.

Song score. A film soundtrack composed primarily of songs that have the potential to be hits.

Soundcarrier. A phonorecord.

SoundScan. A data collection service that tabulates sales of recorded product through POS devices.

Spec, speculation. Employed without assurance of getting paid.

Special material. Music, lyrics, dialogue, and patter specially written for a particular artist's performance.

Split copyright. Copyright proprietor shares his or her ownership with one or more persons.

Split point. Point of cumulative revenue at which the artist and the promoter divide any net income from a concert.

Split publishing. One party shares his or her publishing rights with one or more persons.

Spot. (1) A broadcast commercial announcement. (2) Theatrical spotlight. (3) To place in a particular position, as in "spotting" a film—deciding precisely where a film should be underscored.

Spotting notes. Notes given to a composer of motion picture music by the music editor to specify where each cue will happen in the movie.

SRO. Standing room only, meaning "sold out."

Staff paper. A set of horizontal lines and intermediate spaces used in notation to represent a sequence of pitches, in modern notation normally consisting of five lines and four spaces. Also called a stave.

Station. In radio or television, a station is generally a broadcaster that transmits on one frequency and from one locality. A group of stations airing the same programs is frequently referred to as a *broadcast network*.

Station logo. Broadcast station's musical or visual signature, identification.

Statutory license. The right of a music user to exploit a copyrighted work for specific categories of use for a fee set by a regulatory process and not by negotiation between the copyright owner and the user.

Statutory rate. For a mechanical royalty, the government-established maximum rate paid by the label for the recorded use of intellectual property on a consumer-distributed phonorecord such as a CD. Paid on a per-unit basis, the rate is tied to the individual song or, for longer works (such as some jazz compositions), to the work's length. The rate is periodically adjusted.

Stave. See Staff paper.

Steward. Hires performers and supervises enforcement of their union contract with the producer.

Stick. (1) Music: A baton. (2) Broadcasting: A transmission tower.

Stinger. Accented chord played by an orchestra to underscore a dramatic moment on the screen.

Stock arrangement. Published edition; not a custom chart.

Storyboard. A series of sketches showing the sequence of events for a film or video.

Streaming. The delivery of media content to an end user in a way that allows the end user to start playing the file before the entire file has been transmitted. The content does not permanently reside on the destination device.

Strip show. A series of broadcasts scheduled several times a week at the same hour each day.

Studio musician. Same as session musician.

Subpublisher. Firm affiliated with a prime publisher in providing publishing services, usually abroad.

Subsidiary rights. Exploitation rights that spring from or are secondary to other rights, e.g., the right to produce a motion picture based on a stage musical.

Subsisting. Now in existence, as in subsisting copyrights.

Suggested retail list price (SRLP). The amount of money for which the company that produces a product (such as a record label) recommends that it be sold in stores.

Sunset clause. A provision in a contract specifying that an agreement, regulation, or law will end or be modified in a predetermined way at a future point in time.

Swag. Give-aways—posters, novelties, souvenir items, and the like—as part of a promotion.

Sweeps. Period of the year during which research firms collect data concerning broadcast audience size.

Sweeten. Record additional sounds by overdubbing.

SWOT analysis. Tool for identifying strengths, weaknesses, opportunities, and threats when, for example, developing a marketing or strategic plan.

Synchronization rights/license. The right to use music in such a way that it is timed to synchronize with, or relate to, action on film or video.

Synclavier. Keyboard synthesizer incorporating a computer terminal, digital processor, and storage unit, with which an operator can create, store, retrieve, and re-create musical sounds.

Syncopated. Rhythmic placement of musical tones so that their accent does not coincide with the metric accent.

Syndication. Distribution of programs (produced by a network or syndicator) that individual stations or other outlets transmit simultaneously or at times convenient to them.

Tail. End of a tape or film reel.

Take. One version of a recorded performance, as in "The second take was best."

Technical rider. Addendum to a performance contract stipulating requirements for staging, sound reinforcement, equipment, and so on.

Telecommunications. Production and delivery of all modes of entertainment and information.

Term. The time interval embraced by a legal agreement.

Tessitura. Prevailing pitch and range of a melodic line.

Tight. Slang for a well-rehearsed, cohesive performance.

Timbre. Quality, tone color distinguishing one voice or musical instrument from another.

Time buyer. Advertising agency employee who purchases time to air advertising in an electronic medium such as radio, TV, or cable TV.

Time shift. Capacity of a VCR or digital video recorder (DVR) to record a TV program off the air and move its playback to a time more convenient for the viewer.

Tin Pan Alley. The business of popular music most prevalent in the 1920s in New York. Also, style of popular songs of that era, usually sentimental, with a verse and chorus form in which chorus predominated.

Tour support. Financial resources, such as those provided contractually by a record label, that help underwrite the costs associated with touring a given act.

Track. (1) One recorded portion of combined tracks, as in "24-track" recording; the sound on one track, as in "the bass track." (2) A single selection on an album.

Tracker. Label employee following the progress of a record release—airplay, chart action, sales, and so on.

Tracking. (1) An AFM and SAG-AFTRA payment category in which performers record the same notes more than once and a technician overlaps each version to produce the illusion of a larger ensemble. The performers are supposed to be paid for each taped use of their work. (2) A promotion practice of record companies in which the company has employees call radio stations and record stores to see how often a song is played or a recording is sold.

Tracking scale. Union wage scale for tracking sessions.

Tracking session. Taping session following the recording of basic tracks; overdubbing.

Trading fours. Jazz musicians taking turns improvising alternate four-bar phrases.

Transcription. A copy of recorded music made for purposes other than direct sale to consumers (such as background music in a retail setting, in-flight entertainment, and radio syndication).

Underscore. To compose, record, and mix music into the audio track of a movie or TV program.

Unencumbered. Of or relating to an owned asset that does not have a claim against it.

Union shop. An establishment that hires only members of a labor union or those who promise to join a union within a specified time.

Union steward. An agent who supervises the employment of union artists and provides liaison for them with their employer.

Unison. Music played or sung by two or more people in which instruments or voices perform identical parts simultaneously in the same or different octaves; the interval formed by two tones of the same pitch.

Upfront payment. Money advanced prior to completion of a job or production.

Up full. Background music crescendo to foreground.

Value chain. The linkage of constituent economic contributors in the offering of a product or service. The chain may all be within a single company or viewed more broadly as roles performed sequentially by different entitites. An example of a value chain in the music business would be composer → performer → label → CD replicator → distributor → retailer. Each component of the chain adds value in achieving the ultimate goal of selling the product.

VCR. Videocassette recorder.

Venue. Place of performance or trial.

Verse. A section or stanza of a hymn or song; a section preceding the refrain or chorus of a song.

Videocaster. One who broadcasts, cablecasts, or telecasts videos.

Videogram. Any audiovisual physical medium, such as videocassettes and DVDs, that contains musical compositions.

VJ. Video jockey, analogous to DJ.

VOD. Video on demand. A form of per-program electronic delivery requested by an individual viewer.

Voiceover. Words spoken by an actor or announcer who is not seen on the screen.

Webcasting. Transmission via the World Wide Web; the distribution of media files over the Internet via streaming media technology.

Weighting formula. Evaluations by a performing rights organization used in determining the relative value of various kinds of music performances to judge what royalties are due a rights owner.

Work made for hire. (1) A work prepared by an employee within the scope of his or her employment. (2) A work specially ordered or commissioned for use as a contribution to a collective work.

Working capital. The assets of a business that can be applied to its operation; the amount of current assets that exceeds current liabilities.

Index

MUSIC BUSINESS HANDBOOK
AND CAREER GUIDE

ORGANIZATIONS

Academy of Country Music (ACM)
www.acmcountry.com

Acoustical Society of America (ASA)
acousticalsociety.org

Actors' Equity Association (AEA)
www.actorsequity.org

Alliance of Artists and Recording Companies (AARC)
www.aarcroyalties.com

Alliance of Motion Picture and Television Producers (AMPTP)
www.amptp.org

Alliance for Women In Media (formerly American Women in Radio and Television)
www.allwomeninmedia.org

American Choral Directors Association (ACDA)
www.acda.org

American Composers Alliance (ACA)
www.composers.com

American Federation of Labor and Congress of Industrial Organizations (AFL-CIO)
www.aflcio.org

American Federation of Musicians of the United States and Canada (AFM)
www.afm.org

American Guild of Musical Artists (AGMA)
www.musicalartists.org

American Guild of Organists
www.agohq.org

American Guild of Variety Artists (AGVA)
http://www.agvausa.com/

American Mechanical Rights Agency, Inc. (AMRA) (formerly American Mechanical Rights Association)
www.amermechrights.com

American Music Therapy Association, Inc. (AMTA) (formerly American Association for Music Therapy/National Association for Music Therapy)
www.musictherapy.org

American Musicological Society (AMS)
www.ams-net.org

American Society of Composers, Authors and Publishers (ASCAP)
www.ascap.com

American Theatre Wing
www.americantheatrewing.org

Americans for the Arts (formerly American Council for the Arts)
www.artsusa.org

Amusement and Music Operators Association (AMOA)
www.amoa.com

Archive of Contemporary Music
www.arcmusic.org

Associated Actors and Artistes of America (4As) 165 W. 46th St., Ste. 500, New York, NY 10036-2501 (212) 869-0358

Association of Arts Administration Educators (AAAE)
www.artsadministration.org

Association of Independent Music Publishers (AIMP)
www.aimp.org

Association of Performing Arts Presenters
www.artspresenters.org

Association of Talent Agents (ATA)
www.agentassociation.com

Audio Engineering Society, Inc. (AES)
www.aes.org

Authors Guild (AG)
www.authorsguild.org

Broadcast Music Inc. (BMI)
www.bmi.com

The Broadway League (formerly League of American Theatres and Producers, Inc.)
www.broadwayleague.com

Bureau international des sociétés gérant les droits d'enregistrement et de reproduction mécanique (BIEM)
www.biem.org

California Copyright Conference (CCC)
www.theccc.org

Certification Board for Music Therapists
www.cbmt.org

Chamber Music America (CMA)
www.chamber-music.org

Church Music Publishers Association
www.cmpamusic.org

College Music Society (CMS)
www.music.org

Columbia Artists Management Inc.
www.cami.com

Copyright Society of the U.S.A. (CSUSA)
www.csusa.org

Country Music Association (CMA)
www.cmaworld.com

Country Music Foundation (CMF)
www.countrymusichalloffame.org

Dance/USA
www.danceusa.org

Directors Guild of America (DGA)
www.dga.org

Dramatists Guild of America
www.dramatistsguild.com

Early Music America
www.earlymusic.org

Entertainment Merchants Association (EMA) (formerly Video Software Dealers Association)
http://www.entmerch.org/

Entertainment Software Association
www.theesa.com

Film Musicians Secondary Markets Fund
www.fmsmf.org

Foundation Center
www.foundationcenter.org

Future of Music Coalition
futureofmusic.org

Gospel Music Association (GMA)
www.gospelmusic.org

Guild of Italian-American Actors (GIAA) (formerly Italian Actors Union)
www.giaa.us

Guitar and Accessories Marketing Association
www.discoverguitar.com

Harry Fox Agency, Inc. (HFA)
www.harryfox.com

International Alliance for Women in Music (IAWM)
www.iawm.org

International Alliance of Theatrical Stage Employees, Moving Picture Technicians, Artists and Allied Crafts of the United States, Its Territories and Canada (IATSE)
www.iatse-intl.org

International Association of Venue Managers (IAAM) (formerly International Association of Assembly Managers)
www.iavm.org

International Confederation of Societies of Authors and Composers (CISAC)
www.cisac.org

International Entertainment Buyers Association (IEBA)
ieba.org

International Federation of Actors (FIA)
www.fia-actors.com

International Federation of Musicians (FIM)
http://www.fim-musicians.org/

International Federation of the Phonographic Industry (IFPI)
www.ifpi.org